The Iliad: a commentary

Volume II: books 5–8

THE ILIAD: A COMMENTARY

GENERAL EDITOR G. S. KIRK

Volume II: books 5–8

G. S. KIRK

REGIUS PROFESSOR EMERITUS OF GREEK
IN THE UNIVERSITY OF CAMBRIDGE

 CAMBRIDGE
UNIVERSITY PRESS

PUBLISHED BY THE PRESS SYNDICATE OF THE UNIVERSITY OF CAMBRIDGE
The Pitt Building, Trumpington Street, Cambridge, United Kingdom

CAMBRIDGE UNIVERSITY PRESS
The Edinburgh Building, Cambridge CB2 2RU, UK   http://www.cup.cam.ac.uk
40 West 20th Street, New York, NY 10011-4211, USA   http://www.cup.org
10 Stamford Road, Oakleigh, Melbourne 3166, Australia
Ruiz de Alarcón 13, 28014 Madrid, Spain

First published 1990
Reprinted 1993, 1995, 2000

British Library Cataloguing in Publication Data
The Iliad: a commentary.
Vol. 2, Books 5–8
1. Epic poetry in Greek. Homer. Iliad: commentaries
I. Kirk, G. S. (Geoffrey Stephen), 1921–
883'.01

Library of Congress Cataloguing in Publication data
Kirk, G. S. (Geoffrey Stephen), 1921–
The Iliad, a commentary.
Includes index.
Contents: v. 1. Books 1–4 v. 2. Books 5–8.
1. Homer.–Iliad. 2. Homer.–Iliad. I. Title.
PA4037.K458   1985   883'.01   84-11330

ISBN 0 521 23710 6 hardback
ISBN 0 521 28172 5 paperback

Transferred to digital printing 2005

UP

For N. G. L. Hammond

CONTENTS

PREFACE

This second volume continues the plan outlined in the first, the commentary itself being somewhat denser. Attention is increasingly drawn to typical motifs and themes, which become more marked from book 5 on. At the same time vol. I's emphasis on poetics, especially at the level of rhythm and diction, is maintained; and the analysis of character and motivation, as well as of divine involvement, becomes somewhat fuller than before. The four introductory chapters continue the progressive examination of the background to the *Iliad*; they will be complemented here and there in subsequent volumes, not least chapter 1 on Homeric religion. Reference to modern secondary literature, which some critics have found too slight, has been increased. Subsequent volumes will go further in this respect, although the principle stated in the editorial introduction to vol. I still applies, that neither complete bibliographical coverage nor a generally doxographical approach to Homeric interpretation is sought after.

Two amendments have been made to the list of essential aids (cf. vol. I, xxi). First, Dr Stephanie West's elucidation of *Odyssey* bks 1–4, in the revised, English version of the *Odissea* commentary overseen by Alfred Heubeck, is of exceptional value for many Homeric matters and is cited with corresponding frequency. Second, Ameis–Hentze's commentary, though obviously outmoded in certain respects, still contains much that is both acute and relevant, and in the present volume is cited on a par with Leaf. Other references to works in German are too few, but the influence of Burkert, Erbse, W. H. Friedrich, Latacz, Leumann, Meister, Trümpy and others (not to mention Dörpfeld and Korfmann), if not of Neoanalysis except at its broadest level, is plain enough. In French, the quality and frequency of the guidance provided by Chantraine are equally obvious. Yet the 'commentary for Europe for the 1990s' desiderated by one friend is obviously not to be found in these pages – if it could, or should, be found anywhere. I have also continued to maintain a certain reserve over the ultimate intentions and attitudes, both moral and literary, of the *Iliad*'s monumental composer. That may be frustrating to some, but a commentator's first aim should be, not to provide ready-made answers to all possible questions at whatever level of generality, but to help his users make their own attempts to do so. Meanwhile (as a visit to the recent F.I.E.C. congress in Pisa served to remind one), on many points of Homeric interpretation, not least over questions of religion, a distinctly personal, not to say visceral response is still preferred by many scholars. That is perhaps as it should be; but it gives the author of a commentary like this one a distinct hope that here and there, at least, and even to non-English-speaking scholars, he can offer a certain counter-balancing judgement based on close study (albeit sometimes imperfect) of the Greek text.

My particular thanks are due to Professor R. M. Frazer, of Tulane University, for reading the typescript and saving me from many errors. He had already pointed out a number of corrigenda in vol. 1; a list of these, together with vol. 11's new crop, are enclosed with the next volume to appear (v). Meanwhile certain corrections have already been incorporated in the second printing, 1987, of vol. 1. The more substantial ones affect the following comments: on 2.92–3 *ad init.*, on 2.103 *ad init.* (this I owe to the late Professor Heubeck), on 2.813–14 *ad fin.*, on 3.422, and on 4.228. Owners of the first printing of vol. 1 may find it worthwhile to compare the second printing at these points and amend accordingly.

Dr Neil Hopkinson has once again generously read through the proofs for surface errors, with his accustomed skill. S. Morris, H. von Staden, J. N. Postgate and R. Hägg helped over specific points. R. M. Cook read chapter 4, and my four collaborators have also, of course, made valuable comments. The members of two Yale seminars in the spring of 1988 provided a welcome stimulus; I would thank in particular Shirley Werner, William Johnson, Zlatko Plěse and George Chukinas. Finally Professor Ruth Scodel made me aware, through her paper at the Pisa congress, that more remains to be said about imagined epitaphs in bk 6; we await her published observations with great interest.

Bath and Mauzens, October 1989   G. S. K.

ABBREVIATIONS

Books

Allen, *Catalogue*   T. W. Allen, *The Homeric Catalogue of Ships* (Oxford 1921)

Ameis–Hentze   K. F. Ameis and C. Hentze, *Homers Ilias* (Leipzig 1868–1932; repr. Amsterdam 1965)

Andersen, *Diomedesgestalt*   Øivind Andersen, *Die Diomedesgestalt in der Ilias* (Oslo 1978)

ANET   J. B. Pritchard, ed., *Ancient Near Eastern Texts relating to the Old Testament* (3rd edn, Princeton 1969)

Apthorp, *MS Evidence*   M. J. Apthorp, *The Manuscript Evidence for Interpolation in Homer* (Heidelberg 1980)

Arch. Hom.   *Archaeologia Homerica: Die Denkmäler und das frühgriechische Epos*, edd. F. Matz and H. G. Buchholz (Göttingen 1967–)

Arend, *Scenen*   W. Arend, *Die typischen Scenen bei Homer* (Berlin 1933)

Aspects   Tom Winnifrith, Penelope Murray and K. W. Gransden, edd., *Aspects of the Epic* (London 1983)

Berghold, *Zweikampf*   W. Berghold, *Die Zweikampf des Paris und Menelaos* (Bonn 1977)

Bolling, *External Evidence*   G. M. Bolling, *The External Evidence for Interpolation in Homer* (Oxford 1925)

Burkert, *Religion*   W. Burkert, *Greek Religion: Archaic and Classical* (Oxford 1985); Eng. trans. by John Raffan of *Griechische Religion der archaischen und klassischen Epoche* (Stuttgart 1977); all references, from this volume of the Commentary onwards, will be to the Eng. version

Chantraine, *Dict.*   P. Chantraine, *Dictionnaire étymologique de la langue grecque* (Paris 1968–80)

Chantraine, *GH*   P. Chantraine, *Grammaire homérique* i–ii (Paris 1958–63)

Coldstream, *Geometric Greece*   J. N. Coldstream, *Geometric Greece* (London 1977)

Commentary   *A Commentary on Homer's Odyssey*, vol. i, by A. Heubeck, S. West and J. B. Hainsworth (Oxford 1988); vol. ii, by A. Heubeck and A. Hoekstra (Oxford 1989); vol. iii, by J. Russo, M. Fernández Galiano and A. Heubeck (Oxford 1992); an Eng. trans., with revisions, of *Odissea*

Cook, *Troad*   J. M. Cook, *The Troad: an Archaeological and Topographical Study* (Oxford 1973)

de Jong, *Narrators*   I. J. F. de Jong, *Narrators and Focalizers: the Presentation of the Story in the Iliad* (Amsterdam 1987)

Delebecque, *Cheval*   E. Delebecque, *Le Cheval dans l'Iliade* (Paris 1951)

Denniston, *Particles*   J. D. Denniston, *The Greek Particles* (2nd edn, Oxford 1951)

Desborough, *Last Mycenaeans*   V. R. d'A. Desborough, *The Last Mycenaeans and their Successors* (Oxford 1964)

Edwards, *HPI*   M. W. Edwards, *Homer, Poet of the Iliad* (Baltimore and London 1987)

Erbse   H. Erbse, *Scholia Graeca in Homeri Iliadem*, vols. i–v (+ index vols.) (Berlin 1969–87)

Fenik, *TBS*   B. C. Fenik, *Typical Battle Scenes in the Iliad* (*Hermes* Einzelschriften 21, Wiesbaden 1968)

Fenik, *Tradition*   B. C. Fenik, ed., *Homer: Tradition and Invention* (Leiden 1978)

Foxhall and Davies, *The Trojan War*   L. Foxhall and J. K. Davies, edd., *The Trojan War* (Bristol 1984)

Friedrich, *Verwundung*   W. H. Friedrich, *Verwundung und Tod in der Ilias* (Göttingen 1956)

Frisk   H. Frisk, *Griechisches Etymologisches Wörterbuch* (Heidelberg 1954–73)

Griffin, *HLD*   J. Griffin, *Homer on Life and Death* (Oxford 1980)

Hainsworth, *Flexibility*   J. B. Hainsworth, *The Flexibility of the Homeric Formula* (Oxford 1968)

Hainsworth, *Od.*   Alfred Heubeck, Stephanie West and J. B. Hainsworth, *A Commentary on Homer's Odyssey* vol. 1 (Oxford 1988)

Hesiod, *Erga*   = Hesiod, *Works and Days*

Hoekstra, *Modifications*   A. Hoekstra, *Homeric Modifications of Formulaic Prototypes* (Amsterdam 1965)

HSL   R. Hope Simpson and J. F. Lazenby, *The Catalogue of Ships in Homer's Iliad* (Oxford 1970)

HyDem, HyAp, HyHerm, HyAphr   *Homeric Hymns* to Demeter, Apollo, Hermes, Aphrodite

Janko, *HHH*   Richard Janko, *Homer, Hesiod and the Hymns* (Cambridge 1982)

Kakridis, *Researches*   J. T. Kakridis, *Homeric Researches* (Lund 1949)

Kirk, *Myth*   G. S. Kirk, *Myth: its Meaning and Functions* (Cambridge, Berkeley and Los Angeles 1970)

Kirk, *Songs*   G. S. Kirk, *The Songs of Homer* (Cambridge 1962)

Krischer, *Konventionen*   T. Krischer, *Formale Konventionen der homerischen Epik* (München 1971)

Kullmann, *Quellen*   W. Kullmann, *Die Quellen der Ilias* (Wiesbaden 1960)

Latacz, *Kampfdarstellung*   J. Latacz, *Kampfparänese, Kampfdarstellung und Kampfwirklichkeit in der Ilias, bei Kallinos und Tyrtaios* (München 1977)

Leaf   W. Leaf, *The Iliad* I–II (2nd edn, London 1900–2)

Leumann, *HW*   M. Leumann, *Homerische Wörter* (Basel 1950)

LfgrE   *Lexicon des frühgriechischen Epos*, edd. B. Snell and H. Erbse (Göttingen 1955–)

Lohmann, *Reden*   D. Lohmann, *Die Komposition der Reden in der Ilias* (Berlin 1970)

Lorimer, *HM*   H. L. Lorimer, *Homer and the Monuments* (London 1950)

L–P   E. Lobel and D. L. Page, *Poetarum Lesbiorum Fragmenta* (Oxford 1955)

LSJ   H. Liddell, R. Scott and H. S. Jones, *A Greek–English Lexicon* (9th edn, Oxford 1940)

Macleod, *Iliad XXIV*   C. W. Macleod, *Homer, Iliad Book XXIV* (Cambridge 1982)

Meister, *Kunstsprache*   K. Meister, *Die homerische Kunstsprache* (Leipzig 1921)

Monro, *HG*   D. B. Monro, *A Grammar of the Homeric Dialect* (2nd edn, Oxford 1891)

Moulton, *Similes*   Carroll Moulton, *Similes in the Homeric Poems* (Hypomnemata 49, Göttingen 1977)

M–W   R. Merkelbach and M. L. West, edd., *Fragmenta Hesiodea* (Oxford 1967)

Nilsson, *GgrR*   M. P. Nilsson, *Geschichte der griechischen Religion* I (3rd edn, München 1967)

OCT   Oxford Classical Texts: *Homeri Opera I–V*: I–II (*Iliad*) edd. D. B. Monro and T. W. Allen (3rd edn, Oxford 1920); III–IV (*Odyssey*) ed. T. W. Allen (2nd edn, Oxford 1917–19); V (*Hymns*, etc.) ed. T. W. Allen (Oxford 1912)

Odissea   Omero, *Odissea* (general editor, A. Heubeck; Fondazione Lorenzo Valla, 1981–7); see *Commentary*

Page, *HHI*   D. L. Page, *History and the Homeric Iliad* (Berkeley and Los Angeles 1959)

Parry, *MHV*   A. Parry, ed., *The Making of Homeric Verse*. The Collected Papers of Milman Parry (Oxford 1971)

Reinhardt, *IuD*   K. Reinhardt, *Die Ilias und ihr Dichter*, ed. U. Hölscher (Göttingen 1961)

Risch, *Wortbildung*   E. Risch, *Wortbildung der homerischen Sprache* (2nd edn, Berlin 1973)

Ruijgh, τε *épique*   C. J. Ruijgh, *Autour de 'τε épique': études sur la syntaxe grecque* (Amsterdam 1971)

Schadewaldt, *Aufbau*   W. Schadewaldt, *Der Aufbau der Ilias* (Frankfurt am Main 1975)

Schadewaldt, *Ilias-Studien*   W. Schadewaldt, *Ilias-Studien* (Leipzig 1938)

Schein, *Mortal Hero*   Seth L. Schein, *The Mortal Hero: an Introduction to Homer's Iliad* (Berkeley, Los Angeles and London 1984)

Schmidt, *Weltbild*   Martin Schmidt, *Die Erklärungen zum Weltbild Homers in den bT-Scholien zur Ilias* (München 1976)

Shipp, *Studies*   G. P. Shipp, *Studies in the Language of Homer* (2nd edn, Cambridge 1972)

Shipp, *Vocabulary*   G. P. Shipp, *Modern Greek Evidence for the Ancient Greek Vocabulary* (Sydney 1979)

Stockinger, *Vorzeichen*   H. Stockinger, *Die Vorzeichen im homerischen Epos* (St Ottilien 1959)

Thornton, *Supplication*   Agathe Thornton, *Homer's Iliad: its Composition and the Motif of Supplication* (Göttingen 1984)

Trümpy, *Fachausdrücke*   Hans Trümpy, *Kriegerische Fachausdrücke im griechischen Epos* (Basel 1950)

van der Valk, *Researches*   M. H. A. L. H. van der Valk, *Researches on the Text and Scholia of the Iliad* I–II (Leiden 1963–4)

Ventris and Chadwick, *Documents*   M. Ventris and J. Chadwick, *Documents in Mycenaean Greek* (2nd edn, Cambridge 1973)

Vermeule, *GBA*   Emily Vermeule, *Greece in the Bronze Age* (Chicago and London 1972)

Vernant, *Problèmes de la guerre*   J.-P. Vernant, ed., *Problèmes de la guerre en Grèce ancienne* (Paris, Mouton, 1968)

von Kamptz, *Personennamen*   Hans von Kamptz, *Homerische Personennamen* (Göttingen 1982)

Von der Mühll, *Hypomnema*   P. Von der Mühll, *Kritisches Hypomnema zur Ilias* (Basel 1952)

Wace and Stubbings, *Companion*   A. J. B. Wace and F. H. Stubbings, *A Companion to Homer* (London 1962)

West, *Od.*   Alfred Heubeck, Stephanie West and J. B. Hainsworth, *A Commentary on Homer's Odyssey* vol. I (Oxford 1988)

West, *Ptolemaic Papyri*   S. West, *The Ptolemaic Papyri of Homer* (Köln and Opladen 1967)

West, *Theogony*   M. L. West, *Hesiod, Theogony* (Oxford 1966)

West, *Works and Days*   M. L. West, *Hesiod, Works and Days* (Oxford 1978)

Wilamowitz, *IuH*   U. von Wilamowitz-Moellendorf, *Die Ilias und Homer* (Berlin 1916)

Abbreviations

Wilamowitz, *Untersuchungen*   U. von Wilamowitz-Moellendorff, *Homerische Untersuchungen* (Berlin 1884)

Willcock   M. M. Willcock, *The Iliad of Homer, Books I–XII* (London 1978)

Willcock, *Companion*   M. M. Willcock, *A Companion to the Iliad* (Chicago and London 1976)

Journals

AJP	*American Journal of Philology*
BSA	*Annual of the British School of Archaeology at Athens*
CQ	*Classical Quarterly*
JHS	*Journal of Hellenic Studies*
PCPS	*Proceedings of the Cambridge Philological Society*
TAPA	*Transactions and Proceedings of the American Philological Association*
YCS	*Yale Classical Studies*

NOTE

'*Il.*' means 'the *Iliad*', '*Od.*' 'the *Odyssey*'.

The numbers of occurrences of words and formulas (in the form e.g. '10× *Il.*, 6× *Od.*') are provided for ostensive purposes only, see vol. 1, xxiii. The abbreviation '(etc.)' after a Greek word in such a reference indicates that the total is given of all relevant terminations; '*sic*' in such circumstances means 'in that position in the verse'; '2/11×' means 'twice out of a total of eleven occurrences in all'. In any case, the 'Ibycus' computer and compact disc offer new standards of word-count accuracy to which the 'ostensive' figures just mentioned do not, and perhaps need not, aspire.

| is used to mark the beginning, or the end, of a verse; occasionally, too, the central caesura. 'v.', 'vv.' means 'verse', 'verses', with 'v-e' meaning 'verse-end'.

On 'Arn/bT' (etc.) references see vol. 1, 41f. Σ signifies 'scholium' or 'scholiast'.

INTRODUCTION

1. The Homeric gods: prior considerations

This initial chapter is concerned with the religious background of the *Iliad*: with the ways in which the Olympian pantheon might have developed, and with what aspects of it might be due to Homer himself or the oral heroic tradition on which he drew; with the degree of artificiality and poetic elaboration or suppression consequently to be expected, and the possible awareness of that among his audiences; and especially with the assumptions that might underlie the connexions between men and gods through sacrifice and prayer. The conclusions that can reasonably be drawn are often speculative, and will need to be modified as research on contacts with the Near East, in particular, proceeds; but they are important none the less, affecting as they do the literary and aesthetic impressions made on audiences by divine scenes and episodes in the epic – for example over how far they might be understood as predominantly conventional, and therefore diminished in serious emotional impact. Clearly there are other things to be said, and in greater detail, about the divine characters of the *Iliad*, the individual gods and goddesses as actors and the rôles they play. These will be discussed as they arise in the different commentaries, as also by R. Janko in the introduction to vol. IV. Here, on the other hand, the emphasis is primarily historical and theological.

It is plain, in any event, that our own particular understanding of the nature of Homeric gods greatly affects the ways in which we respond to the *Iliad* as a whole, just as ancient audiences were affected by their own more contemporary reactions. There is no standard and accepted opinion about these matters, and the early stages of Greek religion still lie in darkness, a prey to modern intuition and, occasionally, self-indulgence. Thus, on the one hand, Gilbert Murray's *Five Stages of Greek Religion* of 1925 envisaged the Olympians as the creation of swashbuckling Achaeans, men like the 'real' prototypes of Agamemnon or Akhilleus and possessing their baronial virtues and vices; they were organized as a family and at the same time made more *risqué* and frivolous by Ionians like Homer, before being accommodated to civilized values in Athens and made into 'an emblem of high humanity and religious reform'. Even J. M. Redfield sees them, in a quite different way, as 'literary gods'. Other writers, on the other hand, have inclined to take these gods more seriously, as symbols of permanence against which human ephemerality can be better understood (J. Griffin) or elements in a complex construction for confronting the world at large and keeping disorder at bay (J. P. Gould).[1] Many problems remain, some to be seen with particular clarity when plausible-sounding judgements about ancient religious topics, especially those based on comparative evidence, are subjected to close scrutiny.

Part of the trouble has arisen from a tendency to use one of the earliest pieces of ancient evidence quite uncritically and to prove a variety of inconsistent points. Herodotus' declaration at 2.53 that 'it was Hesiod and Homer that created a theogony for the Greeks and assigned the gods their names and divided out their honours and skills and indicated their appearances' was a not very profound remark based on the survival of Hesiod's *Theogony* and *Works and Days* to describe the earlier phases, and Homer's *Iliad* and *Odyssey* to describe the more recent actions, of the gods, with nothing known from any prior source beyond, perhaps, speculations like that accepted by Herodotus himself that these gods came ultimately from Egypt. His opinion on the operations of Homer and Hesiod is chiefly of interest for the period he placed them in ('not more than 400 years before my time', cf. vol. I, 3f.) and for what it reveals about his own sources and methods of argument. It is worth little in other respects, reflecting a naive view of the situation which probably assigns far too much originality to both the Hesiodic and the Homeric sides of the tradition.

The basic facts are these: that there are *no* Egyptian elements in the Greek divinities of the pre-Classical period; that Zeus, as his name (a form of Sanskrit Dyaus) and his functions as sky- and weather-god show, is an Indo-European import from the north-eastern regions from which the Greek-speaking peoples moved down into Greece about 2000 B.C.; and that the rest of the pantheon consists on the one hand of specific Asiatic adaptations (Aphrodite, Hephaistos, Artemis, probably Apollo) and on the other of local versions of broadly diffused Near Eastern functional archetypes as city-protector, mother-goddess, war-god and so on. That is putting the matter very dogmatically, and further detail will be added later; but these Asiatic and Indo-European associations, together with the later addition of Thracian Ares and Phrygian/Lydian Dionusos, and, more important, the idea of a council of gods under a supreme leader, itself Mesopotamian in origin, show the process of conflation and development to have been a long one, initiated no later than the 2nd millennium B.C. and

---

[1] J. M. Redfield, *Nature and Culture in the Iliad* (Chicago 1975) 76; J. Griffin, *Homer on Life and Death* (Oxford 1980) chs. 5 and 6; J. P. Gould in P. E. Easterling and J. V. Muir, edd., *Greek Religion and Society* (Cambridge 1985) ch. 1.

carried on in largely unreconstructable ways thereafter. The development of heroic poetry and the arrival on the scene of Homer and Hesiod around 750–700 B.C. clearly led the way to increased systematization and personal detail, but scarcely to a radical formulation or reformulation of divine powers as such. Other factors, like the emergence of the names of Zeus, Here, Poseidon, Artemis and a form of Athene (as well as Paian and Enualios) from the Linear B tablets, and the fixed formular status of divine epithets in Homer,[2] demonstrating the widespread acceptance of divine functions and titles at least for the three or four generations necessary for the development of such formular systems, show that Homer must have come at a relatively late stage in the formation of Olympian theology. The same can be said of Hesiod, whose attention to snakes and monsters, to chthonic powers in general which the Homeric tradition preferred to ignore, is unlikely to be due to *recent* contact with the Near East (as part of the Orientalizing movement of the late eighth and seventh centuries B.C., that is) but depends rather on material inherited somehow from Mycenaean times. Some scholars do not agree, for reasons well stated in Oswyn Murray's *Early Greece* (Fontana Paperbacks 1980) 88f.; but references to Kronos imprisoned below the earth in *Iliad* bks 8 and 14 show the Homeric tradition to have been aware of the Succession-myth describing the violent displacement of the first generation of gods, a myth which is closely parallel to the Hurrian–Hittite tale of Kumarbi from the later second millennium B.C. and must have been known in Greece long before 700.

Some of the first generations of gods in those ancient tales are actual embodiments of important world-constituents. Thus Hurrian and Babylonian Anu and Greek Ouranos are the sky, with the 'weather-god' and Zeus as more refined meteorological powers. Such functions are not often emphasized in the Homeric pantheon. Poseidon is closely associated with the sea and perhaps lies behind the Trojan Horse as god of earthquakes, but even Zeus, though he still on occasion deploys the thunderbolt, has lost much of his cosmological force – or rather it has been converted into force of a different kind, authority, that is, over his fellow-gods and mankind. Something similar has happened with other divine functions that are likely to have been of high antiquity and maintained by local cults. Thus Here's rôle as goddess of Argos is equivocal in the *Iliad* in that she is willing to see Mycenae with Argos and Sparta destroyed later, if only Troy can fall now (*Il.* 4.51ff.) – that means that the Judgement of Paris, a developed mythical fantasy with strong folktale characteristics, weighs more heavily upon her, in the minds of these poets, than her traditional cult-status as great goddess

---

[2] Like Παλλάς, 'Αγελείη, 'Αλαλκομενηΐς, Φοῖβος, ἑκαεργός, ἀκερσεκομής, μητίετα, νεφεληγερέτα, αἰγιοχοῖο, βοῶπις, ἐριούνιος, διάκτορος, φιλομμειδής, ἰοχέαιρα, ἐνοσίχθων, ἐννοσίγαιος, γαιήοχος, ἀμφιγυήεις.

of the Argive Heraion. Athene's functional rôle in the poem is rather as war-goddess than as city-protectress, in so far as these can be separated, with her almost contradictory sponsorship of household crafts receiving an occasional mention. Hephaistos performs his function of bronze-smith from time to time but is equally important as a peace-maker among the gods, who on a famous occasion usurps the rôle of Hebe or Ganymede and pours the nectar (*Il.* 1.584ff.). Aphrodite, apart from her rôle as Aineias' mother and protector of her favourite Paris, is largely confined to her basic sphere of love, just as Ares is of war, although both take on broader personalities in their involvement with Diomedes in bk 5 (as well as with each other and Hephaistos in Phemios' song of divine adultery in *Odyssey* bk 8). Hermes is the persistent messenger and escort, though the former function is largely filled by Iris in the *Iliad*. Artemis is sometimes goddess of hunting, but Apollo's connexion with prophecy and healing is only occasionally implied, and he operates more fully as defender of the Trojans and their allies.

As for the rest, they are scarcely mentioned, and the conclusion remains that for the most part these Olympian gods and goddesses behave, under Zeus, as individuals transcending by far the special rôles, functions and local associations that actual cult and tradition might have imposed on them. Admittedly, if more were known about the cults of these deities before Homer, their functions might often appear less specific than they became later, in the Archaic and Classical periods for example; for if every settlement inclined to have its own particular deity, it would be quixotic to expect him or her to confine their interests to metallurgy, medicine or hunting, for instance. Even so, the epic tradition might reasonably be suspected of viewing them not so much through cultic rôles but rather as archetypes of social and sexual relations seen largely in human terms (so e.g. B. C. Dietrich, *Tradition in Greek Religion*, Berlin 1986, 120).

Because of these often quite sophisticated social rôles, most modern critics seem happy to credit most of the idea of the Olympian family to Homer, and to see that as his basic contribution to the development of Greek religion. Yet the Asiatic origins of the concept are virtually undeniable.[3] The Sumerian gods were envisaged in just such a way – as the Igigi, living together on a divine mountain, related to each other under the kingship of Enlil (or Marduk in the derivative Babylonian pantheon), controlling the destinies of men on earth, receiving sacrifices from them. This last characteristic is important, because it is through animal sacrifice that we most clearly discern the pre-Homeric status of the gods conceived as a group. For the Homeric poems reveal sporadic traces of a complicated set of tales about an epoch, preceding that of the Homeric heroes, when men

---

[3] Cf. in general *ANET*; Kirk, *Myth* chs. 3 and 4; H. Ringgren, *Religions of the Near East* (London 1973); Burkert, *Religion* ch. 3.

and gods feasted together, at least on special occasions. More specifically, the gods are occasionally envisaged as absenting themselves from Mt Olumpos, either individually or *en masse*, to go and share in hecatombs – a feast at which many roast oxen were served, that implies – with the Aithiopes (in the *Iliad*) or the Phaeacians (in the *Odyssey*). Those mythical peoples, together, surprisingly enough, with the Cyclopes and the Giants, were part-divine, descended from the gods in some sense, and they, at least, maintained the habit of common dining, of commensality, which had ended so far as ordinary mortals were concerned not all that long before the heroic era described by Homer. Hesiod in the *Theogony* (535ff.) relates the tale of how an agreement was reached at Mekone between Zeus on behalf of the gods and Prometheus on behalf of men about the division of meat which men and gods had until then shared in common. The two races are now to be separated, with gods receiving a share through the act of sacrifice – Prometheus' attempt to fob them off with the inedible portions, mainly the bones, was successful, or equivocally so, since Zeus (according to Hesiod's final version) was aware of what was happening. Presumably he condoned the deceit only because the gods, in a way, no longer had need of the edible portions.

That is interpretation, and Hesiod does not even suggest it; yet it accords with the Homeric purging of some aspects of sacrifice and divine carnality which will be discussed shortly. Exactly why the two sides broke off relations, at least in their communal contacts (for protection of a favourite, as of Odysseus by Athene, can obviously still continue), is uncertain; that forms part of another defective myth, of the Golden Age and the 'reign of Kronos'. He ruled over the golden race of men according to *Works and Days* 109ff.; they were eventually hidden by the earth somehow, but made by Zeus into benevolent daimons over the earth. Kronos was deposed in the wars between generations among the early gods; Zeus managed to escape being swallowed by him as a baby, and so despatched him to Tartaros with the other Titans. Signs of this (as already noted) are present in Homer, but it is alien to his main heroic theme, and it was Hesiod who in his *Theogony* attempted to tie the various tales together into a more or less coherent whole.

The importance of these matters is that there was a quite ancient assortment of tales, on which Homer occasionally drew, about the gods as a group mingling in certain ways with the ancestors of the Homeric heroes. It may or may not be legitimate to conclude with W. Burkert (*Religion* 46) that the Mycenaean tablets reveal 'at least the beginnings of a mythical family of the gods', but the Homeric epics of themselves demonstrate that the idea is not a Homeric invention. The history of divine relations with men is a long and complex one, going back at least several generations (and

5

in view of Mesopotamian parallels probably a very long time indeed) in the oral heroic tradition and the popular sources on which it drew. Even the relation of Phaeacians and Giants is worked out in a way, for at *Od.* 7.54–68 the disguised Athene tells Odysseus how Eurumedon, king of the Giants, was father of Periboie, who gave birth to Nausithoos, king of the Phaeacians, after mating with Poseidon. These Phaeacians are ἀγχίθεοι, close to the gods, who come down and feast with them when they sacrifice hecatombs, or so Alkinoos claims at *Od.* 7.201–6. This is not *ad hoc* invention – the interconnexions between these exotic and half-divine survivors (who live, like the Cyclopes and the twin groups of Aithiopes, at the ends of the earth and out of touch with ordinary mortals) are too complex, too consistent and too casually revealed for that.

Near Eastern influence is obviously a crucial factor. Exactly how, when and to what degree it was exercised on the formation of specifically Greek religious ideas is unknown; clearly Ugarit and Cyprus were important points of contact in the later Bronze Age. But it is most plainly perceived in the case of individual deities. Zeus is shown by his name to be Indo-European, but his functions have significant parallels, too, with those of Babylonian Marduk. Aphrodite is pure Sumerian/Akkadian in type and origin, she is Inanna and Ishtar, Canaanite Anath, the love-goddess, down-graded by the Greeks from her aspect of 'queen of heaven'. Artemis is west-Asiatic, a version of the mother-goddess type; Asiatic also is her mother Leto and her brother (in the developed Greek pantheon at least) Apollo – whose epithet Lukeios is more plausibly connected with Lycia in S–W Asia Minor than with wolves, and whose northern, Hyperborean associations seem to be secondary. Hephaistos is another familiar west-Asiatic representative, the smith-god and divine armourer, localized in lightly-Hellenized Lemnos just off the Asiatic coast. Hades and his consort Persephone have much in common with the Sumerian ruler of the underworld, Queen Ereshkigal – of course the change of sexes and the promotion of Hades to be brother of Zeus himself are important too. Only Here, Athene, Poseidon, Hermes and Demeter (who has few heroic connexions) have strong claims to be predominantly Hellenic in origin and development, or at least to be deep-rooted local versions of common Near Eastern archetypes.

I have drastically simplified, even now, this question of the Asiatic components of the Greek gods; but Mesopotamian influence extends beyond individual types to general themes and ideas about the structure of the world in religious terms, and they are probably even more significant. The idea of a 'golden age' is curiously ambiguous and patchy among the Greeks, and that probably arises from the conflation of Mesopotamian and, in this one case, Egyptian elements. The divine family is an easy product of a group of gods and goddesses belonging to different generations, a Sumerian belief from at least the third millennium B.C. The triumph of the youngest of the gods in a crisis is another motif that connects Zeus and Marduk, though it may also have broader folktale affiliations. The 'lowering of kingship from heaven' is a key Mesopotamian notion which ultimately lies behind the erratically developed Homeric idea of god-reared kings, symbolized by Agamemnon's ancestral sceptre descended from Zeus himself at *Il.* 2.100ff. The realm of the underworld is curiously similar even apart from its rulers – the seven gates of Mesopotamian myths have no exact Greek parallel, but the river of the dead and the infernal ferryman are common to both. The idea of *moira* or destiny as a divine instrument is difficult and confused in many Greek contexts, but is a plausible development of the concrete *me*'s or divine ordinances of the Mesopotamian gods. Olumpos itself is a non-Greek name applied to several peaks in western Asia as well as to the Thessalian mountain that became home of the gods for the Greeks; the Ugaritic divine assembly, too, took place on the 'northern mountain' according to texts of the later second millennium B.C.

The study of the ways in which Greek-speakers adapted some of these common ideas and themes to their own special needs and emphases is one of the most exciting and difficult challenges for the modern student of Greek religion. Many of the blank areas of the mythical map respond to this kind of approach. The myth of the great flood is a concrete example, since it is clear that this is a Mesopotamian idea in origin, one that lacks reality when transposed to largely unfloodable Greece and therefore loses its centrality in the tale of the relations between men and gods. Ambiguities over the Golden Age (what caused its termination? and who had enjoyed it, men in general or just favourites or descendants of the gods?) are similarly caused: in fact there is one particular area in which Mesopotamian themes had to be drastically curtailed or adjusted – precisely, that is, over the relations between men and gods. It was here that the Greeks most radically rethought this Mesopotamian inheritance; for the Mesopotamian gods had created men to be their slaves, to bake their bread and clean out their temples. The 'black-headed ones' were tolerated for just so long as they performed these functions efficiently; if they became noisy or too numerous, a portion of them would be wiped out by the attack of some divinity. Relics of this theme of insubordination and over-population can be seen in the Greek context (specifically in the *Cypria*'s interpretation of 'the plan of Zeus', *Il.* 1.5n.), but generally speaking the Greeks utterly rejected this view of men as slaves of the gods, at least until the rise of Orphism in post-Homeric times. Men had once banqueted with the gods on special occasions like the wedding of Peleus and Thetis, there was no total separation then, and it was for some disputed reason, probably involving bloodshed, that the two had finally separated. But the gods were still seen as concerned over men – indifferent at times, as the epic shows, but ultimately viewing them as very far from slaves and chattels.

Because of this radically different viewpoint many of the Mesopotamian mythical and religious themes had to be bowdlerized or suppressed. The House of Hades is a less destructive and dismal place than the Mesopotamian House of Dust, in which the dead are clad with feathers and feed on dust and can be hung on hooks in front of Queen Ereshkigal; the infernal judges Minos and Rhadamanthus imply a distinct set of values here. We could hardly imagine the Homeric gods agreeing to make a concerted attack on mankind, and not only because of their difficulty in reaching unanimous decisions – even the Mesopotamian gods eventually unite against the murderous Erra and in defence of men, but only because that is where their interest now lies. Most important of all in this context is the Greek ambivalence over the creation of mankind itself. There are specific and graphic Mesopotamian myths on this topic, but the Greeks talked vaguely of Deukalion and Prometheus and concentrated on the safer topic of the creation of women. That is probably because a united divine resolve to create men would lead directly to that unpalatable theme of men designed to be slaves of the gods.

All that adjustment of age-old and widely diffused versions of divine organization and behaviour clearly happened long before the final composition of the *Iliad* – much of it, one might guess, before a poetical tradition had developed at all in any recognizable form. Homer's gods have already lost most of their Asiatic colouring, and in most respects have also lost the contradictions arising from the process of cross-cultural assimilation. That stage in their formation is definitely pre-Homeric.

The *post*-Homeric state of affairs, by contrast, is predictably much clearer. Now the gods of the Greek world are firmly established in temples, they are brought down as far as they can be to earth and anchored again in specific localities – not necessarily within the cities themselves but close to them, where the ancient cult-spots have become enormous sanctuaries like those of Here near Argos and Samos, and of Huakinthos-Apollo a few miles out of Sparta. Homer's Olumpos-based gods, only occasionally associated with specific temples or *temene*, must have seemed very different to his audiences from the gods and goddesses they were already worshipping in their new temples, some of them quite substantial ones; of course the gods were not always present there, but their more or less continuous concourse on Olumpos must already have seemed a slightly artificial idea. The tradition of temple-worship doubtless goes back a long way, but the singers of the epic tradition had turned attention away from it because it did not fulfil their requirements for dramatic, united and unlocalized divine participation.

Other aspects of cult and belief survived the implied diversion of the epic tradition. First, the rituals concerned with agrarian fertility which lay at the heart of some of the organized festivals of the developed *polis* – in Athens the Puanepsia, Anthesteria and Thargelia or, for a more restricted public, the Thesmophoria or Eleusinia. Second, these great religious festivals themselves, whether based on fertility, initiation or the celebration of a particular deity. A Homeric precedent is seen in the gathering of male citizens on the sea-shore of Pulos to make special sacrifices for Poseidon in *Odyssey* bk 3, or in the procession of women to entreat Athene in her temple in Troy in *Iliad* bk 6; but generally speaking these public acts of worship are not, for obvious reasons, a typical epic theme. Third, the cult of the dead, either by offerings soon after death or in the worship of powerful ancestors, is borne out by the cemeteries as well as by literary references from the Archaic age on. This merges with the cult of heroes to which the epics themselves seem to have given an impetus. Lastly, the important household cults of Hestia, the hearth, of Zeus in his aspects of Meilikhios and Herkeios, protector of the store-room and courtyard, of Hermes and Apollo Aguieus, guardians of fertility and property; with these one can join the countryman's worship of nymphs and spirits of mountain, spring, river and forest, though these do find some mention in the *Odyssey*.

These are certainly not post-Homeric *in origin*. Widespread temple-cults, regular veneration of the dead, rituals of fertility and public festivals are firmly established in the Archaic age, and it would be extraordinary if the extremes of public and private worship were not widely known before, as well as after, the acme of the Homeric tradition. The conclusion is therefore inevitable that Homer and the epic tradition suppressed *a great deal* about the ordinary religious practices of their day. That may not be found very surprising: in many respects it reflects the nature of the epic subject-matter itself; but once again the *Odyssey*, with its developed peacetime scenes both of palace and of countryside, provided an opportunity that was broadly rejected.

One act of worship which, as we saw, was definitely not suppressed is the act of animal sacrifice. The process itself is described in typical scenes and seems more or less automatic (although sometimes abbreviated) so far as the human participants are concerned – but is the reaction of the recipients, the gods, so straightforward? The life of these dwellers on Mt Olumpos is modelled on that of a prosperous and artificially extended family: the generations have been concertina'ed, there are too few grandparents and too many half-sisters, but it is all very human. They have their own party-

9

nights at which Apollo plays the lyre and the Muses provide vocal backing (*Il.* 1.601–4), and at which they eat – what? One of the most remarkable and least emphasized paradoxes of 'Homeric religion' is that these transcendent creatures are implied on several occasions to depend on mortals for one thing only, the coarse hunger-allaying smell and smoke of burning suet, spiralling to heaven from the fat-encased thigh-bones roasted in preliminary ritual down below. That is never stated in completely direct terms, but Zeus favours Hektor, for example, because he never fails in such offerings. We might expect them to eat great, god-sized steaks at their own banquets, but of course what they actually consume is ambrosia, 'immortal food' never further specified than that, washed down not with wine but with nectar. And yet that was not always so; it was not so long since the age of commensality and the marriage of Thetis and Peleus – no mention there of separate diets like those of Odysseus and Kalupso at *Od.* 5.196–9! Indeed the Hesiodic tale of the division at Mekone showed that until the end of that golden age of commensality gods and men had eaten, on special occasions at least, the same food: the best cuts, that is, of oxen. That idea is firmly passed over by Homer; his references to ambrosia and nectar are (as will be seen) surprisingly infrequent, but whenever the gods are glimpsed dining on Olumpos that is presumably what they have.

Homer, then, spares his audience any suggestion of meat-savour-sniffing in the golden halls of Olumpos, just as he keeps clear of any signs of drunkenness among the gods – only Dionusos gets drunk, and then not in Homer and not in heaven. In short, there has been a significant degree of what I have elsewhere called de-carnalization of these Olympians in the course of the epic tradition, not least, one might conjecture, by Homer, the monumental composer, himself. That this was not simply a revival of vegetarian cults in the Late Bronze Age (when 'tables of offerings' for grain, honey, oil and wine are far commoner than outdoor altars for burnt sacrifices) is shown by the almost total neglect in the poems of non-animal offerings, apart from occasional libations of wine.

It is important to look more closely for a moment at the Homeric mentions of divine diet. There are four places in the epic where the gods are specifically said to feast on hecatombs. The simplest is *Il.* 9.535, where 'the other gods fed on hecatombs' – but (as Griffin notes, *HLD* 187 n. 22) this lay in the past, in the tale of the Calydonian boar and its aftermath. Two of the other instances show the gods as sharing in a hecatomb-feast with the Aithiopes: *Il.* 23.205–7 and *Od.* 1.25f., to which *Il.* 1.423f. can in effect be added. The first of these is especially explicit: Iris (hardly the most material of these deities) says she is going to the Aithiopes 'where they are sacrificing hecatombs to the immortals, that I too may feast on a share of the sacred offerings'. The fourth case is *Od.* 7.201–3, where king Alkinoos declares that always up to now the gods have appeared plainly to the Phaeacians when they are sacrificing glorious hecatombs, and dined by their side, sitting where they do. Now it is surely no accident that none of these passages is about the gods feasting *on Olumpos*. So far as those feasts are concerned the closest we get to their absorbing sacrifices is when at *Il.* 2.420 Zeus 'received' the sacrifices, δέκτο being a very vague term. That the burning of fat on altars is the gods' entitlement is beyond doubt (cf. *Il.* 4.48f. = 24.69f.); it is plainly stated at *Il.* 1.315–17 that the savour of sacrifices to Apollo rises to the sky: 'and they performed perfect hecatombs for Apollo of bulls and goats beside the shore of the unharvested sea, and the savour reached the sky, whirling round with the smoke'. What is *not* said is that the god sniffed or even relished the savour, let alone that his hunger was allayed by it. In short, all the detail is lavished on the human end of sacrifice, the burning of fat-encased thigh-bones on the altars down below. What might have been the one exception is of the kind that proves the rule, for at the end of bk 8 of the *Iliad* the Trojans are camped in the plain and oxen are brought out from the city to be roasted for their meal. There is no specific mention of sacrifice, but at 549 'the winds carried the savour from the plain to within the sky' – and at this point the pseudo-Platonic author of the second *Alcibiades* (149D) quoted three more verses which no medieval manuscript knew of and Aristarchus evidently proscribed. The first two are as follows: '– the sweet savour, but the blessed gods did not feed on it, were unwilling to, since holy Ilios was very hateful to them'. If these gods had *not* hated Troy (and that is one reason for doubting this addition, since only some of them were of that mind), they would have fed on the savour ascending from the roasting oxen; that is the undeniable implication. It may be that this kind of phraseology was around in the oral tradition, and that our rhapsode or other elaborator drew on it for his unsuccessful supplement; but it was in any case the kind of language that Homer himself evidently preferred to avoid, in his attempt (as I suggest) to reduce the cruder features of these gods and, not least, their diet.

What, then, about the other side of the meat-eating picture, that is, ambrosia and nectar as the regular intake on Mt Olumpos? There is another surprise here, for a closer look at the text of the *Iliad* and *Odyssey* reveals that references to these substances are much rarer than one might think. Ambrosia is really an adjective in origin, describing anything immortal, and is also the name of a kind of divine ointment. It is used of divine food only six times in the *Iliad*, four in the *Odyssey* – but is never described as being consumed on Olumpos, and that is interesting. It is served by Kalupso to Hermes at *Od.* 5.93 and later eaten by her while

Odysseus has mortal food (5.199); otherwise it is only mentioned in that poem as brought by doves through the Clashing Rocks for Zeus, or with nectar as imagined source of the wine Poluphemos so much admired. In the *Iliad* the case is even worse: ambrosia is produced three times as food for divine *horses*, and the other three it is dripped, with nectar, into mortal Akhilleus by Athene to give him magical sustenance. It is nectar that saves the day, in a sense, since of its five Iliadic mentions the other two, at least, show it as being drunk by the gods on Olumpos (at 1.598 and 4.3); in the *Odyssey* its three appearances are when Kalupso serves it to Hermes, then herself, and then the Poluphemos exaggeration.

Add to all this that κνίση, the savour of sacrificial meat, is used only twice in Homer with incontrovertible reference to savour moving skyward for the gods (and even then, as we saw, there is no authentic description of their ingesting it); elsewhere it signifies either the fat itself or its savour as smelled by men. Formulas for this range of ideas are confined to τέμενος βωμός τε θυήεις, 'sacred enclosure and reeking altar', and to the altar which 'has never lacked a generous feast, libation and κνίση, which is our divine prerogative'. All this suggests that the idea of savour rising from sacrifices was traditional, but that its being smelled by the gods on high was not much emphasized by Homer at least, and that there may indeed have been a degree of suppression over that aspect. Then the idea of ambrosia and nectar was introduced, relatively late in the oral poetical tradition judging by frequency and formular status, and even then with little stress on their use on Olumpos itself. Still further developments were the idea of gods not having blood in their veins (too meat-like), but rather a special fluid called ἰχώρ, which is mentioned only when Aphrodite and Ares are wounded by Diomedes in bk 5 of the *Iliad*; and, later than Homer, the introduction of incense as a means of making the burning fat smell sweeter. At all costs the vision had to be avoided of anything resembling that gruesome Mesopotamian scene in the eleventh tablet of the Epic of Gilgamesh in which when sacrifices are restored the hungry gods smell the sweet savour and crowd round the sacrificer like flies.[4]

It may be possible to place this Homeric purification of the gods in a broader perspective. Karl Meuli showed (with certain exaggerations) that assigning part of the slain animal to the gods probably goes back to Palaeolithic hunting customs (*Phyllobolia für P. Von der Mühll*, Basel 1946, 185ff.). It is in the main a symbolic act, not necessarily evoking a keen image of what this implied for the gods themselves. M. L. West was following this view when he wrote (*Theogony* 306) that sacrifice 'may from

---

[4] *ANET* 94f.; see further Kirk in *Le Sacrifice dans l'antiquité, Entretiens Hardt* xxvii (Vandœuvres–Genèves 1981) 75ff. and esp. 77–80.

the start have involved commending the remains to the care of a god... It was only later, when the god was held to come and feast with the men... or when the smoke and vapour was held to carry the god's share of the meal up to him in heaven, that a sense of the unfairness of the apportionment developed and gave rise to the Prometheus myth.' These stages can now perhaps be provisionally fitted into a more detailed historical picture. Thus 'commending the remains to the care of a god' continued into the Neolithic period, and relics of the idea persisted into the 'comedy of innocence' of age-old rituals like the Bouphonia at Athens, in which the sacrificer sought to evade guilt for the slaughter of the animal. Yet this approach was overlaid by the post-Neolithic Mesopotamian idea of the gods as a group feeding on the smoke of sacrifice. That can only have reached Greece in the Late Bronze Age, when outdoor fire-altars begin to be found; of course animals had been sacrificed before that, for example for a particular deity within his or her shrine, but not necessarily burnt, in whole or part, so as to feed gods in the sky. Then the special Greek idea of gods descending to feast with men, associated with the concept of a Golden Age, was developed, to be replaced in its turn by the Homeric view of the Olympians feeding on ambrosia and nectar and reducing the whole 'shared ox' to a mere token of honour and entitlement.

If the epic tradition progressively removed the most carnal aspects of the Olympian gods and goddesses – leaving certain physical activities, sex in particular, conveniently vague in accord with evidently long-standing public taste – and if, in addition, it greatly played down and removed to the background not only fertility-based cults but also public religious festivals, temple-based worship and most of domestic religion, then the resulting 'Homeric' religion has little claim to resemble 'real' cult and belief. And yet, to regard it more positively, the poetic tradition may have contributed a good deal more to the assimilation of the Homeric gods than the sublimation of sacrifice – by diminishing their frightening competitiveness as city-gods, by reducing attention to the more horrific sides of the underworld, by concentrating on the gods-in-conclave motif represented by the Igigi and the Anunnaki, and above all by highlighting Zeus as paterfamilias rather than as thunderbolt-wielder. Possibly by changes in these directions, more certainly by progressive sleight of hand over the divine acceptance of sacrifice, Homer and his poetical predecessors presented their contemporaries with a view of the gods which, artificial and literary as it may have been in certain respects, was neither impossibly archaic nor incapable of further development. Polytheism was presented in its most benign form, with Zeus providing a principle of order – even, for those who consider this an advantage (and the Greeks in their way surely did) a monotheistic nucleus. This is a consideration that needs to be kept firmly in mind as we respond to some of the more human and less elevated rôles and reactions of the gods and goddesses of the *Iliad*.[5]

[5] Cf. J. P. Gould, in P. E. Easterling and J. V. Muir, edd., *Greek Religion and Society* (Cambridge 1985): 'The Homeric image of divinity is an image of marvellous and compelling adequacy... We would be quite wrong... to set aside the model of divinity that we find in the Homeric poems and imagine it as a purely literary fiction and no part of the "sense" of Greek religion.'

2. Typical motifs and themes

The second chapter of volume I was devoted to a summary consideration of the structural elements of Homeric verse – that is, the composition of whole verses from phrases, often standard or formular, that filled the regular colon-slots; together with the formation of longer sentences from distinct verses through various kinds of cumulation and enjambment. Much of the style and language of Homer at the microscopic level clearly depends on an oral repertory of standard but easily varied phrases, whole verses and short passages welded together so as to produce the subtle variety and rich texture of the poems, in which the traditional and the expected are held in tension with the innovative and the individual.

In a sense that is simply an extension, with a strong degree of formalization, of what any composer does with a vocabulary of single words. Oral poetry depends on the practised ability to deploy preformed elements of language and meaning in larger units than those of ordinary utterance or written literature. But this kind of composition also makes use of other standard components on a broader scale: of typical actions and ideas that are used and reused in different combinations and contexts. These may vary in extent from minor and specific motifs, as of a warrior stripping armour from his victim, to major and more generalized themes, as of a prince refusing to fight because of an insult to his honour. Between the two, and often easier to identify, is the 'typical scene' examined in Arend's pioneering study of 1933, in which recurrent actions of everyday or heroic life are described again and again in standard language that can be abbreviated or elaborated where necessary: for example scenes of arrival or departure by land or sea, of meeting, of preparing a meal or a sacrifice.[6]

The use of typical motifs and themes, and to a lesser degree of typical scenes, is extensive in the Homeric epos, as much a part of the singer's essential technique as his use of typical phrases, half-verses or verses in the sentence. It is functionally necessary for the formation and maintenance of a long and complex oral narrative (as is clearly stated, for example, by Krischer, *Konventionen* 9–11). The combination and variation of traditional motifs and thematic material, together with their elaboration by special detail, results in a richness of plot, speech and action that greatly exceeds the expected limits of the traditional and the conventional as such.

[6] These are further examined by M. W. Edwards in ch. 2 of vol. v, where he also carries further the investigation into 'composition by theme'.

The whole *Iliad*, for example, can be analysed in terms of its basic and typical themes and their variants, and shown to be less complicated and unwieldy in structure than first appears. That underlying thematic simplicity, overlaid as it might be by apparent complexity of detail (not least in personnel) and a masterly use of surface variation, and in which the wrath-theme is paramount, will be fully considered by N. J. Richardson in an introductory chapter to vol. vi. Meanwhile the present discussion initiates a progressive examination of typical motifs to which every successive volume will have something to add. It does so mainly by considering in a preliminary way, first the presence of typical elements in the opening 200 verses of bk 5 and, by contrast, a famous speech in bk 6, then the operation of typical patterns in battle-poetry, the characteristic mode of Iliadic action. It is in this last sphere that the use of typical elements is most prominent and has been most fully demonstrated.[7]

In one sense a concentration on battle-scenes for the study of the typical in Homer is misleading, much like the assumption that noun–epithet groups are representative of formularity; these are both exceptional *loci* for the standard, the conventional and the heavily traditional. Yet what is true of fighting and of the epithets of people and things can be seen to apply in a lesser degree to other subjects and contexts also, and demonstration is certainly simplest in their case.

The first 200 verses of the fifth Book, concerned mainly with fighting of an unexceptional kind, provide a reasonable introductory sample. In Table A typical components of each verse or short passage are summarily noted (in what might otherwise appear to be mere paraphrases), being further explained, for the most part, in the commentary:

Table A *Typical themes and motifs in the first 200 vv. of bk 5*
(See further the commentary *ad loc.*, except for entries with an asterisk.)

1–3	a deity inspires hero/army with might/confidence (see also on 125)
4	armour gleams like fire
5–6	autumn star (various applications)
9–26	'The whole incident is composed of typical motifs', Fenik:
	(*a*) seer/priest loses son(s) in battle
	(*b*) pair of brothers as victims
	(*c*) warrior on foot against two in chariot
	(*d*) rescue by god/goddess of a favourite
15	weaker of two warriors throws first

[7] In Bernard Fenik's *Typical Battle Scenes in the Iliad* of 1968, one of the outstanding technical studies of Homer of the last 50 years, to which frequent reference has been made in vol. 1 and which will be widely cited, in particular, in the commentary on bk 5.

16–18   first thrower misses, second hits
18   'missile did not leave hand in vain' (figure rather than motif)
19*   location of wound
25–6   importance of capturing victim's horses
27–9   panic of troops when leader killed
29–35* deity persuades another, or mortal, to withdraw from battle
30   taking someone by the hand (various applications)
37–8   enemy forced to retreat, series of slayings
38–83   painful/horrifying wounds (see also on 66–7)
42   mode of dying (variously expressed)
46–7   spear-wound in shoulder immediately fatal
47   darkness/death envelops victim (see also on 42)
53–4   (a) deity fails to protect favourite
        (b) victim killed despite factor that might have saved him
56–7*   fleeing warrior hit in back
59–64   character has 'speaking', i.e. significant, name
61   special skill as gift of a deity
66–7   exact path of weapon after hit (see also on 73–4)
70–1*   victim a bastard son
73–4   exact path of weapon after hit (see also on 66–7)
77–8*   victim a son of seer/priest (see also on 9–26)
80–1   attacker uses (first his spear, then) sword/stone
84   general fighting as transition from one duel to another
87–94   (a) fire or water as simile for irresistible attack
        (b) ring-form (typical figure rather than motif)
95–120 (a) woundings by arrow-shot
        (b) victor's boast
        (c) archer's ultimate failure
95   run of successes ended when a powerful enemy 'notices' and initiates
        counter-attack
115–20 (a) typical prayers
        (b) wounded man prays for, and gets, relief from wound, then rallies
            troops
116   reminiscences about a father (Tudeus theme)
121–2* deity cures/inspires/lightens a warrior's limbs (see also on 1–3, 135–6 (b))
123*   someone 'stands near' another and addresses him/her (see also on 170)
124*   *parainesis* (speech of exhortation from god/leader)
125*   deity inspires hero/army with might/confidence (see also on 1–3)
127 30 removal of mist (various applications)
130*   dangerous to fight against gods
131*   single exception to a general rule (a narrative figure with folktale
        associations)
134–65 hero's entry into battle marked by simile, then multiple slayings (see
        also on 161–3)
135–6   (a) deity fills favourite with might (see also on 1–3)
        (b) deity/physician rapidly assuages wound (see also on 115–20 (b))

137–42	(typical actions in lion/cattle similes; see also on 161–4)
144–65	(a) victims sharing a chariot (see also on 9–26, 160)
	(b) pairs of brothers (see also on 9–26, 159)
145–7	(a) first spear, then sword (see also on 80–1)
	(b) victims in chariot (see also on 9–26)
148–9	prophet's sons killed (see also on 9–26)
152–8	old father loses both sons (see also on 9–26, 148–9)
156–8	father's grief at death of son(s) (see also on 152–8)
159	pair of brothers as victims (see also on 9–26, 152–8)
160	victims sharing a chariot (see also on 9–26, 144–65)
161–4	simile: victor like lion among cattle (see also on 87–94, 134–65, 137–42)
164–5	(a) plundering victim's armour
	(b) handing over victim's horses to one's companions (cf. on 25–6)
166–70*	hero seeks another to meet crisis in battle
166	run of successes ends when powerful enemy notices (see also on 95)
170	someone 'stands before' another and addresses him/her (cf. on 123)
172–3*	warrior has a special skill
174	prayer before an arrow-shot
177–8	(a) need to recognize gods in battle (see also on 130)
	(b) a god's anger
	(c) failure to sacrifice as reason for anger
182–3	recognition of a warrior by his armour/horses
184–6*	special prowess ascribed to divine help (see on 187–91)
187–91	failure ascribed to divine wrath/support (see on 184–6)
187	deity diverts a missile
188–9	place of missile-strike described (see also on 19)
194–6	storage/care of chariot(s)/horses
197–200	father's injunction as son leaves for war (see also on 124)

Virtually the whole of this passage, therefore, is made up of typical and repeated motifs, patterns and ideas. Perhaps something of the kind is to be expected with predominantly martial narrative, although the sheer extent of the typical component is remarkable. Yet an example from a quite different context will show how the use of the typical is both pervasive and often extremely subtle. One of the most moving scenes in the poem is the argument between Hektor and Andromakhe in bk 6 about whether or not he should seek safety in order to protect his wife and child. Andromakhe's address is deeply pathetic, most obviously where she tells him that he stands in place of her father, mother and brothers as well as being her strong husband; though part of it is devoted to two basically factual accounts, first of the capture of Thebe, then of the weak point in the Trojan walls. There is much standard material in all this, reworked as usual so as to seem fully appropriate to this wholly untypical encounter. But it is in Hektor's reply at 6.441–65 that the way in which familiar ideas occur in every verse, yet with an original effect, is most clearly seen. This is best shown by a verse-by-verse paraphrase in the left-hand column of Table B, with typical elements summarized alongside on the right (for further discussion of motifs identified in the latter see especially the commentary on 6.438–9, 6.207–8, 6.441–3, 6.447–9, 6.455, 6.456–7, 6.459–62 and 2.356):

Table B *Hektor to Andromakhe at 6.441–65:* (a) *paraphrase,* (b) *typical motifs*

(a)	(b)
441 'I too am concerned	(concession, then disagreement)
442 but fear reproach	*aidōs*, fear of public opinion
443 if I hold back like a coward	cowardly behaviour in battle
444 which is against my nature	'heroic code', upbringing
445 and upbringing, to fight like a hero	fighting as *promakhos*
446 to win honour for myself and my father	winning *kleos*; respect for father
447 yet I know full well	(formular v.) firm conviction
448 that Troy will fall	'day will come'; captured city
449 with Priam and all Trojans	(typical inclusive expression)
450 but care not so much for them	fate of citizens (priamel)
451 or Hekabe and Priam	(duty to father and mother)
452 or all my brothers	brother(s) as victim(s)
453 lying in the dust	war-victims defiled
454 as for your suffering, when Achaeans	(rising scale of affection)
455 lead you captive, in tears	captivity, weeping
456 for you will be a slave at the loom	typical servile tasks: loom...
457 or carrying water at an Argive spring	...and water-fetching
458 unwilling, under duress	slavery is hateful
459 and one will say	typical comment
460 "she was wife of Hektor,	past status or reputation
461 greatest among Trojans"	praise of hero
462 causing you fresh grief	(resumptive) widow's grief
463 at loss of husband/protector	mourning a husband: slavery
464 but may I die	('I would rather...than')
465 before I hear your cries as you are dragged away'	captivity, weeping

Despite this heavy use of typical motifs, Hektor's words are clearly far from standard or ordinary in their total effect, and to see how this may be so is to understand something of Homer's art as a creative poet transforming his inherited tradition. In itself the speech's structure, quite apart from typical elements, is straightforward. His nature and upbringing will compel him to fight, yet he knows this will lead to Troy's fall and the suffering of its citizens. But it is his wife's fate that causes him most agony; she will be a slave in the land of the enemy, people will remark on her as Hektor's wife – but may he be dead first and be spared witnessing all this. Clearly his dilemma is a tragic one: he sees what he must do, with all its terrible consequences, but is caught between overwhelming pride and sense of public duty and his love and pity for wife and child. It is a dilemma many soldiers face, yet worse; for Hektor's whole way of being makes him believe in war, even when there is no comforting sense that his cause is just. The one thing he might have done, force Paris to surrender Helen, no longer seems possible; he is caught in an unendurable trap, the worst consequences of which he can only avoid by his own death. That is the ultimate heroic solution, which is also, paradoxically, an ultimately selfish one.

Against this background the imagined comment of 460f., typical as it is, assumes an important function. That she was Hektor's wife is poignant and ironic, but it also seems to justify his escape from the dilemma, since a heroic death will confirm him as ἄριστος and bring her some comfort. Earlier, too, his rhetorical demonstration of Andromakhe's unique place in his loyalty and affections at 450–4 echoes her own statement at 413–30 of the loss of father and brothers at the hands of Akhilleus; for he must face a similar loss, and yet, instead of her remaining as his solace, he himself must die and she face degradation and slavery. To see this simply or primarily as an instance of the rising-scale-of-affection pattern exemplified in the Meleagros-tale of bk 9, and given prominence by Kakridis (*Researches* 19, 49ff.) and others as significant for the structure of the whole poem, is surely a distorted view. S. Schein (*Mortal Hero* 174) can even claim that this ascending scale 'indicates to anyone familiar with the convention that Hektor's wife is dearer to him and more honored than the others' – but this is what Hektor explicitly says, and no knowledge of any convention is needed to make his meaning plain. Other motifs earlier in his speech carry analogous echoes – or more significantly counter-echoes, in which one typical motif is played off against, or used to undermine, another. Respect for a father in 446 is opposed to a relatively diminished concern for him at 451; Hektor's own motivation in 442, a complex of shame, guilt and self-glorification, combines typical elements of αἰδώς and upbringing that are here placed in tension with each other. Finally the implied suppression of one typical motif that is obviously germane can hardly be ignored; for is

Hektor consciously or otherwise deluding himself and Andromakhe about her fate, by avoiding the idea mentioned rather delicately by Nestor at 2.355, that no Achaean should think of going home before he has slept with a Trojan wife?

All the more subtle confrontations between characters in the *Iliad* reveal a similar interplay between the typical and the individual. Yet it is over the whole range of battle-poetry, which is such a large and fundamental component of the poem, that analysis of typical elements is most demonstrably helpful. Books 5 to 8 are still in a sense preliminary, and the heaviest and most continuous fighting comes in the central part of the action from 11 to 17. It is there that special problems of tactics arise. These have been carefully considered by J. Latacz in his *Kampfdarstellung*, and will be fully discussed in vol. IV. Yet the six standard constituents of Homeric battle can be discerned from bk 4 onward:

1. Mass combat
2. Individual contests (i.e. fights between individuals)
3. Speeches (of report, challenge, boast and counter-boast, rebuke, encouragement, consultation, advice)
4. Similes (often to illustrate (1) or lead on to (2))
5. Divine intervention (to inspire an individual or an army; to save a favourite, or remove another god from the scene)
6. Individual movements (i.e. apart from (2), e.g. from or to camp or city, or one part of the battle to another)

Further typical aspects can be added to each of these six components. Thus the prelude to MASS COMBAT is the arming, forming up, marching out and stationing of the armies, most fully described of the Achaean host in bk 2. The two armies engage, first perhaps with a brief phase of long-distance fighting with javelins and arrows; then a front is formed in which the first ranks on each side (στίχες or φάλαγγες, which do not differ in meaning) face each other. As fighting continues they may come into such close contact that, as at 4.446–51 = 8.60–5, shields clash against enemy shields and spears against spears. The front ranks contain the πρόμαχοι or fore fighters, and often individuals among these are imagined as stepping forward and engaging with each other in the space between the two armies.[8] Equilibrium may be maintained for some time, but then, through DIVINE INTERVENTION or particular INDIVIDUAL CONTESTS, one of the armies will be pushed back, a movement that may turn into a rout. Inevitably that

[8] H. van Wees (*CQ* 38, 1988, 1–24) gives a somewhat different interpretation, against Latacz and others, but is not in my view persuasive. He thinks that 'all the fighting is done by πρόμαχοι, and that there is no question of the "multitude" engaging in any kind of mass combat' (12), though he is not entirely consistent on this point.

will be stemmed somehow – since the monumental poet needs to maintain the reciprocal rhythm of battle – and a front will be re-established from which in due course another advance will be made.

Against the background of MASS COMBAT are fought countless – or so it is made to seem – INDIVIDUAL CONTESTS. Developed accounts of these strike the reader, as they must have struck early audiences, as the most memorable and significant kind of battle-description. That is true, but Latacz has shown that the sense of mass fighting (either through formal and typical descriptions such as in 4.446–51 = 8.60–5 cited above, or through the mention of to-and-fro movements as at 6.2, or in recurring brief signals that individual combats are surrounded by general battle, as at 5.84 ὡς οἱ μὲν πονέοντο κατὰ κρατερὴν ὑσμίνην, cf. e.g. 5.699–702n.) is continuously present, and that the poet never neglects for long to restore a feeling of the whole process of warfare. INDIVIDUAL CONTESTS and references to MASS COMBAT show different aspects of the same fighting, and the former are selected or temporarily isolated from the broad sweep of the latter as the poet's eye focuses for a time on one encounter to the exclusion of all others. Often he will describe sequentially combats that must be understood as simultaneous; that is part of the oral narrative technique. In any event Homeric battle is not to be imagined as a set of individual duels with nothing else happening – that is restricted to the two formal confrontations of bks 3 and 7, where the two armies are seated and watching. Rather it is the continuing clash of both sides, either static or with one or other in retreat, either loose or tight, in which the INDIVIDUAL CONTESTS between πρόμαχοι, or the onrush of a particular hero against the helpless troops of the enemy, are singled out to represent all that is fiercest, noblest and most typical of battle.

In fact the number of individual combats and victims is surprisingly small given the enormously varied and cumulative impression made by the whole epic. It is usefully summarized by Martin Müller, *The Iliad* (London 1984) 80–3. There are 140 specific individual contests, of which only 20 involve more than one blow and only 8 (not counting the formal duels of bks 3 and 7) go beyond the first exchange; a dozen or so warriors die as a result of a spear-throw aimed at someone else. About 170 Trojans (and allies) and 50 Achaeans die in these encounters, with a dozen injured. Of about 140 wounds, only 30 are remarkable and described in some detail, and they fill a bare 100 verses in all – how different from the impression we receive that the *Iliad* is replete with long descriptions of gory wounds! Yet in restoring a proper balance between descriptions of mass combat and the focus on individual contests – something that is essential when we are keeping in mind the progress of the battle as a whole, not just within a single Book but in the context of the entire poem – it must not be forgotten, indeed is obvious, that the individual encounters have special literary and human importance quite apart from their contribution to the progress of warfare as such. It is through them, to a notable degree, that the poet sees the changing fortunes of the different heroes and builds up a complex picture of their responses. Hektor is more prominent among the Trojans than any single leader is allowed to be (except Diomedes for a time) among the Achaeans, in Akhilleus' absence; and it is through his constant victories and setbacks (in addition of course to the great Troy-scenes of bk 6), and through his reactions to them, that his subtle and complicated nature is allowed to show through – together with the Trojan dependence on him and a continual sense of the city's impending doom.

Typical causes, typical sequences of events and typical changes of fortune operate in detail against the broad background of battle. Thus a change in mass combat may be caused by an individual *aristeia* or the death or wounding of a particular commander; or by a *parainesis*, human or divine, or some other kind of divine intervention, or by the arrival of a warrior who has seen a danger or been specially summoned. At critical moments one side or the other will adopt tight formation, πυργηδόν 'like a tower'; at other times they are grouped more loosely, as in the fighting round Patroklos' corpse in bk 17. Chariots are used in typical ways, usually for bringing a warrior into battle or waiting close by him in case of retreat, but occasionally in mass pursuit. Individual killings can be either of a sequence of victims distinguished only by name, or by an alternating chain of Trojans and Achaeans, or by the more developed encounters with a fully described victim and details of wound and manner of death. This is the form of Homeric warfare we tend to regard as most typical, and it is also, because of its often pathetic presentation, the most essential, perhaps, to the composer's purpose. Other and less important forms are concerned with whether the encounter is on foot or, partly at least, by chariot; whether the spear is thrown or thrust, or the armour is stripped from the victim, or what happens to his horses if they are nearby; whether there are developed speeches of boast and counter-boast, challenge and reply, exultation in victory. Each of these has its own typical rules. All this takes place within the formalized parameters of the battlefield and the plain of Troy: on one side the citadel itself, on the other the ships and huts with the sea behind them, with the two rivers and occasional markers like the oak-tree or tomb of Ilos in between, and from bk 7 onward the wall and trench, in front of the naval camp.

Within the whole panorama other typical elements and actions stand out. A complex exchange of blows between two opposed fighters is, as we have seen, relatively rare. Usually the stronger one throws or thrusts with a spear that is fatal before any counter-blow can be delivered. Where there *is* an exchange, certain definite rules apply; as always, these are not simply arbitrary but reflect the necessary conditions of combat and the proper display of martial qualities or deficiencies. Thus the following sequences are typical and legitimate:

  i A misses B, B then kills A
 ii A misses B, B hits but fails to penetrate, A kills B
iii A hits B but fails to penetrate, retreats, and is then killed or wounded
      by C
 iv A misses B, B misses A, A kills B with second shot
  v A misses B, kills C
 vi A hits B with spear or stone, then kills B with sword or C with spear.

In i, ii and iv the victor is always Achaean. Missing with a throw is not necessarily fatal (so iv), for B can miss also; but failing to penetrate (with throw or thrust) is fatal or nearly so, as in ii or iii, since it is a sign of inherent weakness or the lack of divine support; so one never finds that A hits B but fails to penetrate, B misses, then A kills B.

Other typical details, some already noticed, are as follows:

(1) A deity lends might to a warrior, or heals a wound; prepares for battle and descends to the battlefield; rescues a favourite, guides a weapon, removes mist or darkness, takes mortal form to deliver a *parainesis*.

(2) A victim is one of a pair of brothers, son of a priest or prophet, or a river; is slain while fleeing; has some special skill, or is rich, or is a bastard, or has a father whose sorrow is described.

(3) One man on foot faces two in a chariot; charioteer is killed instead of spearman, or has to flee when the latter is killed; his horses are captured, or he is told to keep them close by a leader fighting on foot.

(4) A warrior enters battle where fighting is thickest; is divinely inspired or rescued; protects a wounded comrade; makes a decision after soliloquy; addresses an enemy before engaging.

(5) Wounds are cursorily or fully described; teeth shattered, arm or head hacked off; painful wounds to the belly, bizarre and fantastic wounds; passage of missile described, it is stopped or deflected by armour; pain as a wound stiffens.

The following are better characterized as typical narrative patterns:

(6) A sequence of individual contests is ended when an enemy leader notices from another part of the battlefield and rallies support; or by a simile leading to a mass-combat description.

(7) One warrior rebukes, consults or advises another; e.g. Sarpedon rebukes Hektor (for leaving fighting to allies), Glaukos rebukes him (for not defending Sarpedon), Apollo (as Mentor) rebukes him, or (as Periphas)

Aineias. Such rebukes are almost always on the Trojan side and often reflect tension between Trojans and allies or Dardanians.

(8) In developed individual contests the victim is described in the so-called ABC pattern: A, basic information (his name, patronymic, city); B, anecdotal information, often pathetic (e.g. he is rich and hospitable, or an only son, or a bastard); C, resumption, and details of death (he was killed in such-and-such a way).

(9) Three attempts (e.g. at attacking a god) are made, with culmination at the fourth; this is a typical folktale pattern, like the 'sole survivor' motif, but also a typical rhetorical device, like 'then A would have captured Troy, but...'

'As so often in the Iliad, then, the unique is only a new arrangement of the typical': Fenik's sage words (*TBS* 58) are not intended as derogatory, but reveal much about Homer's technique not only of battle-poetry but also in other narrative forms including speech. His conclusions about battle-poetry are hard, or impossible rather, to refute. The examination of the main Iliadic battle-scenes is thorough, its results simple and conclusive: that all such scenes are made up of typical details or motifs and typical patterns. There are variations from time to time, also occasional individual details that are not typical, but these are always deployed among a larger number of standard elements. No one scene is the same as any other (despite the exact repetition of certain passages), not because such unique elements are commonly used – they are not, and are mainly confined to special Books like 5, 8 and 21 – but because the selection and arrangement of typical elements are always under slight variation.

Is the result monotonous? For the modern reader, it can be – but through the sheer mass of martial encounter rather than its typical and repeated elements as such. For the range of the typical is itself substantial both in subject and in tone; for example, from factual statements of who struck whom to pathetic details of the victim's background or the manner of his death. It reflects, in the end, a poetical view of battle, as with other standard epic subjects, and perhaps a deliberate restriction of the range of possibilities in realistic terms. Thus in individual contests a throw can hit, and penetrate or not; it can miss, or hit someone else (or a horse). But it could also bounce off and be deflected onto another victim, yet this never happens in the *Iliad*. An opponent can try to retreat, or he stands firm; but he could also throw while the other is challenging or boasting, or resort to subterfuge, for example by trying to distract the attacker's attention – but these things never happen. Then again archers could be used more widely than they are, and the details of fighting from or against chariots could be greatly supplemented. In mass fighting more use could be made of terrain, which could be more closely visualized and categorized than it actually is. There may have been special reasons for the limitations of possibilities in these and other matters – warfare itself can have certain conventions in an age of chivalry; but from the singer's point of view the material had in any event to be kept to manageable proportions, as well as being made to serve his underlying literary ends.

So far the emphasis has been on minor motifs, together with the looser texture of battle-description as a whole. It is in the combination of typical elements, whether of phrasing or of content, and in their variation in detail, that the oral poet's technique is most unusual and may most rewardingly repay close analysis. Yet the choice and arrangement of broader topics is also important, perhaps even more important, in a different way. Many of these, too, were typical – that is, established in the tradition as themes that could be used for fresh contexts in the composition of a whole poem. Among those themes would be a warrior's abstention from war, attempts to conciliate him, unfaithful wives, quarrels over booty, late-coming allies, funeral games (cf. Fenik, *TBS* 238; the use of these broader themes is more fully discussed by M. W. Edwards in ch. 2 of vol. v). Both this type of material and more specific ideas were likely to have been available for incorporation and development by the monumental composer of the *Iliad*. It is beyond dispute that much of his material was traditional in subject as well as expression; some of it was certainly concerned with the Trojan *geste* itself. Thus the *Iliad* alludes in passing to many events of the Trojan War that lay outside its own strict temporal limits: Paris' abduction of Helen (e.g. 3.443–5), Nestor and Odysseus visiting Peleus on a recruiting mission (7.127f.), the gathering of the fleet at Aulis (2.303ff.), Akhilleus in Skuros (9.666–8, cf. 19.326), the abandoning of Philoktetes on Lemnos and the death of Protesilaos on landing (2.721–5, 2.698ff.), the capture of Thebe and Lurnessos (1.366ff., 2.688–93, 6.415–29), the mission of Odysseus and Menelaos to Troy (3.205ff.). Other and more mythical tales are also known, like the Judgement of Paris (24.28) or Akhilleus' education by Kheiron (11.830–2). The essential extra-Iliadic references were noted by Kakridis (*Researches* 93); Kullman (*Quellen* 6–11) added a number of others, of which several, however, could be Homeric inventions. The *Iliad* and *Odyssey* also know in detail of events that followed the action of the former, like Akhilleus' own death, the capture and sacking of Troy and the difficult returns home of certain Achaean heroes. It is clear that Homer was able to draw on traditional versions of parts, at least, of the whole Trojan War, including its origins and aftermath; as well no doubt as on versions of the Theban Wars and the Argonautic voyage, not to mention other heroic narratives of which traces have not survived. The range of oral poetry before Homer is something that can only be guessed at, but the sophisticated formular language of the Homeric poems themselves, as well as those specific and identifiable references, suggests that it was both extensive and with a long history.

The unpalatable truth remains that we can hardly ever know for certain which particular themes came into the Homeric epos from specific earlier poems, and which – the vast majority, perhaps – from unidentifiable sources over the whole range of the oral heroic tradition. Despite that, the Neoanalytical school (which in one degree or another included Kakridis, Pestalozzi, Howald, Schadewaldt, Reinhardt, Kullmann and Heubeck; see further M. W. Edwards' generally sympathetic account in ch. 2 of vol. v) has argued that many Iliadic themes *can* be demonstrated to come from earlier poetry, as represented by Proclus' summaries (for the most part) of the Epic Cycle, and in particular from the *Aithiopis* ascribed to Arctinus of Miletus or perhaps an earlier version of that narrative. Thus Diomedes saving Nestor at *Il.* 8.80ff. is said to be based on Antilokhos saving Nestor (and being killed by Memnon in the process) in the *Aithiopis*; Paris shooting Diomedes in the foot at 11.369–78 is held to reflect his fatal wounding of Akhilleus in the heel in the *Aithiopis*; Memnon's death at the hands of Akhilleus in the *Aithiopis*, and the preservation of his body at the plea of his divine mother Eos, are claimed as the direct source of Iliadic themes like the death of Patroklos, the removal of the dead Sarpedon by Sleep and Death, and Akhilleus' relation to his mother Thetis.

That there is some connexion between an *Aithiopis* and our *Iliad* is probable enough; but that the latter necessarily imitated the former, rather than vice versa, cannot be proved. A third possibility, as Fenik argued at *TBS* 231–40, is that both poems drew independently, for the most part at least, on a broad reservoir of oral poetry that is now lost and irrecoverable. Neoanalytical approaches are sometimes valuable in suggesting a possible explanation for conjunctions of ideas in the *Iliad* that are otherwise puzzling. In so far as its exponents are simply claiming that the *Iliad* deploys and extends typical themes from earlier poetry, it is impossible to disagree. That is manifestly true – but it may not take the critic very far, and surely does not justify all the insistence on the *Aithiopis* that has been mooted so far. It may well be that most progress in assessing the master-composer's aims and methods is to be made by studying the recurrence and variation of broad general themes within the *Iliad* itself (and the *Odyssey* too, where relevant), where their operation and *differentiae* can be seen in full context, rather than through the barren and arid summaries of Cyclic material in a Proclus or a Eustathius.

3. The speech-element in the *Iliad*

One tends to think of heroic epic as mainly composed of objective narrative; yet nearly half of the *Iliad* consists of direct speech, and the proportion in the *Odyssey* (whatever view one takes of the status of Odysseus' reminiscences in bks 9–12) is still higher. This remarkable statistic means that both Homeric epics are, to a substantial degree, dramas rather than narratives – or rather, narrative expressed as drama, in which the progress and overtones of the action are evoked as much through confrontations and conversations between the characters involved as by the ostensibly neutral descriptions of the poet as observer and narrator.

Narrative itself deserves closer attention than it has traditionally received, and the new approach of 'narratology' in its less schematic forms helps to unravel the different strands of ostensibly straightforward description. This will be discussed by M. W. Edwards in vol. v. But it is the special qualities of speech in the *Iliad* that form the subject of the present chapter, adding an additional dimension to those of formular language, enjambment, colometry and typical themes that have already been summarily examined as elements of the complex totality of Homeric style. Attention to the problem has been spurred by an important article by Jasper Griffin, 'Homeric words and speakers', in *JHS* 106 (1986) 36–57. It may be that differences between speech and narrative – which for him raise difficulties about orality – do not constitute quite the paramount aspect of Homeric style that Griffin at one point suggests. Certainly there are other aspects, of traditional expression versus innovative for instance, which, together with the deployment of typical themes and motifs, determine more completely the characteristic forms of Homeric poetry. Yet the special qualities of the speeches deserve to be more closely studied, following Griffin's lead (and of course, in a different way, Lohmann's), together with the matters considered in the rest of this Introduction, namely religion, historicity and theme. Like them, it can only receive preliminary treatment here, to be supplemented in varying degrees in other volumes of the Commentary; but it is important to suggest some of the broader implications of the topic as well as the more special ones singled out so far.

The obvious sophistication of some of the conversations in the *Iliad* – for example, in bk 6, between Glaukos and Diomedes or, in a very different key, Hektor and Andromakhe – has sometimes persuaded critics that the speeches must be a relatively new element in the Greek heroic epic. That has seemed to be confirmed by certain linguistic features, notably the predominance there of abstract nouns, some of relatively recent formation. Objective narrative, on the other hand, appears at first sight simpler, and instances are not hard to find of 'primitive' forms of epic (for example the folk-epics of the Serbian *guslari*) that are almost wholly in third-person narrative. Griffin (p. 37) thought there was 'some truth' in the idea that 'narrative scenes...were...much more traditional, the speeches much more innovative', and inferred from this that the composition of speeches may be later. But if it really happened to be the case that narrative style and language were highly conservative, speech not so, that would not of course entail that speeches as such were later in composition.

It may be helpful to say at once that the speech-element in Greek epic was probably *not* a late development, at least if we assume the origins of that epic tradition to go back, as seems highly probable, well into the second millennium B.C. That is mainly because the Greek epic was probably affected in its earlier stages by the literary forms of Near Eastern poetry. This probability depends on Near Eastern tendencies in myths and religion as well as on a few special narrative themes, like the friendship of Akhilleus and Patroklos and the latter's passage to the underworld, that can be traced in Sumerian, Akkadian or Hurrian–Hittite myths and tales. M. L. West, at least, in the steps of Walter Burkert, accepts that influence as almost axiomatic (*JHS* 108, 1988, 169). If so, it is relevant to see whether the remains of Near Eastern literature suggest pure narrative as the normal means of presentation of folklore and quasi-epic, with the use of speech as absent, intrusive or a later elaboration.

A simple answer is suggested by some of the longer and more important Sumerian and Akkadian myths and tales, for example as translated in *ANET* (i.e. J. B. Pritchard, ed., *Ancient Near Eastern Texts*) 37–119. The result, crude but not essentially misleading, is as follows:

Sumerian
1. 'Enki and Ninhursag' (*ANET* 38–41, earlier 2nd mill. B.C): at least one-third speech
2. 'Gilgamesh and the Land of the Living' (*ANET* 47–50, earlier 2nd mill.): nearly half speech
3. 'Inanna's Descent to the Underworld' (*ANET* 53–7, earlier 2nd mill.): about half speech

Akkadian
4. 'Creation Epic' (*ANET* 60–72, early 1st mill.): *c.* one-third speech
5. 'Epic of Gilgamesh' (*ANET* 73–99, early 2nd mill. onward): at least half speech.

Proportions are very approximate; many of the speeches are repeated, some in narrative format; the figure for the 'Creation Epic' excludes the (narrative) list of Marduk's fifty names. Yet the conclusion is striking and obvious, that these Sumerian and Akkadian tales, which influenced so much of the rest of Near Eastern literature, are all cast in strongly dramatic form. The predominantly or exclusively narrative form virtually does not exist. The same is true of most Egyptian tales: the 'Contest of Horus and Seth' and 'Journey of Wen-Amon' (*ANET* 14–17 and 25–9) are at least half speech, the 'Story of the Two Brothers' (*ANET* 23–5) about one-third speech. They are from around 1000 B.C.; it may or may not be accident that the earlier 'Story of Sinuhe' (*ANET* 18–22, from *c.* 1800 B.C. onward) is mostly narrative. As for other major Near Eastern tales of the 2nd millennium B.C., Hittite 'Ullikumis', 'Illuyankas' and 'Telepinus' (*ANET* 121–8) have between a third and a half speech; Ugaritic 'Poems about Baal and Anath' (*ANET* 130–42) and 'Keret' and 'Aqhat' (*ANET* 143–55) have a somewhat smaller speech-component overall, but are still markedly dramatic.

The result, therefore, is that the written literature of the ancient Near East in the second and the first part of the first millennium B.C. (apart, of course, from legal, historical and ritual texts) regularly contained a strong dramatic element, with many speeches by, and conversations between, characters set out in full. That was the general cultural and literary background against which the Greek epic tradition appears to have formed itself; it seems highly unlikely, therefore, that *its* strong speech-element was a later development and not the result of second-millennium archetypes.

That still leaves the possibility that narrative was more conservative in its expression than speech. So far as type-scenes like meals, sacrifices, meetings, journeys and many elements of battle are concerned, that may well be so, since speech has little (apart from prayer and short formulas of welcome, boasting, encouragement or rebuke) that is likely to be so timeless and so typical. Here some of the main linguistic differences between speech and narrative need to be illustrated, mainly by selection from the data presented by Griffin. One of the most remarkable is in the use of abstracts, on which P. Krarup (*Classica et Mediaevalia* 10, 1948, 1–17) wrote a valuable study; here the difference between speech and narrative in the *Iliad* and *Odyssey* overall is of the order of 4 or 5 to 1. Most of these abstract forms were obviously more suited to the utterance of characters rather than to the more concrete narrative of the singer himself, who as Griffin stresses is often conscious of his supposedly uninvolved position as mouthpiece of the Muse. Thus nouns ending in -φροσύνη or beginning εὐ- nearly all occur in speech. That is because they belong to the analysis of moral attitudes or mental states; the same can be seen in epithets ascribing gentleness (ἀγανός, ἤπιος,

The speech-element in the Iliad

μείλιχος, ἐνηής), folly (ἄφρων etc.) or justice (δίκη, θέμις), all predominantly in speech. κακός and ἀγαθός reflect the same tendency, the former 253 × speech versus 48 × narrative overall, the latter 58:13 (not counting the special use in βοὴν ἀγαθός). The 'reservation of the crucial moral terms from the narrative to the speeches' (Griffin, p. 40) results in these other Homeric totals: ὕβρις etc. 26:3, ἀτάσθαλος 30:1, σχέτλιος 29:1, τιμή etc. 111:15, αἰδώς 24:1, αἰδέομαι 33:9, ἔλεος etc. 55:23.

More surprising, but again reflecting the more factual and positive side of narrative, is that over 70 negative adjectives, many with ethical or emotional value (Griffin, p. 44), are found only in speeches, including ἄπιστος ἄποτμος ἀπτόλεμος ἀτρεκής ἀεργός ἀκηδής ἀκλεής ἀναίτιος ἀπευθής ἄπρηκτος. Superlatives behave similarly, not only the emotive ἔχθιστος and φίλτατος but even (with only few narrative occurrences) κάρτιστος μέγιστος κάλλιστος. By contrast ἄριστος is a technical term and occurs more equally. On the other hand emphatic particles and adverbs like ἦ and μάλα (let alone ἦ μάλα together, common in Plato's dialogues and plainly colloquial) predictably occur only in speech. So does the use of χρή (55 × in Homer), obviously because the narrator does not have occasion to say that characters, let alone things, ought to or must do such-and-such.

This last point reminds us that much of the linguistic difference between speech and narrative arises simply out of the forms and parts of speech entailed by the two modes of expression. Griffin is perhaps inclined to undervalue this kind of consideration, finding the observation that Virgil may have been compelled by metre to use *Amphitryoniades* rather than *Hercules* to be an explanation 'on a very humble level' (p. 50). That may be why he does not refer to the work of A. Shewan, who as long ago as 1916 stated that 'It is a familiar fact that there are considerable differences, metrical and linguistic, between the general narrative and the speeches of the *Iliad* and the *Odyssey*', and went on to explain some of them in purely grammatical and functional terms. Thus correption (shortening of a final long vowel or diphthong before a succeeding initial vowel) is commoner in speech because it contains more words so ending: 'presents, futures and perfects are of course much more common in speech, and parts in the first and second persons are almost wholly confined to it' (*Homeric Essays*, Oxford 1935, 329), and these often end in long vowels and diphthongs (as do many vocatives, for instance). That is merely one example of the way in which the forms of speech – its far greater use of subjunctives, optatives and even infinitives (cf. Shewan, p. 321) in addition to the above – can differ at a very concrete level from those of narrative. It is inevitable that the language of Homer is, in this respect, not uniform and may even be said in a limited way to involve 'two vocabularies' (Griffin, pp. 40 and 50); yet the

31

singers can hardly have found much difficulty in adjusting their responses to such natural and unavoidable calls for differing modes of expression according to circumstance.

Such matters will be seen in better perspective when the older studies both of verbal forms (reflected in Shewan) and of vocabulary are carried further. Meanwhile it is important to remain aware that narrative, of its nature, tends to be objective, factual, progressive and sequential, with relatively little expression of emotion. Speech, on the other hand, tends to be subjective, evaluative, rhetorical and emotional, with a greater degree of syntactical subordination, and by turns persuasive, interrogative, conditional and wishful. This is, of course, an over-simplification: speech and narrative often overlap, with factual passages in the former and occasional expressions of emotion (often in reporting the behaviour of individuals as I. J. F. de Jong notes, *JHS* 108, 1988, 188f.), as well as the more complex subordination of clauses, in the latter. Thus in bk 6, again, the narrative of Hekabe getting the dress for Athene at 288–95 is emotionally coloured (with the superlatives κάλλιστος, μέγιστος, νείατος) – even more so the description of Andromakhe running up to Hektor at 392–406. Yet when she addresses Hektor at 407–39 the passionate short statements soon give way to a more objective style as she recalls the details of her father's death, with many conventional epithets that belong more properly to narrative. Consideration of a sequence like 15.592–746 reveals that speech and narrative can sometimes maintain a similarly elevated level for a considerable time. Yet it remains generally true that the emotional and expressive needs of speakers, together with the complexity of their thoughts and arguments, impose a different colouring on many speeches from that normally sought by the predominantly remote and objective narrator, who adopts a flowing and progressive style that is sometimes ornate but nevertheless syntactically straightforward.

Thus progressive and temporal conjunctions are frequent in narrative, but particle-complexes and other conjunctions are far commoner in speeches – consider Diomedes' opening remarks to Glaukos at 6.124–30: οὐ μὲν γάρ ποτ᾽ ... τὸ πρίν· ἀτὰρ μὲν νῦν γε ... δυστήνων δέ τε παῖδες ... εἰ δέ τις ἀθανάτων γε ... οὐκ ἂν ἔγωγε ... οὐδὲ γὰρ οὐδὲ ... Moreover speech abounds in subordinate clauses (final, causal, conditional) as well as in disjunctions, wishes and direct addresses. Narrative's typical devices are those of emphasis, especially through word-order, with conventional phraseology varied by figurative language and especially similes; speech's are rhetorical, including antithesis, alliteration and assonance, with frequent irony and even humour. Such generalizations tend to disguise the many different forms that speech and narrative can assume in themselves: for the former, from short comments, commands, messages or challenges to more elaborate monologues, prayers, supplications, and rhetorical addresses, including exhortations (*paraineseis*) and lamentations; for the latter, from simple and relatively undecorated to more elaborate description, depending on sentence-length, enjambment and colometry as well as the disposition of conventional phrases, with results that can range from the matter-of-fact and the dispassionate to the urgent and the sublime. Differences of scale and emphasis, as well of course as the intervention of speeches, have their own effect on narrative colouring, as indeed can be seen in much of the battle-poetry. Only occasionally does the poet allow himself to address a character, or the Muse, directly (cf. Edwards, *HPI* 36–8), but decoration, figurative language and similes more subtly reduce the potential frigidity of objective narrative in its extremer forms.

The technical differences of expression in speeches lead back to the question raised earlier, of how far speech and narrative might have arisen in different periods. Nothing has changed the probability that the dramatic *epos* goes back in specifically Greek forms to as early as the mid-second millennium B.C., when Mesopotamian, Egyptian and Hurrian–Hittite parallels show the combination of speech and narrative to be widely diffused. Most of the *differentiae* of Homeric speech arise out of the need for a more complex syntax and a less impersonal vocabulary, as well as the mechanical implications of particular speech-forms. Yet the proliferation of abstract nouns is only partly explained by the greater emotional range of speech, and suggests that there were specific expressive developments, allied indeed with new forms of rhetoric, in the later phases of the oral style – much, indeed, as the taste for allegorical figures such as Eris, Deimos and Phobos may be held to belong to the later developments of narrative technique.

What is thought-provoking about the use of speech in the *Iliad* is not only that it involves its audience in the action as a kind of drama, but also that it allows – sometimes, at least – its different characters to be presented as individuals, through their own words and the thoughts and feelings they reflect. Many harsh things have been written about the Greek lack of interest in individual literary character, not only in epic but also in tragedy. It is true that the 'heroic character' as such imposes a certain uniformity of reaction over matters of possessions, of pride and reputation, of concern for victims in battle and the rights of lesser figures like servants and women. Yet anyone who reads or hears the *Iliad* knows perfectly well that the main characters (as well as lesser ones like Thersites, Pouludamas or Glaukos) have their own definite personalities, and that these arise not only out of what the narrator says about them but also out of what they themselves do and say. Sometimes action reveals almost as much about character as words themselves – but usually those actions are glossed by the character's own

33

comments, which are often intensely revealing. Again, it is important to distinguish the *content* of speeches from their *style* – except that only too often the two are inextricably intermingled. Thus Diomedes is self-controlled in the face of erratic authority, unlike Akhilleus, and this emerges not only from what they do, and from the actual content or message-element of their speeches, but also in the very words they use and how they express themselves. All this requires close study. Once again the formular style imposes a degree of uniformity, but it is notoriously overridden by the prolix impetuosity of Akhilleus' utterances to the Embassy in bk 9, and can also be tempered in more subtle ways. P. Friedrich and J. M. Redfield analysed some of his speeches in a perceptive article in *Language* 54 (1978) 263–88, briefly summarized by Griffin on his pp. 50f.; they consider, rightly, that too little attention has been paid to 'the general shape of utterances, the use of rhetorical devices, and the choice of particles'. Griffin complements this by a study (pp. 51ff.) of Akhilleus' special vocabulary as against that of Agamemnon. Apart from his predilection for violent and abusive terms, special to him and his circumstances, like ἀσκελέως, βούβρωστις, ἐφυβρίζων, σκυδμαίνω, ὑπεροπλίῃσι, δημόβορος, κυνῶπα, φιλοκτεανώτατε, Akhilleus is especially prone to the use of similes, sometimes pathetic ones, and to the evocation of distant places. There is a grandeur of vision, as well as a cruelty and irony, in his language that sets him apart from other characters in the poem; that is well said by Griffin and will be illustrated in later volumes of the Commentary.

Meanwhile readers will find much in the detailed notes to confirm that particular traits of character are sometimes revealed in particular styles of speech. That must not be exaggerated; many speeches of many characters are not differentiated from those of others, and there is a general 'speech style' that is determined largely by circumstance, by what needs to be said on a particular occasion. Yet reference to the following speeches, and the commentary on them, will confirm the general point as well as suggesting the possibility of distinctions, here and there, between male and female ways of speaking as well as between divine and human:

Pandaros to Aineias at 5.180–216
Sarpedon to Hektor at 5.472–92
Ares and Zeus at 5.872–98
Glaukos and Diomedes at 6.123–231
Paris to Hektor at 6.333–41
Helen to Hektor at 6.344–58
Andromakhe and Hektor at 6.407–93
Athene to Here at 8.358–80
Zeus to Here at 8.470–83.

34

Clearly there are other parts of the poem where conversations are even more revealing: the quarrel between Akhilleus and Agamemnon in bk 1, the Embassy to Akhilleus in bk 9, the final exchanges between Hektor and the dying Patroklos in bk 16 and Akhilleus and the dying Hektor in bk 22, the meeting between Akhilleus and Priam in bk 24.

Character is revealed in these, but more than character; for in circumstances that are especially tragic and pathetic it is direct-speech protestation as such, rather than particular character, that is significant above all. What the characters say does not so much reflect their own particular personalities at this moment as their human and generic responses, often confused and inadequate, to the events in which they find themselves entangled. That may be a salutary note on which to leave this complex and enthralling topic; for it reminds us once again that speech in Homer is no more important as a means of revealing a man's or a woman's (or a god's) particular character and personality than for what it does to impart drama and subtlety to the action as a whole.

4. History and fiction in the *Iliad*

The historicity of the *Iliad* has been a matter of continuing interest and concern ever since antiquity, with new impetus from Robert Wood in the eighteenth century and Schliemann in the nineteenth. It can hardly be ignored in these introductory chapters. Yet at best only a provisional treatment can be offered – it would be 'safer' to avoid the issue and attempt none at all – since so much remains to be discovered and rethought. Further reflexion on the modes of destruction and probable dates of Troy VI and VIIa (see pp. 40f.), further study of the Hittite archives (pp. 42f.), further excavation around Besika Bay on Troy's Aegean shore (pp. 49f.), further consideration of the nature of the oral tradition and its Near Eastern antecedents (pp. 29f.), will all alter the way we look at the *Iliad* in relation to its historical background, as well as the characteristics of the oral tradition as a whole.

One preliminary question can hardly be avoided: does 'historicity' really matter? Clearly in some ways it does. The history of the Late Bronze and Early Iron Ages in the central and eastern Mediterranean is of obvious importance in itself, and there are still many respects in which the Homeric epic affects that history. Archaeologists sometimes suggest that for armour, weapons, buildings and other concrete matters the information of the poems has been overtaken by actual discovery; even that is not yet entirely true, but there are broader concerns which are less easy to resolve. The most obvious question here is whether a Trojan War, in the sense of one in which Troy was besieged and eventually overthrown by a Panachaean expedition, ever really took place. Even that entails a limitation of historical perspective; but the political and military aspects of the *Iliad* have tended to win the limelight, not least because of the excitement of archaeological discovery from Schliemann on, in Mycenae and Pylos as well as Troy itself.

The historical accuracy of the *Iliad* is obviously important from that point of view – but does it affect the poem's *literary quality* so strongly, or indeed at all? The *Iliad*, after all, is more than anything else a great drama, concerned with people and feelings rather than concrete environment or historical background as such. Some critics even resent attention being paid to the material aspects of the poem, or expect them to be excluded from ordinary commentaries and confined to archaeological handbooks. That is absurd, if only because all human affairs are affected by external

36

circumstances and the concrete controls on behaviour; moreover both singers and early audiences clearly devoted careful attention to these matters. But, leaving that aside, can it really be said that historical accuracy affects literary quality in any serious way?

The singers of the Iliadic tradition, and the monumental composer who imposed its form and scale on the whole poem, were clearly much concerned with things like geography, landscape, weather, buildings, weapons, fortifications and military tactics, and described them in all sorts of ways. These were part of the world in which their characters operated. But did it matter if transmission through generations of singers had distorted some of the details? Not, presumably, to the singers or their audiences, who after lapse of time would tend to accept as true even a garbled account of, say, chariot tactics, so long as it did not become poetically distracting. A later historical analyst like Thucydides takes such things more seriously, as will any careful modern reader (and not only literal-minded or pedantic ones). But it is arguable that, although warriors in action – and that is a main subject of the poem – have to be described in detailed tactical situations, it is not especially relevant in literary terms whether these are 'real', provided they seem so to the listening or reading public. By extension, given that the personal drama of an epic may arise partly out of the conditions and tensions of warfare, it would not matter to anyone except the historian whether the war described in the poem actually took place, so long as it is made sufficiently plausible. It merely has to be a *credible* background for the action, whether or not it was 'real' in some stricter sense.

Logically and philosophically, something like that has to be granted. Psychologically, things stand differently, and many readers undoubtedly feel that historical authenticity does matter after all. Even so, there are grades of authenticity to be considered.[9] A work of history can be authentic, or nearly so, when it adequately expresses more or less everything that can reasonably be known about a past event. In a historical novel, on the other hand, one may accept as authentic a constructed historical background that is compatible with known facts, even if it goes further in detail, or in the conjunction of disparate sources or events, than surviving evidence suggests. That kind of authenticity allows for a substantial imaginative contribution, recognizable from the evident fictionality of the characters involved and their immediate circumstances. But what of the case where there is a *bogus* authenticity – a background that professes to be historically accurate, or appears to be so to the audience or reader, but can be shown by historians to be slipshod and inaccurate? Is the reader then entitled to

---

[9] Cf. W. E. Bassett, *The Poetry of Homer* (Berkeley 1938) on 'the illusion of historicity'.

feel disenchanted or cheated in some way? Or is the *plausibility* of the background all that matters? People do, as a general rule, feel deprived or misled when something that implicitly claims to have certain qualities is later found to have different and perhaps inferior ones. In this respect the discovery that the historical background of the *Iliad*, real as it seems, is in fact purely imaginary would inevitably produce a degree of disappointment. This might be mainly a modern consequence, since its historical authenticity was not often questioned by ancient audiences. Yet that is only partly relevant, since our own doubts and feelings are in any case strongly involved.

Still another aspect of 'authenticity' needs to be considered. The things we respond to most keenly are often things that seem intrinsic to the world itself, of which we sense that we form a part. In literature we accept interpreters, intermediaries who can focus certain aspects of the world and of human experience – but only to the extent that they do so without obvious distortion. The creative imagination is admired for just so long as what it creates is in touch with 'life itself', arranged and revealed in a perceptive way that might otherwise escape the audience or reader. If we are made aware of aspects of a narrative that are gratuitously false, that distort history and reality without corresponding gains in understanding, then our faith in the value of the whole work is impaired. If the Trojan War did not take place, then we are compelled to consider the nature and intentions of the personal and private imaginations that invented it – and to ask, for example, whether the insights they appear to show in relation to Akhilleus and Priam or Hektor and Andromakhe are as valid as they seem. In short, and not to press such an argument too far, significant characters and actions are revealed against backgrounds and in circumstances that should possess their own kind of authenticity; and defective presentation of the one weakens, or needlessly complicates, the audience's perception of the other. If that is true of a historical novel, it is no less so of a traditional epic many of the elements of which are almost as ancient as the events it purports to describe. With that, we can turn again to Troy.

That the mound of Hisarlik was the site of Homer's Ilios can no longer be reasonably doubted. It fits so exactly with the poetical description of a great fortress lying close to the Hellespont in one direction, and to the foothills of Mt Ida in the other. It had for many centuries been a powerful and wealthy place even before the development, from *c.* 1800 to *c.* 1250 B.C., of the sixth city; and there is no other fortified site in the whole region that could possibly have given singers the idea of Troy. One is immediately faced, therefore, with a certain degree of historical accuracy. Troy was there, a real place, fortified with great walls 'just as Homer said'. But the geography of the region was filled out with far greater detail than that: the two rivers, Skamandros and Simoeis, that met in the plain between the citadel and the Hellespont; the islands that lay within reach, Tenedos close to Troy, Lesbos to the south, and Lemnos, Imbros and Samothrace marking the approaches to the Hellespont from the west, with the peak of Samothrace visible above Imbros (cf. *Il.* 13.11–14); Sestos and Abydos up the straits; a great artificial tumulus near the shore at Besik-Tepe (cf. p. 49), not strictly on the Hellespont but which singers could loosely identify with Hektor's idea of his own tomb at *Il.* 7.86–91 (q.v. with n.), as well as smaller ones closer to Troy that may have given rise to Homeric landmarks like the tombs of Ilos and Aisuetes and the mound called Batieia. Southwest of Mt Ida were places attacked by Akhilleus in his raids before the action of the *Iliad* begins: Khruse, Thebe, Lurnessos and Pedasos as well as Lesbos offshore. The Catalogue of Trojan allies in book 2 suppresses much of the central part of the Aegean coast to the south of that, because that is where the Ionians landed and where the Iliadic tradition was finally formed; even Miletos is described as Carian, despite its long Mycenaean history, to avoid the appearance of anachronism; but the Troad and the south coast of the Hellespont toward the Propontis are evidently known in some detail. If the singers of the ninth and even the tenth century B.C. knew all that,[10] then surely they also knew whether Troy fell by siege, and if so who constituted the attacking force.

In short, they could have been as correct about the basic fact of the fall of Troy to an Achaean expedition as they were about the position, power and physical aspect of the citadel itself – windy Troy with its wide streets, high gates, fine walls and towers, its steep and beetling aspect. All these are preserved in traditional epithets, some possibly deliberate and specific (though cf. vol. I, 173–7).[11] 'Windy', otherwise applied only to the obscure Enispe, could have special reference to the persistent north-easterlies of Trojan summer; εὐρυάγυια, 'of wide streets', reminds one that the peripheral street inside the great wall of the sixth city was unusually broad and cannot be closely paralleled elsewhere – yet on a single occasion the epithet is called into service for Mukenai also, which it does not fit, and it might be merely honorific. Nevertheless the concept of the citadel as a

---

[10] The famous hot-and-cold springs of *Il.* 22.147–56 are of course omitted from this survey, but it is interesting that J. M. Cook (in Foxhall and Davies, *The Trojan War* 170) thinks that those beneath Bunarbashi, though some way from Hisarlik, could have been remarkable enough to generate the reference.

[11] As argued, rather uncritically, by W. Leaf, *Troy* (London 1912) 150f. For a concrete discrepancy between Hisarlik and the Iliadic version see pp. 47f.; and for a generally sceptical assessment J. Cobet in *Antike Welt* 14 (1983) 39ff. Schadewaldt, *Aufbau* 17, envisages autopsy by Homer.

whole, crowned with palace and temple, is sharp enough, not, as it seems, evidently fictitious. Does the broad outline of an Achaean siege correspond?

First, possible motives for such an attack, if not obvious, are at least perceptible. Not of course to avenge the seduction of an Achaean princess, still less because of a Judgement of Paris that led to all that; those are mythical and folktale elements; but as a by-product of trade through and beyond the Hellespont (for pure copper according to Bloedow in the article cited on p. 41) to refurbish the wealth and prestige of the declining Mycenaean palace-states by plundering a conspicuous foreign target that was relatively accessible – and perhaps rumoured to be so damaged by earthquake as to be there for the taking. Homer does not say that, or even imply it; but fiction notoriously likes to suggest personal reasons for international acts of aggression that are political and economic in origin. Yet Herodotus was an expert in making folktale and myth look like history, and the Homeric tradition could have done something similar. Themes of wrath and abstention, of war for a woman, of a warrior's close companion, were familiar in Sumerian and Akkadian literature from long before the Trojan War, and could have been an unseen influence – compare the more overtly Near Eastern affinities in some of the Lycian material and two or three motifs common to the Gilgamesh-epic.[12]

Second, the *Odyssey* suggests a degree of disruption after the Trojan War, back in the Mycenaean cities of mainland Greece, which accords with an expensive and exhausting failure. That is what a major siege, whatever the result, must have been, since it is extremely improbable that either what remained of Troy's perhaps legendary treasure, or its strategic and economic potential once captured, would have made the expedition economically worth while. No signs of booty that might have come from Troy have been found in Greece, for what that is worth. Third, if Troy–Hisarlik did escape major damage and social collapse from armed attack towards the end of the Bronze Age, then it would have been the *only* great fortified centre in the eastern Mediterranean world to have done so.

Assuming for the moment that Troy fell, who were the aggressors, and which of the successive settlements on the site of Hisarlik did they overthrow? To take the second question first: Troy VIh (that is, the last phase of the long-lasting sixth settlement, with refurbished circuit walls and added gate-towers as they still stand) was held by Professor Carl Blegen and the Cincinnati expedition of the 1930s to have been heavily damaged by earthquake around 1300 B.C.; afterwards Troy VIIa saw the populace crowded into small houses built in the former wide streets, with the earlier

[12] P. M. Warren's passing suggestion (*JHS* 99, 1979, 129) that Iliadic narrative motifs may be prefigured in the 15th-cent. B.C. miniature fresco from Akrotiri in Thera is now interestingly developed by Sarah Morris, *American Journal of Archaeology* 93 (1989) 511f.

great *megara* subdivided and storage jars built into the house floors.[13] According to Blegen this settlement was destroyed by enemy attack around 1240 and perhaps as early as 1270 B.C. For some time his conclusions have been the object of simmering doubts,[14] and it now appears almost beyond dispute that Myc IIIC fragments found in Troy VIIa (actually nearly all of them turn out to be local imitations) put its fall *as late as around 1140*, with latish Myc IIIB in Troy VIh bringing *its* collapse down to around 1250. All this is shown with great clarity in the first and most cogent half of an important article by Edmund T. Bloedow, 'The Trojan War and Late Helladic IIIC', *Praehistorische Zeitschrift* 63 (1988) 23–52. The end of the effective military power of the Mycenaean palaces of the Greek mainland is still judged to be signalled by the sack of Pulos around 1200 (i.e. at the end of Myc IIIB), with Mycenae itself under serious attack not long thereafter.[15] If so, then the only settlement the Achaeans could have captured would be late Troy VI, after all, and not Troy VIIa as the Cincinnati expedition had decided. That is a conclusion of fundamental importance – consoling in its way, since the picture conveyed in the *Iliad* is certainly of a substantially undamaged city without the refugee aspect of Troy VIIa. Some scholars, Schachermeyer and Akurgal prominent among them, had believed that whatever city was actually captured, the Homeric description, in the *Iliad* at least, envisaged the sixth.

Yet the difficulty remains that, according to the Cincinnati excavators, the damage to Troy VIh was caused by earthquake, not human attack. This conclusion is still accepted by Bloedow, partly on the ground that new geological studies by G. Rapp (in *Troy* Supplementary Monograph 4, Princeton 1982) confirm (what was surely known before) that ancient Troy was earthquake-prone. It is admittedly easier to question the excavators' ideas on the date of the fall of Troy VIIa (which depended on a ceramic dating-system since revised because of fresh material from the Argolid, especially Tiryns) than their theory of the causes of destruction of Troy VI (since here their judgement was based on an expert general view of what they found and saw). Yet according to Wilhelm Dörpfeld, the highly competent original excavator of the sixth city (which Schliemann entirely missed), there was evidence there too of extensive fire damage

---

[13] See C. W. Blegen *et al.*, *Troy* III (Princeton 1953) for Troy VI, with *Troy* IV (Princeton 1958) for Troy VIIa. Other accounts or summaries tend to be misleading.

[14] Reported e.g. in Michael Wood's *tour de force*, *In Search of the Trojan War* (London, B.B.C., 1985) 223ff.

[15] Bloedow's survey and its conclusions are based on the recognition, based on E. B. French's almost universally accepted revision of Furumark over LHIIIC, that many of the local imitations of Mycenaean pottery found in Troy VIIa are of the Granary Style, and therefore come near the end of IIIC, after the middle of the 12th century B.C. in a median absolute dating.

compatible with enemy attack: 'This city was thoroughly destroyed by enemy action. Not only were the traces of a great conflagration recognizable in many places, but the upper parts of the city walls and the gates and especially the walls of the buildings inside them underwent a violent destruction which can have happened neither through an outbreak of fire alone nor through an earthquake' (*Troja und Ilion*, Athens 1902, 181). Blegen did not accept this, though he remained ambiguous about the signs of burning, and attributed the destruction of the sixth city entirely to earthquake and not in any sense to enemy attack. But it is notoriously difficult to distinguish between natural disaster and human destruction in the ruins of an ancient settlement, especially where fire damage is concerned; even Blegen could have been wrong, and K. Bittel, who was present during much of the Cincinnati campaign, continued to disagree with the exact form of his diagnosis. Yet a major earthquake surely *was* involved somehow, toppling the great walls in several places. Huge blocks fell from the southern part of the wall into the streets, presumably as the result of seismic shock since the effects are generally held to be incompatible either with dismantling by captors or with the use of a battering-ram (symbolized, according to Pliny and Pausanias, by the Trojan Horse). That the earthquake happened, and was closely associated with the city's collapse, remains relatively certain. It is possible, however, that this is not the immediate cause of the fires detected by Dörpfeld, but that it opened up the city to attack, and that an invading army, whether or not present at that exact moment (unlikely but not impossible), was able as a consequence to enter the city and set it ablaze.

With its successor-settlement Troy VIIa, the main certainty is that it was for most of its existence *prepared* for siege. That is shown by the improvised housing within the walls and around the gates, as well as by the new custom of sinking storage jars into the floors. Mycenaean imports had virtually ceased; the damaged city walls were patched up; eventually this settlement was destroyed by fire, probably (or certainly as the excavators thought, although even here the evidence is thin) as a result of enemy attack. But these attackers cannot have been united Achaeans from the mainland, since by this time, after about 1150 B.C., the Mycenaean palace-states there were already destroyed or on their last legs; they may, on the contrary, have been relics of the Sea-People movements, or pirates, or Thracians.

Thus there is nothing in the archaeological record to controvert the idea that the Achaeans *did* attack Troy, the Troy VIh of around 1250; although nothing in the ruins positively proves it. Before turning to a radically different kind of evidence, that of the heroic tradition itself, something needs to be said about a second type of possible concrete evidence, that of the cuneiform documents excavated from 1906–7 on at the Hittite capital of Hattusas (modern Boghazkoy) in central Anatolia. These have been subjected to continuous discussion since E. Forrer drew attention in 1924 to apparent similarities between some of the proper names there and certain prehistoric Greek names known from Homer: Ahhiyawa ~ Ἀχαι(ϝ)οί, Wilusa ~ (ϝ)Ἴλιος, Taruisas ~ Τροία, Alaksandus ~ Ἀλέξανδρος, Tawakalawas ~ Ἐτε(ϝ)οκλέ(ϝ)ης, Milawanda/Milawata ~ Μίλητος.[16] A few distinguished Hittitologists still believe in some or most of these equivalences, despite serious objections raised by F. Sommer in 1932;[17] others are extremely sceptical, or offer quite different identifications of the events, places, and persons involved.[18] I do not propose to enter into this whole question here, for two perfectly good reasons: first, that only expert Hittitologists can pronounce on these matters; second, that there is still deep disgreement between such experts, and therefore no firm Hittite evidence that can be used to elucidate Homeric problems. That has not prevented, and will not prevent, people from trying to use this fascinating but still essentially mysterious material as ancillary support for theories based primarily on other kinds of evidence: a mistake, perhaps, in principle.[19] That said, the day will come when this rich archive is more fully understood, and then our conclusions may have to be revised.

Now we can turn to consider another and radically different type of evidence, that of the oral tradition itself, which was positive that an Achaean siege took place. Most scholars, it is probably fair to say, feel that this tradition, although it obviously incorporates certain fantastic and fictitious elements, and has in addition been subjected to a degree of distortion, is likely to retain some kind of historical core. Yet that is impossible to prove, and some scholars do not agree. Sir Moses Finley, in particular, insisted that the poetical tradition is unreliable and that by far the most probable aggressors (he was thinking of Troy VIIa rather than Troy VIh, but that does not seriously affect the issue) were the miscellaneous mercenaries and piratical bands (loosely referred to by the generic name of Sea Peoples) who, perhaps with a small Achaean element, carried out raids in many different parts of the eastern Mediterranean, Anatolia and the Levant from *c.* 1300 to *c.* 1150 B.C.[20]

[16] Part of the background is set out in Page, *HHI* ch. 1, though the dating of the Hittite texts has been significantly altered since then; cf. O. Gurney, *The Hittites* (2nd edn, Penguin Books 1981), also Michael Wood, *op. cit.* ch. 6.

[17] Most recently H. G. Güterbock, 'Troy in Hittite Texts?', in M. J. Mellink, ed., *Troy and the Trojan War* (Bryn Mawr 1986) 33ff.

[18] Cf. e.g. D. F. Easton in Foxhall and Davies, *The Trojan War* 23ff.

[19] 'One assumption erected upon another', Bloedow, *op. cit.* 39.

[20] For a relatively recent review of this complex question, one that rightly stresses the widespread disturbances and progressive decline of Mediterranean nations close to the end of the Bronze Age, see N. K. Sandars, *The Sea Peoples* (revised edn, London 1985), especially 197–203. For a less cautious reaction see Mellink's own Postscript in M. J. Mellink, ed., *Troy and the Trojan War* (Bryn Mawr 1986).

In order to believe that, Finley had to undercut, and virtually destroy, the evidential value of the whole Homeric tradition. This he attempted to do by citing the gross historical distortions and chronological displacements of the *Chanson de Roland* and the *Nibelungenlied*, both of them incorporating strong oral elements.[21] Yet all that such comparisons prove is that oral traditions *can* be historically erratic. The degree of error varies enormously according to subject-matter, local conditions and, especially, the tightness, in expressive and retentive terms, of the particular narrative tradition. Neither of those epics had anything like the disciplined form of the Homeric poetry, and therefore the potential for relatively accurate preservation of details over several generations. Mycenaean elements in language, customs and *realien* demonstrate that specific information, whether or not in strictly poetical form, could have been carried down from the assumed time of the Trojan War itself. That greatly reduces the chance of Germanic-type displacements of major historical events and movements. The *Nibelungenlied* illustrates what *could* happen, not what probably did happen with the quite distinct Homeric tradition. In 'The character of the tradition', one of the comments on Finley's paper in *JHS* 84 (1964) 12–17, I argued that both those traditions were heavily infected by the intervention of Latin literate sources, which caused widespread misunderstanding through the scholarly and uncomprehending conflation of separate regional accounts (see also Hainsworth, *op. cit.* in n. 21, 112f.). The Greek oral tradition down to Homer, by contrast, was 'pure' in that it was immune to written sources, depending more or less exclusively on the passage of saga material, mainly in poetical form, from one generation to the next and from close to the end of the Bronze Age on. Moreover, despite the massive perversion in the *Chanson* tradition of the encounter at Roncevaux (from a heroic but minor attack on Charlemagne's rearguard by Christian Basques to a major battle against the Saracens), it is generally true that the largest distortions in this kind of loose tradition affect personnel rather than events; and that major happenings like the battle of Kossovo in the South Slavic tradition, established as they are in widespread public memory, remain substantially untraduced. The Siege of Troy, of course, would be far closer to Kossovo than to the Roncevaux model.

It is important to remember that the Homeric tradition, quite apart from its unparalleled tightness and complexity of poetical expression, was evidently formed not too far from its main scene of action. Here the Aeolic elements, the presence of which in the artificial dialect-mixture of Homer

---

[21] Most clearly in *JHS* 84 (1964) 1–11; see also his later statement in 'Schliemann's Troy – one hundred years after' (Fourth Annual Mortimer Wheeler Archaeological Lecture, 1974). See further J. K. Davies, 'The reliability of the oral tradition', in Foxhall and Davies, *The Trojan War* 87ff., and J. B. Hainsworth, 'The fallibility of an oral heroic tradition', *ibid.* 111ff.

(see vol. I, 5f.) probably entails definite poetical contact over a considerable period with a region abutting via Lesbos on the Troad itself, are of special importance. Aeolic settlers from Methymna in northern Lesbos may not have moved permanently into the coastlands of the southern Troad much before 800 B.C., but they must have encountered Mysian natives long before that, among whom some memory of Troy might, or must, still have survived.

Some kind of saga tradition, indeed, is likely to have been maintained in Lesbos itself, the northern shores of which, in the territory of Methymna, looked across a mere ten miles of water to the southern foothills of Mt Ida.[22] Again, the date and progress of Hellenic occupation in Lesbos is not yet firmly established, but it is hard to consider it as beginning later than around 950 B.C.; before that there had been an important settlement, culturally akin to that of Troy from the Early Bronze Age on, at Thermi just north of the later Mitylene. Just as to the south the first Ionian migrants of around 1000 B.C. would have met Mycenaean descendants familiar with much about the history of Miletos, so Aeolic contacts through Lesbos would have revealed much in the way of local informal tradition emanating from the south-western Hellespont and the southern Troad itself. To all this must be added the possibility that some kind of formalized, i.e. poetical, tradition about the Trojan War already existed in those regions, to be developed and improved by the Ionian and Aeolic *aoidoi* of the new colonial Greek settlements.

This argument is obviously speculative; it may be stronger when put in a negative form. Supposing the idea of a major Achaean attack on Troy to be wholly fictitious, would survivors in the Troad have conspired in a view of their comparatively recent history that went clean against their own memories and traditions? The decline of Troy had proceeded steadily since the end of the sixth city; its last inhabitants before it was finally more or less depopulated were partly Thracian, judging from the Knobbed Ware characteristic of Troy VIIb2, but obviously the farmers round about continued to live and work in the region. Would the fiction of a massive defeat by foreigners, ancestors of those who were stealing their lands to the south, have been readily acceptable to those Dark Age survivors who, like the Mysians to the south of Ida, were numerous and determined enough to have kept Aeolic settlers substantially at bay? And when Greeks finally moved into the northern Troad and founded Troy VIII on the ancient mound of Hisarlik, at just about the time the *Iliad* was becoming known in its monumental form, would these settlers themselves have acquiesced in a version of their new settlement's prehistory that ran counter to all local memory? Perhaps so – perhaps by claiming descent (as those in Lesbos did)

---

[22] Cf. J. M. Cook in Foxhall and Davies, *The Trojan War* 168.

from Orestes and so Agamemnon himself, they were trying to assimilate themselves to the bogus Troy tradition; but their own self-effacement in the perpetuation of a major literary myth, supposing that is what it was, must even so have been remarkable.

On the whole, then, the universal Greek belief in their capture of Troy, founded as it was on an oral heroic tradition extending many generations into the past from Homer's time, is hard to contradict. It was enshrined not only in the *Iliad* and *Odyssey* but in the whole Cyclic tradition, as well as in the complex mythographical syntheses that culminated in the pseudo-Hesiodic *Catalogue of Women*. The Homeric poems may not have taken long to establish themselves as a standard, but even so it is noteworthy that not a single doubt is recorded about the gathering of the fleet at Aulis, the investiture of Troy and its eventual capture. Add to this that the Catalogue of Ships, though far from being a Mycenaean muster-roll, suggests that the concept of a united Greek force can be carried well back into the Dark Age; whereas the Trojan Catalogue contains elements of an Anatolian survey that is likely to be constructed mainly on the basis of Ionic and Aeolic experiences after their migration of *c.* 1000 B.C.; see vol. I, 237–40 and 262f.

Finally among these indirect arguments, the other two great heroic sagas, of the voyage of the Argonauts and the successive expeditions against Thebes, are themselves suggestive. The former is only mentioned once in Homer, at *Od.* 12.70 (where however the Argo is πᾶσι μέλουσα, 'well-known to all'), but is plausibly held to have contributed to the form of some of Odysseus' sea adventures.[23] It is obviously replete with folktale and fantasy, but in so far as it records a voyage through the Hellespont, the Propontis, the Bosporus and into the Black Sea it also appears to possess a core of reality and reflect the experiences of marine explorers from the Late Bronze Age on. The Theban wars, on the other hand, are well known in the *Iliad*, particularly in respect of Diomedes' father Tudeus. They are likely to be historically based – not of course in the individual duels that sealed the fate of the Seven, but in the idea, archaeologically confirmed, of a destruction of Thebes at least a generation before the supposed Panachaean expedition. It was no doubt part of the literary conception of a dynastic war that it should be settled by duels between champions. That would have had its special appeal to noble descendants, but the heroic spirit is displayed most effectively not only in individual duels but also against the clash of great armies. Nestor's reminiscences suggest that regional traditions explored the mass-combat theme in a minor way, and not without a core of historical reality; but the attack on Troy, which was foreign but not distastefully so, remote but still accessible by sea, a powerful citadel on the edge of a natural battlefield, became the obvious focus for this whole more

---

[23] See K. Meuli, *Odyssee und Argonautika* (Berlin 1921).

realistic view of heroic activity, as well as a symbol of Achaean success before the Late Bronze Age semi-feudal world finally collapsed. Not only the analogy of other 'Heroic Ages' (which elevate a *geste* of the recent past to counteract a depressing present), but also the residual historical qualities of the competing Theban epic, suggest that the development of a pure fiction centred on Troy was unnecessary and improbable.[24]

If the *Iliad* retains a certain authenticity, in that it describes a real location and a war which in some form may have taken place there, it also contains fantasy and misunderstanding; that is obvious. The war against Troy did not involve a thousand ships, any more than it lasted ten full years. Moreover the poets of the tradition were sometimes as vague or confused over details of the beleaguered city as they were over details of armament and tactics. Thus knowledge of the citadel and its remains did not extend to its gates. The Scaean gate, it is implied, faces the battlefield; it is flanked by the great tower of Ilios (6.386 with 393), which fits the main gate and tower of Troy VIh (and also Troy VIIa) – except that this faces south, not north towards the Hellespont. Homer mentions another gate, the Dardanian, but it is unclear whether that is really a different one. In any event a multi-gated Troy would be a reasonable assumption, for if Mycenae had only one gate (and a postern), Thebes notoriously had seven. In fact three gates survive in the remains of Troy VI and VIIa, with a postern close to the north-eastern one. The whole northern stretch of the wall has disappeared – collapsed down the escarpment, plundered for stone for the platform of the great Hellenistic temple of Athene, finally obliterated by Schliemann; but it presumably contained no proper gate, and in this respect the *Iliad*'s picture of troops issuing from the Scaean gate straight onto the plain in the direction of the Hellespont is imaginary. In reality Troy–Hisarlik was most vulnerable from the level of the escarpment: that is, from the east, south and south-west. Its three main gates were positioned on those sides for practical access, but had to be heavily fortified against attack across level or only gently sloping ground – or rather, that is so for the north-easterly and the south-facing gates, but not for that on the west side (that is, facing towards Besika Bay), to which no supporting tower or outworks were added in the refurbishment of the defences in the latest phase of Troy VI. Admittedly a minor gate in that section was blocked up, but the distinctly weaker section of wall just to the north of it, built out of smaller stones in an earlier phase of the sixth city, was for some reason left alone. It has always been tempting to identify this, as its discoverer Dörpfeld did (*Troja und Ilion*, 608), with the point mentioned by

---

[24] J. T. Hooker, on the other hand, argued for the attack on Thebes as poetical prototype for that on Troy (*Wiener St.* 13, 1979, 18); whereas G. Nagy (*The Best of the Achaeans*, Baltimore 1979, 140) thought that elements from various tales of conquest were combined.

Andromakhe at 6.434 where the wall was ἐπίδρομον, most open to attack. That is of course pure speculation; but one may still wonder why this weak point in the citadel's defences was allowed to remain, facing as it did precisely in the direction from which an enemy landing was most to be expected – that is, either from the Hellespont (in which case the enemy would have rounded the edge of the escarpment and approached from the west or south-west) or directly from the only possible landing-place on the Aegean shore at Besika Bay. There is no obvious answer to this question.

This particular problem is hardly eased by recent confirmation[25] that the Scamander delta has filled in over the millennia, and that at the time of Troy I the citadel lay on, or very close to, the shore of a deeply intrusive bay. This gradually diminished so as to leave the sixth city, in its later phases, still within a mile or so of the head of a shallow-watered estuary. That the mouth of the Scamander should silt up like those of the great rivers of the Aegean coast had been conjectured at least since the time of Herodotus (2.10), though conditions there (with the currents of the Hellespont sweeping past) are not identical. It was accepted by local writers in the Hellenistic period, notably Hestiaea of Alexandria Troas, who were interested in reconstructing the Homeric battlefield and in particular determining the position of the Achaean naval camp. So far, too few bores have been sunk in the plain to plot exactly the southern shore of the embayment; and it is possible that it was less intrusive in late Troy VI than Rapp and his Turkish colleagues concluded. J. V. Luce has accepted their findings, however, and in *Oxford Journal of Archaeology* 3 (1984) 31ff. offers an interpretation of the *Iliad* on the assumption of a deep bay. This means placing the Achaean camp on a north–south axis along the inner shore of the Sigeum ridge – that is, facing Troy across a body of water. That is not at all the impression we form from the text; specifically it is incompatible with two major Homeric assumptions, first that the Trojans attacked the camp frontally and not from one end, second that the ships were drawn up along the shore of the Hellespont itself.[26] On the other hand, if we suppose that a shallow bay still existed at the end of the Bronze Age, but intruded by only a mile or so from the present shoreline, then the Homeric outlines of the plain, and the relative positions of citadel and camp, can be roughly preserved, at the same time as reducing the impracticable depth of the battlefield on current assumptions.

Detailed speculations of this kind – in which the position of the Achaean camp maintains its importance in a tradition stretching back to Hestiaea

[25] Cf. G. Rapp and J. A. Gifford, edd., *Troy* Supplementary Monograph 4 (Princeton 1982) 11ff.
[26] Later authors used 'Hellespont' loosely, to include its approaches, but there is neither evidence nor likelihood that Homer did so.

and Aristarchus, and beyond them, no doubt, to countless anonymous guides from Troy VIII onward – are especially equivocal at a time when important and perhaps critical archaeological evidence is still under investigation. For the excavation from 1984 on by Professor Manfred Korfmann and the Tübingen expedition at Besika, on the Aegean coast some five miles south-west of Hisarlik, is raising some intriguing new possibilities and perhaps giving fresh support to the idea, propounded by A. Brückner in 1924 and supported by Dörpfeld, that the Achaean camp must have been at Besika Bay and not on the Hellespontine shore to the north of Troy. Comment on these extremely important matters (in the context of historicity, that is) may be confined for the present to the following observations.[27]

(1) An extensive cemetery containing a variety of burials (both interments and cremations or part-cremations), mostly in pithoi but including a cist-burial and a chamber-tomb, and contemporary with the final phase of Troy VI (i.e. the assumed archaeological date of the Trojan War), has been found at the foot of the Besik–Yassitepe promontory which forms the northern end of Besika Bay. Most of the grave-goods had been looted in antiquity, but much contemporary pottery of Mycenaean type (most but not all of it local imitation) was found nevertheless.

(2) The search for the corresponding habitation-site, which must have been more than a mere hamlet, is still in progress.

(3) That may turn out to be more than a Mycenaean entrepôt (though Mycenaean trading-stations of the kind exemplified in the Aeolian islands north of Sicily provide a possible parallel), but in any case can have little directly to do with possible activities at the encampment of a raiding force, since many of the bodies were those of women and children.

(4) At the very least the new discovery (*a*) shows that Mycenaean trading contacts with late Troy VI were more extensive than previously envisaged on the basis of the rather small quantities of Mycenaean-style pottery found at Hisarlik itself; (*b*) provides sounder commercial motives than before for the assumption of close Mycenaean/Trojan contacts towards the end of the Bronze Age, especially in view of (5) below; (*c*) establishes Besika Bay as an important harbour for Troy–Hisarlik for many centuries before that, since a settlement contemporary with early Troy I has been found in the same area.

(5) Korfmann has re-presented the case, with some powerful new arguments even beyond the range of the new finds, for Besika Bay as the place where ships would wait for favourable weather before trying to enter

[27] Professor Korfmann's interim conclusions are to be found in two lucid and penetrating contributions to M. J. Mellink, ed., *Troy and the Trojan War* (Bryn Mawr 1986) 1–28, and his preliminary reports in *Archaeologischer Anzeiger* for 1985 and 1986.

the Dardanelles. C14 dating of marine deposits inland from the present shoreline confirms that the bay was considerably deeper then than now (though for different reasons from those that applied to the lower Scamander valley just round the corner).

(6) Further thought will be needed on commercial and perhaps strategic relations between the Besika embayment and that between Hisarlik and the (true) Hellespont. The importance of Besika Bay as an anchorage (up to a mile offshore) for modern sailing vessels is not identical with its probable importance, for beaching and limited inshore anchoring, for ancient ships, although the factors cited by Korfmann (*op. cit.* 4f.) from the early sixteenth-century Ottoman cartographer Piri Reis are perennial: namely that when wind and current, singly or in conjunction, prevent sail- and oar-driven craft from entering the Dardanelles, as frequently even in summer, then Besika Bay, protected both from north-easterlies and from adverse currents, is the closest safe waiting-point. It may be added that, once Cape Sigeion had been safely rounded, then the Scamander embayment may have been the next waiting-point for further progress up the Hellespont and through the narrows towards the Propontis.

(7) Against all this background it must be borne continually in mind that, even if there was a historical Achaean attack on Troy, the *Iliad* would present a version of it that was not contemporary but based on some 400 years of oral transmission and poetic licence and misunderstanding. Mycenaeans were probably familiar with Besika, and hostile ones among others may have landed there, but the *Iliad* account still firmly envisages the Achaeans as encamped on the Hellespont at the mouth of the Scamander.

These words may make a fitting conclusion to this survey, since they emphasize once again that historical fact and poetical description, although they can seriously overlap – as I believe they did over the Trojan War – are in the last resort separate entities.

COMMENTARY

BOOK FIVE

Battle has been joined at the end of bk 4; now the composer displays its progress through the exploits of a single great hero. In a sense Diomedes reminds us of the absent Akhilleus, combining a certain reserve and prudence with something of the other's demonic quality after Patroklos' death. That, and Athene's continuous support, lead by almost inevitable stages to this Book's special theme of the wounding of gods. After an initial run of lesser victims he is confronted by Pandaros and Aineias, of whom he kills one and wounds the other; Aphrodite enfolds her son Aineias in a new version of the scene in bk 3 where she rescued her favourite Paris; encouraged by Athene, Diomedes attacks and lightly wounds her. Her comforting by Dione is a brilliant interlude, but the dominant theme of attacking gods reappears as Apollo himself has to repulse Diomedes and summon Ares to help the Trojans. Athene and Here decide to intervene and descend to the battlefield; Athene joins Diomedes in a spear-attack on Ares, who is severely wounded and, as Aphrodite had done, retreats to Olumpos where Zeus reluctantly has him cured.

The physical damage to the two immortals is a startling idea; but one of them is the antithesis of war, the other its most contemptible exponent. No other deity could suffer thus, though Dione comforts Aphrodite with historical precedent. Only Diomedes, perhaps, could be the aggressor, and only then with divine support. This gives his triumph a special dimension, but also allows the poet to develop an almost philosophical interest in the confrontation between heroic nature at its highest and divine nature at its most carnal and demeaning – one that reveals itself further in the distinction between divine and human blood and in unique actions like Ares leaning his spear and chariot against a cloud or rushing up to heaven like a tornado. None of these unusual ideas, any more than the prominence of Diomedes himself, justify Analytical doubts of the Book's position in the canon. Its unity of style and structure (cf. Andersen, *Diomedesgestalt* ch. 4) and its many cross-references with bks 3, 4 and 6 (cf. Kirk in *Aspects* 16ff.) integrate it completely into this earlier part of the *Iliad*, in which the monumental composer sets out in brilliant detail some of the background of war, heroism and divinity before moving on to the great battles at the heart of the poem.

1–94 Athene inspires Diomedes with strength and confidence and he begins his triumphant progress by defeating the two sons of Dares. Six other Achaean leaders including Agamemnon each make a kill, but Diomedes scatters the Trojan lines like a river in flood

1–94 The narrative is carefully balanced:

  1–8 The goddess fills Diomedes with might
  9–26 He slays one son, Hephaistos rescues the other
  27–37 Athene persuades Ares to withdraw
  37–84 Six other Achaean leaders kill their opponents in turn
  85–94 Diomedes rages like a river in flood.

Thus Diomedes both begins and ends this initial scene of fighting, with a series of six other encounters in between. The long Pandaros episode will follow at 95–307, with Diomedes wounded but then slaying eight victims in succession before facing the renewed attack by Aineias and Pandaros. Thus one ring-composition episode leads to the next, with conspicuous common patterns like the repeated sequences of six or eight victims and Diomedes as main centre of attention throughout.

1–3 The integrally enjambed opening sentence maintains the flowing style of the closing scene of bk 4. There is no major break, though Athene's inspiring of Diomedes indicates that an important new episode is beginning.

1 ἔνθ' αὖ, 'then again', as often after an interruption such as a generic scene or a summary; so e.g. at 12.182, 16.603, 17.344. Παλλὰς 'Αθήνη is a common v-e formula (with | Παλλὰς 'Αθηναίη 3 × *Il.*, 6 × *Od.*); she was so described only four vv. before at 4.541. Παλλάς may be related to παλλακή, πάλλαξ, mod. Gk παλληκάρι, implying 'youth' (cf. Chantraine, *Dict.*, Strabo 17.816; Hainsworth on *Od.* 6.328, disagrees), rather than to πάλλειν = 'shake' with reference to the aegis (see on 2.446–51; it is shaken by Zeus at 4.166–8 and Apollo at 15.230 and 321, but the verb there is ἐπισσείειν or σείειν). That would fit her later description as Parthenos; the further conclusion that Pallas was a generic maiden-goddess later specified as 'Αθηναίη by her connexion with Athens (so e.g. Burkert, *Religion* 139) may not be warranted. The Palladion, an ancient image of her, was kept in her temple at Troy according to the Cyclic tradition (cf. Dion. Hal. 1. 69) but does little to clarify her special nature; similarly with post-Homeric references to a male Pallas as Titan, Giant or hero (Arcadian or Attic), cf. West on Hesiod, *Theog.* 376.

The exegetical scholia (AbT) reflect an ancient debate (cf. e.g.

M. H. A. L. H. van der Valk, *Mnemosyne* 5, 1952, 269–86) on why Diomedes should be chosen as hero of the first extended *aristeia* (an ancient critical term, literally 'prowess', for an individual warrior's period of special triumph); particularly since at 2.768f. Aias was said to be far the best after Akhilleus. That came in a possible expansion (vol. I, 242f.); but Aias is clearly a powerful fighter, joint first choice with Diomedes and Agamemnon to oppose Hektor at 7.178–80. The scholia reached the right kind of conclusion: that although Aias is without peer in defence, the others are more flamboyant in attack (in fact Aias virtually never leads an attack). In the event each of them will have his triumph: Diomedes here, Agamemnon early in bk 11 and Aias as defender of the ships from bk 13 on.

2–3 A deity filling a hero with special strength is a common Iliadic motif, similar to that by which a whole army is inspired. Often the hero despatches a series of victims, as when Poseidon inspires the two Aiantes at 13.59ff. or Apollo Hektor at 15.262 (= 20.110, of Aineias). Diomedes' inspiration results immediately in his slaying of Phegeus and routing of Idaios at 10ff.; but his *aristeia* will last through the whole Book and indeed into 6, with fresh doses of divine inspiration at 121ff. and 793ff. See further Fenik, *TBS* 10; Krischer, *Konventionen* 24–7. — ἔκδηλος is *hapax* in Homer, and μένος καὶ θάρσος non-formular; κλέος ἐσθλόν, on the other hand, appears 6 × *Il.* and has possible Indo-European overtones (cf. e.g. M. L. West, *JHS* 108, 1988, 153). The poet has decided to devote a long episode to Diomedes' triumphs and seems to offer the warrior's desire for glory as a rather cursory excuse.

4 Armour gleaming like fire is another common motif, cf. e.g. 22.134f. or more loosely 13.340–2 (where there is a blinding brazen gleam from helmets, corslets and shields); nowhere else does fire as a sign of divine inspiration come specifically from helmet and shield (but cf. 18.205–14), though this is another IE motif, cf. M. L. West, *op. cit.* 154. The asyndeton is abrupt and emphatic.

5–6 The simile at 22.26–31 confirms that 'the autumn star which shines brightest of all' is Sirius, there 'Orion's dog'; see also West on Hesiod, *Erga* 417. On 'washing in Okeanos' compare 18.487–9, where Arktos (i.e. the Great Bear) alone is said to have no share in the baths of Okeanos – that is, does not set. Here, however, washing (or bathing) implies brightness rather than setting; Sirius is indeed far brighter; see further J. B. Hainsworth on *Od.* 5.272–7. There is no sinister implication to this simile, unlike that at 22.26–31 which describes a bright autumnal star as an evil sign that brings fever; so too Hesiod, *Erga* 587 and similarly in later poetry.

7 ἀπὸ κρατός τε καὶ ὤμων recurs at 17.205, but of stripping armour from a fallen foe. It is part of a formular cluster for that idea (cf. e.g. 11.580, καὶ αἴνυτο τεύχε' ἀπ' ὤμων |, and 7.122 n.), adapted here to the fire that gleams from helmet and shield in 4. 'Head' refers to the former, 'shoulders' perhaps primarily to the latter (Ameis–Hentze) – this resumptive v. differs partly for variety, partly because of the difficulty of fitting a word for shield, either ἀσπίδος or σάκεος, into the v-e. Zoilus of Ephesus, the so-called 'Homer-lasher' (cf. the D-scholium on 4 and T on 7), thought the hero to be in danger of conflagration.

8 ~ 16.285; κλονέοντο (etc.) is a favourite Iliadic term, 21 × *Il.* (+ κλόνος 7 ×), related to κέλομαι but also to κέλλω = 'push' according to Chantraine, *Dict.* s.v. κέλλω, and implying agitated movement together perhaps with shouting. For κατὰ μέσσον *sic* cf. 4.541.

9–26 Diomedes' inspiration leads to a spectacular clash with the two sons of Dares, in a contest even more elaborate than that of Aias with Simoeisios at 4.473ff. It establishes the beginning of the hero's triumph firmly enough to permit a short run of other Achaean victories at 37ff., the point being to show his feats as set in the midst of, and standing out from, other front-rank encounters. The whole incident is composed of typical motifs, on which see pp. 16–18 and Fenik, *TBS* 11. The most conspicuous are (a) *prophet or priest loses a son or sons in the fighting* (so at 77f. with Dolopion the priest of Skamandros and 148–50 with Eurudamas the dream-interpreter, also 11.329ff., 13.663ff., 16.604f.); (b) *pair of brothers as victims* (cf. the three pairs who will succumb to Diomedes at 148–65, also 4 × bk 11 and twice elsewhere); (c) *fight between a warrior on foot and two opponents in a chariot*; (d) *rescue by a god or goddess of a favourite*, a motif to be reused at 311ff. when Aineias is rescued by his mother Aphrodite – itself anticipated at 3.380f. where Aphrodite similarly removed Paris; so at 20.325–7 (Poseidon and Aineias), 20.443f. (Apollo and Hektor) and 21.596f. (Apollo and Agenor).

9–11 Starting from the victim's father is a conscious literary device, heavily emphatic; similarly at 13.663, 17.575. Dares the priest is not heard of elsewhere, neither is a cult of Hephaistos in Troy, though plausible enough given his Lemnian connexions. Dares' name is Phrygian (cf. von Kamptz, *Personennamen* 338f.); Idaios (who has a herald namesake at 3.248 and elsewhere) is presumably named after Mt Ida; Phegeus is likely to be of Greek derivation, i.e. e.g. from φηγός = 'oak', and therefore even more fictitious.

The dual ἤστην is *hapax* in Homer, though υἱέες ἦσαν/ἦμεν/ἐστόν is formular. So is μάχης εὖ εἰδότε πάσης (4 × *Il.*, not *Od.*), which seems confined to dual subjects and is not used of individuals, i.e. with εἰδότα -ι. Shipp (*Studies* 246) finds a number of mild linguistic abnormalities in this encounter, though 'the first half of [bk 5] is in general free from abnormalities': that is true.

12 Literally 'those two, separated [*sc.* from the mass fighting], leapt to face him'; ἀποκρίνεσθαι not otherwise *Il.*, but intelligible enough.

13 ἵπποιιν, literally 'the two horses', as usual implies the whole equipage (as with the simple plural ἀφ' ἵππων at 19); there have been no less than 8 dual forms in the last 4 verses. ἀπὸ χθονός balances ἀφ' ἵπποιιν, and ὄρνυτο matches 12 ὁρμηθήτην.

14 A formular v., 12 × *Il.*, used both of the approach of armies (as already at 3.15) and of individual encounters – whether in a formal duel or, as here, when the contestants are envisaged as separated (12 ἀποκρινθέντε) from the rest.

15 It is usually the weaker warrior and probable victim that throws first (similarly bT). On δολιχόσκιον ἔγχος see 3.346–7n.

16–17 The runover-word cumulation is forced, but ἀκωκή -ῆ (12 × *Il.*, always at v-e) usually has the gen. of the spear expressed, cf. δουρὸς ἀκωκή -ῆ (6 × *Il.*) — These vv., with 18, recur with different names at 16.478–80 in the fight between Patroklos and Sarpedon, itself begun by the formular v. 462 = 14 here. They are, therefore, Homeric. Yet οὐδ' ἔβαλ' αὐτόν occurs only in these two contexts; missing with first throw is common, but is usually differently expressed, e.g. the spear hits someone else instead. αὐτόν for regular μιν, with no special sense of contrast, is a relatively late usage; van Leeuwen also noticed that δεύτερος, rather than ὕστερος as here, is formular in this kind of situation, and plausibly conjectured οὐδ' ἔβαλεν Ϝ', ὁ δὲ δεύτερος...

18–19 The missile which does not escape from hand in vain is a typical figure, both in this phrase (5 × *Il.*) and in other variants; it is, in its way, a neat cliché, more emphatic than simply saying that the weapon struck. The language in this opening scene is strongly formular, especially at the v-e; thus 14 ἰόντες (etc.) has a strong inclination to come last in the v. (21 × *Il.* even apart from the formular v. 14 itself); similarly with 16 ἀκωκή (etc.), see 16–17n., also 17 χαλκῷ (77/91 × *Il.* at the v-e); in the nom. the v-e tendency is weaker, in the acc. non-existent. In 18–26, also, only 21 and 24 do not end with a common formula. Noun–epithet groups predominate, and they naturally tend towards the final colon. The conventional quality of this sequence of vv. is quite marked.

20–1 Idaios leaps out of the chariot but fails to defend his brother's body (which would have been proper, as with Aineias and Pandaros' body at 297–301, cf. 4.494–7), and evidently begins to run away. Fenik (*TBS* 12) notes that whereas a second man in a chariot regularly tries (usually without success) to escape when his companion has been killed, brothers nearly always defend each other dead or alive; so at 11.248ff., 11.426ff., 14.476f., 16.319–21, cf. 20.419ff. Thus Idaios' inadequacy is untypical, marking off the episode from the impending encounter between Aineias and Pandaros (by chariot) and Diomedes (on foot) at 275ff.

22 οὐδὲ γὰρ οὐδέ κεν αὐτός: the repeated negative is strongly emphatic, cf. e.g. 6.130 and n., 13.269; it is arguable whether the first οὐδέ refers to the event, the second to the person as Did/AbT maintained.

23-4 Divine rescues are a relatively common theme, see 9–26n. The protection by a god of his priest is another typical idea, here interwoven with that of divine rescue; cf. Apollo and Khruses at 1.8ff. 'Hiding with night', equivalent to covering with thick mist as at 11.752, means that Idaios was made invisible (against 13.425 where it implies killing). — V. 24 has a distinctly pathetic ring with its opening long monosyllables and strong emphasis on οἱ (both through δή and by its position): the priest's grief is almost the god's own.

25-6 'Diomedes is always mad about horses': so bT, wrongly; grabbing an enemy's chariot and horses was important whenever possible; here as elsewhere they are handed over to helpers without delay to be driven back to the ships. See Fenik, *TBS* 12.

27-9 The panic of troops (which is what the 'stirring' of their spirit amounts to) when their leader is killed is best paralleled at 16.289–92; πᾶσιν ὀρίνθη θυμός is formular, 3 × *Il.* They notice that Idaios has got away, ἀλευάμενον, rather than his sudden invisibility.

29-36 Athene's intervention to remove Ares is curiously unemphatic, beginning as it does in the middle of a v. (29); it has other surprising aspects, not least Ares' silent acquiescence as the goddess takes him by the hand and leads him away. His presence on the battlefield (where he is a potential menace to the exploits of Athene's protégé Diomedes) takes us back to 4.439–45 where battle was first joined and Ares spurred on the Trojans, Athene the Achaeans. The audience is assumed to remember that he is still around and needs to be disposed of; once again that stresses the relatively light break between the two Books.

30 Taking someone by the hand can imply firmness as well as kindness; it is what the heralds were told to do with Briseis at 1.323. The χειρὸς ἑλοῦσ' formula has just been used of Athene in yet another sense at 4.542 (but see n. there), where she so protects an imaginary figure in the midst of battle.

31-5 Athene supports her proposal by suggesting that Zeus will be annoyed if they intervene – more plausible after his explicit ban early in bk 8, and which recurs, also of Athene and Ares, at 15.121ff. Ares should of course decline, especially in view of the Trojan discomfiture of 29; but being obtuse by nature he does not grasp that Diomedes' successes must be divinely inspired.

31 She addresses Ares formally – presumably he would enjoy the savage epithets. The repetition of the vocative is unique in Homer

(Hrd/AbT); the change of quantity, partly comical (Ameis–Hentze), is justified by the variation of initial alpha elsewhere in the v., always Ἄρης (etc.) in the thesis, Ἄρης in the arsis. Metrical lengthening in the opening syllable is a possible factor, as in e.g. | δῖά, though cf. W. F. Wyatt, *Metrical Lengthening* (Rome 1969) 88. See also 20.150–2n. *fin.* — Of his three epithets βροτολοιγός is straightforward, 'ruinous to mortals', μιαιφόνος means 'polluted by murder', cf. μιαίνω, μίασμα, and τειχεσιπλήτης 'approacher [i.e. attacker] of [city] walls', with -πλήτης connected with πέλας, πελάζω.

32–4 Athene's syntax is varied and soothing, almost obsequious: 'might we not leave them to fight... and let us withdraw, and avoid Zeus's wrath?'.

35–6 θοῦρον Ἄρηα is formular (9 × *Il.*), especially at the v-e; it was used a few vv. back, at 30, when Athene addressed him; therefore one cannot conclude that the choice of epithet, as he is led away like a child, is consciously ironic. Yet his being sat down by the Skamandros at 36 (where he is later found 'on the left of the battle' at 355) is surely humorous. — ἠϊόεντι is *hapax* in Homer, presumably connected (but not necessarily in post-Homeric uses) with ἠϊών = 'bank'. The river's initial σκ- never lengthens a preceding short vowel, by a metrical licence to allow the name to be used in hexameters (as with σκέπαρνον, 2 × *Od.*), cf. Chantraine, *GH* I, 108–10. V. 36 is rhythmically emphatic with its initial sequence of trochaic caesuras and assonance of ἔπειτα καθεῖσεν, the consequent dactylic rush curbed by the equivocal short syllable before Σκαμάνδρῳ.

37 The Greeks (Δαναοί is used where metrically convenient for Ἀχαιοί but 'has no corresponding toponym', S. West on *Od.* 1.350) 'bend' or turn the Trojans, i.e. into flight. ἕλε δ᾽ ἄνδρα ἕκαστος is part of a minor system for a series of quick slayings by one side, cf. 16.306 | ἔνθα δ᾽ ἀνὴρ ἕλεν ἄνδρα, with resumptive 16.351 οὗτοι ἄρ᾽ ἡγεμόνες Δαναῶν ἕλον ἄνδρα ἕκαστος. Similarly, but on a smaller scale, three Trojan leaders will kill three opponents with apparent ease at 7.8ff., and this signifies a major Achaean retreat.

38 Runover-word ἡγεμόνων, not strictly necessary, may reflect standard phraseology exemplified in 16.351 (quoted in 37n.) rather than the singer's convenience in planning the v. as a whole; yet it serves to emphasize the heightened pace of action, followed as it is by another (integral) enjambment (on which see vol. 1, 33f.).

38–83 There are six Achaean victories, the first three by more important warriors, the second by less: Agamemnon, Idomeneus, Menelaos, then Meriones, Meges, Eurupulos. There are two Cretans here, of whom Idomeneus slays at 43 a Maeonian warrior who curiously bears the name of the Cretan palace-town Phaistos, which rivalled his own Knossos.

That probably arises out of a simple association of ideas in the singer's mind; many names of minor victims had somehow to be provided, often, presumably, at short notice. All six victims are of the second or third rank: Odios, Phaistos, Skamandrios, then Phereklos, Pedaios, Hupsenor. Each is described in some detail, either about themselves and their parentage or over the manner of their death. Odios and Phaistos have least of this, and there are signs of a wish to elaborate the lesser victors' victims so as to balance out the six encounters overall. That is surely why the last three die from painful and complicated wounds in contrast with the simpler blows inflicted on the first three; cf. Friedrich, *Verwundung* 77 and Fenik, *TBS* 15 and n. 11, who also observes that 'Of the major heroes only Agamemnon and Achilles are given horrible slayings with any consistency' (but see 66–7n.).

38–40 Agamemnon's victim is Odios, coupled at 2.856 with the equally obscure Epistrophos as leader of the Halizones; this contingent from far-off Alube is in general unconvincing. Here he is termed 'great', and his being chariot-borne, too, is perhaps intended to make him more of an opponent. Nevertheless he turns away and gets a spear in the back, driven through his chest with such force that he is 'thrown out of' the chariot: 39 ἔκβαλε, unique in this application. πρώτῳ γὰρ στρεφθέντι probably means that he was first to turn to flight (cf. Τρῶας δ' ἔκλιναν in 37), rather than with e.g. Willcock that he was first to be hit, corresponding with πρῶτος in 38. Five of the six encounters emphasise in different ways that the victim was in flight, and this is implied for Phaistos too, see 46n. The Achaeans at this point are irresistible.

42 A formular v., 7× *Il.*, with its first half another 12×; see on 4.501–4. It is a probable concordance interpolation (p. 294) at 15.578 and could be here; the best MSS and a late papyrus omit it. Yet the description of the moment of death is carefully varied in this sixfold sequence, even if ἀράβησε δὲ τεύχε' ἐπ' αὐτῷ (with a different formula preceding) comes twice, cf. 58 and n. Although a balance is sought between these killings, it would be made too mechanical by the repetition of whole vv. There was a choice of standard descriptions for common actions like the final collapse in death, and singers evidently varied them deliberately.

43–4 Nothing else is known of Phaistos (cf. 38–83n.) and his father, though an Achaean Boros is mentioned at 16.177, or of Tarne which a D-scholium equated with Sardis.

46 Phaistos is struck while mounting his chariot; the heavy word ἐπιβησόμενον bridges the central caesura and produces a rising threefolder with an undeniably ponderous or majestic effect. The wound in his right shoulder is immediately fatal as commonly in *Il.*, cf. 7.16, 11.421, 13.519f., 14.450–2, 15.341, 15.541–3, 16.289f., 16.321ff., 16.343f. *Arrow*-wounds in the shoulder are not fatal, cf. 5.98ff., 11.506ff.; but the damage a spear-head can do is explicitly described at 16.322–5, where Thrasumedes thrusts at Maris in the shoulder 'and the spear-point sheared the base of the arm away from the muscles and struck it completely off'. This must be exaggerated, but it is what singers had come to accept as possible.

48–50 While Idomeneus' followers were stripping Phaistos' armour, Menelaos 'took', i.e. killed, Skamandrios the cunning hunter. Nothing else is heard of him or his father Strophios; the river Skamandros was named at 36; for Skamandrios as Hektor's son see on 6.402f. It was thought by bT that the name was suitable for a hunter, as one who passes his time by rivers and in woods; but it is the latter, and especially in the mountains, that are relevant as 52 suggests. — The meaning of αἵμονα, only here in Homer, was unprofitably debated in antiquity. It is connected with αἷμα by Euripides at *Hec.* 90, but 'bloody in the chase' is unlikely here; association with αἱμύλος, 'cunning', is debatably spurned by Chantraine. In 50 ἔγχεϊ ὀξυόεντι is formular, 7 × *Il.*, ὀξυόεις being an expansion of ὀξύς as φαιδιμόεις of φαίδιμος at 13.686, even if the primary derivation is from ὀξύα, 'beech', cf. Chantraine, *Dict.* s.v.

51–4 Being taught by Artemis herself means little more than that he was, precisely, a good hunter or rather a noble one. Hunting was always closely connected with Artemis, a strongly functional goddess of relatively narrow range (though also associated, as Apollo's sister, with dancing and with sudden death for women). In her rôle as πότνια θηρῶν she was protectress of animals as well as patroness of their destroyers, cf. the comparison of Nausikaa to her at *Od.* 6.102–4 where she 'goes through the mountains, pouring her arrows over tall Teügetos or Erumanthos, rejoicing in wild boars and swift deer'. That is the goddess who has taught Skamandrios here to 'hit all the wild creatures nurtured by mountain forest'.

53–4 That Artemis did not help him 'demonstrates the inexorability of destiny' according to bT – but also that gods did not always choose to protect their favourites, a common Iliadic motif. It also exemplifies a more general trope, both ironical and pathetic, whereby a victim is killed, despite something that should or might have saved him – e.g. his father being a seer, cf. 2.831–4 = 11.329–32, 5.148–51, 13.663ff.

Zenodotus read χραῖσμεν θανάτοιο πέλωρα for χραῖσμ' Ἄρτεμις ἰοχέαιρα, 'unintelligibly' according to Arn/A; that judgement is surely correct, and the *lectio difficilior* argument does not apply. χραισμεῖν is always in the negative in Homer as Ameis–Hentze noted. — Artemis is ἰοχέαιρα here (and 7 × *Il.*, elsewhere); the epithet seems to mean 'who pours her arrows', from ἰός and χέω, compare δοῦρατ' ἔχευαν at 5.618; and to be unconnected with χαίρειν, 'rejoicing in arrows', even though that is a superficially attractive sense in terms of popular etymology. — The 'far-shootings in which he previously excelled' are given an ironical colouring by γ' after τὸ πρίν: 'previously, at least' (i.e. he might have got in a good shot against Menelaos, if he had been lucky). ἐκηβολίαι should strictly be derived from ἑκών, not ἑκάς as it came to be in later Greek, but association with ἑκάς by popular etymology is easy enough (as Chantraine notes, *Dict.* s.v.) and could have happened within the epic tradition itself. See also on ἑκάεργος, 439n.

58 The description of his collapse maintains the variation of phraseology, see 42n.:

42	δούπησεν δὲ πεσὼν	ἀράβησε δὲ τεύχε᾿ ἐπ᾿ αὐτῷ
47	ἤριπε δ᾿ ἐξ ὀχέων	στυγερὸς δ᾿ ἄρα μιν σκότος εἷλε
58	ἤριπε δὲ πρηνὴς	ἀράβησε δὲ τεύχε᾿ ἐπ᾿ αὐτῷ
68	γνὺξ δ᾿ ἔριπ᾿ οἰμώξας	θάνατος δέ μιν ἀμφεκάλυψε
75	ἤριπε δ᾿ ἐν κονίῃ	ψυχρὸν δ᾿ ἕλε χαλκὸν ὀδοῦσιν
82f.		τὸν δὲ κατ᾿ ὄσσε

ἔλλαβε πορφύρεος θάνατος καὶ μοῖρα κραταιή.

Thus ἀράβησε δὲ τεύχε᾿ ἐπ᾿ αὐτῷ comes twice in alternate deaths, ἤριπε/ἔριπε four times in successive ones, though in differing contexts. The idea of darkness or death enveloping the victim is introduced in 47 and reused in alternate episodes thereafter, being notably developed in the closing occurrence at 82f. This provides a strong conclusion to the series, being longer, more elaborate and distinct in rhythmical effect – since the powerful πορφύρεος θάνατος virtually overruns the main caesura in contrast with the strongly four-colon character of its five predecessors.

59–64 Meriones' victim is Phereklos son of Harmonides ('Joiner') the carpenter – unless τέκτων, carpenter, is also to be taken as a proper name, i.e. Phereklos son of Tekton son of Harmon, cf. *Od.* 8.114 Τεκτονίδαο, which is unlikely. Compare 5.785 Stentor, 6.22 Boukolion, 7.220 Tukhios, 18.592 Daidalos and especially *Od.* 22.330f. Phemios Terpiades for other names indicative of the owner's profession, also 4.394–5n., von Kamptz, *Personennamen* 260f. Phereklos itself is not such a name. The reference of ὅς in 60 and 62 is a longstanding question; Aristarchus (Arn/A) discussed whether it was Phereklos or Harmonides that made the ships for Paris, and bT's conclusion that it was the latter probably derives from him. Leaf on the other hand thought that 'ὅς in 60 and 62 no doubt refers to the principal person, Phereklos'; but the first ὅς most naturally refers to Harmonides, both because of verse-division and because he, not Phereklos, has the 'speaking name'. That points the second ὅς, despite its demonstrative force, in the same direction.

61 As with Skamandrios (51–4n.), his skill is seen as due to the favour of a functional goddess – little more than a cliché.

63 The ships were 'initiators of evil' because they carried Paris to Lakedaimon.

64 Aristarchus athetized (Arn/A), since he believed οἵ τ' αὐτῷ (which refers, of course, to Paris–Alexandros) to be an improper reflexive form; that is wrong as Herodian saw (Hrd/A), cf. especially οἵ αὐτῷ at 16.47 and 23.126. The scholia invoked two different prophecies of doom (if Paris went overseas, or if the Trojans pursued seafaring) to give a special reference to 'he knew nothing of the divine decrees' – which need mean no more than his ignoring the rules of hospitality.

66–7 Meriones will inflict a similar wound on Harpalion at 13.651f. (though with an arrow, which accounts for slight differences of language) soon after another gruesome wound by him at 13.567–9: this seems typical of him, cf. Fenik, *TBS* 18, Friedrich, *Verwundung* 52–7. The exegetical scholiasts certainly went too far in suggesting that 'the wound of fornication's shipbuilder' is deliberately made αἰσχρόν, shameful, i.e. because in the bladder. Willcock, *Companion* 55f., cites medical testimony for the spear's path, but any accuracy in the description is surely due to commonsense appreciation of the rough relation between buttock, spine and bladder rather than to any special technical knowledge. See also on 73–5.

68 Phereklos groans because of the nature of the wound and collapses onto his knees, presumably as he doubles up in agony. Aristarchus (Arn/A) tried here and elsewhere to explain how a victim fell in relation to the blow, on the doubtful assumption that the poet's descriptions were regularly based on close observation.

69–71 Meges is son of Phuleus (cf. 72) and leader of the contingent from Doulikhion and the Ekhinaes islands (cf. 2.625–30); his father had moved to Doulikhion after a quarrel with *his* father, see on 2.625–6 and 2.627–30. His victim here is Pedaios the bastard son of Antenor, whose wife Theano (Athene's priestess at 6.298, see n. there and cf. 11.224) had raised him to please her husband.

73–5 The bronze spear-point hits the back of his head (ἰνίον, the occiput) and cleaves right through, along by his teeth, under the tongue: a good instance of Homer's supposed surgical precision. The contrast is unmistakable between this harsh pseudo-realism and the pathetic implications of Theano's care in 71; it is reinforced by the even less probable detail in 75, 'he took [i.e. bit] the cold bronze with his teeth'.

76–80 If the descriptions of death have been carefully varied (see on 42 and 58), so, less obviously, have the introductory vv. giving the names of victor and victim, also the verbs for killing. Once again the final sentence is the most elaborate: Eurupulos with his patronymic, then his victim Hupsenor occupy 76; 77f. describe the victim's father, then 79 resumes 76 in reverse order (τὸν μὲν ἄρ' Εὑρύπυλος followed by a varied patronymic phrase); the main verb is postponed for all of five vv. to the end of 80 (ἔλασ' ὦμον |).

76–8 Nothing more is heard of Dolopion; he is priest of the river Skamandros (who takes part in the Battle of the Gods, 20.73f., and receives sacrifices, 21.131f.), honoured like a god himself in a hyperbolic phrase (78) but also described by the martial ὑπερθύμου, 'high-spirited', in 77. Typically this epithet belongs to the Trojans (Τρῶες -ας ὑπέρθυμοι -ους 7 × *Il.*), but it can also be used of individuals, sometimes obscure ones – and sometimes, as here, for obvious metrical convenience. A second Trojan Hupsenor, son of Hippasos, will occur at 13.411; see also on 144.

80–1 μεταδρομάδην is *hapax* in Homer, δρόμος itself being virtually confined to the Games in bk 23 (8/9× *Il.*+2× *Od.*). This is a brilliantly imagined scene, with Hupsenor fleeing in front of him, Eurupulos closing at the run and leaping on him with drawn sword to slash away the whole arm. There are standard phrases here, but it is hardly the case that 'the death of Hypsenor... is fully typical' (Fenik, *TBS* 19), since an attack on a single victim with the sword and without preceding use of the spear is unparalleled in *Il*. At 144–7 Diomedes kills one of a pair with the spear, the other with the sword – similarly at 11.143–7 Agamemnon first kills Peisandros with the spear, then attacks his brother and cuts off both arms and the head with the sword; but this is regular enough since the sword is used when the spear has not yet been retrieved. The point is not trivial, owing to the normally strict conventions of Iliadic contests: the spear, thrown or thrust, is the heroic first-strike weapon, the sword being reserved for the *coup de grâce* or for occasions when a spear is not available. Five deaths have been caused by the spear; this unusual sword-blow places even greater emphasis, in this final scene of the six, on a violent and pathetic Trojan demise.

82–3 This powerful description of death, from τὸν δὲ κατ' ὄσσε on, recurs at 16.333f. and 20.476f. The 'purple death over the eyes' is associated with blood in all three contexts, here through αἱματόεσσα δὲ χείρ.

84 The idea of battle as 'labour' is not uncommon (6.522n.), and ὡς οἱ μὲν πονέοντο recurs at e.g. 627. The v. leads back from the other six Achaean victors to Diomedes himself; such transitions, by a v. or brief passage describing general fighting, are a typical device, cf. Fenik, *TBS* 19.

85–6 Here, however, Diomedes is himself part of the general fighting, so much so that you could not tell whether he was among Trojans or Achaeans. That means either (a) that he was 'everywhere at once', or (b) that the front ranks were on top of one another and he in the thick of things – a dramatic expression enhanced by the rising threefold rhythm of 85.

Something similar, including οὐδ᾽ ἂν ἔτι γνοίης, is said of intermingled armies at 14.57–60.

87–94 A powerful simile develops the idea of his irresistible might and the havoc it causes: he is like a river in spate which breaks its banks and destroys the fields. Fire and surging water are Homer's two favourite comparisons for irresistible attacks, whether by individual or whole army. Thus Patroklos' horses are compared at 16.384–93 to a storm that brings trees down the mountain torrents and destroys men's work in the plain, in a passage that has a typical structural similarity to Diomedes' triumph here (cf. Fenik, *TBS* 9), particularly in its circular movement from hero to other victories back to hero.

87–8 The river presumably gained force in the mountains like that at 16.392; it is χειμάρρῳ (from -ρροος), 'winter-flowing', i.e. a torrent. The present simile concentrates, however, on the destruction it causes below, as the emphasis on its artificial banks suggests; thus the comparison with Diomedes 'raging over the plain' is untypically exact. The γέφυραι that are scattered must be embankments or levées, heaped-up mounds of earth alongside the river-bed to keep it under control when winter storms come. In Homer the term is confined to *Il.*, 5 × in the old formula ἀνὰ πτολέμοιο γεφύρας etc., the other 2 × in this simile. The γέφυραι of battle, unlike the 'bridges' of post-Homeric Greek, are presumably passages rather than crossings ('the ways through between the masses of troops', T on 4.371, q.v. with n.). The verbal form γεφύρωσεν (2 × *Il.*) implies something like a causeway at 15.357, γεφύρωσεν δὲ κέλευθον (when Apollo fills in the Achaean trench for the Trojans to pass over); whereas at 21.245 Akhilleus pulls a tree down into the river, blocking its waters and bridging it or making a path out of it somehow. γέφυρα, therefore, is a mound of earth either along or across a ditch or river-bed.

89–90 There is no such etymological connexion between ἐεργμέναι, from (ϝ)έργω, and ἕρκος (cf. Chantraine, *Dict.*) as between ἰσχανόωσιν and 90 ἴσχει, both forms of ἔχειν, and 88 χειμάρρῳ expanded by ὅς τ᾽ ὦκα ῥέων; the phonetic similarity may have been attractive none the less. The river breaks out of its embankments and through the protecting walls of the gardens – rather than orchards or threshing-floors, other possible meanings of ἀλωή, because respectively more prone to damage and better suited by ἐριθηλής, 'very fertile'.

92 αἰζηός, etymology unknown (18× *Il.*, 2× *Od.*), is shown by its contexts to mean a man in his prime, a vigorous man – often, though not here, a warrior. In the similar comparison at 16.392 the corresponding sentence is μινύθει δέ τε ἔργ᾽ ἀνθρώπων. αἰζηῶν is more emphatic as bT suggest, since the choice of word is not in this case due to metrical needs.

There may be an echo of the phalanxes (ranks) which 'moved dense into hostile war', also after a simile, at 4.281; especially since αἰζηῶν occurred in the preceding v. there also. κλονέοντο/κίνυντο φάλαγγες is a formula, 3 × *Il.* with each verb; on κλονέοντο see 8n. 94 is cumulated, not semantically strong in itself but adding emphasis and helping to close off the episode more completely.

95–165   Diomedes' triumph is not without its reverses, for Pandaros temporarily disables him with an arrow-shot; but he prays to Athene who fills him with even greater might, so that he slays four pairs of Trojans in quick succession

95–120 The wounding episode strongly resembles that at 11.369–400, where Diomedes is struck in the heel by an arrow-shot from Paris. That wound is more serious in its consequences and less obviously a Homeric invention, but Fenik, *TBS* 20f., points out that both are typical scenes made out of typical elements, as regularly in Iliadic battle-poetry. As often, too, the differences are significant. Diomedes, accompanied by Odysseus in bk 11, is apparently irresistible in both cases and it takes an archer to stop him. At 11.373–6, however, he is stripping a victim; also the drawing of the bow is described, if briefly, in contrast with the bare account here, see on 97f. The wounds are not dissimilar, but the apparent victor's ensuing words are: here he urges the other Trojans to attack, at 11.380ff. he addresses a typical victor's boast to Diomedes, who replies with an insulting assertion of the triviality of the wound. Other typical motifs are involved, e.g. the ultimate failure of an archer (cf. Teukros at 8.292ff. and 15.458ff., Helenos at 13.593–7; so H. Erbse, *Rhein. Mus.* 104, 1961, 177).

95 A hero's run of victories is often ended when a powerful enemy 'sees' him or 'notices' what is happening and initiates a counter-attack; so too with Diomedes' next run of successes, when Aineias sees him, ἴδεν, at 166 and sets off to find Pandaros again. — Lukaon's son is, of course, the archer Pandaros, last seen in action at 4.88ff. when he broke the truce by shooting and wounding Menelaos. He is to be an important figure in this Book too, both in the present scene and when he meets his death fighting with Aineias against Diomedes.

96 The poet describes what Pandaros sees by combining bits of his previous narrative, lightly adapting the first half of 87, θῦνε γὰρ ἄμ πεδίον, and the last part of 93, κλονέοντο φάλαγγες, and combining the two. The conversion of active κλονέοντα to middle κλονέοντο is grammatically substantial but achieved with deceptive ease, as is the insertion of πρὸ ἔθεν ('before him') to lead from one adapted phrase to the other. This is typical of the singers' skill in formular combination and variation.

97–8 Pandaros simply draws his curved bow (καμπύλα τόξα 5 × *Il.*; ἄγκυλα τόξα and παλίντονα τόξα or τόξα παλίντονα belong to the same system) and shoots Diomedes in the shoulder as he charges. Compare the more elaborate account of his wounding Menelaos at 4.104ff., where he takes his bow, which is described in detail, out of its case; his companions are protecting him; then the arrow is fitted to the string, the bow drawn back and the arrow released with a shrill sound; finally its path is traced in detail. That was a momentous shot with graver consequences, for now Diomedes recovers with Athene's help and quite rapidly. Probably, too, the poet remains aware of his long description some 500 v. before and chooses not to repeat it; moreover the unexpected and briefly described wound might be held to typify the unpredictability of battle. Nevertheless the wounding itself is curiously unemphatic.

99–100 γύαλον is from * γύη, 'curve' or 'hollow'; it can mean a combe or valley, or a curved part of the corslet or breastplate. For Aristarchus (Arn/A) it probably signified the whole curve of the *thorex*; bT assigned it to 'the hollow part around the shoulder', probably because of this particular context; modern scholars usually take it either as the front- or as the back-plate of a bronze corslet. Here the arrow strikes the right shoulder after penetrating the armour; at 13.506–8 ∼ 17.313–15, however, Idomeneus smashes the γύαλον with a spear to the middle of the belly, and at 13.586f. an arrow strikes κατὰ στῆθος, on the chest, but rebounds from the γύαλον – one sees the reason both for Aristarchus' judgement and for the 'front-plate' interpretation. Finally at 15.530 Meges' corslet, admittedly an heirloom, is γυάλοισιν ἀρηρότα, implying at least two γύαλα which form a separate or distinguishable part of the θώρηξ. Once again the two-plate interpretation works. — The piercing arrow keeps right on and the corslet is stained with blood; ἀντικρύ in 100 means 'to the opposite side' as at e.g. 13.652 and 16.346, where the weapon explicitly ἐξεπέρησε, 'passed out', i.e. of the body; see 112–13 n. *init.*

101 Elsewhere | τῷ (τῇ) δ' ἐπὶ μακρὸν ἄϋσε (4 × *Il.*) means that the victor shouted 'over' the victim, that is, in triumph. Here Pandaros is addressing his own side, rather, as in Ἕκτωρ δὲ Τρώεσσιν ἐκέκλετο μακρὸν ἀΰσας (3 × *Il.* +4 similar).

102 'Spurrers of horses' looks like a common formula for the Trojans; in fact it recurs only once, and then of the Thebans.

104 The early (3rd cent. B.C.) papyrus POxy 223 and some MSS have δηθὰ σχήσεσθαι and μένος (the former also in Eustathius 528.5); Aristarchus (Did/A) was clearly right in insisting on δήθ' ἀνσχήσεσθαι (syncopated ἀνασχήσεσθαι from ἀνέχομαι) and βέλος, which became the vulgate readings.

105 Why does Pandaros think Apollo must have caused his coming to Troy? Probably for no other reason than that he himself is an archer and came 'trusting in his bow' (205). On Λυκίηθεν see 2.826–7n.: Pandaros'

Lukie cannot be that of Sarpedon and Glaukos in S–W Asia Minor, because he leads troops from Zeleia under Ida; they are Τρῶες both in the Trojan catalogue and later here at 200 and 211. His patron Apollo is Λυκηγενής at 4.101; see n. there, also for his father's name Lukaon.

107–8 Diomedes is able to withdraw to where Sthenelos has his horses and chariot waiting (both being separately specified in contrast with e.g. 13 and 111, see 13n.).

109 Καπανηϊάδη extends, as a vocative, the formular system outlined in the comment on 4.403 (16.586, | – ∪∪ – Σθενέλαον, can also be added).

110 πικρὸν ὀϊστόν picks up the πικρὸς ὀϊστός | of 99 and is a common formula (10 × *Il.*).

112–13 διαμπερές, literally 'piercing right through' (δι-ανα-πείρειν) but also with a metaphorical meaning, 'completely' or 'continually'. Here the literal meaning applies; Sthenelos draws the swift missile (swift by nature, not at this moment) right through and out the other side. That is, the arrow has indeed gone ἀντικρύ (100); it cannot be pulled back against the barbs and so has to be drawn through the back-plate of the corslet. — The blood was 'darting' up, ἀνηκόντιζε (from ἄκων = 'throwing-spear'; the compound form, used of water at Herodotus 4.181, appears only here in Homer). The (front of the) corslet had been spattered with blood at 100; here more spouts up as the arrow is withdrawn from the back.

χιτῶνος is surprising after the θώρηξ of 99 and 100. Does it mean 'tunic' simply, in which case the corslet is ignored; or the corslet itself, as in the common epithet χαλκοχίτων (31 × *Il.*, 24 × in the formula Ἀχαιῶν χαλκοχιτώνων |)? στρεπτοῖο should help; its general sense is 'turnable', from στρέφειν, thus 3 × *Il.* of the mind, the tongue or the gods; but εὔστρεπτος, εὐστρεφής, εὔστροφος describe ropes or other flexible objects (6 × *Od.*, 3 × *Il.*). This evidence would favour a flexible tunic here, whether linen or leather, as would 21.31, where Akhilleus ties the hands of Trojan prisoners with straps carried 'over their turnable *khitons*', ἐπὶ στρεπτοῖσι χιτῶσι. A two-plate bronze corslet might have had substantial straps, but the Trojan captives can hardly have been envisaged as wearing metallic armour.

Aristarchus is not usually helpful over this kind of problem. According to Apollonius Soph. 145.21 (cf. Erbse, II, 20) he explained στρεπτοῖο in terms of scale armour with 'twisted' threads, or possibly of ring or chain mail (Eust. 528.23) which is certainly much later. Some modern discussions, on the other hand (e.g. Lorimer, *HM* 196ff.; Wace and Stubbings, *Companion* 506ff.), are still vitiated by the obsolete idea inherited from Reichel that all Homeric references to bronze corslets are interpolated. The clumsy corslet of bronze hoops found at Dendra in 1960 (cf. e.g. Vermeule, *GBA* 135) disproved that, even though nothing of this particular type is described in

Homer. Metallic scale corslets were used in Assyria and Egypt in the 2nd millennium B.C. (Lorimer, *HM* 197–9), and other types, of either metal or leather, are illustrated on the Warrior Stele and Warrior Vase from Mycenae (Lorimer pls. II and III; H. W. Catling, *Arch. Hom.* E 74–118, has a full discussion of the archaeological record). In the *Iliad*, apart from formular χαλκοχιτώνων etc., χιτών usually denotes a woven tunic, whether or not as armour; Locrian Aias and a minor Trojan have linen corslets, see on 2.529–30, whereas at 3.358–60 ~ 7.252–4 the spear first penetrates the θώρηξ and then pierces the χιτών underneath. Yet χιτών undeniably refers to a metallic corslet at 13.439f., where Idomeneus shatters Alkathoos' brazen tunic (ῥῆξεν δέ οἱ ἀμφὶ χιτῶνα | χάλκεον); and in two further instances the meaning is ambiguous. On the other hand the all-important χαλκοχιτώνων (etc.) is shown by its frequency to be completely traditional. The comment on 4.135–6 concluded that bronze corslets belonged to the Mycenaean age and were gradually displaced by non-metallic ones, until the development of hoplite armour from Homer's time on. That would account for occasional confusions over corslets and *khitons*, not least for the present apparent inconsistency over what Diomedes is wearing before and after his wounding by Pandaros.

115–20 Diomedes prays in similar terms to those used by Odysseus and himself to Athene (again) at 10.278–91, where at 285–90 he likewise cites the goddess's support of his father Tudeus; but the content of the whole passage is most closely paralleled by 16.508–31, see Fenik, *TBS* 21f. Thus language, content and context of Diomedes' prayer are all typical. Structure is simple, with mainly 'ideal' colometry and cumulative enjambment, until the integral connexion of the last couplet brings the short speech to a rhythmically distinctive end.

115 On Ἀτρυτώνη (5× *Il.*, 3× *Od.*) see 2.157n., and on the form of the prayer itself cf. 1.37–42 with n.

116 That Athene had been Tudeus' supporter in battle was common knowledge, cf. 4.390, and Diomedes assumes it to be so here too. At 800–13 Athene herself will extol Tudeus in comparison with his son and repeat that she was his protectress; indeed she will shortly reply at 125f. that she has filled Diomedes with his father's might. The Tudeus theme recurs several times in books 4–6, see e.g. on 4.389–90, 6.222–3, also Kirk in *Aspects* 26; E. Vermeule, *PCPS* 33 (1987) 142.

117 'Be my friend too'; φῖλαι, here and at 10.280, is middle aor. imperative.

118 δός δέ τέ μ' ἄνδρα: so Herodian and the vulgate, though Aristarchus evidently accepted τόνδε τέ μ' ἄνδρα (Did/A), an earlier variant recorded in the pre-Aristarchan POxy 223 (cf. 104n.). δός begins five other Iliadic vv. including the similar 10.281 (see on 115–20), and is clearly right, even though δέ τε is classed by Denniston, *Particles* 531, as 'awkward' (cf. also 137–42n. *fin.*). — It was debated (AbT) whether the subject of ἐς ὁρμὴν ἔγχεος ἐλθεῖν is Diomedes or Pandaros: 'grant...that I may come to where I can discharge a spear' or 'that he comes within range of my spear': a minor matter, but one that can probably be resolved. The latter involves a change of subject, not serious in itself, but the correlation of ἑλεῖν ἄνδρα and ἐς ὁρμὴν...ἐλθεῖν, with its typical *husteron proteron*, supports the former.

119 ἐπεύχεται: Pandaros' boasting had been addressed to the Trojans rather than Diomedes himself, see on 101; note also the contrast with the other meaning of εὔχεσθαι, 'pray', in 121.

120 'Seeing the light of the sun' to imply 'living' is formular (with φάος ἠελίοιο|), 3 × *Il.*, 5 × *Od.* It is an ancient I-E figurative expression, also in the *Rigveda*, cf. M. L. West, *JHS* 108 (1988) 154.

122 This v. recurs at 13.61 and 23.772, cf. 23.627. The commonest use of γυῖα is when limbs are loosened in death, e.g. (ὑπέ)λῦσε/λῦντο δὲ γυῖα | (12 × *Il.*). In the present quite different application the limbs are specified as legs and arms, to show more vividly the heavy feeling the wound produced. They are now made ἐλαφρά, light, and the unusual verse-rhythm brilliantly illustrates the change: the first half, with its mild breach of 'Meyer's Law' and consequent run of three trochaic breaks, has a light and jaunty sound, whereas the awkward πόδας καὶ χεῖρας ὕπερθεν, with its emphatic spondee in the fourth foot, its gratuitous detailing of γυῖα and its otiose description of the arms as 'above', suggests the heaviness of the limbs before their transformation.

124–32 Athene's response is slightly longer than the prayer itself, but shares the same kind of rhythmical climax, namely integral enjambment in the closing couplet after a series of whole or lightly enjambed vv. before; see 115–20n. *fin.* It is made more dramatic, too, by the rising threefolders (rare so far in this Book) 127 and 130; they form a chiastic statement of the essential preliminaries ('the mist is removed...don't attack gods'), leading into a cumulated couplet (| τοῖς ἄλλοις...), progressively enjambed, which names the crucial exception ('...except for Aphrodite').

124–6 These vv. correspond closely with 115–17; thus an opening v. of address and instruction is followed by two referring to Tudeus. Athene does not mention Diomedes' wound any more than he, since he had simply asked for her loving protection and the ability to kill his opponent (117f.); she makes his limbs light (122) and tells him she has filled him with 'paternal might' (125). The ignoring of the wound is slightly surprising, the typical event being more consistently handled at 16.528f., where after Glaukos' prayer to Apollo the god wipes away the blood as well as stopping the pain and filling him with might. Here, however, the singer evidently plans to reuse the wound as motive for Athene's appearance a second time, at 793ff.

127–30 The removal of the ἀχλύς, 'mist', from Diomedes' eyes so that he can distinguish gods from men is a unique application of a typical if flexible motif, on which see also Fenik, *TBS* 22 and 52–4. At 506f. Ares will cover the battle with night in order to help the Trojans; at 15.668–70 Athene removes a 'divine cloud of mist' from the beleaguered Achaeans' eyes so that they can see their exact situation; at 16.567f. Zeus spreads destructive night over the fighting round Sarpedon's body, and similarly round Patroklos' (with ἠήρ this time) at 17.268–70, cf. 17.368f.; at 17.643–50 Aias prays for this mist (ἠήρ and ὀμίχλη) to be lifted and for sunlight to be restored, and Zeus grants his prayer; at 21.6f. Herē sends a deep mist (ἠήρ) over the fleeing Trojans to hold them back; Poseidon temporarily blinds Akhilleus with a divine mist (ἀχλύς) while he removes Aineias at 20.321 and 341f. The present application is thus distinct from all these; the ἀχλύς is one that prevents Diomedes (like all other mortals, probably) from distinguishing gods from men. For gods often come in disguise – that must be the implication of πειρώμενος in 129, since a god does not *make trial of* a mortal by appearing manifestly on the battlefield. In fact Aphrodite is not disguised when she rescues Aineias and enfolds him in her arms at 314f., and Diomedes' subsequent attack on her is caused by the recognition, not that she is divine not human, but that she is a weak goddess and not one like Athene: 331 γιγνώσκων ὅ τ᾽ ἄναλκις ἔην θεός. Ares, too, is undisguised when Diomedes attacks him at 841ff., even if he is acting like a man and stripping a dead human victim; but here, in any case, the hero has Athene herself to direct his actions. The singer is thus adapting the mist-over-the-eyes motif for a special but temporary dramatic effect. He does not specify very precisely what the mist implies, or concern himself too much about how Diomedes recognizes his divine opponents when they actually appear.

130 ἀντικρὺ μάχεσθαι |, with the final upsilon scanned as short, comes only here and in the related 819. Otherwise ἀντικρύ is scanned as three longs (24 × *Il.*, not *Od.*, which however has καταντικρύ 2 ×, ἀντικρύς 3 ×), as much perhaps through its value as first word in the v., 20 × *Il.*, as because its final upsilon was necessarily long by nature – indeed it is short in Attic ἄντικρυς as later accentuation shows (Chantraine, *Dict.* s.v.). There is no reason to regard ἀντικρὺ μάχεσθαι | as especially late, or interpolated, rather than as a useful if infrequent formular adaptation.

131–2 Many cumulated vv., perhaps most, reflect the singer's progressive and paratactic technique, an almost unconscious one, of adding information as it occurs to him. Here (and at 820), on the contrary, the addition of τοῖς ἄλλοις is very deliberate, and the arrangement of generalization ('don't fight against gods') followed by significant exception ('– any of them, except Aphrodite') is a rhetorical device designed to produce both emphasis and surprise. It is further heightened by the alteration in enjambment and sentence-length noted on 124–32, as well as by γ' (omitted by Zenodotus and about which Aristarchus vacillated, Did/A) in 132.

134 Diomedes had retreated at 107 to where his chariot was held in reserve, for Sthenelos to remove the arrow; now he mixes again with the πρόμαχοι, 'front fighters', i.e. he rejoins the loose fighting between the front ranks of Achaeans and Trojans. Fenik, *TBS* 22f., identifies a typical action-pattern beginning here, whereby a hero's entry into battle is marked by a simile and then multiple slayings produce a strong reaction from the enemy. Yes, but one should also remember that individual successes, and the alternation of advance and retreat by either side, are essential elements in the large-scale conception of the *Iliad* – as well as of most martial epics, oral or not. It is only the frequent use of a *simile* in this pattern that is significantly 'typical' in more than a banal or inevitable sense.

135–6 Eager and dangerous before, he is now, after Athene's injection of 'paternal might' (125), three times as strong (punctuate after μάχεσθαι as in OCT – Leaf followed by Shipp, *Studies* 245, is wrong in taking μεμαώς as *nominativus pendens*). Usually μένος is regarded as a part of oneself which can be urged on and increased, as in the formular v. (9× *Il.*) ὡς εἰπὼν ὤτρυνε μένος καὶ θυμὸν ἑκάστου. Here, however, the extra μένος is said to take hold of him, 136 ἕλεν, as though it were external to himself; it is, of course, injected into him by Athene here, but then it also 'takes hold of' the lion without divine agency. The closest parallels are 22.346 and 23.468; but this remains an individual variation of the traditional usage.

Homeric similes often diverge in elaborated details from the situation they illustrate, but here there is a more serious difference; for it is the wound itself that increases the lion's σθένος (139), whereas the increase of μένος in Diomedes is caused by the goddess, and the wound ignored. That does not mean that the psychological effect of Diomedes' wound is seen in divine terms, exactly; rather there is some imprecision over the wound's immediate effect and whether Athene soothes or heals it or not. That probably arises from the combination of two distinct typical themes: (i) a god or goddess fills a favourite with irresistible power (so Athene at 1ff.); (ii) a god, or a godlike physician like Makhaon at 4.217–19, miraculously cures or temporarily assuages a wound.

137–42 Moulton, *Similes* 60, notes that lions are a prominent subject for similes in this Book, i.e. at 161, 299, 476, 554 and 782 as well as here (though is it really 'effectively balanced and reversed' by 554ff.?). —

Despite uncertainty over the wound itself, there is a detailed correspondence which goes beyond Diomedes' actions and the explicit field of comparison; for the simile must also recall Pandaros (and reveal something new about him), envisaged as the shepherd who has lightly wounded the lion and then perhaps avoids it as it attacks the flock.

Most Homeric similes abound in the use of generalizing epic τε, this more than most; see Denniston, *Particles* 520ff., who cites 15.271–5, 15.630–6, 16.157–63, 17.673–8 as other conspicuous examples, also Ruijgh, τε *épique* chs. 11, 19, 17. ὥς τε, a frequent device for introducing a simile, has already occurred in 136; now 137 has τε, as often, after a relative, ὅν ῥά τε. Denniston 521 observes that although there may be some responsive force in this common epic idiom, 'almost all the examples denote habitual, typical action'. Next, 138 has χραύσῃ μέν τ' followed by οὐδέ. There is a certain emphatic force to μέν here (cf. Denniston 359), but it is mainly preparatory and in contrast with οὐδέ as balancing adversative (Denniston 191); it is coupled with τε which, since it occurs in an antithetical sentence, might still be held to have a certain additive function – yet 'there are strong reasons for believing that here, too, as in the case of relatives, τε generalizes the action' (Denniston 528). The following v., 139, repeats the pattern with τοῦ μέν τε... ἔπειτα δέ τ' οὐ, and 141f. vary it slightly by following αἱ μέν τ' with αὐτὰρ ὁ. Thus it is not only the successive τε's, 6 in 6 vv., that are remarkable, but also the emphatic μέν τ(ε)'s at or near the beginning of three of them.

137 ἀγρῷ: pasturage (as opposed to ἄρουρα, ploughland or cultivated fields), only here in Homer as a simple locative, though cf. ἐπ' ἀγροῦ and ἀγροῦ ἐπ' ἐσχατιήν -ῆς (7 × *Il.*, 4 × *Od.*). ἐπ' εἰροπόκοις ὀίεσσι is another quasi-adverbial appendage, '⟨watching⟩ over wool-fleeced sheep'.

138–9 The shepherd 'grazes (the lion) when it has leapt over into the sheepfold, but does not weaken it; indeed he increases its strength, and afterwards does not try to come to (his flock's) defence'. χραύσῃ and δαμάσσῃ are aor. subjunct. with generic τε in the relative clause, as often; cf. e.g. 9.117 and Chantraine, *GH* ii, 245, as well as 137–42n. αὐλή is a courtyard or open space; the construction of gen. αὐλῆς is a loose one – the lion has not leapt over *it*, exactly, but over its wall so as to be *within it*.

140 The meaning has been debated from antiquity on, or rather taken without argument in one or other of three possible ways. Does it mean (i) 'but he [*sc.* the shepherd] slips among the steadings and shuns in fear the empty [i.e. open] places'? Or (ii) 'but he slips among the steadings and they [i.e. the sheep], deserted [*sc.* by him], flee in panic'? Or (iii), 'but it [*sc.* the lion] enters the steadings and they, deserted, flee in panic'? (iii) is supported by Leaf and Willcock but entails an obtrusive change of subject from 139 προσαμύνει to 140 δύεται; it is more likely that the shepherd continues as subject of the first part, at least, of 140. The main difficulty with (ii), as also (iii), is 'the curiosity of τὰ δ' ἐρῆμα as if of μῆλα replacing ὀίεσσιν, and ἐρῆμος of animals, elsewhere in H. only of places (Leaf)' (Shipp, *Studies* 245). Some slight support for the change of gender is provided by 11.245, but it remains awkward with τὰ δ' ἐρῆμα almost immediately preceding αἱ μέν τ' ἀγχιστῖναι in the next v. Aristarchus commented on the anomaly (Arn/A) but did not athetize. As for (i), whereby the shepherd remains subject of the whole of 140 as of 139, it is supported by T and there is little to be said against it except that Homeric φοβεῖσθαι normally means 'be routed' and not 'fear' – but cf. 22.137, also Trümpy, *Fachausdrücke* 219. It is, in the end, a question of whether the composer pays more attention to the shepherd or to his flock at this moment. Unfortunately the freedom of Homeric similes in the development of details makes that impossible to determine.

σταθμούς connotes the sheep-pens or shelters, though at 2.470 σταθμὸν ποιμνήϊον means a sheep-station in a more general sense, and at 18.589 σταθμούς are distinguished from κλισίας and σηκούς, 'huts' and 'enclosures'. It is clearly a rather vague term for a station or standing (< ἵστημι etc.) for animals, ranging from the whole enclosure to particular stables, pens or shelters within it.

141 The difficulties are not yet over. Does this mean that the ewes (as they now firmly are; ὀίεσσι in 137 could be either masc. or fem.) are 'poured' on top of each other, very close together (ἀγχιστῖναι, cf. ἄγχιστος), in their panic; or that they are heaped together *in death* (so e.g. Ameis–Hentze), i.e. that the lion has killed them? In favour of the latter is that some mention of a victim or victims might be expected (but see next n.), also that τοὶ δ' ἀγχιστῖνοι ἔπιπτον |, 1 × *Od.*, refers to the falling of human casualties; of the former (favoured by b), that κέχυνται seems deliberately chosen as a variation of the ἔπιπτον formula and beautifully describes the almost fluid huddling together of a nervous flock, also that the lion would only kill one sheep, not a whole mass. The choice between the two is difficult, certainty impossible.

142–3 ἐμμεμαώς picks up the μεμαώς of 135 and is itself paralleled by the μεμαώς of 143. Bentley as well as Leaf shared the feelings of bT that the conjunction of ἐμμεμαώς and ἐξάλλεται, viz. of increased courage and implied retreat, is odd; but the lion is assumed to have made his kill, whether or not that is meant by 141, and leaps out of the enclosure to safety in the highest of spirits. — βαθέης -ν is found 4 × *Il.* as a convenient metrical variant for βαθείης etc.; here the yard is deep behind its envisaged high wall, see also on 138.

144–65 Diomedes now kills four pairs, all except the first described as brothers. Willcock rightly notes that 'The reason for them being in pairs is clearly that he was catching them in their chariots', though that is not stated except of the last pair at 160. Agamemnon similarly kills three pairs at 11.92–147, one consisting of two sons of Priam as at 159ff., and Diomedes and Odysseus kill two pairs later in the same Book at 11.320–35; all of these are specifically described as chariot-borne. Victims sharing a chariot constitute a typical motif, as do pairs of brothers (see Fenik, *TBS* 11 and 22), cf. Phegeus and Idaios at 10ff.

144 The first of the four pairs is especially obscure. Another minor Trojan called Astunoos (son of the equally unknown Protiaon) recurs at 15.455; Hupeiron is not heard of elsewhere, his grandiose description as ποιμένα λαῶν being applied to minor as well as major characters. One is reminded of the last victim of the earlier sequence, Hupsenor at 76f., whose father Dolopion was dignified by another grandiloquent formula and whose name seems to have been reapplied like that of Astunoos here; see 76–8n. He, too, had his arm sheared off by a sword-blow.

145–7 First spear, then sword is used, as often when a pair is caught in a chariot. The sword-slash severs (147 ἔεργαθεν, from ἔεργειν, to separate or cut off, with -θε as aor. suffix, cf. Chantraine, *GH* I, 328f.) the whole shoulder; shoulder-wounds are also common with spear and arrow, cf. 46n. Emphasis on the wound makes up for the cursory description of the recipient; this will be reversed in the next three pairs.

148–9 τοὺς μὲν ἔασ' -ε performs a similar transitional function 3 × elsewhere. Diomedes' next victims are Abas and Poluidos; neither recurs, though Abas reminds one of the Abantes of Euboea, and Poluidos of the great Argive seer of that name, cited as father of Eukhenor of Korinthos at 13.663 and 666f. Their father is the aged Eurudamas, as obscure and devoid of precise nationality as his sons. He is, however, a dream-interpreter, as befits a son who is Poluidos, 'much-seer [*or* -knower]', and shares the name of the famous Argive; see on 13.66off. Aristarchus (Arn/A) commented on the coincidence, and claimed that an ὀνειροπόλος interprets his own dreams and not those of others – perhaps an inference from the present context. The father-seer motif recurs in different forms: the Argive Poluidos knew that his son would die at Troy or of disease if he stayed at home, yet Eukhenor went to Troy all the same (13.663ff.; the motif of Akhilleus' fate as foretold by Thetis overlaps, cf. 9.410–16); and at 11.328–34 Diomedes (again) kills the two sons of Merops (again in a chariot), a seer who forbade his sons to fight, and yet they disobeyed him and perished.

150 The meaning has been disputed from antiquity on. Is it 'the old man interpreted no dreams for them for their homecoming' (i.e. they did not come home), or 'he did not interpret dreams on their behalf when they were coming [*sc.* to Troy]', i.e. he did not foresee their fate? Leaf opted for the latter (also supported by bT and presumably Aristarchus), mainly because ἐρχομένῳ at 198 refers to Pandaros coming to Troy and to what his father told him as he left home; also because the regular term for returning home is νίσσεσθαι or νοστεῖν, not ἔρχεσθαι. That is probably correct.

152–8 The note of pathos is strongly sounded once again, with another old father as key figure; for Diomedes' next victims are Xanthos and Thoon the only sons of aged Phainops. As with the preceding pairs their home remains anonymous, and all three look like *ad hoc* inventions. Xanthos as a proper name occurs 22 × *Il.* but nowhere else of a man (5 × of one of Hektor's horses, 16 × of rivers, either Skamandros or the Lycian one). Two other Trojan Thoons are briefly mentioned elsewhere, and Phainops too has two namesakes on the Trojan side – one a contemporary, father of Phorkus at 17.312 (whereas this Phainops will have no surviving sons, 154ff.), the other a friend of Hektor from Abudos at 17.583; this one is Asiades, like the Adamas who fought next to one of the other Thoons at 12.140. Thus the singer seems to be using a stock of relatively uncommon, or even unsuitable, Greek names for minor Trojan victims, of which there have to be many at times like this. Moreover he, and conceivably his predecessors, used some of them again and again; see also on 159–65.

153 τηλυγέτω: 'of tender age' or 'late-born' – but see on 3.174–5, 9.482. Phainops' advanced years are emphasized in the rest of the v., both to increase the pathos and to reinforce the point of the next v., that he could not produce another heir.

155–8 Even their killing is described pathetically, through the 'dear' life-spirit that he took away in 155 and the runover ἀμφοτέρω of 156 (echoing ἄμφω τηλυγέτω in 153). Their father's grief, too, is painfully evoked – both his wailing, 156 γόον, at not greeting their return, 158 δέξατο, and the grievous cares, κήδεα λυγρά, at his lack of heirs; moreover it is Diomedes, rather than they, who 'left' him all this, for he is the subject of λεῖπ' in 157. Thus Phainops receives an ironic legacy that prevents him leaving one of his own to his natural heirs; and his possessions (κτῆσις, accumulated wealth) will be divided among χηρωσταί, a term formed like ἀθληταί (Hrd/A) for those who divide up the bereaved household as lesser inheritors (bT); they are 'heirs of a vacant inheritance' (West on the similar *Theog.* 607), but especially οἱ μακρόθεν συγγενεῖς (Hesychius). Precisely how this evidently ancient term is related to χήρα 'widow' and χῆρος 'deprived of' is unclear, cf. Chantraine, *Dict.* s.v. This particular technical elaboration is in any event unique in Homer and makes more vivid, rather in the manner of a simile, the simple motif of a father deprived of his sons as used briefly of Dares at 24.

159–65 The final pair are sons of Priam (so too with a pair of

Agamemnon's victims at 11.101–3, cf. 144–65n.), and to that extent more real than their shadowy predecessors; they also rate a simile describing their death, one with the additional function of focusing more clearly on Diomedes. They are cardboard characters none the less. Ekhemmon does not occur elsewhere; his name is unusual but correctly formed, the gemination of mu a sign of shortening, viz. from Ekhemenes – as also, curiously enough, with another Priamid, Pammon at 24.250 (von Kamptz, *Personennamen* 21, 62, 164, 196). Khromios is used for several other minor characters, always in lists: a Pylian commander at 4.295, a Lycian one at 5.677, a Trojan victim of Teukros at 8.275, a Trojan ally at 17.218. Only the last of these is more than a battle statistic, earning two more mentions in bk 17; see also 152–8n. *fin.*

161–2 On lion-similes see 137–42n.; this relatively brief one strongly recalls the more elaborate one with which the present run of slayings began. There the lion leapt in among the sheep in their steading and (presumably) killed one or more, see on 141; here he leaps (161 θορών, cf. 138 ὑπεράλμενον) among cattle in their enclosed pasture and breaks the neck of one of them. The point of comparison differs slightly but the balancing effect (or reinforcement, cf. Moulton, *Similes* 61 n.) is unmistakable. — V. 161 is a dramatic rising threefolder, emphasized by the quasi-rhyme of λέων and θορών. The violence of the breaking of the victim's neck (described in more detail at 11.175) is cleverly evoked by ἐξ αὐχένα ἄξῃ, not only by the intensive preverb itself but also, as T noted, by its tmesis from ἄξῃ. V. 162 by contrast is almost gentle in a sinister way, with its leisurely vagueness over whether the victim is calf or cow and the image of them grazing peacefully, βοσκομενάων; they do so in their ξύλοχος, their pasture where they also lie down – the term is used of a deep lair of wild boar or leopard at 11.415 and 21.573, of a lion's lair at *Od.* 4.335 = 17.126. There, the wooded or thicketed aspect is emphasized (the term being a condensed form of *ξυλο-λόχος, Chantraine, *Dict.*); here, the place for lying or sleeping – for we can hardly imagine these cattle as grazing in the middle of a wood. Zenodotus (Arn/A) offered one of his most eccentric readings here, βουκόλου for πόρτιος; predictably it had no effect on the MS tradition.

164–5 He 'made them descend' from their chariot (that is, they fell out of it after fatal blows) κακῶς ἀέκοντας, a further irony based on expressions like 4.43 ἑκὼν ἀέκοντί γε θυμῷ, 7.197 ἑκὼν ἀέκοντα. The substitution of κακῶς for ἑκών neatly retains the alliterative effect while seeming to make further description of their fatal wounding unnecessary – that is, whether he used spear then sword, for example; he can hardly have broken their necks, exactly, as in the simile, and it helps not to press the comparison in detail.

165 Since this is the last of the sequence of slayings Diomedes has time to plunder the armour and hand over the captured horses to his companions, both typical details.

166–240 Aineias seeks out Pandaros in order to stop Diomedes; after long consultation, in which Pandaros deplores his own previous lack of success, they agree on a joint attack in which Aineias is to drive the chariot, Pandaros to be spearman

166 This is Aineias' first appearance in action; he is curiously devoid of patronymic etc. (cf. Reinhardt, *IuD* 128) as he catches sight of (cf. 95n.) Diomedes ravaging the Trojan ranks. στίχας ἀνδρῶν (14 × *Il.*) occurs only here with ἀλαπάζοντα, though together they make a powerful phrase, cf. 11.503 νέων δ' ἀλάπαζε φάλαγγας.

167 This v. recurs at 20.319, with Aineias again involved (not as subject but as joint object of the search). Otherwise κλόνος is used in the formula κατὰ κλόνον (4 ×, rather than ἀνὰ κλόνον as here), and without an awkward defining gen. like ἐγχειάων. Incidentally κλόνος and forms of κλονέω, 28 × *Il.* in all, are conspicuous by their absence from *Od.*; see also on 8.

168–9 Archery is the best means of dealing with someone invincible at close range; the same vv. occurred in similar circumstances at 4.88f. The laudatory terms (168 ἀντίθεον, 169 ἀμύμονά τε κρατερόν τε) are subtly ironical – Pandaros is not, of course, especially godlike, 'blameless' (*vel sim.*; see A. A. Parry, *Blameless Aegisthus* (Leiden 1973); S. West on *Od.* 1.29) or powerful, but his final appearance, in spite of his self-depreciation, has a certain displaced heroic quality. — For the εἴ που ἐφεύροι idiom cf. αἵ κέν πως etc. and 2.72n.; it does not imply that Pandaros is especially hard to find, but throws added emphasis on | εὗρε which immediately follows. On this verb without connecting particle cf. 4.89n. (to which should be added that 2.169 and two of the other four asyndetic uses have ἔπειτ(α) following, somewhat mitigating the abruptness). But 4.327 and 11.197 = 15.239 remain the closest parallels; all are the culmination of a specific movement to find someone.

170 στῆ δ(έ) is an especially frequent way of beginning a v., 48 × *Il.*, 19 × *Od.* (+στῆ ῥ(α) 3 × *Il.*, 7 × *Od.*). ; one person often stands near another and then addresses him or her (though this is not the only application), cf. e.g. 14.297, στῆ δ' αὐτῆς προπάροιθεν, ἔπος τ' ἔφατ' ἔκ τ' ὀνόμαζεν. The present formulation is unique in having plain ηὔδα rather than προσηύδα or προσέειπε, followed by a double accusative, ἔπος...μιν.

171–8 Aineias addresses Pandaros in a typically heroic combination of rebuke (171f.), flattery (172f.), practical observation (174–6) and pious prudence (177f., cf. 174). The exhortation lacks rhythmical emphasis except for 174, but is noticeably cumulative (172, 176, 178), with other progressive enjambments at 173, 175 and 177.

171 Similarly Aias to Teukros at 15.440f., ποῦ νύ τοι ἰοὶ | ὠκύμοροι καὶ τόξον...;, and cf. 2.827.

172–3 The cumulated καὶ κλέος is unusual, with no close parallel in 25 Iliadic uses of κλέος, many formular. Pandaros' reputation is flatteringly emphasized, not least by σέο γ'. For Λυκίη see 105n., on εὔχεται 1.91n., also S. West on *Od.* 1.172.

174 Best heard as a rising threefolder,

ἀλλ' ἄγε τῷδ' ἔφες ἀνδρὶ βέλος Διὶ χεῖρας ἀνασχών,

which makes the instruction more urgent. That separates τῷδ' from ἀνδρί but places more emphasis on *this* man, with Aineias imagined as pointing him out; stressing the main caesura, on the other hand, unacceptably isolates βέλος. Διὶ χεῖρας ἀνασχών is formular (twice elsewhere), prayer before an arrow-shot being a typical motif. There is something random, therefore potentially divine, in the long-distance weapon.

175–6 Sarpedon uses these same vv. of Patroklos at 16.424f.; the unidentifiable enemy is a reminder of the confusion of battle, also a way of stressing his almost superhuman status. ὅδε is predicative, 'who(ever) is acting violently *here*' (for this sense of κρατέει cf. 21.315).

177–8 This at first hearing gratuitous addition underlines a crucial motif introduced by Athene at 127–32, of gods taking part in the battle and the need to recognize them. It also plays on the distinct motif of divine wrath (e.g. Apollo's at 1.75, Poseidon's against Odysseus in *Od.*), itself a special form of the general *menis* theme. Failure over sacrifice is itself a typical reason for divine rage (178 ἱρῶν μηνίσας), cf. 1.65 and 9.533. — ἔπι is for ἔπεστι (Ameis–Hentze), 'follows as a consequence'.

180–216 Aineias' request unleashes a much longer reply, in which Pandaros identifies Diomedes but claims to be unable to do as Aineias wishes (for further thematic resemblances to 20.81–102 see Fenik, *TBS* 27f.). The whole speech is negative and indignant, though logical in its way; rhythmically fairly regular, it contains much progressive enjambment and relatively little internal punctuation. His frustration is expressed not through diction (cf. p. 34) so much as through his unusual and naive personal reactions in themselves. The line of argument, which according to Lohmann (*Reden* 40–3) combines ring-form, parallel and serial elements, is as follows:

181–3 The destructive enemy looks like Diomedes (cf. 174f.)
183–7 He might be a god (cf. 177f.), but, if not, then a god is
    protecting him

188–91 I wounded him in vain, so a god must be angry (cf. 178)
192–204 I have no chariot to attack him with, but left it behind though urged by my father to bring one
205–8 My bow has failed me not once but twice
209–16 It meant bad luck, so I shall smash it if I get home.

180 βουληφόρε implies nothing special about Aineias' position among the Trojans, since the epithet occurs 15 × *Il.*, of various commanders. Out of 7 occurrences in the voc., 4 are applied to Aineias, the other 3 to Sarpedon and Idomeneus, who are metrically equivalent for this purpose.

181 Aristarchus changed his mind (διχῶς, Did/A) over whether μιν or μέν is correct here, but the former is clearly preferable and was accepted by nearly all MSS. — δαΐφρων might seem ill-chosen of Diomedes on this occasion, if it really meant 'intelligent'; it is, however, a general-purpose epithet in *Il.* (28 ×, of which 3 × each of Diomedes and Tudeus), and Chantraine is surely right (*Dict.* s.v.) in arguing for a primary derivation from δάϊς, 'battle': 'of martial intent' or the like. In *Od.*, on the other hand, 5 of its 21 uses are in the formular description of Odysseus as δαΐφρονα ποικιλομήτην, and all the rest could carry the same meaning, presumably 'intelligent'. There the connexion seems rather to be with δαῆναι, 'learn'; thus the tradition vacillated over an evidently ancient term. See also S. West on *Od.* 1.48–9.

182–3 Pandaros claims to recognize Diomedes by his shield, helmet and horses. This is not a fully typical motif, but the idea of recognizable accoutrements is obvious enough. One need not think just of shield-devices (as in Aeschylus, *Septem*), though they are one possibility and were freely depicted in Geometric as in subsequent vase-painting. At 11.526 Kebriones recognizes Aias simply by his broad shield – that is an unusual piece of equipment like Akhilleus' huge spear, but other shields could have carried special decoration like Akhilleus' in bk 18, on a simpler scale, or perhaps a mere emblem. Other elaborate pieces of armour, like Agamemnon's corslet at 11.19–28, would be familiar and recognizable.

For τρυφάλεια as a term for helmet see on 3.371–2 and 3.362; αὐλῶπις (4 × *Il.*) is no less mysterious, see Chantraine, *Dict.* s.v. αὐλός, Trümpy, *Fachausdrücke* 44, Lorimer, *HM* 239–42, Wace and Stubbings, *Companion* 515, J. Borchhardt, *Arch. Hom.* ε 58. αὐλός is a pipe, tube or groove; the -ῶπις element might refer it to a slit or opening for eyes and nose, but is hard to explain if αὐλ- signifies a socket for the plume. Special horses, like special armour, would be generally known, as Diomedes knows those of Aineias at 261–3; though his own are not remarked on elsewhere. — Pandaros thinks it is Diomedes; that is what his appearance suggests (181 ἐΐσκω), but he could be a god, i.e. in disguise. This reference to Aineias' cautious words at

177 caused Aristarchus to athetize (Arn/A) on the (wholly unjustified) ground of inconsistency.

184–6 Another possibility occurs to Pandaros: that the apparent Diomedes is not himself a god, but is the real man (ἀνήρ is predicative) with a god standing close by him and 'wrapped around the shoulders in cloud', i.e. invisible; cf. 127–30n.

187–91 The reason for this conjecture (apart from the 'madness', τάδε μαίνεται, of 185) is that Pandaros had hit him on the right shoulder and knew the arrow to have penetrated the corslet (189, cf. 99–100n.). He was therefore convinced (190 ἐφάμην, cf. 103f., 3.27–8n.) that Diomedes was mortally wounded; yet all the same (191 ἔμπης) he did not in fact subdue him, cf. 104 – *therefore* some god is enraged (or 'this is then an angry god', Willcock), θεός νύ τίς ἐστι κοτήεις (and must have diverted the shot, cf. 187 and n.).

187 However, Zenodotus wanted to athetize this v. (Arn/A) because the arrow was not diverted elsewhere but scored a hit; to which Aristarchus replied that it was diverted to a non-fatal spot. That was so of the wounding of Menelaos at 4.129ff., but is not said to be the case here. There is indeed some confusion in what Pandaros says, since he has seen the arrow strike the shoulder (188) and thinks the wound to be fatal, which is not the case. Divine intervention actually comes later, but Pandaros senses unfairness and misuses the typical god-diverting-a-missile motif to express it. If the v. were a standard one, interpolation might be a possibility; but it is not, and was presumably made for the occasion. — τούτου is ablatival, 'away from him'; κιχήμενον has present sense, 'on course for scoring a hit' (Ameis–Hentze).

190 For Ἀϊδωνῆϊ προϊάψειν cf. Ἄϊδι προΐαψεν at 1.3, Ἀϊδωνεύς being a lengthened form of Ἀΐδης as at 20.61 and later in tragedy. Note the repetition of καί μιν after 188.

192 Pandaros' new line of argument, that he has no chariot with which to renew the attack, ignores the possibility that he might shoot again at Diomedes and have better luck next time; after all, his bow is not broken like Teukros' at 8.327f. He presumably continues to think of Diomedes as god-protected – but in that case a chariot would make no difference. Pandaros is not meant to be a wholly logical man.

193–203 The unusual tale of how he had decided not to bring a chariot to Troy, in spite of all those he had at home and his father's advice, is part of his characterization – unusually deliberate for the *Iliad* – as self-pitying and shallow-minded. Perhaps, too, it serves to gloss over his unsuitability as chariot-partner for Aineias in facing this dangerous foe, by showing him as having some experience with horses.

192 ∼ 14.299. τῶν κ' ἐπιβαίην: 'on which I could mount' in order to confront this enemy, not for running away as T claimed – the exegetical scholia exaggerated Pandaros' bad character, accusing him e.g. of meanness over the horses' rations, a misinterpretation of 202 (q.v. with n.).

193 There is a conversational ring to ἀλλά που: 'but, I tell you'; it could also be ironical (Ameis–Hentze).

194–5 The 11 chariots he left at home are 'fine ones, just joinered, new-made'. The tautology of πρωτοπαγεῖς and νεοτευχέες worried Zenodotus, who according to Aristarchus (Arn/A) μετέθηκεν the v. or the words somehow. There is a probable lacuna in the scholium, and Ludwich suggested that Zenodotus had combined the two vv. into πρωτοπαγεῖς, παρὰ δέ σφιν ἑκάστῳ δίζυγες ἵπποι (thus saving the tautology at the expense of the nice detail about the canvas covers). But μετέθηκεν means 'altered the order of' and does not imply the restoration of a shorter text (some have taken it to be a corruption of ἠθέτηκεν, but omission of 194 leaves the rest of the context in disarray). Actually there is nothing wrong with the passage; the tautology is emphatic as often in Homer, who 'sometimes put words of equal force side by side, παραλλήλως' as Aristarchus remarked. Bolling, *External Evidence* 88, disagreed.

For chariots covered when in store cf. 2.777, 8.441; it is one of several 'familiar details' in this passage, despite being without parallel as a whole (Fenik, *TBS* 28). παρὰ... ἵπποι recurs at 10.473, the only other place where horses are δίζυγες, meaning little more than that they were two to a chariot. The tidy arrangement of the stable might be impracticable in real life, but makes a pretty picture and at least conveys that resources were there in abundance. See also on 2.777–8, where a similar lack of realism may apply.

196 For well-fed horses, another familiar detail, cf. 2.776, 8.188f., 564 (where most of the v. recurs), 13.35. Their diet is a down-to-earth one of barley and spelt (in contrast with the lotus and parsley of Myrmidon horses at 2.776).

197–200 The typical motif of a father's injunction as his son leaves for war is reused here, with some adjustment of regular formular language; compare 6.207 (Bellerophon's father) καί μοι μάλα πόλλ' ἐπέτελλεν and 11.782 (Akhilleus' and Patroklos' fathers) τὼ δ' ἄμφω πόλλ' ἐπέτελλον. Usually, however, the injunction is a general one – for Akhilleus and Bellerophon it is contained in the famous v. αἰὲν ἀριστεύειν καὶ ὑπείροχον ἔμμεναι ἄλλων. Here it also has a more practical side: to be a leader for the Troes (his own particular people, that is, see 105n., also on 2.826–7 and 4.90–1) *mounted on his chariot*. The elevated tone survives in 200, virtually identical with 2.345 where Nestor tells Agamemnon ἄρχευ' Ἀργείοισι κατὰ κρατερὰς ὑσμίνας (the closing phrase 7× *Il.*); in fact ἀρχεύειν, not elsewhere, may be modelled on ἀριστεύειν in the αἰὲν ἀριστεύειν injunction. Shipp, *Studies* 247, counted it as an 'abnormal feature' together with a few others in Pandaros' complaints, which are 'a kind of digression and have often been condemned'. Rather they form part of a rare virtuoso description, built around the revaluation of several minor but typical motifs and designed to show Pandaros in his last hour of life as an unusual and almost comical individual, one in whom the ordinary heroic qualities have become a bit unbalanced.

197 αἰχμητά is not found elsewhere as a nominative singular, but may not be as untraditional as Shipp claimed citing Risch (*Studies* 247). γέρων αἰχμητά Λυκάων is presumably modelled on γέρων ἱππηλάτα Πηλεύς etc. (4 × *Il.*, similarly 4 × with Phoinix and Oineus), and αἰχμητά could have been repeated with other aged warriors with ◡ – – names. See further S. West on *Od.* 3.68.

200 Τρώεσσι: his own people, the Troes, from around Zeleia, as also in 211; see on 105.

201 This v. recurs at 22.103, its last half strongly formular (11 × *Il.*, 16 × *Od.*).

202–3 Pandaros' reason for leaving his horses behind is again unusual, being practical but ill-judged. φειδόμενος looks like a useful form but occurs only here (other forms of the verb 1 × *Il.*, 2 × *Od.*); that the act is also compassionate is shown too by pathetic μοι in 202 and 'being accustomed to eat their fill' in 203. — For ἀνδρῶν εἰλυμένων cf. 782 and 18.287 ἐελμένοι ἔνδοθι πύργων. Ancient critics disagreed about the spelling of ἅδην (Hrd/AbT); the aspiration is strictly correct, cf. e.g. Latin *satis*, but epic psilosis probably applies; metrical lengthening accounts for the long first syllable, which is naturally short (and so in its two other Iliadic uses).

204 The initial digamma of Ilios was usually observed; but ὅτ᾽ ἐς Ἴλιον εἰλήλουθα recurs twice in bk 21 and in irreproachably Homeric contexts, the deaths of Lukaon and Asteropaios (81 and 156).

206–8 'For I already let fly at two of the champions... and from both of them brought forth real blood after scoring a hit, but roused them on the more': the individual words belong to the standard heroic vocabulary but it is an unusual complaint, also quite complex in colometry by the standards of this mainly straightforward speech, with its rising threefolders in 207 and probably 208. The note of self-pity and naive pathos sounds unmistakably once again. Ameis–Hentze unjustifiably athetized, partly on the grounds of repetition after 188f.

208 Editors take ἀτρεκές as adverbial and equivalent to ἀτρεκέως, after bT, but rhythm and word-order argue for its being adjectival. ἀτρεκέως is frequent in the mainly Odyssean ἀλλ᾽ ἄγε μοι τόδε εἰπὲ καὶ ἀτρεκέως κατάλεξον (4 × *Il.*, though in bks 10 and 24, 13 × *Od.*, +variants), and ἀτρεκές is adverbial in its only other occurrence, at *Od.* 16.245. But the meaning of ἀτρεκής is 'true', 'unswerving', from ἀ-*τρέκος, cf. Lat.

torqueo, and the sense here, in any case metaphorical, could be 'real blood', i.e. not illusory or due to over-optimism. — Strictly it was only Diomedes that he stirred on even more, 208 ἤγειρα δὲ μᾶλλον.

209–16 Pandaros ends with the conclusion that his bow has brought him bad luck and a petulant threat that he will smash it if he gets home safely. He is, of course, about to go to his death.

209 κακῇ αἴσῃ also at 1.418; the homely πάσσαλος or peg is used for suspending a variety of objects, a yoke at 24.268, a bow again at *Od.* 21.53, also in *Od.* for a lyre (twice) and a shirt.

211 Τρώεσσι: see 200n.

212 Verbs of seeing accompanied by ὀφθαλμοῖσι(ν) are common in both epics – it was a favourite and indeed formular epic redundance. νοστήσω and ἐσόψομαι are aor. subjunct. rather than fut. indic.

213 καὶ ὑψερεφὲς μέγα δῶμα | recurs at 19.333 preceded by | κτῆσιν ἐμὴν δμῶάς τε; that v. also comes 2 × *Od.* (with its 2nd hemistich 7 ×). Pandaros could have used either version – that is, referred *either* to possessions, servants and house *or* to native land, wife and house. With Akhilleus at 19.333 the former was necessary since he had no wife, so too with Penelope at *Od.* 19.526; but Odysseus too chooses this version at *Od.* 7.225, leading to comments on his materialism (cf. Hainsworth *ad loc.*). Yet both forms of the v. were present in the tradition, and there could be a random element in the selection of either.

214 = *Od.* 16.102, with εἰ μή + opt. ('because subordinate to the wish, τάμοι', Willcock) following at *Od.* 16.103 as in 215 here. — ἀλλότριος φώς, 'some total stranger'; ἀλλότριος etc. is commoner in *Od.* (15 ×) than in *Il.* (2 ×) for obvious contextual reasons. There is a fair amount of primarily Odyssean terminology hereabouts, partly because much of the subject-matter (the contents of large houses and so on) is closer to that poem.

216 ἀνεμώλια: 'of no account', impermanent like the wind, as in its three other Iliadic occurrences. bT compared being snatched away by gales or Harpies (*Od.* 4.727, 1.241), but that implies disappearance and is a different idea.

217–28 Aineias skilfully turns Pandaros' mind to more positive action; his speech, together with Pandaros' reply, contains more integral enjambment than before (here, in 5 out of 12 vv.), but is apparently dispassionate none the less. Yet the idea of attacking such an opponent in such company is highly imprudent.

218 ἀγορεύειν is often used of speaking, in a quite neutral way; here it is tempting to take it more literally, since Pandaros has been holding forth rather, as though in assembly. — οὐκ ἔσσεται ἄλλως, 'no change will be made' (Leaf): the situation will not improve until we face up to him.

219–20 νώ is unique in *Il.* for νῶϊ (as at 224) as acc. of the dual (so

Hrd/A); it occurs 1 × *Od.*, where it can be read as νῶ', at 15.475. Emendation here is difficult, neither Brandreth's πρὶν νῶϊν τῷδ' ἀνδρί nor van Leeuwen's πρὶν ἐπὶ νῶϊ τῷ ἀνδρί being quite satisfactory. — They are to make trial of Diomedes both with horses and chariot and, as one would expect, in full armour, σὺν ἔντεσι. Aineias means that they are to make a regular attack in contrast with that of an archer; there is no implication that Pandaros has to change equipment, that aspect being passed over in silence.

221–3 = 8.105–7. The Τρώϊοι ἵπποι are those of the divine breed started by Aineias' great-great-grandfather Tros; as Diomedes will relate at 265–72, Zeus gave the first ones to Tros in recompense for his son Ganumedes, and Aineias' father Ankhises had later managed to breed from their stock by stealth. These horses are expert at swift movement over the plain in both pursuit and retreat, φέβεσθαι here implying the latter rather than panic or rout. Von der Mühll (*Hypomnema* 94ff.) assigned all references to Aineias' horses to his poet B, an approach ridiculed by Reinhardt, *IuD* 133–5.

225 Aineias forgets both his own idea that Diomedes might be a god in disguise and Pandaros' amendment that he may be supported by an invisible god (185f.) in supposing that divine help must now have ceased, temporarily at least. He ignores Athene, since Zeus has overall responsibility for success or failure.

226–7 Aineias' chariot was mentioned for the first time at 221; before that, especially at 166–70, he was treated as though on foot. Now he offers whip and reins to Pandaros (having already told him to mount, 221 ἐπιβήσεο), adding that he himself will dismount and do the fighting, i.e. when the need arises: ἐγὼ δ' ἵππων ἀποβήσομαι ὄφρα μάχωμαι. That implies nothing about whether he is envisaged as already in the chariot. Zenodotus, however, read ἐπιβήσομαι not ἀποβήσομαι (Did/A), with Aristarchus and most MSS supporting the latter; Aristarchus' reason is wrong, but ἀποβήσομαι is certainly correct. That is demonstrated by 17.479f., where Automedon tells Alkimedon in closely similar words to take the reins; he himself will dismount (ἀποβήσομαι, not queried in the scholia there though ἐπιβήσομαι was read by a small minority of MSS) and fight – which he then does, 17.483 ἀπόρουσε. Zenodotus' reading was probably determined by the assumption that Aineias is talking about an *immediately imminent* action, since they both enter the chariot at 239, ἐς ἅρματα ποικίλα βάντες. The whole passage is indeed a little confusing, (i) through the erratic introduction of Aineias' chariot and a lack of specific information about whether he is in it or not; (ii) through the adaptation of a typical motif whereby a hero offers the reins to another and *immediately* dismounts to engage an enemy, as with Automedon in book 17. The charioteer's function in that case is to keep the chariot close behind him, see on 233–4 below.

228 Alternatively, Pandaros is to face up to ('receive') Diomedes while Aineias manages the horses. Repetition of 'receive' in a wholly different sense is momentarily disconcerting: 227 δέξαι the whip and reins, 228 δέδεξο (perf. imper.) this man, i.e. Diomedes.

230–8 Pandaros accepts Aineias' last suggestion with a graceful statement of his reasons, omitting to note that Aineias is by far the stronger spearman of the two. Compare 17.475f. (see on 226–7), where Automedon refers to horses obeying Patroklos who knew how to control them.

231 On καμπύλον ἅρμα see 6.38–44n.

232 Aineias' claim that his horses are good at pursuit and retreat, something of a rhetorical flourish at 223, is now to be taken literally, since Pandaros sees that they might very well be retreating before Diomedes.

233–4 ματήσετον, 'do nothing' or 'act in vain', cf. 23.510 μάτησεν; also μάτην, 'in vain', first in *HyDem*. This is a variant of the charioteer's typical rôle in close support of a warrior who has dismounted, cf. e.g. 11.339f., 15.456f., 16.367f., cf. 16.657. At 230–2 it was presumably the accustomed touch they would miss; here it is the accustomed voice.

236 μώνυχας -ες ἵππους -οι |: the first occurrence of a common formula (33 × *Il.*, 1 × *Od.*), in which the epithet is generally agreed to derive from * σμ-ῶνυξ from * σεμ-, cf. εἷς, μία, Lat. *semel*: 'with single hoof' (in contrast with cloven-hoofed animals like cattle). See Chantraine, *Dict.* s.v.

237–8 The language remains, as it has for much of the discussion, in a low key; but with individual applications, in accord with the often untypical subject-matter, of some common epic words and phrases. The emphatic 237 is simply constructed ('but *you* drive *your* chariot and *your* horses'), and the finality of these two closing vv. is stressed by their correspondence with those of Aineias' speech just before; compare especially 228 | ἠὲ σὺ τόνδε δέδεξο with 238 | τόνδε δ' ἐγὼν ἐπιόντα δεδέξομαι.

239–40 The rhyme of φωνήσαντες and βάντες (though modified by tonic accent), each at the end of a participial clause and separated by the central caesura, produces a ponderous effect – which makes the rising threefolder of 240 all the more dramatic by contrast, rounding off the scene and evoking, together with ἐμμεμαῶτ', the speed and resoluteness of their advance.

241–310 As Aineias and Pandaros approach them by chariot Sthenelos advises Diomedes to withdraw and is rebuked for it. In the engagement that follows Pandaros is killed and Aineias severely wounded while trying to protect his body

241–2 A fresh phase in the action is initiated in a typical way when

Sthenelos catches sight of the Trojan chariot advancing towards them. A new discussion begins, balancing that of Aineias and Pandaros.

243–50 Sthenelos' speech is tactful, even ingratiating, as he makes the case for prudent withdrawal (a typical theme, Fenik, *TBS* 30) by assessing the opposition in detail. He is seen by the poet as prone to speak too readily, and his indignant words to Agamemnon during the Inspection at 4.404ff. had led to a rebuke from Diomedes such as he will receive here. The disagreement between the two men is once again highly dramatic.

243 Diomedes is addressed in this intimate way ('joy of my heart' almost) by Athene at 826 and Agamemnon at 10.234, and so too Patroklos by Akhilleus at 11.608, cf. 19.287.

244 A sense of urgency is conveyed by the alliterative μεμαῶτε μάχεσθαι preceded by two rhyming anapaestic words, ὁρόω κρατερώ, with emphatic ἐπὶ σοί as short third colon.

245–8 ἀπέλεθρον: 'immeasurable', cf. Chantraine, *Dict.* s.v. πλέθρον; note too the repeated εὔχεται (1.90–1n.). Genealogy is as important here as martial skills. The implication of 246 that Pandaros' father Lukaon is well known is not confirmed elsewhere, see on 105 and 4.101.

249–50 Aristarchus (Did/A) strangely took ἐφ᾽ ἵππων to mean 'towards the horses (or chariot)'; but obviously χαζώμεθ᾽ ἐφ᾽ ἵππων simply means 'let us withdraw by chariot', ἐφ᾽ ἵππων having that sense in its three other Iliadic occurrences. Diomedes was last seen fighting on foot (134ff.), his chariot and Sthenelos presumably close by (183). Zenodotus athetized both vv., irrationally since they are directly taken up in the first words of Diomedes' reply, μή τι φόβονδ᾽ ἀγόρευε. They are rather moving, in fact, with μηδέ μοι οὕτω | giving a pleading effect to the formular v. 250, which recurs with minor adjustment at 11.342 and 20.412.

251–73 Diomedes gives him a fierce look (just as at 4.411) and delivers a long reply, first rejecting the idea of retreat as out of the question and then outlining a plan for capturing Aineias' priceless horses.

252 'Say not a word about turning to flight' (Leaf compared 16.697, φύγαδε μνώοντο), 'since I don't think you will persuade me'; the last phrase being not exactly ἠθικόν, attuned to the character as bT remarked (i.e. a gentle rejection between friends), but rather a typically Homeric idiom of understatement.

253–6 Diomedes works himself up in the course of this exercise in self-justification, which moves from calm progressive enjambment (although with violent ἀλυσκάζοντι and καταπτώσσειν) to short passionate assertions and integral enjambment.

253 γενναῖον only here in Homer (from whom γέννα, γεννάω are also absent); γένος and γενεή, however, are common enough, and the connexion of γενναῖον with 'race' or 'family' is obvious: 'it is not in my blood (or family tradition) to fight by seeking escape'.

254 The cumulated v. adds the idea of his μένος being still sound, with probable reference to his wound.

255–6 He refuses to mount his chariot as Sthenelos has urged; ὄκνος is a strong term, implying revulsion as much as hesitation. He will face them αὔτως, nevertheless; ἀντίον (rather than ἀντίος) is unobjectionable, cf. 17.69, 19.70, 22.195; anaphoric αὐτῶν is by no means unparalleled, if a little weak. τρεῖν makes up in emphasis what it lacks in elegance (unlike τρεῖ at 11.553 = 17.663, its contraction cannot be resolved); but neither ἔα nor ἐᾷ with synizesis, favoured by Herodian (AbT) and most editors, can be directly paralleled as epic forms of ἐάω, cf. Chantraine, *GH* 1, 305. V. 256 has its possible blemishes, then; ἀντίον εἶμι, τρέειν μ' οὐκ εἴα Παλλὰς Ἀθήνη, after van Leeuwen, is a possible restoration. Shipp, *Studies* 268, finds similar 'features from later Greek' in Akhilleus' impassioned speech at 9.308ff., and a degree of superficial modernization of such lapidary statements of the heroic code would not be surprising.

257–8 Their horses will not carry both of them, at any rate, to safety – the expression provokes Diomedes' afterthought about the need to capture the horses themselves (see next n.). In πάλιν αὖτις the first term is local, 'back again' (Arn/A). For the emphatic repetition of γε in 258 cf. 287f., 16.30, 22.266; the resemblance to Attic γοῦν is coincidental, εἴ γε being thoroughly Homeric (cf. also ἐπεὶ οὖν, ὡς οὖν, Denniston, *Particles* 416f., 448).

259–61 Diomedes' new idea (for the formular v. 259 see on 1.297) continues his previous line-of-thought: if Athene (cf. 256) lets him kill both opponents, not just one (cf. 257f.), then and only then will Aineias' horses be available for capture. — κῦδος ὀρέξῃ | (etc.), 9 × *Il.*, is part of a long formular system, with κῦδος ἄροιτο, ἔδωκεν, ὀπάζει, ἔθηκε (etc.) another 28 × in all. πολύβουλος Ἀθήνη, by contrast, is totally unformular, indeed anti-formular. The epithet recurs only at *Od.* 16.282 (see next para.), also of Athene but more pertinently. There, Athene is last word in the v., and separated from the epithet which remains positioned as here. That is the regular formular position for this name, which out of 88 Iliadic occurrences in the nom. comes 86 × at the v-e (15.123, where no epithet is involved, being the other exception). In the *Od.* Athene comes 107 × at the v-e, only once (at 16.260, and then without epithet) elsewhere. The upshot is that πολύβουλος Ἀθήνη straddling the main caesura, which looks at first sight merely unusual, is a unique case among almost two hundred; it goes completely against the established tendencies of one of the strongest and most voluminous formular systems in the Homeric epos. Apart from removing Athene from her established position at the v-e – something which may only be done, it seems, and then extremely rarely, when she is devoid of epithet – this usage separates personal name from epithet by the main caesura in an unaccustomed and perhaps violent way. The ancient critical tradition noticed nothing awry, modern editors likewise.

What conclusion should be drawn – that the v. is interpolated or corrupt? Interpolation is unlikely, since the whole instruction is integral to what happens next. Corruption, or expansion rather, is possible, though without obvious purpose. *Od.* 16.281–3 remains as conceivable model (with 281 = 259 here):

> ἄλλο δέ τοι ἐρέω, σὺ δ' ἐνὶ φρεσὶ βάλλεο σῇσιν·
> ὁππότε κεν πολύβουλος ἐνὶ φρεσὶ θῇσιν Ἀθήνη,
> νεύσω μέν τοι ἐγὼ κεφαλῇ, σὺ δ' ἔπειτα νοήσας...

Yet the question remains why an Iliadic singer should choose to model his v., and distort formular usage to this extent, on a wholly different Odyssean passage about hiding armour. Perhaps the desire to use κῦδος ὀρέξῃ displaced Athene from the v-e; but the sentence could easily have been formed differently so as to avoid such anomalies. – τούσδε μέν is in contrast with 263 Αἰνείαο δ'; they are his own swift horses, though ὠκέες ἵπποι just 4 vv. before referred to those of Aineias.

262–4 μεμνημένος in 263 applies to the whole sequence of events: he is to remember to tether his own horses and drive Aineias' away to the Achaean camp. V. 263 (with the similar 323) remains rhythmically awkward, a rising threefolder complicated by a breach of 'Meyer's Law', i.e. trochaic break in the second foot.

265–72 The merits of the horses descended from those given by Zeus to Tros have already been touched on by Aineias at 222–3 (see n.), and their history is now expounded by Diomedes who evidently knows all about them (either from prisoners or through Argive tradition, bT).

265–9 γενεῆς in 265 and 268 is partitive, with 265 ἧς ablatival: 'For of that race (I tell you) from which Zeus gave to Tros... of that race Ankhises stole ⟨some⟩, by mating mares [*sc.* with them] without Laomedon's knowledge.' On Ganumedes (Tros's son, υἱος in 266 being gen.) see 20.231–5 with 4.2–3n., also 2.819–20n. for the descendants of Dardanos. Ankhises was a generation younger than Laomedon, in the other branch of the family.

270–2 Of the resulting brood Ankhises kept four in his stable and gave two to his son; they now draw Aineias' chariot. ἀτίταλλ', cf. ἀταλός, means 'nurtured' either of horses or of children (5 × *Il.*); see further Leumann, *HW* 140. — Aristarchus (Did/A) read dual μήστωρε, of the two horses, in 272; others, including Plato, *Lach.* 191B and a few MSS, read μήστωρι to agree with Αἰνείᾳ (cf. Did(?)/T on 8.108). The choice is not easy, since μήστωρα φόβοιο | occurs 4 × *Il.* of warriors ('deviser of rout' obviously) and that is probably the traditional meaning of the phrase; but these horses 'know how to...pursue and retreat', διωκέμεν ἠδὲ φέβεσθαι, at 222–3, and the formula could have been applied to them in that sense. At 8.106–8 Diomedes will describe them in similar terms; in fact 8.105–7 = 5.221–3, and are then followed by 108 οὕς ποτ' ἀπ' Αἰνείαν ἑλόμην, μήστωρε φόβοιο (where immediately preceding φέβεσθαι favours μήστωρε rather than the minority reading μήστωρα).

273 Capture of a valuable prize of horses or armour is important not only for their usefulness and material worth but also for the κλέος they bring, cf. 8.192, 10.436–41 and 17.130f.

275–80 Meanwhile the horses in question draw near, and Pandaros, after a brief preliminary taunt, casts his spear from the chariot. Compared with the lengthy conversations that preceded, the encounter itself, as often, is cursorily described.

277–9 Diomedes is addressed without overt abuse, then Pandaros simply adds that having failed once with the arrow he will try again with the spear; yet the introductory | ἦ μάλα lends special significance to his words, cf. 3.204 and 11.441. The effect is threatening and intimate at the same time, complicated as it is by the leisurely addition of πικρὸς ὀϊστός after βέλος ὠκύ. The poet thus chooses to make him echo his earlier words to Aineias rather than involve him in a major heroic exchange or develop his portrayal as petulant and ineffective.

281–2 The throw is accurate but lacks power; it penetrates the shield but not the corslet, which it merely gets close to, πελάσθη. That lack of power is significant and usually fatal (p. 24).

283–5 But Pandaros is once again (cf. 102–5) foolishly confident that his hit has been mortal. V. 283, with his shout of premature triumph, repeats 101, but his words this time are a definite boast over his supposed victim, cf. 101n. On both occasions his description as ἀγλαός increases the irony, as his sanguine nature causes him to exaggerate to the point of absurdity the probable effects of his throw. All he can have seen is the spear penetrating the shield, but now he claims 'you are hit in the midriff, right through', and will not long survive the blow.

μέγ' in 285, as at 11.288, must be adverbial (so Leaf), since taking it closely with εὖχος breaches 'Hermann's Bridge' and creates a marked trochaic break in the fourth foot. To put it another way, normal colometry, for good reasons of euphony, requires a fourth colon consisting of εὖχος ἔδωκας after the bucolic caesura; moreover εὖχος nowhere else has an epithet in its quite extensive formular system with parts of διδόναι (10 × *Il.*, 2 × *Od.*). The difference in sense, not rhythm, is admittedly small: 'you have abundantly given me glory' rather than 'you have given me great glory' – εὖχος in any case signifying something like κλέος rather than 'wish' or 'prayer'.

286 The same v. recurs when Diomedes is wounded by Paris at 11.384; here at least he can be genuinely unperturbed since there is no damage (except to the shield, that sort of detail being regularly ignored).

287–9 ἤμβροτες οὐδ' ἔτυχες is a typical epic polar construction, here insultingly emphatic. Diomedes' response balances Pandaros' boast: each begins with an abrupt statement or claim followed by a complicated and sarcastic opinion about the consequences (284 οὐδέ σ' ὀίω |, 287 ἀτὰρ οὐ μὲν σφῶϊ γ' ὀίω |; οἴω or ὀίω at the v-e 31 × *Il.*). This kind of boast and response constitutes a typical motif, cf. e.g. 11.380–90 and Fenik, *TBS* 32. — πρίν is often followed by γε as Leaf remarked, but the accumulation of no less than four γ(ε)'s in 287f. is exceptional; it gives the assertion a distinctly sinister tone, as does Diomedes saying that at least one of them will fall (i.e. if not both). — V. 289 is formular, recurring twice elsewhere; sating Ares with blood is a powerful and gruesome figure sharpened by the probably archaic ταλαύρινον, 'hide-supporting', i.e. shield-bearing, see on 7.238–9.

290 Diomedes throws, προέηκε; he is on foot but evidently not close enough to thrust. The encounter resembles his initial fight with Dares' sons at 9ff. – they were in a chariot, he on foot, he killed one and the other was divinely rescued. The spear is lethally guided by Athene; as usual, there is no sense that this lessens the human drama or the victor's part in it; the very fact that the hero is helped by a deity establishes his power and his triumph.

291–3 'The slaying itself is both grisly and unrealistic', Fenik, *TBS* 32. Such bizarre deaths and *Scheinrealismus* are not uncommon in *Il.*, cf. Friedrich, *Verwundung* passim and especially 23f. Here the spear enters by the eye, passes the teeth and severs the base of the tongue before emerging by the lower part of the chin. The explanations given by b are that Pandaros must have lowered his head to avoid the blow, or that Athene being taller directed the shot downward, neither being very persuasive. The minute description of the spear-head's path depends more on the singer's desire to create an effect (for the spear-head as ἀτειρής see on 660–2) than on any special keenness of observation, cf. 66–7n. This is an important death, the culmination of lengthy preliminaries; the poet chooses not to moralize over Pandaros as truce-breaker (perhaps because Athene herself had persuaded him, 4.93ff.), but the audience may reasonably expect particular emphasis on the manner of his destruction. — Aristarchus (bT) seems to have taken 293 ἐξελύθη to mean 'lost its force', against Zenodotus' ἐξεσύθη (Did/AT), 'hastened out'. Both are awkward, but the majority of

MSS may be right in preferring Zenodotus – unless Ahrens, Leaf, Willcock and others are justified in emending to ἐξέλυθε, simply 'came out', 'emerged'; but that form with ε for η is not found elsewhere.

294 This v. recurs only at 8.260, and is compounded of two formular halves: ἤριπε δ' ἐξ ὀχέων 9 × *Il.*, ἀράβησε δὲ τεύχε' ἐπ' αὐτῷ 10 × *Il.* (7 × with | δούπησεν δὲ πεσών); cf. e.g. 42 and 47 for the two halves, separately, and the comment on 58. The elements of the first hemistich, again, are strongly formular, | ἤριπε 20 × *Il.*, ἐξ ὀχέων (*sic*) 23 × *Il.* On ἀράβησε see 4.501–4n. *fin.*

295–6 Each v. is cumulated in a characteristic manner, first with an otiose pair of epithets to lead into new information about the horses, then with an otiose runover epithet leading to a formal but inessential statement of death. The cumulation is unobjectionable, serving to emphasize the encounter's climax at least so far as Pandaros is concerned – for apart from a brief reference at 795 he will not be heard of again. Yet the language is adapted from other formular uses with less than accustomed ease. Thus αἰόλα παμφανόωντα, the second component of which gravitates most naturally to the v-e (11 × *Il.*), does not recur; παρέτρεσσαν is *hapax* in the epic, presumably meaning that the horses shied away, but is an obvious replacement, to avoid hiatus after preceding short vowel, for ὑπερώησαν from ὑπ-εροέω, 'recoil', the reading in equivalent contexts at 8.122f. and 314f. That may be acceptable, but λύθη ψυχή τε μένος τε in 296 (also at 8.123 and 315) is less so; λύθη is found with μένος at 17.298 and with γυῖα 3 ×, but nowhere else of ψυχή, to which it is not obviously appropriate. There were traditional phrases for the departure of the life-spirit, but the poet here prefers his own fresh adaptations, which are not always successful. Yet rhapsodic elaboration can probably be discounted.

297–310 The culmination of the encounter, more important in the dramatic plan of the Book than Pandaros' death itself, is the subsequent wounding of Aineias – which leads in turn to Aphrodite's rescue and Diomedes' devastating attack on her. It is described in a balanced narrative of 14 vv., of which the first $5\frac{1}{2}$ show Aineias full of defensive fire, the next $2\frac{1}{2}$ Diomedes easily subduing him, the last 6 Aineias struck down and sinking into unconsciousness.

297 Ancient critics (perhaps not Aristarchus himself) fussed about Aineias' spear and shield, thinking he must have lent his own to Pandaros when he himself took the reins. Attempts to punctuate after ἀπόρουσε and make Aineias take the dead man's armour after leaping from the chariot were countered by Ptolemaeus of Ascalon followed by Herodian (Hrd/AbT). Obviously the singer was none too precise about the armour here, particularly how Pandaros armed himself when he mounted the chariot at

238f.; Aineias must have kept his own on, or near him, after taking over as charioteer.

298–9 Cf. 8.330f. ~ 13.419f., 17.4–8 and 17.132–7 for the typical motif of a warrior defending a dead companion's body by standing over it with his shield; and the last two of these for the typical use of a simile as in 299 (Fenik, *TBS* 33).

300–1 = 17.7–8. πρόσθε is adverbial (*contra* Aristarchus, Arn/A), with οἱ 'ethic' as in 298. In 301 τοῦ γ' ἀντίος struck Leaf as 'very strange', since τοῦ must refer to the dead Pandaros, whereas ἀντίος implies an attack on a live opponent; yet the attempt to remove a defended corpse would itself entail the aggression implied by ἀντίος.

302–10 Correspondences with bk 17 are supplemented by others with 8.320–9 and 20.283–8. In the former (where 8.321 = 302 here and 329 στῆ δὲ γνὺξ ἐριπών ~ ἔστη γνὺξ ἐριπών in 309) Hektor leaps from his chariot with a terrible cry and hurls a stone which badly wounds Teukros, who is subsequently rescued; see 8.320–2n. In the latter (where 285–7 ~ 302–4 here) the subjects of ἰάχων and λάβε in 285 (= 302) are different, as here: Akhilleus rushes at Aineias with a terrible cry, then the latter picks up a stone (and *would* have hit him, except that Poseidon rescued him). These are typical scenes, therefore, which can be varied in arrangement and detail, especially where the victim is wounded but later rescued; see further Fenik, *TBS* 33–5.

302–4 These are formular vv. (see previous n.). σμερδαλέα etc. is always first word in the v., 21 × *Il.*, 9× *Od.*, | σμερδαλέα (ϝ)ιάχων (on which see further Hoekstra, *Modifications* 53) occurring 7 × *Il.*; σμερδαλέος (its ending -αλέος epic and Ionic, cf. e.g. θαρσαλέος ἀργαλέος λευγαλέος) clearly means something like 'terrible', 'frightening' but is of debatable etymology. Woundings by stone-throw are not uncommon in *Il.*, recurring in six specific incidents and five general descriptions. χερμάδιον is a stone or boulder (cf. later χερμάς, 'sling-stone'); the idea that it derives from χείρ, i.e. as something held in the hand, is probably wrong, despite χειρί in this formular v. (its purpose being emphatic and alliterative rather than etymological, to reinforce the assonance of σμερδαλέα and χερμάδιον).

303 It is tempting to take μέγα ἔργον as 'a monstrous affair' in apposition to χερμάδιον, but Leaf was right to insist that it describes the whole action of picking up the stone. ἔργον is not used in a purely concrete sense in Homer (as it came to be in later Greek, cf. the similar development of πρᾶγμα), and LSJ is mistaken in classing instances like 1.294 or 2.38 under II, 'thing, matter'. ἔργον in its many Homeric instances still has strong action-content as 'work' or 'deed', something carried through rather than the simple product of action; that is so even of e.g. *Il.* 6.289, where πέπλοι are ἔργα γυναικῶν. But the strongest evidence in the present case is the formular meaning of μέγα ἔργον as 'great deed' in all other Homeric uses (7 × *Il.*, 11 × *Od.*). — On the potential optative φέροιεν without ἄν or κε see Chantraine, *GH* II, 216–18.

304 bT commented that the poet 'was much later than heroic times'. 'Such as mortals now are' (4 × *Il.*) does indeed contrast heroic strength with that of the singer's contemporaries, perhaps surprisingly in a tradition where the singer's own *persona* is so carefully suppressed. The idiom may have developed in speech, as when Nestor says at 1.272 that none of mortals as they now are (i.e. the younger heroic generation he is addressing) could have fought with those he defeated in his youth.

305–6 The boulder struck Aineias on the hip, just where the top of the thigh turns in the hip-socket known as the 'little cup'. This kind of anatomical knowledge must have been common enough from the cutting up of sacrificial animals, quite apart from warfare.

307–8 It shattered the joint and broke both tendons, on which see 4.521 and n. There the tendons were connected with shin and ankle; again a stone-throw caused the damage and 'utterly crushed them', 4.522. Here in 308 the rough stone tears (literally ὦσε, 'pushed') off the skin – a deliberately milder description, since Leto and Artemis at 447f. will have to heal this wound, which ought to be fatal.

309–10 See on 58 for other variants of the falling-to-the-ground and moment-of-death formulas. ἔστη is surprising at first, but must mean that he collapsed (ἐριπών) onto his knees (6 × *Il.*) and remained like that, leaning (ἐρεισάμενος) with one hand on the ground. bT suggested that this was for Aphrodite to gather him up the more easily – see on 68 for Aristarchus' concern with such matters. That is not so, cf. especially 8.329 where Teukros is hit by a boulder and στῆ δὲ γνὺξ ἐριπών, but is not killed or rendered unconscious; and 11.355f. (~ 309f. here), part of an episode in which Hektor is struck on the helmet, retreats, collapses and loses consciousness but soon recovers. In neither case is a special posture for divine rescue in question. Rather, and more obviously, the στῆ δέ (or ἔστη) γνὺξ ἐριπών formula was developed to describe a temporary bringing to the knees without final collapse – that is the force of στῆ; and this was then loosely applied to the present situation, which is slightly different.

τὸν δὲ σκότος ὄσσε κάλυψε | (11 × *Il.*) normally implies dying rather than fainting; but the more elaborate whole-v. formula τὸν (τὴν) δὲ κατ' ὀφθαλμῶν ἐρεβεννὴ νὺξ ἐκάλυψε(ν) occurs 3 × *Il.*, and this shorter version has elements of both. It is undeniably moving and makes a strong ending to the episode, helped by the alliteration and assonance of κελαινὴ νὺξ ἐκάλυψε. Similar effects can be heard in the rest of these two vv. with their γ's, κ's and χ's, the repetition of ἐρ- in ἐριπών καὶ ἐρείσατο, and the mournful sound of ει and η in ἐρείσατο χειρὶ παχείη | γαίης.

311–430   Aineias is saved from death by Aphrodite, who is recognized and attacked by Diomedes and wounded in the hand; she drops her son who is then protected by Apollo. With Ares' help she retreats to Olumpos and complains to her mother Dione, who comforts her with a list of other human attacks on gods, and cures her wound as Athene and Here make fun of her to Zeus

311–17   Aphrodite's intervention is briefly stated; it is the prelude to events which have their comic side, but here the goddess's love and divinity are suggested in a flowing and romantic style, especially in 313–15.

311–12   See on 3.373–5 for the | καί νύ κεν... | εἰ μὴ ἄρ' ὀξὺ νόησε construction; the context there (where 374 = 312 here) is similar, with Aphrodite rescuing Paris from Menelaos. καί νύ κεν ἔνθ' ἀπόλοιτο recurs at 388 of Ares, and εἰ...νόησε appears 6 × *Il.* in all, of which thrice in bk 5, twice in bk 8 (which has a number of stylistic details in common with 5) and once in a similar context at 20.291, where Aineias is again rescued by a god, this time Poseidon. — Reinhardt tried to establish a relative chronology for the three divine rescues (*IuD* 137f.); but Fenik is surely right (*TBS* 36f.) that they are variant forms of a single theme, with the present version closer to bk 20 than bk 3; priority of composition cannot be established in such a case.

Aineias usually comes as first word in the v., and only here (because his spondaic name is awkward in the fifth foot) as last. He acquires for the occasion the ἄναξ ἀνδρῶν formula that properly belongs to Agamemnon (44 × *Il.*) but is applied 5 × to miscellaneous other characters, including Ankhises at 268, whose names happen to fit. — On Διὸς θυγάτηρ Ἀφροδίτη, and the system of v-e formulas for this goddess, see on 3.424.

313   A cumulated v., designed to stress Aphrodite's maternal motives as well as to convey a certain pathos – heightened by the rising threefolder – by recalling the passionate encounter with Ankhises that led to Aineias' birth.

314–15   Aphrodite's rescue technique is unparalleled (cf. Fenik, *TBS* 39); elsewhere when a god rescues a mortal it is by casting cloud or darkness over the attacker's eyes, or over the endangered warrior so as to make him invisible, as Aphrodite herself did with Paris at 3.380f. She 'poured her pale forearms' around her son in a unique and beautiful phrase, not least through the repetition of ευ and κ sounds in ἐχεύατο πήχεε λευκώ, apparently a development of λευκώλενος as the regular epithet for Here (24 × *Il.*). Presumably she enfolds him in her arms and simultaneously covers him with a fold of her robe (epic καλύπτειν implies covering as often as hiding). Ancient critics argued whether the idea was to make him invisible (cf. ἐκάλυψεν in 3.381 = 20.444) or to protect him with the divine garment; bT thought the former, 316 ἕρκος supports the latter.

316–17 Cf. ἕρκος ἀκόντων | of μίτρη and shield at 4.137 and 15.646 respectively.

318–30 While Aphrodite is carrying her unconscious son to safety (318), Sthenelos is mindful of Diomedes' instructions (319f., cf. 259–73) to tether his own horses and capture those of Aineias.

319–20 συνθεσιάων: 'agreement(s)' as at 2.339; Sthenelos did not forget the agreement enjoined on him, i.e. Diomedes enjoined and he agreed.

321–4 As often in the epic, the language of an instruction (at 261–4, q.v. with nn.) is closely followed, though with necessary changes, when the instruction is carried out. Only νόσφιν ἀπὸ φλοίσβου (as at 10.416, where φλοίσβοι' cannot be restored as it can here) is new and provides a fresh and vivid detail. In 323 the substitution of a straightforward formular epithet, καλλίτριχας, for 263 μεμνημένος restores fluency to the rising threefolder.

326 ὅτι οἱ φρεσὶν ἄρτια ᾔδει | recurs at *Od.* 19.248; in *Il.* ᾖσι φρεσὶν ἄρτια βάζειν (14.92, also 1 × *Od.*) is the only parallel. Literally 'because he [i.e. Deipulos] knew in his heart things joined to [i.e. harmonious with] himself [i.e. Sthenelos]'.

327–30 Meanwhile Sthenelos brings up his chariot in support of Diomedes' attack on Aphrodite, who had begun withdrawing Aineias at 318 but can still be overtaken here. — She is named Kupris in 530, 5 × in this Book but never again in Homer; though she had an altar and precinct at Paphos according to *Od.* 8.362f. Hesiod (*Theog.* 191–200) called her Κυπρογενέα in his account of her birth from the foam from Ouranos' severed genitals, and seems to have explained her cult in Cyprus (and indirectly the later one in Kuthera) through this tale. Yet why is this Paphian connexion – certainly pre-Homeric in origin, late-Mycenaean or earlier and based on an ancient Near Eastern cult there, cf. Burkert, *Religion* 153 – alluded to in *Il.* only in this episode? Wilamowitz argued (*IuH* ch. 14, esp. pp. 283 and 286) that bks 3, 4 and 5 had once formed a separate small epic with some special sources: on the one hand for Menelaos' visit to Idomeneus and the death of the Dioskouroi in book 3 (these also in the *Cypria*), on the other for Aphrodite as Kupris in bk 5, cf. Lorimer, *HM* 442. Yet Aphrodite's connexion with Paphos and Cyprus was probably available to *any* singer in the formative stages of the Trojan epic. It has also often been urged that there is a stylistic connexion between Demodokos' sophisticated song of the love of Ares and Aphrodite at *Od.* 8.266ff. (where the reference to Aphrodite in Paphos occurs) and the present Book – also perhaps with the Theomachy of bks 20 and 21, which display a comparably irreverent attitude to gods in general and Aphrodite, with Ares, in particular; see further W. Burkert, *RhM* 103 (1960) 130ff.

Yet might there not be some other and more concrete, i.e. linguistic or stylistic, reason for the choice of Kupris rather than Aphrodite? One possibility is that she is so named because the poet wants to mention her *in the first part of the verse*. She has a well-developed formular system under her name of Aphrodite; but that operates exclusively in the second hemistich, see on 3.424. The reason is clear, that ∪∪–– will not fit into the first half (except, intolerably, after an initial monosyllable and ending with the second foot). Therefore, if the singer needs to place her in the first hemistich for reasons of emphasis or sentence-structure, he has to find another name for her – not difficult, since Κύπρις was evidently available and conveniently short. The five occurrences in this Book are not inconsistent with that idea. Thus in 330 the narrative is rapid and concise; subject and object of attack are identified as soon as possible after the runover word, | ἐμμεμαώς· ὁ δὲ Κύπριν, the second hemistich being devoted to the attacking action itself. In 424 subject and object are again placed first, | ἦ μάλα δή τινα Κύπρις, not only for emphasis but also because Ἀχαιϊάδων will not fit, together with necessary particles, into the v.'s first half. In 458 ~ 883 Κύπριδα comes first for emphasis (as Ares says, first her, then himself). Fifthly in 760 Here complains that Aphrodite and Apollo are rejoicing: τέρπονται is emphatic first word, which forces Ἀπόλλων into the second half and leaves room for Κύπρις, not Ἀφροδίτη, in the first: τέρπονται Κύπρις τε καὶ ἀργυρότοξος Ἀπόλλων.

Thus there are good functional reasons for adopting a short name for the goddess in some and perhaps all of these five instances. It may be noted that the oral style favours the clustering of unusual terms, which tend to become lodged for a while in the singer's unconscious mind. Aphrodite bears her regular name in five other places in this Book, but she requires an epithet for both stylistic and semantic reasons in three of them; then in 248 a straightforward naming of the goddess is required by Sthenelos' reference to her, and in 370 her mother is Dione and Cypriot affiliations would be distracting. — Obviously this kind of argument can be abused; placing her in the first half of the v. might have been convenient in a few, at least, of the 23 direct Iliadic references to her outside bk 5, yet Κύπρις does not recur. The wounding of gods by a mortal is a theme unique to this Book, and this special name could be part of that. Much remains doubtful, but the metrical and functional explanation deserves serious consideration.

331–3 Diomedes was attacking her, as bT noted, because Athene had told him to do so back at 131f., having removed the mist from his eyes at 127f. so that he could recognize, γιγνώσκης, god and man, i.e. distinguish the two. The hero had recognized Aphrodite easily enough, but the point here is that he also knows that she is not a formidable opponent even though divine. — In 332 ἀνδρῶν must belong with πόλεμον, 'men's warfare', despite the main caesura; so does anastrophic κάτα (*contra* Hrd/A), which prevents one from phrasing the v. as a rising threefolder exactly. V. 333 is saved from being merely pedantic, and a possible addition if so, if taken almost colloquially: 'not an Athene or an Enuo' (the latter appearing briefly with Ares, also known as Enualios, at 592).

334 Another slight impreclsion, since he was probably already attacking her in 330. The second half recurs at 17.462, with ὀπάζων meaning 'follow' rather than 'make follow', its usual sense.

336–8 He reaches out and strikes the extremity of her hand with his spear; the hand is ἀβληχρήν, 'soft' or 'weak' (also of walls at 8.178), a word related to μαλακός (Chantraine, *Dict.* svv. ἀβληχρός, βλάξ), the contrary of the warrior's χειρὶ παχείη at 309. The spear has cut through her robe εἶθαρ, 'immediately', i.e. without resistance, in a parody of its path through shield and corslet in more regular combat. The robe is ambrosial (see 2.19n., also S. West on *Od.* 4.445) and made by her attendants the Graces, emphasizing both her feminine weakness and her divinity. — Neglect of digamma in 338 ὅν (ϝ)οἱ (contrast 14.178) may reflect a formula with neuter antecedent, τό/τά (ϝ)οἱ; Aristarchus' view is not available, since the scholia for 335–636 are missing in A.

339 The 'hand's extremity' of 336 turns out to be the wrist, cf. 458. θέναρ, *hapax* in Homer, is 'the hollow of the hand' (bT), i.e. the palm; adjectival πρυμνός means 'at the base of', cf. γλῶσσαν πρυμνήν at 292. Here it is used as a noun, the base of the palm where it joins the wrist.

339–42 The wound draws blood, but it is ἄμβροτον αἷμα, a phrase reused only of Ares at 870, the spilling of divine blood being confined to this Book. The uniqueness of the event elicits the notion that divine blood is not really αἷμα at all but a special substance called ἰχώρ (only again at 416, see n. there for its literal meaning). This leads to the aetiology of 341f.: gods do not consume bread and wine, therefore they are bloodless and hence are called (i.e. actually are) immortal. Far from being 'a very poor interpolation', with 342 'a meaningless *non sequitur*' (so Leaf), 341f. are a dramatic theological innovation, cast in epigrammatic and quasi-hieratic form, wholly in accord both with the Homeric tendency to minimize many of the more carnal aspects of the gods and with the needs of this particular theme of divine wounding. That gods live on ambrosia and nectar is not specifically mentioned but is a related and relatively recent idea, repeated several times in both *Il.* and *Od.* though not consistently applied, designed to play down the ancient Mesopotamian concept of the gods actually feeding on sacrificial animals offered by mortal worshippers, either directly on their flesh or on the savour therefrom: see pp. 9–13. In these vv., then, it is implicitly argued that the gods are immortal, ἄμβροτοι; that βροτός is connected with blood (cf. βροτὸν αἱματόεντα |, 4 × *Il.*); that human life is sustained by food and drink, and spilling out the blood means death; that gods are deathless and therefore bloodless, and that if blood is sustained by mortal food, then their food must be immortal, ἀμβροσίη, their drink nectar, and what flows in their case (340 ῥέει, *sc.* in their veins) something distinct, namely *ikhor*.

343–6 Despite the *ikhor*, gods evidently feel pain; as Aphrodite flings down her son with a shriek (343 ~ *Od.* 10.323) Apollo is conveniently there to rescue him once again, and conceals him in dark cloud (cf. 314–15n.). Vv. 345f. (from μή τις...) reproduce 316f. and emphasize the repeated action.

347 τῇ/τῷ δ' ἐπὶ μακρὸν ἄϋσε 4 × *Il.*, of which thrice in this Book, once in bk 8.

348–51 Diomedes' 4-v. taunt is typically concise and epigrammatic, carefully composed for the occasion and not especially formular, at least after 348. Firm injunction in the opening v. is followed by sarcastic enquiry in the next (349), with more complex irony in the enjambed vv. at the close.

349 'Some refer it to Helen' (T), surely with reason, cf. 3.399. ἀνάλκιδες is usually applied to warriors as a rebuke, ἀλκή being the great martial quality, 'heroic stamina' (ἀλκή and ἄλκιμος *c.* 100 × *Il.*). Obviously women, Amazons apart, do not have it.

350–1 The repetition of πόλεμον sounds awkward at first – less so if it implies 'the very mention of war' (as γε suggests): 'If you do enter warfare in the future, then I think you will shudder at its very name, even if you hear it somewhere else.' That is still unclear, but presumably the underlying sense is 'If you persist in meddling with war, then you will come to hate it so much [i.e. because you will get similar punishment and worse] that you will shudder at its very name...'

352 Attention turns to the wounded goddess as she departs in an unhappy state, ἀλύουσ', 'beside herself', cf. ἀλύων of Akhilleus at 24.12 and ἀλάομαι, 'wander'.

353–4 Iris is useful for this sort of thing. Last seen persuading Helen to watch the single combat at 3.121ff., she now leads Aphrodite out of battle, in agony and with her skin darkening with the blood-like substance.

355 The three preceding vv. have been 'ideal' four-colon ones or nearly so; 355 maintains their strongly dactylic quality (as will 356), but is given an added bouncing effect, in contravention of 'Meyer's Law', by the two successive trochaic breaks produced by ἔπειτα: an effect which echoes, whether intentionally or not, Iris' presumed speed of action here. — Ares is 'towards the left of the battle'; there is little point in trying to relate this to where Athene had left him by the Skamandros at 36, since as Fenik observes (*TBS* 41) 'This is the normal orientation when there is movement from one part of the battlefield to another', as at 11.498, 12.118, 13.326, 675, 765, 17.116, 682, all with ἐπ' ἀριστερά and 4/8× preceding the bucolic diaeresis as here.

356 The runover-word varies the flow of narrative and leads to the curious and unparalleled information that the god's spear was leaning on 'air' (presumably a cloud with which he had surrounded himself to make him invisible), as also, by a rather awkward zeugma, were his 'swift horses', which must imply his chariot. Leaning a spear against mist or cloud (which even Presocratics, Anaximenes especially, were to regard as having a degree of solidity) could be convenient – but does one need to lean a chariot against anything whatever? Only if it is unharnessed (cf. 8.435), which this one is not. This is the first extreme example of the untypical and bizarre details, associated with Ares and Aphrodite in particular, that are an undeniable feature of this Book (see also on 314–15). Its effect is debatable, but the idea of a war-god isolated in a cloud of invisibility on the edge of battle is striking none the less.

357–8 For ἡ δὲ γνὺξ ἐριποῦσα cf. 309 ἔστη γνὺξ ἐριπών and 309–10n.; the spondaic first foot of this and the following v. is in marked contrast with the preceding dactylic runs, emphasizing both her heaviness and her persistence as she asks for her half-brother's horses and chariot (they were also lovers, e.g. in Demodokos' song at *Od.* 8.266ff., or, later, husband and wife). | πολλὰ λισσομένη -ος recurs at 21.368, with its two components also formular at the v.-beginning in other combinations; for lengthening of a short final vowel before initial λ, μ, ν or ρ see Chantraine, *GH* I, 175ff.

359–62 Her words do not of themselves reflect her suffering; her 4-v. request (on 359 φίλε see 4.155n.) matches Diomedes' boast at 348ff. in its relaxed style as well as in length, notably in the hendiadys of 'convey me and give me your horses' in 359 and the leisurely description of Olumpos in 360. The closing couplet is, again, more complex, the first of a series of divine complaints about Diomedes' impious aggression.

362–9 The style is paratactic with much progressive enjambment, and heavily formular; several phrases recur in other divine chariot-scenes, especially in this Book.

363 The epithet–noun formula picks up χρυσάμπυκας ἤτεεν ἵππους | in 358; that was evidently the more regular use, with epithet and noun separated by – ∪ ∪ (cf. 720 = 8.382), the present adaptation being metrically less fluent. χρυσάμπυκας is a special epithet for divine horses (cf. 4.2–3n.), the mortal equivalent being κρατερώνυχας, cf. καλλίτριχας.

364–9 A heavily formular passage: the first half of 364 recurs at 837 of Athene; the second half of 365 recurs at 17.482 = 24.441. Then 366 comes

6 × *Il.*, 3 × *Od.* (including with ἵππους for ἐλάαν); 367 is a formular assemblage, with θεῶν ἕδος αἰπὺν Ὄλυμπον recurring at 868 (+ *HyAp* 109). The first half of 368 appears 4 × *Il.* (including 775), always of divine subjects; in 369 (~ 13.35, of Poseidon), λύσασ᾽ -ας ἐξ ὀχέων recurs 3 × *Il.* (including 776, + 1 variant), ἐξ ὀχέων *sic* being particularly common (23 × *Il.*).

370–2 The typical element diminishes in this moving scene, which is also gently humorous, where the wounded goddess falls into her mother's lap (like a child as bT remark). ἐν γούνασι πῖπτε comes here only, though with a variant ἐφέζετο γούνασι in the parallel passage at 21.506 (see 373–4n. *init.*); whereas holding or taking someone ἀγκάς, in various senses, is found 5 × *Il.*

The mother–daughter relation is heavily stressed in 371, not only for itself but also because Dione is unique in the heroic epos. Aphrodite is daughter of Zeus often enough, cf. her formular description as Διὸς θυγάτηρ, but a mother for her is mentioned only here. Homer evidently wished to gloss over the savage old tale of her birth in the sea from Ouranos' genitals (cf. Hesiod, *Theog.* 188ff.), even though her description as Kupris indirectly recalls it – see on 327–30, also on 339–42 for the down-playing of carnal extremes. Dione appears in an eclectic list of divinities hymned by the Muses at *Theog.* 11–21, and at 353 there as one of a catalogue of Nymphs; as West comments, she 'was an important goddess only at Dodona: there she was the consort of Zeus νάϊος, Zeus of the flowing water, whose oracular spring issued forth at the base of the famous oak'. In the present context Aphrodite could have resorted directly to Zeus like Ares at 869ff. (and indeed Artemis at 21.505ff.). Yet a mother is an apt comforter for a goddess, as well as further varying these two broadly parallel scenes in bk 5; therefore the poet provides Olumpos with this new but temporary addition, rooted in Greek cult and a possible consort for Zeus through her very name Dione, a feminized form of his own; Ameis–Hentze compared 14.319 Akrisione for the termination implying 'wife of'.

373–4 Dione's 2-v. question is repeated by Zeus to Artemis at 21.509f.; the two contexts are similar, Artemis in the Theomachy being thrashed by Here and resorting to Olumpos for complaint and comfort. Trying to identify the 'original' of such near-doublets is notoriously hazardous, see e.g. on 311–12. One must admit, however, that here the Theomachy text, despite the difficulties of that episode, is the more satisfactory, because of the awkward and avoidable echoing of κατέρεξεν and ἔρεξε in 5.372 and 373. These must be different verbs (despite J. Casabona, *Recherches sur le vocabulaire des sacrifices en grec*, Aix-en-Provence 1966, 44), since the former means 'stroke' or 'pat' with the hand (4 × *Il.*, 3 × *Od.*), the latter 'do', 'perform', from ῥέζω < (ϝ)έρδω, cf. ἔργον. In both passages ἔρεξε is already echoed, without obvious point, by ῥέζουσαν in 374 = 21.510; to add a preliminary κατέρεξεν in 372 by choosing that particular formular v. of address (4 × *Il.*, 2 × *Od.*), apposite to the situation as it may be, seems gratuitous. It is perhaps best accounted for as unconscious word-association.

Dione speaks as though to a child; she assumes that the wound must have been inflicted by a god or goddess (there is no special nuance to Οὐρανιώνων (etc.), 8 × *Il.*, always at the v-e). μαψιδίως is an expanded form, here and 1 × *Od.*, of μάψ, 'pointlessly' or (as here) 'foolishly'; ἐνωπῇ apparently means 'in full view', i.e. in public. Willcock's suggestion that this is a 'playful and rather sly dig at Aphrodite, whose misdemeanours tend to take place in private' is an ingenious way of accounting for a rather odd expression which may, however, have a merely colloquial origin.

376–80 Aphrodite's reply combines indignation, pathos and cunning. After the abrupt οὖτά με it proceeds in 377f. to stress her innocent motherly concern and ends with an indirect attempt to involve the other gods on her side. The style remains uncomplicated, with strong progressive enjambment continued in the first part of Dione's speech which follows.

376 On ὑπέρθυμος see 76–8n. – it is especially appropriate to Diomedes here, at least if ὑπερ- is taken as implying excessive, rather than simply high, courage.

379 The components are formular, but the whole phrase 'dread combat of Trojans and Achaeans' recurs only (with one slight change) at 6.1.

380 The language recalls Athene's words at 130, μή τι σύ γ᾽ ἀθανάτοισι θεοῖς ἀντικρὺ μάχεσθαι.

382–415 Dione responds with a short list of other gods, down to 404, who had suffered injury at the hands of mortals. The style, as in other such abbreviated versions of tales outside the Trojan saga, is succinct and allusive (see Kirk, *Songs* 164–6), though with the occasional expansion of detail (389f., 401f.). She ends, by contrast, with a brilliant and intricate threat against Diomedes (406–15).

382 τέτλαθι is the first of five successive uses of τλάω (see on 385); here it means 'endure' rather than something closer to 'suffer' as in the other instances.

384 Divine involvement with men is stated as fact, without moral implications as e.g. at *Od.* 1.32ff.

385–7 Another part of the story of the Aloadai is given at *Od.* 11.305–20, where their mother Iphimedeia appears among the heroines seen by Odysseus; she was married to Aloeus but bore Poseidon twin sons. They were of monstrous size (nine fathoms tall at age nine) and threatened to pile Mt Ossa on Olumpos, then Pelion on Ossa, to attack the gods in the sky, but Apollo killed them before they reached maturity. They are equivalent, therefore, to Tuphoeus and the Titans as rebels against Zeus, and have much in common with the giant Ullikummi in the Hurrian-Hittite myth (see *ANET* 121–5; Kirk, *Myth* 214, 217). This primeval aspect is not remarked in the present reference, where they tie up Ares in a bronze jar for 13 months. According to bT this was in revenge for Ares killing Adonis, placed under their charge by Aphrodite – this looks like Hellenistic aetiology, yet enclosure in a jar or chest is an ancient idea (*Myth* 195, 198, 200), and Eurustheus taking refuge from Herakles in such a jar was a popular theme of 6th-cent. B.C. vase-painting. The tale as it appears here may be too bizarre to be a plausible Homeric invention as Willcock suggests *ad loc.*; yet other versions did not survive, judging at least by the lack of other hard information in the mythographical tradition.

385 The repetition of | τλῆ μὲν... | τλῆ δ'... | τλῆ δ'... (here and at 392, 395) after the τλῆμεν of 383 (note also the rhyme) is a typical rhetorical device especially in lists; compare repeated | οἳ δ(έ) in the bk 2 catalogues as well as the repeated | τὴν δὲ μέτ' and | καὶ...εἶδον of the heroines appearing before Odysseus at *Od.* 11.260ff.

388–91 'Ares would have died'; he was *in extremis* according to 391, but Moira would surely have prevented such a theological absurdity, since, like Hades in 402, and despite his inferior status and late entry into the pantheon, he was not 'made to be mortal': οὐ μὲν γάρ τι κατάθνητός γε τέτυκτο, cf. 901. Mythographers differed, or were silent, about Eeriboia, the stepmother of the Aloadai, and her relation to Hermes; no doubt he did the rescue because of his legendary skill as a thief, cf. 390 ἐξέκλεψεν and S. West on *Od.* 1.37ff.

392–4 The next divine victim is Here, introduced in a v. that corresponds with 385; Herakles is the attacker both here and at 395ff. According to bT some thought that Here and Hades (at 395ff.) were wounded in the same incident, others that the infant Herakles wounded her for withdrawing her breast.

395 Hades himself is wounded ἐν τοῖσι, i.e. as one of those divine victims, again by arrow-shot (that is emphasized at 404, Herakles' club being a post-Homeric invention). He is πελώριος, 'huge', a term applied 14 × to a variety of individuals including Ares (twice) and especially appropriate here. The arrow, on the other hand, is swift (rather than the more exotic 'triple-barbed', in the dative, of 393, cf. 11.507n.) in accord with regular formular rules for ὀϊστός -v.

396–7 ὡυτός is an Ionic contraction not otherwise in Homer, not necessarily because unknown in the oral tradition but because this unparalleled phrase, 'the selfsame man', is designed to be unusually emphatic and ironical. Here he is son of Zeus, at 392 of his human father Amphitruon. Homer's source for his misdeeds is obscure – perhaps some predecessor of Panyassis' *Herakleia* (though τλῆ μὲν Δημήτηρ in Panyassis frag. 16 is clearly derived from Homer as W. Kullmann noted, *Das Wirken der Götter in der Ilias*, Berlin 1956, 13 n. 1; cf. also H. Erbse, *RhM* 104, 1961, 162 n. 10). The scholia, drawing on earlier discussions e.g. by local historians of the Argolid, offered a variety of explanations: (i) the reference is to Herakles' attack on the Pylians, either (*a*) for supporting Orkhomenos against Thebes (T on 11.690) or (*b*) when he slew Neleus' sons at Pulos as recalled by Nestor at 11.690–3 (bT on 5.392–4), the Pylians being supported by Poseidon, Here and Hades according to the D-scholiast on 11.690; or (ii) the incident occurred when Herakles became angry with Plouton–Hades for his opposition to the removal of Kerberos from the underworld (bT on 5.395–7, cf. Σ on Pindar, *Ol.* 9, 33). Aristarchus (Arn(?)/T) evidently took 397 ἐν Πύλῳ as equivalent to ἐν πύλῃ, i.e. at the gate (*sc.* of the underworld), an interpretation supported by ἐν νεκύεσσι *if* this implies 'among the dead in Hades' (as when Helios at *Od.* 12.383 says he will go down to Hades καὶ ἐν νεκύεσσι φαείνω) rather than 'among the corpses on the battlefield' (cf. e.g. 10.349 and ἐν αἰνῆσιν νεκάδεσσιν, of Ares, at 886). Rhythmical criteria are ambiguous; the former is favoured if the v. falls into two parts, with ἐν Πύλῳ ἐν νεκύεσσι as a single phrase; but then it could be a rising threefolder. Πύλῳ of the gate of the underworld is abrupt, and Herakles dealing death and destruction at Pulos at 11.690–3 seems against it. The violent penetration of the underworld was an essential part of the mythical biography of Herakles, but the exact nature of the Pulos reference remains obscure. Pausanias (6.25.2) even assigned the incident to the Eleian Pulos, where Hades had a temple in his time.

398–402 Hades reacts as Aphrodite has done and Ares will do by rushing to Olumpos to be cured (comforting is not mentioned; unlike the childish Ares, he is too formidable for that). The versification is sophisticated: 398 is a rising threefolder (since πρὸς δῶμα Διός is indivisible); 399 is technically four-colon but again falls into three (non-rising) parts; integral enjambment leads into 400, with matching punctuation at the bucolic break. The emphasis on Hades' physical suffering is strong: already 'given over to pains' in 397, he is now 'grieving in his heart, pierced with pains' (πεπαρμένος alliterative like δῶμα Διός) – for the arrow had been 'driven', ἐλήλατο, into his shoulder (i.e. was lodged there, a unique expression) and distressed his spirit, κῆδε δὲ θυμόν |, cf. 11.458. Alliteration becomes still more emphatic with the π's and φ's of 401 (repeated with 402 at 900f. of the curing of Ares), cf. ἐπὶ δ' ἤπια φάρμακα πάσσεν -ειν, twice in bk 11. The abrupt | ἠκέσατ', in integral enjambment, emphasizes the rapidity of the cure, especially after the long words of 401 where Paieon smoothes on his unguents (which are ὀδυνήφατα, countering the ὀδύναι of 397 and 399).

Paieon as a god of healing occurs only in this Book and at *Od.* 4.232, but a *Pajawone* was known in Mycenaean Knossos, cf. Burkert, *Religion* 43; see on 1.473 for the Paieon as song of rejoicing for Apollo. That was sung after the god had ended the plague, and it is a short step to connect this, and Apollo himself, with healing in general; but Apollo and Paieon are still distinct in Hesiod frag. 307 M–W, i.e. the scholium on *Od.* 4.231; see further Burkert 44. The exact status of this Paieon on Olumpos remains in doubt, the oral tradition itself being probably flexible on the matter. At any rate Hades is cured, and his immortality asserted in a typically emphatic generalization in 402 to mark the end of the list of divine victims. One is only surprised that his removal from the underworld to Olumpos, temporary as it is, does not provoke more comment.

403–4 Or rather, there *is* a sense of outrage, but it is all directed against Herakles (to whom the exclamatory nominatives of 403 refer, right back to 396f.). The language is unusually violent: ὀβριμοεργός recurs only at 22.418, where Priam applies the term to Akhilleus who is defiling his son's body; and περὶ δ' αἴσυλα ῥέζεις is what the enraged river Skamandros says to Akhilleus, again, at 21.214 – this hero has, after all, something of Herakles' manic quality at times. Aristarchus, however, read αἰσυλοεργός (Did/T); that could be correct, since ὃς οὐκ ὄθετ' αἴσυλα ῥέζων would then be the kind of etymological appendage not uncommon in Homer, with ῥέζων picking up -εργός.

406–9 Diomedes is a fool if he does not see that attacking gods means imminent death: 407 is a solemn pronouncement, prepared for by the formality of οὐδὲ τὸ οἶδε κατὰ φρένα in 406 and with 407 μάλ' adding weight to the whole sentence. Its theology, however, is complex. Being supported by one god does not necessarily save one from punishment by another; but then Athene is a powerful goddess, one who can regularly protect Odysseus against Poseidon in the *Odyssey*. Yet physical attacks on gods are a different matter; they are against the basic order of things and therefore contravene Moira itself. Attacks on Zeus or the gods as a whole (as for example by Tuphoeus and the Aloadai) are punished by death; Herakles survived his attacks on Apollo, Hades and others, but then he was Zeus's son; ordinary mortals are different and the general rule applies. Nevertheless Diomedes himself, despite the graphic and pathetic vv. which follow, will survive unharmed; the tradition did not record a violent death for him, and Athene's support was evidently crucial.

The intimacy of παππάζουσιν, 'call (him) papa' (as Nausikaa does Alkinoos at *Od.* 6.57) is acceptable from a mother comforting her daughter, i.e. not in a heroic context: so bT. But the meaning is not (as they also thought) that impiety is punished by ἀτεκνία, but rather that such a one does not return from war at all to his wife and family, cf. *Od.* 12.42f.

410–11 εἰ καὶ μάλα καρτερός ἐστι(ν) | recurs at 13.316, but a more significant parallel is 1.178, where Agamemnon tells Akhilleus | εἰ μάλα καρτερός ἐσσι, θεός που σοὶ τό γ᾽ ἔδωκεν. Diomedes should consider (says Dione) whether a better god than Aphrodite (*sc.* at fighting) might not confront him – perhaps a forward reference to Ares, as T asserts, but perhaps also to Apollo.

412–15 The threat has been veiled so far, now the possible consequences are openly envisaged: Diomedes' wife Aigialeia (᾽Αδρηστίνη, daughter of Adrestos, cf. e.g. 9.557 Euenine for the patronymic, also E. Vermeule, *PCPS* 33, 1987, 136) will wake her household with wailing for her dead husband. Dione's tone is disturbing and ironic as she describes in measured terms this aristocratic young wife distraught with grief. V. 412 δήν, 'for long', echoes adjectival δηναιός in 407 – this waking of the household will persist for many nights. φίλους οἰκῆας is significant too: the servants are dear to her because they are all she has. V. 414 is rhythmically distinct, probably a rising threefolder; there is something passionate about alliterative ποθέουσα πόσιν, especially after the tender κουρίδιον, with τὸν ἄριστον ᾽Αχαιῶν like an epitaph at the end, ironic as bT suggest and with demonstrative τόν equivocally tacked on to the ancient formula. Finally 415 (hardly interpolated as Leaf thought, but touching in its formality) reverts to Aigialeia; she is not only περίφρων as in 412 but also ἰφθίμη, a stalwart wife, in chiastic balance with Diomedes as ἱπποδάμοιο.

416 Aphrodite's wound is only a graze despite the agony (352, 354); medical treatment is unnecessary, and Dione just wipes away the blood-equivalent with both hands. ἰχῶ, acc. of masc. ἰχώρ at 340 (see on 339–42 and 353–4 *fin.*), is the divine equivalent of blood in these two Homeric passages alone. Of unknown etymology, it means lymph or serum in Plato, Aristotle and Hippocratic writers, something similar at Aeschylus, *Ag.* 1480. It was used in spoken Ionic according to Shipp, *Vocabulary* s.v., and must have struck the poet as a suitable pseudo-technical term.

417 A specially composed v., conspicuously asyndetic. ἄλθετο literally means 'nourished itself', i.e. grew whole, from ἀλδαίνω (q.v. in Chantraine, *Dict.*) – nothing to do with αὔξω as bT thought but from root αλ-, 'nourish', cf. Lat. *alo*.

418–21 Athene's departure from the battlefield was not specially noted, but cf. 510f. That the goddesses are replying in kind to Zeus taunting them at 4.5–12 (so bT) is confirmed by verbal echoes:

418 | αἱ δ᾽ αὖτ᾽ εἰσορόωσαι   4.9–10 εἰσορόωσαι | τέρπεσθον
419 | κερτομίοις ἐπέεσσι Δία   4.5–6 ἐπειρᾶτο Κρονίδης ἐρεθιζέμεν
Κρονίδην ἐρέθιζον   ῞Ηρην | κερτομίοις ἐπέεσσι

At 762 Here will address Zeus with similar apparent hesitation to that of 421 here; both vv. draw on an interlocking formular system, cf. e.g. 20.301

κεχολώσεται αἴ κεν Ἀχιλλεύς |, 23.543 κεχολώσομαι αἴ κε τελέσσῃς | and *Od.* 1.158 ἦ καί μοι νεμεσήσεαι ὅττι κεν εἴπω;

422–5 The taunt itself is expressed in a complex 4-v. sentence in which two participial clauses, with a relative clause interposed, lead in an almost Latin style through three enjambments to delayed main verb and direct object. 'Assuredly Kupris, in inciting some Achaean woman to follow the Trojans whom now she terribly loves, caressing one of those fine-robed Achaean women, on a golden pin has scratched her slender hand': subtleties only apparent in Greek are the separation of τινα from Ἀχαιϊάδων in 422, the resumptive τῶν τινα and addition of ἐϋπέπλων to Ἀχαιϊάδων in 424 and the sarcastic ἀραιήν as epithet of χεῖρα in 425. καρρέζουσα is a syncopated form of καταρέζουσα, cf. 372 κατέρεξεν and 373–4n. All this is close in spirit to 3.406–9, where Helen invited Aphrodite (who was trying to get her into bed with Paris) to 'go and sit at his side, renouncing the path of the gods...be for ever grieving over and guarding him, until he makes you either his wife – or his concubine'. The implications of 422f. are unmistakable: Aphrodite *had* sent one of the Achaean women, namely Helen, to follow the Trojans whom she 'terribly loved' – as she loved Paris according to Helen's sneer at 3.408f.; the very words are used by Aphrodite herself in that same context at 3.415, but of Helen, ὡς νῦν ἔκπαγλα φίλησα. Behind all lies the Judgement of Paris, specifically mentioned only at 24.28–30 but underlying the whole relationship between Paris and Aphrodite and the hostility towards Helen of Here and Athene.

426–7 The goddesses had 'muttered against' Zeus at 4.20 after his little joke; here the father of men and gods merely smiles as at 15.47, then summons Aphrodite and addresses her kindly, perhaps to annoy the others.

428–30 His benevolent words make a dignified conclusion to the episode as he restores order by reminding Aphrodite of her true function, and foreshadows further involvement by the other two.

431–518 Now Diomedes attacks Apollo, who is holding the wounded Aineias, and is repulsed. The god makes an image of Aineias over which the two sides fight, and tells Ares to put an end to Diomedes' rampage. Ares stirs up Trojan resistance (as does Sarpedon through a rebuke to Hektor), and Apollo sends the real Aineias, now divinely cured, back into action

431 A standard v. for closing off a conversation and moving to a different scene of action.

432–3 Diomedes rushes at Aineias, the concealing cloud of 344–6 irrelevant as he recognizes both him and the god holding him (γιγνώσκειν again, cf. 128, 182, 331, and later 815, 824).

434–5 His lack of respect even for the powerful Apollo goes against the spirit of Athene's instruction at 129–32; but he is passionate to finish off and plunder his victim – ἵετο δ' αἰεί | is stronger than it may seem, being used at 13.424 of Idomeneus' desire to kill a Trojan or die in the attempt.

436–9 Diomedes hurls himself thrice against the god and is thrice repulsed; a fourth attempt leads to a dramatic rebuke. The climactic | τρὶς... | τρὶς...τὸ τέταρτον pattern recurs 3 × more, at (*a*) 16.702–6, (*b*) 16.784–6 and (*c*) 20.445–9, all very like the present passage; the oral predilection for 'thrice' is also exemplified at 18.155, 21.176 and 22.165 (with τὸ τέταρτον at 22.208). (*a*) is equivalent to 435f. but slightly fuller:

> τρὶς μὲν ἀπ' ἀγκῶνος βῆ τείχεος ὑψηλοῖο
> Πάτροκλος, τρὶς δ' αὐτὸν ἀπεστυφέλιξεν Ἀπόλλων
> χείρεσσ' ἀθανάτῃσι φαεινὴν ἀσπίδα νύσσων.

The next v. in each case is the same, so too | δεινὰ δ' ὁμοκλήσας in 439 and 16.706; a pungent divine rebuke follows in both, with χάζεο as a common element. The rebuked hero retreats in fear in an almost identical pair of vv. (443f. ~ 16.710f.). (*b*) is not quite so close; Patroklos leaps thrice like Ares (| τρὶς μὲν ἔπειτ' ἐπόρουσε recurs exactly) with a great shout, killing thrice nine mortals in the attack; then 16.786 = 438 here ('but when for the fourth time...'). (*c*) begins with Akhilleus attacking in the same formula, τρὶς...ἐπόρουσε; the next v. relates details particular to the episode, then comes 'but when for the fourth time' and | δεινὰ δ' ὁμοκλήσας as at 439 and 16.706, followed by ἔπεα πτερόεντα προσηύδα | as in the latter. The subsequent rebuke is to Hektor not the god, though Apollo is also involved.

Fenik (*TBS* 46–8) concludes that 'Although the three scenes are related, it is futile to try to establish a chronological relationship between them... they belong to a common type that is older than them all.' That is correct, and Analytical attempts to establish priority for one or the other have proved vain both here and with most other scenes sharing typical details or patterns or both. Yet 'common type' is almost too abstract a description. Some singer or teller of tales on some definite but unreconstructable occasion must have initiated the 'three times... then the fourth' pattern, building perhaps on three as a typical number for multiple events. Similarly some particular but unrecoverable act of imagination must have initiated the physical-attack-on-a-god idea, though that certainly lay far in the past, perhaps in a Mesopotamian rather than a Greek context. Various versions of such attacks were no doubt tried and developed, and at some point the triple pattern was incorporated. The result is intensely dramatic and so became part of the typical repertoire of heroic poetry, to be expressed in formular language as the tradition developed, with omissions or extra details appropriate to different occasions and personnel.

439 ἑκάεργος Ἀπόλλων | 10 × *Il.*, understood as from ἑκάς ('working from afar') by the poets, though probably from ἑκών ('working at will') in origin: cf. Chantraine, *Dict.* svv. ἑκάεργος, ἑκηβόλος, and 53–4n. *fin.*

440–2 Apollo's warning comes in a compact and closely enjambed 3-v. sentence, proceeding from sharp deterrence (through the rhetorical assonance of φράζεο … καὶ χάζεο) to broader prohibition ('don't think on a par with gods') justified by an epigrammatic general rule ('there is no similarity between the races of gods and men'). φράζεο is formular as first word, 7 × *Il.*, 2 × *Od.*, a position occupied by χάζεο in its other two occurrences (including 16.707). The rhyming combination of the two, cf. ἆσσον … θᾶσσον at 6.143, is naive but effective; an equally homely touch is the dismissive description, unique in Homer (though cf. χαμαιγενέων), of men as χαμαὶ ἐρχομένων, 'that walk on the ground'.

445–8 A unique and striking episode: Apollo places Aineias out of harm's way in his temple in Troy, where he is miraculously healed. On Pergamos see 4.508n.; it is the acropolis of Ilios (cf. also 460), on which any temple would obviously be imagined; Athene's was there (6.88) as bT remarked, as indeed in Hellenistic times – the foundations are still visible – and no doubt also in Troy VIII. Pergamos is 'sacred' for this reason perhaps, though Ilios itself is regularly so described, e.g. Ἴλιος -ν ἱρή -ν 16 × *Il.*, cf. S. West on *Od.* 1.2. Apollo's mother and sister are imagined as healing Aineias' shattered thigh in the god's ἄδυτον or inner shrine (only here and at 512). Their presence there is unparalleled in Homer, but the three deities seem to have had a common cult at Dreros in Crete as early as around 725 B.C. That is the probable foundation-date of the temple there, its three hammered bronze cult-statues being perhaps slightly later (see J. N. Coldstream, *Geometric Greece*, London 1977, 297f. and 291 n. 49; for circumstantial evidence from Delphi and Delos cf. Burkert, *Religion* 48–9 and *HyAp* 158f.). The wound was a drastic one (cf. 305–10) requiring something more than the healing powers even of a Makhaon, for whom there was in any case no Trojan equivalent. The cure had to be divine, therefore; Apollo was otherwise occupied (and see on 398–402, second para.), and his mother and sister, as goddesses, balance Dione who had earlier cured Aphrodite. They not only cured him but also κύδαινον, literally 'gave him glory': hardly medical encouragement (bT), even though *Od.* 14.438 κύδαινε δὲ θυμὸν ἄνακτος means 'cheered his heart', but closer akin to Ares κύδεϊ γαίων after *his* cure at 906.

449–50 Another untypical incident follows (though not wholly un-paralleled in *Il.* as Fenik, *TBS* 48, claims) as Apollo makes an image of Aineias over which the two sides fight. εἴδωλον etc. (4 × *Il.*, 9 × *Od.*) is usually a wraith of the dead as in the formula ψυχαί, εἴδωλα καμόντων |; at *Od.* 4.796, however, Athene created an εἴδωλον of Iphthime who appeared to Penelope as though in a dream; and at 21.600f. Apollo makes himself 'in all respects like Agenor himself' and so draws Akhilleus away from the fleeing Trojans. εἴδωλον does not appear there, though ἐοικώς does, and the basic idea of Apollo making a hero's image as a distraction (whether or not by disguising himself) is the same. | αὐτῷ τ' Αἰνείᾳ resembles | αὐτῷ... Ἀγήνορι at 21.600, but καὶ τεύχεσι τοῖον |, 'and such as him in armour', has no close parallel – there is a different use of τοῖον at the v-e at 483. The assonance and alliteration of τεῦξ', -τοξος and τεύχεσι τοῖον add little and are somewhat distracting.

452–3 These vv. recur at 12.425f., but 453 contains difficulties none the less. βοείας | is usually taken as an adjective, but its other 5 Iliadic instances are substantival, i.e. as ox-hides. Separation of epithet and noun over the v-e is rare and nearly always inelegant; far better, then, to take βοείας as a noun here ('shields', simply, cf. βῶν for shield at 7.238), with 453 as elaboration. λαισήϊα are mentioned nowhere else in *Il.*; they are long as opposed to round according to Arn/A on 12.426, but that is probably just a guess. Other comments in the scholia are equally unhelpful, as also with πτερόεντα. According to Herodotus 7.91 the λαισήϊον was a Cilician ox-hide shield; Lorimer (*HM* 195) accordingly took them as Trojan here, with τε distributive, but that seems doubtful. ἀσπίδας εὐκύκλους (etc.) recurs 3 × elsewhere, despite which v. 453 looks like a rhapsodic gloss.

455–9 Apollo's invitation to Ares to re-enter the fighting corresponds closely with Athene's invitation to him to leave it at 31–4; and draws on her language there. The same v. of address (see on 31) is followed in each case by the same sort of polite question, | οὐκ ἄν δή with aor. optative. Ares is to get rid of Diomedes – 457 repeats Aphrodite's indignant description of him at 362, then 458 specifies her wound more clearly (see on 339), while ἐπέσσυτο δαίμονι ἴσος repeats the wording of the actual attack at 438.

461 Apollo has withdrawn to his temple (445–8n.); now in this rising threefolder Ares goes among the Trojans and urges them on. Aristarchus (Did/T) reported divergence over Τρῳάς or Τρῶας, the Sinope, Cyprus and Antimakhos texts (vol. 1, 42f.) having the former, the 'common' text the latter. Despite that, Τρώων became the vulgate reading and may well be preferable to either.

462 Akamas will be killed at 6.7f.; meanwhile he is a suitable disguise for Thracian Ares (cf. 13.298–303).

463–4 The god addresses Priam's sons in particular, perhaps as prelude to Sarpedon's rebuke to Hektor which follows – where at 475f. Hektor's brothers and brothers-in-law are said to be conspicuous by their absence from the fighting. Fenik (*TBS* 48f.) points out the typical elements in this brief *parainesis*, comparing 466 with 15.735f. (which is not quite the same, however).

465 An organic but untraditional v. Neither κτείνεσθαι nor ἐάσατε exactly recur and the short dat. plur. Ἀχαιοῖς cannot be easily amended; λαὸν Ἀχαιοῖς | looks like an awkward adaptation of the common formula λαὸς -ν Ἀχαιῶν |, 19 × *Il.* Shipp (*Studies* 248n.) is probably right that the dat. depends on ἐάσατε rather than being, irregularly, 'of the agent' (so too at 8.244 and 21.556f.): '…leave the troops to the Achaeans to be killed [*sc.* by them]'.

466 Zenodotus and most MSS read ποιητῆσι, Aristarchus (Did/T), wrongly, ποιητοῖσι.

467 | κεῖται ἀνὴρ ὅς -ν recurs at 16.558, cf. also | κεῖται Σαρπήδων/ Πάτροκλος at 16.541, 18.20.

468 According to bT it was right not to mention Aphrodite here as at 248, since Ankhises is the parent who matters to the Trojans. That is true, since Ares' tone is undeniably businesslike.

470 This (probable) rising threefolder occurs 10 × *Il.* (+3 × θυμὸς -ν ἑκάστου | only) and must have been well established in the oral tradition; yet it ignores the effect of digamma in (ϝ)εκάστου. The pronunciation of the semi-vowel must have been under change for at least two or three generations; see further Hoekstra, *Modifications* 42ff.

471 Sarpedon, appearing for the first time after his entry in the Trojan Catalogue (see 663n. for his name), now strongly rebukes Hektor, μάλα νείκεσεν, in a typical scene that complements Ares' rebuke of the sons of Priam just before and is structurally similar to it. Fenik has a useful discussion of this 'rebuke pattern' (*TBS* 49–52; cf. 24–6 for the broader 'consultation pattern'), of which the strongest other instances are 16.536ff. and 17.140ff.; in both of these it is Glaukos that rebukes Hektor. In other and less impressive examples Kebriones or Apollo disguised is the rebuker, Hektor or occasionally Aineias the one rebuked. In every case the result is that the Trojans advance, but not for long, with Aias prominent among those that check them; often darkness is cast over the battle by a god as at 506f. here. Clearly we are dealing with an established archetype varied according to circumstances. Since the three most elaborate instances all involve Lycian rebukes to Hektor for ignoring the allies, it looks as though this was a fundamental application, therefore that the broader theme of quarrelling between Trojans and allies was stronger in the old poetical tradition than *Il.* suggests. Such rebukes are often unjustified (see also on 800–34), with Hektor simply engaged elsewhere. Yet he has played almost no part in the fighting since the truce in bk 3 (there is a passing mention of him at 4.505), and the typical rebuke pattern may well have struck the composer as a convenient way both of involving him once more and of introducing Sarpedon as a sympathetic and ultimately pathetic figure.

473 φῂς που: 'I suppose you kept telling yourself'; ἐξέμεν may refer to Hektor's own name (so Willcock). No adequate reason is suggested for

Hektor's imagined, and by realistic standards improbable, neglect of the allies, which may be a purely rhetorical or typological device (but see previous n.).

475–6 Actually two sons of Priam had died in action quite recently, at 159f.

477–86 Sarpedon's praise of allied devotion becomes increasingly emotional. V. 478, a rising threefolder emphasized by the colon-end rhyme ἐγών... ἐών, develops the idea of ἐπίκουροι in the preceding v.: 'For I am an ally, and have come from very far afield', as 479 then demonstrates by apparently adapting the relevant entry in the Achaean Catalogue, 2.877, τηλόθεν ἐκ Λυκίης, Ξάνθου ἀπὸ δινήεντος. For a similar reference to allies fighting far from home and family cf. 16.538–40. Next in 480f. comes a typical heroic combination of sentiment and materialism: he has left behind a wife, a baby son – and desirable property. Integral enjambment and excited assonance follow with τοῖον... οἷον... φέροιεν... ἄγοιεν before this agile speaker returns, through 485 τύνη δ᾽ ἕστηκας, to Hektor's stolid and spondaic non-involvement.

478 ἥκω may be Attic as Shipp claims (*Studies* 248); it recurs at *Od.* 13.325 and in a few MSS elsewhere, but ἵκω (etc.) is usually preferred.

481 κάδ, as though he had said κατέλιπον in the previous v., exemplifies a regular idiom, cf. 3.268, 7.168, 23.755.

483–4 Shipp, *Studies* 249, calls the hiatus after μαχήσασθαι and 'Αχαιοί 'comparatively uncommon', wrongly, since hiatus at colon-breaks is both regular and frequent. φέρειν καὶ ἄγειν became standard Greek for taking booty, the former referring to portable goods, the latter to people and cattle.

485 For τύνη see 16.64–5n.

486 ὤρεσσι: hiatus is more acceptable before the initial long vowel of the contracted form (which Aristarchus accepted, Arn/A on 18.265, cf. bT here) than it would be with ὀάρεσσι which one might otherwise expect (cf. 9.327 ὀάρων).

487–8 The second of these has strong formular content and is harmless, but the first, on which it depends, presents grave difficulties. The long α of ἁλόντε is surprising (cf. ἁλοῦσα at e.g. 2.374, and Chantraine, *GH* I, 18) and its dual termination inexplicable (though see further on 9.182) – it cannot refer to wives as well (bT), and only under strain to his troops. OCT's λίνοι᾽ is unjustified for vulgate λίνου (before (ϝ)αλόντε); Bentley's λίνου πανάγροιο ἁλόντες is one remedy, not especially convincing. Then Leaf's feeling about λίνον πάναγρον, that it sounds un-Homeric as periphrasis for a net, will be shared by many. Elsewhere λίνον means 'thread' rather than 'net', until Hellenistic poetry at least; neither πάναγρος nor ἀψῖδες recurs in Homer, and the latter does not otherwise mean 'mesh' before Oppian. Major corruption of 487, or interpolation of both vv., seems probable. Again, since the A scholia are missing for 335 to 636, Aristarchus' opinion, which would be helpful here, is not available.

490–2 Sarpedon's rebuke ends strongly: 490 should probably be heard as a rising threefolder, placing even more stress on | σοὶ δὲ χρή; the four ponderous words which constitute 491 reinforce the earnest effect, and 492 provides a distinctive and more dactylic ending which reverts to the initial reproach motif, κρατερὴν...ἐνιπήν.

493–7 Such speeches of reproach or advice usually result in direct action, without further comment, by those to whom they are addressed. In 493 δάκε is from δάκνω, literally 'bite'; afterwards the expression becomes very standard, 494 recurring 4× *Il.*, 495f. 2× and 497 3×. Indeed the whole of 494–7 recurs at 6.103–6 in a similar context, with Hektor again springing into action after lengthy advice from Helenos.

497–8 ἐλελίχθησαν means 'were turned round', from ἐλίσσειν, in a form perhaps affected by confusion with ἐλελίζειν = 'shake' (cf. Chantraine, *GH* I, 132). 497 = 17.343, and 498 recurs at 15.312 down to ἀολλέες, with φόβηθεν | 5× *Il.*

499–505 As often, a simile is used to focus part of the description of mass fighting: 'As the wind carries chaff over the holy threshing-floors when men are winnowing, when golden-haired Demeter separates the grain and the chaff under the hastening winds, and the heaps [of chaff] gradually whiten, so then did the Achaeans become white with dust above, which the horses' hooves kicked up between them to the brazen sky as they fought at close quarters and the charioteers made the horses wheel.' The image is redolent of peaceful activity and rural charm in contrast with the fighting here; the threshing-floors are holy because Demeter herself presides over them (cf. bread as Δημήτερος ἀκτή at 13.322, 21.76); she is golden like the colour of ripe corn. As the winnowers throw the corn up with their fans the winds blow the pale chaff to one side, and whitened heaps are formed. This is likened by the poet to the white dust that covers the Achaeans; at 3.13 it had risen from their feet as they marched, here they are stationary and it is the horses that produce it. The effect is vigorous if a little forced, 503 being rhythmically abrupt and the whirling chariots otherwise out of place among these static ranks (497f.). ἄχναι and ἀχυρμιαί are probably related, cf. Chantraine, *Dict.* s.v. ἄχυρα; ἂψ ἐπιμισγομένων is sometimes taken as referring to the horses in 504 rather than δι' αὐτῶν in 503. For another winnowing simile see 13.588–92.

506–18 The quite complicated style continues, with long sentences, noticeable subordination and four integral enjambments in 506–11. The whole passage was suspected by Leaf and parts of it by others; it contains a few unusual features but the restitution of the real Aineias to the battle needs to be mentioned somehow, moreover the episode as a whole has a certain vigour.

506–7 οἱ δέ could refer to the Trojans, or to both sides together, not to chariot-borne warriors as bT proposed. 'Carried straight on the might of their hands' is clumsy, but little more so than μένος δ' ἰθὺς φέρον αὐτῶν | in impeccable surroundings at 16.602, cf. also 519–21n., 4.447n. and 20.108. Commentators are divided over whether to take μάχη with ἐκάλυψε or Τρώεσσιν; 1.521 μάχη Τρώεσσιν ἀρήγειν | strongly suggests the latter, and Leaf's idea that μάχη might be taken ἀπὸ κοινοῦ can be firmly rejected. Covering the combatants in darkness supports, rather than casts doubt on, the authenticity of the context, since this is a typical consequence of a rebuke-scene as Fenik shows, *TBS* 52–4, paralleled at 16.567, 17.268ff., 17.368f., 17.591 and 17.644. The curious view that the dust-whitened Achaeans would stand out as targets is recorded by bT.

508–11 A short résumé of Ares' reasons for action, inessential but not alien to the oral style; such summaries are especially common with divine actions or intentions, cf. 11.74–7, 13.347–60, 15.593–5. This one is not completely accurate over what Apollo had told Ares at 455–9, also Athene's departure is not remarked elsewhere; again that kind of looseness over details is easily paralleled. — | Φοίβου Ἀπόλλωνος χρυσαόρου recurs only at 15.256. There is nothing unusual in the relative rarity of a name–epithet group at the v.-beginning, but 'with golden sword' is an unexpected attribute for a god whose typical weapon is the bow; it recurs at *HyAp* 395. Apollo saw that Athene had gone, οἰχομένην (*contra* Fenik, *TBS* 55 n. 44); she was Δαναοῖσιν ἀρηγών | to balance Apollo as Τρώεσσιν ἀρήγων | 4 vv. earlier, but here ἀρηγών is a noun, cf. 4.7 δοιαὶ μὲν Μενελάῳ ἀρηγόνες εἰσὶ θεάων.

512–18 The restoration of Aineias to battle is inconspicuously achieved by Apollo (αὐτὸς δ' in 512), the εἴδωλον of 449 ignored.

514–16 His companions rejoice – τοὶ δὲ χάρησαν |, with the whole of 515, recurs at 7.307f., see 7.308–10n. *init.* The half-v. cumulation in 516, καὶ μένος ἐσθλὸν ἔχοντα, a unique and surely a feeble phrase, serves to distinguish the position from that in bk 7: there the Trojans are glad to welcome Hektor back from danger, here Aineias is ready for action (at 541ff.).

517 πόνος ἄλλος recurs only at *Od.* 11.54 and could be emended to πόνος αἰπύς (3 × *Il.*). Yet πόνος frequently means 'toil of battle', cf. 84n. and e.g. 13.344, and πόνος ἄλλος may therefore simply mean 'fresh toil', cf. e.g. 4.334. More difficult is ἀργυρότοξος by itself of Apollo; Shipp (*Studies* 249) is correct against Leaf that there is no exact Homeric parallel. ἐννοσίγαιος is closest.

518 For Ἔρις τ' ἄμοτον μεμαυῖα see on 4.440–1.

Book Five

519–710 *The battle continues; despite individual successes the Achaeans are slowly forced back as Ares supports the Trojans. Agamemnon, Aineias, Menelaos, Antilokhos and Hektor all have their moments of triumph; then Tlepolemos succumbs to Sarpedon in a major episode, and Hektor becomes even more of a danger*

519–21 | τοὺς δ': the Achaeans. Aias, the great defensive fighter, is always prominent when the Achaeans are under pressure; on Αἴαντε see 2.406n. οἱ δὲ καὶ αὐτοί |, 2 × *Od.*: their own resistance hardly needs stressing, and 521 perhaps tries to make up for this by its unusual expression in the style of 506, q.v. with n. The plurals are rhetorical; βίας recurs only 2 × *Il.* and of winds, but 7 × *Od.*; ἰωκάς is found only here (and the singular twice, once as a personification at 740). ἰωκή and related ἰωχμός imply no more than 'battle-throng' elsewhere, but 'pursuit' is a likely meaning here and supports the probable connexion with διώκω.

522–7 Unyielding resistance is often described by a simile; the present one is striking and unusual, with the four warriors like still clouds set by Zeus over the high peaks of mountains (cf. *Od.* 19.205) in windless weather. One sees it often in the Aegean, each island peak topped by its own white cloud. The shrill winds that can blow up and scatter them suggest the tensions among which Aias and the others remain sublimely unmoved. Cloud similes are found elsewhere, but not to represent stillness – Zeus *removes* the cloud from a great peak at 16.297f. Moulton may be right (*Similes* 63) to balance the present instance against the mist and clouds of Ares' rapid ascent to Olumpos at 864ff., though that image is obscure in contrast with great simplicity and clarity here. — 523 νηνεμίης, a temporal genitive (Ameis–Hentze), begins a series of peaceful words that continues with ἀτρέμας and εὕδησι before the onset of violence with ζαχρειῶν, πνοιῇσιν λιγυρῇσι and ἀέντες. On | ζαχρειῶν (= 'violent', 3 × *Il.* of warriors) cf. Chantraine, *Dict.* s.v. ζαχρηής; a compound of ζα = διά (intensive) and a form related to aor. ἔχρα(ϝ)ε (cf. χραύειν, 'attack'), it should presumably be spelled ζαχραέων.

527 = 15.622; P 41 omits, wrongly (*contra* Bolling, *External Evidence* 88). The simile is now referred to the Achaeans in general.

528–32 The exhortation is a typical component of general battle scenes; here the Achaeans are standing firm (cf. 527 μένον ἔμπεδον) around their other leaders, with Agamemnon moving through the throng. The exhortation recurs in Aias' mouth at 15.561–4, with καὶ αἰδῶ θέσθ' ἐνὶ θυμῷ for καὶ ἄλκιμον ἦτορ ἕλεσθε here. The commoner address is ἀνέρες ἔστε, φίλοι, μνήσασθε δὲ θούριδος ἀλκῆς (7 × *Il.*), but variation was sometimes sought in repetitive formal elements. — The vulgate spelling αἰδεῖσθε in 530, retained in OCT despite Leaf, should probably be changed to αἴδεσθε from αἴδομαι (cf. αἰδομένων in the next v.), and similarly elsewhere when metrically possible; αἴδομαι is the older form, cf. Chantraine, *GH* I, 310f.

The epigrammatic quality of 531f. in particular is typical of such short protreptic speeches. Beneath the fine words lies a severely practical message: stick together, look after each other, it's safer that way; those who retreat win no glory and risk their lives as well.

533–40 Agamemnon throws immediately after his *parainesis* (like Hektor at 15.429) and hits Deikoon in the lower belly – he specializes in painful wounds, not least in his *aristeia* early in bk 11 (Friedrich, *Verwundung* 59ff.), though nothing is made of the victim's agony here.

534–5 Deikoon and his father Pergasos appear only here. Their names sound authentic enough: Deikoon is literally 'enemy-watcher', from δήϊος and κοέω, cf. Koon, Demokoon, Hippokoon, Deipulos, Deiphobos, von Kamptz, *Personennamen* 107, 167; Pergasos has an Asiatic suffix, cf. Pergamos at 446 and 460 and Pergases as Carian place-name (but also Pergase as Attic deme), von Kamptz 157f., 341–3.

535–6 Imbrios at 13.171–6 similarly stands out among the Trojans and is honoured by Priam like his own sons; he comes from Pedaios, which has the same name as Antenor's illegitimate son at 69f., and Aineias' Dardanian lieutenants at 2.822f. are also sons of Antenor. Such coincidences are often due to unconscious association, especially over minor and more or less fictitious characters and places. Here the Trojans honour Deikoon for his quickness among the front fighters, a routine description conferring little individuality.

537–40 537–9 ~ 17.517–19; other similarities between bks 5 and 17 have already been noticed, e.g. in 471n., 506–7n. *fin.* At 17.517 occurs the more regular form, καὶ βάλεν Ἀρήτοιο κατ' ἀσπίδα πάντοσ' ἐΐσην, since the standard way (9 × *Il.*) of saying that A hit B's shield, with βάλε, is to have the verb in the first half of the v., the κατ' ἀσπίδα... formula in the second. Here, however, Agamemnon's long name has to go in the second half (even | Ἀτρεΐδης would present difficulties); the result is conspicuously less fluent. — On νειαίρῃ, also νείατος, νέατος, all meaning 'lower part of', cf. Chantraine, *Dict.* s.v. νειός; on ζωστήρ see 4.132–3n.; on 540 see 42n.

541–9 Aineias does not try to attack Agamemnon, who has just killed his friend, but slays Diokles' twin sons; for similar patterns cf. Fenik, *TBS* 57. Their genealogy is in strict ring-form:

542 The sons of Diokles were Krethon and Orsilokhos;
543 their father lived in Phere
544f. and was descended from the river Alpheios
546 who fathered Ortilokhos
547 who fathered Diokles

548   who had twin sons,
549   Krethon and Orsilokhos.

Phērē is the same as Phērai at 9.151 = 293 (and distinct from Thessalian Phĕrai), one of the seven Messenian cities promised by Agamemnon to Akhilleus, probably on the site of modern Kalamata: cf. vol. I, 181f., also S. West on *Od.* 3.488. Telemakhos stops overnight with this same Diokles son of Ortilokhos to break his journeys from Pulos to Lakedaimon and back (*Od.* 3.488f. = 15.186f.); and Odysseus had once stayed with Ortilokhos in Messene according to *Od.* 21.15f. Diokles was clearly an important figure in the tradition, and the seven towns, all of which appear to correspond with Mycenaean sites round the head of the Messenian gulf, were of some historical status.

Critics from antiquity on have been puzzled by the variation in spelling between grandfather Ortilokhos and grandson Orsilokhos, given that it was common, later at least, to name the one after the other – Glaukos has a *great*-grandfather Glaukos at 6.154f. The MSS predictably reflect attempts to make the names identical, and Zenodotus read Κρήθων 'Ορτίλοχός τε at 549 (Σ on *Od.* 3.489, cf. Erbse II, 79 on 549). Yet Aristarchus ruled 'the ancestor with a *t*, the offspring with an *s*' (Did(?)/T on 542), and most editors rightly accept this. Both forms are legitimate derivatives of ὄρνυμι (von Kamptz, *Personennamen* 213), indeed Orti- is the earlier form from which the -s- form developed, cf. J. Wackernagel, *Sprachliche Untersuchungen zu Homer* (Göttingen 1916) 236f. and Chantraine, *Dict.* s.v. ὄρνυμαι. It was probably represented in Mycenaean. The -t- pronunciation may well have been felt appropriate to an older generation (cf. προτί > πρός), and the adoption of a newer spelling (assigned to two other minor characters at 8.274 and *Od.* 13.260) would scarcely infringe the honorific connexion between grandson and grandfather.

544–8 Several of the details are typical as one would expect: the victims are brothers, cf. e.g. 148f. and 152, and twins, cf. 6.21–8; their father is a rich man, cf. 612f. (and the victims themselves are often rich, cf. e.g. 707f., 6.13f.); they are descended from a river, cf. 16.174, 21.157f.

545 On the extent of Pylian territory see 2.591–4n.

550–3 bT note the pathos of their youth, as of their being twins in 548; the 'black ships' add to the effect, though not perhaps deliberately since the formula is in itself neutral. εὔπωλος recurs as an epithet for Ilios at 16.576.

554–8 The brothers are compared with two lions reared in the mountains who ravage the flocks until they are killed. Fenik, *TBS* 58, notes typical elements here (pairs of wild beasts, two lions on mountain peaks, attacks on cattle etc., a lion killed by men) and remarks that 'As so often in the Iliad... the unique is only a new arrangement of the typical.' But he also observes that nowhere else is the lion's *death* the main point of resemblance; indeed concentration on the typical can disguise the fact that this simile is rather different from others. The language and much of the detail are unusually formular (ὄρεος κορυφῇσιν; βαθείης ... ὕλης; βόας -ες καὶ ἴφια μῆλα; ἐν παλάμῃσι; ὀξέϊ χαλκῷ; and cf. σταθμοὺς κεραΐζων of a lion at 16.752); neither the actual killing nor the implied pathos (for the lions too are young) is much emphasized. In particular the rearing of the cubs by their mother 'in the mountain peaks ... in the thickets, τάρφεσιν, of a deep forest' seems almost too dramatic for the bald statements that follow of the damage they cause and their death merely 'at men's hands'. Yet 557 ὄφρα καὶ αὐτώ stresses the apparent inevitability of their own deaths, and it is perhaps this aspect of warfare that the poet wishes to emphasize in a deliberately flat and sombre conclusion. Moulton (*Similes* 60f.) sees the simile as 'effectively balancing and reversing' that at 136ff. (q.v. with nn.), in which Diomedes' might is compared to that of a lion leaping into a steading.

560 Similes are often grouped to illustrate different phases or aspects of an action, cf. the famous sequence at 2.455–83 with a good discussion by Moulton (*Similes* 18–33). Here the poet may feel that the brothers' actual death has not been much illuminated by the main lion simile, and so adds a short and pathetic reference to their collapsing like pine-trees. Elaborated tree-similes occur at 4.482ff., 13.178ff., 13.389ff. (= 16.482ff.), 14.414ff., 17.53ff.

561 The transition to a fresh episode is deftly managed, with | τὼ δὲ πεσόντ' picking up | καππεσέτην in 560. Such mediated transitions (as also at 590 and 596) are interspersed with more casual ones introduced e.g. by ἔνθ' αὖτ' or ἔνθα as at 541, 576.

562–4 562 is formular, 7 × *Il.*; with | σείων ἐγχείην in 563 compare 3.345, of Menelaos and Paris, | σείοντ' ἐγχείας. Menelaos' reaction here is bold, compassionate and imprudent; Agamemnon had shown at 4.169–82 what a disaster his death would be to the whole expedition, yet here he is attacking Aineias who, if no Hektor, at least is Menelaos' superior as a fighter. Some hesitation may be felt over the addition that Ares encouraged him with the intention of leading him to his death. Its expression is harmless, though μένος as object of ὄτρυνεν is unusual; | τὰ φρονέων is formular, with τά as antecedent of ἵνα. Fenik, *TBS* 59, compares Athene persuading Pandaros to break the truce at 4.92ff. and Apollo urging Aineias to attack Akhilleus at 20.79ff.; neither is quite similar, and each is a developed episode. The brief and off-hand character of the present suggestion, together with the inorganic nature of 563f., makes later elaboration a possibility.

565–7 Antilokhos ('always sharp in emergencies', bT) comes to help him, fearing 'lest he should suffer some ill and wholly frustrate them of their toil'; on σφας see Chantraine, *GH* I, 267. This has been thought by Neo-analytical critics (cf. e.g. Von der Mühll, *Hypomnema* 100) to be copied from the scene in the Cyclic *Aithiopis* where the same Antilokhos, at the cost of his life, saves his father Nestor – an idea ably dealt with by Fenik (*TBS* 59f.), who notes both the differences of the two scenes and the typical elements in both; see further on 373–4 and 436–9, also pp. 26f.

568–9 'The two of them were holding χεῖρας and sharp spears against each other' is intelligible but strained. ἔγχεα ὀξυόεντα is a rare adaptation to the plural of a formula designed for the dat. sing. (7 × *Il.*). For similarly vague expressions cf. 506 μένος χειρῶν ἰθὺς φέρον and 13.134f. ἔγχεα δὲ πτύσσοντο θρασειάων ἀπὸ χειρῶν | σειόμεν'.

570–2 The language becomes more regular. For a warrior's retreat when his opponent is reinforced cf. Hektor at 17.128ff.; there is nothing unheroic about it.

573–5 With Aineias in tactical retreat, Antilokhos and Menelaos drag back the corpses of Krethon and Orsilokhos before returning to the fight. τὼ μὲν ἄρα δειλώ continues the pathetic tone, to which the dual forms, extended now to their killers, contribute. δειλώ is more than a euphemism for 'dead' as Leaf and Ameis–Hentze suggest; δειλός in Homer always has a strongly pathetic ring.

576–89 The joint endeavour continues, as is stressed by the dual ἐλέτην in 576; actually it is Menelaos that kills Pulaimenes, while Antilokhos goes for Mudon whose dramatic death provides a climax to the episode.

576–7 This same Pulaimenes, leader of the Paphlagonians at 2.851, is represented as still alive, and mourning his dead son, at 13.658f. (cf. 643). Those two vv. are cumulated and inorganic; their author overlooked the present passage as ancient critics were fond of pointing out. The four-word 577 gives an impression of importance, especially with its spondaic ending, but the sustained coincidence of word and colon is ungainly.

579 νύξε connotes thrust not throw; ἑσταότ' suggests that Pulaimenes had left his chariot.

580–3 His charioteer Mudon, just turning the horses for flight, is first incapacitated by a stone-throw and then finished off by sword; 4.517–26 is similar, but first strike by stone is unusual. Both Mudon and his father Atumnios have probably Asiatic names (von Kamptz, *Personennamen* s.vv.) assigned to two minor characters elsewhere; on the latter cf. 16.317n. In 582 ἀγκῶνα...μέσον is object of 580 βάλ', with a gen., 'hitting (him)', understood after τυχών, cf. e.g. 4.106. Mudon drops the reins which are 'white with ivory'; see 4.141f. with n. for another kind of ivory horse-trapping. The reference could be to decorative ivory discs (rather than a kind of handle, bT) – or the poet's fancy could have run away with him, cf.

Artemis as χρυσήνιος at 6.205. The almost contemporary Nineveh bas-reliefs of Ashurbanipal's lion-hunt show the reins as plain though the other harness is richly decorated; yet nothing is impossible – the palace of Shalmaneser III at Nimrud produced a mid-9th-cent. B.C. *horse-blinker* made of gypsum (Metropolitan Museum, Rogers Fund 62.269.12)!

584 A rising threefolder marks the climax of Antilokhos' attack as he strikes Mudon on the head with his sword; on κόρσην see 4.501–4n. The difficulty of reaching up to deliver this blow against a man standing in a chariot is remarked on by bT – see next n., however.

585–8 Mudon's end is dramatic and grotesque, a 'phantasma' in the modern critical term. Expiring, ἀσθμαίνων, he falls head-first out of the chariot and sticks upright in soft sand until his horses knock him over. V. 585 = 13.399, in a somewhat similar passage also involving Antilokhos (who spears Asios' charioteer, frozen with fear at his master's death, so that he falls from the chariot, then sends away the horses as at 589 here). But there is no phantasma in the bk 13 passage; for that one compares 16.401–10, where Patroklos hits Thestor, crouched in fear in his chariot, in the jaw and then pulls him over the rail on the end of his spear like an angler with a fish. Fenik (*TBS* 60–2) deals well with these three scenes, pointing out their overlaps and their special details – e.g. the charioteer is struck with terror in the other two passages but not here. Attempting to establish a copy–model relationship, cf. Friedrich, *Verwundung* 11–16, is, as usual, unsound, and Fenik is right to think in terms of a general type-scene (cf. also 11.128f.) of which these are all representatives. Even so, the difficulty of striking a man in a chariot on the head with one's sword may be resolved (*contra* Fenik, *TBS* 64f.) by comparison with 16.403, where the victim has slumped down in fear, ἧστο ἀλείς. The singer, that is, retains this detail in mind though he does not directly express it here. — Attempts to remove the impossible elements, either by envisaging an attack of cataleptic rigor mortis or by imagining Mudon as caught up in and held upside-down by the chariot somehow (bT, Leaf), are a waste of time. This is a pure flight of fancy, like Patroklos dangling his victim from the end of his spear in bk 16.

586 κύμβαχος recurs at 15.536 as a noun meaning the top of the helmet *vel sim.*; here it means 'head-first', and there is a probable connexion with κυβιστάω, 'dive' or 'somersault'. βρεχμός is *hapax* in Homer, a relation of later βρέγμα = 'forehead'. Falling on forehead and shoulders is a remarkable feat in itself.

587 The deep sand would have made the chariot impossible to manoeuvre. Many MSS omitted ῥ' before ἀμάθοιο or read ψαμάθοιο instead. Since ψάμαθος etc. occurs 10 × *Il.*, ἄμαθος only here (though cf. 9.593 ἀμαθύνει), the former might seem correct; but Aristarchus (Arn/A on

9.385) distinguished the two, with ψάμαθος connoting sand on the shore and ἄμαθος dust inland.

590–5 Hektor 'notices' them and rushes at them, though no specific contact ensues. The passage is a version of 11.343–5, expanded by the cumulation of Ares and his companions in 592–5 – if it is not the present version that is 'basic' with bk 11 presenting an abbreviation. Yet the singer appears to draw quite frequently on battle descriptions elsewhere, especially in bks 11, 13 and 15–17, and elaborate them with special effects. Fenik (*TBS* 64) again warns against the model–copy fallacy, but the elaboration of an existing description by the addition of two or three vv. could be a special case, not necessarily susceptible to the type-scene argument.

591 κεκληγώς, not κεκλήγων is the vulgate reading in all six Iliadic occurrences and should be retained (OCT notwithstanding), the Aeolic termination -οντες being correct in the plural (4 × *Il.*); see Chantraine, *GH* I, 430f.

592–5 Ares is attended by Enuo, the spirit of war named also in 333. She in turn 'has', 593 ἔχουσα, Kudoimos, perhaps leading him by the hand or even, as bT suggest, holding him *in* her hands as Eris holds the πολέμοιο τέρας at 11.4 – more probably the former, since Kudoimos ('Uproar') appears with Eris and Ker in almost human guise at 18.535f. Here he is 'shameless in ⟨the sphere of⟩ carnage', a unique phrase loosely formed after the near-rhyme ἐν αἰνῇ δηϊοτῆτι | (6 × *Il.*). δήϊος ranges in meaning from 'hostile' to 'slaughterous', apart from its special (perhaps original) sense 'blazing', cf. δαίω, as in δήϊον πῦρ | (4 × *Il.*); see Chantraine, *Dict.* s.v. — Even more dramatic (with alliteration in 594 as in 593) is the vision in 594f. of Ares wielding a huge spear and moving now in front of Hektor, now behind. The whole allegorical elaboration is brilliantly conceived and strongly recalls 4.439–45, where Ares, and Athene accompanied by Deimos, Phobos and Eris, rally the two armies. Both belong to the latest phase of composition rather than to that of rhapsodic elaboration, cf. 4.444–5n.

596–606 Nothing has been heard of Diomedes (except for a brief ref. at 519) since his repulse by Apollo at 443, cf. 457. Now he reappears, not to continue his own *aristeia* but as a foil for Hektor; even he finds withdrawal prudent in the face of Hektor supported by a god. The Trojan is pre-eminent for a while until Athene and Here contrive to remove Ares, when Diomedes comes into his own again.

596 | τὸν δέ: Hektor perhaps, or Ares according to Ameis–Hentze, since Diomedes sees him too, cf. 604.

597–600 Cf. 3.33–5 where Paris catches sight of Menelaos and recoils like one who sees a poisonous snake. ἀπάλαμνος is predicative – this anonymous traveller stands helpless by the river; formed from παλάμη =

'palm of the hand', it implies 'unable to do anything', not 'indolent' as at Hesiod, *Erga* 20. The details, as usual, bring the comparison brilliantly to life: crossing the great plain, which increases his isolation and alarm; the repeated stress on the rush of water (swift-flowing, flowing into the sea, roaring and foaming); the progression from standing (598) to running backward (599). Moulton, *Similes* 62, rightly contrasts all this with the earlier rushing-river simile at 87ff., where Diomedes is irresistible, like a torrent from the mountains as it surges out of control through the plain – whereas here he is stopped, fearful and helpless, and Hektor and Ares, rather, are like the swift-flowing river.

601–6 Diomedes' symmetrically arranged little speech urges his troops to give ground before Hektor. The six vv. form three couplets: (i) Hektor is always formidable, (ii) and supported by a god, as now; (iii) therefore give way to him and avoid fighting with gods. (i) and (iii) are enjambed, with varied colon-emphasis; (ii) consists of rhythmically parallel rising threefolders.

601–2 The syntax is awkward, since the formular 602 depends elsewhere (at 16.493, 22.269) on a preceding χρή. Here, οἷον δή is presumably exclamatory: 'How we marvelled at...' (θαυμάζομεν being probably imperf.), with the infinitive implying '*for being* a spearman and bold fighter'.

603–4 'But there is always a god at his side ⟨which is why even his superiors, like me, have to treat him carefully⟩ – as Ares is just now, in the likeness of a mortal.' κεῖνος ('Ares there') strongly suggests that he is fully visible, not just to Diomedes who has had the mist removed from his eyes (127f.) but also to the others. He is not, therefore, simply a rhetorical flight by the poet, though his more abstract attendants of 592f. may be.

605–6 The Achaeans are not to turn tail, but to retreat while facing the enemy. ἶφι μάχεσθαι is part of a loose formular system constructed on μάχεσθαι at the v-e:

ἶφι μάχεσθαι	(7 × *Il.*)
Τρώεσσι μάχεσθαι	(10 × *Il.*)
Δαναοῖσι μάχεσθαι	(1 × *Il.*)
μεμαῶτε (etc.) μάχεσθαι	(9 × *Il.*)
π(τ)ολεμίζειν ἠδὲ μάχεσθαι	(9 × *Il.*).

Diomedes' hesitation over attacking gods (also at 6.128ff.) is broadly consistent. Athene at 127–32 gave him the power to recognize them and told him to attack only Aphrodite; since then he has wounded her, and been frightened off by Apollo as he tried to reach Aineias (432–44). He will soon, at 815–34, be authorized by Athene to attack Ares too, but here he obeys orders and ordinary prudence. — Fenik (*TBS* 63f.) notes that the few

major Greek retreats are nearly all brought about by Hektor with strong
divine support; so also at 15.306ff. (Apollo with aegis), 17.592ff. (Apollo.
and Zeus with aegis), cf. 8.130ff. (Zeus with thunderbolt).

607 For μάλα σχέδον ἤλυθον, which has a threatening ring, cf. 13.402
and a similar phrase at 611.

608–9 Two victims in the same chariot form a typical motif, cf. 159f.,
11.101ff. and 11.126f. (all with | εἰν ἐνὶ δίφρῳ ἐόντας). Skill in battle is often
attributed to otherwise obscure victims to make them seem more important,
cf. e.g. Deikoon at 536; even so, it is worth noticing how much more
attention is paid to Aias' single counter-victim at 611–18 than to Hektor's
success at this point. Menesthes, like Menestheus, -ios etc., is a shortened
form of Menesthenes.

610–11 Pity activates Aias as it did Menelaos at 561 after the death of
another pair; the first parts of 610 and 561 are identical. 611 = 4.496, with
| στῆ δὲ μάλ᾽ ἐγγὺς ἰών 4 × *Il.*, an expansion of frequent | στῆ δ(έ). Though
formular, the v. gives an accurate and vivid description: he gets close, takes
a firm stand and then throws.

612–14 Amphios of Paisos is puzzling; he looks as though he ought to
be the same as Amphios of Apaisos (though his father is Selagos not
Merops) in the Trojan Catalogue at 2.830, see n. there. This Amphios is led
by destiny to come as an ally; the other one, too, with his brother, was
brought to Troy by the dooms of black death (2.834 = 11.332). But this
Amphios is in full armour whereas the other was λινοθώρηξ; and the sons
of Merops are killed, with clear reference to the catalogue-entry, at
11.329–32. Aristarchus (Arn/A) noted on 2.830 that 'there is another
Amphios of Perkote, son of Elatos', which assumes that Paisos is the same
as Apaisos (and in Perkote), but reading Elatos for Selagos scarcely helps.
There is clearly some confusion, perhaps mainly in the Catalogue.
'Unconscious word-association in the choice of a name for a minor figure'
(Willcock) is one possibility. Typical motifs (rich victim – cf. 544–8n.;
destiny leading one to Troy) will continue in the description of his wound
and the attempt to strip him.

616–17 The first half of each v. is the same as in 539f., the death of
Deikoon. δούπησεν δὲ πεσών, without the addition of ἀράβησε δὲ τεύχε᾽ ἐπ᾽
αὐτῷ as in 540, allows new action to be initiated in the second hemistich;
so 9 × *Il.* against 7 × for the whole v., exemplifying one type of formular
flexibility.

618–19 Strong break at the main caesura is twice repeated, giving an
urgent impression as the short sentences are displaced so as to run from
mid-v. to mid-v. Enjambment is progressive; the sense of disruption would
be still greater if it were integral as at 653f.

620–2 Two integrally enjambed vv. now provide contrast with the preceding sentence, which is echoed, however, in the strong mid-v. punctuation of 622. That a victor is prevented from stripping the corpse by concerted enemy action is a typical motif, cf. 4.531ff., 13.509ff. (where 510f. = 621f.). Here it is emphasized by successive and rather repetitious cumulations of detail: 618 the Trojans shower spears on Aias; 619 many hit his shield; 620 he withdraws his spear; 621–2 but cannot strip off the armour, being pressed by missiles.

620 λὰξ προσβάς (as at 16.863) means that he put his foot on the corpse to withdraw his spear, λάξ implying 'with the flat of the foot' (cf. λακτίζειν), or possibly the heel, cf. Lat. *calx*.

623–4 Standard elements are here constrained to new uses: πολέες -ας/πολλοί -ούς τε καὶ ἐσθλοί -ούς 7 × *Il*. but only here not at the v-e; bare ἔγχε' ἔχοντες | only here, jejune in comparison with 4.533 δολίχ' ἔγχεα χερσὶν ἔχοντες |, cf. 12.444 and 17.412 ἀκαχμένα δούρατ' ἔχοντες |; κρατερήν goes better with ὑσμίνην as at 627 (10 × *Il*.) than with unique ἀμφίβασιν in 623. Editors usually take this term to imply 'defence' (cf. 299 ἀμφὶ δ' ἄρ' αὐτῷ βαῖνε) rather than 'surrounding', because of κρατερήν; but see next comment.

625–6 = 4.534–5, where in a similar incident Thoas has killed Peiros but can do no more than retrieve his own spear because the Thracian companions 'stand around', 532 περίστησαν, the body. Indeed that, or something like it, is the probable origin of ἀμφίβασιν in 623, especially since δολίχ' ἔγχεα χερσὶν ἔχοντες, as probable source for the weak ἔγχε' ἔχοντες of 5.624, immediately follows. Thoas' frustration is more energetically described than that of Aias here, and the killing of Amphios is in retrospect flat and derivative.

627–69 A far more substantial encounter follows, between Sarpedon and Tlepolemos 'son and grandson of cloud-gathering Zeus' (631). The former is leader of the Lycians (for his name see on 677–8, also on 16.419), son of Zeus and Laodameia, the latter of the Rhodians and son of Zeus's son Herakles. 'They say the Lycians were always enemies of the Rhodians' (bT on 639), and many have suspected the present encounter of reflecting historical conflict between Rhodes and the Lycian mainland some sixty miles eastward (cf. Page, *HHI* 148, with refs.). Opinions differ about whether such Rhodians would be Mycenaean or Dorian – compare the description of Tlepolemos as Rhodian leader at 2.653–70, with 2.655–6n. which concludes slightly in favour of a post-Bronze-Age origin for the catalogue-entry. Nothing in the present description in itself suggests specific historical reminiscence, but see further on 6.168–70. — The episode does little to sustain the idea of relentless Trojan advance, even though Sarpedon emerges as victor; yet it enlivens the palate after the rather routine taste of the last 50 vv. Wilamowitz (*IuH* 281) and others have regarded it, like Sarpedon's rebuke at 471–96, as a palpable insertion.

628–9   The heavy patronymic bridges the main caesura to make a rising threefolder, and the solemnity is increased by postponing the subject μοῖρα κραταιή to the end of the sentence.

632   Vulgate καί is awkward as Leaf observed; μέν would be better, cf. e.g. 2.657.

633–46   Tlepolemos makes a typical challenge: an initial taunt of cowardice (633–7) leading to a boast about his own lineage (638–42), then to Sarpedon's supposed weakness again and a prediction of his imminent death (643–6). The accusation of cowardice is obviously unfair, Sarpedon being regularly presented as an exemplary warrior; the point of such taunts was to put one's opponent off his stride as well as to bolster one's own ego.

634–7   The insulting enquiry recalls Agamemnon's to Diomedes in the Epipolesis at 4.371, | τί πτώσσεις, followed by an unflattering comparison with his father Tudeus; the issue of parenthood is central here also in relation to Zeus and Herakles. Athene will renew the Tudeus comparison at 800ff. in a structurally similar address. For μάχης ἀδαήμονι φωτί cf. 13.811 μάχης ἀδαήμονές εἰμεν and 3.219 ἀΐδρεϊ φωτὶ ἐοικώς; the preceding ἐνθάδ' ἐόντι is otiose, but generally speaking the style of this speech (638 perhaps apart) is exceptionally fluent, even if formular content is relatively low. That is illustrated by 635–7, a complex and carefully enjambed sentence, in which the elegant ψευδόμενοι... and πολλὸν...ἐπιδεύεαι constructions are unique in Homer and ἐπὶ προτέρων ἀνθρώπων recurs only at 23.332.

638–9   ἀλλ' οἶον is an ancient puzzle. Taking it as exclamatory, 'but what a man do they say mighty Herakles was!', with Aristophanes, Aristarchus and Heracleo (Arn, Nic, Hrd/A), is preferable to supplying something like 'an offspring of Zeus must be...'; but the strongest sense is given by reading ἀλλοῖον with Tyrannio (Hrd/A). The periphrasis βίην Ἡρακληείην (on which see 2.658–6on.) counts as masculine, as regularly (cf. e.g. 11.690). θρασυμέμνονα comes only here and, also of Herakles, at *Od.* 11.267 where θυμολέοντα also occurs (the latter of Akhilleus at 7.228 and twice of Odysseus in *Od.*). With θρασυμέμνονα von Kamptz (*Personennamen* 81, 263f.) compares Memnon, Agamemnon, connecting it with μήδομαι etc. rather than μένος or μένειν; he may be right, but in any case this particular compound makes the latter connexion seem likely as popular etymology at least.

640–2   Laomedon's horses are those partly divine ones described at 265–70. The tale of Herakles saving Hesione from a sea-monster is alluded to at 20.145–8 (cf. also 14.250–6, 15.26–30); her father Laomedon had promised some of his horses as reward but cheated him of them (as explained by Sarpedon at 648–51), whereupon the hero sacked Troy. The 'fewer men' of 641 recalls Sthenelos' boast at 4.407 that the sons of the Seven had destroyed Thebes with παυρότερον λαόν, another recollection of the Epipolesis, see on 634. — χήρωσε δ' ἀγυιάς | in 642 is a powerful phrase unparalleled in the epic.

643 κακός of a warrior means 'cowardly' quite specifically; it is not found elsewhere with θυμός.

646 Cf. 23.71 πύλας 'Αΐδαο περήσω |, also 9.312 for the gates of Hades as hateful. Sarpedon counters with a similar expression at 654.

649–54 He freely concedes (ἦτοι...) that Herakles sacked Troy, but adds that this was the result of manifest injustice by Laomedon. The implication is that Tlepolemos' argument has no force – perhaps that Herakles had justice on his side, his grandson not (T).

649 ἀγαυοῦ (always *sic*; cf. 11.1n.) is always applied to the wicked Laomedon not in relation to his possible physique (T) but because of his polysyllabic name (so too of Τιθωνοῖο |, Δευκαλίδαο |, 'Ιλιονῆος |, Πανθοΐδαο |). ἀφραδίῃσιν signifies folly, not mere thoughtlessness.

650 Laomedon's evil response adds insult to injury; the detail, allusive and incomplete though it is, helps to sharpen the description as well as setting up the contrast of εὖ and κακῷ.

651 τηλόθεν ἦλθε is a harsh assonance, but echoes Sarpedon's own claim at 478, μάλα τηλόθεν ἥκω, cf. 645 ἐλθόντ' ἐκ Λυκίης.

652–4 The same threat is made by Odysseus to Sokos at 11.443–5, except that ἐξ ἐμέθεν τεύξεσθαι here (middle with passive sense, cf. e.g. 13.346) places even greater emphasis on ἐγώ and its forms, 4 × in this sentence. In 652 = 11.443 φόνον καὶ κῆρα μέλαιναν, not elsewhere, is a typical formular combination of φόνον καὶ κῆρα φέροντες (etc.) (3 × *Il.*) and κῆρα μέλαιναν | (9 × *Il.*). This closing threat is even more energetic than Tlepolemos' equivalent, helped by its two integral enjambments, the alliteration of δουρὶ δαμέντα | ... δώσειν and the neat pairing of εὖχος and ψυχήν as objects of δώσειν. Instead of passing through Hades' gates as in 646 the victim is to give up his life-soul to Hades 'famed for his horses' (e.g. in the rape of Persephone, *HyDem* 18f.; they may have chthonic aspects, cf. Burkert, *Religion* 138); the expressions are deliberately varied, each making a suitably impressive dénouement to the taunt.

655–62 As often with elaborately prepared encounters the actual fight is quickly over, here with a single spear-throw from each side. The distinctive feature is that these throws are simultaneous (the closest parallel being 13.584f. where spear and arrow are discharged together). Parallels can be found for other details (cf. Fenik, *TBS* 67), but the effect is unusual nevertheless. The present account may be closer to what happened in battle than the usual Homeric convention by which first one throw or thrust is described, then the other, though that makes for a more dramatic narrative. The ultimate in simultaneity is at 21.162f., where Asteropaios throws a spear with each hand.

656–9 There are pauses after the runover names at 656 and 658, similarly after the enjambed first part of the intervening v. This strong internal punctuation gives a sense of rapid action, culminating in the smooth and lingering whole-sentence 659 as death covers Tlepolemos' eyes.

657 Compare 11.553 = 17.662 for spears rushing from hands; that this is not a dead metaphor is confirmed by 661, see on 660–2.

659 On night covering the eyes see 309–10n., last para.

660–2 For a moment it is as though Tlepolemos were still alive, then the pluperf. βεβλήκειν helps remove the illusion (though at 4.492 it had a simple aor. sense). Sarpedon's αἰχμή at 658 had been 'painful' (fatally so, in fact); this one hastens on (cf. 657n.) eagerly, μαιμώωσα, like a person almost, as at 15.542 (cf. spears as λιλαιόμενα 3 × elsewhere). It grazes the thigh-bone but Sarpedon's father Zeus is still protecting him, ἔτι being a hint of what lies ahead in bk 16.

663–7 His comrades began to carry the wounded Sarpedon away from the fighting; the spear was being dragged along with him and weighing him down – no one noticed it nor thought of drawing it out of his thigh (so that he could hobble on his feet, ἐπιβαίη), because of their haste and the trouble they were having in attending to him. The urgent rhythms and rhetoric continue, with three integral enjambments and as many strong internal punctuations.

663 Σαρπηδόνα -ος -ι falls conveniently between the main (masc.) and bucolic caesura (18/20 × *Il.*, 6 × preceded by ἀντίθεον -ῳ); -ντος, -ντι are alternative forms for gen. and dat. The name has been associated ·with ἅρπη, which fits the Cilician place of that name (on a sickle-shaped bay) if not the Thracian town. -ηδων is a common place-name suffix, but the Lycian personal name Serpodis is suggestive, *zrppeduni* on the Xanthos stele even more so; see von Kamptz, *Personennamen* 312f., with refs. to Kretschmer and Sundwall. Sarpedon seems to be a real character from west-Asiatic saga, though see on 627–69 and 677f.

665–7 τὸ μέν refers not to the spear but to μηροῦ ἐξερύσαι: 'no one thought of that, namely drawing the ash-spear from his thigh'. σπευδόντων is partitive gen. after 665 οὔ τις.

668–9 The carrying of Tlepolemos' body balances that of the wounded Sarpedon at 663f., with | ἐξέφερον πολέμοιο exactly repeated and ἑτέρωθεν in 668 emphasizing the symmetry. Here, however, the description ends with Odysseus 'noticing' what has happened (cf. 95n.), which superficially echoes 665 οὐδ' ἐνόησε.

670 Assembled for the occasion, not without signs of strain, to show Odysseus as keen for action. The closest to | τλήμονα θυμὸν ἔχων is 806 θυμὸν ἔχων ὃν καρτερόν, cf. 16.209 ἄλκιμον ἦτορ ἔχων. Odysseus is τλήμων twice in bk 10; Leaf was probably right to take this as based on his standard epithet πολύτλας, but the present context calls for 'courageous' rather than 'enduring'. φίλον ἦτορ | is formular (12 × *Il.*, 19 × *Od.*), nowhere else as subject of μαίμησε etc.

671–3 Decisions between alternative courses of action are presented either through monologue or by objective narrative as here (and at 13.455ff., 14.20ff., 16.713f.): so Fenik, *TBS* 67f., after Hentze. The question is whether to pursue Sarpedon (and the small group carrying him), or to attack the main body of Lycians; it is worked out in uninterrupted vv., in contrast with those that preceded, down to 681. — προτέρω in 672 implies 'forward' rather than 'further', adding little to διώκοι. 673 ~ 10.506, ἦ ἔτι τῶν πλεόνων Θρηκῶν ἀπὸ θυμὸν ἕλοιτο (with the concluding phrase 6 × *Il.*, 1 × *Od.*), where Athene again makes up his mind for him. τῶν in τῶν πλεόνων has demonstrative or contrastive force, and emendation is unnecessary.

674–6 The second option is chosen as usual (though not at 13.458f.), here because Sarpedon is not destined to die at Odysseus' hands. This is a clear foreshadowing of the famous scene beginning at 16.433f. where Zeus laments that Sarpedon is destined to be killed by Patroklos:

> ὤ μοι ἐγών, ὅ τέ μοι Σαρπηδόνα, φίλτατον ἀνδρῶν,
> μοῖρ' ὑπὸ Πατρόκλοιο Μενοιτιάδαο δαμῆναι.

Destiny (on which see 16.434n.) is normally enforced by a god, here Athene at 676. She does not appear and address him as sometimes happens (as e.g. with Apollo and Patroklos at 16.703–9), but works on his mind, τράπε θυμόν; for comparable acts of divine mental influence see 7.44, 8.218.

677–8 If Sarpedon may have a genuine Lycian name (663n.), his troops, the ordinary soldiers, πληθύς, certainly do not. Of Odysseus' seven victims only Khromios and Prutanis are conceivably Asiatic by name, and they have been Hellenized; the other names are thoroughly Greek and thoroughly fictitious, some applied to several different minor characters. Thus Koiranos reappears elsewhere as a Cretan; there are four other occurrences of a Khromios (Neleid, Priamid, Trojan and Mysian); Halios is a son of Phaeacian Alkinoos in *Od.*, cf. the Nereid Halie at *Il.* 18.40; there is a Pylian Noemon, too, and an Ithacan in *Od.*, son of Phronios. Noemon like Phronios (cf. S. West on *Od.* 1.113) is a 'speaking name' – the compiler of the present list has a *penchant* for such, whether appropriate or not: Alastor, Khromios ('thunderer') and Alkandros belong to the battlefield, but Koiranos ('ruler'), Noemon and Prutanis ('leader') are social or political, while Halios is a man of the sea. An eighth Lycian will be named at 695, Sarpedon's friend Pelagon – he has a tribal name, Illyrian in origin, though with a superficially marine appearance.

679–82 For the standard construction | καί νύ κ'... | εἰ μὴ ἄρ' ὀξὺ νόησε see on 311–12 and 3.373–5. The whole of 681, too, is formular, 7 × *Il.*; but 682 δεῖμα (for δέος), only here, may belong to the latest stage of oral language (since | δεῖμα φέρων and δεῖμα φέροντες | would both be useful), recurring at *HyDem* 293 and later; though personified Deimos is found 3 × *Il.*

682–3 Sarpedon's joy at Hektor's approach is natural though not without irony, since this is their first contact after Sarpedon's rebuke at 471ff. The affecting ἔπος δ' ὀλοφυδνὸν ἔειπε (cf. ὀλοφύρομαι, 'groan' or 'lament') recurs at 23.102 and *Od.* 19.362; an ἔπος can otherwise be described in *Il.* as πυκινόν (4 ×), ἅλιον (3 ×) or κακόν (2 ×), but this emotive epithet is paralleled only by Odyssean θυμαλγέα, twice.

684–8 Sarpedon's plea is cumulative and complex. The tone is ingratiating, naturally so in the circumstances, and the desire to die inside Troy softens his earlier remarks (472ff.) about relations between Trojans and their allies. οὐκ ἄρ' ἔμελλον (cf. 18.98, 22.356) shows he has had no previous idea of impending death, cf. Denniston, *Particles* 36, but believes his wound to be a fatal one. The audience is reminded of his real destiny, foreshadowed at 674, of dying at the hands of Patroklos; see further on 16.419–683. The renewed mention at 688 of his wife and baby son (after 480) marks him as a sympathetic figure; does it foreshadow Hektor with *his* wife and baby in bk 6, where they are described in the same formular terms at 366? It is, after all, Hektor he is addressing here; but then Hektor will not reply. What is certain is that both of them are deliberately shaped by the poet as men of feeling.

Fenik (*TBS* 69f.) has argued after Friedrich, *Verwundung* 103ff., that the whole speech loses its impact because Sarpedon is, in fact, mistaken; it was probably designed, therefore, for a context where the speaker really *is* dying. When one compares Sarpedon's similar but slightly longer appeal to Glaukos at 16.492–501, when he is indeed mortally wounded, it is hard not to admit a difference in emotional authenticity. Even Agamemnon's lament over the wounded Menelaos at 4.155–82 is moving by comparison, though Menelaos is not, in fact, seriously hurt – but that is a longer and more elaborate speech. Yet Sarpedon's words here are brief and to the point; they have their own particular pathos through their reference to his wife and son; in any case the wound is not immediately fatal, at least if he can envisage dying back in Troy, and the appeal to Hektor has to be put as strongly as possible.

689–91 Hektor does not waste time answering but runs straight past (cf. 8.98) to keep the enemy at bay. He does not attack Odysseus, who has been laying into the Lycians, since the incident is modelled on 669–76 just before. There Odysseus had noticed Tlepolemos being carried back but decided to turn on the Lycians in general; now Hektor notices the whole situation (not just Sarpedon), and turns on the Argives. In each case the intention is to kill as many as possible of the enemy rather than one great warrior:

673 ...τῶν πλεόνων Λυκίων   ἀπὸ θυμὸν ἕλοιτο
691 ...'Αργείους, πολέων δ'   ἀπὸ θυμὸν ἕλοιτο.

692–3 Meanwhile his *goodly* companions set *god-like* Sarpedon down under the *exceedingly beautiful* oak-tree of *aegis-bearing* Zeus. 692 = 663, where the same comrades carried Sarpedon away from danger, suitably resumes his tale, but the addition of another v. rich in epithets makes an unusually stately impression. ἀντίθεον is regular for Sarpedon in this position and case (663n.), but ἑταῖροι are only δῖοι in these two contexts. After bucolic diaeresis they are regularly ἐσθλοί; where an initial consonant is needed, then πιστοί (after πιστός -ν ἑταῖρος -ν |, 7× *Il.*) might be expected, and δῖοι seems a direct response to Sarpedon being godlike, the son of Zeus in fact, and to the importance of the occasion. That is supported by 693 περικαλλέϊ, this oak-tree being nowhere else so described in its other six uses. That it belongs to aegis-bearing Zeus is stated at 7.60 also, where it is no more than 'tall'. αἰγιόχοιο Διός is standard for this position in the v. (11× *Il.*), and it is hard to see how Shipp (*Studies* 249f.) could term it 'untraditional'. — The oak-tree is one of the poet's few fixed points on the battlefield and this is its first appearance. A thrice-used v. describes it as close to the Scaean gate (on which see 3.145n.): Σκαιάς τε πύλας καὶ φηγὸν ἵκανεν/ἵκοντο (6.237, 9.354, 11.170). Here and at 7.22, 7.60, 21.549, however, the gate is not mentioned. It is surprising to learn that Sarpedon has been carried back so far from the open field of battle, but Leaf and others are probably wrong in taking this as another oak-tree altogether; see further Thornton, *Supplication* 151f.

694–5 ὥσε θύραζε after the model of ὥσε χαμᾶζε, 4× *Il.* There is nothing to be said for Ptolemaios' reading, Selagon (cf. 612) for Pelagon (Did/AT), on whom see 677–8n. *fin.*

696 That formular flexibility can be confusing is shown in this description of a warrior losing and then recovering consciousness, since the soul 'leaving' the body, 696 λίπε ψυχή, normally implies death (16.453, *Od.* 14.134, 14.426, 18.91). Sometimes it leaves from the limbs or a wound (e.g. 14.518f.); more often it is envisaged as breath, like θυμός, or as like smoke, 23.100. Close to the present use is Andromakhe fainting as she sees Hektor dragged behind Akhilleus' chariot,

22.466 τὴν δὲ κατ' ὀφθαλμῶν ἐρεβεννὴ νὺξ ἐκάλυψεν,
ἤριπε δ' ἐξοπίσω, ἀπὸ δὲ ψυχὴν ἐκάπυσσε,

where κατύω means something like 'breathe', cf. καπνός; the ψυχή 'leaving' implies much the same. Then in the structurally similar scene at 14.409ff. Hektor is hit by a stone from Aias; his comrades revive him by pouring water over him; he spits out blood, then sinks down again and 'black night covered his eyes', τὼ δὲ οἱ ὄσσε | νὺξ ἐκάλυψε μέλαινα (438f., similarly of Aineias fainting at 5.310) – that is, he loses consciousness again. The language is close to that of the first v. of the Andromakhe passage, which twice elsewhere, however, signifies death (including Tlepolemos' at 659), like most other references to night or darkness covering the eyes. ἀχλύς works slightly differently; it causes a kind of blindness at 127 and 3 × *Il.* elsewhere (cf. 127–30n.), but death, in the same phrase as here, at 16.344 and *Od.* 22.88. Thus the four main descriptions in *Il.* of losing consciousness, in respect of Aineias, Sarpedon, Hektor and Andromakhe, draw in different ways on a formular terminology primarily designed for describing death.

697–8 Sarpedon regains consciousness aided by the breeze; whether it literally restores his breath-soul is debatable. The alliteration of π's, πν's and κ's is prominent and deliberate. ἐμπνύνθη, Aristarchus' preferred reading (Erbse *ad loc.*), is followed by OCT, but the vulgate's ἀμπνύνθη is probably correct (despite ἐμπνύνθη at 14.436), cf. 22.222 ἄμπνυε, from ἀναπνέω = 'regain one's breath'. Attempts after Schulze to dissociate the word, together with πεπνυμένος, πινυτός etc., from πνέω may be misdirected (so Chantraine, *Dict.* s.v.), though cf. Hainsworth on *Od.* 8.388. The process of recovery is more fully described at 22.475, of Andromakhe, ἡ δ' ἐπεὶ οὖν ἄμπνυτο καὶ ἐς φρένα θυμὸς ἀγέρθη. — ζωγρεῖν means 'capture alive' in its three other Iliadic occurrences, from ζωός and ἀγρεῖν, cf. ζωάγρια = 'spoils'; here it means 'revive' with the -αγρεῖν element understood as ἀγείρειν. This is apparently perverse, but evidently came within the limits of acceptable adaptation. κεκαφηότα recurs at *Od.* 5.468; one would like to connect it with 22.467 ἐκάπυσσε (with Ameis–Hentze), though the aspiration is difficult as Chantraine noted s.v. Context favours a more general sense, 'being distressed', θυμόν in either case being acc. of respect.

699–702 This kind of brief survey of the general situation is often inserted to keep individual incidents, which necessarily predominate for dramatic purposes, in perspective (cf. p. 22). Hektor is still accompanied by Ares (cf. 592–5; here the rhetorical embellishments of Enuo and Kudoimos are dropped); the Achaeans are in steady but controlled retreat (cf. 605f.), aware that Ares is still against them. The emphasis on the god is consistent with what has preceded and the rôle he will later play with Diomedes. To define what his presence in the fighting meant to the audience is difficult; Ares is sometimes, no doubt, little more than a metaphor for martial power, as Willcock suggests on this passage. Yet Greek gods *are* anthropomorphic, after all, and were often envisaged as appearing in human form; one can hardly withhold this capacity from primarily functional deities like Ares and Aphrodite. Here bT remarked quite acutely that Ares' involvement in the slaughter may be balanced by his own physical wounding later, which is certainly not a metaphor.

703 The formular v. recurs at 11.299, again of Hektor, and 16.692 of Patroklos. A still more elaborate way of introducing such a list of victims is by calling on the Muses, ἔσπετε νῦν μοι Μοῦσαι..., as at 11.218 and 14.508, cf. 2.484n. — Aristarchus (Did/A) rightly insisted on plur. ἐξενάριξαν; many MSS have the singular, reflecting an attempt to exempt the god from actual slaughter; but cf. 842 where he is stripping a victim (ἐναρίζειν can mean either that, or killing).

705–7 The list corresponds with the even barer one of Odysseus' victims at 677f. Here a few epithets appear, mainly formal, and the final name is elaborated at 708–10. The other two occurrences of 703 are followed, as here, by lists of names contained in exactly three vv. – a good example of typical patterning. The Achaean victims are not such an obviously makeshift group as those of Odysseus (677–8n.). This Teuthras is not found elsewhere, though Axulos Teuthranides is killed by Diomedes at 6.12f., cf. also Teuthrania in Mysia which the Achaeans mistook for Troy according to the *Cypria*; Teuthras was Telephos' father. Another Orestes is found on the Trojan side, fighting alongside Asios at 12.139 and killed at 12.193f. Trekhos has no namesake and is said to be Aetolian, but seems to be derived from Trekhis in southern Thessaly. Another Oinomaos, like the other Orestes, is with Trojan Asios at 12.140 and is killed at 13.506. Helenos has a more famous namesake in the Priamid seer, and there is an Ithacan Oinops, his father's name, at *Od.* 21.144. Oresbios occurs only here; 'Mountain-life' looks wholly invented, but the next 3 vv. add that he lived in Hule, a rich man, by the shore of the Kephisian lake (i.e. Lake Kopais), in a prosperous Boeotian community. That elaborated description, with several typical elements (708–10n.), is no doubt designed to round off this whole section rather than supply accurate biographical information. It is remarkable that none of these six victims recurs elsewhere in the poem, still more so that four have *Trojan* (or allied) associations. The other two, Trekhos and Oresbios, are at least located in Greece, but have particularly fictitious names. It looks once again as though the singer raided his repertory for minor names, particularly Trojan or allied ones and especially those involved in Asios' attack on the Achaean wall in bk 12 – for Teuthras too has a connexion with Asios, in that Axulos at 6.13, whose father was also a Teuthras, came from Arisbe on the Hellespont which contributed to Asios' contingent according to 2.836–9.

707 See on 4.137–8 for Oresbios' gleaming μίτρη.

708–10 On Hule as contributor to the Boeotian contingent see 2.500 and vol. 1, 192 and 196. The victim who is rich, or has a rich father, is a typical detail, cf. 543f., 612f., 16.594–6, 17.575f. and 544–8n. The association of prosperity with rivers or lakes is also typical, cf. e.g. 2.825, 2.854; for κεκλιμένος, 'by the shore of', cf. especially 15.740. The rich community of Hule is reminiscent of Ὕδης ἐν πίονι δήμῳ at 20.385 – presumably a coincidence, since Hude is under Mt Tmolos and πίονι δήμῳ | a formula, 5 × *Il.*, 4 × *Od.*

711–834   Athene and Here determine to stop Ares; Here looks after the preparation of horses and chariot while Athene dons her armour. They get permission from Zeus before descending to the battlefield, where Here, disguised, encourages the Achaeans, and Athene rebukes Diomedes and urges him to attack Ares

711 τοὺς δ', i.e. Hektor and his troops. Again the 'noticing' device is used for a change of scene or action, this time from the field of battle to Olumpos; the consequences of Here's noticing will fill the remainder of the Book. There will be a similar episode at 8.350ff., where Here similarly sees Hektor raging and invokes Athene's support. τὸν/τὴν/τοὺς ὡς οὖν ἐνόησε(ν) followed by different epithet–name groups occurs 9 × *Il.* (+2 variants), including at 95.

712 = 7.18, after a similar preceding v.

714 Another formular v. |ὦ πόποι, 29 × *Il.*, is often followed by ἦ; cf. 8.352 and 8.427, also addressed to Athene but without Atrutone (on which see 2.157n. and S. West on *Od.* 4.762). There will be an unusual proportion of repeated vv. in this whole episode, at least down to the goddesses' arrival on the battlefield, partly due to typical scenes of preparing a chariot and arming. The style is spirited none the less.

715 For ἄλιον τὸν μῦθον ὑπέστημεν cf. *HyHerm* 280, ἄλιον τὸν μῦθον ἀκούων; it is a relatively late and slightly awkward adaptation of e.g. 2.286 ὑπόσχεσιν ἥν περ ὑπέσταν – since to promise a promise is one thing, to promise 'that saying' quite another.

716 No specific promise need have been made to Menelaos, but he is clearly involved.

718 = 4.418, likewise the concluding v. of a brief exhortation, cf. 24.618.

719–52 The two goddesses initiate a major new episode, culminating in the wounding of Ares and his retreat to Olumpos, which is obviously a close parallel to the earlier wounding of Aphrodite. We shall expect, therefore, to find certain repetitions of theme and language. What is surprising is that the preparations for action by Here and Athene are closely reproduced in bk 8, where once again they decide to intervene in order to curb Hektor's devastations, only to be frustrated at the last moment by terrible threats from Zeus. That scene begins at 8.350 when Here once again expresses horror to Athene about the Trojan success, and asks whether they are to stand idle. Athene replies by first railing against Zeus, but at 374ff. she accedes and tells Here to harness the horses while she herself goes to Zeus's palace to put on armour. Herē obeys, at 8.381–3 ~ 5.719–21 here; then the bk 8 version moves straight on to the arming of Athene, where 8.384–96 = 5.733–7 and 745–52. In other words, bk 8 does not have *either* the elaborate description of the preparation of the chariot at 5.722–32 *or* that of Athene donning the aegis and helmet at 5.738–44.

Modern critics have debated the matter at length: is the bk 5 passage here an expansion of bk 8, or is the bk 8 version an abbreviation and re-adaptation of bk 5? That question is not so pointless as model–copy arguments usually are; for it can be urged that, though both scenes contain typical elements as Fenik showed (*TBS* 72–4), they are not type-scenes like many others but 'are so long and so specifically grounded in the action of the Iliad that they appear to be especially devised for this particular poem' (p. 72). Moreover close attention to 719–21 reveals, surprisingly, that this part of the common description has been adapted from the bk 8 version (or something very like it) and does not naturally fit its present context.

719–21 ~ 8.381–3, except that the subject of 719 ἀπίθησε is Athene not Here. That is because Here is now the immediately preceding speaker, whereas her speech of protest and exhortation at 8.352–6 had been followed by a long reply from Athene which is absent here. That reply had contrived to distract attention from Zeus's ban on divine intervention; no such consideration operates here. The consequence is that | ἡ μέν at 8.382 is quite undoubtedly Here; that is what the run of the sentence suggests, and in any case Here has just been told by Athene to harness the horses; she obeys this instruction (381) and goes off to do this very thing (382). The next v., 383, however, is clearly otiose, and many good MSS omit it. Now compare these three vv. in their bk 5 context. The previous speaker has been Here, so it is now Athene who obeys – what? Not a specific instruction to harness as in bk 8, but a general exhortation, 'let us, too, take thought for battle'. But that means that the subject of | ἡ μέν in 720 is ambiguous, or rather refers most obviously to Athene. Actually it is Here who is to harness the horses (as the other context had made plain through 8.374), and this now has to be established by the addition of 721. This, as we saw, is otiose in the bk 8 context and omitted by many MSS; here it is essential, and with no sign of doubt in the MS tradition – yet its makeshift nature is confirmed by its apparently being designed *for use in the vocative not the nominative*. That is strongly suggested by 14.194 and 243 (despite 19.91 and *Od.* 3.452) as well as by the whole-v. type of address with full titles, perhaps also by the form πρέσβα itself (Shipp, *Studies* 252, *contra* Risch, *Wortbildung* 68).

Thus these introductory vv. seem to have been adapted and elaborated from the bk 8 scene – either that, or some closely similar archetype. A further difficulty from which the bk 8 version is free will be discussed on 734–7; all of which suggests that further differences between the two, over the preparation of the chariot and the aegis of Athene, *are caused by elaboration here rather than simplification there* – a conclusion which may have important consequences for our view of bk 8 as a whole.

722–3 The horses are harnessed by Here, the chariot is assembled by Hebe, on whom see 4.2–3n.; she will wash and clothe the revived Ares at 905. Chariots were stored indoors with covers over them (2.777–8, 5.194–5, 8.441 and nn.), often with wheels removed as 8.441 also implies. The Linear B chariot tablets show this to have been regular Mycenaean practice (Ventris and Chadwick, *Documents* 361–9). καμπύλα κύκλα, here only, is modelled on καμπύλα τόξα (5 × *Il.*); these wheels (the original meaning of κύκλος) are of bronze and fit onto an iron axle, both metals being exotic choices for these functions (*contra* bT); the axle of Diomedes' chariot at 838 is φήγινος, 'of oak', which is realistic (4.485–6n.). The eight-spoked wheels are a great rarity (Lorimer, *HM* 319), probably a pious exaggeration likewise, since nearly all Bronze Age and Early Iron Age depictions of wheels show four spokes, a few six.

724–6 The tyres were of bronze, the felloes (i.e. the rims inside them) of gold. Real felloes were of wood, see the simile at 4.485–6 with n.; the formula θαῦμα ἰδέσθαι | refers primarily to gold rather than bronze; for a parallel in the *Rigveda* cf. M. L. West, *JHS* 108 (1988) 155. The silver πλῆμναι of 726 are the hubs or naves; they are περίδρομοι, that is, they revolve, see also next n. *fin.* The temporary change to the present tense, εἰσί, is eased by the lack of copula in the previous sentence.

727–8 The δίφρος is the chariot's bodywork, the part in which the charioteer and his companion stand; it can also connote the whole equipage. Its earlier sense is 'chair', see 6.354n. – apparently one that can be carried on each side (δίς + φέρειν), Chantraine, *Dict.* Here it is 'stretched with gold and silver straps'; the materials replace more mundane leather – but does this mean that the floor is made out of straps under tension, or that the front and sides are so constituted? Critics differ; artistic depictions, rough and ready for the most part (cf. Lorimer, *HM* 310ff.), show various types including the latter; the former is surely impracticable, since the leather would stretch and a foot find its way through somehow. As for the two rails, ἄντυγες, running round (περίδρομος has three different applications in its three Iliadic occurrences, cf. 726 and 2.812), that may again be a divine doubling of the usual single rail; or it may count each terminal (often looped) as a separate unit, which is not implausible if the derivation of δίφρος is right.

729–31 The assemblage of a cart, not a chariot, is described at 24.266–74; there too the yoke is separate, but the pole, ῥυμός, is permanently attached to the chassis (δίφρος) as evidently here (and in the Linear B chariot-ideogram), and the two are bound together at the pole's extremity. λέπαδνα are breast-collars attached to each end of the yoke; divine metals are greatly in evidence, with impressive effect. Finally Here yokes the horses and the ring-composition vignette is complete.

734–7 Meanwhile Athene pours her supple gown onto her father's floor – a voluptuous description and movement, tempered by the reminder that she had made it herself, i.e. as goddess of handiwork. ἑανός, 'pliant' *vel sim.*, seems distinct from (ϝ)εανός, 'garment', cf. ἕννυμι. Then she puts on the χιτών (112–13n.), Zeus's own as it seems, and the rest of her (his?) armour; the actions symbolize her transformation from peaceful goddess to goddess of war. Her 'father's floor' in 734 comes as a surprise, since the description lacks the essential preliminary instruction in the corresponding episode at 8.374–6: '*You* harness the horses for us, while I enter Zeus's house and arm for war.' In bk 8 Zeus is away on Ida; here he is still on Olumpos (753f.), which makes entering his house even more risky. Aristarchus retained these vv. against Zenodotus (Arn/A), athetizing them at 8.385–7 (Arn/A *ad loc.*) since no fight ensued there and an elaborate arming scene was therefore superfluous. Aristophanes had felt the same, and Zenodotus omitted 8.385–7 entirely (Did/A). Aristarchus also discussed whether only the *khiton* belonged to Zeus, or all the τεύχεα of 737, and appears to have favoured the latter (Nic/A).

738–42 On the aegis see 2.446–51n.; it is deployed by Zeus at 4.167 and by Athene at 2.447–9, 18.204 and 21.400. In 742 Διὸς τέρας applies to the gorgoneion rather than the aegis as a whole, cf. 11.4 but also 11.36, with nn. The allegorical figures of 739–40 are strongly reminiscent of the decoration of Agamemnon's shield at 11.32–7 (Phobos and Deimos, and Gorgo with dreadful gaze); also of Eris as companion of Ares at 518 and Phobos (with Deimos) and Eris as spirits of war at 4.440. Alke and Ioke are not personified elsewhere (on κρυόεσσα see 6.344n.); Γοργείη -ν κεφαλή -ν δεινοῖο πελώρου recurs at *Od.* 11.634 and is imitated at ps.-Hesiod, *Aspis* 223f., cf. also Hesiod, *Theog.* 856.; Shipp, *Studies* 250, categorizes the whole phrase as 'a typically Aeolic combination of adjective and genitive'. The possibility of rhapsodic elaboration may be stronger here than at 4.440ff. (cf. 4.445n.), especially since some kind of expansion seems involved

(719–21n. *fin*.). Yet the elaboration of this particular arming-scene, despite its straining after effect, does succeed in increasing the majesty of the two goddesses, especially Athene, as prelude to the attack by her and Diomedes on Ares himself.

743–4   743 = 11.41, in Agamemnon's arming-scene; on κυνέη see 3.336n., on ἀμφίφαλος 3.362n. Here and at 11.41f. the φάλοι or ridges are on each side of the helmet, which is ἀμφίφαλον; but the four φάλαρα implied by τετραφάληρον were probably different – though nothing to do with cheek-pieces (A), since at 16.106 Aias' helmet is constantly struck by spears κὰπ᾽ φάλαρ᾽ εὐποίηθ᾽ (see also on 13.132f.). φάληρος in later Greek means 'with white markings' (and waves at 13.799 are φαληριόωντα), see Chantraine, *Dict.* s.v. φαλός. Lorimer, *HM* 242, sees them as metal plates, but great uncertainty remains; see also D. H. F. Gray, *CQ* 61 (1947) 117–19. V. 744 is even more mysterious. The equivalent v. in the arming of Agamemnon is 11.42, ἵππουριν, δεινὸν δὲ λόφος καθύπερθεν ἔνευεν; this could have stood here too, with χρυσείην for ἵππουριν if the poet was still anxious to emphasize precious materials for the divine helmet. As things stand, Athene's golden helmet is 'fitted with foot-soldiers of a hundred towns', suggesting both the huge size of the helmet and its wearer (so bT) and the comprehensiveness of its decoration. Willcock's 'hardly intelligible' is too severe, but the expression is both unparalleled and imprecise. πρυλέες, 5 × *Il.*, are distinguished from ἱππῆες at 11.49–52 (as Aristarchus remarked there, Arn/A). It meant 'foot-soldiers' in the dialect of Gortus in Crete according to Eustathius 893.34, and may indeed have been an ancient term even if absent from the Linear B texts; it recurs at ps.-Hesiod, *Aspis* 193, having become part of the more grandiose vocabulary of warfare. See Chantraine, *Dict.*, Trümpy, *Fachausdrücke* 178f.

745–7   Most of this powerful description of the goddess, cumulative in structure and increasingly sonorous as it proceeds, recurs at *Od.* 1.99–101 though without the flaming chariot. It seems probable that the main poet himself created these 3 vv. for the general context here and at 8.389–91, since the style is strong and accomplished but with conspicuous non-formular elements. Thus acc. ὄχεα is infrequent (5 × *Il.* against ὀχέων 30 ×, ὄχεσφι(ν) 22 ×, cf. ὀχέεσσι at 722 and once else); φλόγεα is not found outside these vv.; βριθὺ μέγα στιβαρόν appears thrice elsewhere, but of Akhilleus' 'Pelian ash-spear' or its equivalent; στίχας ἀνδρῶν | is formular, but 'subduing the ranks of heroes' is not; and ὀβριμοπάτρη, 'with mighty father', is found only here (and at 8.391) in *Il.* though 3 × *Od.* In 745 ποσὶ βήσετο is especially interesting. This sort of repetitive expression is part of the oral style, cf. 3.161n. and 3.437n., but 'went with the feet', with no epithet signifying e.g. swiftness, is unique to this context (whereas ἴδεν ὀφθαλμοῖσιν, e.g. at 770, and 'answered with words' are relatively frequent). It is absurd in a way, but suggests a solemn and measured movement nevertheless.

748 A less successful v. (here and at 8.392) than 17.430 from which, or something similar, it seems to be adapted: πολλὰ μὲν ἄρ μάστιγι θοῇ ἐπεμαίετο θείνων. That rising threefolder uses ἄρ quite naturally – here the position of ἄρ' is awkward, its evident purpose to avoid hiatus. ἐπιμαίομαι can mean 'touch' as well as 'reach out towards'.

749–52 The parallel passage in bk 8 ends with these 4 imposing vv.; after that the action diverges, though the Horai will be on hand again at 8.433 to deal with the goddesses' chariot and horses when their expedition is aborted. The concept of the entrance to Olumpos being guarded by gates formed out of cloud is striking and original; it does not accord exactly with Homeric descriptions elsewhere, but these are in any case fragmentary and inconsistent; on the whole question, and especially Aristarchus' understanding of it, see Schmidt, *Weltbild* 81ff. and especially 84. As with the preceding vv., the idea and its expression seem to have been developed for the occasion. The gates creak in opening (cf. 12.460) – μύκον from μυκάομαι, usually of the bellowing of bulls but also of a spear-point against a shield. They open αὐτόμαται, 'of their own accord', but are under the general control of the Horai, the Hours or Seasons, to whom (entry to) Olumpos is here entrusted. Hesiod describes them as daughters of Zeus and Themis at *Theog.* 901f., where they are unexpectedly named as Good Rule, Justice and Peace. More to the point, they were worshipped in Attica as Thallo and Karpo (West, *Theog.* on 901, cf. p. 32) and were spirits of life and growth, probably agricultural in origin but incorporated in the epic pantheon in a vaguer form, much like the Nymphs and particularly the Graces (cf. *HyAp* 194). Leaf commented on the freedom of imagery which made these clouds creak; Aristarchus (Arn/A) had justified the idea of clouds by their being the gateway to the sky, so to speak, since the οὐρανός strictly speaking is set above the atmosphere. See also on 1.315–17; at 13.523, however, Ares can sit 'on Olumpos' peak under golden clouds'. The exact relation of Olumpos to the sky is in any case left vague (as noted above), or differently conceived on different occasions.

753–4 The Olympian gods inhabit the top of Mt Olumpos; Zeus has his palace there (cf. e.g. 398) but spends much of his time apart, on its very highest peak; it is there that Thetis found him at 1.499f. (in identical vv., see n. there), and Here and Athene find him here now. Similarly when he wants to overlook the battlefield he sits on the highest peak of Ida (14.157), much as Poseidon watches from the highest peak of Samothrace, 13.12f.

757–63 Here addresses Zeus with two heavily tactful and rather amusing questions, each beginning with Ζεῦ πάτερ. The first is long (5 vv.)

and relatively complex, with mainly progressive enjambment, and is designed to arouse his indignation; the second, short and to the point, seeks permission to chastise Ares. Formular elements are not conspicuous, and the speech seems once again to have been composed for the context.

757 An ancient variant, ἔργ᾽ ἀΐδηλα |, was rejected by Aristarchus (Did/A,T) here and at 872; neither it nor καρτερὰ ἔργα is formular.

758–61 ὁσσάτιον, only here in the epic, was copied by Hellenistic writers; for its suffix cf. 8.353 ὑστάτιον. The whole phrase ὁσσάτιόν τε καὶ οἷον is rhetorically effective, its limited survival perhaps accidental. ἔκηλοι | (8 × *Il.*, 9 × *Od.*) adds a certain complacency to 760 τέρπονται; 761 is less successful, colometrically ambiguous since τοῦτον goes closely with ἄφρονα and leaves an awkward trochaic break in the second foot, infringing the spirit, at least, of 'Meyer's Law'. Acc. sing. θέμιστα does not recur (except of the personified Themis), though plur. θέμιστας occurs 6 × *Il.*

762–3 On the polite form of question in 762 see 418–21n., and for the metrical lengthening in ἀποδίωμαι compare 16.252 ἀπονέεσθαι.

764 There was an ancient variant, τὴν δ᾽ αὖτε προσέειπε πατὴρ ἀνδρῶν τε θεῶν τε, according to Arn/A (while some MSS have τὴν δ᾽ ἡμείβετ᾽ ἔπειτα πατὴρ...). Standard vv. of address, with name–epithet groups to fit them, are easily interchangeable at any stage of transmission; here the vulgate version has the advantage of a stronger epithet in context, 'cloud-gatherer'.

765–6 Zeus laconically accedes to his daughter's request, as to similar requests from her at 8.39f. (if genuine) and 22.183–5. The brevity reflects his authority and decisiveness, but also glosses over his acting against his promise to avenge the insult to Akhilleus. — ἄγρει, cf. ἄγρα = 'prey', means 'seize'; as an interjection preceding another imperative (4 × *Il.*, 2 × *Od.*, usually followed by μάν, νῦν or δή) it signifies 'well then', 'seize the moment' almost. Leaf compared French *tiens*, but the idiom may be different. On Athene as ἀγελείη cf. 4.128n.; whether meaning 'bringing booty' or 'leader of the host' it was designed for her martial aspect, but is also a regular way of describing her in an oblique case: Parry, *MHV* 55–63. πελάζειν, 'bring close to', cf. πέλας, is frequent in different forms (18 × *Il.*, 13 × *Od.*), but only here is it used metaphorically and with abstract object; 'bring him close to evil pains' is an unwieldy expression, though perhaps all the more emphatic for that.

768–9 Once again Here lashes the horses; the couplet recurs at 8.45f., its first v. (sometimes with ἐλάαν for ἵππους) 8 × in all.

770–2 The divine horses at a single stride cover as far as a man can discern from a high place over the wine-dark sea. Divine journeys are often illustrated by similes, and the ὅσσον...τόσσον construction is useful for comparisons of distance: thus 3.12 (as far as a stone's-throw), 16.589–92 (spear-throw), 23.431–3 (discus-throw), 24.317–19 (width of a door). The style is typically concise, with a few elevated words suitable to the divine subject; on ἴδεν ὀφθαλμοῖσιν see 745–7n. ἠεροειδές should probably be taken with τόσσον, i.e. 'as far into the misty distance as...' The observer is a herdsman, perhaps, like the goatherd who at 4.275 sees a cloud coming over the sea. Sea and the view-point high above it are common elements, realistic so far as they go but also emotive through the high place, the solitary observer, the mist or cloud over the water. There might even be an echo of 1.350 where Akhilleus looked out ἐπὶ οἴνοπα πόντον as here, but the phrase is formular at the v-e, see n. there. οἴνοπα implies something very like its famous translation: 'wine-dark', 'wine-like in appearance' (cf. ὄπωπα), i.e. in colour, also of cattle at 13.703. ὑψηχέες must mean that these horses held their heads high as they neighed or whinnied – a curious epithet even for divine steeds, and perhaps ὑψαυχένες, as in bT's gloss, should be read both here and at 23.27. The singer's choice of epithet to precede ἵππους -οι | was in fact a wide one: ὠκέας or μώνυχας, then for a longer word καλλίτριχας, κρατερώνυχας, χρυσάμπυκας, ἐριαύχενας, ἐρυσάρματας.

773–4 The goddesses descend to earth at 'the flowing rivers' – according to 6.4 it is 'between the streams of Simoeis and Xanthos' that the general fighting takes place. Little is said about the Simoeis elsewhere (whereas Skamandros is a major landmark); it is mentioned by itself at 4.475 and 20.53 and together with Skamandros/Xanthos at 6.4 and 12.22. Confirmation that the two rivers met is provided by 21.307ff., where Skamandros calls on Simoeis to help contain Akhilleus (fighting in the river itself) by increasing its own flood; thus there is no reason for suspecting 774. The Simoeis is commonly identified with the modern Dümrek Su which flows in from the east and joins the Skamandros or Menderes, flowing northward down from the foothills of Ida, quite near the Hellespont, with Ilios–Hissarlik enclosed in the angle between the two; see also pp. 38f.

775–7 Herē still has charge of the horses. The first v. is formular with different divine subjects, as is λῦσασ' ἐξ ὀχέων in 776 ~ 8.50, followed elsewhere (in 369 and 13.35) by παρὰ δ' ἀμβρόσιον βάλεν εἶδαρ, an idea elaborated in the whole of 777. Thus the passage is an elaborate expression of a typical motif, expanded to include the unique but charming detail of the river pushing up ambrosia, presumably on its fertile banks, for the horses to feed on. The special food of the gods (2.19n., see also pp. 9ff., 96f.) becomes that of their horses too; nowhere else is it implied to be a kind of plant, though the idea is plausible since it corresponds with mortal σῖτος or cereal. — ἠέρα in 776 confers invisibility; it is thick mist rather than air though others cannot see it, so the horses are left to graze unnoticed. The gender of πουλύν has caused discussion: is it intended as feminine, or is ἠήρ to be counted as masculine only here in Homer? The formula ἠέρι πολλῇ | (5 × *Il.*) shows the latter to be unlikely. M. L. West favoured ἠέρι πολλῷ as *lectio difficilior* at Hesiod, *Theog.* 9, but on the basis of a doubtful assessment of Σ on 697 (Aristarchus' opinion being revealed by Arn/A on 10.27 πουλὺν ἐφ᾽ ὑγρήν | and 19.97 θῆλυς ἐοῦσα). The truth is that πουλύν, like θῆλυς -ν, can be masculine in form but feminine in function (cf. Chantraine, *GH* I, 252f.), the epic lengthening of -ο- to -ου- providing singers with a useful metrical variant, πουλύν πολλήν.

778 Surprisingly, the two goddesses 'went like pigeons in their gait', a phrase imitated at *HyAp* 114. ἴθμαθ᾽ (< ἰέναι) is not found again before Callimachus, but τρήρωνα πέλειαν | occurs 4× *Il.*, 1× *Od.* τρήρων is glossed as 'light' and 'swift' by Hesychius, and the connexion with ὀτρηρός cannot be ruled out; that with τρέω seems more probable. πολυτρήρωνα at 2.502 and 582 shows that τρήρων can also be a substantive, the name of the genus as LSJ suggest, cf. συσὶ κάπροισιν at 783 and ἴρηξ κίρκος at *Od.* 13.86f.; or it may be the wild rock-pigeon, πέλεια the tamer dove. At all events the goddesses seem to be imagined as strutting or waddling – hardly a dignified motion, but gently humorous rather than downright comical. Often it is the swiftness of birds that is attributed to gods (cf. 13.62–5, 15.237), yet ungainly disguises can also be assumed, as when at 7.59 Athene and Apollo sit in a tree like vultures; see the full discussion there. Von der Mühll (*Hypomnema* 103) thought the application to Iris and Eileithuia at *HyAp* 114 to be more natural, Ameis–Hentze that the reference is to short, quick female paces; N. J. Richardson suggests that quietness, rather, may be implied.

780–3 Diomedes is found in the thick of battle. πλεῖστοι καὶ ἄριστοι, properly of an élite contingent (e.g. Agamemnon's at 2.577, 817, Hektor's at 12.89, 197), is here more loosely applied as the Achaeans huddle together on the defensive, cf. 12.38 ἐελμένοι. They are like lions or boars (782f. ~ 7.256f.), the latter a regular exemplar of aggression under attack as at 11.414–18, 17.281–3, 17.725–9. At 12.42–8 it is either a boar or a lion, as here, that resists the hunters; that is a developed description in which the offer of an alternative, boar or lion, tends to be diffuse and distracting; here the simile is a brief amalgam of the main elements of all those more elaborate images – hunter, hounds, lions, powerful boars – and the alternative does not weaken the effect.

784–6 Herē takes the guise of Stentor and shouts a rebuke at the Achaeans. Surprisingly, this is the only Homeric mention of a figure destined to become proverbial (cf. Aristotle, *Pol.* H 4.1326b6–7). He has a 'speaking name', cf. στένειν (von Kamptz, *Personennamen* 253f.), and a 'brazen voice' like Akhilleus, whose ὄπα χάλκεον is compared to a trumpet at 18.219–22; it is as loud as that of fifty others according to 786, a cumulated v. omitted by some texts (so Did/AbT, also by P. Bodmer 1; Aristarchus probably athetized, cf. Apthorp, *MS Evidence* 49) because of its hyperbole; but see K. J. McKay, *AJP* 80 (1959) 383–8. Such powers might be appropriate in a god, cf. Ares at 859–61, but are bizarre in an otherwise obscure mortal and belong to the list of odd details in this Book. The exegetical tradition supposed him to be a Thracian killed by Hermes for boasting of his louder voice, or inventor of the conch-shell war-trumpet (AbT).

787 Agamemnon will begin his rebuke at 8.228ff. with the same words, one of several points in common between bks 5 and 8. | αἰδώς, Ἀργεῖοι and εἶδος ἀγητοί etc. ('admired for your looks') each recur twice; κάκ' ἐλέγχεα is part of Thersites' insult at 2.235.

788–91 Reproach, often violent, is a regular ingredient of heroic encouragement. These 4 vv., carefully varied in enjambment and internal punctuation and culminating, as often, in a concise whole-v. conclusion, make a single and telling point: that while Akhilleus was still fighting the enemy never ventured beyond their gates, but now they are close to the Achaean ships. That is a typical motif as Fenik notes (*TBS* 75), restated by Akhilleus himself at 9.352–4 and 16.69ff.; here it serves in addition to bring him briefly to mind (bT). Poseidon will develop the same idea in a speech likewise beginning | αἰδώς, Ἀργεῖοι at 13.95–110; indeed 791 = 13.107 and is more suitable there, since the Trojans at this point have not reached the ships themselves. That they previously 'never moved in front of the Dardanian gates' (789f.) is not very precise but clear in general purport; at 9.353f. Akhilleus will say that Hektor was previously unwilling to fight away from the wall, or only as far as the Scaean gate and the oak-tree. On the Scaean and Dardanian gate(s), perhaps identical as Aristarchus thought (Arn/bT), see 3.145n. and pp. 47f. — Shipp, *Studies* 197f. and 250, describes οἴχνεσκον as 'late', citing with approval Leaf's judgement that its context verges on the grotesque; but it is entirely harmless, not heavily traditional but firmly rooted in both epics. Its frequentative form is neatly balanced against 788 πωλέσκετο.

792 See on 470.

793 Athene 'rushed at' Diomedes, ἐπόρουσε, in an untraditional application of a verb used to suggest aggressive movement in all but two of its 24 Iliadic occurrences. The other exception is 17.481 where it connotes leaping onto a chariot, corresponding with 17.483 ἀπόρουσε. Twice it describes someone rushing towards a corpse to strip the armour, but everywhere else it implies a rapid attack. In its single Odyssean occurrence sleep rushed at, i.e. suddenly overcame, Odysseus at 23.343 – at least that is another *metaphorical* use. Admittedly Athene here is about to criticize Diomedes, to attack him with words, but that does not really justify the odd choice of verb; and the following v., where she discovers him by his chariot, suggests that ἐπόρουσε may have been intended to mean 'rushed to find him', which is no less clumsy.

794–5 She finds 'that lord' by his chariot cooling off his shoulder-wound. She had lightened Diomedes' limbs at 122 but did not really heal the wound, cf. 124–6n. The surrounding throng of 781f. is now disregarded; it is an epic narrative convention that long, isolated conversations can take place in the midst of battle; 'the bystanders are forgotten' as Fenik remarks (*TBS* 75), as in the exchanges between Diomedes and Glaukos at 6.119ff. and Akhilleus and Aineias at 20.176ff. — Aristarchus (Arn/AbT) noted the idiomatic compression of 795, 'the wound...which Pandaros hit with [i.e. made by hitting with] his arrow'; cf. 16.511.

796–8 The wound was in the right shoulder, cf. 98, and that is the one the τελαμών or shield-strap crosses, at least with this round ἀσπίς (for which P 41 has ἀμφιβρότης in place of vulgate εὐκύκλου); see Lorimer, *HM* 182 and pl. II. 4. The κοιναί or 'common' texts had τρίβετο for τείρετο, but Aristarchus accepted the latter (Did/A); its regular epic use is metaphorical but rubbing is its literal sense, cf. Lat. *tero*. As he lifts the strap and wipes off the blood the θώρηκος γύαλον of 99 is disregarded; on κελαινεφὲς αἷμ(α) see Leumann, *HW* 202ff.

799 bT remarked on the close observation of this gesture of grasping the yoke, which 'happens even now'.

800–34 At 124–6 Athene had promised the wounded hero 'might...such as his father Tudeus once had'. Now the wound is weakening him again; there is no prayer this time, but Athene reappears and rebukes him directly for slackness, saying he is very different from Tudeus about whom she recounts a laudatory anecdote. That same tale had been summarized in the Epipolesis by Agamemnon, whose un-warranted rebuke of Diomedes there was typologically similar to the present one: see vol. I, 368–72 and esp. 4.389–90n. Clearly the Tudeus theme is in the singer's mind in these two Books as a mechanism for spurring Diomedes into action, and Diomedes himself will refer to it again at 6.222f. The two rebukes are especially elaborate, representing a different dimension of the pattern discussed on 471, and might seem repetitious if Athene's tone were not so different from Agamemnon's, half-humorous rather than pompous. Then her version omits the background of Tudeus' solitary mission to Thebes (indicated with a certain vagueness at 4.376–84) and begins at 803f. with his arrival there. At 4.385f. he had found the Cadmeans dining in Eteokles' palace; now 805 adds that Athene had told him to join them peaceably and not provoke them – but he does just that in both versions by challenging them to athletic contests which he wins. Finally the bk 4 version added the typical folktale consequence that the Thebans try to ambush him on leaving, whereupon he kills all but one of the fifty ambushers. That version is therefore more complete, but the present one will emphasize, in line with its general context, Athene's unsuccessful attempt to control Tudeus' habitual boldness. See further on 807–8 below.

In the Epipolesis scene Agamemnon's rebuke was answered by Sthenelos, then himself rebuked by Diomedes. Here there is no third speaker and Diomedes defends himself, with Athene urging him on a second time. The ring-form of her first speech is exact and conspicuous (so Lohmann, *Reden* 14): (A) You are not like your father Tudeus, (B1) who was courageous even when I discouraged him; (B2) but you hang back even when I encourage and protect you, (A) therefore you are no true son of Tudeus. A similar form is artfully suggested in Diomedes' reply (through γιγνώσκω in 815, q.v. with n., and 824), but is absent from Athene's second speech.

800–1 Not living up to one's father is a typical reproach, exemplified not only at 4.372 but also in Tlepolemos' challenge to Sarpedon at 635–7. V. 801 adds that Tudeus was short in stature, μικρός, a rare word in epic (2 × *Il.*, 1 × *Od.*), the regular Homeric terms for 'small' being ὀλίγος (40 × +compounds) and τυτθός (32 ×). μείων too is Homeric (Myc. *me-u-jo*) and was regarded as the comparative of μικρός in later Greek, but despite Szemerényi may be from a different root: see Chantraine, *Dict.* svv. with refs. The etymology of μικρός, at least, is obscure, and even the analogy with μακρός doubtful. Chantraine assigns to it 'a more expressive, concrete and sometimes familiar' sense, but Shipp's 'lacking in epic dignity' (*Studies* 196f.) is excessive, especially in view of τυτθός. Actually ὀλίγον appears in the immediately preceding v., and that more than anything may have prompted the use of a less familiar term here.

No less unusual is the idea itself, details of physique being rare in the epic except for anti-heroic characters like Thersites (2.216–19) and Dolon (10.316). The Viewing from the Walls in bk 3 is a special case, and Odysseus is described there by Priam, for purposes of identification, as a head shorter (μείων) than Agamemnon but with broader shoulders (3.193f.). Such physical details as are given are usually designed to emphasize other qualities by contrast: thus Odysseus is not outstanding in height or posture when he speaks, but a brilliant speaker none the less (3.209ff.); Tudeus here is 'small in stature but a real fighter'; even Dolon is 'evil in appearance but a swift runner'. Later, Pindar can describe Herakles himself as μορφὰν βραχύς, ψυχὰν δ' ἄκαμπτος, '(relatively) short [surely not 'of little account'] in physique but unswerving in heart' (*Isthm.* 4.53). This, then, is a rhetorical figure which may reflect little in the way of positive information about the heroic subject. Yet 4.389–90n. concluded that the Tudeus tales were probably derived from a hexameter source, some predecessor of the Cyclic *Thebais*, in which case Tudeus' short stature could have come independently from there.

802–8 Probably to be taken as a single sentence, with 805 parenthetical and αὐτάρ in 806 resumptive. Athene's point is that Tudeus could not help being a fighter even when she told him not to be, despite which she kept on supporting him.

802–4 παιφάσσειν implies 'darting', cf. 2.446–51 n. *fin.*, and ἐκπαιφάσσειν 'darting out', i.e. rushing forward into the battle. Athene has forbidden him to make war, πολεμίζειν οὐκ εἴασκον, reflecting the language of 4.376 where Tudeus came to Mukenai with Poluneikes ἀτὲρ πολέμου. According to 4.380–4 the Argives were kept back by Zeus but sent Tudeus ahead from the Asopos river on a solitary mission, presumably to see if Eteokles would make terms (cf. Tudeus' μειλίχιον μῦθον in Diomedes' summary at 10.288). ἄγγελος in 804 recalls the ἀγγελίην of 4.384, in itself ambiguous, just as 803 νόσφιν Ἀχαιῶν recalls μοῦνος ἐών in 4.388; similarly Καδμείωνες, Καδμεῖοι for Thebans, here and at 807, reflect 4.385 and 388.

806 Pandaros had addressed Diomedes as καρτερόθυμε at 277.

807–8 Closely related to the equivalent couplet at 4.389f.:

ἀλλ᾽ ὅ γ᾽ ἀεθλεύειν προκαλίζετο, πάντα δ᾽ ἐνίκα
ῥηϊδίως· τοίη οἱ ἐπίρροθος ἦεν Ἀθήνη.

Differences are due to objective narrative in bk 4 as against Athene's first-person account here. It is hard to assign priority, since 4.389 has ἀεθλεύειν which 5.807 lacks (and is necessary for complete understanding), whereas 4.390 has ἐπίρροθος which is unique in Homer and seems to be syncopated from ἐπιτάρροθος here and at 828 (but see on 4.389–90). Probably both are variants of a specific poetical predecessor. Aristarchus omitted 808 (*contra* Zenodotus, Arn/A and Did/bT; cf. Apthorp, *MS Evidence* 4–6) as inconsistent with Athene's prohibition just before. That fails to recognize the complexity of her argument: 'I told him to behave peacefully, but he made challenges nevertheless; I stood by him even so, as always, and helped him win – just as I stand by you, too, and encourage, not discourage, your fighting; despite which you hold back.' — πάντα δ᾽ ἐνίκα must mean 'he won all the contests'; bT's other suggestion, πάντα κοῦρον, is hardly possible.

809–10 The goddess underlines her efforts to support and activate Diomedes: παρά θ᾽ ἵσταμαι, φυλάσσω, προφρονέως κέλομαι.

811–13 The language has formular elements but is unusual none the less: πολυάϊξ occurs once elsewhere, in the *Od.* and of πόλεμος; limbs can be seized by weariness as by trembling, but only here is δεδύκεν, acceptable in itself, used with κάματος; δέος ἴσχει ἀκήριον recurs only at 13.224

(ἀκήριον presumably from κήρ ~ θυμός, i.e. 'without spirit'). After Athene's predominantly progressive and narrative style the sharp internal break and integral enjambment of 812 make a decisive ending, especially with the emphatic ring-reference back to its opening v. at 813.

815–24 Diomedes defends himself calmly and skilfully, partly by quoting back at Athene her earlier instructions. His words, though awkward in places through adaptation of phrases from elsewhere, are carefully constructed in rhythm and rhetoric, moving from whole-sentence vv. (815, 816) and progressive enjambment (817–18) to more complex sentences (819–23) and the concise whole-v. conclusion about Ares, the important new subject, in 824.

815 Ability to recognize gods is a *leitmotiv* of the whole Book (cf. 128), which is why Diomedes reverts to it here, perhaps with a touch of irony; Athene's words, after all, not to speak of her appearance, make her identity unmistakable. He will repeat the emphatic γιγνώσκω at 824, giving an impression of completeness to his whole address by means of apparent ring-form reversion; but see further on 816 *ad fin.*

816 οὐδ' ἐπικεύσω | is a primarily Odyssean formula (8 × + 3 variants), recurring in *Il.* only in the linguistically untypical bk 10, at 115. Among Odyssean uses 4.350 and 17.141 ἔπος οὐδ' ἐπικεύσω and 5.143 πρόφρων... οὐδ' ἐπικεύσω show further similarities. This does not mean that the speech or the whole scene is by the main composer of the *Odyssey*, exactly; there are Odyssean patches in bks 1 and 24, for example, which are determined by particular kinds of subject commoner in *Od.* than in *Il.*, see e.g. on 1.312 and 434. Here it might be argued that intimate conversations between goddess and hero are a primarily Odyssean topic, just as seafaring or night-journeys with Hermes might be. Athene's speech adds some support to the idea, since her words in 809, παρά θ' ἵσταμαι ἠδὲ φυλάσσω, are also used by her to Odysseus at *Od.* 13.301: ἐν πάντεσσι πόνοισι παρίσταμαι ἠδὲ φυλάσσω (the phrase does not recur, though cf. *Il.* 4.54 for a probable echo). Moreover she had begun that same sentence with οὐδὲ σύ γ' ἔγνως | Παλλάδ' Ἀθηναίην, which may even have a bearing on Diomedes' address to her here, 815 γιγνώσκω σε, θεά, otherwise a little mysterious.

817 Takes up Athene's δέος ἴσχει ἀκήριον at 813, but also reveals its close connexion with 13.224 where the phrase recurs. That is superficially similar but grammatically quite different:

οὔτε τινὰ δέος ἴσχει ἀκήριον οὔτε τις ὄκνῳ
εἴκων ἀνδύεται πόλεμον κακόν...

It is hard not to envisage a model–copy relationship in a case like this, as against an archetype of which both are derivatives; and the model here is likely to be bk 13. Athene has not mentioned ὄκνος; *her* alternative to δέος is 811 κάματος, and the singer might be expected to have repeated that, even if it required an extra v. As it is, he seems to have chosen the easier course of adapting an existing v. from his repertory, even at the cost of imprecision.

818 This, on the other hand, seems composed for the occasion, though not without traditional elements; thus ἐπέτειλας (etc.) always comes at the v-e as here. Aristarchus (Did/T) read σέων, rightly; the vulgate σῶν is a needless modernization, conceivably Attic, since e.g. σφέων with similar synizesis is regular (and contracted σφῶν appears only with αὐτῶν, cf. Chantraine, *GH* I, 63). Van Leeuwen emended, needlessly; for the general sense cf. 1.495 οὐ λήθετ' ἐφετμέων.

819–21 = 130–2, except for 819 οὔ μ' εἴας μακάρεσσι in place of 130 μή τι σύ γ' ἀθανάτοισι – an instructive instance of the adjustment of epithet for purely functional and metrical reasons. See on 124–32, also on 130 for the scansion of ἀντικρύ and on 131–2 for the cumulation of τοῖς ἄλλοις.

822–4 In fact the immediate reason for Diomedes being as Athene found him (i.e. standing by his chariot) is that he is cooling off his wound, cf. 794f. That wound is mentioned neither by Athene (despite her reference in 811 to κάματος) nor, perhaps surprisingly, by Diomedes himself. Instead he names the general reason for the Achaeans' retreat, namely Hektor's success and their awareness that Ares is supporting the Trojans, cf. especially 702.

826–34 Athene's reply is benevolent and encouraging; she seems to have forgotten her previous insults – perhaps Diomedes' demeanour, patient as ever, has helped. Now he is to go straight for Ares, whom she abuses in an elegant and highly subordinated sentence (829–34).

826 Also at 243; see n. there.

827–8 τό γε, 'on this account' (Willcock) rather than 'for that matter' (Leaf), cf. the similar 14.342. She now claims to be Diomedes' ἐπιτάρροθος, lightly adapting her language of 808, q.v. with n.

829–31 πρώτῳ, 'straightaway', without delay; there is no implication that he would then turn against someone else. σχεδίην, adverbially, 'at close range'. θοῦρον Ἄρηα | is a formula, 7 × *Il.*; at 30 it similarly triggered off a following v. full of opprobrious epithets, also by Athene. His madness, i.e. in indiscriminate killing, is a standard criticism, e.g. at 717, but ἀλλοπρόσαλλος, 'all things to all men' ('unreliable', *LfgrE*), appears only here and at 889 (where it is Zeus that so rebukes him); he is also τυκτὸν κακόν, literally 'a wrought evil', purpose-built as it were – not only by nature but also through practice as bT suggest.

832–4 This earlier promise to side with the two goddesses against Troy is referred to briefly at 21.413f. but not elsewhere. It may be an *ad hoc* invention, since, despite Ares' mythical connexions with the foundation of

Thebes, his affiliations as Thracian are Trojan rather than Achaean – and with his mistress Aphrodite, herself mother and protectress of Aineias. That may over-simplify a complicated and defective mythological tradition, and the salient fact may be that he represents a different and more savage view of warfare than Athene, and is unlikely to remain for long as her accomplice. — Leaf rightly noted the ambiguity of 834 τῶν δὲ λέλασται; apparent correspondence with the preceding v. would suggest τῶν δέ as the Argives, but it may mean 'those undertakings', cf. στεῦτ' in 832.

835–909 Athene joins Diomedes in his chariot and helps him wound Ares, who with a roar of pain rushes up to Olumpos. He complains bitterly to Zeus, who does not conceal his dislike but has him healed. Athene and Here return to Olumpos having achieved their aim

835–6 Sthenelos has been standing silent (in contrast with the Epipolesis scene) in the chariot; now Athene ejects him and takes his place. ἀφ' ἵππων ὦσε χαμᾶζε | (itself based on ἀφ' ἵππων ἆλτο χαμᾶζε |) occurs 3 × *Il.* elsewhere, but of toppling warriors from their chariot with a fatal blow. That is clearly its traditional application. No hearer could take that to be the meaning with Sthenelos now, but the image evoked is imprecise none the less, so | χειρὶ πάλιν ἐρύσασ' is cumulated in the next v. as a correction almost – she draws Sthenelos backward, that is, out of the rear of the chariot. ἐμμαπέως (1 × *Il.*, 1 × *Od.*) is of debated origin but most probably connected with μάψ, the meaning being virtually the same. A verbal form μαπέειν is found thrice in the pseudo-Hesiodic *Aspis* and is surely an artificial creation.

838–9 Aristarchus athetized these striking vv. as unnecessary, absurd and illogical (Arn/A). It was probably the theological implications of Athene's sheer weight that distressed him; they are indeed a little shocking, and were perhaps intended to be so. Concrete physical gestures like Athene tugging Akhilleus by the hair at 1.197 (or indeed her robust displacement of Sthenelos just now) show that the gods can be conceived as having many corporeal attributes – including a kind of blood, indeed, in the present Book. She and Diomedes will shortly come upon Ares plundering a man he has killed in battle, and she will personally ram home Diomedes' spear into the divine belly. The theme of physical attack on gods is uniquely exploited in this Book, and now the creaking axle (which is realistically φήγινος, 'of oak', cf. 722–3n.) emphasizes Athene's purely physical presence in graphic detail. It is hard for a modern reader not to detect flashes of humour, as indeed in parts of the conversation that preceded (in which Fenik, *TBS* 77, refers to Athene's 'banter', comparing Apollo's words to Hektor at

15.244f.). Yet 839 at least is a solemn and serious statement, with ἄνδρα τ' ἄριστον matching Diomedes as true hero (and stalwart figure, that implies) with the terrible and superhuman goddess. The elevated diction and dramatic rhythms from 835 to 839, with the portentous runover words of 838 and 839, strengthen the scene's majestic effect.

840 Shipp may be right (*Studies* 252) that this has been abbreviated from καρπαλίμως μάστιγα καὶ ἡνία λάζετο χερσί (2 × *Il.*) to incorporate the epithet–name formula – but that does not indicate 'late composition', simply normal oral practice. Consequent lengthening of δέ before the mu of μάστιγα is perfectly acceptable, cf. e.g. 19.395.

841 Repeats the language of Athene's instruction at 829, with αὐτίκ' for ἀλλ' ἄγ'. That accounts in part for the asyndeton (because of lack of room for a connective), which is dramatic in itself; also for πρώτῳ, less natural here than there, see on 829–31.

842–3 Ares is discovered stripping Periphas whom he has just killed, cf. 848: a unique event, though his epithet μιαιφόνος shows him as liable to do this sort of thing. Other gods kill from afar, so are not directly polluted by blood. The victim here is created for the occasion; neither this Periphas nor his father Okhesios are heard of elsewhere, though a Trojan Periphas, a herald, is fleetingly dreamed up at 17.323 (his patronymic Eputides is a speaking name, and so perhaps Periphas too, von Kamptz, *Personennamen* 26). Okhesios is likely to be a literary formation, cf. von Kamptz 12; Nicander declared him to be a son of Oineus (bT) and so Diomedes' uncle. In any case the poet makes unnecessary difficulties for himself by terming Periphas 'far the best of the Aetolians', since that title belonged to Thoas both in the Achaean Catalogue and elsewhere in the poem.

844–5 The resumptive phrase τὸν μὲν Ἄρης... comes quickly, after only a single v. of contextual detail, but is forceful in its repetition of the shocking ἐνάριζε and the addition of μιαιφόνος, a standard epithet for the god but exemplified in drastic action here. It leads into Athene's unparalleled donning of the cap of Hades, yet another of the exotic details for which this Book is famous. Unlike others, *ikhor* for example, this has little to do with the special theme of wounding gods, and departs from the usual divine means of invisibility, namely covering with cloud or mist. The cap of invisibility, a widely diffused folktale concept, is enshrined in the Perseus myth (cf. Apollodorus 2.4.2), which is especially rich in folktale motifs and devices; but this is naturally its earliest testimony in a Greek context, followed by *Aspis* 227. Its description here obviously draws on the popular etymology of Hades as ἀ-ϝίδης, the unseen one; that is emphasized by μή μιν ἴδοι and the repeated ὡς δὲ ἴδε of the next v. Perhaps the cloud mechanism seemed too unwieldy for a divinity in motion and with a mortal close beside her; moreover the idea of one deity joining a mortal in physical action against another is highly untypical, one that might seem to call for untypical details in its description.

847–9 The obscure Periphas is again dignified with the epithet πελώριος (assigned to Ares' spear at 594 and to Hades at 395) in 847 which repeats most of 842. A typical runover-word cumulation enables the singer to dwell once more on this unnatural act of killing by extending ἐξαίνυτο θυμόν | (3 × *Il.*) through κτείνων; moreover κεῖσθαι ὅθι sets up a sharp conceptual contrast between the god's inert and abandoned victim and his own rush at Diomedes in 849. βῆ (βάν) ῥ' ἰθύς is standard, one of several formular elements in these 3 vv., which succeed however in conveying a sense of ruthless determination.

850 The third occurrence in this Book of this standard v.

851–2 Ares, on foot, strikes first at Diomedes, who remains in his chariot with the goddess invisible beside him; it is a thrust not a throw as he reaches forward with his spear over yoke and reins.

853–4 The untypical action is loosely expressed, for ἀϊχθῆναι suggests a spear in flight rather, cf. 11.552f. = 17.661f., θαμέες γὰρ ἄκοντες | ἀντίον ἀΐσσουσι, and 3.368 ἤχθη παλάμηφιν ἐτώσιον. Athene's diversion of the thrust reminds one of the even more miraculous feat where she *blows back* Hektor's spear-shot at Akhilleus at 20.438–41.

855–7 ὡρμᾶτο, always implying 'rushing at (*or* toward)', suits a fighter on the ground better, but must be intended here to describe Diomedes' lunge from the chariot. Athene ἐπέρεισε, pressed the spear on, into Ares' lower belly; for the μίτρη (which Aristarchus wrote in the dat. here, probably rightly against the acc. in Herodian and the vulgate, Did/AbT) see 4.137–8n. It is noted by bT that Ares is not conceived as a giant as at 21.407, otherwise Diomedes could not have reached even his lower belly. Neither singer nor audience would be likely to calculate this sort of thing very closely, but even so the god was probably felt to be larger than life, just like Athene with her exceptional weight (838f.).

858 The second hemistich is repeated in the Theomachy at 21.398, when Ares reminds Athene of this incident as he tries to attack her. A definite physical wound is inflicted, though its immediate effects are not stated until 870. δάπτειν has a general meaning, 'consume', 'devour' (cf. Lat. *daps, damnum*, Chantraine, *Dict.*) as of fire at 23.183; and a more specific one, 'tear' (in the process of devouring?), as of beasts feeding in the similes at 11.481 and 16.159. The latter sense is especially implied in διαδάπτειν as here (by tmesis).

859–61 The wounded god (cf. 870–1n.) shrieked, ἔβραχε, a verb implying a loud, harsh sound as of the axle creaking at 838, armour squeaking somehow at 4.420 and 16.566 and doors being unbarred at *Od.*

21.49; also of the noise made by a horse or a bull. The short quantitative simile 'as loud as nine or ten thousand warriors' recurs at 14.148f. of Poseidon shouting – but in encouragement not pain and rage as here, where the effect is bathetic, as is the recurrence of Ἄρης in the general sense of 'war' (cf. e.g. 2.381).

862–3 Both sides are seized by terror as they hear the great god roar; it is, after all, something inhuman and unnatural. | δείσαντας is a typical runover-word, its main purpose to lead into the formal conclusion of the simile (τόσον ἔβραχε...). The wounded and demoralized Ares is still ἆτος πολέμοιο, 'insatiate of war' (a phrase applied to him alone, 4 × *Il.*, in which the uncontracted spelling ἄατος could be restored), either ironically or through the automatic use of a regular name–epithet group.

864–7 After his great shout the god's departure needs to be described in no less striking terms. Striking this simile certainly is – but also curiously obscure, both in what it describes and in the exact point of comparison. Two other cloud similes in bk 16, one comparably opaque, appear in contexts which as a whole bear the stamp of the main composer: 16.297ff., 'as when Zeus moves thick cloud from a high mountain-top, and its look-out places, ridges and gorges are revealed, and from heaven the limitless upper air is torn asunder, so did the Danaans take respite for a little...', and 16.364ff., 'as when cloud comes from Olumpos into [*lit.* within] the sky out of the clear upper air when Zeus spreads a storm, so was their shouting and panic from the ships...' Part of the former recurs with a clearer application at 8.557f.; the latter was denounced by Leaf and others, wrongly, as a poor doublet of 16.297ff., and is not made entirely clear by Moulton, *Similes* 35. The present simile belongs, then, to a particular category and is not unique to this Book; it confirms a certain poetic tolerance over precise matters of comparison, not least in weather-images which tend of their nature to be impressionistic.

It may help to start out from a very literal translation:

5.864 Such as dark mist appears out of clouds
865 after heat when a harsh wind rises
866 such to Diomedes son of Tudeus did brazen Ares
867 appear as he went together with clouds into broad sky.

In 864 ἐκ is probably to be taken locally as at 11.62, whereas in 865 the majority opinion is surely correct that | καύματος ἔξ goes together, with ἔξ meaning 'after' or 'as a result of' and ἄνεμοιο...ὀρνυμένοιο gen. absolute. Winds do often arise after great heat (bT); but can 864 merely indicate gathering clouds (cf. Herodotus 1.87) with accompanying gloom towards east or west (so Eustathius 615.29f.)? And does τοῖος in 866 mean no more than 'so dark' (Ameis–Hentze)?. 867 and 868 show Ares' exit as both rapid and upward, εἰς οὐρανόν; a more promising idea is of some kind of whirlwind, as in Willcock who translates 864, after E. V. Rieu, as 'like a black (column of) air which appears out of the clouds'. This may be correct, especially in view of the strict meaning of ἀήρ (more properly spelled ἠήρ in Homer) as mist or tangible darkness – hence 'column'. The phenomenon would be neither a 'fiery whirlwind' (πρηστήρ in Greek) nor Leaf's 'whirlwind of dust raised by the scirocco', but something more like a tornado, which is dark in appearance and, after descending, then rapidly ascends into the sky. Compared with e.g. Moulton's likening of Ares' disappearance to 'the dissolution of the clouds in the sky after a thunderstorm', which appears to depend on Lattimore's translation of 164, such an interpretation has much in its favour.

869 καθέζετο is formular *sic* in all 11 of its Iliadic occurrences. At 906 Ares will similarly sit next to Zeus, but glorying, κύδεϊ γαίων (4 × *Il.*), rather than grieving as here.

870–1 'Immortal blood' is still flowing from the wound – *ikhor* is not mentioned here, see on 339–42 and 416. Ares' wounding is of course parallel to Aphrodite's, where ἰχώρ was introduced, but differs in detail. There is no real contradiction in any case, since even at 339f. the fluid was first described as ἄμβροτον αἷμα θεοῖο, cf. ἄμβροτον αἷμα here, and only then specified as ἰχώρ. Therefore bT are justified in saying 'He did not add "ikhor" a second time, having instructed us before on what it is.' — Ares formally displays his wound to Zeus; at 370f. Aphrodite had rushed straight into her mother's arms. In both cases the theme of divine sufferings at the hands of mortals will follow. V. 871 recurs at 11.815 of Patroklos and 18.72 of Thetis; ὀλοφύρομαι signifies lament in all three cases, though through pity, rather than pain and rage, in the other two.

872–87 Ares' complaint is curiously lacking in passion, at least until near its end, reflecting an ingratiating persuasiveness as much as his temporary debility. After an initial whole-v. question that seeks to establish his rôle as innocent victim he resorts to a series of bland couplets, from 873 to 884, of which four are cumulative with progressive enjambment, only 877f. and 881f. being periodically enjambed. V. 885, with stark internal punctuation and integral enjambment, introduces a harsher and less artificial tone and leads into the alliterative and emphatic 886. Finally its cumulated appendage 887 (if authentic, see n.), a possible rising threefolder, reverts to Ares' blander style with self-pity well to the fore.

872–4 A summary version of the old complaint about men's awful behaviour towards the gods, most fully made by Dione at 383–404, cf. also Zeus at *Od.* 1.32ff. Aphrodite had complained to her mother, here Ares complains to his father and calls on him to feel moral indignation (οὐ νεμεσίζῃ...;) about Diomedes' violent acts. Ironically 872 is a close adaptation, with ὁρῶν for Ἄρη, of Here's words to Zeus at 757, where it was Ares' own deeds that Zeus was asked to deplore. — ῥίγιστα is the only Homeric occurrence of this superlative form, though ῥίγιον 5 ×; not unnaturally it occurs in speech not narrative, see next n. *ad fin.*; it is from ῥῖγος = 'cold' (which makes one shiver, as with terror) as ἄλγιον ἄλγιστος from ἄλγος. ἀλλήλων ἰότητι, 'by each other's will'; ἰότης is of obscure derivation but perhaps connected with ἴεμαι, 'wish for'.

875–80 Ares tries to turn Zeus against Athene by saying that all the gods are against him for favouring her as his own child. In 875 σοί can hardly mean διὰ σέ as Aristarchus thought (Arn/A), and the phrase simply means 'we are all at war with you'; then σὺ γὰρ τέκες is taken further by 880 αὐτὸς ἐγείναο, with clear reference, as bT suggest, to Zeus giving birth to Athene from his head (cf. Hesiod, *Theog.* 924). Criticism of Athene is no less extreme – she is hardly ἄφρονα, 'mindless', and 'destructive, always concerned with unfair deeds' (ἀήσυλα being a form of *ἀϝίσυλα). Nor is it true that Zeus never confronts or opposes her, for that is what 879 προτιβάλλεαι must mean. Ares' language is indeed slightly unusual in places; that is due to his passionate resentment (like that of Akhilleus in bk 9, see on 9.307ff.) rather than to the style of speech as such (though see J. Griffin, *JHS* 106, 1986, 49 and 37 on ῥίγιστα and ἰότητι, also pp. 30ff.).

881–2 Aristarchus read ὑπερφίαλος (Did/A), whereas the 'popular' texts, αἱ δημώδεις, and the medieval vulgate had ὑπέρθυμος as e.g. at 376, q.v. with n. μαργαίνειν is found only here in *Il.*, though 3 × *Od.*

883–4 'It is a rhetorical characteristic to begin not from one's own accusations but from the others already agreed' (AbT); hence Ares mentions the attack on Aphrodite first. In fact these vv. are repeated from *Apollo*'s complaint to Ares himself at 458–9, q.v. with n., and draw on language used in the description of Diomedes' earlier attacks. On Kupris see 327–30n.

885–7 Once again language, as well as content, is unusual in places. Even ὑπήνεικαν does not exactly recur, though the verb itself is common. ἦ τέ κε δηρόν is strongly emphatic (on ἦ τε see Denniston, *Particles* 532; ἄν is commoner than κε here, cf. Chantraine, *GH* ii, 246): 'Assuredly ⟨otherwise⟩ I should for long have suffered woes there [i.e. on the battlefield] among the piles of dead.' πήματ' ἔπασχον looks formular but is not, though alliteration with πῆμα is often sought; what one suffers, πάσχειν etc., is usually ἄλγεα. νεκάδεσσιν, unique in Homer, is more graphic than the common νεκύεσσιν (cf. ἐν Πύλῳ ἐν νεκύεσσι in 397) since it probably adds the idea of *piles* of corpses. There is a strong thematic connexion, moreover, with what Ares will say at 15.115–18, when he wants to avenge his dead son Askalaphos even if it means being struck by a thunderbolt and 'lying together with corpses among blood and dust', 118 κεῖσθαι ὁμοῦ νεκύεσσι μεθ' αἵματι καὶ κονίῃσιν. Clearly the idea of the savage god of battle being struck down among his victims lies deep in the poetic tradition.

887 The v. is inorganic, and its expression, and indeed its logic, arouse suspicion even apart from Ares' untypical turns of speech: (i) the contraction ζώς is unusual and belongs to the latest stage of the epic language; it is paralleled however by ζών at 16.445. Similarly ἔα for ἦν occurs only at 4.321 and 2 × *Od.* (ii) ἀμενηνός is unparalleled in *Il.* and seems to be derived from the Odyssean formula νεκύων ἀμενηνὰ κάρηνα, 4 ×, cf. *HyAp* 188 ζῶντ' ἀμενηνόν. (iii) τυπή = 'blow' is found nowhere else before Apollonius Rhodius and Nicander; moreover χαλκοῖο, as against χαλκοῦ, happens not to recur in Homer, which reinforces the idea of χαλκοῖο τυπῆσι | as a special invention. So much for expression, which is distinctly untraditional; what of meaning? Does it make sense to say 'I *would long have suffered woes among the piles of dead there, or I would have been alive, but devoid of strength, through blows of bronze*'? Surely not; either this god is thoroughly confused as Leaf suggested, or the composer of this v. must have taken ἐν αἰνῇσιν νεκάδεσσιν to imply 'among the dead in Hades' *vel sim.*, cf. e.g. 397 – but that is specifically excluded by 886 αὐτοῦ. In either case inept rhapsodic or later embellishment is distinctly possible, even though the ancient critical tradition noticed little amiss.

889–98 Zeus's angry reply is in marked stylistic contrast; against Ares' ingratiating couplets are set a sequence of abrupt whole-v. sentences, broken only by cumulated 893 and the concluding two-v. sentence, periodically enjambed, of 897f., which reflects Zeus's partial relenting as well as the preference for rhythmical contrast at the end of a speech.

889 ἀλλοπρόσαλλος was first used of Ares by Athene at 831, see 829–31n.

890–1 Agamemnon at 1.176f. had told Akhilleus in similar terms that he was most hateful to him, and for the same reason. Vv. 891 and 1.177 are identical, but the v. belongs more appropriately here, see 1.177n. Ares, whenever he is most fully personified in *Il.*, represents the worst and least heroic side of warfare.

892–4 The idea of strife reminds Zeus of Here; it is to her, he suggests, that Ares' predicament is mainly due. That is partly correct, though Ares had come closer to the truth in blaming Athene (875f.). Zeus chooses to ignore that accusation, probably because it implicates himself too closely; Here, he implies, is notoriously uncontrollable, whereas he could not so easily defend himself over failure to control Athene. The treatment of divine psychology is especially thoughtful here.

892 Cf. 16.549 | ἀάσχετον, οὐκ ἐπιεικτόν; diectasis of -α conveniently allows the phrase to fit into the second hemistich. ἐπιεικτόν, passive in form, is active in meaning, 'unyielding', in all 4 Iliadic occurrences.

894 ἐννεσίῃσιν recurs at Hesiod, *Theog.* 494, but not elsewhere in Homer. It is one of the several relatively recent words and forms in the conversation between Ares and his father.

895–8 Zeus gives paternity as his reason for saving Ares from prolonged suffering, saying nothing about the impropriety of a god being close to death, remarkable as that idea may seem to us.

897 He applies the very term, ἀΐδηλος, destructive, to Ares that Ares himself had used of Athene at 880. The v. is rhythmically and phonetically ungainly, with γένευ a unique Ionism (i.e. from γένε(σ)ο, cf. Attic ἐγένου) promoted perhaps by the commoner ἐμεῦ and τευ which precede.

898 'You would long since have been lower than the children of Ouranos', i.e. Kronos and the other Titans confined by Zeus to Tartaros or below. The tale is given by Hesiod at *Theog.* 716ff. but is also known to Homer, cf. 8.479–81, 14.279, 15.225. Admittedly Οὐρανίωνες elsewhere (6 × *Il.*, 3 × *Od.*) are the Olympian gods, those who dwell in the οὐρανός or are descended from Ouranos in the second generation. Zenodotus, who read ἐνέρτατος, seems to have accepted that interpretation (Arn/A, Did/T), which gives a feeble sense, not least because Ares is in any case lowest of the Olympians. Aristarchus was probably right in taking the reference as to the Titans.

899 On Paieon as divine healer see 398–402n.; he is associated with, but usually distinguished from, Apollo (so Aristarchus, Arn/A, cf. bT on 1.473). Aphrodite's wound had been superficial and was easily soothed by her mother at 417; Ares' is more serious and needs the attention of Paieon himself, whose services were in the nature of things seldom required and whose status on Olumpos is left undefined.

900–1 = 401–2, of Paieon curing Hades when wounded by Herakles. Aristarchus probably read πάσσεν not πάσσων (Did/A), as did a substantial proportion of the medieval MSS including A, B and T; that meant he must have omitted or athetized 901 (which is absent from several good MSS, though not from A). Presumably he felt the v. to be suitable for Hades but not for Ares here, and was thinking of 388 where Ares 'would have died' had Hermes not rescued him; but see 388–91n.

902–4 Formally it is the speed (904 ὡς ἄρα καρπαλίμως) of Paieon's cure that is illustrated by this striking and homely simile, but the real point of comparison is more detailed – also (as Shirley Werner reminds me) the whole thing ironically describes how *human* blood behaves, cf. 870–1n. ὀπός is 'juice', especially the acid juice of the wild fig that was used as a rennet for curdling milk (902 was imitated by Empedocles frag. 33 D–K):

'As when juice, hastening on, compacts white milk, which is liquid but is very swiftly thickened all round as it is stirred, so swiftly...'; for τρέφω = 'thicken' or 'make into curds' cf. *Od.* 9.246.

905 Now Hebe washes him and dresses him in clean clothes. She is not envisaged as bathing him, exactly, as was the Homeric custom with a guest arriving from a journey, especially before a meal (see S. West on *Od.* 3.464ff.). Several such baths are briefly described in *Od.* (cf. Arend, *Scenen* 124ff.), being usually administered by a female servant or servants (as at *Od.* 8.454ff., 23.154f.) or the mistress of the house (Kirke at *Od.* 10.361 and 450, Helen at *Od.* 4.252f.). It is not quite true, therefore, that washing a guest is a maiden's job as Aristarchus claimed (Arn/A), though maidens could do it if available; thus at *Od.* 3.464ff. Nestor's youngest daughter Polukaste bathes Telemakhos. Hebe here is unmarried (being personified girlhood, her eventual union with Herakles unknown in *Il.*), but she is also maid-of-all-work, pouring wine for the gods at 4.2f. and preparing Here's chariot at 5.722f.

906 See on 869, where Ares, fresh from his damaging encounter with Diomedes, first took his seat by Zeus – but 'grieving in spirit' rather than 'exulting in glory' as now; the contrast is amusing and surely deliberate. For κύδεϊ γαίων see on 1.405, where the formula (4 × *Il.*) first appears of Briareos/Aigaion. Probably devised for Zeus himself as at 8.51 and 11.81, it brilliantly suggests Ares' posturing self-satisfaction – but also, after all, his ultimate divinity. Aristarchus could not quite accept the apparent inappropriateness and athetized here (Arn/A, Did/T), obviously wrongly.

907–9 The singer turns briefly to the two goddesses; he chooses neither to involve them with Zeus or Ares at this point (in contrast with 418ff. where they saw Aphrodite and jeered at her to Zeus), nor to concern himself with details of their chariot (cf. 775–7), nor even to revert to Diomedes himself, but rather to bring the whole episode to a swift and formal close.

908–9 See on 4.8, where 908 recurs. There Zeus named the goddesses in provocative tones; here their solemn epithets and the heavy spondaic opening, matched by the four ponderous words of 909, provide a solemn ending to one of Homer's most daring, and at times most humorous, compositions.

BOOK SIX

After the great *tour de force* of Diomedes' *aristeia* in the previous Book, the poet reverts briefly to a series of more ordinary combats. Even now it is not part of his plan to develop the theme of full-scale warfare, and Hektor's brother Helenos is soon telling him to return to the city to organize prayers for the hard-pressed Trojans. The awkwardness of this in strategic terms is disguised by a long digression in which Diomedes faces Glaukos and elicits the tale of Bellerophon. That encounter has the ethos of an arranged contest rather than real battle, and acts as an emotional transition to Hektor's meetings in the beleaguered town, first with the womenfolk at large, then with his mother, then with Paris and Helen, finally with his wife and baby son. The Book ends with Hektor and Paris preparing to sally out once more, the latter temporarily in high spirits.

Glimpses of life in Troy have already been given in bk 3, with Helen and Priam on the walls and Paris reunited with a reluctant Helen after his failure against Menelaos. Now the poet explores this civic and domestic dimension more deeply, especially through the women and their reactions to Hektor. The Achaeans are all warriors, their concubines almost faceless, and conditions in the naval camp martial rather than domestic; it is through the Trojans that much of the pathos and moral complexity of warfare has to be presented, and it is they who will suffer when the city falls. Meanwhile there is no attempt to show physical hardship; on the contrary, Troy and its houses, streets and palaces are described in conventional and almost cosy terms.

Few have doubted the completely Homeric quality of this Book, except perhaps for the technically inorganic Glaukos-and-Diomedes episode which, as Aristarchus noted, was sometimes placed elsewhere. The conclusion of this is ironic and idiosyncratic, but it serves a purpose here as well as being historically and mythically intriguing; moreover it recalls (rather than contradicts, as Analysts claimed) the bk 5 motif of the need to recognize gods. The scenes in Troy are enthralling, including the procession to Athene in her temple that is planned and recounted with full oral precision and motivates the encounter with Hekabe. But it is Hektor's other movements across the city, his meetings with Paris and Helen, and even more with Andromakhe, that are most brilliantly conceived, the former developing further the ambiguities in Helen and her lover (and therefore in the whole *casus belli*), the second revealing Andromakhe's helplessness and

Hektor's paradoxical capacity for love and compassion – and, through both of them, the tragic conflict between public and private duty that the heroic nature is least able to resolve.

1–72 The battlefield is left to men, and the Achaeans, with Aias and Diomedes predominant, score a run of victories. Menelaos is dissuaded by Agamemnon from sparing Adrestos, and the scene ends with a brief injunction to the troops by Nestor

1 The dreadful strife was 'left on its own', οἰώθη, i.e. by the withdrawal of the gods; the v. summarizes the conclusion of the preceding Book and makes a slight break, not a drastic one, before a new, brief phase of fighting. This has much in common with the initial encounters of bk 5, and so forms a kind of ring-form conclusion to the main part of Diomedes' *aristeia*.

2 The rhythm is irregular, perhaps deliberately, with trochaic word-break in the fourth foot between ἴθυσε and μάχη. This breaks 'Hermann's Bridge' (vol. I, 19) and gives a 'bouncing' effect which, together with the initial dactyls stopped by the harsh break after ἔνθ', serves to reinforce the spasmodic, to-and-fro aspect of the fighting. πολλά is adverbial, 'in many directions' or 'often'; ἴθυσε, 'advanced', cf. ἰθυνομένων in a different application in the next v.; πεδίοιο, 'over the plain'.

3 By contrast the heavy words of this v. suggest the dour determination of both sides.

4 On the confluence of Simoeis and Skamandros cf. 5.773–4n. Aristarchus first accepted a different reading, μεσσηγὺς ποταμοῖο Σκαμάν-δρου καὶ στομαλίμνης (Arn/A, Did/bT), but afterwards preferred the vulgate version which better suited his views on the position of the Achaean camp, on which he wrote a treatise. (The variant reading was ἐν τοῖς ἀρχαίοις *sc.* ἀντιγράφοις, Arn/A, such 'ancient' texts being barely mentioned elsewhere; Leaf's ἐν ταῖς ἀρχαίαις *sc.* ἐκδόσεσιν is persuasive, i.e. referring to earlier Hellenistic editions of no great authority.) The compound form στομαλίμνη, *hapax* in Homer, looks Hellenistic and is twice used by Strabo of the Rhône delta and at 13.597 of the Skamandros lagoon. S. West (*Ptolemaic Papyri* 72f.) rightly concludes that 'It is difficult to believe that this version of the line is the original.'

5–6 It is Aias, not Diomedes, who first breaks the Trojan line; he is the great defensive fighter as ἕρκος Ἀχαιῶν suggests, and this move in the to-and-fro battle is a relieving one since he 'made light for his comrades' (cf. the formula φόως Δαναοῖσι γένηαι -ωμαι | in a defensive sense).

7–8 On this Thracian Akamas see 2.844–5n.; he is relatively inconspicuous, though Ares chose to assume his likeness at 5.462.

9–11 In this first individual encounter the same 3 vv. are used to describe the fatal blow as at 4.459–61, the opening combat between

Antilokhos and Ekhepolos after battle was first joined; see n. there, with 5.743–4n. and 3.362n. for the φάλος.

12–19 Emphasis is on the victim rather than Diomedes himself; even the nature of the wounds he inflicts (both on Axulos and on his squire Kalesios, 18f.) goes unspecified.

12–13 Axulos of Arisbe appears only at the moment of his death. His name is unusual (von Kamptz, *Personennamen* 131), but his father Teuthras has an Achaean namesake at 5.705. The leader of the Arisbe contingent was Asios according to the Catalogue, cf. 2.837–9n.

14–15 | ἀφνειὸς βιότοιο recurs twice, at 5.544 (with ἔναιεν *sic* in the preceding v.) and 14.122. His friendliness, i.e. hospitality, is not precisely paralleled, though cf. 17.584 where Phainops (of Abudos next to Arisbe, cf. 2.836) ξείνων φίλτατος ἔσκεν (*sc.* of Hektor) Ἀβυδόθι οἰκία ναίων. Riches 'are a favourite theme in the anecdotes about slain warriors' (Fenik, *TBS* 57, who compares 5.613 as well as 544 and 708, 16.595f. (also with οἰκία ναίων, cf. 17.584) and 17.576). Victims 'distinguished by some outstanding skill or excellence, but who perish nonetheless' (Fenik 15f.) are another typical motif, e.g. at 2.858f., cf. 871–3, 5.50–4.

16–17 Compare 2.873 of the gold worn by Amphimakhos (or Nastes), οὐδέ τί οἱ τό γ᾽ ἐπήρκεσε λυγρὸν ὄλεθρον. Here it is none of those that Axulos had helped who 'come up in front of him', i.e. to defend him; the compound appears only here in Homer. ἄμφω, accusative, is explained in the next v. and resumed by nominative ἄμφω in 19.

18–19 As often the charioteer succumbs as well as his fighting companion. θεράπων and ἡνίοχος tend to go together, cf. ἡνίοχον θεράποντα | 3 × *Il.*; here the compound ὑφηνίοχος is unique, its prefix, as Aristarchus noted (Arn/A), otiose. Odyssean ὑποδμώς and ὑποδρηστήρ provide no real parallel (*contra* Ameis–Hentze) since the terms themselves indicate inferiority, which the prefix merely accentuates; ἡνίοχος is different, since 'holding the reins' or acting as driver is not necessarily a menial task – cf. e.g. the discussion at 5.226–38 about whether Aineias or Pandaros is to drive. The whole relative clause from ὅς ῥα to ὑφηνίοχος is a little forced, like the name Kalesios itself if (as Aristarchus evidently thought, Arn/A) it is from καλεῖν and intended to stress the idea of Axulos' hospitality, i.e. as 'Inviter'. γαῖαν ἐδύτην | is also unique (cf. 411 χθόνα δύμεναι), a simple and perhaps even primitive expression.

20 The next victor is Eurualos son of Mekisteus, a more distinguished figure than his rôle in the poem suggests. Mekisteus was one of the Seven against Thebes, his son an Epigonos and third in command of Diomedes' Argive contingent, see 2.565–6 and n. He kills two pairs of victims following on Diomedes' pair; in the first, Dresos occurs only here, but there is an Achaean Opheltios in a bare list of Hektor's victims at 11.302.

21–2 The next pair have names elsewhere assigned to a river and a town: Aisepos is a river below Ida at 2.825, and Pedasos, home of another minor victim, lies on the Satnioeis river at 34f. It belonged to the Leleges at 21.86f. and was sacked by Akhilleus at 20.92, but was also the name of a different, Messenian town (also of one of Akhilleus' horses). The Satnioeis may have triggered other details in the present passage, since Aias' victim at 14.442–5 will be Satnios 'whom the blameless water-nymph bore to Enops when he was herding cattle [βουκολέοντι, cf. 22 Boukolion here] by the banks of the river Satnioeis'. Thus Pedasos bears the name of a town on the Satnioeis, and Satnios, like Pedasos, has a water-nymph as mother and a herdsman as father – except that Pedasos' father is actually called Boukolion whereas Satnios' father Enops was βουκολέοντι, and his mother is Abarbaree whereas Satnios' mother is unnamed. About Abarbaree we know nothing more. She and Boukolion may be fictitious details designed to vary the general theme, of which Simoeisios at 4.473–89 and Iphition, born to a water-nymph under Mount Tmolos at 20.382–5, provide other versions. But they may also have a story behind them as Willcock suggests; a foundation-legend would be an obvious source. Pedasos must lie somewhere in the southern Troad (Cook, *Troad* 245f., 267), and the Aisepos, though it flows into the western Propontis, rises not too far away. Abarbaree is a curious name for a water-nymph even if understood as ἀ-βόρβορος, 'unmuddy', as Leaf suggests; while Boukolion adds to the aura of conscious fiction.

23–4 His being Laomedon's eldest son does little to make him more credible. Illegitimacy conveniently removes him from the normal genealogy of the race of Dardanos (cf. 2.819–20n.); but Laomedon was king of Troy, whereas Boukolion, through his association with Pedasos, is Dardanian – like Aineias, indeed, who was herding cattle on the foothills of Ida when nearly caught by Akhilleus in the raids on Pedasos and Lurnessos (20.89–92). Aineias' father Ankhises had made love to Aphrodite in the same region (2.820f.), and is yet another probable contributor to Boukolion's complex literary *persona*.

25–6 All the elements of these mellifluous vv. are found elsewhere: cf. 11.106 | ποιμαίνοντ' ἐπ' ὄεσσι λαβών, 3.445 ἐμίγην φιλότητι καὶ εὐνῇ |, 20.225 | αἱ δ' ὑποκυσάμεναι (of Erikhthonios' mares!), 5.548 διδυμάονε παῖδε γενέσθην.

27–8 φαίδιμα γυῖα | is formular (7 × *Il.*), not elsewhere in association with μένος; but the rising threefolder, together with the heavy patronymic which follows, brings the description to a distinctive close.

29–36 Seven Achaean successes follow, with Polupoites, Odysseus, Teukros, Antilokhos, Agamemnon, Leïtos and Eurupulos each claiming a minor victim. Even the victors seem a slightly random selection, which excludes both Aiantes (though Teukros is there) as well as Idomeneus; Menelaos is to follow in the next episode. Polupoites is the Lapith leader prominent in bks 12 and 23, Leïtos a Theban commander grouped with Teukros and Antilokhos (again) at 13.91–3. On Eurupulos, one of the volunteers for the duel at 7.167, see 2.736n.; his contingent precedes that of Polupoites in the Catalogue (2.734f.). The Trojan victims all have Greek-based names except Ableros (but cf. εὔληρα = 'reins' at 23.481 and von Kamptz, *Personennamen* 279f.) and are not mentioned elsewhere in *Il.* – though the last three names are also used for characters in *Od.* Pidutes and Elatos at least have places of origin, the former being from Perkote near the southern Hellespontine shore (see on 2.835–6), the latter from Pedasos, see 21–2n. On such lists and their random origins see also on 5.677–8 and 5.705–7. — No details of wounds are offered; killing with the spear is specified in automatic phrases (31 ἔγχεϊ χαλκείῳ, 32 δουρὶ φαεινῷ), and ἐξενάριξεν | is repeated at 30 and 36 (after 20). Brief contextual information about Pedasos and the Satnioeis river provides the only diversion in this bare list – which is carefully varied, however, in enjambment, sentence-length and internal punctuation.

37–65 In contrast with the rapid and arid sequence of deaths, a full and pathetic episode follows as Menelaos takes Adrestos alive but is then persuaded to kill him. This Adrestos is not identified by place or patronymic, though one of the two leaders of the contingent from around Adresteia on the Hellespont was so named (see on 2.830); another Adrestos is slain by Patroklos at 16.694. The name may be an all-purpose one; yet this developed episode calls for a specific subject (not necessarily a well-known one, cf. Simoeisios in a comparable scene at 4.473ff.), especially in contrast with the obscure persons listed just before.

38–44 A complex and dramatic sentence explains how Adrestos came to be captured, γραφικῶς, 'as in a picture', as the D-scholium remarks: his horses flee in terror, they are caught up in a tamarisk-bush, break the pole near the yoke and run off towards Troy; Adrestos is flung out of the chariot ('the Oinomaos accident', E. Vermeule, *PCPS* 33, 1987, 143), Menelaos stands over him with spear outstretched. ἀτυζομένω, 'being terrified', is of unknown etymology; tamarisks grow in and around the river-beds, cf. 10.466f., 21.18 and 21.350; the accident causes the pole-end to snap, much as with Eumelos in the chariot-race at 23.393, allowing the horses to escape. — A chariot is ἀγκύλον, 'curved' (no doubt from its shape in front), only here, as it is καμπύλον only at 5.231, both epithets normally applying to bows. Vv. 41 and 42 recur more or less exactly, the former at 21.4 (cf. 21.554), the latter of Eumelos' crash at 23.394. Vv. 43 and 44 are composed of formular elements, the understated ἔχων (cf. 21.139) being wonderfully sinister, nevertheless, in this context.

45 'No Hellene does this' (T) – not in *Il.* that is, though it is a regular gesture of supplication, cf. 1.512–13n. The usual formula is λάβε (or ἥψατο) γούνων |, but cf. 21.71 ἑλὼν ἑλλίσσετο γούνων. Only Trojans are taken prisoner in *Il.* (at 10.374ff., 11.126ff., 16.330–2, 20.463ff., 21.27ff.; cf. Fenik *TBS* 83), and they are invariably killed, usually after a supplication. It is a typical theme which can be used either summarily or in a developed scene as here – most brilliantly and at greatest length in the death of Lukaon at 21.34–135. This is one of the several ways in which the superiority of the Achaeans, despite reverses, is suggested.

46–50 Adrestos' plea is carefully persuasive, if hopeless, rather than passionate; these progressively cumulated vv. show none of the intensity of the beginning and end of Lukaon's equivalent plea to Akhilleus at 21.74–96. The same plea, with minor adjustments, is made by the sons of Antimakhos at 11.131–5, where 'son of Atreus' is Agamemnon not Menelaos.

46–7 ζώγρει, 'take me alive', cf. 10.378 and 5.697–8n. The equivalent v. at 11.132 has ἐν Ἀντιμάχοιο δόμοις and not ἐν ἀφνειοῦ πατρός as here; Leaf may be right that the version with father's name runs more smoothly. Perhaps the singer is indeed unwilling to identify this Adrestos more closely.

48–50 These vv. form part of Dolon's plea at 10.379–81 and that of Antimakhos' sons at 11.133–5; 48 also recurs 2 × *Od.* The elements of typical scenes can vary, but similar elements tend to be expressed in similar language. — Iron is relatively valuable in the epic, a prize in the funeral games at 23.826ff., cf. 850ff. Smelting techniques were primitive at first, which is why it is 'much-worked'; according to Lorimer, *HM* 118, 'πολύκμητος implies knowledge of the new method of mild steel production with its day-long hammering'. — ἀπερείσι᾽ ἄποινα | in 49 is the regular phrase (11 × *Il.*), in subtle contrast with the ἄξια...ἄποινα | of 46. The repetition of κεν in the protasis in 50 serves to stress the hypothetical nature of such suggestions.

51 ὅρινε, 'was stirring up', is found for ἔπειθε, 'was beginning to persuade', in a minority of MSS and may be correct. It is thus that the v. recurs 5 × *Il.*, 1 × *Od.*, though 9.587 θυμὸν ἐνὶ στήθεσσιν ἔπειθον provides some support for the vulgate.

52 θοάς...Ἀχαιῶν is formular, 9 × *Il.* (with simple θοάς ἐπὶ νῆας another 4 ×), compare ἐπὶ νηυσὶν Ἀχαιῶν in 50; so is τάχ᾽ ἔμελλε -ον, 3 × *Il.*

53–4 The postponement of καταξέμεν for so long after ἐπὶ νῆας causes a particularly sharp pause, making Agamemnon's intervention (ἀλλ᾽...) all the more abrupt. The tension is increased by his arriving θέων, at the run, and ἀντίος, as well as by ὁμοκλήσας; this usually implies strong reproach, e.g. 3 × elsewhere with δεινά, rather than the 'calling out', cf. -κλή, καλεῖν, which its etymology suggests, Chantraine, *Dict.* s.v. ὁμοκλή.

55–60 Agamemnon's rebuke is remarkable not only for its ruthlessness, which is in character (compare his 'implacable voice' at 11.137), but also for its use of runover cumulation, which advances his argument spasmodically, almost as though he were out of breath, at least until the integral enjambment of 58 and 59 leading to the uninterrupted closing v. 60.

55 ὦ πέπον, ὦ Μενέλαε similarly reflects concern at 17.238. In the singular, πέπων (13 × *Il.*, 3 × *Od.*) is a term of familiarity or endearment (literally 'ripe'), though πέπονες implies excessive softness in its two occurrences at 2.235 and 13.120, and that could be an added implication here.

56 ἄριστα is subject of πεποίηται, not adverbial.

57–60 After the ironical enquiry comes a powerful and rhetorical injunction, its repeated negatives, μή τις ὑπεκφύγοι... μηδ' ὅν τινα... μηδ' ὃς φύγοι, culminating in the positive and all-inclusive ἀλλ' ἅμα πάντες... After what the Trojans (i.e. Paris) did to Menelaos, every one of them – every male at least, even unborn – deserves to be utterly wiped out, ἀκήδεστοι καὶ ἄφαντοι, unmourned (or unburied) and leaving no trace – the phrase, not elsewhere, has a threateningly legalistic ring. The notion of killing male embryos is rhetorical rather than realistic, powerful enough in its way and typical of Agamemnon at his nastiest.

61–2 The repeated π- and ει- sounds confer an epigrammatic quality. Objective comments like αἴσιμα παρειπών are unusual, this one additionally so because Homer normally condemns excessive cruelty and violence – compare 'he planned evil deeds in his heart' at 23.176 as a judgement on the killing of twelve Trojans for the pyre of Patroklos. Yet the same phrase occurs at 7.121, where moral disapproval does not arise; for Agamemnon simply dissuades his brother from standing up to face Hektor. It had been noted at 7.104f. that Hektor is far stronger, which is why Agamemnon's words are αἴσιμα, 'justified'. Assonance and alliteration are even more marked in the bk 7 passage (where αἴσιμα παρειπών is followed by ὁ δ' ἐπείθετο· τοῦ μὲν ἔπειτα), of which this looks like a shorter adaptation. Thus the element of moral judgement should not be exaggerated, as by bT and most modern commentators; the poet is simply noting that Agamemnon's words, extreme as they are, reflect the regular heroic view that Paris' treachery, condoned by all Trojans, spares none of them the normal consequences of defeat. αἴσιμα is what is apportioned or destined, and refers to Agamemnon's invocation of the laws of hospitality in 56 more than anything else. See further B. Fenik, *Homer and the*

Nibelungenlied (Harvard 1986) 22–7. — ἥρως is used of minor as well as major figures among the leaders, often at the v-e (cf. e.g. αὐτὰρ ὅ γ' ἥρως |, 7 × *Il.*) and as a matter of convenience as here; but cf. 62–5n. Its post-Homeric application to demi-gods confirms the general connotation of nobility and high birth (Chantraine, *Dict.* s.v.).

62–5 The strong stops at the main caesura continue, no longer through runover cumulation but in a series of integral enjambments. The result is intense and dramatic as the suppliant is ruthlessly despatched, yet with the violence of the action given a leisurely and almost timeless feeling by the traditional formular groups: ἥρω' Ἄδρηστον, κρείων Ἀγαμέμνων, λὰξ ἐν στήθεσι, Ἀτρεΐδης δέ, μείλινον ἔγχος. The matching demonstrative pronouns in 62–4, each at the start of a new sentence at the central caesura, mark the rapid sequence of events (Menelaos pushes Adrestos away, Agamemnon spears him, Adrestos falls back in death) and echo the pattern of μή τις... μηδ' ὅν... μηδ' ὅς in Agamemnon's speech just before, at 57–9. Here too, as at 59f., the fragmented short sentences culminate in a flowing ending (from 59 ἀλλ' ἅμα πάντες | and 65 Ἀτρεΐδης δέ |).

65 On λὰξ... βάς cf. 5.620n. The vision of Agamemnon treading on Adrestos and dragging the spear out of his guts underlines the triumph of heroic ruthlessness over Menelaos' humane approach.

67–71 For Nestor's various bits of tactical advice see on 2.360–8; they are mostly succinct, as here, unlike his speeches of reminiscence. This *parainesis* is used typically to mark a break in the action (cf. Fenik, *TBS* 49). Stopping to collect enemy armour was evidently common practice, as at 11.755, and had to be warned against (as by Hektor at 15.347, ἐὰν δ' ἔναρα βροτόεντα) when a rapid advance was in progress.

67 This form of address is formular, 4 × *Il.*

68 ἐπιβαλλόμενος, 'reaching after', not otherwise Homeric but graphic enough; so too πλεῖστα φέρων, 'with the greatest possible load'.

70–1 The distinction between 'let *us* kill men' and '*you* shall plunder' is rhetorical; Aristarchus played down such changes of number as a figure of speech, citing 5.877f. and 18.297f. (Did/A, bT), against Zenodotus' different text Τρώων ἂμ πεδίον συλήσομεν ἔντεα νεκρούς (perhaps designed to explain τά in 70, which must otherwise refer to 68 ἐνάρων as a double acc.). Yet Nestor himself is presumably above joining in such plunder even on a suitable occasion.

73–118 Hektor's brother Helenos urges him and Aineias to stop the Trojan rout; Hektor is then to withdraw to Troy and tell Hekabe to arrange formal prayers to Athene in her temple. The troops rally and Hektor leaves for Troy

73–101 'The situation seems to change rather suddenly here; the words of Helenos in 96–101 would naturally follow some such account of Diomedes' exploits as we have had in E rather than the detached combats of the last 72 lines, in which he has appeared only as one among many Greek heroes' (Leaf). But Homeric situations can change suddenly at any time; just when a hero, or either side in general, begins to take charge of events, then something happens to prevent it – either a great warrior on the other side notices what is happening and rallies his troops, or a god, perhaps, does something similar. Moreover the degree of response does not always correspond with the seriousness of the threat; and in any event the sequence of Achaean victories, even though Diomedes is no longer so prominent, symbolizes Achaean invincibility in the wake of his earlier successes.

What *is* a little forced, perhaps, is not the timing of Helenos' suggestion but its nature. For the commanding officer to withdraw from the field to organize prayers for his army's safety is unusual by Homeric standards. Yet Helenos is a prophet and may know something the others do not, as at 7.44ff.; moreover divine support must be properly sought in times of crisis. In any case he recognizes that Hektor, with Aineias, must first stabilize the troops in front of the gates (80–5). That is easier said than done, but the details are omitted and the rally is achieved quite smoothly (103–9). In all this the singer is plainly determined to get Hektor back into Troy; the organizing of prayers is a subsidiary mechanism, not without a certain importance in itself, but it is the great scenes with Hekabe, Paris and Andromakhe that must have been his main narrative aim. In short, the introductory encounters of this Book had served to taper off Diomedes' *aristeia*; that left the Achaeans predominant, but some special motive is needed for Hektor's withdrawal to Troy. Special prayers to Athene are the device used, after the troops have been temporarily rallied. Helenos' suggestions allow for all this, though with occasional traces of compositional expediency.

73–4 = 17.319f., where the Trojan retreat is stopped when Apollo urges Aineias into action.

75–9 The association of Aineias with Hektor is on the face of it surprising; he is second-in-command of the home troops (Ameis–Hentze), but the two of them are said to bear the chief burden on behalf of Trojans *and Lycians* (presumably representing the allies in general), so that the powerful Lycian leader Sarpedon might seem a more suitable choice. Yet Helenos' advice is part of the typical 'advice pattern', itself a variant of the rebuke pattern discussed in the note on 5.471, and such rebukes are typically directed either to Hektor or to Aineias. Moreover they are typically made by either Glaukos or Sarpedon, which excludes the latter as Hektor's associate here. On Helenos see further 7.44–5n.

79 πᾶσαν ἐπ' ἰθύν, not elsewhere but easily intelligible as 'in every initiative', literally 'direction' or 'way of going'.

81–2 'Fall in flight into the womenfolk's arms' is unusual in Greek if less so in English; closest is 13.653f. where a victim 'breathed out his life in his companions' arms', or Andromakhe's wish at 22.426 that Hektor had died in her arms. Usually χερσί are the hands of an enemy by which one succumbs; here the idea of rescue is substituted, but grim echoes remain, as well perhaps as the demeaning idea of women as rescuers.

86–98 Helenos' recommendations continue in this very long sentence, mainly cumulative and periodically or progressively enjambed. It contains a few unusual details and terms, but what has mainly exercised critics has been the number of minor divergences from subsequent references to the events envisaged. These are the principal points of the five different passages concerning the prayers to Athene, with details italicized that are peculiar to any one passage:

(1) Helenos' instruction to Hektor at 86–101: he is to go to Troy, tell Hekabe to lead the older women to Athene's temple on the acropolis, open its gates *with a key*, place the finest dress on her knees and promise twelve oxen if she takes pity and keeps Diomedes away – *the insatiable fighter who surpasses even Akhilleus*.

(2) Hektor's words to his troops at 113–15: he is off to Troy to tell *the counsellors* and 'our wives' to pray to *the gods* and *promise hecatombs*.

(3) Hekabe's guess at 256f. about why Hektor has returned to Troy: *to raise his hands to Zeus* from the acropolis (refuted at 269–80).

(4) Hektor's instruction to Hekabe at 269–80: to gather the senior women, go *with offerings for burning* (θυέεσσιν) to Athene's temple, place the finest dress on her knees and promise twelve oxen if she takes pity and keeps Diomedes away (271–8 = 90–7 with minor adjustments).

(5) Hekabe carries out these instructions at 286–310: she *tells her servants* to gather the senior women, *goes to the storeroom* and takes the finest dress (*with much detail*), they go to Athene's temple on the acropolis, *Theano* opens the gates, they hold up hands to Athene *with a ritual shriek*, *Theano* places the robe on her knees and prays her to *make Diomedes fall before the Scaean gate*, and so receive twelve oxen.

Of the italicized details, the mention of hecatombs in (2) and of θυέα in (4) are minor variations rather than true divergences, since the twelve oxen are a hecatomb in the broad sense (1.65n.), and it seems probable that 270 σὺν θυέεσσιν refers to them and not, as usually, to lesser burnt offerings. The only substantive difference is that in (4) the offerings are to accompany the procession, whereas elsewhere they are promised for the future: see on 269–70.

In (1) the mention of a key (the Odyssean sense of κληΐς, which in *Il.*

usually connotes a bar or bolt) is not repeated in (4) or (5); and only here is Diomedes described in such strong terms as even more fearful than Akhilleus (99–101, see on 94–101). In (2) the addition of βουλευτῆσι, 'counsellors', is surprising, especially since the term does not recur in Homer (even if βουλή is common). Presumably Hektor is adjusting the definition of his mission to make it more palatable to his troops. That is confirmed by his substituting 'our wives' for the γεραιαί, older women, of 87; in fact when he does return to the city he is at once surrounded by wives and daughters asking about their loved ones (237–40). He is in any case generalizing his intentions, as is shown by the substitution of 'the gods', δαίμοσιν, for Athene. In (3) Hekabe's conjecture that Hektor has returned to Troy to pray to Zeus (rather than organize prayers to Athene) is merely a natural misapprehension, a psychological refinement that hardly conflicts with the rest. Hektor's instructions to her in (4) generally accord with Helenos' recommendations in (1), except for the specification of the θύεα discussed above. That leaves (5), the actual narrative of events as they happen. Here the divergences are mainly a matter of expanded detail: Hekabe can hardly gather the women herself, and uses her servants to do so; the selection of the dress is carefully described, both her going to the storeroom and the history of the dress itself; the ritual shriek in 301 is a graphic addition to the prayer (for its function see *Entretiens Hardt* XXVII (Vandœuvres–Genève 1981), 66, and cf. 1.447–68n.); that Diomedes should be killed before the Scaean gate is a dramatic embellishment of the basic requirement of 96, for him to be 'kept away from sacred Ilios'. But the most obvious departure is the introduction of Theano as priestess of Athene, and her performing the important actions, of opening the temple and making the prayer, specifically envisaged in (1) and (4) as carried out by Hekabe.

Theano represents the one serious departure from a generally consistent idea of the gathering of women for prayer to the goddess. Even Hektor's command to his mother shortly before explicitly envisages Hekabe herself as presenting the dress and making the prayer. Theano, then, is a curious innovation. Conceivably the poet seeks an element of surprise or variation to give freshness and force to the event itself; but this is contrary to normal oral practice, whereby the same terms are used to describe an action and the anticipations and instructions that lead up to it. It may be that the poet inclines to be more precise now about ritual matters, as indeed with the ὀλολυγή. No other priestess is mentioned in Homer; but the idea of a specially chosen one (300 τὴν γὰρ Τρῶες ἔθηκαν...), rather than the king's wife *ex officio*, may belong to a later stage of the tradition: see e.g. Burkert, *Religion* 46, 96.

86 | Ἕκτορ, ἀτὰρ σύ is emphatic as at 429. εἰπέ here, and εἴπω in

Hektor's version at 114, meaning 'tell' in the sense of 'order' or 'instruct', are unique in *Il.*; but the development is a natural one, clearly seen in *Od.* at e.g. 15.76 and 22.262, 431, with transitional stages at e.g. 14.497f.

87–98 An exceptionally long and complex sentence, for the oral style at least, with two successive participial clauses (87 ξυνάγουσα..., 89 οἴξασα...), then an imperative clause enclosing an elaborate relative clause (90–2, πέπλον ὅς...θεῖναι), then an indirect statement depending on a second imperative (93 ὑποσχέσθαι) leading to a condition (94 αἴ κ᾿ ἐλεήσῃ), followed by purposive ὥς κεν...ἀπόσχῃ in 96 and a concluding relative clause (98 ὅν...). Despite all that the sequence of thought is progressive and the subordination of clauses chronological rather than logical.

87–94 The gathering of the women, the procession to Athene's temple on the highest part of the citadel, the solemn opening of its doors, the laying of the finest available garment on the knees of the seated cult-image, the prayer for salvation accompanied by the promise of rich burnt offerings: this impressive scene is a fitting reflexion of Diomedes' great burst of destructive energy – even apart from its function, clearly the singer's primary concern, of taking Hektor back to Troy. Despite inconsistencies, the details are important for the understanding of Greek cult: (i) Athene has a free-standing temple on the acropolis; (ii) it is normally kept closed; (iii) it contains a seated cult-image large enough to receive a large πέπλος on its knees (see on 90–2); (iv) burnt offerings are to be made within the temple, 93 ἐνὶ νηῷ – unless Ameis–Hentze were right that this denotes the whole *temenos*. All these are plausible for Homer's time, when the development of independent temples as homes of the deity was proceeding rapidly (Coldstream, *Geometric Greece* 317). The first temple at Samos, the Hekatompedon or 100-footer, was *c.* 800 B.C. (*op. cit.* 327), or at latest 700; that had an external altar, but several early temples (not only at Dreros and Prinias in Crete but also Megaron B in Apollo's sanctuary at Thermon in Aetolia, dating back at least to the 8th and perhaps to the 10th cent.: Coldstream 280, 324) contained hearths and pits which showed that sacrifices were performed inside the temple. For Apollo, at least, these cannot have been chthonian. Such details may have been combined imaginatively by the singer; whether or not the cult of a city-goddess went back to the 8th cent. B.C. in Ilios itself is uncertain, but there was an apsidal temple in nearby Lesbos (at Antissa in the north-west of the island) as early as around 800, and its successor of a century or so later contained a sacrificial hearth (Coldstream 263). Phokaia is another early Aeolic temple-site, and there were several Geometric-age temples in Ionia even apart from Samos.

87 γεραιός is frequent (21 × *Il.*, 4 × *Od.*), though only the present context elicits the feminine form (here and at 270, 287, 296). bT record an ancient variant γεραιράς here and at 270; the title was given to priestesses of Dionusos according to [Demosthenes] 59.73 (cf. Burkert, *Religion* 173, 239). That hardly reduces the mild inconsistency with 114f. and 240f., where Hektor envisages all the women as praying, since even γεραιράς implies a select body of senior women.

88 *Apollo*'s temple on the acropolis of Ilios has already been mentioned at 5.445f. (and will recur at 7.83); see on 5.445–8. He is well established in the Troad, cf. 1.35ff., and it is natural he should have a temple in Troy itself, of which he is the main divine defender. With Athene the case might seem different – she is, after all, Troy's sworn enemy. But (*a*) she is a city-goddess, protector of the citadel, by function, and Theano will pray to her as ἐρυσίπτολι at 305; (*b*) her enmity towards the Trojans is conceived as dating only from the Judgement of Paris; (*c*) a special image of her, the Palladion, was kept in her shrine in Troy according to the Cyclic tradition (*Little Iliad* frag. 9); and (*d*) the main temple on the acropolis was hers in historical times. — Shipp, *Studies* 254, wrongly took ᾿Αθηναίης γλαυκώπιδος as a sign of post-Homeric composition; in the nominative γλαυκῶπις ᾿Αθήνη | is regular and common, but other cases, as often, require a different word-order; similarly ᾿Αθηναίη γλαυκώπιδι (*sic*), 3 × *Il.*

89 κληΐς is a key of some sort (perhaps no more than a kind of hook), rather than a bar or bolt, 3 × *Od.* but only here in *Il.* It is, therefore, one of several 'Odyssean' characteristics in the supplication of Athene, partly explicable on contextual grounds, namely that descriptions of buildings, civic behaviour and so on are commoner there. Yet other details of Hektor's return to Troy will not be noticeably Odyssean; and the meaning 'key' is not in any case a late development, at least in the light of Myc. *ka-ra-wi-po-ro* = κλαϝι-φόρος, cf. Burkert, *Religion* 45, Chantraine, *Dict.* s.v. κλείς.

90–2 E. Bethe, *Homer* II (Berlin 1922) 314ff., persuaded Lorimer, *HM* 445, that temple and statue are an Athenian interpolation – a wholly unjustified conclusion. The Panathenaea was admittedly a famous classical example of the ritual offering of new clothing for a cult-image; yet this was a widespread and ancient custom, and Pausanias noted the weaving by women of a *khiton* for Apollo at Amuklai each year, as well as of a *peplos* for Here at Olumpia every four years (3.16.2; 5.16.2). The *peplos* will be described in detail at 288–95. Placing it on the goddess's knees in 92 presupposes a seated statue, but there is nothing 'late', peculiar or post-Homeric about this as has often been maintained. Standing cult-statues are indisputably older as a type, but even Lorimer conceded that the statue of Athene Lindia in Rhodes was seated and 'very possibly goes back into the eighth century' (443f.). Almost certainly, one might say; and an irrefutable 8th-cent. representation of a seated goddess appeared on a late-Geometric cup (now lost) from the Kerameikos cemetery in Athens, fig. 10 in *Athenische*

Mitteilungen 18 (1893) 113, where a figure seated on a throne is approached by four female worshippers holding garlands. Lorimer attempted to discredit this by categorizing the throne as 'of Assyrian type with a footstool' and noting two winged centaurs on the same band of decoration. All that means is that the cup has orientalizing elements (cf. e.g. Coldstream, *Geometric Greece* ch. 15); it is no less Greek for that, and is certainly of the 8th cent. and not the 7th; and the scene of worship must be one that made sense to Greeks, i.e. was familiar to them. The ancient seated images of Here at Samos and Tiryns, as well as the old seated statue of Athene Polias at Athens, almost certainly go back to the 8th cent. and perhaps beyond (cf. Burkert, *Religion* 90). Finally θεῶν ἐν γούνασι κεῖται (2 × *Il.*, 3 × *Od.*) presupposes a knowledge of seated deities and is shown by its formular status to be Homeric.

93–4 Imperative ὑποσχέσθαι continues the construction of θεῖναι in the preceding v. Twelve is a favourite epic choice for a substantial number; a prize is worth 12 oxen at 23.703, 12 horses are among the recompense offered by Agamemnon to Akhilleus at 9.123 etc., Neleus had 12 sons (11.692), 12 victims and twelfth dawns are common enough, and so on. These oxen are | ἤνις ἠκέστας (here and at 275 and 309), probably 'one year old' (cf. ἐνι-αυτός) and 'not knowing the goad'; Schwyzer's suggestion (*Rh. M.* 80, 1931, 213) that the formula arose out of a false division of the singular ἤνιν * νηκέστην (cf. νηκερδής etc.), thus avoiding an irregular lengthening of ἁ-privative, is attractive as Chantraine notes, *Dict.* s.v.

94–101 The whole of 90–7 will be repeated as part of Hektor's instructions to Hekabe at 271–8, but 98 (with its development in 99–101) is unique to the present passage. Helenos seems to give an extreme and personal view here (98 ἐγώ... φημι), in the heat of battle or of argument; Diomedes is indeed a fierce fighter, but the description of him as strongest and most formidable of all Achaeans, including even Akhilleus, exceeds anything in the rest of the poem, where Akhilleus is always supreme. The poet has set out in Diomedes' *aristeia* to show him as ultimately formidable, a true substitute in terror for the sulking Akhilleus, but here he makes Helenos go beyond that. — The language from 94 αἴ κ' ἐλεήσῃ contains many formular elements: that phrase itself after a verb of prayer or sacrifice, 3 × *Il.* elsewhere (apart from repetitions later in this Book), 1 × *Od.*; ἄλοχοι -ους καὶ νήπια τέκνα 5 × *Il.* elsewhere (apart from 276 and 310); on 96 ὥς κεν see 277n.; Ἴλιον ἱρήν | etc. 12 × *Il.*; μήστωρα -ε φόβοιο 4 × *Il.* elsewhere (apart from 278), with κρατερόν at 12.39; ὄρχαμος ἀνδρῶν | 2 × *Il.* elsewhere, cf. ὄρχαμε λαῶν | 4 × *Il.* Even the hyperbolic assessment of Diomedes is fluently expressed and completely Homeric in style; Shipp, *Studies* 254, is too subtle in picking on 100 φασι, of mythological fact, as 'unpoetical'.

96 Aristarchus (Did/AT) and a minority of MSS read ὥς κεν for αἵ κεν – probably to avoid repetition after 94 αἵ κ', but see on 277.

101 Bentley's ἀντιφερίζειν is probably right for MS ἰσοφαρίζειν, cf. 21.411 and 488 ὅτι μοι μένος ἀντιφερίζεις; in the former many MSS have ἰσοφαρίζεις and there was obvious confusion between the two.

103–6 These vv. recur, also of Hektor, at 5.494–7 and 11.211–14, after a rebuke and a divine instruction respectively. They are, therefore, a typical way of showing the hero's concurrence and his acting directly to rally his troops.

107–9 Hektor moving through the ranks and encouraging his men in 104f. ('a standard tactic', Fenik, *TBS* 177) results in an immediate Achaean retreat, as they tell each other – wrongly in this case – that some god must have rallied the enemy. The 4 preceding vv. have been formular, these by contrast are probably made for the occasion: unaugmented φάν (3 × *Od.*), ὑπεχώρησαν, ἀλεξήσοντα and ἐλέλιχθεν do not recur exactly in *Il.* (though other parts of these verbs do), and even such a useful and standard-looking phrase as λῆξαν δὲ φόνοιο | in 107 is paralleled only at *Od.* 22.63. As with 98–101, the style is nevertheless completely Homeric, with 107 a rising threefolder and 109 ἐλέλιχθεν referring back in ring-form to 106 ἐλέλιχθησαν.

110 This v. recurs at 8.172 and 15.346 (with its second half another 6 × and μακρὸν ἀΰσας 5 × more).

111–12 112 is standard, though Zenodotus (Arn/A) had an inept variant, ἀνέρες ἔστε θοοὶ καὶ ἀμύνετον ἄστεϊ λώβην. For 111 (twice elsewhere), Τρῶες καὶ Λύκιοι καὶ Δάρδανοι ἀμφιμαχηταί is a common alternative, 7 × in all.

113–16 The closest parallel is 17.186f., where after a similar prelude Hektor again introduces his own departure from the front line with ὄφρ' ἂν ἐγώ(ν), cf. Fenik, *TBS* 169f. There he leaves to put on Akhilleus' armour; here, to organize prayers. In each case the v. describing his departure is the same, i.e. 116 = 17.188. On βουλευταί and hecatombs see pp. 164f.

117–18 The scene is rounded off with a brilliantly observed detail as the shield-rim taps Hektor's neck and ankles as he goes. Partly this is to suggest his haste, so keen is he to bolster morale in Troy, but the evocation of heroic armament is unusual and rewarding for its own sake. He is clearly carrying a huge body-shield, slung on a *telamon* or baldric across his shoulder over his back. Two main shield-types are envisaged in *Il.* (they are discussed at length by Lorimer, *HM* 132–92, and H. Borchhardt in *Arch. Hom.* E 1–56, and clearly and briefly by F. H. Stubbings in Wace and Stubbings, *Companion* 510–13; see also on 3.335): first the long body-shield, oblong or figure-of-eight in shape, which more or less encloses a man; second the round or nearly round shield which was probably somewhat smaller (but is paradoxically the only recipient of the formular epithet ἀμφιβρότη, 4 × *Il.*). Both are primarily of leather, but a bronze facing is frequently assumed, e.g. when shields are said to shine, or to gleam with bronze; cf. *Arch. Hom.* E 1–4, 48–52. The former is called σάκος and has its own formular epithets, μέγα τε στιβαρόν τε ('huge and stout'), ἠΰτε πύργον ('tower-like', only of Aias' σάκος which is exceptionally large) and ἑπταβόειον ('of 7 ox-hides'), also of Aias – see on 7.219–23. The latter is the ἀσπίς, which is πάντοσ' ἐΐση ('equal in all directions', i.e. circular), ὀμφαλόεσσα (with 'navel' or central boss) and εὔκυκλος ('well-rounded').

These two shield-types are amalgamated in various ways in Homer but originally derived from different periods. The long body-shield is typically Early Mycenaean and illustrated on objects from the Shaft Graves at Mycenae, most clearly on the Lion Hunt dagger from grave IV (e.g. Lorimer, *HM* 140 fig. 1). By 1200 B.C. the smaller and more manoeuvrable round or nearly round shield, as on the Warrior Vase from Mycenae (e.g. *HM* pl. III, 1b), seems to have superseded the long body-enclosing models. By Homer's own time, some 500 years later, shields were normally of medium size, with handles as well as baldrics, but in all the old shapes (cf. e.g. *HM* 161 fig. 14); compare the exaggerated figure-of-eight of the 'Dipylon' shields depicted by Geometric vase-painters and emblematic of heroic equipment (so T. B. L. Webster, *From Mycenae to Homer*, London 1958, 169f.).

Hektor's shield is simply a 'black skin' in 117, in itself a unique description reminiscent of his archaizing claim at 7.238, οἶδ' ἐπὶ δεξιά, οἶδ' ἐπ' ἀριστερὰ νωμῆσαι βῶν. It has a rim, ἄντυξ, of the kind clearly shown in Mycenaean depictions of body-shields, which strikes his neck and ankles and unambiguously suggests the huge σάκος of Early Mycenaean times. Yet in 118 it becomes ἀσπίδος ὀμφαλοέσσης, a bossed, i.e. round, ἀσπίς. This is a typical confusion of traditional formular descriptions deriving from different stages of the tradition; similarly in the duel between Aias and Hektor in bk 7 the former's σάκος, described in some detail at 219ff., becomes μέσσον ἐπομφάλιον, i.e. with central boss and so circular, when it is struck at 267 (see also 3.335n. on the changing description of Paris' σάκος, as well as 4.448–9n.). Hektor's shield there and twice elsewhere is specifically an ἀσπίς, and that association intrudes upon the rare detail of the body-shield which the poet chooses to portray here. There is a close parallel at 15.645f., where Periphetes trips over the rim of an ἀσπίς which is uniquely described as ποδηνεκέ', reaching to the feet.

119–236 In a long interlude while Hektor returns to Troy, Diomedes encounters the Lycian Glaukos and professes not to know who he is, which elicits a long account of Glaukos' descent from Sisuphos, and especially of the deeds of Bellerophon. Diomedes

salutes him as a guest-friend through their grandfathers, so they exchange armour and
agree to avoid each other in subsequent combat

119–236 The whole episode is inorganic, and Hektor's arrival at Troy
could follow directly on 118 – for example through the adjustment of 237
| Ἕκτωρ δ᾽ ὡς to | αὐτὰρ ἐπεί. According to Aristarchus (Arn/A) 'some
transpose this composition elsewhere', μετατιθέασίν τινες ἀλλαχόσε ταύτην
τὴν σύστασιν – probably in response to its self-contained character rather
than as evidence that some other context suited it better, and reflecting the
selective propensities of Panathenaic rhapsodes before the stabilization of
the text (vol. 1, 5 and 38). There is no good reason for regarding either the
episode itself or its position here as un-Homeric, especially as the
interruption of a narrative by an intrusive episode or diversion is typical of
Iliadic composition, cf. e.g. the Catalogues in bk 2 and Schadewaldt, *Ilias-*
Studien 77. At the same time the abbreviated style (see Kirk, *Songs* 164–6)
suggests that Homer is drawing on longer and earlier versions. See further
Andersen, *Diomedesgestalt* ch. 5.

119 The adversaries' names and patronymics fill the whole v., giving
special weight to the encounter; so too at 20.160 with Aineias and
Akhilleus, to introduce an episode which has further echoes of the present
one (see also on 120, 143, 150–1, 192–5, 209–11). Thus at 20.178f. Akhilleus
similarly asks why Aineias (whom he does of course recognize) has come
forward; then 20.184f. ~ 6.194f.; and for 6.133 | σεῦε κατ᾽ ἠγάθεον
Νυσήϊον cf. 20.189 | σεῦα κατ᾽ Ἰδαίων ὀρέων. Then Aineias rejects
Akhilleus' taunts by reciting his own genealogy (cf. 20.213–41), in which
Tros's three sons recall Bellerophon's three children at 6.196–211. The two
episodes then go different ways. — Glaukos has so far been mentioned only
as Sarpedon's second-in-command at 2.876, but will be prominent later,
including 6 × with this patronymic. His descent from Bellerophon is in one
sense the main point of the encounter, but he is also an effective foil for
Diomedes and provides an unusual conclusion to the latter's *aristeia*.
Diomedes' pre-eminence in bk 5 has admittedly receded, but now his
professed concern at 128ff. about fighting against gods strongly recalls his
recent exploits against Aphrodite and Ares.

120 = 20.159, of Aineias and Akhilleus; the isolation of the pair of
individuals implied by ἐς μέσον ἀμφοτέρων συνίτην almost suggests a formal
duel, compare 23.814. μεμαῶτε -ι μάχεσθαι is found 4 × elsewhere, with
μάχεσθαι | over 90 × *Il.*; here the alliteration is conspicuously carried
through the whole v.

121–2 121 is a standard v., 12 × *Il.*, which here merely repeats the sense
of συνίτην; its main function is to introduce the subsequent v. of address,
as also at 20.176f., 21.148f., 22.248f.

123 The compound form καταθνητῶν occurs only here in *Il.*, but 6 ×
Od. The system of generic epithets for humankind in the genitive case is
quite extensive:

θνητῶν ἀνθρώπων (5 × *Il.*, 4 × *Od.*)
μερόπων ἀνθρώπων (7 × *Il.*, 2 × *Od.*)
καταθνητῶν ἀνθρώπων (1 × *Il.*, 6 × *Od.*)
ἐπιχθονίων ἀνθρώπων (1 × *Il.*, 4 × *Od.*)
πολυσπερέων ἀνθρώπων (1 × *Il.*, 1 × *Od.*)
χαμαὶ ἐρχομένων τ' ἀνθρώπων (1 × *Il.*).

There is some evidently 'uneconomical' duplication here; yet πολυσπερέων
is context-specific (differently from καταθνητῶν), and θνητῶν is usually
found in contrast to gods, unlike μερόπων. In the present use κατα- may be
felt to emphasize Glaukos' special liability to death as part of his opponent's
threatening posture.

124–7 Diomedes expands his assertion, possibly untrue but properly
insulting, that he does not know Glaukos. He has never seen him in battle
(124) – up to now, that is; runover τὸ πρίν leads to the observation that
now, by contrast, Glaukos has advanced far beyond the rest (125) –
through over-confidence, indeed (with runover σῷ θάρσεϊ matching that of
the preceding v.), to await Diomedes' spear (126). The whole threat is
carefully devised, not only in the antithesis of τὸ πρίν and the elaborate
ἀτὰρ μὲν νῦν γε but also in the sinister overtones of δολιχόσκιον ἔγχος,
signalled by the displacement of this common formula from its regular
position (20/21 × *Il.*) at the v-e. Finally the whole-v. sentence in 127 (=
21.151), balancing 124 with two runover lines between, crowns the
argument with a cryptic and witty generalization.

128–43 Diomedes had begun by assuming his opponent to be mortal,
but now adds complacently, or perhaps sarcastically, that he would not
fight against a god. The singer makes him avoid all reference to recent
exploits against gods in bk 5, where he was given special sanction by
Athene, but rather adduce, in accord with the lighter and more reminiscent
tone of this encounter as a whole, the unfamiliar *exemplum* of Lukourgos and
Dionusos.

Ring-composition is prominent and unmistakable, maintaining the
rhetorical style of Diomedes' remarks so far (cf. Lohmann, *Reden* 12f.):

123	What mortal man are you...?	A
127	Mortals who face me, perish	B
128	but if you are a god	C
129	I would not fight gods	D
130–1	Lukourgos did not live for long after	
	angering the gods	E

132–9	(story of Lukourgos)	F
139–40	He did not live for long, since he	
	was an enemy to the gods	E′
141	I would not fight gods	D′
142	but if you are mortal	C′, A′
143	come close and perish	B′

128 Aristarchus (Arn/A) observed that the mist, ἀχλύς, of 5.127 can only have been lifted in part. That is obvious: it was an exceptional device, and by now we are back to the normal state of affairs whereby divine intervention in the guise of a mortal is always a possibility – one discussed by Aineias and Pandaros at 5.174ff. Aristarchus also read οὐρανόν for οὐρανοῦ, strangely, both here and in the similar *Od.* 7.199, followed by a few lesser MSS; T compared 11.196, βῆ δὲ κατ᾽ Ἰδαίων ὀρέων, but the similar passage at 20.189 is closer to home.

129 A delightful air of self-satisfaction is conveyed by ἔγωγε and by the repetition of θεοῖσιν ἐπουρανίοισιν after ἀθανάτων γε κατ᾽ οὐρανοῦ.

130 The paradeigma begins with the heavily emphatic οὐδὲ γὰρ οὐδέ, cf. 5.22n., also 2.703 = 726 οὐδὲ μὲν οὐδ᾽ (and 5 × elsewhere) and Chantraine, *GH* II, 337f. — Lukourgos (or Lukoorgos in his uncontracted form here) was king of the Thracian tribe of Edones according to Sophocles, *Antig.* 955 (and in any case was clearly not related to, or the same as, the slayer of mace-man Areithoos at 7.142ff., any more than his father Druas was to the Lapith of 1.263). Dionusos was at home in Thrace as well as Phrygia, and his cult spread from there down into Greece. The present tale therefore reflects an early stage of resistance to it, parallel with Pentheus in Thebes, Minuas in Orkhomenos and the daughters of Proitos in Argos; see Burkert, *Religion* 165–7. References to Dionusos are rare in Homer – in *Il.* only otherwise at 14.325 (incidentally to his mother Semele whom Zeus had loved), and in *Od.* in relation to Ariadne and Thetis at 11.325 and 24.74 – and only in contexts which are allusive and incidental. His membership of the Olympian pantheon is marginal at this stage (the occurrence of the name, with no context, on Pylos tablets Xa 06 and Xa 1419 being uninformative), though the case of Demeter, who is equally rare in Homer, suggests his role as *non-heroic* rather than necessarily *post-Homeric*. The present tale makes a diverting illustration of the need to avoid physically resisting gods where possible; the more elaborate paradigm of the wrath of Meleagros, recounted by Phoinix to Akhilleus in bk 9, similarly draws on an equally restricted regional myth never elsewhere mentioned in the epic.

131 The heavy and spondaic | δὴν ἦν provides a sudden, emphatic and threatening completion of the sense of the flowing and dactylic threefolder which preceded; see also on its altered recurrence at 139–40. Imperf. ἔριζεν describes his habitual opposition to deity in contrast with the particular act in the second ὅς-clause which follows (so Ameis–Hentze).

132–7 Lukoorgos' attack on the 'nurses of raving Dionusos' (so described according to Aristarchus, Arn/A, either because he makes others mad or because he is himself envisaged as filled with bacchic frenzy) is placed at holy Nuseion, elsewhere called Nusa (see E. R. Dodds, *Euripides, Bacchae* (2nd edn, Oxford 1960), on vv. 556–9). There were many mountains of that name – from India to Babylon, Arabia and Libya according to Hesychius – associated with or named after the god, but bT were right in taking this one to be in Thrace because Thetis is nearby (136), since she lived in an underwater cave between Samos, i.e. Samothrace, and Imbros according to 24.77–84. — The τιθῆναι are so named probably because of the tale alluded to in Homeric Hymn xxvi that the local nymphs received Dionusos from his father Zeus and nurtured him in the glens of Nusa. That might be an elaboration of the present episode (especially in the light of xxvi. 4 δεξάμεναι κόλποισι, cf. 136 here), but seems to go further; or both could embody phraseology and ideas from some common version. At any rate the god leaps into the sea after Lukoorgos lays into the women with a βουπλήξ, whether ox-goad or axe, and they throw down their θύσθλα as they run – again the precise meaning of the term is obscure, branches, vine-shoots or thyrsi being alternative interpretations recorded by bT. The last is probably correct, i.e. from *θύρσ-θλα according to Chantraine, *Dict.* The terrified child-god is comforted in the sea-goddess's bosom: Thetis with Eurunome similarly 'receives' a falling victim, Hephaistos, at 18.398, where ὑπεδέξατο κόλπῳ recurs; but a special association with Thetis is confirmed by *Od.* 24.73–5, where the golden amphora she provided for Akhilleus' bones had been a gift from him – as a thank-offering for the present occasion according to Stesichorus, *PMG* 234; see on 23.92.

138–43 Diomedes' language becomes smoother and less spasmodic as he relates the culmination of the tale and the conclusion he draws from it.

138 ῥεῖα ζώοντες | only here and 2 × *Od.*; the long vowel-sounds and lengthened -α give an almost voluptuous impression in contrast with their anger, ὀδύσαντο (twice in bk 8, 2 × *Od.*, cf. S. West on *Od.* 1.62), against someone who infringes the laws of nature and threatens their peace.

139–40 Blinding is a traditional punishment for impiety, as with Teiresias. Though bT assumed that it was for seeing the god's secret rituals, it was probably for his violent and impious behaviour in general. τυφλός comes only here in Homer (though also of the 'blind man' who claims authorship of the Delian hymn at *HyAp* 172), for whom ἀλαός is the slightly commoner term – in *Il.* only in the formula οὐδ' ἀλαοσκοπίην εἶχε(ν) (3 ×,

+ 1 × *Od.*, which also has the simple epithet 3 ×); it was also regular in the choral lyrics of tragedy. One cannot be sure, nevertheless, that τυφλός is 'later, for Homeric ἀλαός' (Shipp, *Studies* 255), nor does it mark the Lukourgos narrative as post-Homeric. Neither word is clear in derivation (though τυφλός seems to be connected with τύφομαι, 'burn' or 'make smoke'), and both could be old (cf. Chantraine, *Dict.* s.v. ἀλαός: 'Les termes désignant des infirmités, notamment la cécité, sont difficiles, obscurcis par des tabous ou des substitutions').

The emphatic δὴν ἦν of 131 now recurs in a no less powerful and deliberately distorted rhythmical context as the narrative ring is completed; the assonantal effect is reduced, perhaps, but the separation of adverb and verb by the v-e, in a violent and unusual enjambment, engenders a new kind of harshness to emphasize the conversion of 131 ἔριζεν into ἀπήχθετο here: *strife* against gods makes *enemies* of them.

141 This v. reverts to Diomedes' profession of 129 in slightly different language, in which the repetition of θεοῖς so soon after 140 θεοῖσιν, with the variation of epithet to the pious-sounding μακάρεσσι, reinforces the sense of complacency. B. Marzullo, *Atene e Roma* N.s. 1 (1956) 164, adduced the repetition of 129 in 141 as one of several indications that 119–236 is interpolated, but this is controverted by the ring-composition analysis in 128–43n.

142 ἀρούρης καρπὸν ἔδουσιν -οντες recurs only in the Theomachy at 21.465, again contrasting mortals with gods, in a possible derivative of the present passage (since the comparison with leaves also occurs there, cf. 21.464 with 146ff. here). A common source is also possible, though this application would certainly be the earlier. The idea of mortals as cereal-eaters recalls the distinctions of diet, and of blood versus ἰχώρ, emphasized in bk 5, see e.g. on 5.339–42.

143 The climax of Diomedes' rhetorical extravaganza recurs as a single-v. utterance by Hektor to Aineias at 20.429; it is emphasized by the sinister rhyme of ἆσσον...θᾶσσον (cf. 5.440–2n. on φράζεο...χάζεο, also 20.428–9n. and examples listed by Macleod, *Iliad XXIV* 51), developed from formular elements like ἆσσον ἰόντες | (6 × *Il.*) and ὄφρα κε θᾶσσον (2 × *Il.*), with a change here to ὥς κεν to avoid sounding too sprightly.

The striking ὀλέθρου πείραθ' provides a suitably portentous conclusion. The meaning of πεῖραρ (< *πέρϝαρ) has been much debated: 'end', 'limit' or 'boundary' is certain for some Homeric uses (notably πείρατα γαίης, 4 ×), but 'bond' for others (especially where Odysseus is tied to the mast by πείρατα at *Od.* 12.51). Schulze thought they were two different words, but Chantraine and others, especially after Björck (refs. in Chantraine, *Dict.* s.v.), found it possible to derive both meanings from Sanskrit *parvan*, meaning 'knot', 'joint' or 'section'. (LSJ s.v., II, i, are

certainly wrong in creating a further concrete sense 'instrument' or 'tool'
to explain Hephaistos' anvil etc. as πείρατα τέχνης at *Od.* 3.433f.) Here
ὀλέθρου πείραθ' ἵκηαι appears to entail the first meaning, 'limit', i.e. 'reach
the limits of destruction'; but more often the ὀλέθρου πείρατα are
'fastened', ἐφῆπται, to someone (2 × *Il.*, 2 × *Od.*), which implies the second
meaning, 'bond'. Either the substitution of ἵκηαι for ἐφῆπται involves a
shift from one sense to the other, or, more probably, ὀλέθρου πείρατα is on
the way to becoming a dead metaphor and has lost its literal and concrete
force. The scholia remain silent on the topic. See further on 13.358–60, and
A. Bergren, ΠΕΙΡΑΡ *in Early Greek Poetry* (American Philolog. Ass., 1975),
21–62.

144 On Hippolokhos see 197 and 206. φαίδιμος υἱός | recurs 3 × *Il.*;
normally the epithet goes with a proper name, usually Hektor (24 ×). Here
it helps put Glaukos on an equal footing with his enemy.

144–51 Glaukos' reply to Diomedes' taunts is both witty and clever:
'Why bother about who, precisely, I am? Men come and go like the leaves
of the forest; but, if you insist on learning my genealogy – which is in fact
quite widely known – then here it is.' The reflective tone makes Diomedes'
sarcasm sound cheap, and the addition that most people *do* know casts
doubt on his veracity. Finally, he is placed in the annoying position of
having to listen to his rival's ancestry at unusual length (as Akhilleus will
be by Aineias at 20.213–41). — The likening of human generations to the
fall of leaves in autumn and their growing again in spring carries no
suggestion of rebirth, but means that life is transient and one generation
succeeds another. It was a poetical commonplace (cf. e.g. Mimnermus 2.1f.,
Aristophanes, *Birds* 685, with Clement, *Strom.* 6.738) and recurs in Homer
in a slightly different but no less striking form at 21.464–6.

148 τηλεθόωσα, 'burgeoning', from θάλλω: cf. Chantraine, *Dict.* s.v.,
B (3). In references to the number of leaves in spring at 2.468 ∼ *Od.* 9.51,
φύλλα... γίγνεται ὥρη perhaps favours Aristophanes' reading (Did/A) of
dat. ὥρῃ here too, against the vulgate; though nom. ὥρη makes a neat
parataxis, 'and [i.e. when] the season of spring arrives'.

149 Intrans. φύει, unparalleled in Homer in the present stem, follows
harshly on its regular trans. use in 148; Brandreth's φύεθ' is attractive.
ἀπολήγειν is quite a favourite Homeric verb (5 × *Il.*, of which 3 × at the
v-e as here, 3 × *Od.*), with a pathetic ring in the present context.

150–1 The καί of καὶ ταῦτα, as well as the εὖ of εὖ εἰδῇς, may comically
imply that Diomedes has a deep interest in knowing about these things.
Von der Mühll, on the other hand, following H. Fränkel, took καί to mean
that Glaukos is now answering Diomedes' *first* question, namely 'Who are
you?' (*Hypomnema* 114). There are several ways of construing these vv.
(which recur in the Aineias–Akhilleus encounter at 20.213f., see on 119):

(i), with Aristarchus (Nic/A), to punctuate after εἰ δ' ἐθέλεις and take the infinitive δαήμεναι as imperative; (ii) to make δαήμεναι depend on ἐθέλεις, which is rhythmically smoother, in which case either (a) ὄφρ' εὖ εἰδῇς is parenthetical and the object of δαήμεναι is γενεήν (Ameis–Hentze); or (b) πολλοὶ δέ is the apodosis (with δέ redundant, i.e. 'apodotic'), leaving 'and you shall know it too' *vel sim.* to be understood; or (c), with Leaf, the apodosis is 152 ἔστι πόλις..., i.e. the beginning of the genealogy itself. This would be the case if, with Bentley, we excised 151 altogether. It is true that 150 εἰδῇς could be absolute, also that ἴδε etc. nearly always observes digamma; but Homeric practice here is notoriously irregular, and one is reluctant to lose the nice touch of πολλοὶ...ἴσασιν.

152–211 The tale of Bellerophon and his descendants is narrated in a simple and workmanlike style, with little integral enjambment (only at 156, 161, 179, 203, 209) or internal punctuation but much progressive and periodic enjambment and a corresponding tendency towards medium-length sentences. The 12 whole-sentence vv. are unremarkable except for the sequence at 183–7. Colometry is generally regular, though with a higher number of rising threefolders than one might expect in plain narrative (at 169, perhaps 178, then 181, 197), and also a heavy majority of 4-colon vv. of which no less than 37 (out of 60 for the whole passage) are 'ideal', cf. vol. 1, 18 – a much higher proportion than average. Figurative language is rare (164, perhaps 189 and 201), though certain phrases are unusually allusive or compressed: see on 168–9, 192–5, 200.

152–3 Several Ephures were identified in the later grammatical and geographical traditions, though Homer only refers to two or conceivably three: (a) in Thesprotia in western Greece (cf. e.g. bT on 152), at *Il.* 2.659 and 15.531. (b) In *Od.* as a source of poison at 1.259 and 2.328, said by the scholiasts to be in either Thesprotia or Elis – see W. W. Merry and J. Riddell, *Homer's Odyssey* (2nd edn, 1886) on 1.259; S. West on *Od.* 1.257ff. prefers the former, probably rightly. (c) The present Ephure, as Aristarchus noted (Arn/A), must be an old name for Korinthos (on which see 2.570–5n.), for that is where Sisuphos is located in the mythographical tradition, and where Bellerophon tamed the horse Pegasos who became the symbol of Corinth on her coins. The story is told by Pindar at *Ol.* 13.63ff., cf. E. Vermeule, *PCPS* 33 (1987) 137. Leaf and others (including E. Bethe, *Thebanische Heldenlieder*, Leipzig 1891, 182; L. Malten, *Hermes* 79, 1944, 8) saw difficulty in the description of Korinthos as 'in a corner, or recess, of Argos', 152 μυχῷ Ἄργεος ἱπποβότοιο; but that is appropriate provided we take Argos to refer either mainly to the Peloponnese (see on 2.108) or to Agamemnon's kingdom as defined in the Catalogue (vol. 1, 180f.).

This is the only Homeric reference to Sisuphos, the famous trickster-figure (hence κέρδιστος here), except for his appearance in a probably rhapsodic expansion (*pace* A. Heubeck *ad loc.*) at *Od.* 11.593ff., undergoing punishment in the underworld. The Corinthians were regarded as of Aeolic descent (Thucydides 4.42), so Sisuphos here is Aiolides, one of the sons of Aiolos, eponym of the race; his brothers Kretheus (Aiolides at *Od.* 11.237), Athamas, Salmoneus and Perieres (cf. [Hesiod], *Ehoiai* frag. 10 M–W) were Thessalians and thus Aeolic, cf. Herodotus 7.176. Pausanias reported a sanctuary of Bellerophon between Korinthos and Kenkhreai (2.2.4), and credited to the early Corinthian poet Eumelus a story that Neleus (Thessalian by origin), as well as Sisuphos himself, was buried on or near the Isthmus (2.2.2). — Aristarchus, Arn/A on 154, noted the epanalepsis of Sisuphos and that the figure is common in *Il.* but comes only once (actually twice) in *Od.*; see S. West on *Od.* 1.23–4.

154–5 Nothing else is known of Bellerophon's father Glaukos, great-grandfather of the speaker. 'Bellerophon' is a later form, e.g. in Theocritus and in Latin; Homeric Βελλεροφόντης is a Greek formation, 'slayer of Belleros', with -φόντης (cf. -φάτης, -φονος) paralleled in Lukophontes, Poluphontes (see on 4.394–5, 3rd para.), cf. Antiphates: so von Kamptz, *Personennamen* 186. Belleros is either Lycian (so L. Malten, *Hermes* 79, 1944, 11, with further refs.) or, according to Kretschmer's attractive suggestion, a local daimon of Pelleritis on the borders of Corinthia, a region mentioned in *IG* IV 926.27f. (3rd cent. B.C.). In this case Bellerophon would derive his name from a feat parallel to his own slaying of the Chimaera, cf. 179–83 below. The D-tradition, however, asserted that Belleros was a Corinthian nobleman slain by Bellerophon, until then called Leophontes (so also bT) or Hipponoos, who was thereby forced to flee. His name clearly invited all sorts of speculation, mostly based on the Homeric context itself; Zenodotus' preference for Ellerophontes (so Eustathius 289, 38 etc.) remains mysterious.

τίκτειν, 'engender', is used in Homer both of the male and of the female parent, though aor. middle forms as with τέκεθ' are commoner of the father, aor. active (as e.g. at 1.36 and 352) of the mother. The imperf., as with τίκτεν here, is also more commonly found of the father; see further A. Hoekstra, *Epic Verse before Homer* (Amsterdam 1981) Appendix II. τίκτειν is one of those reduplicated present stems in -i- which have a determinative rather than a continuative value, i.e. act as aorists (Chantraine, *GH* I, 313); thus τίκτω (τί-τκ-ω) with aor. ἔτεκον, cf. πίπτω, aor. ἔπεσον, γίγνομαι, aor. ἐγενόμην, ἴσχω beside ἔχω, μίμνω beside μένω, ἵζω beside ἕζομαι. Aristarchus (Did/A), followed e.g. by OCT, reads τίκτεν, but most MSS have ἔτικτεν; the use of the temporal augment is generally inconsistent in our texts, the medieval tradition confused. Homer's practice was flexible, as with the observation of digamma. Aristarchus avoided the augment where possible, especially after masc. caesura and before the v-e (cf. Chantraine,

GH I, 481). Here its retention avoids a heavy and pointless spondaic opening to the v., and is to be preferred.

156–7 That he was physically attractive (not necessarily implied by the routine epithet ἀμύμονα, see 5.168–9n.) supplies the motive for the tale that follows. ἠνορέην ἐρατεινήν in 156 is a unique phrase, though ἐρατεινή etc. is regular at the v-e, 15/16× *Il.*, 10/11× *Od.*

157–9 Proitos was legendary king of Argos, then of Tiryns; the community out of which he drove Bellerophon was either Argos or even, perhaps, if the political geography of the Achaean Catalogue in bk 2 is envisaged (vol. I, 180f.), Corinth itself. If the former, then Bellerophon must previously have been forced to leave Corinth by some such reason as discussed on 152–3 (end of first para.). Apollodorus 2.3.1 reports versions by which he killed his brother or some other person (including Peiren, cf. the Corinthian water-nymph Peirene) by accident. V. 159 looks like a gloss designed to show that Argos itself was in question; and, if the object of ἐδάμασσε is the Argives rather than Bellerophon (Proitos' power over the latter having already been stated in 158), then the reference may be to the conflict with his brother Akrisios, cf. Apollodorus 2.2.1. There, Proitos is king in Tiryns rather than Argos, but a certain flexibility over rôles and places is typical of this kind of folktale material and the handling of it in the arbitrary and speculative mythographical tradition.

κακὰ μήσατο θυμῷ | (etc.) in 157 is a formular group of sinister implication which comes 3/4× *Il.* in abbreviated references to earlier tales: here to Bellerophon, at 10.289 to Tudeus, at 14.253 to Here and Herakles, cf. κακὰ μήσατο ἔργα | of Klutaimestra at *Od.* 24.199. Its remaining Iliadic occurrence, also in bk 10 (at 52, of Hektor), has the same rhetorical ring to it; it seems to be favoured in relatively late phases of composition, i.e. both when non-Trojan myths were worked into the monumental structure in an abbreviated form and when the Doloneia was composed.

160–2 Proitos' wife Anteia (Stheneboia in post-Homeric accounts) was mad for Bellerophon, ἐπεμήνατο, namely for secretly mingling with him in love – that is the construction of inf. μιγήμεναι. The Potiphar's-wife theme is a widespread folktale one, represented in Greek mythology by Peleus and the wife of Akastos (Apollodorus 3.13.3, cf. [Hesiod], *Ehoiai* frag. 208 M–W, Pindar, *Nem.* 4.54–8) as well as by Hippolutos and Phaidra. Bellerophon is wisely (rather than kindly, the usual meaning of the phrase) disposed: he is also δαΐφρων, which might also seem to imply intelligence, as in *Od.*, but see on 5.181 for the probable earlier meaning 'with martial intent'. The application is in any case a routine one, Bellerophontes being described as ἀμύμων (as at 155, 190, 216) when the preceding word ends with a consonant, δαΐφρων when it ends with a vowel, cf. 196.

163–5 Anteia's false accusation is made in two concise and ingeniously constructed vv. of direct speech. 'May you be dead, Proitos, or [i.e. if you do not] kill Bellerophon': the harsh apocope of κάκτανε intrudes brutally on the complicated figure, then 165 maintains the rhetorical tone with φιλότητι μιγήμεναι repeated from 161 and neatly sandwiched between ἔθελεν and οὐκ ἐθελούσῃ. Both deployments of this verb are typical (ἔθελε(ν) sic 5/6 × *Il.*, ἐθελούσῃ (etc.) | 8 × *Il.*), but the closest parallels are ἐθέλων ἐθέλουσαν and especially παρ' οὐκ ἐθέλων ἐθελούσῃ at *Od.* 3.272 and 5.155 (cited by bT after Porphyry).

166–7 Anger, χόλος, seized him (τὸν δέ), the lord, at what ⟨a dreadful thing⟩ he heard; yet he avoided killing Bellerophon outright (because he was a ξένος, so T, or for some similar reason). χόλος is much commoner in *Il.* than μῆνις/μηνιθμός, 46 × against 15 × and similarly with verbal forms; it overlaps the sense of μῆνις as long-term anger, but its connexion with bile gives it a special sense of sudden rage, see e.g. on 4.23; also on 18.107–10 (with J. Griffin, *JHS* 106, 1986, 43). σεβάσσατο...θυμῷ recurs at 417 of Akhilleus refraining from plundering the body of Andromakhe's father. σέβομαι etc. connotes reverence or respect, cf. the Odyssean σέβας μ' ἔχει εἰσορόωντα | (5 ×); also, as here, refraining from doing something because of such respect. It overlaps the sense of the more frequent αἰδέομαι, αἰδώς etc.; the etymology of both words is uncertain, cf. Chantraine, *Dict.* s.vv. σέβομαι and αἴδομαι, the former perhaps connected with a Sanskrit root signifying 'leave' or 'abandon', the latter with one signifying 'respect'.

168–70 If Proitos himself is prevented by some unspecified inhibition (167) from directly avenging the affront to Anteia, then her own family needs to be involved – specifically her father, Proitos' father-in-law (170 πενθερῷ), ruler of Lycia. Homer does not give his name; T identified him with Amisodaros, who brought up the Chimaera according to 16.328f. and is said there to be father of two of Sarpedon's captains; later sources according to Aristarchus (Arn/A) called him Iobates. Thus the Lycian king has two daughters, one of whom marries Proitos, the other (cf. 192) Bellerophon – a strange conflation of families but not unparalleled in the matching up of tales from different regions; compare Tudeus and Diomedes, who as father and son both married daughters of Adrastos king of Argos. One does not know how Anteia reacted to having Bellerophon as her new brother-in-law.

The family connexion between Argos and Lycia may reflect some kind of historical relationship, either in the late Mycenaean period when settlers were penetrating the south-western corner of Asia Minor, especially perhaps from Rhodes (see e.g. Page, *HHI* 147–9; C. B. Mee in Foxhall and Davis, *The Trojan War* 50), or during the Dorian migration into the same area two or three centuries later. The Tlepolemos entry in the Catalogue seems to reflect both, see vol. I, 224–7. Tlepolemos is killed by the Lycian prince Sarpedon at 5.627–59 (see on 5.627–69), another possible sign of a tradition of hostility between Greeks and Lycians; though Sarpedon is cousin of Glaukos and son of Zeus, and therefore represents Achaean immigrant stock rather than native Lycian. We shall learn at the end of the present encounter that Bellerophon had been entertained by Diomedes' grandfather Oineus, presumably in Kaludon; that strengthens the Mycenaean background of these interwoven Lycian references. They are obviously not precise historical reminiscences, but it is hard to disagree totally with Nilsson, *Homer and Mycenae* (London 1933) 263, that 'the most probable explanation of the great rôle played by the Lycian heroes [*sc.* in *Il.*], is that the fights of the Lycians and the Greeks in the Mycenaean Age were chanted in epics, of which fragments were incorporated into the *Iliad*, just as fragments of the Pylian epos were incorporated into it.' Gilbert Murray had already noted that the tale of Lukourgos' attack on Dionusos, just recounted by Diomedes at 130ff., was associated with Eumelus of Corinth in the D-scholium on 131 (*The Rise of the Greek Epic*, 4th edn, Oxford 1934, 176f.); and supposed that a *Europia* or *Korinthiaka* assigned to Eumelus was Homer's source for all or most of the exotic details in this Diomedes–Glaukos encounter (cf. also the scholium on Pindar, *Ol.* 13.74).

168–9 'He bestowed on him baneful signs, inscribing many life-destroying things in a folded tablet': the only definite reference in Homer to writing (see also on 7.175–7), and generally taken as a memory of Mycenaean Linear B (or Hittite hieroglyphs or Cypriot syllabary) rather than a reference to the new alphabetic script – which, however, must have seemed no less mysterious on its first introduction to the Greek world, probably in the late 9th cent. B.C. The present allusion is vague and indirect, perhaps intentionally so rather than through progressive mis-understanding in the poetical tradition. The σήματα λυγρά could be any kind of message-bearing signs, not necessarily pictograms (οἶον οὖν ἐγχαράξας εἴδωλα, Aristarchus (Arn/A)) or Linear B symbols; and γράψας, though its literal meaning is 'scratching' (as in Homeric references to wounds), which would suit clay tablets well enough, would also fit writing on a wooden diptych coated on its inner sides with wax. The balance may be tipped towards alphabetic writing by the 'folded tablet' itself, something probably not unknown to the Mycenaean world (see G. F. Bass, *National Geographic*, Dec. 1987, 730f. on the Kaş wreck) but far more familiar from Assyrian reliefs and in developed uses of the alphabet, cf. L. H. Jeffery in Wace and Stubbings, *Companion* 555, who thought Phoenician prototypes unlikely. W. Burkert (in R. Hägg, ed., *The Greek Renaissance of the Eighth Century B.C.*, Stockholm 1983, 52ff.), gives a useful bibliography and opts for the Phoenician–Greek δέλτος as prototype, assigning the present reference to it (together with the alphabetic σήματα, the Potiphar's-wife theme and the Chimaera), to as late as the early 7th cent. B.C. See further A. Heubeck, *Arch. Hom.* x 141ff.

170–1 Quite why Bellerophon accepted the idea of a trip abroad, carrying an unusual and unknown message, especially after Anteia's embarrassing advances, is left obscure. That is typical of folktales, which are often applied to different local contexts in very uncircumstantial forms, with only the crucial details (involving the particular ingenuity-motifs which gave them permanent appeal) properly filled in. Imprecise and allusive expression, already exemplified in 168 σήματα λυγρά and to an extent in 169 θυμοφθόρα πολλά, is continued in 171 θεῶν ὑπ' ἀμύμονι πομπῇ. Though πομπή occurs only here in *Il.* it is common, for obvious contextual reasons, in *Od.* (25 ×), where escort by gods is occasionally mentioned in general terms, e.g. *Od.* 3.376 θεοὶ πομπῆες ἕπονται and 11.332 πομπὴ δὲ θεοῖς ὑμῖν τε μελήσει. No specific deity (like Athene protecting Tudeus or Odysseus) need be envisaged, but something more than a safe voyage seems to be meant.

172 River Xanthos runs through Lycia and defines the homeland of Glaukos and Sarpedon at 2.876f. and 12.313.

174–5 For the standard locution 'for nine days... and then on the tenth' cf. 1.53f. (Apollo's plague), 24.610–12 (Niobids unburied), 664f. (mourning for Hektor), 784f. (making his pyre); also nine nights followed by a tenth, 9.470–4 (watch over Phoinix). In *Od.* the same turn of speech is regularly used for Odysseus' progress between landfalls during his sea adventures (7.253 = 14.314, 9.82f., 10.28f., 12.447). On expressions for dawn see 2.48–9n.

It was *de rigueur* not to raise matters of business and identification with a ξεῖνος until he had been sufficiently entertained, cf. Alkinoos' delay in establishing Odysseus' identity in Skherie until *Od.* 8.550f. (cf. Jason at Pindar, *Py.* 4.127ff.). The nine-day interval, routine for other actions, is exceptional here, but Bellerophon is a relative and in any case the folktale atmosphere predominates. Moreover the Lycian king's lavish reception, with a banquet each day, establishes a dramatic contrast with his concealed anger once the tablet is opened and read.

176–7 The σῆμα of 176 is the tablet as a whole rather than the specific σήματα within it. | ὅττι ῥά οἱ is formular, 5 × *Il.*, 2 × *Od.*

178 This rising threefolder adapts language already used, with some awkwardness; γαμβροῦ makes an unpleasantly ponderous ending (in contrast with e.g. χαίρων in δέξατο χαίρων |, 4 × *Il.*, 1 × *Od.*).

179–86 Three tasks are set for Bellerophon, all obviously dangerous and without stated reward or purpose, e.g. the offer of a bride if successful as often in folktale. Here the bride and half the kingdom will come later at 192f., and only when the king recognizes Bellerophon's divine connexions.

The prizes could have been falsely offered before that, and fuller versions might have made that clear. Yet this sort of folktale medley tends to gloss over motive and distort character, as for example with Perseus. Bellerophon's involvement with Anteia, however innocent, hardly suggests the swashbuckling type who undergoes tests and quests almost at random.

179–83 The first task is the slaying of the Chimaera, of which the text reveals (i) that it was of divine race, not human; (ii) that it was lion in front, snake behind, goat (i.e. χίμαιρα in its everyday application, one that has survived a winter, cf. χειμέριος) in the middle; (iii) that it breathed out fire. From 16.327–9 we learn also (iv) that it was reared by Amisodaros, father of two companions of Sarpedon, and therefore presumably in Lycia. As for (i), Hesiod at *Theog.* 295–322 made Khimaira the offspring of the Lernaean Hydra (multi-headed), or perhaps of her parents Ekhidna and Tuphaon (the one half-snake, the other perhaps envisaged as breathing fire, though cf. M. L. West on *Theog.* 845), themselves descended from Pontos through Phorkus and Keto. Such monsters are rare in the Homeric epic, which steers clear of animal mixtures (Centaurs are an exception) and other Near Eastern *exotica*; but something like the Chimaera would be envisaged as descended from primeval powers and therefore divine in a sense, cf. 1.403–4n. on Briareos. οὐδ' ἀνθρώπων is a 'polar' addition simply for emphasis, since there can be no question of such a creature being human in origin. On (iii), fire-breathing monsters are also exemplified in the brazen fire-breathing oxen of Aietes in the Argonaut legend, cf. Pindar, *Py.* 4.225. Representations of the orientalizing period (7th cent. B.C.) and later show the goat's head as the fire-breather (so also Apollodorus 2.3.1, Ovid, *Met.* 9.647; cf. West on *Theog.* 321); in fact 182 ἀποπνείουσα could agree either with 181 χίμαιρα or with 180 ἡ δ', i.e. the creature as a whole, which might suggest its front end, the lion's rather than the goat's head, as emitting fire – which is what bT assumed. T adds that there was a Mt Khimaira in Lycia which spurted fire from its centre and had many wild creatures at its edges; this is of possible interest in relation to the Homeric monster's Lycian origin, for Strabo 14.665 associated the mythical creature with a gorge behind Kragos in southern Lycia, whereas Pliny 2.236, after Ctesias, noted two places in the mountains there where flammable vapours emerged from the earth.

179 ἀμαιμάκετος occurs here and at 16.329 of the Chimaera; at Hesiod, *Theog.* 319, in a metrically inept adaptation, of the fire it breathed; and at *Od.* 14.311 of the unbroken mast to which the shipwrecked Odysseus clung. Probably 'invincible', cf. μάχομαι, was the meaning commonly accepted for an old and obscure term (possibly related to μαιμάω, cf. bT and Chantraine, *Dict.* s.v.).

181 On the rising threefolder see 152–211n.

183 Bellerophon slew the monster θεῶν τεράεσσι πιθήσας; the nature of these divine portents is obscure, and the phrase probably signals once again the abbreviation of a longer account. It occurred at 4.398 with reference to Tudeus' defeat of a Theban ambush, again in a summary version of an earlier myth and, significantly, in a form of the ambush-motif shortly to be applied to Bellerophon at 187ff.; see on 4.398, 381, 408. The summarizing technique is similar to that of the Tudeus-references in bks 4 and 5 (see on 4.389–90, 5.802–4) – further evidence that the present account is not post-Homeric.

Could these 'portents of the gods' contain a veiled reference to the winged horse Pegasos, who is the most prominent element of the Bellerophon story in all post-Homeric accounts, and whom he had bridled at Corinth with Athene's help according to Pindar, *Ol.* 13.65ff., cf. Pausanias 2.4.1? That hardly seems likely; yet one of the most puzzling aspects of this episode is Homer's suppression, first of Pegasos (as Aristarchus noted, Arn/A on 183), and secondly of other details of Bellerophon's ultimate offence against the gods, which in the non-Homeric tradition was his attempting to fly up to Olumpos itself, either to enjoy its pleasures or to confront Zeus. Hesiod specifically involved Pegasos in the attack on the Chimaera, *Theog.* 325 τὴν μὲν Πήγασος εἷλε καὶ ἐσθλὸς Βελλεροφόντης, cf. [Hesiod], *Ehoiai* frag. 43a.81–7 M–W; according to Pindar, *Ol.* 13.87–90, Pegasos was involved in all three tests – Pindar here follows Homer in suppressing the reason for the hero's end, but states it openly at *Isthm.* 7.44–7. Scholars have reached no firm conclusion. E. Bethe (in the Pauly–Wissowa article on Bellerophon) thought the Pegasos-theme to be an old one that was not carried overseas with the Bellerophon story, of which Homer followed a Lycian version. L. Malten, on the contrary, took both Pegasos and the Chimaera as Asiatic elements that may have been unknown on the Greek mainland in the 8th cent. B.C. E. Howald, *Der Mythos als Dichtung* (Zürich 1937) 88ff. conjectured that Homer knew about Pegasos but suppressed the idea as somehow unsuitable or inconsistent; that seems reasonable, even if W. Kullmann (*Das Wirken der Götter in der Ilias*, Berlin 1956, 22–5) added that Homer's audience would realize the Pegasos ride to be the delusion of a disappointed man. Lorimer, *HM* 473f., followed Malten in regarding Pegasos as a Carian or Lycian creation, adding that it was excluded by Homer not so much as too oriental but because horseback riding was omitted from the epic as an anachronism. See also J. Gaisser, *TAPA* 100 (1969) 170–4.

184–5 Note the simple and clear ordering of the three main feats, 179 | πρῶτον μέν...followed by 184 | δεύτερον αὖ and 186 | τὸ τρίτον αὖ, with κατέπεφνε(ν) of the first and third (also of the ambush, 190). Its omission from the second is not only for chiastic effect, since Bellerophon probably did not slay all the Solumoi if his son Isandros lost his life against them according to 204. His survival is what matters, the heroic quality of the encounter being adequately shown by the emphatic claim καρτίστην δὴ τήν γε μάχην... of 185, cf. Nestor's description of the Lapiths at 1.266f., | κάρτιστοι δὴ κεῖνοι... | κάρτιστοι μὲν ἔσαν καὶ καρτίστοις ἐμάχοντο, and for φάτο cf. 6.98 ὃν δὴ ἐγὼ κάρτιστον Ἀχαιῶν φημι γενέσθαι. — The Solumoi were indigenous inhabitants, later called Miluai, of Lycia according to Herodotus 1.173, driven out by Lycians coming from Crete under Sarpedon (grandfather, that is, of the Homeric hero, though see on 16.317–29). Solymian mountains are mentioned at *Od.* 5.283, and it is a reasonable conjecture (cf. Strabo 13.630) that the natives were driven into the mountains to the north-east but made incursions into colonized Lycia from time to time.

187–90 The fourth attempt on Bellerophon's life is of a more direct kind; yet the ambush-motif is also at home in folktale, especially when a single survivor is left to report disaster. The chief interest of the present feat is that it is so similar, including its expression, to that of Tudeus with the ambush set by the Kadmeioi at 4.392ff.; see on 4.392, and compare

4.392 ἂψ ἄρ' ἀνερχομένῳ πυκινὸν λόχον εἷσαν ἄγοντες
with 6.187 τῷ δ' ἄρ' ἀνερχομένῳ πυκινὸν δόλον ἄλλον ὕφαινε;
also 4.397 πάντας ἔπεφν', ἕνα δ' οἶον ἵει οἰκόνδε νέεσθαι
with 6.190 πάντας γὰρ κατέπεφνεν
and 6.189 τοὶ δ' οὔ τι πάλιν οἰκόνδε νέοντο.

Here the ambush is composed not of 50 youths but of specially selected φῶτες ἄριστοι, whose leaders are not named; but the same composer seems to have been at work on both summary accounts. Leaf suggested that the present version is a rhapsodic reworking of the Tudeus ambush, since the Lycian king's object had been to avoid directly killing Bellerophon. Yet it is only when all else had failed that he resorted to ambush; and the ingenious conversion of λόχον to δόλον may be too simple for rhapsodic taste.

191 Bellerophon's triumphs suggested the highest kind of heroic ancestry; there is no need to see a reference to the idea, unexpressed in Homer, that Poseidon was his father.

192–5 The royal reward is extravagant but in the folktale manner; the Lycians themselves added a generous landholding, perhaps because he had delivered them from great dangers as bT suggested. A minimally adapted form of 194–5 occurs at 20.184–5, where Akhilleus addresses Aineias, and Sarpedon and Glaukos enjoy a similar estate that is καλὸν φυταλιῆς καὶ ἀρούρης by the Xanthos river at 12.313f. φυταλιή, 'land for planting', implies either orchard or vineyard, the latter perhaps more probable in view of 9.578–80.

196–206 The account of the three children born to the Lycian princess (whom later sources named Alkimedousa or Pasandre, cf. T on 192) is straightforward, though interrupted by 200–2. Laodameia bore Sarpedon to Zeus, succumbing later to Artemis' wrath (she being responsible for sudden death for women, as in 428, especially in childbirth); Isandros was killed in warfare against the Solumoi, see on 184–5; Hippolokhos was Glaukos' own father.

199 Aristarchus (Arn/A) noted that the Homeric Sarpedon is son of Laodameia, not Europe as οἱ νεώτεροι said (e.g. [Hesiod], *Ehoiai* frag. 141.14 M–W); but might have added that Sarpedon must have had a grandfather of that name who was brother of Minos and offspring of Europe and Zeus.

200–2 There are two problems here: (i) these vv. seem to break the logical sequence, and (ii) they are so mysterious about Bellerophon's end. On (i), this information interrupts the account of the three children, and would fit better, if not perfectly, after 205 as Leaf thought. That would have the merit of explaining 200 καὶ κεῖνος (in a hemistich recurring at *Od.* 3.286), which is unaccountable in the present sequence of vv. (though Ameis–Hentze's reference of it to the fate of Lukourgos back at 138–40, presupposing the disruption of an earlier text in which the two men were listed consecutively as sinners, is interesting); for Bellerophon's unhappy end would then follow that of the two of his children who were comparably unfortunate. Even so the narrative is not entirely straightforward; this may be primarily due to (ii), and to the poet's feeling, perhaps, that Bellerophon's own fate could not be passed over in complete silence. Presumably Glaukos, especially in the light of 209f., was concerned to magnify his grandfather's prowess and minimize his defects; and though Pegasos might be suppressed for special reasons (183n.), Bellerophon's eventual ruin through some excess against the gods was probably too familiar to be denied. With the suggested transposition, of which there is admittedly no hint in the ancient or medieval tradition, his misfortune, and therefore his crime itself, would be subtly diminished by being rated with that of his two children, unexceptional victims of Artemis and Ares respectively.

200 | ἀλλ' ὅτε δή is a recurrent v.-beginning in this speech, also at 172, 175, 191.

201–2 'He wandered alone over the Aleian plain, devouring his own life-spirit, avoiding the steps of men': the exegetical tradition could do no better than suppose this to be through grief at the loss of two of his three children (bT, against οἱ νεώτεροι again who talked of Bellerophon's μελαγχολία); but some specific affliction by the gods must surely have been the reason for his avoidance of men. Ἀλήϊον is deliberately connected with the similarly-sounding ἀλᾶτο as 'the plain of wandering'; there seems to have been a real plain so named in Cilicia, to the east of Lycia, in later times at least, cf. Herodotus 6.95. For ὃν θυμὸν κατέδων cf. *Od.* 9.75 θυμὸν ἔδοντες |.

205 No specific reason for Artemis' anger need be envisaged – hardly that Laodameia had slept with Zeus as e.g. Ameis–Hentze suggest. χρυσήνιος is found only here and once of Ares in *Od.*; the connexion with chariots presumably depends on her rôle as huntress. She requires an epithet only three times in this position, with χρυσόθρονος at 9.534 and *Od.* 5.123.

206 On ἔτικτε see 154–5n.; the second hemistich, repetitive though it is, emphasizes Glaukos' pride in his family in a rather touching way. Nothing else is known of this Hippolokhos; a Trojan namesake surfaces briefly in bk 12.

207–8 Another father, Peleus, gives the same typically heroic advice to his son at 11.783f. (where 11.784 = 208 here); ἐπιτέλλειν is regular for this kind of instruction, cf. 5.198 (Pandaros' father), 11.782–5 (Peleus and Menestheus). ἀριστεύειν means much the same as 'be superior to others' in the second hemistich, quite literally always to be best (rather than be a gentleman).

209–11 Living up to one's forefathers is part of the same code and no less élitist, since they were 'far the best' both in Lycia and in Ephure–Korinthos, and Glaukos reasserts his own worth by the pride he shows in them. Language as well as content is typical; 211 recurs as 20.241, in the parallel scene where Aineias recites his genealogy to counter a sneer by Akhilleus, and 209 is similar to *Od.* 24.508.

212–14 Diomedes' joy is unexpected, and the emphatic γήθησεν δέ seems designed to show that; yet the first half of the v. is formular (2 × *Il.* elsewhere, 5 × *Od.*). He sticks his spear into (Bekker's ἐνί for ἐπί may be right) the ground, the 'bountiful earth': the epithet is regular for χθών in the acc. or dat. (12 × *Il.*) but also brilliantly echoes the exuberance of this unique action – itself a sign of peace (so AbT), but also equivalent perhaps to the English cliché of 'slapping the thigh' in amazement or pleasure. Finally μειλιχίοισι (without ἔπεσσι or μύθοισι, cf. 4.256n.) confirms his positive response – which he has not necessarily concealed so far, as bT imply, since epic narrative technique does not encourage interjections to describe a listener's passing reactions.

215–31 Diomedes' reply to Glaukos' elaborate speech is as straightforward in construction as in feeling, consisting mainly of whole-sentence or progressively enjambed vv., with only 4 integral enjambments and little internal punctuation; 219 and 228 are rising threefolders. The argument is logical, with reversions to the central idea of guest-friendship in modified ring-form:

1. You are my guest-friend
2. because my grandfather entertained yours in his home
3. when they exchanged gifts – Bellerophon's is still there.
4. (My father Tudeus I do not remember.)
5. So I am your host in Argos, you mine in Lycia.
6. Let us therefore avoid each other in battle,
7. since there are other opponents for us to fight,
8. and exchange armour as sign to the others of our guest-friendship.

Thus 1, 5 and 8 repeat the theme of ξεινίη, with 2 and 3 giving the historical reasons for it, and 6, 7 and 8 its immediate consequences.

215 For | ἦ ῥά νύ μοι cf. Priam's equally emphatic | ἦ ῥά νύ τοι at 3.183. Athene–Mentes tells Telemakhos ξεῖνοι δ' ἀλλήλων πατρώϊοι εὐχόμεθ' εἶναι at *Od.* 1.187, echoed by 231 below.

216–17 The chiastic arrangement and the juxtaposition of δῖος and ἀμύμονα give great formality to the announcement. — Oineus' city Kaludon is barely far enough from Korinthos or Argos to make such a prolonged stay plausible; 20 is a typical number for long intervals (for example Odysseus' years of absence from home), but 10 days might seem more appropriate here as with the entertainment of Bellerophon, on which see 174–5n. Perhaps metrical convenience determined an interval which is in any case unimportant provided it seemed lavish enough.

218–19 πόρον: literally 'passed over' to each other (as Aristarchus observed, Arn/A, the καί is redundant). The ξεινήϊον was an integral part of the heroic institution of guest-friendship, the concrete symbol of a tacit pact (see M. I. Finley, *The World of Odysseus*, 2nd edn, London 1977, 64–6); the gifts Glaukos and Diomedes are about to exchange are a kind of renewal of that original gift-giving. For the ζωστήρ or girdle see on 4.132–40 and 132–3; that was metallic, but according to Leaf here 'The material of the belt is, of course, leather.' This is because it is bright with purple, but purple-stained ivory attachments could be meant, see on 4.141–2. In any case a girdle is similarly exchanged by Aias with Hektor after their duel at 7.305 (~ 219 here); Hektor offers his sword, these being the kind of gifts available on the battlefield – which is where the girdle Bellerophon received, too, might properly belong. As for his own gift of a golden cup, Nestor took a valuable δέπας on campaign, 11.632–5, and Akhilleus two,

16.225–7 and 23.194–6. It may be that bT are right in finding one a suitable gift for a resident, the other for a traveller.

221 That Diomedes 'left it behind' when he came to Troy serves to make it, and the bond it represents, seem more real. The repetition of κατέλειπον in 223 κάλλιφ' is not significant.

222–3 T had some justification for finding these vv. ἄτοποι, 'out of place'. The mention of Tudeus does seem rather forced, an interruption of the argument; but Diomedes evidently feels the need to show how his father fitted into the tradition of guest-friendship, and to explain, perhaps, why he did not specifically hand on information about Bellerophon's descendants. The theme of Tudeus at Thebes is in any case important wherever Diomedes is concerned.

224–5 The simple and almost child-like language continues as Diomedes looks forward, apparently without irony, to a future in which Glaukos could be in Argos or he himself in Lycia. The addition of φίλος to ξεῖνος and of μέσσῳ to Ἄργεϊ sharpens the intimate effect, and the second half of 225, though strictly unnecessary, makes a visit seem more likely: not 'if ever' but 'whenever', with Lycia glossed in human terms, '*their* community'.

226 Ancient critics made heavy weather of this v.: Zenodotus read ἔγχεσι δ' ἀλλήλους (Did/AbT), to which Aristarchus responded by defending ἀλλήλων; but he too may have accepted ἔγχεσι (Nic/A, a reading which found its way into a majority of MSS). In fact ἔγχεα δ' ἀλλήλων ἀλεώμεθα is unobjectionable. καὶ δι' ὁμίλου compounded the confusion, for Aristarchus (Nic/A) seems to have concluded that the troops of both contingents were to be involved, and that this has something to do with ἀλλήλων. But the phrase means 'even in the thick of the battle' (Willcock) and applies solely to the two principals.

227–9 For anaphoric | πολλοὶ μὲν... πολλοὶ δ' cf. | τούτῳ μὲν... τούτῳ δ' at 4.415–17 (so Ameis–Hentze). The expression is original and cleverly varied: 'There are many Trojans for me to catch and kill, God willing, and many Achaeans for you to slay – whomsoever you can', with ὅν κε δύνηαι an amusing indication of the superiority Diomedes evidently still feels.

230–1 The suggestion of an exchange of armour is made confidently and somewhat abruptly; one compares Hektor's proposal at 7.299–302 for an exchange of gifts to mark the friendly conclusion to their interrupted duel. In both cases what others will think is important. But the gifts at the end of the duel in 7 are individual items, sword and girdle; the exchange of complete sets of armour, confirmed by 235f., is more drastic, and unrealistic even by epic standards. — γνῶσιν in 231 is a unique contraction of γνώωσιν (4× *Il.*); van Leeuwen's γνώωσ' ὁ ξεῖνοι is attractive. For the rest cf. *Od.* 1.187 (quoted on 215); εὐχόμεθ᾿ -ομαι εἶναι | is formular, 10 × *Il.*

232 The v. is composed of standard elements; for καθ᾿ ἵππων ἀΐξαντε -α cf. 11.423, 20.401. Here a rather inelegant rhyme is produced after φωνήσαντε and echoed by 233 πιστώσαντο. That they were in chariots is not suggested by the introduction to their encounter at 119–21.

233 For shaking hands on an agreement compare 'the right hands in which we trust' at 2.341. The terminology of 21.286 is closer, χειρὶ δὲ χεῖρα λαβόντες ἐπιστώσαντ᾿ ἐπέεσσι, but the meaning there is that they took Akhilleus' hand (for comfort, rather) and reassured him by what they had to say. Here πιστώσαντο is different, 'they gave each other assurances'.

234–6 No critic, ancient or modern, has satisfactorily explained this bizarre incident and its unexpected change in ethos; for a useful survey of the various attempts to do so see W. M. Calder III in *Studies presented to Sterling Dow* (Durham, N.C., 1984) 31–5. Most readers, including Plato and Aristotle, have been sufficiently amused by the strange turn of events to refrain from further analysis. The following are relevant considerations, none the less.

(1) There has been no hint up to now of Glaukos wearing golden armour, an extravagant conceit so far as mortals are concerned; nor did Diomedes comment on this remarkable equipment when he met, and ostensibly tried to identify, his opponent. Later, at 8.191–5, Hektor will tell *his horses* that Nestor has an all-gold shield and Diomedes a corslet made by Hephaistos. That is another odd passage (see on 8.191–7); but the corslet there is not of gold, and cannot be intended as the one handed over by Glaukos.

(2) τεύχεα regularly implies the whole set of armour, not just the defensive armour: see Trümpy, *Fachausdrücke* 75ff. Leaf suggested that the term may not include body-armour at 3.89 (where the onlooking troops are invited by Hektor to put their τεύχεα on the ground), but that is feeble support. This substantially rules out bT's suggestion that what were exchanged were single items as with Aias and Hektor at 7.303–5.

(3) The valuing of golden armour at a hundred oxen's worth, bronze armour at nine, makes a neat and epigrammatic conclusion but throws little light on the main problem. The ox as a standard of value is familiar throughout the epic: each golden tassel of Athene's aegis is worth 100 oxen at 2.449, Lukaon was sold into captivity for the same sum and ransomed for three times as much at 21.79f., a bronze tripod is worth 12 oxen at 23.703, Laertes had given the equivalent of 20 oxen for Eurukleia at *Od.* 1.431, Eurumakhos proposes the same amount of gold and bronze as repayment by each suitor at *Od.* 22.57. One suspects an arbitrary element in these equivalents, as well as some influence by metre; E. V. Rieu had some

justification for translating ἑκατόμβοιος, in the case of Lukaon, as '(for) a good price' rather than literally. That gold armour was worth over ten times as much as bronze seems credible, but does not justify Ameis–Hentze's assertion that the gold must have been solid; since even gold plating (which would make the 'golden' armour just believable, though it is not suggested by the simple epithet χρύσεα) would presumably be enormously expensive.

(4) Exchanging armour regardless of physique is envisaged at 14.381f., but that does not make it an appropriate action here in realistic terms.

(5) Nothing in epic psychology suggests that Glaukos would be so easily carried away by Diomedes' ebullient distortion of the rules of guest-friendship (or by wishing to match Oineus' earlier gift as T suggests). He is said to be deluded by Zeus, but that is no more than a light-hearted *façon de parler* – since Zeus would hardly operate so trivially, least of all on a friend of his son Sarpedon.

(6) A cheap success for Diomedes is out of key with the episode as a whole, which is surely intended to crown his extended *aristeia* with a memorable display of magnanimity and heroic relations at their finest.

Such considerations preclude any *literal* and *realistic* understanding of the exchange. That is hardly surprising, since the action and its implications are self-evidently intended to be humorous in some way, at the very least *piquant* and paradoxical, and certainly not serious or heroic in the ordinary epic sense. The poet, it seems, withdraws for a moment from his regular narrative mode and proposes a typical folktale-type transaction containing all the fantasy and exaggeration that are proper to that genre and alien to the normal epic genre. In other words, he substitutes for the expected ending (e.g. a simple exchange of the Aias–Hektor kind) a fantasy which the audience will recognize as such, and which has no particular bearing on the 'real' rôles and characters of the two participants.

Such an effect would be virtually unique in the *Iliad*, a rare intrusion into the epic of an individual flight of fancy. As such it might arouse a suspicion of rhapsodic interference. Yet (i) the mere *addition* of 234–6 can be discounted, since some description must have been given of the exchange of armour envisaged at 230f. – and the suppression of those two vv. also (for which, of course, there is no evidence) might leave the episode's ending looking distinctly threadbare; (ii) the complete *replacement* of a simpler account of the exchange would be unparalleled (or at any rate unprovable), and is probably not the sort of thing that rhapsodes did or audiences would easily accept. It continues to look, therefore, as though Homer himself, who plainly shaped the important Diomedes-and-Glaukos episode with exceptional affection and care, risked a rare virtuoso conclusion to it, perhaps to mark even more clearly the transition to a different world as Hektor makes his way into the city.

*237–311   Hektor arrives back at Troy, converses with his mother Hekabe and tells her
to organize the supplication of Athene at her temple. Theano as priestess opens the
temple and offers the prayers (which are unsuccessful)*

237–41 This 5-v. description of the women crowding round Hektor at the
Scaean gate is as carefully constructed in its way as the preceding 5-v.
group had been. That was a sequence of uninterrupted 4-colon vv., with
only the initial rhyming of φωνήσαντε... ἀΐξαντε in 232 to disturb the gentle
flow. Here the rhythm is more varied, but with a formal chiastic pattern;
the first two vv. are rising threefolders, the last two (240–1) have runover
cumulation followed by a strong stop, and the central 239 is distinctive in
sound if not sense – a *falling* threefolder almost, with the τε's marking the
end of each diminishing colon.

237 For the Scaean gate facing the battlefield see on 3.145, and
for the oak-tree thrice associated with it in Σκαιάς...ἵκανεν -οντο see on
5.692–3.

239 εἴρομαι with direct object, 'ask about', as at 10.416, 24.390. (F)ἔται
in Homer are usually distant male relatives, cf. S. West on *Od.* 4.3 and
Hainsworth on *Od.* 8.585–6; they are distinguished from cousins at 9.464.
Yet a broader sense, closer to 'companions' merely, is suggested here and
there, and a connexion with ἑταῖροι is still sometimes mooted. Chantraine,
Dict. s.v. ἔτης (who untypically misstated the context of 16.456 = 674)
thought it a social rather than a kin term; certainly in later Greek the sense
is no more than 'citizen' or 'fellow-citizen'. Here, where children, brothers
and husbands are specified, more distant male relatives are not inappropriate; but ἀμύνων σοῖσιν ἔτῃσι in 262 may favour 'fellow-citizens'
here too.

241 πᾶσι μάλ' ἐξείης was a variant known to Aristarchus (Arn/A), and
could be correct in view of *Od.* 11.134 = 23.281 (sacrifice to the gods)
| πᾶσι μάλ' ἐξείης – a stronger application of ἐξείης than with πάσας here.
According to bT the meaning is that Hektor told each woman in turn to
pray; that is the most natural interpretation of the present word-order, but
the resulting sense is odd and ἐξείης should probably be taken with θεοῖς
εὔχεσθαι nevertheless, with πάσας a slightly awkward *ad hoc* conversion of
πᾶσι μάλ'. — Τρώεσσι δὲ κήδε' ἐφῆπται occurred at 2.15, q.v. with n.,
where κήδε(α) bears its general sense of 'woes'. It can also imply, more
specifically, 'mourning', cf. κηδείους and κήδεος at 19.294 and 23.160, and
that is the probable sense here. Mourning is 'tied' to the Trojans, is
inescapable, even though they do not yet know it; compare ὀλέθρου πείρατ'
ἐφῆπται, 2 × *Il.*, and cf. 143n.

242–50 Hektor's itinerary inside the city wall will be (1) to Priam's
palace, where he meets his mother; (2) to the house of Paris, where he meets

his brother and Helen (313ff.); (3) to his own house (370ff.), where he hears that Andromakhe has gone to the walls for news of the fighting; (4) back to the Scaean gate, where he finally meets Andromakhe and where Paris catches up with him (390 to end). The two will then sally forth at 7.1–3. The rise in intensity as one visit succeeds another is striking and impressive, and has been noted as a typical narrative device.

There is a distinct air of unreality about this charming and naive description of Priam's palace ('fanciful and romantic', A. J. B. Wace in Wace and Stubbings, *Companion* 489), and it would be a mistake in principle to relate the details too closely either to the layout of the Odyssean palace at Ithake or to actual Mycenaean sites, Pulos and Tiruns in particular, even if the Bronze-Age *megaron* fronted by a courtyard provides a general model. — δόμον in 242 is the whole complex; it is fitted with 'polished porches' (which could be of wood or stone); *in it* (243 ἐν αὐτῇ) are 50 rooms of polished or dressed stone, built close to each other – that is, presumably, attached. This is where Priam's sons sleep with their wives. On the other side, 247 ἑτέρωθεν, and facing them, ἐναντίοι, within the courtyard, are 12 similarly attached rooms where the sons-in-law sleep with Priam's daughters. There are imprecisions here. Are the 50 rooms conceived as 'inside' the palace itself, i.e. beyond the courtyard, in contrast with the 12 that are specifically said to be ἔνδοθεν αὐλῆς? That would not accord with the most obvious sense of 247 ἐναντίοι. And does 248 τέγεοι (which must mean 'roofed' and not, as bT thought, 'on the roof') distinguish these 12 rooms from the other 50? Surely not: this is simply a decorative epithet to fill out the hemistich corresponding with 244 | πεντήκοντ' ἔνεσαν. If all the rooms are round the courtyard, and there is no implied contrast between 243 ἐν αὐτῷ and 247 ἔνδοθεν αὐλῆς, then it is hard for the 12 to be 'facing' the 50. We might like to think of one range down one side, the other down the other, but the unequal numbers do not really fit. Perhaps this is being too literal; that the rooms are all in the courtyard, and that the αἴθουσαι of 243 are the colonnades around it, with the rooms built into the colonnades, is a tempting hypothesis. In Aiolos' palace at *Od.* 10.5–12 things were better arranged; admittedly this is an overtly fantastic affair on a floating island, but Aiolos has six sons and six daughters married to each other, eating with mother and father and sleeping together at night, presumably in their six rooms. — Lorimer, *HM* 431, thinks that knowledge of dressed-stone buildings may derive from Egypt or Phoenicia, and even considers the possibility of interpolation (since 243–50 are inorganic). But Priam's palace needs to be actualized somehow, just like the houses of Paris and Hektor later, and the unequal number of sons and daughters presumably reflects legendary tradition; it would have been architecturally and poetically simpler to have had them equal.

244–50 The two sets of chambers are described in identical terms as far as possible:

244 πεντήκοντ' ἔνεσαν } θάλαμοι ξεστοῖο λίθοιο
248 δώδεκ' ἔσαν τέγεοι

245   ⌈ ἔνθα δὲ παῖδες
     πλησίον ἀλλήλων δεδμημένοι, {
249   ⌊ ἔνθα δὲ γαμβροὶ
246 = 250 κοιμῶντο Πριάμοιο παρ' αἰδοίης ἀλόχοισι.

There is much to be said for reading αἰδοίης for μνήστης in 246, to match 250, a variant noted by Aristarchus (Did/A) and accepted in some MSS; μνήστην -ης -η ἄλοχον -ου -ῳ occurs 3 × *Il.*, 1 × *Od.* in mid-v. and with functional lengthening of a preceding short syllable, but never again at the v-e (where αἰδοίης ἀλόχοισι | recurs at 21.460 and *Od.* 10.11, i.e. in the Aiolos passage).

251–2 ἠπιόδωρος, 'of kindly gifts', is *hapax*; the regular epithet for μήτηρ is πότνια, but the singer may have felt the need for something more specific here, to sound the sympathetic note of Hektor's other encounters in Troy. On a mechanical level, ἐναντίη ἤλυθε could not be fitted in if μήτηρ were preceded by πότνια. A more powerful factor may be the equivalent language of Hektor being met by Andromakhe at 394, ἔνθ' ἄλοχος πολύδωρος ἐναντίη ἦλθε θέουσα. The situations are broadly the same and both vv. begin with ἔνθ(α); by the adaptation of ἦλθε to ἤλυθε and πολύδωρος to ἠπιόδωρος the singer is able to substitute 'mother' for 'wife' – supposing, that is, the later and more elaborate encounter to be earlier in terms of conception. At any rate ἄλοχος πολύδωρος *sic* occurs 2 × *Il.*, 1 × *Od.*, and is likely to be the origin of the unique ἠπιόδωρος.

Hekabe is accompanied by Laodike, who adds nothing here; she was mentioned more purposefully at 3.124, of which 252 seems to be an adaptation with ἐσάγουσα in place of Πριάμοιο. But the natural implication of 251 is that Hekabe came out of the *megaron* into the courtyard and met Hektor there (so e.g. Ameis–Hentze); the addition of 252, which Leaf would have liked to expunge, needlessly complicates this, nor is any special motive needed for Hekabe's movements. Where, or into what, rather, is she leading her daughter? Perhaps into Laodike's room, one of the set of twelve in the colonnade, though that would be rather forced. Aristarchus (Arn/A) was driven to reading ἐς ἄγουσα, 'going to Laodike', i.e. to call on her, but the intransitive use is unparalleled and the prepositional phrase awkward. Andromakhe will be accompanied by another person (the nurse who carries the baby) at 399f., and that might once again affect the shape of the present encounter.

253 The first occurrence of this energetic and moving v., 6 × *Il.*, 5 ×

Od., with its second half another 12 × *Il.*, 21 × *Od.* φῦ is aor. of φύομαι, from which ἐν is separated by tmesis (cf. 1.512–13n. on ἐμπεφυυῖα); the meaning is 'grew into', perhaps implying that she clung tightly to him (οἱ) *with her arm*, embraced him closely, rather than that she took a firm grasp *on his hand*; though *Od.* 2.302 with 321 (see S. West *ad loc.*) shows the latter to be envisaged there.

254 πόλεμον θρασύν similarly at 10.28; otherwise the epithet is applied, more naturally, to persons, except in the phrase θρασειάων ἀπὸ χειρῶν (6 × *Il.*). εἰλήλουθα (etc.) is formular at the v-e.

255–7 | ἦ μάλα δή is common and emphatic in speech, not of course in narrative (cf. J. Griffin, *JHS* 106, 1986, 45), here introducing a confident conjecture. δυσώνυμος occurs only 2 × *Il.* (at 12.116 of an evil destiny), 1 × *Od.* (of an evil dawn), and is a violent expression, almost a curse; cf. κακοΐλιον οὐκ ὀνομαστήν, 3 × *Od.* (Griffin, *op. cit.* 42). They are fighting περὶ ἄστυ, 'round the city' as at 16.448. Hekabe's conviction about Hektor's motive for returning is only partly right: the Trojans were τειρόμενοι at 85, but Hektor himself seemed irrepressible; it was not his θυμός but Helenos' intuition and advice that brought him back to the city, and not personally to supplicate Zeus but to tell the women to pray to Athene. Homer's characters are not averse from imputing motives aloud to those they are talking to; the imputations are often hotly rejected, and this lends a disputatious liveliness (heroic, or convenient for the composer?) to the interchange.

In 257 χεῖρας ἀνασχεῖν | (etc.) is formular for prayer, 7 × *Il.*, 3 × *Od.* She imagines Hektor as praying 'from the city's summit', its acropolis in later terms, not because there was a temple of Zeus there (*pace* Leaf) but because that was its highest place. Compare 22.170–3, where Zeus pities Hektor 'who had burned many ox-thighs for him on the peaks of Ida or at other times on the very highest part of the city, ἐν πόλει ἀκροτάτη'. Both Priam's palace and Hektor's own house are in the upper part of the town, ἐν πόλει ἄκρῃ, according to 317, but that is probably not where Hekabe envisages her son praying.

258–60 A typically constructed sentence: main clause in the first v. (here, with an associated ὄφρα-clause; ὄφρα κε = 'till I have brought', Leaf), dependent clause in the second, qualifying runover-word cumulation in the third, its function to introduce a fresh point. Tone and syntax are heavily persuasive, with Hekabe behaving like a true mother as bT observe. Ameis–Hentze rightly noted that 260 ὀνήσεαι is fut. indic. and no longer depends on 259 ὡς, and this too adds to the coaxing tone: 'Wait for me to bring wine for you, to make libation to Zeus... and then you shall benefit yourself, too, by taking a drink.' The last phrase, a remarkable conversion of the v-e formula αἴ κε πίθηαι, has further persuasive overtones.

261–2   Hekabe rounds off her maternal remarks with what resembles a proverb; this she cleverly relates to her son's special case by sound rather than logic, through the anaphora of κεκμη- and the continuing alliteration of μ's. In 261 μέγα goes adverbially with (ϝ)οῖνος ἀ(ϝ)έξει, itself another probably alliterative effect. It is wholly unjustified to suspect 262 (with Nauck, Leaf, Shipp, *Studies* 255) on the grounds that τύνη is elsewhere (5 × *Il.*) first word, if only because ὡς hardly counts in this respect. On ἔτῃσι see 239n.

263   Hektor retains his fullest formular description as μέγας κορυθαίολος, though it is not really appropriate to this conversation with his mother – see on 359.

264–85   Hektor makes three points in reply: (i) I cannot stay and drink wine, (ii) but you are to organize prayers to Athene, (iii) while I go and find my wretched brother. The tone throughout is practical, harsh at times rather than filial.

264–5   His opening vv. balance Hekabe's concluding pair in assonance and alliteration, with | μή ... | μή (ϝ)οῖνον ἄ(ϝ)ειρε and the recurring m-sounds; for | μή μοι cf. 9.612. ἄειρε may imply little more than 'bring' after 258 ἐνείκω; 'offer', in the sense of raising the cup for him to drink from, cannot be excluded. For 265 ἀπογυιώσῃς μένεος cf. γυιόω 'make lame' at 8.402 and 416. — The differing effects of wine were probably a familiar *topos*, perhaps of Near Eastern origin. Hektor uses any available excuse, since he is in a hurry.

266–8   The two integral enjambments after a run of end-stopped vv. help convey a sense of pious indignation, strengthened by 267 οὐδέ πῃ ἔστι (cf. 24.71). There is of course no reason why Hektor should not wash his hands (a normal ritual preliminary; Telemakhos does so before prayer at *Od.* 2.261) – which is perhaps why he adds the more drastic claim of being spattered with blood and gore.

269–70   The wording varies that of 87, with a necessary change of epithet for Athene (cf. 287, and 87n. for γεραιάς) and σὺν θυέεσσιν as an important addition. It is hard not to refer it to the oxen of 93 and 274; if so, the present version is the only one which graphically envisages the animals as processing up to the temple with the women. Yet θύος would be being used loosely, since elsewhere in Homer it applies to minor burnt-offerings, not animals. ἱερεύειν σφάζειν ῥέζειν (ἔρδειν) are the Homeric verbs for animal sacrifice (so bT), whereas 9.219f. θῦσαι and θυηλάς, 9.499 and *Od.* 15.261 θύεα refer to other burnt offerings; so West on *Erga* 338, but cf. θυσίαισι ... ἔρδοντες at *HyDem* 368f. There is in any case some uncertainty over when the sacrifice is to happen: at 93 and 115 it is to be promised, ὑποσχέσθαι; at 308, when Theano makes the actual prayer, she undertakes to sacrifice the oxen 'straightaway, now', αὐτίκα νῦν, if the goddess grants the prayer (which does not happen).

271–8 = 90–7, with necessary adjustments into direct speech, i.e. 271f. ὅς τίς τοι…ἔστιν for 90f. ὅς οἱ δοκέει…εἶναι (with τοι for οἱ again in 272), and 273 τὸν θές for 92 θεῖναι. See on 86–98, especially under (4); also on 87–98, 87–94, 90–2, 93–4, 94–101.

274 The imper. inf. is here retained unchanged, unlike e.g. θές just before; ὑπόσχεο would have involved a certain amount of recasting, not difficult in itself but undesirable, especially given the free use of such infinitives elsewhere.

277 In the equivalent v. 96 Aristarchus (Did/A) preferred ὥς κεν, a reading found in a small minority of MSS, but no such doubt is recorded here. The two vv. were obviously identical and αἵ κεν should be read in both.

279 This v. is repeated in ring-form after 269, to round off Hektor's instructions and lead on to his own movements.

280–3 His rising agitation as he thinks of his brother Paris is suggested in the interrupted syntax and broken rhythms of these vv., with ἔρχευ (Ionic contraction of ἔρχεο) held over in integral enjambment, which is repeated in 281 and (more weakly) in 282, and ὥς κέ…χάνοι left as an almost incoherent interjection. As often the final v. seems flowing by contrast.

280 μετελεύσομαι ὄφρα καλέσσω: cf. the probable adaptation at *Od.* 17.52, ἐσελεύσομαι [*sc.* ἀγορὴν] ὄφρα καλέσσω (with the object of καλέσσω in the next v.). καλέσσω here means 'summon', simply.

281–3 Hektor instantly doubts whether Paris will consent to listen, and this leads to the wish (similar to 4.182) 'may the earth gape for him αὖθι, where he stands'. For he is a 'great woe' like Helen at 3.50; compare 22.421f. where Priam says of Akhilleus that Peleus ἔτρεφε πῆμα γενέσθαι | Τρωσί, very much as here. τοῖό τε παισίν | recurs at 4.28; thus the language is thoroughly Homeric.

281 ὡς with the optative for a wish is regular, as e.g. at 18.107, but accompanying κε is not (and *Od.* 17.546 presents no real parallel). Emendation to δέ with Bekker, approved by Leaf, is unacceptable; κέ presumably emphasizes the wish's unreality.

284–5 These vv. repeat and develop the wish of 281f.; 284 is straightforward (understanding e.g. δῶμα with Ἄϊδος, cf. 8.367), but the text of 285 is in disarray. The vulgate reading, retained in OCT, is ἀτέρπου, surely a solecism even allowing for poetic licence, the Homeric form (1 × *Il.*, 3 × *Od.*) being not ἄτερπος but ἀτερπής – in any case Willcock is right that the expression would be 'rather mannered for

Homer'. Aristarchus (Arn/A) simply divided differently, ἄτερ που, but that gives an exceptionally clumsy sense. Zenodotus (Did/AT) on the other hand had grasped the nettle by reading φίλον ἦτορ for φρέν᾽ ἀτέρπου, a blatant conjecture no doubt; but something of the kind was demanded by a corruption that seems to have been firmly established by his time. One has some sympathy with Leaf, who wrote that 'The whole end of the speech, from 281, has something strange about it in sentiment as well as expression, and doubts must go further than the word ἀτέρπου'; but Akhilleus' speech to the embassy at 9.308–429, and especially 335–45 and 372–8, shows the degree to which Homer can contrive to make extreme passion distort language.

286–96 Hekabe tells her servants to assemble the womenfolk while she goes to her storeroom (θάλαμος can mean that as well as a bedroom) to choose the finest dress for Athene. The narrative is simple and the style relaxed, with much cumulated detail about the dress and its history. The scene as a whole is varied at *Od.* 15.99ff.

286 Hekabe has been in the courtyard and now goes into the palace.

288 The v. recurs twice (with αὐτός for αὐτή): (i) of Priam at 24.191f., who goes down to the same storeroom (as it must be), which is of cedar-wood and with a high ceiling; κατεβήσετο shows it to be envisaged as a basement, since neither Priam nor Hekabe is upstairs. There he takes out as ransom for Hektor's body a dozen each of dresses, cloaks, rugs, shawls and tunics, as well as ten talents of gold, two bronze tripod-cauldrons, four basins and a valuable Thracian cup. (ii) Of Menelaos at *Od.* 15.99, accompanied by Helen and Megapenthes; he takes a cup, Megapenthes a silver bowl and Helen a dress that she herself has made, all as gifts for Telemakhos. That whole context seems to be modelled on the present one: apart from 99 = 288 here, 106–8 ~ 293–5, and 105 partly matches 289 (see n.). — On κηώεντα (cf. 483 κηώδεϊ...κόλπῳ) see Chantraine, *Dict.* s.v. κηώδης and Hoekstra on *Od.* 15.99. The conventional translation 'fragrant' is probably correct, the meaning arising from *κῆϝος (cf. καίω), fragrant wood for burning.

Aristarchus had a different v. altogether (recorded in P 1 and a few medieval MSS) in one of his editions (Did/A): ἡ δ᾽ εἰς οἶκον ἰοῦσα παρίστατο φωριαμοῖσιν, of which the latter half seems to be taken from *Od.* 15.104 and the former from 490 here. The mention of coffers is unobjectionable, quite vivid even, but the trouble is that Hekabe cannot go into the 'house' when she is already in the palace according to 286.

289 = *Od.* 15.105 as far as παμποίκιλοι (which should be the reading here with the great majority of MSS, *contra* OCT), but then οὓς κάμεν αὐτή replaces ἔργα γυναικῶν here. Some MSS read the latter in the *Od.* passage also, wrongly, since Helen refers specifically at 15.126 to her own handiwork – it is a very personal gift, as is appropriate there but not here. ἔργα γυναικῶν recurs at *Od.* 7.97, where it ends the sentence; it looks like a formula and probably is so, developed here by the cumulation of Σιδονίων in the following v. See Hoekstra *ad loc.*, who has a long but inconclusive discussion of the exact nature of πέπλοι, on which H. P. and A. J. B. Wace were properly agnostic (Wace and Stubbings, *Companion* 501).

290–2 According to Homer here Paris and Helen returned to Troy by way of Phoenicia. Herodotus at 2.116f. cites this passage (also *Od.* 4.227–30 and 4.351f., which however concern Helen with Menelaos rather) against the *Cypria* (frag. XII), which made the lovers reach Troy on the third day, and concludes correctly that the *Cypria* was not by Homer; see also Eustathius 643.1–5. Ancient critics were mystified and suggested that the diversion was to put pursuers off the scent (AbT); a storm was another obvious explanation, neither according with the bland ἐπιπλὼς εὐρέα πόντον of 291. — Aristarchus evidently accepted τάς in 290 without comment, and AbT (on 291) attributed it to Paris' fussiness that he brought back the women as well as the garments. For that is what τάς, the MS reading, unambiguously says; Welcker's τούς, referring to the garments, was approved by Leaf but has elicited curiously little response otherwise. ἄγειν is usually used of persons, but cf. 11.632 of Nestor's cup, ὃ οἴκοθεν ἦγ' ὁ γεραιός. — εὐπατέρειαν is found only here in *Il.*, but twice, of Turo and Helen, in *Od.*; it is an artificial compound formed from πατήρ, and means 'well-born' or the like; cf. Chantraine, *Dict.* s.v. πατήρ and Risch, *Wortbildung* 126.

294–5 These vv. are more detailed and striking than the equivalent description in Helenos' and then Hektor's instructions at 90f. ~ 271f., where the dress was simply 'the loveliest and largest in the palace, and the one she liked best'. Here its 'decorations', ποικίλμασιν, are probably woven (see on 3.125–7) rather than embroidered; it gleams like a star (as Akhilleus' helmet does at 19.381, cf. 6.400–1n.), and lies beneath the others – not only because as the most precious and least used it is at the bottom of the chest (so bT), but also because being at the extremity, or beyond others of its kind, was a poetical figure for something of value or beauty. So Sappho frag. 105 (*a*) L–P of the ripe apple at the top of the bough which the apple-pickers could not reach (though cf. D. L. Page, *Sappho and Alcaeus*, Oxford 1955, 121 n. 3).

296 She leaves the storeroom and is joined by the crowd of senior women, presumably outside the palace.

297 For the expression cf. 88.

298–9 Compare 89, of Hekabe, οἴξασα κληῖδι θύρας ἱεροῖο δόμοιο. For the key see on 89; the unlocking of the temple is omitted in Hektor's instruction to Hekabe at 269ff., no doubt because the poet does not wish to emphasize the change of plan. See p. 165 and the conclusion there that the introduction of Theano may reflect a historical change of practice, away from the idea of the Mycenaean ruler as high priest; certainly 300 appears to emphasize the idea of public choice. Theano is still the wife of a prominent citizen and an established Homeric character; as daughter of Kissēs and wife of Antenor she recurs at 5.70 and 11.224.

301 The ὀλολυγή is a ritual female shriek or wail, often joyous; it occurs only here in *Il.* At *Od.* 3.450 (ὀλόλυξαν) it accompanies the axe-blow that paralyses the sacrificial animal before its throat is cut (cf. Burkert, *Religion* 56, *Homo Necans* 12 and 19, with Kirk, *Entretiens Hardt* xxvii (Vandœuvres–Genève 1981) 66); cf. Aeschylus, *Sept.* 268f., ὀλολυγμὸν ἱερὸν εὐμενῆ παιώνισαν, | Ἑλληνικὸν νόμισμα θυστάδος βοῆς, with Herodotus 4.189.3. It accompanies prayer at *Od.* 4.767, where Penelope shrieks after rather than before the prayer as here; and Eurukleia is about to give the shriek when she sees the slaughtered suitors at *Od.* 22.408 and 411. — χεῖρας ἀνέσχον | as at 3.318 = 7.177 (and in a quite different sense at *Od.* 18.89); cf. 257n.

303 ~ 92 and 273; see on 90–2.

304 The conjunction of εὔχεσθαι and ἀράομαι comes only here; there is no distinction in meaning.

305–6 The vulgate reading ἐρυσίπτολι should probably be retained; the A and T scholiasts preferred ῥυσίπτολι, cf. e.g. 15.141 ῥῦσθαι, but the ἐ- is not pleonastic as they thought, see Chantraine, *Dict.* s.v. ἔρυμαι. — The prayer is less formal than usual (see e.g. on 1.37–42), and Theano proceeds without delay to an impassioned demand for Diomedes' death, going beyond what either Helenos or Hektor had envisaged (96f., 277f.). ἆξον δὴ ἔγχος, 'break his spear', is a unique expression; one is reluctant to displace emphatic ἆξον from its opening position, but van Leeuwen noted that elsewhere (100× *Il.*, 22× *Od.*) ἐγχ- does not coincide with the beginning of the metrical foot. That looks like a serious departure from the instinctive formular deployment of a common term; Payne Knight's ἔγχος δὴ ἆξον has the additional advantage of avoiding hiatus through the sensed digamma of (ϝ)ἆξον.

307–10 For αὐτίκα νῦν see on 269–70; the remainder ~ 83–5 (see on 93–4 and 94–101) and 274–6.

311–12 Aristarchus (Arn/A) athetized 311 as pointless, unusual, redundant in view of 312, and absurd in implying (but does it?) an actual physical gesture. It is true that the goddess could have refused Diomedes' death but granted the Trojans relief from him (as actually happens), just as at 16.250 Zeus grants one part of a prayer and rejects the other. V. 311 could have been added at any point, and there may be a lingering doubt over relevance and taste; but syntax, at least, is unexceptionable, the repetition both of εὐχομένη...εὔχοντο and of initial ὥς (for which see also 17.423f.) being justified by the observation that 311 ends one episode and 312 begins another, exactly as with the last v. of bk 22 and the opening one of bk 23.

312–68 While the women are at the temple Hektor proceeds to the house of Paris, who accepts his reproach and agrees to join him on his return to battle. Helen's invitation to linger is courteously declined by Hektor, who explains that he must hurry on to see his family

313–15 Meanwhile Hektor was on his way, βεβήκει, to his brother's house, which Paris himself had built with Troy's finest craftsmen; the syntax of ἀνδράσιν...ἄνδρες is awkward but acceptable.

316–17 The grouping of bedchamber, hall (or house) and courtyard loosely follows that of Priam's palace, with bedrooms somehow inside the courtyard; see on 242–50. The most important houses would naturally be in the upper town. That can be illustrated from the physical remains of an earlier Troy, for Troy II had an imposing row of six *megara*, the biggest of them (building IIA) at the highest point of the citadel. No remains of the sixth city (or Troy VIIa) survive in this area, since they were swept away with successive enlargements of Athene's temple and its surrounding colonnades in the Hellenistic and Roman eras (not to mention Schliemann's Great Trench), but it is a reasonable conjecture that the grandest dwellings would have been there too, since the city was planned on a radial basis, with surviving Troy VI houses in terraces around and below the same upper area – which is where any prehistoric sanctuary must also have been. The palace at Mycenae is likewise placed at the top of the citadel, and other Late Bronze Age sites, e.g. Athens, were similar. Indirectly Homer's description reflects the late Mycenaean age rather than the intervening centuries down to his own time, in which secular monumental building was virtually unknown.

318 ἔνθ': the poet is at pains to make these quite complicated movements through the city absolutely clear; compare 237, 242, 286–8, 297, 313, 365f., 369f., 390–5, 495, 503–5, 515f., and see on 242–50 *init.*

319–20 Hektor's 11-cubit spear is mentioned again only at 8.494, in a repetition of these vv. when he addresses the Trojan assembly. Aristarchus found the passage more appropriate there, in the more martial context, against Zenodotus (Arn/A on 8.493). Choice of one or the other as original is not of course necessary; here the great spear is obviously designed, with its gleaming tip and golden ring, to give him a special glow of authority as he confronts his unheroic brother. — It is Akhilleus that traditionally had a huge spear, the heavy Pelian ash of 16.141–3 etc.; Aias wields one of 22 cubits (twice the length of Hektor's) at 15.677f., but that is a special naval weapon and not a regular infantry one. The πόρκης, a term of unknown derivation, is evidently a ring that tightened the socket of the bronze spearhead onto the shaft; it would have to be of bronze or iron (see Lorimer, *HM* 260) and could have been gilt, though the epithet χρύσεος (also in *Little Iliad* frag. 5) is again, presumably, to make it sound more regal.

321–4 The θάλαμος, often a bedroom as at 3.391, sometimes a storeroom as at 288, must here be a living-room where Helen can work surrounded by her maids and Paris can bring his armour. The τεύχεα consist of shield and corslet, with the bow mentioned separately – all three would not be carried together, at least according to 3.17f. and 332f. (so Ameis–Hentze). Paris is handling his armour and touching his bow: on ἔπω see Brent Vine, *Indogermanische Forschungen* 93 (1988) 52ff., *contra* Chantraine; ἀφάω is related to ἀφή and ἅπτομαι, only here uncompounded in early Greek but cf. ἀμφαφάασθαι (etc.), 6 × *Od.* (T records the eccentric reading τόξα φόωντα, not of course Aristarchan (Nic/A) but surviving in the **h** family of MSS). The implication may be not that he is simply playing with the armour ('turning it over and admiring it', Leaf, cf. bT), but rather that he is indeed, as he claims at 337–9, preparing to return to the fight. Meanwhile Helen was enjoining, κέλευε, work on her maidservants – the addition of περικλυτά to ἔργα confirms that this was spinning and weaving (cf. 490f., *Od.* 7.105f.) rather than more basic household tasks. Despite Paris' claim, the whole scene is obviously relaxed and lacks urgency.

325 = 3.38, also of Hektor and Paris, q.v. with n.; it is phrased as a rising threefolder, and earlier versions of the text would have had νείκεσσε ϝιδὼν αἰσχροῖσι ϝέπεσσι. 'Shameful words' recur in 13.768, of the same principals, and 24.238, where they precede an opprobrious address in the following v. Here the rebuke, shameful enough in itself, will be less overtly violent (but does not justify Aristarchus' censure, Arn/A, of negligent composition).

326–41 The brief remarks exchanged by Hektor (6 vv.) and Paris (9 vv.) are typical of both men and resemble those at 3.38–75, where Hektor reproached Paris for his despicable behaviour and Paris excused himself. Hektor is less obviously incensed here; his brother's reply is as calm and ingratiating as before.

326–31 Hektor begins and ends with a practical whole-v. sentence: 'You are wrong to sulk' and 'Come on now, lest the city burns.' These are separated by a more passionate statement of the issues, in which, similarly, the interrupted and enjambed central pair of vv. (328 and 329) is enclosed by flowing ones (327 and 330), the last a rising threefolder: (i) our troops are dying and the city is in danger; (ii) the war is for your sake; (iii) you yourself would reproach another who was holding back. Here (iii) is substituted, as an appeal to Paris' better nature, for the expected and harsher conclusion 'therefore you should be fighting harder than anyone else'.

326 οὐ μὲν καλά: for the idiom compare 8.400. Hektor's mention of χόλος comes as a surprise (as it did to Aristarchus, Arn/A), since he might be expected to mention cowardice, slackness or effeminacy as his brother's motive; compare his reproach at 3.39–45. Yet at 521f. he will concede that Paris is not contemptible in battle, is ἄλκιμος even. That is an attempt to be conciliatory, and here, too, he seems anxious not to offend (see preceding n.); the city is, after all, in crisis. Emphatic τόνδ' might seem to suggest a more specific cause for resentment, like Antenor's proposal at 7.347–53, q.v. with nn.; that is improbable, but see e.g. Fenik, *TBS* 122, 238. At 335f. Paris says it is not so much through anger and indignation Τρώων that he stays home: does that mean anger *at* the Trojans or anger *belonging to* them, i.e. against himself? The Trojans were furious with him after the duel in book 3, see especially 3.451–4, where they would gladly have handed him over to Menelaos; but then he might equally have resented that fury (as Arn/A suggests), and that is probably what his χόλος refers to here.

328–9 | μαρνάμενοι is a typical use of the cumulated runover-word to lead to a new subject or idea. ἀϋτή τε πτόλεμός τε | as at 1.492, 16.63; it is the war rather than its din that can be said to 'blaze around' the city (-δέδηε, intrans. perf. of δαίω).

331 Again the emphatic vision of the burning city. 'Burn in blazing fire' recurs of the Achaean ships at 11.667; θέρηται = 'is hot' (cf. θερμός), 'burns'; πυρὸς δηίοιο *sic* is found 5× *Il.*; for the partitive gen. see Chantraine, *GH* II, 52, Monro, *HG* 146, also 16.80–1n. It is debated whether the two Homeric applications of δήϊος, as 'blazing' and 'hostile', arise from different stems; or whether the former, with obvious connexion with δαίω, leads to the latter or *vice versa* (so Risch, *Wortbildung* 105): Chantraine, *Dict.* s.v.

332–41 Paris begins his reply as he did on an earlier occasion at 3.59; but does not continue here, as he had at 3.60–3, by calling Hektor relentless, since the present criticisms are less violent. Typical excuses follow: his unspecified sorrow, and that he was on the point of returning to the fight anyway – encouraged by Helen, he has the grace to add. Then the closely enjambed short statements of 337–9 give an effect, not of indignation or urgency as with Hektor at 327–30, but of hurried invention culminating in the complacent *sententia* about victory. Finally he briskly tells Hektor to wait for him, or that he will easily catch him up.

333–4 'Since you have rebuked me in due measure and not beyond it' – in the equivalent passage at 3.59 the sense is interrupted there, but Lehrs and van Leeuwen were surely hypercritical in suspecting 334. There is no good reason why τούνεκα should not take up 333 ἐπεί (*contra* Leaf), even though the apodosis to an ἐπεί-clause can be missing as at 13.68–70. V. 334 is a formular one, thoroughly suitable for the context and typically disingenuous: '*You* have been fair, so I will respond likewise, and deserve your full attention.'

335–6 The repetition of τοι after 334, the shift of construction after τόσσον, the 'curious' (Shipp, *Studies* 256) dative νεμέσσι and the vivid and unusual ἀχεῖ προτραπέσθαι ('turn myself headlong to grief') all exemplify the lively colloquialism of these exchanges.

337 For μαλακοῖς ἐπέεσσιν see on 325 αἰσχροῖς ἐπέεσσι. Paris seems to be hinting at a contrast between Helen's tone and Hektor's.

338–9 No doubt her words to him were not as 'soft', μαλακοί, as Paris says; his own response, dubiously credible, is suggested in artificially humble language, 'and this seems to me too to be the better course'. He finishes with a typical piece of self-deceiving sententiousness, 'victory goes now to one, now to another', expressed in vague, abstract and epigrammatic terms; for the use of (ἐπ)αμείβεσθαι compare 15.684, θρῴσκων ἄλλοτ' ἐπ' ἄλλον ἀμείβεται. He thus attributes success in battle to more or less random factors, discounting his personal responsibility and performance.

340–1 | ἀλλ' ἄγε νῦν ἐπίμεινον is addressed 2 × *Od.* to a guest; the syntax may reflect a deliberate coaxing tone, 'but wait a little, let me don my armour' (as Willcock suggests *ad loc.*), rather than the epic tendency to parataxis (as against e.g. an ὄφρα-clause, though not as at *Od.* 4.587f. *pace* Ameis–Hentze), illustrated by this v. in countless grammars. The tone of these last 4 vv., each punctuated at the central caesura, is ingratiating but consciously efficient; here the alternative Paris offers demonstrates how quick he will be.

342 Hektor does not reply: the v. recurs exactly at 5.689 (where he is in too much of a hurry to respond to Sarpedon), and with different name–epithet phrases at 1.511 (where Zeus is not snubbing Thetis but pondering her request), 4.401 (where Diomedes is too gentlemanly to defend himself against Agamemnon's reproach), 8.484 (where Here is silent in response to a threatening speech from Zeus) and 21.478 (where Apollo similarly does not defend himself against Artemis' abuse). Hektor may well be showing his disdain in a parallel application to these; that gives a strong sense, supported perhaps by the next v. The formulation has, of course, a purely functional use in tripartite conversations in which A finishes addressing B, then C intervenes, as at 4.401–3 and 21.478–80.

343 Helen's 'soothing words' could indeed suggest that Hektor is showing displeasure. As often in such introductory descriptions, her words are not immediately and directly applied to soothing (or whatever) but start with a different topic – here, self-reproach; that was the probable reason for an ancient variant, δῖα γυναικῶν for μειλιχίοισι (Did/A).

344–58 Helen's address to Hektor flows smoothly, with long and well-formed sentences. Enjambment is correspondingly frequent, being progressive (6× in the 15-verse speech) or periodic (2×) rather than integral (3×); strong internal punctuation comes only at 353. Her tone is depressed rather than passionate, in contrast e.g. with her reproach of Paris at 3.428–36. The initial self-denunciation resembles the way she speaks of herself to Priam in the Teichoscopia, 3.172–5, and the apparent calmness is conspicuous once again there when she identifies Aias and Idomeneus but cannot see her brothers at 3.229–42. It was noted on 3.234–5 that her whole speech 'is cast in a plain cumulative style...with uninterrupted verses and frequent progressive enjambment. Her manner...is melancholy rather than agitated.' The similarity in demeanour to the Helen of bk 6 here is quite striking, a further indication that the monumental composer was responsible for both scenes in the finest detail (cf. A. Parry, 'Have we Homer's Iliad?', *YCS* 20, 1966, 197–201). See also on 24.762ff.

344 Compare 3.180 with n., where δαήρ -ερ (there, not her Trojan brother-in-law but her legitimate Achaean one) and Helen herself as somehow bitch-like (there, κυνώπιδος) recur. She will repeat her description of herself as κύων at 356. κυνὸς ὄμματ' ἔχων, of Agamemnon, signified shamelessness at 1.225 (q.v. with n.) and similarly elsewhere, but such terms may be less violent in their application to women: as West notes on Hesiod, *Erga* 67, the bitch-like woman at Semonides 7.12–20 is merely inquisitive, noisy and unmanageable. — The two epithets that follow have won more comment for their spelling than for their content. ὀκρυοέσσης is meaningless (and distinct from ὀκριόεις, 'jagged', 4× *Il.*, 1× *Od.*), and Payne Knight pointed out that the correct word-division, with restoration of the uncontracted -οο form of the genitive (Chantraine, *GH* I, 45), is κακομηχάνοο κρυοέσσης, cf. κρυόεις, 'chilling' or 'frightful', as of personified Attack and Rout at 5.740 and 9.2. Leumann, *HW* 49f., argued that although ἐπιδημίοο κρυόεντος as an old description of war should be read at 9.64 (cf. Hesiod, *Theog.* 936 πολέμῳ κρυόεντι), the false division had already taken place, and the bastard form ὀκρυόεις been accepted, by the date of the present passage.

345–8 Helen's regrets tend to take the form of these ὀφέλλειν constructions, also at 350; see 3.173 with n., where she wishes she had preferred to die rather than run off with Paris. Here she wishes she had been swept into oblivion as soon as she was born.

346–7 At *Od.* 20.61–5 the unhappy Penelope prays that either Artemis would slay her with an arrow, or a storm (θύελλα again) would come and carry her off (| οἴχοιτο προφέρουσα, cf. | οἴχεσθαι προφέρουσα here) and cast her at the mouth of Okeanos (65). There the poet continues 'as when storms seized up the daughters of Pandareos... [77f.] and the Harpies snatched them up and gave them to serve the hateful Furies', which means that they disappeared (cf. 79). This develops the basic idea of storm-winds and interprets them as the mythical Harpies, who are also said to have snatched away Odysseus (*Od.* 1.241). Thus the Odyssean poet uses the same basic idea and some of the same terminology but relates it specifically to the Harpies (known to the main composer of *Il.* also, since the Harpy Podarge is mentioned at 16.150); incidentally ἅρπυιαι ἀνηρείψαντο |, 3 × *Od.*, breaks 'Hermann's Bridge' and is rhythmically inelegant, but see S. West on *Od.* 1.241. Here the storm-wind would have carried Helen to mountain or sea (347); the latter recalls the mouth of Okeanos at *Od.* 20.65, the former perhaps the traditional place (in later literature, but the idea and practice must be old) for the exposure of unwanted babies.

348 ἀπόερσε, aor. indic. without κε, is part of the past impossible wish after ὄφελ'; on ἀπό(ϝ)ερσε, 'snatched away', see Chantraine, *Dict.* s.v. ἀπούρας. The first hemistich again has an Odyssean flavour, containing the only Iliadic instance of elided κῦμ' against 29 × unelided (as e.g. in the formula of 347), whereas *Od.* has three instances, not exactly similar but all rhyming with the present use: κῦμ' ἐπὶ χέρσου | (2 ×), κῦμ' ἀποέργει |. — It may be that bT are right in saying that the formular phrase τάδε ἔργα is a convenient way of glossing over the shameful past.

349 τεκμήραντο, 'decreed'; see on τέκμωρ at 1.526.

350–1 Her second and less remote wish is that she had got a better man; ἄκοιτις, literally 'bed-mate', is often used of a legal wife, e.g. by Hektor of Andromakhe at 374, but does not necessarily imply one. Paris' fault according to her is that he takes no notice of public moral indignation (351); Helen herself must have incurred some of it, as she recognizes almost hysterically with her bitch-language of 344 and 356, but at least she is aware of it.

352–3 A decisive condemnation, from the initial and derisive 'this man here' (compare Hektor's τοῦτον at 363; they speak as though Paris were not even present) to the contemptuous definition of his mental and moral inadequacy. Its comprehensive nature is reflected in οὔτ' ἄρ νῦν... οὔτ' ἄρ' ὀπίσσω, made almost deliberately clumsy through the harsh but necessary enjambment of ἔσσονται as runover-word. Some parallel to the idea and its expression can be found at 3.107–9 (see on 3.108–10). — ἐπαυρήσεσθαι, 'will enjoy the fruits', ironically, i.e. of his criminal folly, as at 1.410. ὀΐω is also ironic, or threatening rather, as e.g. at 5.350, cf. 1.169–71n.; it occurs at the v-e 23/32 × *Il.*

354 The first hemistich recurs at *Od.* 16.25; ἀλλ' ἄγε is a frequent introductory formula, 29 × *Il.*, even commoner in *Od.* often followed by νῦν or δή. δίφρος meaning 'stool' recurs at 3.424 (again in Helen's house) and 24.578, but is commoner in domestic scenes in *Od.* The *Iliad* mostly uses the word as 'chariot' (5.727–8n.), preferring the grander θρόνος (14 ×) for divine and heroic seats, cf. κλισμός for women's; see further S. Laser, *Arch. Hom.* P 34ff., 45ff.

355 φρένας ἀμφιβέβηκεν also at *Od.* 8.541, but of ἄχος which is more natural; πόνος is strained here, though cf. 77f.

356 On κυνός see 344n. Several MSS read ἀρχῆς for ἄτης, misled no doubt by argument over 3.100 (see n. there). Helen here shares responsibility with Paris, though Hektor had blamed only him (bT).

357–8 Compare 2.119, where Agamemnon says retreat is αἰσχρὸν...καὶ ἐσσομένοισι πυθέσθαι; *Od.* 8.580 (the gods ordained disaster at Troy) ἵνα ἦσι καὶ ἐσσομένοισιν ἀοιδή; and *Od.* 24.200f., (Klutaimestra) στυγερὴ δέ τ' ἀοιδή | ἔσσετ' ἐπ' ἀνθρώπους. ἀοίδιμος, 'subject of song', occurs only here in Homer but also at *HyAp* 299. Troy, Helen and Klutaimestra were obviously among the subjects of earlier poems on which Homer built (cf. the κλέα ἀνδρῶν of 9.189, *Od.* 8.73, Hesiod, *Theog.* 100), but it is interesting to find traces of the singer's sense of vocation in preserving these legendary *exempla*.

359 The v. of address is that used by Hektor to his mother in the parallel scene at 263; in neither case is the singer tempted to replace the formidable μέγας κορυθαίολος by the less martial φαίδιμος (29 × of Hektor, cf. Parry, *MHV* 39). The latter occurs in a shorter speech-formula at 16.858, προσηύδα φαίδιμος Ἕκτωρ |, and the present v. could of course have been easily recast to accommodate it or something similar. Yet | τὸν/τὴν/τοὺς δ' ἠμείβετ' ἔπειτα + epithet–name group is firmly established as an answering-formula; moreover Hektor's helmet will come into its own, in a paradoxically peaceful way, in the scene with his baby son at 469ff.

360–8 . Hektor is courteous but decisive: (i) Do not try to make me stay, since I must return to my hard-pressed troops; (ii) but rather urge on Paris to catch me up; (iii) for I must see my family, perhaps for the last time. The urgent initial v. fires off four distinct thoughts in each 'ideal' colon: 'Do not make me sit / Helen / though you mean kindly / you will not persuade me.' The rest consists of four 2-v. sentences, of which the first maintains the spasmodic tone of the opening, with runover Τρώεσσ' almost violently emphatic; the others, echoing a changing mood, are more relaxed, their balance marked by threefolders at 364 and 366.

361 θυμὸς ἐπέσσυται (3 × *Il. sic*) is strengthened by ἤδη, meaning that his mind is already made up. ὄφρ' ἐπαμύνω is tantamount to an infinitive as in the similar *Od.* 15.66, ἤδη γάρ μοι θυμὸς ἐέλδεται οἴκαδ' ἱκέσθαι; cf. 4.465f. and 5.690f. for the ὄφρα-construction after another verb of strong feeling, λελιημένος.

363 Is there a hint in the reciprocal form that Hektor, courtesy notwithstanding, assigns to Helen a little of the blame?

366 For the association of wife and οἰκῆες see on 5.412–15, and for the structure cf. 5.688 εὐφρανέειν ἄλοχόν τε φίλην καὶ νήπια τέκνα, also ἄστυ τε καὶ Τρώων ἀλόχους καὶ νήπια τέκνα (at 6.95, 276, 310). Here Hektor does not need to see the *city* since he is there already; οἰκῆας provides a convenient alternative opening. The servants are an integral part of the οἶκος, but their apparent priority is the more or less accidental result of formular adaptation (rather than, as bT suggest, a case of duty before pleasure).

367–8 His final words are full of pathos and foreboding, not least in the placing of σφιν and the refrain of ἔτι and αὖτις: a reminder of the city's doom and a prelude to Andromakhe's fears when at last he finds her. The ὑπότροπος phraseology will be repeated more brutally at 501f. ἤδη in 368 underlines the all-powerful influence of the gods as he senses they may already have decided his fate.

369–502 Hektor does not find Andromakhe in their house; hastening to the Scaean gate, he meets her with their son. She begs him not to risk his life; he gently tells her where his duty lies. The baby is frightened by his helmet, and husband and wife part with tenderness and sorrow, she to return to her household where she mourns his impending death

369–70 369 = 116; the singer does not concern himself with varying such functional statements, just as 370 will recur at 497. Houses as well as towns can be 'well inhabited', 'good to dwell in', cf. 415.

371 His not finding Andromakhe at home comes as a small shock to the listener as well as to Hektor, and helps prevent his carefully detailed movements from becoming routine. The reason for her absence highlights the tension in the city and the crisis outside the walls.

373 Andromakhe is on the tower above and to the side of the Scaean gate, already implied at 3.149 and a place of ill omen, for it is from there that Priam will see Akhilleus approaching at 21.526f. Such towers are conspicuous beside the surviving eastern and southern gates of late Troy VI, see pp. 47f. — 'Wailing and lamenting' seems rather overdone of Andromakhe, who is unhappy but controlled when Hektor finds her; it is a phrase used of Patroklos' ψυχή at 23.106, and applies more aptly to the Trojan women generally.

374–80 Hektor's enquiry to the women servants is expressed in curiously stilted terms.

375 The description of these actions finds close parallels in *Od.* (e.g. at 20.128, 8.433), where household scenes are commoner. It is wrong to decide too exactly (*pace* Ameis–Hentze), on the basis of such other scenes, which threshold Hektor is now standing on.

376 Similarly the demand for an accurate answer is predominantly Odyssean (the only close Iliadic parallel being in an ironic address at 14.470), partly but not wholly because the eliciting of special information is more frequent there; see on 379–80. Thus νημερτέα etc. (from negative νη- and ἁμαρτάνω: 'not missing the mark') occurs 20 × *Od.*, 5 × *Il.* The servants will vary the expression (for metrical reasons) at 382 with ἀληθέα μυθήσασθαι (3 × *Od.*, only here *Il.*; ἀληθέα etc. 15 × *Od.* against 4 × *Il.*).

377 The question begins abruptly but takes on literary colouring with λευκώλενος and even ἐκ μεγάροιο, since the poet has simply put the wording of his own narrative at 371 into the speaker's mouth ('the epithet is the poet's, not his character's', bT). Speakers can and do use standard decorative epithets, but here a certain artificiality is apparent. λευκώλενος is regular for Here at the v-e (24/28 × *Il.*), but is used *sic* of Andromakhe at 24.723 as well as 371 here. Otherwise it is applied to Helen at 3.121, but more generally in *Od.* – to Helen, Nausikaa and Arete as well as to maidservants. Thus an almost hymnodic term is gradually extended to more general use.

378 The repetition of πη, now as an enclitic, is unusual and effective, and specifying different relatives-by-marriage maintains the air of precision. γαλόῳ are husband's sisters (cf. 3.122), εἰνάτερες husband's brothers' wives (εἰνατέρων ἐϋπέπλων recurs at 24.769), part of the terminology of the Indo-European system which carefully distinguished the husband's kin (Chantraine, *Dict.* s.vv.).

379–80 ἔνθα περ ἄλλοι | is formular (2 × *Il.*, 4 × *Od.*), with ἔνθα περ *sic* 2 × *Od.* and ἄλλοι (etc.) common at the v-e. On the other hand Trojan women are not elsewhere described as ἐϋπλόκαμοι as in 380, nor is this appropriate here; it is a serviceable epithet used elsewhere of minor figures and maidservants. But, as with λευκώλενος in 377, the application is widened in *Od.*, and its association there no less than 7 × with δεινὴ θεός (for which in *Il.* cf. only the slightly different 5.839), as e.g. in the thrice-used Κίρκη ἐϋπλόκαμος δεινὴ θεὸς αὐδήεσσα, makes it fair to categorize Hektor's short speech here as distinctly Odyssean in manner; see also on 376 and 377. That suggests either that the encounter with the maidservants has been elaborated, perhaps rhapsodically, in an Odyssean style, or more probably that the monumental composer himself could draw on predominantly Odyssean expressions and ideas even when his subject (as in ship-scenes, see on 1.312 and 434) did not particularly require it. Yet δεινὴν θεόν is well chosen for Athene in present circumstances.

381–5 The 'bustling housekeeper' upsets any further Odyssean expectations, since her regular description in the later epic is as αἰδοίη ταμίη (7 ×, *sic*). That could have been used here, except that *Il.* reserves αἰδοῖος etc. for aristocratic figures (15 ×), and prefers ὀτρηρός here, as also of heralds, quite appropriately. — The first half of her reply repeats the terms of Hektor's enquiry with necessary adaptations (ἀληθέα for νημερτέα, -ασθαι for -ασθε, οὔτε... οὔτ' for ἠέ... ἦ). This standard oral practice lends an antiphonic and almost theatrical quality to the exchange, which might indeed require some kind of special emphasis to justify the crossing and recrossing of the city and the otherwise abortive visit to Hektor's home.

386–9 The second part of the reply develops the narrative information of 372f.; the tower is 'the great tower of Ilios', and Andromakhe's precise motive for leaving is added: she has heard that the Trojans are being worn down and that the enemy has great κράτος, domination – a slightly laboured combination of μέγα κράτος ἐγγυαλίξω | etc. and τοῦ γὰρ κράτος ἐστὶ μέγιστον | etc., both formular. Ilios' initial digamma is ignored, as at 5.204 and elsewhere – no excuse for van Leeuwen's unlikely μέγα νήπιε instead. She has rushed to the fortifications like a madwoman (cf. 132 μαινομένοιο), a maenad that is, just as she will μαινάδι ἴση at 22.46off., when she runs out of her palace to the tower as she suddenly realizes Hektor must be dead. Deliberate cross-references by the singer over long intervals are often implausibly urged by scholars of the printed text, but in this case the echo is unmistakable and the poet's foreshadowing both subtle and pathetic.

388–9 ἀφικάνει, present with perfect meaning; δή preceding implies 'must have arrived'. She might have had two servants with her, as at 3.143 and even 22.450 and 461; here she (or the poet) just needs the baby and her nursemaid.

390–1 Hektor rushes out of the house and retraces his steps through the streets; these are ἐϋκτιμένας, a formular epithet but maintaining the stress on the quality of the city and its buildings (cf. 370 δόμους εὖ ναιετάοντας, with n., 386 πύργον... μέγαν Ἰλίου, 392 μέγα ἄστυ), both to dignify Troy and Hektor's mission there and in contrast with its impending doom.

392 Initial εὖτε is often asyndetic, cf. Chantraine, *GH* II, 254.

393 Again the careful description of the different stages of his passage. ἔμελλε surely does not imply that he was about to return to the field of battle at this moment, and would have done so had not his wife intercepted him, as Willcock and others have thought; merely that he was eventually to pass through the gate and out of the city once again. It is inconceivable that, having been told precisely where Andromakhe was, he should rush past without even looking for her.

394–9 Andromakhe comes running to meet him, i.e. having descended from the tower; she is ἄλοχος πολύδωρος (see on 251–2), probably a wife who brought many gifts in the form of a dowry (though cf. 22.472) rather than merely a generous one. The brief narrative is a striking instance of both ring-composition and cumulative technique:

394 she came to meet him
395 Andromakhe did – daughter of Eetion
396 Eetion who dwelt under Mt Plakos
397 in Thebes-under-Plakos, ruling Cilicians;
398 his daughter was Hektor's wife –
399 she came to meet him…

395–7 Eetion, king of Thebe, is Andromakhe's father and mentioned quite often in *Il.* Akhilleus sacked Lurnessos and Thebe and captured Briseis in the former, Khruseis in the latter (1.366–9), after slaying Eetion himself and his seven sons as Andromakhe will recall at 416–28. Her mother was captured and later ransomed; Andromakhe had married Hektor by this time (cf. 22.471f.) and was safe in Troy. Among the loot from Thebe is the phorminx played by Akhilleus at 9.188, his horse Pedasos at 16.152f. and an iron weight offered by him as a prize at 23.826f. and previously thrown by Eetion. In other words, the sack of Thebe had already been elaborated in some detail, and perhaps before Homer's time; see also on 425–8.

Eetion's name is probably non-Greek (von Kamptz, *Personennamen* 135 and 372; it is applied fleetingly to two other characters, a Trojan at 17.575 and 590 and an Imbrian at 21.43). Thebe gave its name to a plain between Adramuttion and Antandros (Herodotus 7.42.1) and has been identified with a Bronze Age and later site at Mandra Tepe (cf. Cook, *Troad* 267; Strabo 13.612) just inland from Edremit–Adramuttion. Plakos was presumably a southern spur of Ida; the scholia reported various guesses about its name and that of Thebe itself. Finally these Kilikes, only here and at 415, are clearly distinct from those of S–E Asia Minor; compare Pandaros' Lycians, also in the Troad and also different from those of the south coast (2.826–7n.).

396 Ἠετίων is an emotive epanalepsis, noted by Aristarchus for its attraction to the case of ὅς which follows (Arn/A).

398 ἔχεθ᾽, was held as wife, with Ἕκτορι a true dat. rather than of the agent.

399–403 Again, like 395ff., a strongly cumulative sentence, this time with undisguisedly pathetic effect: she met him, and the servant accompanied her | – with the child at her bosom, still a baby (cf. 22.484) | – Hektor's son, like a star | – whom he called Skamandrios, but the others | Astuanax, for Hektor preserved the city |. The integral flow from 402 to 403 makes a typical closing contrast after the preceding progressive enjambments.

400–1 The sympathetic idea of the child held close to his nurse's breast is deepened in successive words and phrases, each touching and carefully chosen: tender-hearted (ἀταλάφρονα), a baby still, beloved child of Hektor, like a beautiful star. — Leumann, *HW* 139–41, offered a different explanation of ἀταλάφρων here, i.e. as ἀ-ταλάφρων, '*not* enduring in spirit', cf. τλάω, therefore easily frightened (as he will be by Hektor's helmet); yet the connexion with ἀταλός, 'playful', cf. ἀτιτάλλω, seems more probable (Chantraine, *Dict.* s.v.). αὕτως, as at 22.484, gives νήπιον an especially pathetic ring, maintained in the attachment implied by the patronymic Ἑκτορίδης (only here); ἀγαπητός of a child appears 4 × *Od.* but only here in *Il.*

Finally the baby is like a star, a fair one like that to which the dress chosen by Hekabe for Athene was compared at 295 for its gleaming brightness. Stars can be sinister too, as at 11.62, and Moulton, *Similes* 27, argues that since that dress was connected with a prayer rejected by the goddess, and since a prayer will be made on behalf of the baby at 476–81 – which the audience knows will not be fulfilled – then 'the foreshadowing of evil effected by the associated images is unmistakable'. That is just possible, given the tight construction of this whole Troy episode and the undoubted foreshadowing of Hektor's own doom and that of the city. Yet one main aim of these vv. is to show the child as sweet and lovable (τὸ χάριεν τοῦ παιδός, bT), and the star that is emphatically characterized as καλῷ seems chosen to emphasize that. The irony of his name (on which see next n.), and of Hektor's fast-receding ability to protect the city, remains.

402–3 Skamandros is the main river of Troy, and Hektor must have named his son after it, or its god, as an act of local piety. Simoeisios (4.474 with n.) is named after the other Trojan river, an exact parallel, cf. also Satnios (21–2n.). Astuanax looks like a special honorific name used by the other Trojans as a sign of respect for his father and his part in their defence. This is supported by Andromakhe's lament for Hektor at 22.506f.:

Ἀστυάναξ, ὃν Τρῶες ἐπίκλησιν καλέουσιν,
οἶος γάρ σφιν ἔρυσο πύλας καὶ τείχεα μακρά.

ἐπίκλησιν καλέουσιν | is used of a secondary and informal name at both 18.487 (Ἄρκτον θ᾽, ἣν καὶ ἄμαξαν ἐπίκλησιν καλέουσιν) and 22.29; cf. 7.138f. where Ereuthalion is called 'mace-man', τὸν ἐπίκλησιν κορυνήτην | ἄνδρες κικλήσκουσιν... Therefore 22.506 makes it clear that *in that passage*, at least, Astuanax is a nickname (even though Andromakhe herself had just used it at 22.500). Yet bk 22 does not mention Skamandrios at all; it is only here in the whole of *Il.* that this name is applied to Hektor's son, who is always Astuanax in the Cyclic and later tradition; and a doubt remains whether it was not *Skamandrios*, rather, that was the informal name,

especially remembered or invented for this tender passage between Hektor
and his baby son; there was a Trojan Skamandrios at 5.49. Here
frequentative καλέεσκε suggests something other than an officially given
name – significantly it is used of the nickname in the parallel case of
Kleopatre, called Alkuone by her parents at 9.562. If so, the wording of the
present passage, αὐτὰρ οἱ ἄλλοι | 'Αστυάνακτ', has been reinterpreted in its
(obvious) development at 22.506f.; what it means is that Astuanax is his
proper name, what everyone else calls him, and that it was appropriately
chosen for the son of Troy's chief protector (cf. 478 where Hektor will pray
for the child 'Ιλίου ἶφι ἀνάσσειν).

The matter is complicated, but there is no reason for suspecting the
present passage with Leaf; Plato, *Crat.* 392c–393A, confines Socrates'
remarks to the bk 22 version, but that signifies nothing in itself. — On
thematic imperf. ἐρύετο (from ἐρύομαι rather than ῥύομαι with temporal
augment) see 305–6n. and Chantraine, *GH* I, 294; the form is hardly
'isolated' and peculiar, *pace* Shipp, *Studies* 256.

404–6 The tender moment is described in the simplest traditional
language but at the same time with brilliant freshness. σιωπῇ is formular
at the v-e, 16× *Il.*, but nowhere else conveys quite the same feeling;
παρίστατο *sic* comes 7× elsewhere (with ἄγχι preceding at 5.570 and in
the formula ἄγχι παραστάς |), but the addition of δάκρυ χέουσα (itself a
formula, 9× *Il.*) gives the phrase a unique intimacy. On 405 bT remark,
with some frigidity, on the pictorial effect, γραφικῶς.

406 See on 253 for this formular v., and 440–65n., 2nd para., for the
encounter as a whole.

407–39 Encouraged no doubt by his feeling for the child, Andromakhe
makes a serious attempt to deter Hektor from returning to battle,
emphasizing her total dependence on him. Her speech falls into three parts:
(i) 407–13, emotional prediction of his death and her own misery, with
impassioned short sentences and heavy overrunning of the v-e; (ii) 414–29,
calmer and more remote narration of the death of her parents and brothers;
(iii) a second appeal to Hektor, quieter and even more moving than the
first, leading to the suggestion that he should remain on the walls and
station his troops before their weakest point. — Of these, (i) ends with the
statement that Andromakhe has no father or mother, (ii) explains why, and
(iii) begins with her saying that Hektor is father, mother and brothers to
her as well as fine husband. Thus the argument is simply but neatly
articulated.

407–13 In the opening section 4/7 vv. are integrally enjambed, another
2 progressively so; the sentences are a careful mixture of syntactic and
paratactic, with internal breaks and continuous overrunning of the v-e
suggesting excitement and unhappiness.

407–9 On δαιμόνιε see 1.561n. μένος here is not so much his physical strength as the rash and heroic attitude it gives rise to. — Helen will describe herself similarly as ἔμ' ἄμμορον *sic* at 24.773; this belongs to the special language of laments, and implies that no (good) destiny or portion remains; compare δύσμορος αἰνόμορον, of Eetion and Andromakhe respectively, at 22.481 and δυσάμμοροι of her and Hektor 4 vv. later. This part of Andromakhe's speech, not surprisingly, will have striking verbal echoes in part of her lament on Hektor's actual death at the end of bk 22:

6.408	παῖδά τε νηπίαχον	22.484	πάϊς δ' ἔτι νήπιος αὔτως
6.408	ἔμ' ἄμμορον	22.485	σύ τ' ἐγώ τε δυσάμμοροι
6.408f.	ἢ τάχα χήρη | σεῦ ἔσομαι	22.484	χήρην ἐν μεγάροισι
6.411	σεῦ ἀφαμαρτούσῃ	22.505	φίλου ἀπὸ πατρὸς ἁμαρτών
6.411	χθόνα δύμεναι	22.482f.	Ἀΐδαο δόμους ὑπὸ κεύθεσι γαίης | ἔρχεαι
6.413	ἀλλ' ἄχε'	22.483	στυγερῷ ἐνὶ πένθεσι λείπεις.

Finally, the repetition of τάχα reinforces the feeling of doom as she spells out her plight in simple and even naive terms.

410–12 κέρδιον εἴη/ἦεν/εἶναι is a common v-e formula (11 × *Il.*, 16 × *Od.*), with ἐμοὶ δέ κε κέρδιον εἴη recurring exactly at *Od.* 2.74. For σεῦ ἀφαμαρτούσῃ, like 'losing someone' in English, cf. 22.505; for χθόνα δύμεναι cf. 19 γαῖαν ἐδύτην, with comment on 18–19 *ad fin.* πότμον ἐπίσπῃς (etc.) comes 6 × *Il.*, 2 × *Od.*; ἐφέπω means 'encounter' or similar, cf. Chantraine, *Dict.* s.v. ἔπω.

413 The runover phrase ἀλλ' ἄχε' adds little to the force of οὐ...θαλπωρή in 411f., but cf. 22.483 and 407–9n. above. Its main function is to lead on to a new idea by a typical cumulative technique. πατήρ καὶ πότνια μήτηρ \| is a self-contained formular unit (10 × *Il.*, elaborated from πότνια μήτηρ, 21 ×); it may have been convenient to have the sense of οὐδέ μοι ἔστι confined to the second colon only – leaving room, therefore, for expansion from the previous sentence in the first colon.

414–28 Eetion was introduced by the singer at 395–8, and now Andromakhe describes his death. It is a pathetic and rhetorical embellishment (since Hektor, in quasi-realistic terms, must know it all), serving to illustrate her sense of abandonment as well as the tragic consequences of the city's fall. The respectful treatment of Eetion's corpse is deeply ironical in view of what Akhilleus will do to Hektor's; her brothers' death belongs to the same tale (for one is made to feel that a

longer account is being drawn on). Finally she reverts to her mother (cf.
413), whose capture and subsequent demise complete her own isolation and
dependence.

414 On ἀμός or ἁμός see Chantraine, *GH* I, 272 and *Dict.* s.v. ἡμεῖς, also
Shipp, *Studies* 79f.; it is equivalent to ἡμέτερος, perhaps after Aeolic ἄμμος
rather than a Doric form, but was later equated with ἐμός.

415–16 On these Kilikes see on 395–7 *ad fin.* Akhilleus gave his own
summary version of the attack at 1.366f. (cf. vol. I, p. 91),

ᾠχόμεθ᾽ ἐς Θήβην, ἱερὴν πόλιν Ἠετίωνος,
τὴν δὲ διαπράθομέν τε καὶ ἤγομεν ἐνθάδε πάντα,

specifying loot rather than casualties. ὑψίπυλον in 416 (2 × elsewhere of
Troy) contains an (accidental?) echo of 4.406 Θήβης ἕδος...ἑπταπύλοιο,
that is, of the more famous Boeotian Thebe(s). — κατὰ δ᾽ ἔκτανεν Ἠετίωνα
after 414 πατέρ᾽ ἀμὸν ἀπέκτανε is both emphatic and pathetic, as well as
setting up the opposition with οὐδέ μιν ἐξενάριξε in the next v.

417–20 Akhilleus treated Eetion honourably: he did not strip his
corpse, οὐδέ μιν ἐξενάριξε, but felt that would be wrong – σεβάσσατο γὰρ
τό γε θυμῷ was used of Proitos, too, at 167, see 166–7n. That was not an
invariable view: Hektor envisages removing his opponent's τεύχεα at
7.82–6 even though he intends handing over the corpse for burial and a
funeral mound; moreover nothing is said about armour at his own
cremation, 24.786f. For Elpenor at *Od.* 11.74f., however, the burning of his
armour is important:

ἀλλά με κακκῆαι σὺν τεύχεσιν, ἄσσα μοί ἐστι,
σῆμά τέ μοι χεῦαι...

It can hardly be the spread of cremation that caused a change in viewpoint
(as e.g. Leaf thought), since the burning of the armour is stressed both with
Eetion and with Elpenor; see further M. Andronikos, *Arch. Hom.* w 23f. —
σὺν ἔντεσι δαιδαλέοισιν recurs at 13.331 and 719, though not in connexion
with cremation. See 24.799 for | – ∪ ∪ σῆμ᾽ ἔχεεν, also the description of the
'pouring' of Patroklos' σῆμα at 23.256f. with 23.245–7n.

| νύμφαι ὀρεστιάδες are paralleled by *Od.* 13.356 | νύμφαι νηϊάδες and *Od.*
17.240 | νύμφαι κρηναῖαι, both followed as here by κοῦραι Διός; other
mountain nymphs are κοῦραι Διὸς αἰγιόχοιο at *Od.* 6.105 and 9.154, but
only here (and at *Hy* xix.19, cf. *HyAphr* 257) is the term ὀρεστιάδες used.
Iliadic trees are often associated with mountains, though elms are otherwise
found on the banks of Skamandros; presumably they have funereal
significance as also for Virgil at *Aen.* 6.283. They are added to confirm
Eetion as a great man, cf. the sea-nymphs at Akhilleus' funeral at *Od.* 2₄.47;
there is no need to envisage (with Wilamowitz, *IuH* 313) a particular tree-

encircled mound, known to the poetical tradition, to account for this touching and exotic detail.

421–2 The transition to her brothers' fate is marked by a rising threefolder with a pathetic ring. Their departure for ⟨the house of⟩ Hades on a single day (for ἰῷ, here only, cf. 18.251 ἰῇ δ' ἐν νυκτὶ γένοντο) is especially sad.

423 The first part is repeated from 190, of Bellerophon.

424 Compare 5.137 for the shepherd ⟨watching⟩ over, ἐπί, his sheep. The cattle here are εἰλιπόδεσσι (cf. horses as ἀερσίποδες, sheep as ταναύποδα; also S. West on *Od.* 1.92), a brilliant and traditional epithet, often in the phrase εἰλίποδας ἕλικας βοῦς. Meaning 'of rolling gait' or similar, it is formed from (ϝ)ειλέω (despite ignored digamma, cf. Hoekstra, *Modifications* 67f.), 'turn' or 'roll' (διὰ τὸ ἐλίσσειν τοὺς πόδας, Hesychius); whether a particular circular movement of the rear feet is meant, or their generally shambling walk, remains uncertain. For the capture of herds and flocks cf. 1.154, 18.527–9 and especially 20.90f., where Aineias recalls how Akhilleus chased him from Ida when he fell upon the cattle and destroyed Lurnessos and Pedasos. The isolated herdsman is exposed to attack, and this was a convenient and typical motif – extended here, a little cursorily perhaps, to no less than seven victims.

425–8 It was not the custom to kill women in a captured city; Andromakhe's mother is taken to Troy and then ransomed; she returns to her father's home and dies there. In v. 425 βασίλευεν is unusual, though cf. *Od.* 11.285, the sense being that she is wife to the βασιλεύς Eetion. Now she is almost part of the inanimate spoils, 426 ἅμ' ἄλλοισι κτεάτεσσι |, which recurs (with σύν for ἅμ') only at 23.829 – again in connexion with Eetion and the Thebe booty, though the subject there is an iron weight. The idea of Thebe seems to trigger the same phrase in the singer's mind. — The language and motifs of 427f. are typical, e.g. ἀπερείσι' ἄποινα 10 × *Il.*, ἐν μεγάροισι 10 × *Il.*, Ἄρτεμις ἰοχέαιρα | (cf. 5.53–4n.) 5 × *Il.*; and cf. 205, 19.59 and 24.606 for this goddess as cause of sudden death for women.

429–30 Ἕκτορ, ἀτὰρ σύ was used in a more practical context at 86; here it is deeply pathetic as Andromakhe concludes her argument – 'I have lost father, mother and brothers; *you* stand in their place for me, as well as being my strong husband.' V. 429 takes up the language of 413, with ἀτὰρ σύ μοί ἐσσι in place of (‿) οὐδέ μοί ἐστι; on ἀτάρ (equivalent to αὐτάρ but retained in conversational uses in later Greek), both adversative and progressive, see Denniston, *Particles* 51–4. She means that Hektor is all the family she has, that she depends entirely on him, and her moving words have found many later imitations (e.g. Tekmessa to Aias at Sophocles, *Ajax* 514ff.). It is tempting but wrong to read modern psychological insights into this, of the wife as mother and sister as well as lover. In any event there is passionate affection here, as well as the formal point about the duty Hektor now owes her. So much emerges from the whole passage, and here not least from the emotional repetition of σὺ δέ μοι and even the particular deployment of the standard phrase θαλερὸς παρακοίτης. — For | ἠδὲ κασίγνητος as a case of 'amplifying a formula by enjambment' see V. di Benedetto, *Rivista di Filologia* 114 (1986) 265.

431–2 νῦν reinforces the plea of ἀλλ' ἄγε rather than being strictly temporal as Ameis–Hentze suggest, i.e. in contrast with his attitude so far. All the same, these 2 vv. deliberately hark back in ring form to 407–9: 'You do not pity us...but you are all I have...therefore you must pity us', repeating the thought of her widowhood (typical of her, cf. 22.484, 499, 24.725) but adding that of the baby as orphan, also the important notion of Hektor remaining on the tower (from which, presumably, he is to direct his troops) rather than returning to the battlefield. — αὐτοῦ in 431 does not mean that they are actually *on* the tower now; they are below it, but close enough. The chiastic structure of 432 is against articulating it as a rising threefolder.

433–9 These 7 vv. were athetized by Aristarchus (Arn/A) 'because the words are inappropriate to Andromakhe, since she sets herself up against Hektor in generalship (ἀντιστρατηγεῖ). Also, they contain an untruth; for it was not recorded that the wall was easy to attack in this sector, nor is the fighting so close to the wall. Also, Hektor directs his answer [i.e. at 441] to the earlier points.' It might also be argued that 431f., taking up 407–9 at the beginning of Andromakhe's speech, may suitably bring it to a ring-form conclusion; and that the tactical suggestion is too concrete in tone, anticlimactic even (so e.g. Leaf), after the personal and emotional vv. that precede. Yet (i) the idea of Hektor remaining inside the city, more plausible in the different circumstances of 22.84f., where Hekabe will urge ἄμυνε δὲ δήϊον ἄνδρα | τείχεος ἐντὸς ἐών, requires some kind of rational support from Andromakhe, who is far from hysterical; (ii) the three probing moves by the Achaeans are envisaged as quite recent in that Akhilleus is not mentioned among their leaders at 436f. – even though T's 'she saw them during the time she spent on the wall' is absurd; (iii) even if no very clear picture has emerged about precisely how close the fighting has come, Helenos had instructed Hektor at 80 to station the army *in front of the gates*, and Hektor told Paris at 327f. that the troops are fighting and dying *around the city and its steep wall*; (iv) when Hektor replies that he is concerned with 'all these things', τάδε πάντα, he could be referring to tactical possibilities as well as to Andromakhe's predicament; (v) both the ring-composition and the anticlimax arguments are inconclusive and subjective.

A more positive reason for accepting the passage as authentic – Aristarchus' doubts had no effect, incidentally, on the medieval tradition

– is that it is competently composed and interesting and suggestive in itself. Willcock concluded that 'Probably the whole idea is a momentary invention of the poet, to give Andromakhe an excuse for asking Hector to stay near the city wall', and I am inclined to agree (cf. his '*Ad hoc* invention in the Iliad', *HSCP* 81, 1977, 51f.), with the reservation that the *Augenblickserfindung* concept has its dangers – since the present passage, at least, is carefully constructed as it stands and was presumably refined, like other passages, from performance to performance.

Two final points: (i) Pindar, *Ol.* 8.31–46, mentions that a weak section of the walls was built by the mortal Aiakos, whereas Apollo and Poseidon had built the rest. This may or may not have come from the epic Cycle; as Leaf noted, it could have arisen from the present passage (bT on 438 say the city was destined to be captured through that section) together with the Laomedon tale. (ii) The mention of a weak spot could conceivably reflect a historical fact, namely that the Troy VIh refurbishment of the walls was not quite completed, notably over a short section of the surviving western part (pp. 47f.).

433 This fig-tree is mentioned thrice in the poem and, like the oak-tree (5.692–3n.), is one of the fixed points of the plain. However, it is not immediately clear how close to the walls it stands: (i) the present passage suggests that it is very close (as the oak-tree is to the Scaean gate); (ii) at 11.166–8 the Trojans in full retreat 'rushed from the tomb of Ilos...over the middle of the plain past the fig-tree heading for the city'; (iii) at 22.145ff. Hektor pursued by Akhilleus 'rushed past the look-out place and wind-tossed fig-tree, always out from under (ὑπέκ) the wall, along the cart-road' and past the springs where the Trojan women did their washing. Of these (ii) implies that the fig-tree is between the middle of the plain and the city, not necessarily very close to it, and (iii) that it is fairly close to the walls although a little way out into the plain. The poet evidently did not envisage all these fixed points with complete precision, but it emerges that the oak-tree was very close to the Scaean gate, the fig-tree fairly close to the walls, but obviously at a point somewhere away from the gate; see further Thornton, *Supplication* 152f. That makes a reasonable indication, at least by poetic standards, of where the army might be regrouped to defend a weak section of wall behind them.

434 Neither ἀμβατός nor ἐπίδρομος recurs in the poem (the former 1 × *Od.*), but they are neat enough in context. Difficulties have been made about the change from pres. ἐστι to aor. ἔπλετο, but the former states a permanent fact about the city, the latter implies a particular occasion or occasions.

435 οἱ ἄριστοι is a developed use of the definite article, a relatively late but not infrequent phenomenon in *Il.*

436–7 For the omission of Akhilleus, and its implication, see on 433–9.

438–9 Her concluding vv. are peculiarly Homeric both in conception, viz. the listing of possible alternative motives (cf. e.g. 5.811f.), and in expression: e.g. ἐΰ εἰδώς | 10 × *Il.*, mostly with τόξων; ἐποτρύνει καὶ ἀνώγει 3 × *Il.*, at 15.43 also with θυμός, cf. θυμὸς ἀνώγει (etc.) 11 × *Il.* Helenos at 76ff. is a recent instance of an expert in prophecy.

440–65 Hektor responds quite fully to his wife's pathetic address, though without answering her in detail. The conventional κορυθαίολος is significant here, cf. 469f. and 359n. His words are gentle but unyielding as he declares that pride and upbringing compel him to take his place again in the fighting, that he knows Troy's ruin to be inevitable, that what grieves him most is not so much the fate of his parents and brothers as that of Andromakhe in captivity. The style is melancholy rather than impassioned; medium-length sentences enclose the longer one at 450–5; there is little internal punctuation and much enjambment, integral to begin with, then mainly progressive. The subtle interplay between typical and untypical elements is discussed at length in ch. 2 of the Introduction, pp. 18–21.

Readers will react in their own way to this most famous of all Homeric scenes, on which see e.g. Schein, *Mortal Hero* 173–9; D. Lohmann, *Die Andromache-Szenen der Ilias* (Zürich 1988) 38–47. *Ex cathedra* aesthetic assessments are to be avoided here, but one general aspect may be noted. The recurrent and deliberate conjunction of two styles normally kept distinct, even if not completely so, is certainly significant: the severe and heroic on the one hand, the intimate and compassionate on the other. That emerges not only in the contrasting attitudes of Hektor and Andromakhe themselves but also in the alternation of heroic themes (the capture of Thebe, Andromakhe's tactical advice, Hektor's statement of heroic commitment and his vision of the fall of Troy) and more personal ones (Hektor as her father, mother and brothers; his imagining her slavery). A similar contrast can be found in the narrative background, too, and is symbolized in the baby's reaction to Hektor's great helmet at 467–70 as well as his mother's division between tears and laughter at 484. An analogous counterpoint operates between the rhetorical scale and style of the speeches and the naturalistic detail of certain elements within them; as also between the use of the traditional formular language of epic description and its adaptation from time to time to give startling moments of human insight.

441–3 Hektor is no less concerned than she, but states his own position without prevarication. ἀλλὰ μάλ' αἰνῶς | is followed elsewhere (3 ×) by | δείδω μή..., here by αἰδέομαι in a v. that recurs at 22.105. There, he will fear reproach for having lost most of the army; here he fears the accusation of cowardice if he avoids battle; cf. J. T. Hooker, *Greece and Rome* 34 (1987)

121–3, S. West on *Od.* 2.64–6. Then 443f. recall Diomedes' words to Sthenelos at 5.253f., οὐ γάρ μοι γενναῖον ἀλυσκάζοντι μάχεσθαι | οὐδὲ καταπτώσσειν, a further statement of the 'heroic code' as Fenik notes, *TBS* 31. — ἑλκεσιπέπλους appears only here (with 22.105) and at 7.297, likewise of the Trojan women; cf. Ἰάονες ἑλκεχίτωνες at 13.685 and *HyAp* 147. The unexpected form ἑλκεσι- (from ἕλκειν) is presumably determined by metrical requirements. Parry, *MHV* 99, observed that 'peoples other than the Trojans and Achaeans play no important role in the poems', which no doubt accounts for the restriction of this epithet; it could hardly apply e.g. to the metrically similar Amazons, who are by nature ἀντιάνειραι.

444–6 His own feelings are no less important than public opinion. οὐδέ με θυμὸς ἄνωγεν recalls θυμὸς ἐποτρύνει καὶ ἀνώγει at 439, q.v. with n. (indeed as a typical oral echo it may support the authenticity of that v. and its predecessors). μάθον need not be taken too literally; it is partly a question of family and class (cf. 5.253 γενναῖον), though general upbringing and specific paternal instruction like that to Glaukos at 208 and Akhilleus at 11.784, αἰὲν ἀριστεύειν καὶ ὑπείροχον ἔμμεναι ἄλλων, must have played their part. Indeed that formulation may have influenced the shape of 444f. (which has both ἔμμεναι – x | and initial αἰεί/αἰέν), and could account for the awkward runover of αἰεί here (cf. Nic/AbT).

446 ἀρνύμενος, 'seeking to gain', as at 1.159, cf. *Od.* 1.5: to gain glory for himself and Priam, i.e. for the ruling house of Troy. This is still part of the heroic code, and does not of itself imply, despite the 3 vv. that follow, that he had to concentrate on reputation since he knew the city could not be saved.

447–9 These famous lines have already occurred at 4.163–5; see comments there for the passionate and prophetic tone, also for ἔσσεται with ἦμαρ. The two contexts could hardly be more different: in bk 4 Agamemnon thought Menelaos might die as a result of Pandaros breaking the truce; he proclaimed that Zeus would bring vengeance in time and adduced these vv. as part of that conviction. The effect is no less powerful than here, but its tone, confident and assertive rather than pathetic and resigned, shows how repeated language can take on different colouring according to context, without awkwardness or loss of impact. To decide which of these two contexts is 'original', and declare the other to be derivative in some sense, is obviously wrong in principle. — It is notable how Hektor admits his foreboding here but will be full of confidence later, in the excitement of battle.

γάρ in 447 is inconsequential unless one places an improbable interpretation on 446 (see n.). Several MSS have μέν instead, which is probably correct; Hektor fights for glory yet knows Troy will perish in the end. μέν would then be partly adversative, cf. Denniston, *Particles* 359: 'The primary function of μέν...is emphatic... But, as this process naturally entails the isolation of one idea from others, μέν acquires a concessive or antithetical sense, and serves to prepare the mind for a contrast of greater or lesser sharpness.'

450 Ameis–Hentze classed Τρώων and the genitives that follow as 'objective', i.e. my grief *for* the Trojans etc. Translators like Lattimore, Rieu and Fitzgerald were right to reject the idea; it is the future sufferings *of* the Trojans that mean less to him than Andromakhe's. So much is strongly suggested by 462 σοὶ δ' αὖ νέον ἔσσεται ἄλγος, where the 'new' or additional grief shows that σεῦ (ἄλγος) in 454 also meant *your* grief.

452–3 Many of Hektor's brothers have fallen already, others like Lukaon and Poludoros will fall before his own death; the special mention, in a cumulated pair of vv., of still more who will die when Troy is captured not only continues the scale-of-affection theme but also echoes Andromakhe's brothers who succumbed to Akhilleus during another sack. For the wording cf. 17.428, ἐν κονίῃσι πεσόντος ὑφ' Ἕκτορος ἀνδροφόνοιο (ἐν κονίῃσι(ν) 34 × *Il.*, usually at the v-e but 4 × *sic*).

455 Subjunct. ὅτε κέν τις...ἄγηται contrasts with opt. after κέν in 453 πέσοιεν, 456 ὑφαίνοις and 457 φορέοις, signifying a more vivid eventuality than those secondary consequences; cf. also the prophetic plain subjunct. of 459 εἴπῃσιν. — δακρυόεσσαν ἄγηται breaches 'Meyer's Law' but is not noticeably unrhythmical. ἐλεύθερον ἦμαρ, also at 16.831, 20.193, belongs to a varied group of formular phrases with ἦμαρ at the v-e, most of evil import like 463 δούλιον ἦμαρ, see 4.164n. ἐλεύθερος is found in Homer only in this phrase and the κρητῆρα...ἐλεύθερον of 528; like its opposite δούλιος (both are Mycenaean) it is a technical term and restricted in usage. — T remarks on the generally shaming treatment of female captives, citing 2.355 where Nestor encourages all the Achaeans to sleep with a Trojan wife. Hektor suppresses this ugly possibility and concentrates on the demeaning side of domestic service. According to the post-Homeric tradition Andromakhe was to become mistress first of Neoptolemos and then of Helenos.

456–7 Critics have argued whether this Argos is the Thessalian one, or the Argolid, or the Achaean homeland as a whole, and about precisely where the springs Messeis and Hupereia were situated. This whole approach is probably wrong, apart from understanding Argos in its most general sense. Admittedly a κρήνη Ὑπέρεια is listed in the Achaean Catalogue, surprisingly, as though it were the name of a town; it is among the Thessalian places that supplied Eurupulos' contingent (see on 2.734–5), and Pindar, *Py.* 4.125 mentions a spring of that name near Pherai (which does, indeed, contain a conspicuous fountain); cf. Strabo 9.439, though at 9.432 he placed both Hupereia and Messeis in Pharsalia. The latter was also located in Messenia (!), the former in Laconia (Pausanias 3.20.1 saw one so named at Therapne). But surely the probability is that, despite the obscure Catalogue entry, Messeis ('Middle Spring') and Hupereie ('Upper Spring') are generic and descriptive names that could be given to many springs in many different places, and were chosen for precisely that reason by the poet. — Weaving is a common epic pursuit for maidservants, water-fetching another; the latter is harder work and became typical of Andromakhe in captivity (so Arn/A), as e.g. in Euripides, *Androm.* 166f.

458 The description of her rôle and feelings is abstract but curiously effective. ἀεκαζομένη (etc.) comes only here in *Il.* but 3× *Od.*; for κρατερή... ἀνάγκη cf. *Od.* 10.273, where δέ μοι ἔπλετ' looks like an awkward adjustment of ἐπικείσετ' here.

459–62 κατὰ δάκρυ χέουσαν | picks up the | δακρυόεσσαν of 455. Such comments by unnamed persons are a typical and successful Homeric device, often for drama and variety but also to reflect the heroic need – and especially Hektor's – for public approval. One group follows an introductory v.-beginning ὧδε δέ τις εἴπεσκε(ν), as at 2.271–7 (q.v. with 271n.), 4.81–5, 17.414–19, 420–3, 22.372–5; these are actual comments on present circumstances, or reports of prayers to gods as at 3.297–301, 3.319–23 and 7.178–80, 7.201–5. A smaller group envisages comments that might be made in the future, as here; so 479 (enclosed within a prayer), 4.176–82 (resumed as here by ὥς ποτέ τις ἐρέει), 7.87–91 (introduced as here by καί ποτέ τις εἴπῃσι and resumed by ὥς ποτέ τις ἐρέει), 7.300–2, 22.106f. (see n. there) and 23.575–8. Of these, 7.87–91 is closely related to the present passage not only in the wording of its introduction and resumption but also as spoken by Hektor and including the idea of ἀριστεύειν. Ironically it envisages a happier event, someone commenting in the distant future on the tomb of the man Hektor hopes to kill in a duel. — The epigrammatic quality of 460 was noted by bT, and indeed it and 461 convey a feeling of timelessness and distance that elevated not only Hektor but also the whole *geste* of Ilios. From another point of view his reaction to Andromakhe's imagined fate might seem strangely self-centred; that would be typically heroic, but Hektor also knows she will be remembered mainly through himself. See further Preface, p. x.

462–3 Cross-currents continue: Hektor will *not*, evidently, be quite the man for warding off the 'day of enslavement', nevertheless the memory of him will increase her grief.

464–5 Again his words are ambivalent, but outwardly he means no more than that he could not bear to hear her cries, and would rather be dead first. χυτή κατά γαῖα καλύπτοι -ει recurs of Tudeus' funeral mound at 14.114, cf. 23.256 χυτὴν ἐπὶ γαῖαν ἔχευαν of Patroklos' burial. It signifies an honourable funeral, therefore, one that Hektor needs and expects.

Andromakhe's fate is paralleled at 22.62 and 65, where Priam foresees his daughters and sisters-in-law being dragged along (ἑλκηθείσας, ἑλκομένας) if Hektor is killed and Troy falls. It is tempting to compare ὁρμήματά τε στοναχάς τε at 2.356 and 590, but they are probably struggles and groans *for* Helen, see 2.356n. Here, Ameis–Hentze note that σῆς is subjective, σοῦ objective.

466–70 The description of the baby's fright as his father reaches out to him deserves all its fame, giving a sparkling impression of these intimate events and reactions (cf. bT) in simple, traditional language – only ὄψιν ἀτυχθείς, 'amazed at the sight of', is untypical; it may or may not be intended to recall Hektor's effect on his enemies (Schein argues for the former, *Mortal Hero* 175). The regular and honorific epithets, φαίδιμος, ἐϋζώνοιο, ἱππιοχαίτην (but not, as it happens, κορυθαίολος), maintain the heroic quality of the scene for all its informality; ἄψ, ἐκλίνθη and ἰάχων are familiar from quite different contexts, but finely evoke the baby's response. No special rhythmical effects are sought, but 470 is remarkable for its alliteration, with ν's at beginning and end (δεινόν is adverbial with νεύοντα) enclosing the abrasive κ's, extended in 472 and 473, of ἀκροτάτης κόρυθος.

Dating the frightening horsehair plume is precarious; E. Vermeule (*PCPS* 33, 1987, 146 and fig. 5 on p. 144) opts for a pre-1400 B.C. type of Mycenaean helmet – significant if so, but a Geometric model is also possible (Lorimer, *HM* 239). ἱππιοχαίτης comes only here, but cf. ἵππουριν, δεινὸν δὲ λόφος καθύπερθεν ἔνευεν, 4 × *Il.*

471–5 Emphatic | ἐκ δὲ γέλασσε suggests the parents' release from tension as well as their love of the child. Traditional epithets persist (φίλος, πότνια, φαίδιμος again) with similar effect. Repetition of φίλος (468, 471, 474) underlines the family affection, and, though weapons and armour are often gleaming, predicative παμφανόωσαν in 473, instead of expected πουλυβοτείρῃ (Edwards, *HPI* 211), gives special significance to the helmet as Hektor lays it down and dandles his child. In 475 Aristarchus (Did/A) rightly read (apodotic) δ᾽ in εἶπε δ᾽, rather than εἶπεν.

476–81 Hektor's prayer is more complicated in rhythm and syntax than the narrative just ended. It is addressed to Zeus and the other gods as at 3.298, the addition of others being simply precautionary. In v. 476 τόνδε suggests that Hektor holds the child skyward as he prays: 'Grant that this child of mine too, as well as I, may turn out to be eminent among the Trojans' (Τρώεσσιν being locative dat., cf. Chantraine, *GH* II, 80). In v. 478 βίην τ᾽ ἀγαθόν is a probable adaptation, slightly strained, of the common v-e phrase βοὴν ἀγαθός etc., with ἶφι ἀνάσσειν also depending a little awkwardly on ἀγαθόν. On imagined comments see 459–62n.; heroic ideology reasserts itself as Hektor foresees his son returning from his first kill, bringing back the bloody armour he has stripped from the foe, to the joy rather than horror of his mother.

480 ἀνιόντα loosely after εἴποι, an acc. of relation or respect, cf. Chantraine, *GH* ii, 46f.

482–5 482 is a rising threefolder, after which abrupt παῖδ᾿ ἑόν is doubly emphatic. She takes the child to her fragrant bosom (on κηώδεϊ see 288n.), δακρυόεν γελάσασα, weeping and laughing all at once, and he pities her as he notices it (νοήσας | as also in 470). Stroking, κατέρεξεν, in 485 is a tender and usually feminine gesture, as 5/7× in this formular v.

486 Andromakhe had likewise addressed Hektor as δαιμόνιε at 407 as a term of affectionate remonstrance, see on 1.561; μοι is ethic dat., 'I beg you'; ἀκαχίζομαι, 'distress oneself', cf. ἄχος.

487–9 προϊάπτειν in all 4 Iliadic occurrences is used of casting into Hades, cf. 1.3; on ὑπὲρ αἶσαν and similar expressions see 2.155n. αἶσα and 488 μοῖρα are equivalent, both meaning 'share' or 'portion' and so fate or destiny. Each man is born with a certain general portion, notably mortality, cf. 489 (= *Od.* 8.553) ἐπὴν τὰ πρῶτα γένηται 'when once he is born'; also a special one, assigned (after Homer) by the Moirai, cf. Hesiod, *Theog.* 904–6 with M. L. West's comment. In v. 488 φημι is solemnly declarative, the periphrastic perf. πεφυγμένον ἔμμεναι conveying the sense of completeness: '*No* man, I say, ever escapes his destiny, not the coward nor again the brave', where μέν in οὐ...οὐδὲ μέν is regular and emphatic (Denniston, *Particles* 362). Hektor's tone so far is rhetorical and prophetic.

490–3 Now he gently turns to practical matters and sends her on her way. These 4 vv. recur 2× *Od.* with certain changes, appositely at 21.350–3 but as an interpolation according to Aristarchus (Arn/A) at 1.356–9, on which see S. West *ad loc.* They seem to have been so well known in this Iliadic context that their Odyssean recurrences were quotations, almost; in this case a single lost archetype, or typical use, is improbable. The last 2 vv. could be modified according to context; μῦθος, πομπή and τόξον were substituted for war as men's concern at *Od.* 1.358, 11.352 and 21.352 respectively (though πόλεμος δ᾿ ἄνδρεσσι μελήσει recurs at *Il.* 20.137), and τοῦ γὰρ κράτος ἔστ᾿ ἐνὶ οἴκῳ is the regular Odyssean substitute for τοὶ Ἰλίῳ ἐγγεγάασιν. — The MSS read πᾶσιν ἐμοὶ δὲ μάλιστα in 493 but the Odyssean versions (as well as Epictetus and one papyrus, P 21, of no great authority) have πᾶσι μάλιστα δ᾿ ἐμοί, which, for what it is worth, preserves the digamma of Ἰλίῳ as in the similar use at 17.145. — Andromakhe is to return home and attend to, κόμιζε, her particular tasks with loom and shuttle (like Helen at 3.125; she herself will be thus occupied when news of Hektor's death reaches her at 22.440ff.), as well as giving instructions to the maidservants. Leaf may not be right that ἐποίχεσθαι was 'properly of weaving only', despite 1.31 ἱστὸν ἐποιχομένην; movement *towards* a task is probably implied.

494–6 Hektor picks up his plumed helmet – its significance not forgotten – as his wife starts off homeward in tears (cf. *Od.* 4.556). Once again the routine language is interrupted by an unusual term, ἐντροπ-αλιζομένη, 'continually turning round', in a last fleeting image of tenderness and regret.

497 497 = 370, of Hektor, where it is admittedly more appropriate in that he was in a hurry, whereas Andromakhe is not (496). | αἶψα δ' ἔπειθ' ἵκανεν -ον occurred at 3.145, cf. 20.341, and the language is typical enough to explain any minor looseness of application.

498–9 ἀνδροφόνοιο comes as a shock after Hektor's tender domestic encounter – perhaps it is a deliberate recall to the realities of battle, since an epithet is not essential here (plain | Ἕκτορος 17 × *Il.*); it is standard for Hektor in the gen. at the v-e, but its two other occurrences at the beginning of the v., at 17.638 and 24.724, both have particular point. — πολλὰς | ἀμφιπόλους is an awkward enjambment. Parry, *MHV* 264, noted that πᾶς, πολύς and ἄλλος are sometimes separated from their noun by the v-e, but other instances of πολλαὶ | (etc.) are smoother, cf. 9.97 ~ 9.116, 13.797, 23.520, 24.163. The gravitation of ἔνδοθι to a convenient position, and consequent lack of room for ἀμφιπόλους or even δμωάς in that v., may have been a contributory cause.

500 This premature mourning for Hektor is prophetic and sinister, a foreshadowing of 22.473ff., 24.719ff.; the women perceive from Andromakhe (as bT remarked, 499 ἐνῶρσεν implies either by her tears or because she told them) that he will never return alive. ζωόν is separated from γόον by verse-rhythm and is less of a jingle than it looks, with verbal γόον echoing the substantival γόον of the previous v. and ᾧ ἐνὶ οἴκῳ further underlining the pathos and the paradox: they mourned him in his own home, although he was still alive and elsewhere.

501–2 A final couplet expands the idea of their mourning and premonition, but also provides a formal and epigrammatic conclusion to the whole scene of Hektor in Troy (since what remains is concerned solely with his return to battle). For μένος καὶ χεῖρας Ἀχαιῶν cf. 13.105, 17.638, for προφυγόντα μένος καὶ χεῖρας cf. 7.309.

503–29 Paris runs like a proud stallion and overtakes his brother, who is cool but less hostile as they prepare to leave the city

503–5 δήθυνεν, 'took a long time', cf. δήν, δηθά and τάχα > ταχύνω. The decorative epithets are standard ones, but their number, together with the stallion simile that follows, helps present Paris in a more glamorous light: ὑψηλοῖσι, κλυτά, ποικίλα χαλκῷ, κραιπνοῖσι. The whole scene, including the simile, has something in common with the briefer description of Akhilleus himself at 22.21–3:

> ὡς εἰπὼν προτὶ ἄστυ μέγα φρονέων ἐβεβήκει
> σευάμενος ὡς θ᾽ ἵππος ἀεθλοφόρος σὺν ὄχεσφιν
> ὅς ῥά τε ῥεῖα θέῃσι τιταινόμενος πεδίοιο.

506–11 The simile will be exactly repeated, but of Hektor returning to battle after being revived and inspired by Apollo, at 15.263–8, q.v. with n. Aristarchus (Arn/A) judged it to be interpolated there, but it is equally effective, in a slightly different way, in that context, and the probability is that the monumental composer liked it well enough to use it twice. That is unusual; Moulton, *Similes* 94 and n. 16, observes that 8 developed similes are repeated in *Il.* and *Od.* together, but the fact is that most of them are very short; only 11.548–55 ~ 17.657–64 and *Od.* 4.335–9 = 17.126–30 exceed 2 or 3 vv. (apart from the present one), both of those being lion similes.

Much of the language, as often in similes, is untypical, partly as a consequence of special kinds of subject; but as a whole it is both energetic and sumptuous. στατός: 'stalled' or stabled; κοστή or ἀκοστή is 'barley' according to Hesychius (a Cypriot word, or Thessalian according to AbT), and ἀκοστήσας (ἀκοστέω) therefore 'having had his fill of barley', cf. Chantraine, *Dict.* — In v. 507 κροαίνων is evidently connected with κρούω, and with θείη means 'runs with stamping feet' (ἐπικροτῶν τοῖς ποσὶ διὰ τοῦ πεδίου, Arn/A): 'gallops over the plain in thunder' (Lattimore) conveys just too much, 'canters down a field' (Fitzgerald) far too little. — The 'fair-flowing river' of 508 is formular, the rest of the v. not; though the other two Homeric instances of participial εἰωθώς (etc.) likewise apply, curiously enough, to horses. Whether the observation of equine behaviour is as close as the scholiast thought (φιλόλουτρον γὰρ τὸ ζῷον, T) is arguable. λούεσθαι is contracted from λοέεσθαι, presumably the correct Homeric spelling; Shipp's objections to this and other forms hereabouts, *Studies* 257, seem overdone. ἀμφὶ δὲ χαῖται in 509 recurs by ironic contrast of the dead Hektor's hair dragged in the dust at 22.401; here the mane 'springs out on either side, on the shoulders' (an awkward expression, due no doubt to lack of special vocabulary for this sort of detail), i.e. it streams in the wind as the horse gallops. Confident in his pride and glory, his knees carry him swiftly to the accustomed pasture of horses – the change of subject is expressive, as also, in a different way (though cf. next n.), is the galloping dactylic rhythm. γοῦνα φέρει may strike us as stilted but is typically Homeric, cf. λαιψηρά τε γούνατ᾽ ἐνώμα (3 × *Il.*); feet and knees are often associated in the act of rapid movement, cf. 514 ταχέες δὲ πόδες φέρον and p. 248 *fin.* – Virgil's version (*Aen.* 11.494) opts for mares rather than horses, *in pastus armentaque tendit equarum*; Leaf rejected the social implication as inappropriate.

512–16 It is through the streets of Troy, down from his house in its highest quarter (for κατὰ Περγάμου ἄκρης cf. 4.508n., also 5.460 ἐφέζετο Περγάμῳ ἄκρῃ), that Paris runs in glory like the stallion. The opulent language continues: he is all-gleaming in his armour, like Elektor, the Shining One, i.e. the sun, and laughing aloud as his swift feet carry him along. — V. 513 recurs as 19.398, of Akhilleus, though with Ὑπερίων for ἐβεβήκει; which tends to confirm 'sun' as the meaning of ἠλέκτωρ, as also at *HyAp* 369 and Empedocles frag. 22.2 D–K (where its usual interpretation as 'fire', e.g. by Chantraine, *Dict.* s.v., is inaccurate). The etymology is unknown, but ἤλεκτρον as amber *or* an alloy of gold and silver confirms gleaming brightness as the core sense. καγχαλόων plainly implies 'laughing out loud' with sheer joy, as at 3.43 and 10.565; it is either an onomatopoeic creation or possibly developed from χαλάω, cf. Chantraine, *Dict.* s.v. For the feet that carry him see 506–11n. *fin.*; 514 is another strongly dactylic verse like 511, and once again may be expressive of rapidity, though 515 is equally dactylic and yet conveys no special idea of motion – Leaf on 511 rightly recommended caution in assessing such rhythmic effects. At all events 516 comes as a marked contrast, bringing the sentence to a calm conclusion after these two rather bouncing vv., as he catches up with Hektor on the point of turning away from the spot near the Scaean gate where he had been conversing (ὀάριζε, cf. 22.127) with his wife.

517 πρότερος might seem to suggest that Paris, in his impulsive self-confidence, 'got in first' as it were. That is just possible, but this is a standard half-v. (10 × *Il.*) meaning that when two people met one of them spoke first, and is usually without special significance.

518–19 Athene disguised as his brother Deiphobos twice addresses Hektor as ἠθεῖ᾽ at 22.229 and 239 (on the first occasion followed by ἦ μάλα δή as here); so too Menelaos to Agamemnon at 10.37. The term may be particularly suitable between brothers, but means no more than 'familiar friend', from ἦθος 'custom'. — AbT (followed e.g. by OCT) took Paris' remark as a question, but ἦ μάλα δή usually prefaces a confident conjecture (see on 255–7) or heavily ironical affirmation, cf. Athene of Aphrodite at 5.422 and Denniston, *Particles* 285. δηθύνων echoes δήθυνεν in 503, while ὡς ἐκέλευες refers specifically to Hektor's ἀλλ᾽ ἄνα at 331 but more generally reflects Paris' own claim at 341 that he would catch him up.

521–9 The earlier part of Hektor's response is complex in thought and expression as he analyses his brother's paradoxical nature and his own shame at the reproaches he has to hear. Then at 526 his words become more philosophical as he defers such matters until later and summons them both to action.

521 ἐναίσιμος after 519 ἐναίσιμον is unexpected, given that the adjective only occurs 5 × *Il.*; it is an unconscious repetition (a not uncommon oral phenomenon), and there can be no deliberate punning effect since the two uses are so different: 519, did I not come in due order, i.e. according to what was agreed, and 521, a man who is fair, i.e. judges things in due order.

522 ἔργον...μάχης, 'your performance in battle' (Ameis–Hentze), a special application of the general concept of fighting as work, cf. 4.470–2n., 6.522n. and the φυλόπιδος μέγα ἔργον of 16.208. No one could question Paris' valour when he put his mind to it, since he was ἄλκιμος: this term usually comes in epithet–name formulas, especially of Patroklos; it is the opposite of δειλός at 13.278; even the stout fighter, the ἄλκιμος, can be put to flight by Zeus at 17.177; troops are exhorted to have an ἄλκιμον ἦτορ – it is not something one necessarily has all the time, but can be summoned up even by quite ordinary fighters in a crisis. Yet the description comes as a surprise as Hektor strains to be affable, especially in view of his words to Paris at 3.45, ἀλλ' οὐκ ἔστι βίη φρεσὶν οὐδέ τις ἀλκή.

523 ἑκὼν μεθιεῖς is formular, cf. *Od.* 4.372 | ἦε ἑκὼν μεθιεῖς, *Il.* 13.234 ἑκὼν μεθίῃσι μάχεσθαι |, also 23.434. οὐκ ἐθέλεις is puzzling at first after ἑκών, since no paradox of the ἑκὼν ἀέκοντί γε θυμῷ kind (cf. 4.43) can be intended; but it seems to depend on an aural reminiscence of 10.121 *vel sim.*, πολλάκι γὰρ μεθιεῖ τε καὶ οὐκ ἐθέλει πονέεσθαι. — Editors rightly warn that τὸ δ' is demonstrative, and object of ἄχνυται: 'my heart grieves for that, when I hear...'; ἐμὸν κῆρ | is again formular (3 × *Il.*, 2 × *Od.*), its connexion with θυμός unusual but not to be analysed too closely, since the different terms for heart and emotions are used by Homer quite loosely.

526 Compare Agamemnon's words to Diomedes at 4.362, similar in structure as well as in the ἀρεσσόμεθ' idiom ('we shall make amends to each other for these things'): ἀλλ' ἴθι, ταῦτα δ' ὄπισθεν ἀρεσσόμεθ', εἴ τι κακὸν νῦν...; and for the final words cf. 1.128f., αἴ κέ ποθι Ζεὺς | δῷσι.

527–8 Hektor's preceding vv. have been tight and a little awkward, with forced adaptations of phrases used elsewhere. Now the style becomes more expansive in a long sentence which, unusually for the oral style, can only be construed after some delay and when ἐλεύθερον is reached – for a moment it sounds as though Zeus is granting something to the heavenly gods. Actually it is for them that the 'mixing bowl of freedom' is to be set up, i.e. in a celebratory feast, in a unique figurative phrase; cf. 9.202, κρητῆρα καθίστα, and on ἐλεύθερος 455n.; S. E. Bassett, *The Poetry of Homer*

(Berkeley 1938) 78f., thought such phrases (cf. e.g. the 'stone tunic' of 3.57) characteristic of Hektor in particular.

529 The final whole-v. cumulation has a suitably formal and terminal ring to it, as well as a certain irony that makes an appropriate conclusion to these splendid but ambivalent scenes in the beleaguered city.

BOOK SEVEN

So far every Book of the *Iliad* has contributed in different ways but with strong effect to the monumental plan of the poem, either through establishing the central theme of the wrath of Akhilleus, or by preparing for, and delaying, the great battles to come, or by presenting major figures like Diomedes, or essential background like the behaviour of individual gods and goddesses or the characters in the beleaguered city. The seventh Book, by contrast, seems to falter slightly in its monumental rôle, as well as in the coherence of events generally – this is reflected in the clumsy Hellenistic title of the Book, Ἕκτορος καὶ Αἴαντος μονομαχία. Νεκρῶν ἀναίρεσις (on which see also p. 277, (3)). Hektor and Paris return to battle as indicated at the end of bk 6, but are soon interrupted by Apollo and the proposal for a second formal duel, curiously like that of bk 3 but without stated or accomplished purpose. It is bizarrely curtailed by the heralds, and Hektor survives. At the celebratory dinner for Aias, Nestor proposes a truce for the collection and burning of the dead; Priam independently proposes the same, and the Achaeans take the opportunity of building a huge defensive wall and trench around their camp. The Book ends with nightfall and the arrival of wine-ships from Lemnos.

There is, needless to say, much that is fascinating in all this. The Achaean reluctance to respond to Hektor's challenge, Menelaos' quixotic offer and the subsequent selection of a champion by lot are especially dramatic. The details of the duel itself as well as Nestor's reminiscence which precedes it are in their different ways wonderfully Iliadic. Yet a new kind of arbitrariness in the selection and preparation of topics begins to reveal itself; and the succeeding bk 8, too, where battle is re-engaged, will be replete with shifts of fortune that sometimes appear weakly motivated and contribute little to the progress of the epic as a whole. Achaean reverses are admittedly needed to justify the despatch of the Embassy to Akhilleus in bk 9, and that episode is a central element in the poem – one that leads on (after a special interlude in 10) to the grand and indispensable bks 11 and 12, from which point the dynamic of the large-scale conception continues unimpeded. Yet the commentator on bks. 7 and 8 must come to terms with a sequence that is both less powerful and more full of minor structural and stylistic problems than most of the rest. Some of the difficulties have been exaggerated; but in bk 7 the relation of the duel to that of bk 3, and certain aspects of the Achaean wall and trench, require careful consideration, as does the possibility that a few details reflect Athenian influence.

These matters have been extensively discussed, primarily from the Analytical point of view, e.g. by Bolling (*External Evidence* 92–4) and Page (*HHI* 315–24 and 335–40) on the wall and trench, on which see also Thornton, *Supplication* 157–60, and by Von der Mühll (*Hypomnema* 129–43) on the duel, on which see also W. Berghold (*Die Zweikampf des Paris und Menelaos*, Bonn 1977, which has a useful appendix and bibliography on bk 7 at 183ff.). Shipp, *Studies* 258–62, conveniently summarizes the claimed linguistic anomalies. My own tentative conclusions (for which see especially on 8–13, 74–5, 327–43, 334–5 below) will be roughly these: that we cannot know exactly why Homer decided to introduce, somewhat cursorily in places, a second version of the duel theme; that the truce and the associated building of wall and trench are a valid compositional device, given that the wall is to fulfil an important function later (notably in bk 12), and permit a probable reapplication of motifs used in traditional accounts of the landing at Troy ten years before; and that apart from 334f. there is little sign of special Attic influence.

1–43 Hektor and Paris regain the battlefield, where each slays a minor Achaean and Glaukos a third. Athene notices what is happening and descends from Olumpos to Troy. Apollo intercepts her and proposes a stop to fighting for the day; she agrees to his suggestion that Hektor should challenge an Achaean champion to a duel

1 ἐξέσσυτο, 'rushed out of', cf. 2.809 = 8.58 πᾶσαι δ' ὠΐγνυντο πύλαι, ἐκ δ' ἔσσυτο λαός. The scansion of πυλέων as an anapaest is unusual (Chantraine, *GH* I, 64; Janko, *HHH* 49f.), paralleled only at 12.340 and by θυρέων at *Od.* 21.191. Emendation of |καὶ πυλέων to | ἠδὲ πυλέων is possible in the former, but here Bentley's ⟨ῥά⟩ πυλέων can be dismissed, since no particle follows | ὡς εἰπών in any other of its over 70 Iliadic occurrences. πόλεως, πόλιος and πύργων are especially unattractive. Trisyllabic πυλέων should probably be accepted, therefore, as a rare metrical resource; after all, -έων for -άων is regular enough, and synizesis not mandatory.

2–3 For ἐν δ' ἄρα θυμῷ... μέμασαν cf. 13.337 μέμασαν δ' ἐνὶ θυμῷ |. The plethoric πολεμίζειν ἠδὲ μάχεσθαι is formular, 8 × *Il.* (and not specially 'to emphasize their eagerness', bT).

4–7 Other similes involve sailors at sea, but as observers of a star or a fire (4.76, 19.375); the closest parallel (bT) is *Od.* 23.233, ὡς δ' ὅτ' ἂν ἀσπάσιος γῆ νηχομένοισι φανήη, after a shipwreck. Hektor had rallied his troops at 6.110–15 but their position remains acute, cf. 6.327f. The point of comparison is simple and exact, both parties getting the relief they long for (4 and 7, ἐελδομένοισιν, discussed in vol. v, ch. 4 (ii) a). It is unusually simple, indeed, for a Homeric simile, of which this is not typical (*pace* Willcock) – it is a little plain and obvious even, stylistically more Odyssean than Iliadic.

They 'drive the sea' with their oars, a vivid and unique phrase. ἐλαύνειν is regularly used in *Od.* of driving a ship along (and in *Il.* of driving horses); compare also ἅλα τύπτον ἐρετμοῖς, 7 × *Od.*, as well as *Od.* 12.172 ἑζόμενοι λεύκαινον ὕδωρ ξεστῆς ἐλάτῃσιν. The ancient variant ἐρέσσοντες for ἐλαύνοντες (Did/A) has little to commend it. The language so far is markedly Odyssean, as often with maritime details (see on e.g. 1.432–9), but γυῖα λέλυνται -ο is firmly established in *Il.* too, cf. e.g. 13.85.

8–16 Paris and Hektor each kill a victim as does Glaukos; perhaps he is added to represent the allies (as Λυκίων ἀγὸς ἀνδρῶν, though cf. 13–16n. *init.*) in this brief and symbolic rout, or perhaps bT on 13 were right that he is allowed to demonstrate the bravery that was inhibited in his meeting with Diomedes. The three encounters are perfunctorily described and hardly justify Athene's urgent response.

8–13 ὁ μέν is Paris, picking up, as often, the last of a pair to be mentioned (Arn/A). His victim is Menesthios son of Areithoos, κορυνήτης or 'mace-man', specifically a nickname in Nestor's account of his demise at 137ff. This Menesthios occurs only here (there is a Myrmidon namesake at 16.173, cf. also Menestheus, Menesthes and 5.608–9n.), as does his mother Phulomedousa. She is given the epithet βοῶπις which regularly belongs to Here and is used elsewhere of a mortal woman only at 3.144, almost certainly an Athenian interpolation – see n. there; also not infrequently in the pseudo-Hesiodic *Ehoiai*. This could be significant in a Book in which Athenian influence is mooted for other contexts; though nothing else about this particular episode, or the Areithoos tale, looks Attic. The family is ostensibly a Boeotian one from Arne, a town mentioned in the Achaean Catalogue but otherwise obscure (vol. I, 194 and 197); Nestor's victim of 136ff. is Ereuthalion, squire of Lukourgos who had managed to kill the mace-man in a narrow passage – so both Ereuthalion and Lukourgos were presumably Arcadian. Areithoos and his son could still in theory have been Boeotian; yet that would go against the general parochialism of Nestor's reminiscences, and it remains probable that the poet is drawing loosely on his own memory and imagination here, in pre-empting material he has in mind for Nestor shortly.

There is also an apparent chronological difficulty about Menesthios fighting at Troy. If Nestor is around seventy (see on 1.250–2), then his fight against Ereuthalion, when according to 153 he himself was very young, say twenty, was some fifty years back. By then Lukourgos had killed Areithoos and had time to pass on his arms to Ereuthalion; that puts Areithoos' death, and therefore the birth of his son, at least some years earlier. A 55-year-old Menesthios seems improbable, but we should remember that the tradition was imprecise over Nestor's chronology (see on 1.250–2 again). Aristarchus (Arn/A) seems to have distinguished Areithoos father and son, the former the mace-man and the latter the father of Menesthios; in which case ὄν in 9 would refer not to Menesthios but to 'lord' Areithoos, i.e. Areithoos junior, in 8. That is too contrived a solution (as Leaf remarked on 149) to be easily accepted.

13–16 Glaukos is introduced in standard terms (13 = 17.140), his victim made no more interesting than his predecessors. Neither Iphinoos nor his father Dexios, the object of wild speculation in AbT, recur, and they look like *ad hoc* inventions; like Eioneus in 11 they are placeless as well as faceless. Iphinoos is struck in the shoulder as he mounts his swift chariot, ἵππων... ὠκειάων (to flee, that implies); the wound is fatal, see on 5.46. The second half of 16 recurs at 15.435. — Hiatus within 15 ἐπι-άλμενον is nothing surprising in itself, despite the objections of Leaf, Shipp and others, since the original initial σ of ἅλλομαι, Lat. *salio*, of which this is middle aor. participle, was still erratically felt, cf. Chantraine, *GH* I, 184. Yet ἐπιάλμενος recurs only at *Od.* 24.320, and the common form is undoubtedly ἐπάλμενος, 6 × *Il.* (+ κατεπάλμενος 1 ×). It regularly follows the fem. caesura; here a masc. caesura, and so the earlier form, is needed.

17–18 τούς, viz. the Trojans, with Ἀργείους object of ὀλέκοντας. These vv. were first used at 5.711f. with Here as subject. Hektor's formidable attack and the steady Achaean retreat there provided a far more serious reason for divine intervention, which underlines the casual and perfunctory quality of these three conquests and their undistinguished victims.

19 The composer uses much typical material hereabouts; the present v. occurs 4 × *Il.*, 2 × *Od.* of Athene (and once of Thetis). Even the more sedate Here will rush similarly, ἀΐξασα, at 14.225 = 19.114, where the divine progress is made more dramatic by details that might be out of place here, as she passes over Pierie and Emathie to Thrace, and from over Athos crosses the sea to Lemnos.

20 'Holy' is a standard epithet for Troy, cf. Ἴλιος ἱρή | (etc.), 20 × *Il.*, and on 1.366; see further M. L. West, *JHS* 108 (1988) 163 and 157f.

21 ~ 4.508 (see n. there for Pergamos), but with βούλετο νίκην (4 × *Il.*) for κέκλυτ᾽ ἀΰσας.

22 God and goddess meet by the oak-tree, a little way out in the plain facing the Scaean gate; see on 6.237 and 433. Clearly Athene was not about to enter the city itself, and Apollo descends from its heights to intercept her before she can rally the Achaeans.

23 A few MSS, including Ge ~ D, have ἑκάεργος for Διὸς υἱός, as 5 ×

in the formula προσέφη ἑκάεργος Ἀπόλλων |. It is not particularly suitable here, but may reflect (unrecorded) scholia and attempt to avoid a kind of repetition with Διὸς θύγατερ in 24.

24–32 He addresses her with a brotherly mixture of courtesy and sarcasm, and is anxious to persuade her of the reasonableness of his proposal. Changes in tone and approach are subtly reflected in the carefully varied enjambments. His motive is obvious: to prevent Athene from completely turning the tide of battle, even though Hektor is temporarily victorious. Berghold, *Zweikampf* 185f. n. 1, develops Reinhardt's dictum that Apollo does not actually hate the Achaeans (as Here and Athene do the Trojans) but only wishes to protect the Trojans; and maintains that the god's actions in *Il.* show him mainly as a preserver of measure and destiny and agent of Zeus's will. That is a useful corrective to seeing Apollo simply as the Trojan god (and see on 26–7 *fin.*); but at the same time this is a rôle the poet often imposes on him, if only to strike a balance of power. V. 21, indeed, was quite categorical, Τρώεσσι δὲ βούλετο νίκην.

24–5 Compare Zeus's question to Here at 14.298, Ἥρη, πῇ μεμαυῖα κατ' Οὐλύμπου τόδ' ἱκάνεις; in which, as here, μεμαυῖα has a strong sense, 'eagerly wishing' rather than 'intending' (Willcock; though see on 36). δὴ αὖ (with synizesis; the vulgate has δ' αὖ) is ironical or resigned, cf. δὴ αὖτε at 1.340, 7.448 and the echo in Sappho frag. 1.18 (etc.), τίνα δηῦτε πείθω; Apollo asks 'why have you come *this* time [*sc.* after your previous intervention of bk 5] in such eagerness?' — θυμὸς ἀνῆκε(ν) | (6 × *Il.*, not *Od.*) is preceded here and at 21.395, also of Athene, by μέγας, giving it a distinctly ambiguous flavour, flattering but also ironic.

26–7 ἦ ἵνα δή introduces 'a suggested answer to a question already asked' (Denniston, *Particles* 283), as with Akhilleus to Athene at 1.202f., τίπτ' αὖτ' εἰλήλουθας; | ἦ ἵνα δὴ ὕβριν ἴδης..., with the addition of δή stressing the inevitability of the motive. — ἑτεραλκέα νίκην | comes 4 × *Il.*, the sense apparently no more than that superiority is now given to the side that was losing before (AbT). It is not at all clear why the poet chose stark monosyllabic δῷς in an enjambment of some violence (on contracted subjunct. forms see Monro, *HG* 50), except perhaps to throw more weight on the rhetorical addition 'since you have no pity for the Trojans dying'. This is a theme the god is to develop in 31f.; see also 24–32n. *fin.*

28–9 τό is demonstrative and refers forward to the suggestion in 29 (rather than backward to the idea of obeying him): 'But, if you care to listen to my suggestion, this would be much better – for us to put a stop to war...'. πόλεμον καὶ δηϊότητα (etc.) is a standard phrase, 6 × *Il.*, and an emphatic one.

30–2 The runover-word cumulation is logically necessary, as well as serving its usual function of leading into a fresh idea or elaboration, since Apollo can hardly expect to have Athene end the war altogether. Preventing Athene from actively supporting the Achaeans at this moment is the best he can hope for. Indeed his tactic seems successful, since, when fighting resumes next day, at first it is equal but then the Trojans prevail (8.72ff.). — 'Until they find the *tekmor* of Ilios', cf. 9.48.; on τέκμωρ see 1.525–7n. – it is the 'end' or 'boundary' of Troy, that which determines its fate, an indirect and abstract expression which sets the fate of Troy as somehow objectively fixed, with the contestants struggling and suffering until they eventually discover it. Apollo in his next words seems to accept that the two goddesses' wish is final, 'to destroy this town utterly' (διαπραθέειν, thematic aor. inf. of διαπέρθειν), and that this is its τέκμωρ; yet the complex syntax may conceal a certain disingenuousness on his part.

33 An ancient variant, τὸν δ' ἠμείβετ' ἔπειτα, was known (Did/A); the difference is minimal, though this would afford a degree of variety in view of 37, see on 3.199.

34–5 Athene makes a quick decision and agrees, but disguises the real reason for her descent to Troy – which was presumably not only to counter the threat posed by Hektor with Paris and Glaukos but also to help the Achaeans take the offensive again.

36 πῶς μέμονας, 'how do you intend...?' cf. Lat. *memini*; the impetuosity implied in most uses of μενοινάω, μεμαώς etc. (cf. μένος) is absent here (cf. Chantraine, *Dict.* s.v. μέμονα). πόλεμον καταπαυσέμεν ἀνδρῶν effortlessly varies the language of 29 to suit the new grammatical context.

38–42 Apollo's 5-v. reply, an initial statement of suggested action followed by two balancing and closely-enjambed explanatory couplets, is undramatic and almost flat. The effect may be intended to suggest divine dispassion, though it accords with the curiously low-key treatment of this whole meeting.

38 Ἕκτορος...κρατερὸν μένος is a grandiose periphrasis for Hektor himself, cf. 16.189 Ἐχεκλῆος κρατερὸν μένος and 23.837 Λεοντῆος κρατερὸν μένος: a variant of the Πριάμοιο βίην or βίην Ἡρακληείην idiom on which see 2.658–60n. It is no objection to the locution that it 'splits the formula Ἕκτορος ἱπποδάμοιο' (Shipp, *Studies* 258), cf. Hainsworth, *Flexibility*, *passim*.

39 ἤν τινα: cf. e.g. 2.72 αἴ κέν πως θωρήξομεν, with comment; the conditional idiom does not entail any real doubt about the gods' ability to achieve their aim. The form ἤν is surprising, and Chantraine, *GH* 1, 282, found its many occurrences (19× *Il.*, 17× *Od.*) 'all suspect'. Often εἰ, or εἴ(αἴ) κ', can be restored; the former was supported here by Heyne and

Brandreth, but Leaf's objection seems just, that this common construction requires κε or ἄν. ἥν may well be a relative innovation, but it is questionable whether this presumably Ionic contraction has in all ineradicable cases to be regarded as post-Homeric. — οἰόθεν οἶος recurs only at 226; with the similar αἰνόθεν αἰνῶς of 97 it is a particular mannerism of this Book (see also on 5.440–2, 6.143; and for the clustering of formulas vol. III, ch. 2), in which the -θεν formation is used intensively (developed from many other Homeric adverbs in -θε(ν) with an ablatival sense, perhaps by the medium of more abstract formations like πεδόθεν); see Chantraine, *GH* I, 241f. and M. Lejeune, *Les Adverbes grecs en* -θεν (Bordeaux 1939) 89f. Arn/A interprets as μόνος πρὸς μόνον (bT give οἴως as an alternative), but is unlikely to reflect Aristarchus here.

The emphasis on a duel (which one would have thought was plainly implied by προκαλέσσεται and ἀντίβιον μαχέσασθαι, but see next n.) is further developed by οἶον of his opponent in 42.

40 The same v. is used of Paris' challenge at 3.20 and is the first of several detailed similarities; but whether Paris at that point intended single combat is open to question, see 3.19–20n. Certainly ἐν αἰνῇ δηϊοτῆτι would normally suggest general fighting.

41 ἄγαμαι implies a strong or excessive reaction (cf. post-Homeric ἄγαν; also 3.224n. and Chantraine, *Dict.* s.v. ἀγα-) and developed two contradictory meanings, 'admire' on the one hand, 'grudge' on the other. The latter is more probable here, since the Achaeans would resent the idea of Hektor's boastful challenge going unanswered. — χαλκοκνήμιδες occurs only here, to take the epithet–name group back to the masc. caesura, in place of regular and frequent εὐκνήμιδες. It is now clear that bronze greaves were not particularly uncommon in the Late Bronze Age, see on 3.330–1, and that objections to the present epithet (e.g. Shipp, *Studies* 258 n. 2) are no longer cogent.

43 Athene's further agreement is cursorily noted, and might seem to follow logically from her words at 34f. Actually a duel might not suit her plans at all well unless she was set on rigging the outcome, which does not appear to be the case. Once again the poet's desire to proceed with a second duel, without too much concern for motivation, is the determining factor.

44–122   Helenos conveys the divine intention to Hektor, who stands between the two armies and makes his challenge. The Achaeans are embarrassed; eventually Menelaos rises to accept, but is dissuaded by Agamemnon

44–5 This is the only place in *Il.* where παῖς must be scanned as a monosyllable (as against over 50× as two naturally short uncontracted syllables). The *Odyssey* differs, with 6 monosyllables against 28 dissyllables.

ἐφήνδανε comes only here, cf. τοῖσιν δ' ἐπιήνδανε μῦθος | (7 × *Od.*), also 13–16n. on ἐπ(ι)άλμενος.

Helenos' previous appearance has been at 6.76, as Πριαμίδης Ἕλενος, οἰωνοπόλων ὄχ' ἄριστος, where he suggests Hektor's withdrawal to Troy to organize prayers to Athene. No special act of divination, or supernatural understanding of divine wishes or conversations, is credited to him on that occasion, which in some respects exemplifies the typical 'advice pattern', see on 6.75–9; yet his suggestion is of a religious kind, and Hektor accepts it from him without question (see also on 6.73–101). His later appearances will be simply as commander (at 12.94) and warrior (at 13.576–99, cf. 758–82 where he is wounded by Menelaos) or as one of the sons rebuked by Priam at 24.249. In the post-epic tradition he reveals by prophecy that Troy can only be taken by means of Herakles' bow (Sophocles, *Phil.* 604–13), and escapes to Epeiros to become Andromakhe's second husband (Euripides, *Androm.* 1243–5, cf. Virgil, *Aen.* 3.294ff.) – these are exotic developments perhaps of no great antiquity. The tale that he and his sister Kassandre gained the power of hearing divine voices when their ears were licked by snakes as babies (cf. Melampous) is recounted in the D and bT scholia on the present passage and credited to the inventive 3rd-cent. B.C. writer Anticleides (*FGH* 140 F 17). It is salutary to remember that Kassandre's own prophetic powers are passed over in silence by Homer, indeed by all surviving sources until Pindar (*Py.* 11.33).

Yet the Trojans need a prophet, if only to balance Kalkhas, and Helenos is assigned the rôle at 6.76 (where, however, he makes no prophecy) and here, where intriguing hints are given of his technique. He intuits the divine plan, σύνθετο θυμῷ, 'put it together for himself [the literal meaning being more apt here than 'gave heed to' *vel sim.* as at e.g. 1.76] in his heart' (or mind). Aristarchus (Arn/A) interpreted this as meaning that he understood by prophecy, not by hearing their conversation: μαντικῶς συνῆκεν οὐκ ἀκούσας αὐτῶν τῆς φωνῆς. It is true that 44f. need not imply that he perceived their actual words in some way (though they do not exclude it), or did any more than a μάντις usually does when he divines a god's thoughts or intentions, as Kalkhas with Apollo's at 1.93ff. Yet 52–3 will completely alter the picture; see the comment there.

46–53 Helenos finds Hektor (in a formular v., = 8.280) and conveys his advice in a simply organized short speech: 2 vv. of address and persuasion, 3 about what exactly he is to do, then 2 of justification and credentials. Colometry is fourfold and simple, enjambment light.

47–8 Διὶ μῆτιν ἀτάλαντε (etc.) is a flattering formula used 4 × of Odysseus, twice of Hektor (so addressed at 11.200 by Iris herself); it is not found in *Od.*, but cf. θεόφιν μήστωρ ἀτάλαντος (etc.), 2 × *Il.*, 2 × *Od.* ἦ ῥά νύ μοί τι πίθοιο (2 × *Il.*, cf. 28) confirms that Helenos is being as persuasive as possible; so does his addition that he is, after all, Hektor's brother. It is strange that he does not mention his prophetic status, even though it is implied at 53.

49 = 3.68 in the first, Paris vs. Menelaos, duel.

51 = 40, repeating the terms of Apollo's proposal – which does not of course prove he had heard it *verbatim*.

52–3 The solemn spondaic opening of 52 leads to an only slightly less impressive phrase for dying, a formula found 4× *Od.* (with θανέειν for θανεῖν) though not exactly elsewhere in *Il.* (but cf. θάνατον καὶ πότμον ἐπίσπῃ, etc., 3×). V. 53 was athetized by Aristarchus (Arn/A) on the ground that Helenos understood the gods through prophecy, 'as already stated' (viz. in his note on 44, q.v. with comment). This is plainly a personal judgement based on his reluctance to accept overhearing the gods as a valid form of prophecy. That may or may not be justified, but a more concrete reason for suspicion is not mentioned by Aristarchus: that the content of 52 does not form part of the divine conversation as reported. This could be mere oversight, or the conversation could be fuller than the poet chose to record. Yet it remains true that, even if Helenos is speaking loosely, ὅπ' ἄκουσα θεῶν, after σύνθετο θυμῷ | βουλήν in 44f., and following on the report of an actual divine conversation, implies quite strongly that he heard or intuited (or whatever) *what they were saying to each other*, and not a message addressed by a god to him *qua* prophet. That kind of prophetic eavesdropping on divine plans is unparalleled in Homer; yet it is clear that in the present instance the gods could hardly resent it, indeed must have intended some device for putting their scheme into effect. In short, Helenos' intuition involves an unusual view of the way the gods might convey their wishes to a human intermediary (cf. Berghold, *Zweikampf* 186), but one that may merely attempt to lend detail, in particular circumstances, to a form of communication that is normally left mysterious or undefined. This poet (or the poet at this juncture) may reveal a special interest in – or indifference to the niceties of? – such similar responses to fate or circumstance: compare Priam independently making to the Trojan assembly at 375–8 the same untypical suggestion of a truce for collecting the dead as Nestor had made to the Achaean chieftains at 331–3.

54–6 = 3.76–8, q.v. with n., and the conclusion that 'In its present form this three-verse passage is specific to the two formal duel-scenes and was probably composed for one or both of them, or for a close archetype'; also that Hektor 'greatly rejoicing' seems more natural in the earlier instance, since there Paris has agreed to make a move towards ending the war whereas here he himself will have to face an unknown and probably formidable opponent, for no very obvious advantage, and with no more than Helenos' few confident words to encourage him. The exegetical scholia on this second occurrence of the 3 vv. reflect a complex scholarly analysis of Hektor's actions and motives. The silent signal of holding up his spear with a grip half-way up its shaft (to show that his intentions are not warlike, A) was held to be more necessary here, when the armies are locked in noisy conflict, than in bk 3 when they were not yet fully engaged (bT). — In 56 the vulgate reading is τοί as at 3.78, but one group of MSS including A, D and Ge favours οἱ, accepted in OCT. Usually the MSS replace the older form τοί with οἱ (etc.) except where metre demands the former (cf. Chantraine, *GH* I, 275f.), which is not so here. The repeated passages were probably at some stage identical and τοί should be preferred; but with the partly modernized and incompletely systematized spelling of our texts even that is debatable.

57 In the equivalent scene in bk 3 the Achaeans continued to hurl arrows and stones at the Trojans until Agamemnon ordered them to stop (3.79–83). That is condensed here, and Agamemnon bids them be seated, like the Trojans, as though he had been through all this before.

58–61 Epanalepsis of initial κάδ (apocope of κατά) in 57 and 58 links the pair of deities to the pair of armies. The Trojans sat, then the Achaeans likewise, then the gods did something similar. It is primarily a rhetorical device, but the divine interest is confirmed and the forthcoming duel given a special and unworldly status. As T put it, the poet is elevating the proceedings, ὑψῶν τὰ πραττόμενα, by making the gods spectators.

59–60 Athene and Apollo sit on the high oak-tree (presumably that of 22, q.v. with n.) to watch; they are 'like vultures' – is that just a simile, or have they actually taken vulturine form? The question is not merely pedantic and has literary interest; unfortunately ancient critics left no opinion on the matter. There are several other contexts in both *Il.* and *Od.* where gods, and especially Athene, move rapidly like birds and on occasion take their form (cf. F. Dirlmeier, *Die Vogelgestalt homerischer Götter*, Sitzungsberichte der Heidelberger Akademie der Wissenschaften, Phil.-hist. Kl., 1967, 2): (i) Dr S. West's first thoughts were probably correct (i.e. in *Odissea* I, not the English revised version) that *Od.* 1.320, of Athene, ὄρνις δ' ὥς... διέπτατο, is simply a simile to express rapidity of movement, which is characteristic of Homeric deities. (ii) Her second thoughts (in the Eng. version) are preferable over *Od.* 3.372, where φήνη εἰδομένη cannot simply be equivalent to φήνη δ' ὥς – indeed εἰδόμενος -η specifically means 'disguised as' or 'taking the form of' in *all four* of its Iliadic occurrences and *all remaining eight* of its Odyssean ones, as in the repeated v. Μέντορι εἰδομένη ἠμὲν δέμας ἠδὲ καὶ αὐδήν (5 ×). (iii) When Apollo descends from Ida ἴρηκι ἐοικώς at *Il.* 15.237 he obviously goes as swiftly as a hawk, not in the likeness of one. (iv) Hainsworth may or may not be right in *Odyssey* I that αἰθυίῃ δ' εἰκυῖα of Leukothee at *Od.* 5.337 means 'in the manner of' and not 'in the form of'. It should be noted that ἐοικώς -ότες usually connotes 'like' in a general sense, but 'in the likeness of' at 2.20, 5.604, 13.357, 14.136, 17.725, 21.600, 24.347. (v) Again, at *Od.* 22.240 Athene darts up into the roof of the *megaron* and sits there, ἕζετ' ἀναΐξασα χελιδόνι εἰκέλη ἄντην, like a swallow. The bird-comparison might apply simply to her movement, ἀναΐξασα, but word-order as well as the addition of ἄντην suggests she has temporarily disguised herself. (vi) There is one passage, and that in *Il.*, where a minor deity goes up into a tree and almost certainly takes the form of a bird; for at 14.286–91 Sleep, Ὕπνος, climbs the highest tree on Ida to observe Zeus without being seen by him and sits there, covered by the pine-branches, like the bird gods call χαλκίς and men κύμινδις. Movement is not in question here, and the obvious interpretation is that Hupnos not only sits concealed like the bird, but has taken the bird's form (the term for 'like', ἐναλίγκιος, could imply either; for the latter cf. 17.583).

A degree of uncertainty remains. No doubt vultures (αἰγύπιος is a poetic and generic name, φήνη perhaps *Gypaëtus barbatus*, cf. D'Arcy W. Thompson, *A Glossary of Greek Birds*, 2nd edn, London 1936, s.v.) did from time to time sit in trees in pairs when battle was on; and if the gods are set on watching from such a position, then they might simply be likened to them. The poet may, after all, consider them as invisible to men in any case, which reduces the possible absurdity. But the Hupnos passage favours a temporary metamorphosis – a regular stratagem for gods, these two more than most. All in all that appears the most likely interpretation; the poet had in any case some specific sense in mind for this striking and unusual image. At least theriomorphism can be left out of the account, since neither Athene nor Apollo, presumably, was originally a vulture (!), cf. 1.551n.

61–2 The cumulated | ἀνδράσι τερπόμενοι makes the image of the two gods in the tree even more striking. Probably in an incongruous form, certainly in an incongruous place, they sit there 'rejoicing in men': that is, in the opposed armies now seated and waiting for single combat to be arranged. The model, ironically, is the Zeus of 8.51f. and 11.80–2, seated in splendid isolation, rejoicing in glory, watching the city of the Trojans and the ships of the Achaeans. These gods are not at heart so objective as that, but for the time being they take pleasure in the mortals spread out before them, whose immediate destiny they have jointly determined.

The seated ranks are πυκναί, densely packed, and πεφρικυῖαι, either 'shivering' or 'bristling', with shields, helmets and spears. The relation of these two senses of φρίσσω etc. is less than crystal clear (cf. Chantraine, *Dict.* s.v. φρίξ). Cold causes shivering, and hair to bristle; but the real connexion may be in the idea of an apparently rough surface, whether spiky or through oscillation. The *Iliad* uses both senses: fields bristle, φρίσσουσιν ἄρουραι, with corn at 23.599, people shiver or shudder, πεφρίκασι, in fright or horror at 11.383 and 24.775. Sometimes the senses overlap. Here 'bristling' is only strictly appropriate to the spears, but in any event *the description properly belongs not to a seated army but to one advancing*: the crucial comparison is with the dense, dark phalanxes that move into battle σάκεσίν τε καὶ ἔγχεσι πεφρικυῖαι at 4.281f. — As bT remark, 62 even by itself stirs the imagination as well as elaborating the narrative; and the visual aspects of the scene are further developed in the simile that follows. The equivalent scene at 3.84f. had nothing similar, but proceeded directly to Hektor's speech.

63–6 The simile is typically sharp and brilliant but provokes further reflexion on the meaning of πεφρικυῖαι and φρίξ. In the last n. it was seen that the (seated) troops are 'bristling' with weapons because that was the way advancing armies are usually envisaged, especially in relation to their spears. Now the ranks of Achaeans and Trojans are seated 'as the φρίξ of the west wind pours over the sea, when it [*sc.* the wind] first springs up, and the sea darkens because of it [*sc.* the φρίξ]'. The φρίξ is the rippling or ruffling of the surface: it is a movement of the water but presents a static rough appearance when seen from a distance. Whether the whole mass of troops is itself envisaged as tensely moving, as oscillating in anticipation as it were, is doubtful; more probably it is simply the ruffled surface, akin to bristling, that is so visualized. But their ranks are πυκναί (61), and in the comparable 4.282 they are also κυάνεαι, purple or dark; the blackening of the sea evokes that same density and darkness. So too at 21.126 a fish will dart up through the black ripple, μέλαιναν φρῖχ' ὑπαΐξει; at *Od.* 4.402 the old man of the sea will emerge 'covered by' black ripple, as though it were something tangible, μελαίνῃ φρικὶ καλυφθείς. These applications appear to extend and loosen the terms of the present simile, cf. also 23.692f., ὡς δ' ὅθ' ὑπὸ φρικὸς Βορέω ἀναπάλλεται ἰχθὺς | θίν' ἐν φυκιόεντι, μέλαν δέ ἑ κῦμα κάλυψεν. Leumann, *HW* 62 n. 30, argued that the author of those vv. misunderstood the genitive Ζεφύροιο in the present passage, taking it as possessive whereas it is actually absolute with ὀρνυμένοιο νέον in 64. That is ingenious, but the separation of Ζεφύροιο from ὀρνυμένοιο is strongly against it, and both descriptions seem to be syncopations of longer ones in which the φρίξ is specifically caused by the wind; so that the φρίξ of the west (or north) wind means the ripple belonging to, or emanating from (so Ameis–Hentze), that wind.

Finally Aristarchus (Did/A) read πόντον ὑπ' αὐτῇ, taking Ζέφυρος as subject of μελάνει – verbs in -αίνειν being usually transitive in Homer, but cf. 20.42 κύδανον; the vulgate πόντος ὑπ' αὐτῆς is widely preferred. μελάνει for μελαίνει seems to be a variant *metri gratia*, for which other forms in -άνω offer no good parallel (Shipp, *Studies* 85f.).

67–91 Hektor's speech begins with the same formular v. as in the equivalent passage at 3.86, but is followed correctly by ὄφρ᾽ εἴπω...κελεύει; whereas 3.87 misapplies a v. used twice later in bk 7, suggesting priority at this point for the present version of the duel, see on 3.86–7. The speech as a whole is simply expressed, cumulative in style and with heavy progressive enjambment (10 instances), with 4 vv. in periodic enjambment and only one (79) in integral, against a mere 3 whole-v. sentences. The latter part, in which he sets out the details of returning the loser's body, is especially discursive and reflects his constant concern with this theme, which is to become an obsession from bk 22 on. The formular epithets stand out more than usual from this rather plain style, and give a relaxed and almost ingratiating impression to his words: 67 ἐϋκνήμιδες, 69 ὑψίζυγος, 71 εὔπυργον, 72 ποντοπόροισιν, 75 δίῳ, 77 ταναήκεϊ, 78 κοίλας, 82 ἱρήν, 83 ἑκάτοιο, 84 ἐϋσσέλμους, 85 κάρη κομόωντες, 86 πλατεῖ, 88 πολυκλήϊδι, οἴνοπα, 90 φαίδιμος.

His overtly stated main points form a coherent argument if they are glossed somewhat as follows: (i) the oaths made for the previous duel have not ⟨yet⟩ been fulfilled; (ii) ⟨therefore⟩ Zeus must be determining destruction for one side or the other; (iii) ⟨therefore⟩ let a champion face him, Hektor, in renewed single combat ⟨to see which side is really at fault⟩; (iv) moreover ⟨Zeus's involvement demands that⟩ the loser's body should be handed over for proper burial, (v) in the case of a ⟨probable⟩ Achaean loser, with a mound that will perpetuate their ⟨and especially Hektor's⟩ *kleos*.

69 The reference to the oaths is unambiguous; only extreme Analysts have questioned its authenticity. The oaths were those solemnly taken by Agamemnon (with Odysseus) and Priam at 3.275ff., before the previous duel that day, to the effect that if Paris killed Menelaos, then the Achaeans were to give up Helen and leave forthwith; if the reverse, then the Trojans were to hand over Helen, the goods she brought with her and proper reparations. To this Agamemnon added that in the absence of reparations the war would continue. Both sides cursed oath-breakers (3.298–301), but the duel ended in an unforeseen way with no clear decision. It is only the truce that is formally broken (when Pandaros wounds Menelaos at 4.125ff.), and it is then that Agamemnon claimed naturally enough that the Trojans had trampled on the oaths, 4.157 κατὰ δ᾽ ὅρκια πιστὰ πάτησαν, and predicted that Zeus would destroy Troy as a consequence – words echoed by Idomeneus at 4.269–71. The Trojans made no comment – nor is there any reference to Pandaros' treachery (admittedly at the behest of Athene) at his death in bk 5. Now at last Hektor mentions the oaths, and, as one might expect, in an egregious manner that makes the whole affair look like an act of god: 'The son of Kronos, who weighs the balance on high, did not bring the oaths to completion.' In short, some reference to the abortive outcome of the previous duel can hardly be avoided, and he deals with the matter brilliantly. What is surprising is that the Achaeans let him get away with it, making no rebuttal even when it would help them out of their embarrassment when none of them is anxious to accept Hektor's challenge.

70 τεκμαίρεται, 'decrees', as with τεκμήραντο at 6.349 (literally, establishes a τέκμωρ or end, see on 30–2): Zeus is decreeing, with evil intent, κακὰ φρονέων, for both parties, until one or other suffers defeat. κακὰ φρονέων is a self-contained formula, 5 × *Il.*, cf. e.g. 16.373 Τρῶσι κακὰ φρονέων; which makes it difficult to take κακά with τεκμαίρεται also, ἀπὸ κοινοῦ as Willcock suggests. Rather the quality of Zeus's decree is revealed by the state of his mind, κακὰ φρονέων.

73 Aristarchus read δ' ἐν for μέν (Did/A), almost certainly correctly. A second μέν after ὅρκια μέν in 69 is unlikely (except for those who like Leaf would like to expunge the oaths altogether), whereas δ' balances that μέν; moreover 'there are among you ἀριστῆες' is preferable to 'you have ἀριστῆες...', simply. In any case the function of γάρ (in ὑμῖν δ' ἐν γὰρ ἔασιν) is complicated; Denniston, *Particles* 73, calls it an isolated Homeric instance of 'fusion of clauses'; that presumably implies, what seems to be the case, that γάρ presupposes the sentence which actually follows: '(let someone face up to me,) *for* you have among you the chieftains of all the Achaeans'.

74–5 Hektor now challenges an Achaean champion to face him; his ostensible purpose is suggested in the supplements of 67–91n. *fin.*, but he must know, all the same, that Zeus would probably *not* determine the previous oaths in his favour. Perhaps he feels that to kill one of the enemy leaders in single combat would be worthwhile in itself, and more effective than pursuing his recent advantage in general fighting; or perhaps the poet has no fully worked-out motive for him in mind, but proceeds for his own purposes with a second formal duel. What those purposes might be, however, is itself unclear: (i) further delay, given that there is to be another major distraction in the building of the wall and trench, seems unnecessary; (ii) the single-combat theme is hardly rich enough to encourage further deployment so soon, given the poet's apparent difficulty in varying it (e.g. over how the duel is to be terminated); (iii) foreshadowing of Hektor's final encounter with Akhilleus (except for the ironical concern shown over the fate of his body) is not sufficiently stressed to be a plausible motive; (iv) the emphasis thrown on Aias and his rôle as the Achaeans' main defensive fighter could be achieved in other ways, and in any case emerges in bk 12 and later; though it undoubtedly helps justify his membership of the embassy in bk 9. — If the composer's materials and motives remain a little mysterious at this point, at least his character Hektor can be said to be successful in disguising his weak moral stance as challenger.

In 75 πρόμος was evidently taken by Aristarchus (Arn/A) as a syncopated form of πρόμαχος (i.e. 'front fighter' in a special sense), and Chantraine, *Dict.*, was inclined to agree. It has been noted that no other human character in Homer applies an honorific epithet to himself as in Ἕκτορι δίῳ (cf. φαίδιμος Ἕκτωρ in 90); yet δίῳ is not in any case very emphatic, and Hektor is doing no more than use formal and grandiloquent language appropriate to his challenge and his temporary self-confidence.

76 The solemn declaration and invocation correspond formally with the prayers and oaths of 3.276ff. They were to do with the ending of the war, but now Hektor is concerned solely with the disposition of the loser's corpse. That might reflect the composer's uncertainty of purpose; or it could be Hektor's way of further distracting attention from the ambivalent implications of the proposed encounter: 'he abbreviates and distorts the matter of oaths, since they had recently transgressed them' (T).

77–85 There is close correspondence between the main elements of the two conditional sentences: 77 εἰ μέν κεν ἐμὲ κεῖνος ἕλη and 81 εἰ δέ κ' ἐγὼ τὸν ἕλω; 78 τεύχεα συλήσας φερέτω and 82 τεύχεα συλήσας οἴσω; 79 σῶμα δὲ οἴκαδ' ἐμὸν δόμεναι πάλιν and 84 τὸν δὲ νέκυν ἐπὶ νῆας ἐϋσσέλμους ἀποδώσω; 79f. ὄφρα πυρός με | Τρῶες...λελάχωσι and 85 ὄφρα ἑ ταρχύσωσι...Ἀχαιοί.

79–80 These vv. recur at 22.342f. when Hektor lies mortally wounded: his request will be brutally rejected by Akhilleus. He had already tried to reach agreement over the treatment of the loser's corpse at 22.254ff., with some similarity to the present passage at 258f.:

> ἀλλ' ἐπεὶ ἄρ κέ σε συλήσω κλυτὰ τεύχε', Ἀχιλλεῦ,
> νεκρὸν Ἀχαιοῖσιν δώσω πάλιν, ὡς δὲ σὺ ῥέζειν.

Both direct repetition and loose similarity are probably deliberate, underlining Hektor's obsession with this matter and giving ironical point to his emphasis on the present occasion. — Inf. δόμεναι is used as 3rd-person imper. here, 'let him give', but (as more commonly) as 2nd-person imper. at 22.341; the change of reference is minor and says nothing about priority. σῶμα, not otherwise of a human corpse in *Il.* (though 3× *Od.*), is an acceptable metrical variant for the commoner νέκυς as in 84. πυρός λελάχωσι (etc.) 'allot one's share of fire', i.e. in cremation, is a brilliantly figurative phrase, 4× *Il.*

81–3 Hektor knows he has divine support (52f.) and credits it to Apollo, partly no doubt to depress his challenger. Dedicating trophies on temple walls was a common later custom mentioned only here in *Il.*

85   The verb recurs at 16.456 = 674 of Sarpedon, ἔνθα ἑ ταρχύσουσι κασίγνητοί τε ἔται τε, followed by the significant words τύμβῳ τε στήλῃ τε. Here too the act of ταρχύειν is to be followed by building a mound (86 σῆμα); but there the tomb and gravestone are specifically part of the ταρχύειν process – which cannot, therefore, be solely concerned with the immediate disposal of the body (as with corresponding πυρὸς ... λελάχωσι at 79f.). That is important, because ταρχύειν has naturally often been connected (and still is, e.g. by Willcock) with ταριχεύειν and τάριχος, 'dried (or smoked) fish', and held to connote some special treatment of the corpse, e.g. a kind of embalming for those killed overseas. The close relation of ταριχεύειν (used by Herodotus no less than 12 × of mummifying) to ταρχύειν is in fact doubtful (Chantraine, *Dict.* s.v. τάρῑχος; he seems to deny the possibility s.v. ταρχύω), the suppression of the former's long iota being inexplicable. In any event ταρχύειν in Hellenistic uses, as well as in Hesychius and the garbled scholia on this passage, retains the implication of solemn burial rather than any peculiar treatment of the corpse, and M. Andronikos (*Arch. Hom.* w 6) rightly stresses this as the Homeric meaning. See also G. Nagy in C. A. Rubino and C. W. Shelmerdine, edd., *Approaches to Homer* (Austin 1983) 197ff.

86   As part of the formal burial of his victim Hektor envisages the Achaeans as 'pouring a conspicuous mound', a σῆμα, for him. Only one of the tumuli along the shores near Troy can be said to have been certainly there in Homer's time; that is Beşik Tepe above Besika Bay on the Aegean shore, of which J. M. Cook in his exemplary survey concludes that 'we cannot tell whether the Aeolians who came to settle on this coast saw a broad low mound or a tall tumulus at Beşika. In either case, however, they must have been aware of a massive artificial barrow there' (*Troad* 174). The other surviving tumuli seem from their (sparse) contents to have been later; the prominent Üvecik Tepe, three kilometres inland from Besika Bay, is probably the Roman 'Tomb of Festus' built over a tumulus of classical date (Cook, 172f.), and the three tumuli between Sigeum and Kum Kale, i.e. close to the promontory at the southern entrance to the Dardanelles, were probably built in the later 6th or earlier 5th cent. B.C. (Cook, 159–65). None of these is strictly 'over the flat Hellespont', the only survivor to fit that description being the conspicuous In Tepe, the 'Tomb of Ajax', to the east of the mouths of the Skamandros and near Rhoeteum, which is of Hadrianic date though it had a predecessor closer to the sea (Cook, 88). — It is possible, therefore, that a prominent mound behind Besika Bay (where there was also a cemetery with Mycenaean connexions, see pp. 49f.) was indeed a landmark familiar to sailors who passed this way, 'sailing in many-tholed ship over wine-dark sea' (88), and so gave Homer or a predecessor the idea. There may, of course, have been other early tumuli that have not survived, even perhaps along the strictly Hellespontine shore.

87–91 καί ποτέ τις εἴπῃσι followed (in 91) by ὡς ποτέ τις ἐρέει follows the pattern of 6.459 and 462, likewise a comment imagined by Hektor; see on 6.459–62, also on 300–2 below. The second καί in 87 could mean either 'even' or 'also', the point being that the mound will last long into the future.

88 νηΐ πολυκλήϊδι recurs at 8.239 and 3 × *Od.*, and πλέων ἐπὶ οἴνοπα πόντον 2 × *Od.*; ἐπὶ (εἰς) οἴνοπα πόντον by itself is found 3 × *Il.*, 4 × *Od.* Sailing the sea is a more common Odyssean pursuit, but this particular combination of established phrases, with its plangent repetitions of π, ν and κλ, is a unique and brilliant evocation of the timeless remoteness of this unknown passer-by.

89–90 The style of the comment is that of funerary epigrams, in which every word counts. The onlooker, as Hektor imagines, will sense that 'splendid Hektor' is the victor, and that his unnamed heroic victim is himself ennobled thereby. See further on 300–2, also Preface p. x.

91 Hektor now specifically claims what he has so far only hinted at (in words that won the disapproval of the exegetical scholiasts, who accused him of ambition, pretension and barbarism): that as winner of the duel he will attain glory for ever – cf. the κλέος ἄφθιτον conceived as Akhilleus' destiny at 9.413.

92 = 398 and 3.95, where a similar silence greeted Hektor's equivalent proposal for a duel. The v. is formular, 10 × *Il.*, 5 × *Od.*

93 Technically a rising threefolder, though colometry is overridden by the strong antithesis of the exactly matched μέν and δέ clauses. Such rhetorical phraseology is prominent here and there in this Book, see on 39, 120–1.

94 | ὀψὲ δὲ δή is formular, 7 × *Il.*, 5 × *Od.*, often following the formular v. 92; so also at 399. Together they neatly express a thoughtful or nervous reaction to a serious proposal. There is no ὀψὲ... after 3.95, since Menelaos there accepts the proposal with confidence; here his offer is delayed and reluctant.

95 νείκει ὀνειδίζων, obtrusively redundant and not found elsewhere, is scarcely improved by reading νείκε' as in 'some of the commentaries', Did/A. The rest is more straightforward, though apparently unique to the occasion, and makes Menelaos' unhappiness unmistakable.

96–100 His reproaches are expressed with unambiguous severity which needs no support from unusual colometry, punctuation or sentence-length.

96 ἀπειλητῆρες is *hapax*; Ἀχαιΐδες οὐκέτ' Ἀχαιοί repeats Thersites' insult of 2.235.

97 For αἰνόθεν αἰνῶς see on 39 οἰόθεν οἶος.

99–100 'May you all become water and earth' is a unique expression. These are the components from which human beings are made according to one popular view (so Hesiod, *Erga* 61, Xenophanes frag. 33, cf. Hesiod, *Theog.* 571 with M. L. West's comment), and the Achaeans' inertia makes it an appropriate form of curse. ἀκήριοι, from κῆρ = 'heart', means 'lifeless' or 'spiritless' (6 × *Il.*; in its two Odyssean uses it has a different sense akin to that of ἀκήρατος). ἀκλεές is neuter acc. used adverbially; nom. plur. ἀκλέες, so accented, had some support (cf. Eustathius 669.1) but is probably an incorrect form (Chantraine, *GH* 1, 74). αὕτως intensifies: 'in an utterly inglorious way'.

101–2 Internal punctuation and light integral enjambment, leading to the pointed general statement about the gods, stand in effective contrast to the periodically and progressively enjambed couplets just before. τῷδε is not 'harsh' (Leaf) (nor is its dative force hard to understand), but emphatic and derogatory. On πείρατ' see 6.143n.; here the sense must be not 'bonds' but 'limits' – not that victory is manipulated as though on strings, but that the ends or decisions about who shall win are held above, in the sky, among the gods.

103 bT were right to note the minor oversight that Menelaos would already have been in armour, wrong to suggest that perhaps he now puts on special armour for the purposes of a duel.

104 This v. is almost identical with 16.787, ἔνθ' ἄρα τοι, Πάτροκλε, φάνη βιότοιο τελευτή, where in moving terms the poet announces Patroklos' imminent death. Here the emotional level is lower and the statement conditional – yet Menelaos *is* in danger, and the rather staid narrative of events so far needs to be made more dramatic. On the poet's use of apostrophe, direct address in his own voice to one of his characters, see on 4.127, also Edwards, *HPI* 37f.; Patroklos (no less than 8 ×, all in bk 16) and Menelaos (7 ×) are the main recipients of this kind of address, which can be metrically useful (as with Eumaios in *Od.*) but also seems to reveal a special sympathy by the poet for these particular characters. Menelaos was twice apostrophized, at 4.127 and 146, when he was wounded by Pandaros, at first sight fatally; now, too, he is on the verge of great danger.

105 Hektor's superiority will be defined by Agamemnon at 111–14.

106–8 The other chieftains restrain him, but Agamemnon takes him by the right hand in a solemn and intimate gesture, cf. e.g. 4.154. ἔπος τ' ἔφατ' ἔκ τ' ὀνόμαζε(ν) is a common form of emotional address, 17 × *Il.*, 26 × *Od.*, often accompanied by touching with the hands. δεξιτερῆς ἕλε χειρός occurs in such a context here only, but cf. 14.137 δεξιτερὴν δ' ἕλε χεῖρ' Ἀγαμέμνονος – Bentley preferred the acc. form at 7.108 also, to observe the digamma of ἔπος.

109–19 Agamemnon's reply begins with an excitably punctuated and closely enjambed couplet, after which the style becomes calmer as he explains his reasons. He ends, like Menelaos, with a clause or sentence beginning at the bucolic diaeresis: 118 αἴ κε φύγῃσι, 101 αὐτὰρ ὕπερθε.

109–10 ἀφραίνειν only elsewhere at 2.258 and *Od.* 20.360, in abuse of Thersites and by the suitor Eurumakhos respectively. The abstract form ἀφροσύνη seems concocted to strengthen ἀφραίνεις; like χρή with the gen., it is otherwise Odyssean. Menelaos' madness consists in fighting unnecessarily against a stronger opponent.

111 ἐξ ἔριδος: 'out of rivalry' as at *Od.* 4.343, i.e. just to make a contest (rather than out of rivalry with the other Achaeans as bT claim). That is not, of course, Menelaos' true motive for standing up, which is likely to have been shame at the failure of the others and a feeling of responsibility for the war on his own part – issues Agamemnon may prefer to avoid.

112 στυγέουσι, 'abhor', conveying strong physical revulsion (so Chantraine, *Dict.* s.v.); the idea of fear is clearer in the recurrence of this hemistich at 15.167, of the other gods' feeling about Zeus.

113–14 'Even Akhilleus' – but not elsewhere in *Il.*, and this must be a piece of persuasive exaggeration by Agamemnon to assuage his brother's pride. Akhilleus himself will say at 9.352–5 that while *he* was fighting Hektor never dared move far from the walls. It is in fact no insult to Menelaos to say that Akhilleus is greatly his superior, πολλὸν ἀμείνων, in war. The language is fairly standard at this point, though ἀντιβολῆσαι etc. comes at the v-e in its other 8 Iliadic uses.

117–19 The subject changes to Hektor: he will have a hard task whoever the Achaeans set against him – Agamemnon's peroration is rhetorical in style and occasionally strained in expression. Thus ἀδειής comes only here; admittedly ἀδεής is not easily accommodated in hexameters, except e.g. in the formula κύον ἀδεές (3 ×). μόθος is a relatively unusual term for the moil of battle; three of its occurrences are in the phrase κατὰ μόθον, the other two relate to Hektor, here and at 240, q.v. with note. ἀκόρητος is regular, also with πολέμου, ἀϋτῆς and μάχης. 118–19 are reminiscent of Akhilleus's threat at 19.71ff.,

>   ἀλλά τιν' οἴω
> ἀσπασίως αὐτῶν γόνυ κάμψειν, ὅς κε φύγῃσι
> δηΐου ἐκ πολέμοιο ὑπ' ἔγχεος ἡμετέροιο.

γόνυ κάμψειν, 'to bend the knee', i.e. probably to sit down after the strains of fighting, is confined to these two contexts (with the more drastic ἄμφω γούνατ' ἔκαμψε when Odysseus is washed ashore at *Od.* 5.453), though not uncommon in tragedy. Homeric knees can be touched, unloosed, speedily wielded, or subdued, all in standard phrases, and there is no reason why they should not be bent also – though the precise implications of that are not made so clear. At any rate critics have not been disposed to question the

vv. in their bk 19 form. Yet 119 here involves a clumsy adaptation, suggesting that bk 19 may indeed be the model; for ὑπ' ἔγχεος ἡμετέροιο there is unsuitable and has to be replaced. This is done nearly but not quite in the form of 5.409, ἐλθόντ' ἐκ πολέμοιο καὶ αἰνῆς δηϊοτῆτος – here, however, ἐλθόντ' gives way to δηΐου. Leaf found the repetition with δηϊοτῆτος 'disagreeable' and thought these 3 vv. probably added; ancient critics noticed nothing amiss, moreover 119 recurs as 174, where it appears necessary. In any event Greek audiences did not find verbal repetitions so jarring as we sometimes do; cf. P. E. Easterling, *Hermes* 101 (1973) 14ff.

120–1 These words, down to παρειπών, occurred at 6.61f. (with the possible toning down of παρέπεισεν to ἔτρεψεν), likewise of Agamemnon to Menelaos – see n. there; but now assonance and alliteration are made even more extreme by the addition of the ὁ δ' ἐπείθετο· τοῦ μὲν ἔπειτα. No one who heard these lines could doubt that they were being treated to a display of aural fireworks which had no particular relation to meaning but was, on the other hand, consonant with the sporadic rhetorical *tours de force* of the present Book; see also on 39, 93.

122 Appears regular in expression, and well describes an action which makes a firm and rather touching conclusion to Menelaos's brave intervention. Yet it happens to involve a unique application of the formula ἀπ' ὤμων τεύχε' ἕλοντο (4 × *Il.*, cf. αἴνυτο τεύχε' ἀπ' ὤμων 2 × *Il.*), elsewhere used of stripping the armour off a victim (cf. 5.7n.), as in the unambiguous variant ἀπ' ὤμων τεύχε' ἐσύλα, 3 × *Il.* There is, of course, no reason why a gesture, e.g., should not have different applications according to context. Thus χεῖρε (...) πετάσσας, 'stretching out both arms', in *Il.* describes a victim collapsed on the ground or imploring succour from his comrades (twice each); in *Od.* an embrace, or the Cyclops guarding the exit from his cave, or a kind of dive (once each). That gesture of itself has multiple implications; even so, its martial uses in *Il.* can create a kind of resonance in *Od.* When a particular use becomes established by repetition, exceptional applications become noticeable and may create distinct overtones. Thus the peaceful action of Menelaos' servants 'taking' armour off shoulders *could* carry a residual echo of the more violent removal from corpses in battle. That seems unlikely; but by temporarily abandoning traditional martial associations the singer has done something noteworthy by oral standards.

123–205 Nestor rebukes the other Achaeans for their reluctance, relating a long exemplary tale of events in his youth. As a result nine chieftains volunteer, of whom Aias is then selected by lot

123–60 The poet is clearly interested in varying this duel from its precursor in bk 3; essential ancillary themes appear in both, but they are differently developed. Thus the very idea of a challenge leads to alternative possibilities of response: immediate and straightforward, delayed and complicated. Delay inevitably elicits a rebuke, itself a common theme (see on 5.471); indeed rebuke followed by acceptance or self-justification is a classic Homeric device for dramatizing attitudes and elaborating confrontations. Even in bk 3, where Menelaos accepts the challenge, the rebuke theme made an appearance; for Paris makes an implicit challenge and then retreats from it, to be rebuked by Hektor who then makes a formal challenge on his behalf. Here in bk 7 the rebuke theme is even more prominent. First Menelaos rebukes the other Achaeans for their cowardice; then Agamemnon lightly rebukes him for his rashness; finally Nestor makes a developed rebuke based on his own exploits when young.

It may well be that, as Schadewaldt felt (*Ilias-Studien* 82ff.), this type of *parainesis* is extremely ancient; yet we can know little about it in earlier forms, and it is not prominent in e.g. the Gilgamesh epic. Nestor's reminiscences about warfare and skirmishing in the western Peloponnese (perhaps reflecting conditions after the collapse of the Mycenaean empire, cf. vol. I, 215f.) have an air of authenticity and may represent a particular strand of local saga, entirely separate from the Trojan or Theban material, that became available to Homer or his predecessors; see now M. L. West, *JHS* 108 (1988) 160. Together with his own seniority and rôle as counsellor, with a *penchant* for reminiscence even apart from exemplary aspects, it has been developed into an important minor *genre* within the poem as a whole. The *Iliad* contains four such speeches by Nestor: (i) 1.254ff., where he intervenes in the quarrel between Agamemnon and Akhilleus and tells them to take his advice, as the Lapiths did when he helped them in their war against the Centaurs; (ii) the present speech, in which he starts by saying how Peleus would lament if he knew what was happening, then recalls how he himself readily responded to the Arcadian Ereuthalion's challenge and slew him; (iii) 11.656–803, where, addressing Patroklos, he criticizes Akhilleus for his indifference to the Achaean plight and remembers his own prowess in the skirmishes between Pylians and Epeians, culminating in his devastation of the Epeian chariot-force; he recalls how Peleus and Menoitios instructed their sons as they left for Troy, and urges Patroklos to use his father's advice against Akhilleus; (iv) 23.626ff., where he thanks Agamemnon for awarding him a prize and recalls how he won every contest but one at the funeral games for Amarunkeus. Of these, (i) and (iv) are shorter and relatively simpler than the others, of which (iii) is longest with 158 verses. (i), (ii) and (iii) are all rebukes, and (ii) and (iii) both refer at some length to Peleus. A somewhat similar *parainesis* (with Peleus-reference, youthful reminiscence and developed *exemplum*) is

Phoinix's speech to Akhilleus at 9.434ff. There, however, allegorical elements are added and the main *exemplum* is not autobiographical but an independent tale of the wrath of Meleagros.

The present speech is regularly expressed, though with a necessary concentration of proper names at 133–7. The style is cumulative and progressive, only the death of Areithoos at 142–5 giving rise to shorter, less sedate sentences. Finally it may be noted, against the doctrine often advanced by scholars about Homeric digressions in general, that the length and complexity of Nestor's *paraineseis* do *not* for the most part correspond with differing needs for emphasis on their particular contexts, but vary according to their own interest and internal associations. Further study is needed, but meanwhile the facile idea that length and elaboration necessarily reflect structural or emotional importance should be treated with caution.

123 The other Achaeans still need spurring into action; Nestor is the obvious person to do it, especially since he cannot take up the challenge himself.

124–5 His rebuke begins like his reproach to Akhilleus and Agamemnon at 1.254ff.; 124 here = 1.254, and at 1.255 Priam would rejoice, | ἦ κεν γηθήσαι, whereas here Peleus would lament, | ἦ κε μέγ᾽ ὠμώξειε (in contrast with μέγ᾽ ἐγήθεεν at 127). The exegetical scholia fussed about why Nestor should adduce *Peleus'* grief to persuade the Achaeans, since he was father of Akhilleus who was causing all the trouble. But Peleus was a respected figure who typically filled the rôle of the father sending off his son to Troy, and whom Nestor once visited (127–8n.). — 'Horseman' is usually applied to heroes of the previous generation (so e.g. Willcock); see on 2.336 for ἱππότα (21 × of Nestor, also of Peleus (twice), Phuleus, Tudeus and Oineus); ἱππηλάτα, with γέρων usually preceding, goes with Peleus (4 ×), Phoinix (3 ×), Tudeus and Oineus. Clearly -eus names predominate, but these epithets are also useful for preceding *dissyllabic* names beginning with a consonant or digamma, and the old -eus names are often dissyllables. Horsemanship is not an attribute peculiar to them: Patroklos is ἱππεύ(ς) (4 ×), and ἱπποδάμοιο is most frequently used of Diomedes.

126 The description is unique, though composed of standard elements; e.g. Nestor himself is (λιγὺς) Πυλίων ἀγορητής (2 ×).

127–8 Nestor will describe the occasion more fully in another reminiscence at 11.769ff.: he and Odysseus were visiting Peleus in Phthie to recruit his son (and Menoitios') for the war against Troy. Zenodotus' μέγα δ᾽ ἔστενεν for μέγ᾽ ἐγήθεεν, and consequently μειρόμενος for εἰρόμενος, would be incredible had not Aristarchus said so (Arn, Did/A, Arn/T). In 128 τόκος probably means much the same as γενεή, i.e. parenthood (as also, probably, in the same phrase at 15.141 and *Od.* 15.175), rather than 'offspring' as often in later Greek.

130 The poet is straining to make the imagined scene an unusual one. Neither ἀείρειν nor ἀναείρειν are used elsewhere in Homer of raising arms in supplication (or, as here, indignation) to the gods – the regular formula is χεῖρας ἀνέσχον (etc.) as in 177, 9× *Il.*, 3× *Od.*; nor are χεῖρας usually φίλας (only at *Od.* 12.331), though the epithet somehow suits Peleus' imagined despair. Aristarchus (Did/A) and a few late MSS read βαρείας for φίλας ἀνά, unappealingly.

131 | θυμὸν ἀπὸ μελέων; so *Od.* 15.354, cf. *Il.* 13.671f. = 16.606f., 23.880. Its combination with the δῦναι δόμον formula (3.322 + 3 variants) is casual, not to say careless, since it is the ψυχή not the θυμός that normally descends to Hades.

132–3 The invocation in 132 was used by Agamemnon, rhetorically, at 2.371 and 4.288. Nestor's wish that he were young again is a typical way of introducing his reminiscences, but at 11.670 and 23.629 it takes the form of the v. that will be used resumptively at 157, εἴθ' ὡς ἡβώοιμι... That is precluded here since αἰ γάρ has just occurred, hence ἡβῷμ' simply.

133–5 The setting of this encounter between Pylians and Arcadians (on ἐγχεσίμωροι cf. 2.692 and 4.242n.) is described with notable vagueness. Pheia is said to be on or by two different rivers, Keladon and Iardanos (of which Keladon might be a tributary, Ameis–Hentze); yet classical Pheia was not on any river worth the name, neither was a Keladon or Iardanos known in the Peloponnese. According to Strabo 8.348 some thought the town was Khaa and the river Akidas (the latter mentioned by Pausanias 5.5.8 as joining the Anigros somewhere near Arene/Samikon). Aristarchus (Arn/A), on the other hand, took κελάδοντι to be an epithet like ὠκυρόῳ, with a change of case by the time their noun, 'Ιαρδάνου, finally appears in 135. That is unacceptable, even if one suspects that ῥόῳ κελάδοντι (cf. ῥόος κελάδων at 21.16) lies at the root of the problem. As for Iardanos, the same phrase 'Ιαρδάνου ἀμφὶ ῥέεθρα | denotes a river in western Crete at *Od.* 3.292 (see S. West *ad loc.*), and the poet may have repeated the name almost automatically – though a river as such is not required by the context. Strabo, *loc. cit.*, talked of a *tomb* of Iardanos.

Acc. plural Φεάς appears at *Od.* 15.297; it is in or near Elis, passed by Telemakhos on his voyage home from Pulos to Ithake. The MSS there have Φεράς, a common confusion, and Didymus argued for it here too; but Aristarchus, Strabo and others show Φεάς to be the right reading in *Od.*, and Φειᾶς is probably correct here. Pheia is most likely to be the predecessor of the classical *polis* on a hill near modern Katakolo, by the northern end of the Cyparissian Gulf, but the rivers remain mysterious (despite HSL 94); the mouth of the Alpheios lies some ten miles down the coast. If the western

Arcadians were in Parrhasia (vol. 1, 218), then they might have interfered as far to the N-W as Pheia; though somewhere further south, around Arene indeed, might have been a more plausible area for border clashes with Pylians.

136 Nestor had mentioned Ereuthalion back at 4.319, where he told Agamemnon that he wished he were as young as when he slew Ereuthalion. Now comes the full story.

137–50 Similarly Areithoos has had a brief mention at 9f. where Paris kills his son Menesthios. That passage named Areithoos' wife Phulomedousa, perhaps an *ad hoc* invention; see on 8–13, which also considers possible chronological difficulties. Here we learn that Areithoos was given the sobriquet 'mace-man' (also at 9) because he was armed not with bow or spears but with an iron mace; that one Lukourgos killed him by trapping him in a narrow place where he had no room to swing the club, and spearing him to death; and that Lukourgos wore his victim's armour until he grew old and gave it to his squire Ereuthalion, who challenged the Pylians. The tale is narrated in clear ring-form: would I were young, Ereuthalion, Areithoos, Ereuthalion, would I were young.

137 That Ereuthalion was wearing Areithoos' armour is emphasized again at 150; quite why it, as opposed to the iron mace, was important is unclear, except perhaps as a means of introducing the tale of Areithoos' death. More probably a longer version is being abbreviated.

138–41 According to 9, Areithoos' son Menesthios lived in Arne, presumably the one in Boeotia; see on 8–13. Here bT say that Areithoos, though Boeotian, was an ally of the Arcadians – obviously mere guesswork. His name is Greek but his weapon (probably related to κόρυς) is Near Eastern, perhaps Assyrian, in type. Its being of iron differentiates it from primitive Early Bronze Age maces with stone heads from Troy and northern Greece (cf. H. G. Buchholz's ultimately inconclusive discussion, *Arch. Hom.* ε 319–38). It also suggests that it is not merely a development of e.g. the Centaurs' branches, compare Herakles' (post-Homeric) club and Orion's bronze one, ῥόπαλον παγχάλκεον, at *Od.* 11.575. Any kind of club would be relatively useless in organized battle, precisely in the φάλαγγες he is supposed to have smashed according to 141, since anyone with a thrusting-spear, let alone a throwing-spear, lay out of range. One possibility is that Areithoos was originally an Arcadian brigand, the subject of saga after the end of the Bronze Age, whose rôle gradually developed so that he was credited with armour and involved in formal warfare; another, that Homer got the idea from Near Eastern sources, perhaps poetical and perhaps via Cyprus (so Lorimer, *HM* 119f.).

138 Epanalepsis of the proper name casts further emphasis on the whole digression; also, through δίου, on the heroic status of Areithoos.

142–5 Like 147, 142 can be phrased as a rising threefolder – perhaps should be, in contrast with the emphatic central caesuras of the intervening verses. Areithoos' death has a folktale aura: how do you deal with a club-swinging enemy? Get him in a place where he has no room to swing. That is done by trickery, 142 δόλῳ, i.e. the narrow passage is planned and not just a fortunate accident. Again the lack of realism reminds one of folktale: he could have shot him down almost anywhere, but the mace-man has to be overthrown specifically in relation to his idiosyncratic weapon. This Lukourgos (no relation to the Thracian king of 6.130ff.) is said in the later tradition to be an Arcadian hero, son of Aleos or Amphidamas, father of the Argonaut Ankaios; his grave was shown at Lepreon (Pausanias 5.5.5).

143–4 A narrow defile at a place called Phoizon was remembered as site of the ambush in Pausanias' time (8.11.4). στεινωπῷ ἐν ὁδῷ looks unique, but recurs in the context of the chariot-race at 23.416. ὄλεθρον | χραῖσμε entails a loose extension of the regular meaning of χραισμεῖν, 'help': 'ward off destruction, οἱ, to his benefit'.

145–6 The killing is described in totally formular language, with the first half of 145 recurring at 13.397, the second at 11.144 and 12.192, and | τεύχεα δ' (τ') ἐξενάριξε 4 × *Il.*; τά (etc.) οἱ πόρε sic is also formular, 6 × *Il.*, as is χάλκεος Ἄρης, 5 × .

147 μετὰ μῶλον Ἄρηος |: so also at 16.245.

149 δ' is apodotic. This is the first time we hear that Ereuthalion was Lukourgos' θεράπων (on which see 165n.).

150 For the emphasis on Lukourgos' armour, quite apart from the mace, see on 137. Whatever Ereuthalion's degree of fictionality, his challenge may be specially created by the poet here to provide Nestor with his *exemplum*.

151 οὐδέ τις ἔτλη | 7 × *Il.*; the rest of the v., though regular in vocabulary, is not exactly paralleled.

152 θυμὸς ἀνῆκε(ν) 6 × *Il.*, elsewhere at the v-e. πολυτλήμων (cf. πολύτλας) comes only here in *Il.* and once in *Od.*; it is emphatic in contrast with 151 οὐδέ τις ἔτλη (so Ameis–Hentze).

153 | θάρσεϊ ῷ is apparently parallel to | σῷ θάρσεϊ at 6.126, with ῷ equivalent to ἐμῷ, 'through my own boldness'; that may be correct since it leads on more consequentially to the mention of Nestor's extreme youth. So Zenodotus, but Aristarchus disagreed (Arn/AT), evidently taking the phrase to refer to Ereuthalion, '*his* rash self', after the model of βίην Ἡρακληείην etc. on which see 38n. Extreme youth is a typical element of this kind of David-and-Goliath encounter; cf. Nestor's other youthful triumph at 11.717ff.

154 δῶκεν...'Αθήνη |: cf. εὖχος ἔδωκε -ας | 3 × *Il.*, δώη δέ μοι εὖχος Ἀπόλλων 2 × *Il.* Nestor has not previously mentioned this prayer, but such omissions and compressions are common enough, especially in the abbreviated-reference style and in relation to gods, cf. e.g. 6.183n. *init.*

155–6 155 is solemnly spondaic. μήκιστος does not recur in *Il.* but is used of the giants Otos and Ephialtes at *Od.* 11.309; Nestor applied κάρτιστος with triple emphasis to the great Lapiths and Centaurs of his youth at 1.266f. (cf. also 6.185, 9.558). Such superlatives typically belong to speech not narrative, see p. 31. Nom. πολλός is rare (3 × *Il.*, 2 × *Od.*) compared with πολύς; in association with τις, only here in Homer, it is a distinctively Ionic idiom, and like ὀλίγος τις is frequent in Herodotus, see J. E. Powell, *A Lexicon to Herodotus* (Cambridge 1938) s.v. τις, III.3. Thus a poet who could have used κεῖτο μέγας μεγαλωστί as at 16.776 (with some adjustment to provide a connecting particle) ventures on a new and partly colloquial description in which ἔνθα καὶ ἔνθα is traditional enough (cf. e.g. 2.812, 5.223, 6.2) but παρήορος, evidently intended to mean 'sprawling' *vel. sim.* (as in a possible imitation at Aeschylus *Prom.* 363), probably entails a wholly idiosyncratic reapplication of a traditional term.

For it is one of Manu Leumann's *tours de force* to have shown in detail (*HW* 222–31) the curious background to Homeric uses of παρήορος, παρηορίαι. The former is properly the trace-horse, the latter the traces; the derivation is from ἀείρομαι (Chantraine, *Dict.* s.v. ἀείρω 2), 'be suspended from', 'be attached to', in the special sense of 'harnessed', as e.g. with συναείρεται at 15.680. The παρήορος is the horse that is harnessed παρά, to the side. That is unmistakable at 16.467ff. when Sarpedon hits and kills Patroklos' trace-horse Pedasos (specifically said to have been put ἐν παρηορίῃσιν, in addition to the yoked pair, at 16.152; see n. there); the other two horses leap apart, the yoke creaks, the reins are entangled, ἐπεὶ δὴ κεῖτο παρήορος ἐν κονίῃσι – 'since the trace-horse lay in the dust' (471). Automedon then cuts the horse clear and order is re-established. Leumann argues that ἔκειτο παρήορος ἔνθα καὶ ἔνθα here in bk 7 is a reapplication of κεῖτο παρήορος ἐν κονίῃσι at 471 there, and thus that the singer has misunderstood as 'sprawling' a phrase that had lodged in his memory out of proper context.

One thing is certain: that παρήορος here cannot mean 'trace-horse'. At 23.603 it must mean 'reckless' or the like, which could be a metaphorical derivative of the trace-horse meaning; could 'sprawling' be a different one, i.e. running out to the side ἔνθα καὶ ἔνθα, in two directions, namely very extended? That is just possible, but now (at 227f.) Leumann adduces another argument: for at 8.80–90 a horse of Nestor's (no less) is wounded; it is disturbing his other horses, and Nestor cuts away the traces, παρηορίας ἀπέταμνε. It is a trace-horse, therefore – but the poet curiously refuses to use the term παρήορος itself, even though clarity and context demand it. Is that because he is the same as the composer of the Nestor-reminiscences, and so takes παρήορος to mean something different? Leumann thought so; the matter will be further discussed in 8.87–91n.; meanwhile it is difficult to treat his contention as anything less than a strong possibility, and an intriguing one.

157 A typical v., see on 132–3, used here to close the ring.

158 ἀντήσειε μάχης, an adaptation of traditional language to produce a colloquial effect: 'would have a fight on his hands'.

159–60 159 οἵ takes a 3rd-person verb, 160 οἵ a 2nd-person one (there is nothing unnatural about the latter, *contra* Leaf); Ameis–Hentze compare 5.878, 17.250 and *Od.* 9.275f. for the change of number, but the main factor may be that 159 retains as much as possible of 73, ὑμῖν δ' ἐν γὰρ ἔασιν ἀριστῆες Παναχαιῶν.

161–8 Nine stand up at Nestor's rebuke (they are imitated in the metrically awkward *Od.* 8.258), with Agamemnon remembering his kingly rôle and volunteering first – though he could have done so sooner, one remembers, when dissuading his brother. The list is more complex than at first appears. V. 162 ∼ 23.288 (with Eumelos for Agamemnon) and 163 = 23.290, both from the list of volunteers for the chariot-race. The next 4 vv. recur at 8.262–5 in a list of eight Achaeans who follow Diomedes in driving the Trojans back from the trench: they are Agamemnon, Menelaos, the two Aiantes as here, Idomeneus and Meriones as here, Eurupulos as here, and lastly Teukros. The four repeated vv. are hardly typical or traditional, and one or other context is borrowing from the other; bk 8 takes many repeated lines from elsewhere and is *prima facie* candidate as borrower (τοῖσι δ' ἐπ' may fit better in 8.262, which has two heroes named in the previous v., but then τοὶ δ' ἐπί in 7.164 would make an awkward hiatus). Diomedes replaces Agamemnon as first and Teukros is included, though see on 164 below; Menelaos is of course added, though excluded here for special reasons.

The chariot-race list has a further affinity with the present one in that it leads to a drawing of lots (at 23.352–7, though for places rather than to find a single name). There, Eumelos, Diomedes, Menelaos, Antilokhos and Meriones are involved, of whom Eumelos is known primarily for horsemanship and would not be a suitable opponent for Hektor; Antilokhos provides an excuse for his father Nestor to give advice, but is too young for the present rôle – even though he is among the volunteers for the spying expedition at 10.227–32, q.v. with n. Eurupulos and Thoas are the least powerful candidates, but the former is to be prominent in bk 11 (though his contingent rates only 4 vv. in the Catalogue) where he is wounded, whereas Thoas wins high praise later, see on 2.638. There are no other obvious absentees, apart of course from Akhilleus, Patroklos and Menelaos, since

Tlepolemos is dead and e.g. Meges, Menestheus or Leïtos are clearly less effective; for Teukros see on 164, and for Odysseus on 8.261–5.

164 The Aiantes are 'clothed in fierce defence' as at 18.157, cf. ἀναιδείην ἐπιειμένε at 1.149 and the common formula θούριδος ἀλκῆς |; for a possible IE parallel see M. L. West, *JHS* 108 (1988) 154. They are probably the two Aiantes, rather than the greater Aias and Teukros (who are sometimes meant, by the old use of the dual Αἴαντε which is also extended to simple plural forms, see on 2.406); that is suggested by the recurrence of this v. at 8.262 in a list in which Teukros is specifically named (see previous n.) – unless that v. is indeed borrowed from here and its implication misunderstood. In fact neither the lesser Aias, sometimes envisaged as light-armed (see on 2.527), nor Teukros who is usually an archer, makes an ideal champion, though both are often seen fighting in regular armour.

165 ὀπάων occurs only 6 × *Il.*, not *Od.*, of which 5 × of Meriones as companion of Idomeneus (and once, at 23.360 in a probably secondary use, of Phoinix). The word is Mycenaean and signifies a companion in warfare especially (Chantraine, *Dict.* s.v.; C. J. Ruijgh, *Minos* 9, 1968, 124); but Meriones is also called Idomeneus' θεράπων (6 × *Il.*), a far commoner term which can, but need not, express a more subservient relationship. ὀπάων Ἰδομενῆος | (3 ×) and θεράπων ἐΰς Ἰδομενῆος | (3 ×) serve different metrical purposes; the possibility of a specifically Cretan origin for the former cannot be discounted. See further S. West on *Od.* 1.109–12.

166 This formular description of Meriones (4 × *Il.*) may be of considerable antiquity – cf. M. L. West, *JHS* 108 (1988) 156 on the scansion of Ἐνυαλίῳ ἀνδρεϊφόντῃ.

168 Odysseus comes last, almost as an afterthought – not because he is clever (bT) but because he can hardly be omitted after such as Eurupulos and Thoas (neither he nor Thoas appears in the bk 8 list).

170–4 Nestor now tells them to draw lots; that is succinctly conveyed in 171, the other 3 vv. being general exhortation. Is this to divert attention from the possible disadvantages of a lottery (religious beliefs apart) when the paramount need is to choose the best man? The problem was noted by bT (171,*e*) and they suggested some psychological reasons for doing it Nestor's way.

171 πεπάλασθε (rather than -εσθε, cf. εἶπας etc.), from πάλλειν = 'shake', is correct against the impossible πεπάλαχθε which found its way into many MSS despite Aristarchus (Arn, Did, Hrd/A). 'Shake now with the lot, successively, to see who gets it' must not be taken quite literally. What actually happens is that they each throw their marked lot into Agamemnon's helmet and then Nestor does the shaking – not to mix the lots, or not only that, but until one jumps out (175–82). In the less developed drawing of lots in the first formal duel Hektor and Odysseus at 3.316 'took lots in the helmet and shook them', presumably to mix them up – for at 324–5 (q.v. with n.) it is Hektor alone who performs the final shaking that makes the winning lot jump out. Like much technical vocabulary in Homer, that of drawing lots tends to be loosely deployed from time to time; thus 3.316 recurs at 23.861, but there the two contestants, not the umpires, do the shaking. Yet the same syntax as here is implicit in 24.400, τῶν μέτα παλλόμενος κλήρῳ λάχον ἐνθάδ' ἕπεσθαι – which confirms that 'shaking with the lot' is a general expression for casting a lot, and λαχεῖν etc. for winning.

172–3 ὀνήσει... ὀνήσεται: he will benefit the Achaeans and also himself, if he survives; αὐτός, ὃν θυμόν and the middle form of the verb emphasize the personal advantages, obviously in gifts and honour.

174 For the repetition δηΐου... δηϊοτῆτος see 117–19n. *fin.*

175–7 Each of the nine made his mark on, ἐσημήναντο, the lot (presumably a potsherd, see on 3.324–5) and put it in the helmet – the regular receptacle, cf. 3.316. There is no question of any kind of writing being used as at 6.169, since each can recognize only his own σῆμα (183ff.); Aristarchus rightly remarked that they used signs not letters (Arn/A).

177–8 The prayer occurs at the same point, and is introduced in the same terms, as in the equivalent drawing of lots in bk 3, see on 3.318–23. In 177 ancient grammarians (cf. Hrd/A) and medieval MSS were divided between θεοῖσι δέ and θεοῖς ἰδέ, the former being preferable. V. 178 will be repeated at 201; | ὧδε... εἴπεσκε(ν) is strongly formular, see on 6.459–62.

179–80 The prayer is unusually succinct; for the use of the infinitive (perhaps assuming δός, T) cf. 2.413, 3.285. The three names are in order of preference as 182f. show; yet a favourable view of Agamemnon (cf. 162) is maintained, since Odysseus or Idomeneus might well have been preferred. He is 'king of Mukene of much gold', which recurs, in even more honorific circumstances, only at 11.46 and 1 × *Od*.

181–2 The same v., though with a different name–epithet group, appeared immediately after the prayer in bk 3 also, at 324. Now in 182 the winning lot leaps out of the helmet as it is shaken; ἐκ δ' ἔθορε κλῆρος recurs at *Od.* 10.207 (cf. 23.353), but in 3.325 the idea is held over to the v-e and a different phrase, ἐκ κλῆρος ὄρουσεν |, used. That is to accommodate a unique and attractive detail, | ἂψ ὁρόων, 'looking away', of the lot-shaker at the verse's beginning.

183–9 This part of the description is unparalleled elsewhere; the showing of the winning lot for identification is unnecessary in bk 3, where only two parties are involved, and is passed over in the cursorily described lottery for the five chariot-drivers at 23.352ff. Here the herald has to carry the lot around all nine (who are in the throng rather than forming one, 183 and 186, φέρων ἀν' ὅμιλον ἀπάντη); it is rejected by each one until it is placed in the hand of the man who had scratched his mark on it (187 ἐπιγράψας) and now recognizes his σῆμα.

184 ἐνδέξια, to the right, is the formal as well as the propitious way to circulate, cf. Hephaistos pouring wine for the gods at 1.597.

188 Handing over the lot for inspection is described in detail to make the moment of recognition even more dramatic. ὑπέσχεθε is *hapax* in Homer, though ἔμβαλε is common, and Aphrodite placed her girdle in Here's hands, ἔμβαλε χερσίν, at 21.47. There is an appealingly naive quality about the herald 'standing close' (6 × *Il.*) and dropping the lot onto Aias' hopefully outstretched hand.

189 Can be heard either as four-colon or as a kind of threefolder, perhaps the latter (in contrast with the regular colometry of the preceding vv.) since a climax is intended.

190 Aias' joy is reflected in a heroic and almost rustic reaction, not a typical one, as he flings the lot to his feet.

191–9 He announces that the winning lot is his and expresses his joy (cf. 189); then, with successive afterthoughts in cumulated vv., tells the others to pray for his success. Vv. 195–9 were athetized by the ancient critics, probably wrongly, see n. *ad loc*. Admittedly 191–4 alone would have constituted a short, practical statement, but the remainder turns into a justifiable and almost expected boast, ending with integral enjambment providing a typical rhythmical climax.

191–2 καὶ αὐτὸς | θυμῷ is mainly for emphasis, though θυμῷ also performs the runover-word's common function of introducing a fresh thought – here, that he will win. δοκέω meaning 'think' is found in Homer only here and at *Od.* 18.382; it is categorized by Shipp, *Studies* 259, as a 'common prose usage'. That is correct, but the verb appears only 8 × *Il.* even in its regular meaning 'seem'.

193 δύω is aor. subjunct. (Aristarchus' δύνω, Did/A, failed to carry conviction); compare Paris' ἀρήϊα τεύχεα δύω at 6.340.

195–9 Aristarchus (Arn/A) athetized these vv. (so too Zenodotus and Aristophanes, Did/AT on 198) as out of character with Aias and making him absurdly contradict himself; even Leaf found that hypercritical. In fact Aias' series of qualifications enables him to lead from the idea of the prayer to a typical piece of self-projection, to be echoed by Hektor at 237–43.

195 For silent prayer cf. Odysseus' at 23.769, ὃν κατὰ θυμόν. The idea is not commonly expressed in *Il.* but is reasonable in the circumstances, for the Trojans are assumed to be observing proceedings closely. The motive for silence is presumably to avoid their frustrating events by a counter-prayer. For σιγῇ ἐφ' ὑμείων cf. 19.255 ἐπ' αὐτόφιν ἧατο σιγῇ, where the Achaeans listen in silence to (and partake in) Agamemnon's prayer.

196–9 Wilamowitz, *Untersuchungen* 244 and n. 6, thought 195 to be authentic but to have generated these next 4 vv. as interpolations; his real objection was to 199 ἐν Σαλαμῖνι, q.v. with n.

196 Aias' amendment is reasonable enough, since a silent prayer might suggest that he is afraid. ἀμφαδίην is an obvious polar alternative to σιγῇ (cf. λάθρη... ἀμφαδόν at 243); the ἐπεί-clause recurs at *Od.* 2.199.

197–9 Now he proceeds to say why fear is out of the question: no one will put him to flight, either (i) by force, βίῃ, against his will, or (ii) through skill, ἰδρείη, i.e. through lack of skill on his own part, since he is no ignoramus in the arts of war. — δίηται, 5 × *Il. sic*, is related to διώκω, cf. Chantraine, *Dict.* s.v. δίεμαι; for the subjunct. as remote fut. cf. e.g. 6.459. ἑκών ἀέκοντα is a rhetorical flourish to strengthen βίῃ, for being driven back by force is obviously against one's will (ἑλών is an ancient variant for ἑκών, preferred by Aristarchus, Did/A, but not compelling). The vulgate then has τ' ἀϊδρείη, wrongly; both ἰδρείη and νήϊδα are connected with (ϝ)οῖδα, νη- being a negative prefix. Hektor in turn will boast of his technical knowledge in the successive οἶδα's of 237–41.

The acc. and inf. construction is unusual where the subject is unchanged, but cf. e.g. 13.269. ἔλπομαι is directly paralleled only at 15.110, but the meaning is not merely 'think' or 'consider' as commentators say; rather the ironical use of 'expect' is natural enough, 'I should be surprised to find that...' Finally that Aias was raised in Salamis is mentioned in Homer only here and in the notorious catalogue-entry at 2.557. That v. was found to be probably authentic despite later objections, and it was suggested in the n. on 558 there that the Salaminian origins of Aias and Teukros may have been played down because of ambivalence in the oral tradition over their Aeacid connexions. The mention of *a* birthplace here is typical and effective, and the v. is probably reflected in Pindar, *Nem.* 2.13f.; γενέσθαι τε τραφέμεν τε is formular, also at 18.436, *Od.* 3.28 (τραφέμεν being 2nd aor. act. inf., intransitive).

200–5 The prayer's introduction is standard (201 = 178), and the invocation in 202 the same as in two separate prayers in the first formal duel at 3.276 and 320, also 24.308. It is especially relevant because Zeus looks down from Ida and is the prime enforcer of justice. Like several prayers in the bk 3 duel it is 4 vv. long, see on 3.351–4. δός here takes first a direct object, νίκην, as at 16.524 δὸς δὲ κράτος, then its usual infinitive construction, here with ἀρέσθαι which adds little to the sense beyond emphasis; there is a loose parallel at *Od.* 2.116f. Another refinement follows, a prudential wish for a draw in case Zeus happens to be favouring Hektor; εἰ in 204 is to be taken with περ, 'even if', with καί emphasizing Ἕκτορα (cf. Denniston, *Particles* 488). φιλέεις καὶ κήδεαι is lightly formular, κῦδος ὄπασσον (etc.) strongly so.

206–312   Aias arms and is terrible to see. After an exchange of boasts they fight: Aias has the advantage but the heralds intervene, and he and Hektor exchange pieces of armour

206–13 Aias arms (the standard details being omitted here, though see 220–3n. *init.*) and advances like huge Ares: the style is majestic, with elaborative phrases like 207 περὶ χροΐ, 209 μετ' ἀνέρας, 212 νέρθε δὲ ποσσίν, 213 μακρὰ βιβάς effectively supplementing the portentous epithets, 206 νώροπι, 208 and 211 πελώριος, 210 θυμοβόρου, 212 βλοσυροῖσι, 213 δολιχόσκιον.

206 κορύσσετο νώροπι χαλκῷ is used of Patroklos at 16.130, cf. κεκορυθμένος αἴθοπι χαλκῷ, 7 × *Il*. The verb, cf. κόρυς 'helmet', came to imply arming in general. νώροπι is a relatively rare metrical substitute for αἴθοπι and probably means much the same, 'gleaming' *vel sim.*, see on 2.578, also Chantraine, *Dict.* s.v. (νηλέϊ, of course, which is metrically equivalent, can only go with χαλκῷ when it connotes an offensive weapon, 'pitiless' spear(-head) etc.).

207 τεύχεα | is surely right against vulgate τεύχη, probably a later Attic spelling; cf. 22.322 ἔχε χρόα χάλκεα τεύχεα | and for the synizesis 4.113 σάκεα. It is nevertheless an uncommon form, probably the result of careless formular adaptation:

(1)   14.187 αὐτὰρ ἐπεὶ δὴ πάντα περὶ χροΐ θήκατο κόσμον
(2)   14.383 αὐτὰρ ἐπεί ῥ' ἕσσαντο περὶ χροΐ νώροπα χαλκόν
(3)   23.803 τεύχεα ἑσσαμένω...
(4)   7.207 αὐτὰρ ἐπεὶ δὴ πάντα περὶ χροΐ ἕσσατο τεύχεα.

Thus (1) seems to be a laboured attempt to convert (2) to a singular subject (see n. there); (4) is perhaps another such attempt (for πάντα...κόσμον would be wholly unsuitable here), in which the initial formula of (3), perhaps, is displaced and its first dactyl revalued as a spondee – νώροπι χαλκῷ has in any case been used in the preceding v., which may help confirm that (2) is somehow implicated in (4) here.

208–11 An unusual simile, close to that at 13.298ff. (see n. there), οἷος δὲ βροτολοιγὸς Ἄρης πόλεμόνδε μέτεισι... Both are elaborations of the common short simile of a hero advancing etc. like Ares, e.g. 13.802 Ἕκτωρ δ' ἡγεῖτο βροτολοιγῷ ἶσος Ἄρηϊ. Ares is πελώριος, 'huge', also at 5.594, as is Aias in the resumption at 211 here; in fact the whole phrase πελώριος, ἕρκος Ἀχαιῶν had been used of Aias by Helen at 3.229 (πελώριος etc. of various subjects, always *sic*, 16 × *Il.*).

209–10 πόλεμόνδε comes in its standard position (13/16 × *Il.*), but μετ' ἀνέρας does not exactly recur elsewhere – for μετά + acc. = '⟨so as to be⟩ among' cf. 13.301. They are men whom Zeus has 'brought together to fight' in, or with, strife (*pace* Willcock), 210 being an elaboration of 1.8 ἔριδι ξυνέηκε μάχεσθαι, with ἔριδι expanded to θυμοβόρου ἔριδος μένεϊ; cf. 19.58 | θυμοβόρῳ ἔριδι μενεήναμεν, also 16.476. The couplet is a little laboured but contributes to the grand style of the whole passage.

212 μειδιόων βλοσυροῖσι προσώπασι is one of Homer's most brilliant and powerful phrases, surely created for this context or for another exercise in the grand style at 15.605–10. There Hektor rages like Ares (again!) or blazing fire; froth surrounds his mouth, his eyes blaze out under savage brow, 608 λαμπέσθην βλοσυρῇσιν ὑπ' ὀφρύσιν, and his helmet shakes terribly around his forehead as he fights. βλοσυρός is of uncertain etymology and means 'terrible', 'savage' or 'imposing' rather than 'shaggy' as LSJ suggest, see Leumann, *HW* 141ff. and Chantraine, *Dict.*; for the plural προσώπασι cf. *Od.* 18.192. 'Smiling with terrible countenance' (Ameis–Hentze compare Here 'laughing with her lips' at 15.101f.) suggests a savage joy in battle that Homer rarely expresses, an ominous culmination, perhaps, of Aias' rejoicing at 189 and 191f.

212–13 The majestic language continues; neither νέρθε nor ποσσίν is strictly necessary (the phrase recurs at 13.78), but they add weight to μακρὰ βιβάς, again of Hektor at 15.307 and Aias at 15.686. The vision of Aias taking huge strides forward, wielding his great spear and smiling dangerously, is unforgettable...

214–16 ...and produces immediate effects on those present: joy for the Achaeans, terror for the Trojans, a quaking of the heart for Hektor himself.

217–18 A hero is allowed to feel panic, but not to turn and run before a single opponent – though Akhilleus will overwhelm Hektor's moral resistance, and so outdo even Aias here, in bk 22. The first half of 217 is formular but the compounds ὑποτρέσαι and ἀναδῦναι do not recur – the singer may wish to distinguish between running away in panic and retreating in relatively good order into one's own ranks, a typical motif for which standard language was available, some of it used here: e.g. 17.129 Ἕκτωρ δ' ἂψ ἐς ὅμιλον ἰὼν ἀνεχάζεθ' ἑταίρων. Paris at 3.31ff. had suffered near heart-failure like Hektor and retreated forthwith into his own ranks, cf. 36 καθ' ὅμιλον ἔδυ Τρώων, thereby earning Hektor's violent condemnation.

προκαλέσσατο χάρμη |, cf. χάρμη προκαλέσσατο at 285: χάρμη is from χαίρειν, but J. Latacz, *Zum Wortfeld 'Freude' in der Sprache Homers*

(Heidelberg 1966) 20–38 and 127, shows that it means 'will to fight' rather than 'joy in fighting' (the distinction is sometimes a fine one) – certainly not 'combat' merely as implied by most editors, who have taken the dat. as one of aim or direction ('Dativ des Zweckes', Ameis–Hentze), i.e. 'challenged to combat'. 'Will to fight' makes sense in all 22 Iliadic occurrences, including 17.161 (q.v. with n.); Hektor made the challenge through his will to fight.

219–23 V. 219 recurs at 11.485 and 17.128. Aias carries his σάκος 'like a tower', and it is ἑπταβόειον, 'made from seven ox-hides': on Homeric shields, and how the *sakos* differed from the *aspis* but was often confused with it, see on 3.335, 6.117–18, and the discussion of the Shield of Achilles in vol. v. Here the question is how Aias' shield may have differed from others in the poem. Page, *HHI* 234f., developing Lorimer, *HM* 181ff., held that it differed greatly, being the sole Homeric instance of a true Mycenaean body-shield as represented on the Lion Hunt dagger from the fourth Shaft Grave (cf. e.g. Lorimer 140, fig. 1). Other *sakea* (he thought) are broad, of leather, and, like the *aspis*, wielded by hand and much smaller than the tower shield. It is true that *sakea* are sometimes confused with the round *aspis*, which itself can occasionally be thought of (as at 6.117f. and 15.645f.) as a body-shield. Yet Aias is the only first-rank warrior who is consistently and often described as armed with the *sakos*, just as to a lesser degree Hektor is with the *aspis* – see the Table in Trümpy, *Fachausdrücke* 30f. His shield is so termed on 22 occasions spread over 10 different Books; only at 267, later in the present encounter, is it fleetingly conceived in *aspis*-terms when struck μέσσον ἐπομφάλιον. It also carries the unique descriptions ἠΰτε πύργον (3 ×, all in the formular v. represented by 219 here) and ἑπταβόειον (5 ×), the latter suggesting great size or at least thickness (since even Akhilleus' divine shield has only five layers at 18.481). This *sakos* is undoubtedly bigger and more conspicuous than all the rest, just as Akhilleus' great Pelian ash-spear (see on 16.143) is bigger and heavier than other spears. Whether that makes Aias a subject of poetry from 'long before the Trojan War', as Page claimed, is questionable (though see now M. L. West, *JHS* 108, 1988, 158f.), if only because knowledge of the oblong tower-shield and its operation could undoubtedly have survived through representations, e.g. in frescoes, at least until the end of the Bronze Age. Moreover Aias' association with the tower shield may have been maintained by his special rôle as provider of cover for Teukros as archer as at 8.266–72, q.v. with n.

219 Does ἠΰτε πύργον primarily connote *function*, or *visual aspect* (i.e. size and/or shape), or both? Language makes this difficult to determine: ἠΰτε is a special Homeric term, a 'conjunction of comparison' (Chantraine, *GH* II, 250), its possible adverbial effect in certain contexts hard to gauge.

Thus in 235, μή τί μευ ἠΰτε παιδός... πειρήτιζε, one might wonder how far the force of ἠΰτε παιδός extends from μευ to πειρήτιζε, if at all. Here, the shield might be *carried* 'as a tower' – manoeuvred, perhaps, so as to provide total protection for the warrior while in motion. Even if ἠΰτε... has no close relation to φέρων, 'like a tower' might imply more than great size and strength (as in σάκος μέγα τε στιβαρόν τε, 3 × in arming-scenes, e.g. of Paris at 3.335f.). If so, this shield could be tower-like in specific appearance, e.g. tall, rectangular (seen from the front) and protectively enclosing.

220 χάλκεον: 'gleaming', 'shining' and 'brazen' are common epithets of shields in general, see on 6.117–18, 1st para.; but the bronze facing (cf. 223) is not emphasized in relation to Aias' shield elsewhere, in contrast with Sarpedon's round *aspis* of 12.295–7, which has stitched oxhides on the inside and beaten bronze on the outside, and Hektor's of 13.804. Doubtless it is an *ad hoc* poetical embellishment; Tukhios, the shield's fictitious maker, is described in 221 as a leather-worker, not a craftsman in metal like Hephaistos in bk 18.

220–3 Detail is elaborated as in a simile; it emphasizes still further the formidable nature of Aias and his equipment. Elements of the typical arming-scene, passed over at 206f., appear at this later stage in contrast with Paris' full-scale arming at 3.330–8. — Nothing more is known of the leather-worker (literally '-cutter') Tukhios beyond the typical fantasies of Hellenistic writers. His is a 'speaking name' (cf. vol. 1, 283 and 371f., also 5.59–64n.), evidently created from τεύχειν as the laboured Τυχίος κάμε τεύχων suggests (von Kamptz, *Personennamen* 267). He is said to be a native of Hule, presumably the Boeotian town of the Catalogue, see on 2.499–500. Aristarchus (Arn/A) observed that the upsilon is long there but short here and at 5.708, where Hule is said to be on the Kephisian lake, and home of wealthy Oresbios. Hude, mentioned at 20.385 as beneath Mt Tmolos near Sardis, was likewise associated with wealth; this may have been noticed by Zenodotus, who read Ὕδη for Ὕλη at 5.708 (Arn/A) – if that is not merely a visual confusion of (majuscule) lambda and delta. In any case, as Strabo observed (9.408), Aias would hardly have got his shield from Lydia. The matter was further exploited in the foolish tale recorded by T on 220 and by Eustathius 678f. that Homer when blind lived for a time in Kume's colony Neon Teikhos near Sardis, where he was cared for by a leather-worker called Tukhios whom he immortalized out of gratitude (so too in the ps.-Herodotean *Life* 7f., OCT Homer v, 196f.).

222 αἰόλον: either 'rapid', its original sense, or 'scintillating', 'gleaming'; presumably the latter here in view of the shield's brazen surface and huge size. The well-fed bulls are loosely cumulated onto ἑπταβόειον both as further embellishment and to lead on to the top layer of bronze. The application of metal sheeting to such a large and presumably unstable surface is hardly realistic (though ἥλασε is a technical term of bronze-working, cf. 12.295f. ἐξήλατον... ἥλασεν) – yet another detail of Homeric armament that depends more on poetic imagination than on actuality.

224–5 These vv. resume 219 at greater length in a kind of ring-form: 'Aias came close carrying tower-like shield... carrying that shield he stood close and addressed him.' πρόσθε στέρνοιο, as at 22.313, is more suitable for a smaller shield, an *aspis*, perhaps, as at 20.163. — ἀπειλήσας does not mean exactly 'threatening' here, or at least no explicit threat will be made. These typical initial speeches of challenge and taunt are normally introduced by a neutral v. of address as at 5.632, 6.122, 11.429; sometimes εὐχόμενος, 'boasting', occurs in the resumptive v. at the end. ἀπειλεῖν, etymology unknown, basically seems to imply vigorous assertion (Chantraine, *Dict.*), usually 'threaten' but simply 'promise' at 23.863 and 872, 'boast' at 8.150 and (more ambiguously) *Od.* 8.383. | ὣς φάτ' ἀπειλήσας is used of an actual threat, though not in battle, at 23.184, but recurs in its looser sense at 21.161, where Asteropaios has made no threat other than mentioning his ancestry and saying 'let us fight'.

226–43 Taunt and counter-taunt are kept short, perhaps in response to the unusual scale of the duel itself, and differ strongly in style and content. Aias makes the point that many Achaeans could face Hektor even in Akhilleus' absence; Hektor resents an imagined slight and boasts in unusual terms about his skill at warfare. Aias' 7 vv. are heavily enjambed (integral at 226, 229, progressive at 227, 231), Hektor's 10 lightly so (no integral, progressive at 235, 238, 242, with 3 whole-sentence vv. as well as an introductory v. of address); his short statements seem sententious rather than practical. Thus 5 out of Aias' 7 vv. have an 'ideal' fourth colon (and therefore bucolic diaeresis), against only 3 of Hektor's 10. Each has a rising threefolder, at 232 and (probably) 236; the former comes as final v., as often, to provide rhythmical climax. Paradoxically the corresponding climax in Hektor's reply consists in a final hemistich that is 'ideal', i.e. with the formula αἴ κε τύχωμι occupying the fourth colon after bucolic diaeresis, in contrast with 8 preceding vv. each of which has either the 'alternative' longer fourth colon or a relatively rare spondaic ending. V. 238 is rhythmically unusual in any case, see 238–9n. *init.*

226–7 οἰόθεν οἶος as in 39, see n. there; this is not quite 'an ironical repetition of Hector's own words' (Leaf), since 39 was spoken by Apollo, though with reference to Hektor's challenge. V. 227 is a more straightforward repetition, cf. 73.

228–30 The second formal duel, unlike the first, is dominated by the sense of Akhilleus' absence. ῥηξήνορα (etc.), 'smasher of men', is specific to him (4× *Il.*, 1× *Od.*); θυμολέοντα | again goes beyond usual heroic epithets, elsewhere of Herakles (2 ×) or Odysseus in his wife's estimation (2 × *Od.*). Vv. 229f. recurred in the digression on the outstanding Achaean warrior and horses at 2.771f., but that could be an afterthought (vol. 1, 242f.); at all events they are perfectly in place here, with ὁ μέν met by 231 ἡμεῖς δέ. Aristarchus (Did(?)/T) seems to have preferred ἐπιμηνίσας, wrongly; ἀπο- is intensive (cf. Leaf on 2.772).

232 | καὶ πολέες is a convenient runover phrase, with more point here than at 10.171. The curt invitation to commence hostilities contrasts strongly with the drawing of lots for first throw in the earlier duel. Presumably the motif is suppressed here because a more complex lottery has been needed to select the champion; but priority of strike was not necessarily regarded as an advantage in ordinary battle (cf. 3.313–17n., also on 235–6 below).

234 Hektor begins with an honorific whole-v. address (twice elsewhere, by friends) in contrast with Aias' abruptness in 226.

235–6 In what respect is Aias 'making trial of him' as though he were child or woman (see on 219)? Because of the offer of first strike according to most editors following bT; that may normally have been granted to the younger and less experienced warrior where it was not either ignored or settled by lot, cf. Poseidon to Apollo at 21.439, | ἄρχε, σὺ γὰρ γενεῆφι νεώτερος. But perhaps it is just Aias' condescending tone that annoys his adversary; compare Aineias' response to Akhilleus, 'don't expect to frighten me with words as though I were a baby' (followed, as here, by 'since I *know* how to...') at 20.200f.

236–41 The sixfold deployment of οἶδεν, οἶδ(α) is highly rhetorical, developing the contrast of ignorance and skill initiated by Aias in 198. The woman who does not know about martial matters is a convenient foil for Hektor's recital of all *he* knows; the οὐκ ἴδεν... εὖ οἶδα antithesis of 236f. leads to balanced repetition of οἶδ' within 238, then to a pair of co-ordinate vv. with initial οἶδα at 240f. Thus under the general rubric of 237 (I know battles and manslayings) Hektor divides his skills into (i) with the shield, (ii*a*) at rushing forward in attack and (ii*b*) in the standing fight. The analysis is not so logical as its formalism suggests, since (ii*b*) certainly overlaps (i). Further ambiguities are discussed below.

236 Already noted on 226–43 as a rising threefolder; ἡ is shortened only here.

237 μάχας τ' ἀνδροκτασίας τε | as at 24.548; the latter, 5 × *Il.*, tends to be used in rhetorical contexts, cf. also 11.164.

238–9 Rhetoric overpowers rhythmic norms in 238, with the two corresponding dactylic pairs overriding the central caesura, no 4th-foot break and heavy spondaic νωμῆσαι βῶν to conclude. Yet the stress on οἶδ(α) throughout may have allowed the singer to pause after its second occurrence, and so reactivate the central word-break. βῶν, here only, has caused surprise from antiquity on, but Aristarchus' justified acceptance of it (Did/A) as a form of βοῦν, itself supported by Aristophanes and a few MSS, established it in the vulgate. It survived in Doric and is probably Aeolic in Homer according to Leumann, *HW* 201, but is now attested for Simonides in Photius' *Lexicon* (cf. vol. IV, ch. 3). βοῦς (βῶν), masc. or fem., means 'ox' or 'cow', hence 'a leather shield', cf. Trümpy, *Fachausdrücke* 36f.; ἑπταβόειον is usually taken as signifying *ox*hides, but βῶν | ἀζαλέην, 'dry cowhide', is exactly paralleled by 12.137 βόας αὔας, cf. 12.105 τυκτῇσι βόεσσι.

Hektor knows how to wield his leather shield to right and left. This probably implies dexterity in defence, though bT cite the ingenious idea that δεξιά entailed pursuit, ἀριστερά flight – depending, that is, on how the shield is slung across the body. That dexterity, according to 239, is ταλαύρινον πολεμίζειν for Hektor, i.e. 'that is what I call real shieldman-ship': compare the thrice-used description of Ares as ταλαύρινος πολεμιστής, the fighter who carries the leather shield (cf. 5.287–9n.; on * ταλάϝρινος cf. Chantraine, *Dict.* s.vv. ῥινός and ταλάσσαι, and for ῥινός as shield, rather than skin or layer of a shield as at 248, cf. 4.447 with n., 13.406, 804). But can Hektor claim so much in the way of skill for simply moving the shield from side to side? Sense would be stronger if there were a concealed reference to the war-god and his seemingly archaic description: 'that for me is serious fighting, ⟨like that of shield-bearing Ares himself⟩', rather as with μέλπεσθαι Ἄρηϊ in 241; cf. Bechtel, *Lexilogus* s.v. ταλαύρινος, Trümpy, *op. cit.* 38, who however is doubtful about the implied reference to Ares. Leumann, *HW* 196–201, offers full discussion and a slightly different explanation.

240–1 Both vv. have elicited various interpretations, sometimes arbitrary. ἐπαΐξαι in 240 can only mean 'charge at', 'attack' as in all other martial uses of this common verb. μόθος, 5 × *Il.*, of disputed etymology, seems to imply mêlée rather than din; ἵππων (despite being swift, see on 3.265) connotes chariots. Therefore Hektor means he is skilled at attacking the mêlée of chariots; whether that might imply 'attacking ⟨so as to stir up⟩ a mêlée of chariots', as Trümpy, *Fachausdrücke* 158 suggests after Ebeling, seems doubtful.

The main question is whether Hektor is now envisaged as himself fighting from a chariot (so e.g. Leaf, Ameis–Hentze) – it is a typical accomplish-ment, after all, of the Homeric warrior – or whether he is skilled at charging the enemy, still on foot, as they take to their chariots in flight (cf. Willcock, p. xiv). Against the former is that it is irrelevant to the skill required in a duel, and moreover would seem to involve a mass chariot action, on which see 4.297–300n. Then 240 and 241 are clearly intended to set out different and complementary aspects of the warrior's skill; and the reference of 241 is beyond argument, i.e. to the standing or stationary fight, ἐνὶ σταδίῃ, which tends to confirm 240 also as concerned with the foot-soldier's skills. The content and language of 18.158ff., where the subject is again Hektor, are also relevant:

> ὁ δ' ἔμπεδον ἀλκὶ πεποιθὼς
> ἄλλοτ' ἐπαΐξασκε κατὰ μόθον, ἄλλοτε δ' αὖτε
> στάσκε μέγα ἰάχων...

This, like ἐν σταδίῃ at 13.514, describes a warrior under pressure; here, on the other hand, the phrase implies something less necessarily defensive – that is shown by the ironical 'dance for Ares' (cf. 16.617, where Aineias describes Meriones as a dancer, ὀρχηστής, for avoiding his spear), as well as by the contrast at 15.282f. and 13.314 between ἐν σταδίῃ or σταδίῃ ὑσμίνῃ and long-distance fighting with the bow. What seems intended, therefore, is fighting at close quarters in general, static as opposed to mobile warfare as Willcock puts it. Thus Hektor claims to be skilled with the shield and at fighting both in pursuit and at close quarters. The language has been less untypical than at first appears: βῶν is unusual, but 'dry skin' for shield is paralleled elsewhere, as are ταλαύρινον πολεμίζειν, charging into the μόθος and dancing in standing fight. Only wielding to right and left and the chariots themselves are exceptional. βῶν may be an archaizing form, but the language is high-flown and rhetorical rather than rhapsodic or otherwise 'late'.

242–3 In ἀλλ' οὐ γάρ the ἀλλ' goes with a main clause (here, understood), γάρ with the dependent clause (Denniston, *Particles* 99): 'but (I shall not begin until you are ready), for...' Hektor ends with a sentiment already sketched by Aias at 195f. (cf. 196 ἀμφαδίην with ἀμφαδόν here), that stealth is unheroic: he will not eye him secretly – the phrase has distinctly voyeuristic overtones, cf. *Od.* 19.67 – but make his throw openly.

244–73 The fight is longer and more elaborate not only than its bk 3 counterpart but also than almost any other Homeric combat. Most of the expression is typical (though see 260–2n.), with several vv. and hemistichs recurring elsewhere; comment will be correspondingly briefer. The distinction between Aias' *sakos* and Hektor's *aspis* (cf. 219–23n.) is maintained with unusual care, as is that between spears that are first *thrown*, then retrieved and *thrust*; yet it remains a conceptual, not a realistic sequence of events. Colometry and (mainly progressive) enjambment are straightforward and, with the possible exception of rising threefolders at 253 and 263, unremarkable.

244 The bk 3 duel began with this same v. at 3.355 (and continued with 3.356–60 = 250–4 here, see n. *ad loc.*). There, Menelaos attacks with his sword directly after the initial spear-throws.

245–8 Hektor's throw hits Aias' shield on its outer layer of bronze, which it pierces together with six of the seven layers of hide, to stop (σχέτο, aor. middle) in the seventh. This all accords with the description of the σάκος ἑπταβόειον at 219–23. χαλκὸς ἀτειρής, 'unwearying bronze', recurs at 5.292; this is its regular and perhaps proper application, namely to bronze weapon or spear-head, though at 14.25 it is used of bronze armour struck *by* swords and spears, cf. simple χαλκός at 267.

250–4 = 3.356–60, with 251–2 = 11.435–6 and 251 also recurring at 4.136; see on 3.355–60, especially in relation to 253f., where the spear uniquely 'beside his flank sheared the tunic, and he swerved and avoided black doom' – a couplet sometimes suspected but here accepted as fully Homeric. In v. 252 ἠρήρειστο (pass. pluperf. of ἐρείδω, 'was pressed') reproduces, with its heavy syllables and repetition of ε's and ρ's, the force of the blow as bT commented, probably also its tearing penetration. Then the rising threefold rhythm of 253, stopped by abruptly enjambed ἔγχος in the following v., may seem to evoke the weapon's further but ineffectual progress.

255–60 ἐκσπασσαμένω: various forms of σπάω are used (6 × *Il.*) of withdrawing a spear from a victim's body, though σπασσάμενος at 16.473 and 2 × *Od.* refers to drawing a sword from the scabbard, more usually ἐρυσσάμενος etc. Here, rather, the spears are withdrawn from the shields they have nearly or completely penetrated. The progress from throw to thrust is clearly articulated: προΐει δολιχόσκιον ἔγχος for the former (at 244 and 249), then withdrawal (255), then falling on one another (256 σύν ῥ' ἔπεσον), i.e. at close range, then smiting or piercing the enemy's shield (258 μέσον σάκος οὔτασε δουρί, 260 ἀσπίδα νύξεν), both verbs being reserved for close-range thrusting, cf. Trümpy, *Fachausdrücke* 92f. and 96f. — ἅμ' ἄμφω | σύν ῥ' ἔπεσον recurs at 23.686f. in the boxing match in the Funeral Games; this duel, too, will end as though it were a friendly competition (cf. Kirk, in Fenik, *Tradition* 38f.).

The simile of the clash of lions or boars recurred at 5.782–3, q.v. with n. Boars are a regular symbol of counter-attack, cf. e.g. 11.414–18; that justifies the alternative here, to complement the unprovoked aggression of lions. Zenodotus and others omitted 256f. (Did/A), which may have been added, as Bolling thought (*External Evidence* 91f.), 'through a wish to do away with the distributive apposition, and its gratification by the ordinary cento technique'; but more probably Aristarchus and the vulgate were right to retain them here.

259 χαλκός is the bronze spear-head, see on 245–8, also on 3.348–9 where the v. recurs; it is the reading of Aristarchus (Did/A) and a minority of MSS, though the specious χαλκόν entered the vulgate.

260–2 These vv. are not typical (despite ἐπαλμένος *sic*, 4 × *Il.*, and μεμαῶτα | 7 × *Il.*), unlike most of the rest of this description, but were evidently constructed for this or a specifically similar occasion; 26of. recur almost exactly at 12.404f., but οὐδέ there for ἡ δέ looks like secondary adaptation. Aias leapt forward and stabbed, νύξεν, the shield; the spear penetrated and 'pounded Hektor back in his fury' (Lattimore), στυφέλιξε δέ μιν μεμαῶτα; then it reached and grazed (τμήδην, cf. τέμνω) his neck so that blood spurted up (κηκίω).

263 The rising threefolder (confirmed by the recurrence, down to the 4th-foot break, at 11.255) gives a sense of Hektor's resilience despite the blow.

264–5 His retreat to get the stone is well observed, as is his 'thick hand', cf. 3.376n.; both vv. recur at 21.403f. of Athene against Ares, where an extra v. describes the stone even more closely: τόν ῥ᾽ ἄνδρες πρότεροι θέσαν ἔμμεναι οὖρον ἀρούρης. Here the poet does not wish to make the stone too massive, since Aias is about to pick up another even bigger. Even so, it is rough and large and black (suggesting death and doom rather than because it is meteoric?).

267 A non-standard cumulation to suggest the accuracy of the blow and its impressive if limited effect. Neither ἐπομφάλιον nor περιήχησεν recurs, though ἀσπίδες ὀμφαλόεσσαι etc. are frequent (11 × *Il.*), and cf. 13.192 ὁ δ᾽ ἄρ᾽ ἀσπίδος ὀμφαλὸν οὖτα. The boss belongs properly to the round *aspis* and is applied to Aias' tall *sakos* by courtesy or carelessness (cf. 219–23n.); χαλκός is now the shield, in particular its bronze surface.

268–9 Only here is a stone-throw met by a counter-throw; Aias' stone is not only bigger, but 269 suggests that he threw it even harder. πολὺ μείζονα...ἀπέλεθρον recurs at *Od.* 9.537f. of Poluphemos bombarding Odysseus' departing ship. For | ἧκ᾽ ἐπιδινήσας cf. | ῥῖψ᾽ ἐπιδινήσας at 3.378 and 19.268, of hurling Aineias' helmet and a goat's corpse respectively; the former is the 'proper' application, i.e. swinging a relatively light object before releasing it, as with a discus. A boulder, on the other hand, would be projected as in putting the weight, and that is clearly suggested by ἐπέρεισε: 'he *put forth* great strength' ('put his weight behind it', Willcock, cf. bT). (ϝ)ῑ́ς, only in epic, cf. ἶφι, Lat. *vis*; the whole phrase 'immeasurable force' also at 5.245.

270 He broke the shield inward, εἴσω, cf. 13.553 and *Od.* 18.96 (though neither is exactly similar).

271–2 Short sentences mark increasing tension as Hektor's knees give way and he is stretched flat on his back beneath the shield. Vulgate ἀσπίδι ἐγχριμφθείς is right against Aristarchus' ἀσπίδ᾽ ἐνιχριμφθείς (Did/A), designed to avoid a (not unusual) hiatus. χρίμπτομαι signifies coming close to something, often forcibly (cf. Chantraine, *Dict.*): 'being brought into close contact with his shield' is something of an understatement, in pointed contrast with Apollo's simply expressed action of instantly raising him. The god was ostensibly still watching, with Athene, from the oak-tree, cf. 58ff., but we are not meant to envisage this too keenly, still less to wonder what *her* reaction might be. The main point is that Hektor is on his feet again by a recovery that must be supernatural, though the poet does not wish to dwell on its details. In the corresponding duel Aphrodite intervenes to save Aineias – she is closely involved in the aftermath, but the actual rescue is dealt with in almost equally cursory terms, 3.380f. τὸν δ' ἐξήρπαξ' Ἀφροδίτη | ῥεῖα μάλ' ὥς τε θεός; nor is the adversary's response directly noted.

273–81 They would be smiting each other with swords in the final culmination of this elaborate contest, which has proceeded through all possible stages from spear-throw to thrust to stone-throw, had not the heralds intervened. It is a startling anti-climax, and the language of the wrestling-match in bk 23 suggests that this kind of intervention was typical of the Games-model the poet is using here (cf. 255–60n.):

Bk 7		Bk 23	
273	καί νύ κε δὴ ξιφέεσσ'	733	καί νύ κε τὸ τρίτον αὖτις
274	εἰ μὴ κήρυκες	734	εἰ μὴ Ἀχιλλεύς
279f.	μηκέτι... ἀμφοτέρω γὰρ	735f.	μηκέτ'... νίκη δ' ἀμφοτέροισιν.

The surprise is the greater since Aias is apparently winning, having suffered no real damage from his opponent.

274–6 'Messengers of gods and men' is a standard description, cf. 1.334; πεπνυμένω ἄμφω in 276 is applied to heralds again at 9.689, but to other pairs at 3.148, *Od.* 18.65; on πεπνυμένος etc. see 5.697–8n. On Talthubios see 1.320n.; Idaios is his only named Trojan counterpart, who appears repeatedly in this Book and also at 3.248, 24.325 and 470. They are mentioned in chiastic order, i.e. the Trojan last.

277–8 For the various uses of the σκῆπτρον see on 2.109; here the heralds use their staves as a symbolic and sacred barrier between the contestants. Were they acting under orders, or simply as umpires? Such questions, irrelevant in a sense, underline the improvised nature of this device for terminating the duel. Renewed emphasis on their wisdom (278 πεπνυμένα μήδεα εἰδώς, as at *Od.* 2.38, after 276 πεπνυμένω ἄμφω) may be designed to distract attention from this.

279–82 Idaios' remarks are brief and a little incoherent, their tone intimate and ingratiating. That these bitter enemies should be addressed as 'dear children' comes as a shock – φίλα τέκνα at 10.192 is different, being addressed by the aged Nestor to young warriors of his own side, and Akhilleus' calling Priam γέρον φίλε at 24.650 is remarkable in another way. πολεμίζετε μηδὲ μάχεσθον is adapted from πολεμίζειν ἠδὲ μάχεσθαι, 8 × *Il.*;

280 recurs at 10.552, but is at least as well in place here. The idea of Zeus favouring Hektor, and therefore of a draw, has already been mooted at 204f., but the present assertion that he loves both equally is unexpected in view of what has actually happened, namely that Aias would have killed Hektor were it not for Apollo's miraculous intervention. For Zeus's special regard for Hektor see on 4.48–9.

281 αἰχμητής can be qualified by an epithet like κρατερός but is used by itself to mean a good spearman, cf. 5.602 (+2 × elsewhere) αἰχμητήν τ' ἔμεναι καὶ θαρσαλέον πολεμιστήν. Ameis–Hentze were probably right to take ἴδμεν ἅπαντες as implying 'we know it now, because of the present fight'; even so the whole v. is bland, almost vacuous, testifying to the singer's difficulties in making the intervention plausible rather than to a subtle characterization of heraldic style.

282 'Night is already here' – this additional motive for interruption is no more plausible than the rest. The duel would not have been started if darkness had been imminent, and though complex in its successive stages can hardly have lasted long. The portentous and proverbial 'it is good to obey night' underlines Idaios' efforts to sound convincing; καί here may imply 'in addition to other factors', or be emphatic as with περ in the formally similar generalization at 24.130f., ἀγαθὸν δὲ γυναικί περ ἐν φιλότητι | μίσγεσθ'. For 'obeying' night cf. 8.502 = 9.65 πειθώμεθα νυκτὶ μελαίνη.

282–6 Aias replies to Idaios (but κελεύετε invokes both heralds together): let Hektor as challenger – 285 merges 218 and 150 – accept or reject the interruption, and he will do likewise. This seems generous in the circumstances; again the tone and language are those of an exhibition match rather than a duel to the death.

287–302 Hektor starts with flattery, then points out the benefits to both of stopping the fight, and finally proposes an immediate exchange of gifts to provoke public approval. His style is prolix and conciliatory, rhythmically regular and with much periodic and progressive enjambment.

288–9 μέγεθός τε βίην τε | is not formular despite appearances (μέγεθος only 3 × *Il.*), though cf. ἠΰς τε μέγας τε | (etc.), 8 × *Il.* Martial prowess as a divine gift can sound grudging, as at 13.727, and the addition of 289 makes the tribute more generous. πινυτή and adjectival πινυτός are otherwise Odyssean, especially of Penelope; the term covers wisdom (cf. the related πεπνυμένος) as well as prudence, and takes up the claim of both men to be wise or knowledgeable in warfare (198f., 237ff.). For the rest of the v. cf. Helen's sneer at Paris who had claimed to be Menelaos' superior, 3.431 σῇ τε βίῃ καὶ χερσὶ καὶ ἔγχεϊ φέρτερος εἶναι.

290–3 This Book makes threefold use of the typical pattern 'now let the fighting stop – for today; it can continue later, until…': (i) at 29f. when

Apollo proposes an interruption to Athene; (ii) here; and (iii) when Priam at 376–8 (= 395–7) proposes to the Trojans a truce to gather the dead. The language of all three overlaps:

(i)   29 νῦν μὲν παύσωμεν πόλεμον καὶ δηϊοτῆτα
      30 σήμερον· ὕστερον αὖτε μαχήσοντ᾽ εἰς ὅ κε τέκμωρ...
(ii) 290 νῦν μὲν παυσώμεσθα μάχης καὶ δηϊοτῆτος
      291 σήμερον· ὕστερον αὖτε μαχησόμεθ᾽, εἰς ὅ κε δαίμων
      292 ἄμμε διακρίνῃ, δώῃ δ᾽ ἑτέροισί γε νίκην
(iii) 376 παύσασθαι πολέμοιο δυσηχέος εἰς ὅ κε νεκροὺς
      377 κήομεν· ὕστερον αὖτε μαχησόμεθ᾽, εἰς ὅ κε δαίμων
      378 ἄμμε διακρίνῃ, δώῃ δ᾽ ἑτέροισί γε νίκην.

The variations between παύσωμεν, παυσώμεσθα and παύσασθαι, with consequential changes from acc. to gen. and πόλεμον to μάχης, or the move to another πόλεμος-formula (πολέμοιο δυσηχέος) in 376 to accommodate an extra εἰς ὅ κε clause, are typical of oral ingenuity in adaptation. Given the amount of reduplication which is clearly acceptable to this singer, there is nothing in (ii) as a whole to mark it as interpolated – except that ἑτέροισι in the plural fits (iii), where it refers to both sides, better than (ii) where strict logic might demand ἑτέρῳ. This persuaded Leaf and Ameis–Hentze among others that 291 and 292 (to which they added 293 as a repetition of 282), are suspect. That is possible but, in the light of the frequent repetition of vv. and half-vv. in this Book, unlikely; especially since ἑτέροισι can be justified by taking Aias and Hektor as representing each side. V. 293 is a different matter, and Aristarchus too suspected this second occurrence (Arn/A on 282 and 293); yet it provides a useful pivot for the final clause ὡς σύ τ᾽ εὐφρήνῃς which follows. If it is to be omitted, then 290 παυσώμεσθα must be the main verb and 291f. treated as parenthetical. Yet a repetition of Idaios' words would accord well with the ingratiating generalizations and excuses to which Hektor seems to have resorted.

294–8 εὐφραίνειν is used typically, of surviving battle and bringing joy to one's wife and friends. παρὰ (ἐπὶ) νηυσὶν Ἀχαιῶν | is a common formula; for 295 ἔτας see on 6.239; 'lord Priam's great town' and 'Trojans and Trojan women with trailing robes' are equally typical. Yet the passage gains a certain piquancy from Hektor's loving description of his own reception, as the dignified men and women of Troy are set against the anonymous and repetitive ἔτας καὶ ἑταίρους of 295 – to whom the addition of οἵ τοι ἔασιν, 'those that you have', lends an almost dismissive ring.

Finally he ventures on the remarkable statement that the women of Troy 'will pray to me' when they enter the θεῖον...ἀγῶνα, the 'divine concourse', i.e. the sacred place of assembly (Willcock) rather than where the gods gather as at 18.376. Commentators have shied away from taking μοι εὐχόμεναι literally, as 'praying to me', namely as a god, and have hopefully described μοι as 'ethic', i.e. 'praying on my behalf'. Yet phrases like θεὸς δ' ὡς τίετο δήμῳ (5 × *Il.* of Hektor and others), and even Akhilleus' ironic description of Hektor at 22.394 as ᾧ Τρῶες κατὰ ἄστυ θεῷ ὡς εὐχετόωντο, show that the literal version here deserves consideration; Nestor's boast at 11.761, πάντες δ' εὐχετόωντο θεῶν Διὶ Νέστορί τ' ἀνδρῶν, 'all prayed to Zeus among gods and Nestor among men', may turn the balance in its favour. Such locutions are on the face of it extraordinary, almost unbelievable, contradicting the whole Greek distinction between mortals and immortals. Yet their sense is certainly figurative in some degree. In the moment of victory a hero really could be honoured like a god, but addressing prayers to him would be conceived in a special sense; 'who as they gather to give thanks to the gods will include me in their prayers' is the sort of compromise interpretation that has to be considered. V. 298 remains curious in expression nevertheless, since the idea of prayer is subordinated to that of 'entering the divine assembly', itself oddly reinterpreted. Rhapsodic elaboration is a possibility, but for Hektor to magnify his own reception over Aias' is very much in the heroic style.

299–305 Finally an exchange of gifts is proposed, to complete the resemblance to a friendly competition rather than a serious duel – indeed the gifts will be a girdle like that given by Oineus to Bellerophon as a ξεινήϊον at 6.219, and a sword with sheath and baldric like that given Diomedes as prize after the fight-in-armour in the Games at 23.824f. The closest similarity is to Diomedes and Glaukos in bk 6 (but with different gifts); though there was good reason for some kind of honorific exchange there, since they had discovered they were guest-friends through their grandfathers.

300–2 Hektor ends with an imaginary comment to help justify the action he is recommending. He had done exactly the same at 87–91, also at the end of a speech, and a similar remark, if with a different purpose, concludes his address to Andromakhe at 6.459–62. Such comments by imagined observers are a not uncommon rhetorical device in Homeric speeches, cf. 6.459–62n. and e.g. 12.317ff., where ὄφρα τις ὧδ' εἴπῃ(σιν) recurs; but Hektor makes exceptional use of them, and this must be intended to reveal something about his character – a special susceptibility to public opinion, at least, reflecting his keen sense of duty but also akin to his special concern over the treatment of his body after death. Here, as at 89f., his imagined comment has strong epigrammatic quality: 'they fought; they parted in friendship', with the antithesis pointed by initial ἠμέν and ἠδ' and echoed by διέτμαγεν ἀρθμήσαντε. For the formula ἔριδος πέρι θυμοβόροιο cf. 209–10n., also 20.253. ἀρθμήσαντε, *hapax* in Homer (ἄρθμιοι 1 × *Od.*), means 'being unified', 'being in harmony', cf. Chantraine, *Dict.*

s.v. ἀραρίσκω; in combination with ἐν φιλότητι it produces the extra-ordinary idea – to which Hektor's rhetoric and the poet's skill have almost conditioned us, temporarily at least – of Hektor and Aias as *good friends*!

303–5 In the fight-in-armour at the Funeral Games Agamemnon will award Diomedes a sword (μέγα φάσγανον rather than ξίφος ἀργυρόηλον, obviously for metrical reasons) 'together with scabbard and well-cut baldric' (where 23.825 = 304 here). A 'girdle gleaming with ivory', the same phrase as in 305, was Oineus' gift to Bellerophon at 6.219, q.v. with n. The friendly context of those gifts is a further indication of the present duel's ambivalent status. — Leaf must be right that imperf. δίδου (against 303 δῶκε) shows the actions as simultaneous: Hektor gave while Aias was giving.

306–7 As usual ὁ μέν refers to the last-named of a pair, here Aias. Hektor returns to the ὅμαδος of the Trojans, their 'gathering' as at 15.689 rather than their 'din' which is the usual Homeric meaning. There might just be an implied reference to the idea of the Trojans as noisy, cf. 3.2 and 3.8–9n., in comparison with the Achaeans; but 'gathering' seems to be the original sense, cf. e.g. ὁμάς and Chantraine, *Dict.* s.v.

308–10 307 τοὶ δ' ἐχάρησαν and 308 recur at 5.514f. — ἀρτεμής (also 1 × *Od.*) is of uncertain etymology but clearly means something like 'unharmed', the graze of 262 being ignored. V. 309 echoes Aias' formidable appearance at 208ff. and explains the Trojan relief. ἀελπτέοντες, 'despairing (of his safety)', is unique in Homer, a derivative of ἄελπτος (first in *HyAp* and Hesiod) which recurs at Herodotus 7.168.2, where one is less surprised to find it. σόον εἶναι | is adapted from σόον -οι ἔμμεναι – ∪ ∪ – – |, 3 × *Il.*, 1 × *Od.*

311–12 Both sides carry off their champion in procession, 310 ἦγον, 312 ἄγον; Aias is κεχαρηότα νίκῃ, rejoicing in the victory that was his by rights (after all, as bT noted, Hektor had been wounded and had fallen). Agamemnon had claimed a similar victory for Menelaos at 3.457, when his opponent was snatched to safety by Aphrodite as Hektor has been raised by Apollo. Yet Aias might be thought to have spurned real victory here by accepting the heralds' intervention, see 282–6n.

313–411   At the celebratory feast Nestor proposes a truce for burying the dead and a subsequent fortification of the camp. Simultaneous Trojan discussions lead to an offer, conveyed by Idaios, to return the riches Helen had brought with her, and more in addition, and also of a truce for burial. The Achaeans reject the first but accept the second

313–26 The description of the feast in Agamemnon's quarters is entirely composed of vv. used elsewhere. The scene is, of course, a typical one and many of its vv. are typical also; even so the cursory quality, and the wide range of contexts from which vv. appear to be drawn, are unusual. On the suppression of sacrificial details see 314–15n.; one might have expected Agamemnon to speak, but the scene's main purpose is to provide a stage for Nestor. The chief repetitions are: 313 = 9.669; 314–15 = 2.402–3; 316–18 ~ *Od.* 19.421–3; 317–20 = 1.465–8, 2.428–31; 321 ~ *Od.* 14.437; 322 = 1.102, 13.112; 323–6 = 9.92–5.

313 Plural κλισίησιν etc. is often used of a single warrior's hut, sometimes for metrical convenience but also to confer grandeur.

314–15 These vv. occurred at 2.402f. of a similar feast for the leaders, with Nestor likewise conspicuous. There the sacrificial aspect is described at 410–29, with them standing round the ox, throwing barley, listening to Agamemnon's prayer, preparing the divine offering (cf. 2.410–31n.). Not all these details are necessary here, and sacrificial scenes are often selective over such points, see on 1.447–68. Yet the sacred side of the slaughter is conveyed only by the term ἱέρευσεν and the mention of Zeus as recipient, whereas the secular parts of the standard account are given more or less in full. Brief versions of the preparation of meals may omit the sacrificial aspect, as at 9.89–91, but of more detailed descriptions only that of the dinner prepared by Autolukos' sons for Odysseus at *Od.* 19.418–25 is entirely secular. It is notable that 316 recurs only there.

316 Skinning the animal is mentioned in the phrase καὶ ἔσφαξαν καὶ ἔδειραν at 1.459 = 2.422, also *Od.* 12.359; the present v. recurs only at *Od.* 19.421, on which see previous n., with the first hemistich also at *Od.* 8.61. διέχευαν (only here *Il.*, 3 × *Od.*), aor. of διαχέω (with the notion of spreading, though cf. Chantraine, *Dict.* s.v. χέω *ad fin.*) implies jointing, preliminary to 317 μίστυλλον, cutting into pieces of edible size; ἄπαντα is not adverbial (*pace* Monro, Willcock) so much as proleptic, 'divided it into all its parts'. ἀμφί θ' ἕπον, handled or prepared it, perhaps refers to a stage between skinning and jointing, e.g. cutting off the head, feet and tail.

321 Agamemnon offers Aias the prime cut, the chine complete with ribs, as Eumaios does Odysseus (though of pork not beef) at *Od.* 14.437. Similarly at *Od.* 4.65 Menelaos presented the νῶτα βοός, his own privileged portion, to his guests, and at *Od.* 8.475 Odysseus cut off a piece of the chine for Demodokos; cf. also *Il.* 9.207.

323–6 These vv. recur at 9.92–5, where at another of Agamemnon's dinners Nestor makes a different proposal. The structure of the two scenes, whose purpose is to introduce an important new course of action, is similar.

327–43 Nestor introduces quite out of the blue the idea of burying the dead; it is typical, perhaps, of his tactical initiatives, but nothing that has just occurred particularly calls for it. No doubt the real point is the building of the wall and trench, which is presented as incidental; but even that is not particularly motivated by present circumstances, the Achaeans being under no special pressure. His speech contains other unexpected features, as well as some odd turns of language: the omission of any mention of a truce for burying the dead, the idea of taking the bones home, and the vagueness of the proposed connexion between mound and walls.

There is also an external difficulty which has much exercised critics. According to the received text of Thucydides 1.11.1 the Achaeans had built the wall *on their arrival*, nearly ten years earlier: ἐπειδὴ δὲ ἀφικόμενοι μάχῃ ἐκράτησαν (δῆλον δέ· τὸ γὰρ ἔρυμα τῷ στρατοπέδῳ οὐκ ἂν ἐτειχίσαντο)..., 'but since they won a battle on their arrival (that is manifest, since they would not otherwise have built the fortification-wall for the camp)...' It was G. Hermann who first concluded that Thucydides' *Iliad* cannot have contained the present account of the wall-building (see Bolling, *External Evidence* 92ff.), and D. L. Page took the matter to extremes by arguing that the whole of bk 7 from now on is an Athenian interpolation (*HHI* 315–24 with 335–8). Page's discussion, though defective and misleading in its conclusions, presents the evidence clearly enough. The following points may be made.

(1) Akhilleus will specifically state at 9.349f. that the wall and trench have been built in his absence, i.e. during the Wrath. Attempts (e.g. by Wilamowitz) to dismiss this passage as an interpolation were rejected even by Bolling (*op. cit.* 98f.) and Page (*op. cit.* 338), who, however, failed to explain away this crucial piece of support for the bk 7 description.

(2) The Thucydides text may have suffered surface corruption: R. M. Cook's ἀνετειχίσαντο for ἂν ἐτειχίσαντο may be untenable for reasons adduced by Page on his p. 338, but D. S. Robertson's 'brilliant' conjecture οὐκ ἂν ⟨ἔτει ι'⟩ ἐτειχίσαντο cannot be dismissed so easily. Page claims that it does not fit Thucydides' argument (which he sets out in full); that is true on Robertson's own interpretation, but the meaning could be somewhat different: 'that is clear – for they would not have fortified it ⟨in the tenth year⟩ [*sc.* as Homer said, but on arrival]'. In that case Thucydides would be accepting the tradition of a wall protecting the ships, but rejecting as unhistorical Homer's account of it as built in the tenth year: 'the wall was there – they must have built it on arrival, which presupposes a successful battle on landing – Homer's version in the seventh Book being simply a dramatic elaboration'.

(3) The Alexandrian editors, judging from the extant scholia, did not doubt the authenticity of the wall-building episode. At the same time the Hellenistic title of bk 7 (on which see p. 230) refers only to the collection of the dead, suggesting that versions were around *without* the wall-building.

(4) There might be a trace even in Homer of some kind of wall built up against the beached ships on some earlier occasion. Willcock (n. on 337 *ad*

fin.) followed Paley in thinking that 14.31f., according to which the Achaeans had 'dragged up the first ships towards the plain, and built a [the?] wall up against their sterns, ἐπὶ πρύμνῃσιν', refer to a different wall from that now envisaged in bk 7 (he finds the same distinction at 13.683, but that is unlikely). If so, then Thucydides could have been referring either to that passage or to the tradition reflected by it (for he demonstrably used non-Homeric sources and traditions, including of course the *Cypria*, for certain other deductions in his opening Book).

The comment on 14.31f. will tend to reject the Paley–Willcock interpretation, but there is something to be said for it nevertheless. Nestor's wall is a grand affair equipped with towers and built so as to meet the burial mound. It can hardly be right up against the ships' sterns (in any case 334 τυτθὸν ἀποπρὸ νεῶν must be disregarded as part of a probable interpolation, see on 334–5); the question is whether ἐπὶ πρύμνῃσιν in 14.32 can be taken so loosely as to imply something similar. Literally it describes a wall 'at' or 'against' their sterns, moreover one built when the ships were first drawn up (since εἴρυσαν and ἔδειμαν are co-ordinate). That being so, it is not quite out of the question that the monumental composer, when he came to plan and develop the large-scale fighting around the ships from bk 12 on, realized that the wall built close to their sterns, and which he found in the tradition, was inadequate to justify and accommodate the kind of combat he needed to elaborate; and so decided to supplement or virtually replace it with a more formidable construction, the idea of which would then be typically credited to Nestor.

328 For anticipatory γάρ followed by τῷ (in 331) see also 13.228; Denniston, *Particles* 70f., makes it plain that the construction is not especially Attic as Shipp suggests (*Studies* 260).

330 | ἐσκέδασ' ὀξὺς Ἄρης entails an easy adaptation of standard terminology and is hardly 'untraditional' (Page, *HHI* 339) or 'late' (Shipp 260). For the rest of the v. (~ *Od.* 10.560 = 11.65) cf. 1.3 ψυχὰς Ἄϊδι προΐαψεν and 16.856 = 22.362, in deeply Homeric contexts, ψυχὴ δ'...Ἄϊδόσδε βεβήκει.

331 Surprisingly, nothing is said about a truce, which would be essential and is presupposed by the oaths Agamemnon mentions at 411.

332 κυκλήσομεν (aor. subjunct.) is a unique use of this verb (not otherwise found before tragedy) to mean 'let us wheel' the corpses in carts; cf. Page, *HHI* 339 – this *is* surely untraditional.

334–5 Aristarchus athetized (Arn/A) on the grounds that collecting the bones is not customary and that individual ones would not be recognizable in the common pyre. F. Jacoby (*JHS* 64, 1944, 37ff.) showed that bringing back bones or ashes of fallen warriors from abroad was an

Attic custom only instituted in 464 B.C., and Page (*HHI* 323) took this as further proof of the Attic origin of the whole wall-and-trench episode. *This couplet* must surely be accepted as interpolated, probably indeed Athenian (since the idea goes far beyond that of 23.252, of Patroklos' bones being retrieved from his pyre for later burial with those of Akhilleus). That does not implicate the whole context, however; the vv. are inorganic, as Aristarchus saw, leaving ἀτὰρ κατακήομεν αὐτούς | to close the sentence – admittedly a little abruptly. Nothing will be said about this bone-collecting in the actual narrative of events at 430–2.

336–7 ἐξαγαγόντες | ἄκριτον ἐκ πεδίου has been much debated. Aristarchus (Nic/A, Porph. bT) preferred to take the participle as intrans., 'marching out', but such a use is unparalleled, cf. 6.251–2n. *fin.*; also that meaning is unacceptable when the v. is repeated in the actual narrative at 436f. (which seems prior in composition, see on 338). But if ἐξαγαγόντες is transitive, what is its object? (i) Scarcely 'corpses', since in the repetition at 436 the burning of the corpses (and their prior collection) has clearly been done on the previous day. (ii) τύμβον has its supporters: 'extending it in an unbroken line from the plain', Willcock – that is a possible sense of the verb, but this particular interpretation is really meaningless; see, however (iv) below. (iii) That leaves ἄκριτον, which must then be translated as 'indiscriminate material', i.e. they brought earth back from the plain 'not selecting the suitable stones as for a regular wall' (Leaf). Such an application of ἄκριτος is completely unparalleled. (iv) On the repetition at 436 we learn that Aristophanes had read ἐν πεδίῳ for ἐκ πεδίου (Did/A), and that this was regarded by Aristarchus as perhaps preferable. If this *was* the right text in both places, then ἐν πεδίῳ is firmly disconnected from ἐξαγαγόντες. Supposing we take this with τύμβον, after all, but without the restriction of that adverbial phrase: could it mean 'drawing out its circuit', cf. 23.255? There is no direct Homeric parallel, but the later sense of 'lead on' or 'induce' presupposes some such application of the preverb ἐξ-. In that case τύμβον... ἕνα... ἄκριτον ἐν πεδίῳ would mean 'one communal mound in the plain' (for τύμβον... ἄκριτον must mean 'undiscriminated' in relation to individual corpses, not 'indistinguishable from the plain' as Porphyry argued, cf. bT).

338 Nestor mentions only towers here, but how can they be built against the mound? We have to understand, with some awkwardness, a wall in which the towers are set (the two are normally distinguished as at 12.36, but cf. 8.213, 12.333). Clarification comes at 436f. where the wall is specifically added: ποτὶ δ' αὐτὸν τεῖχος ἔδειμαν | πύργους θ' ὑψηλούς. This suggests that the *narrative* of the wall-building was shaped first, with Nestor's proposal, though prior in our text, following it with light adaptation where necessary (see next n.). Yet τεῖχος ἔδειμαν cannot be altered to τεῖχος δείμομεν or the like, therefore τεῖχος is suppressed and ὦκα substituted to give δείμομεν ὦκα, leaving θ' to be omitted in the next v. and πύργους to do the work, with some strain, of τεῖχος...πύργους θ'.

339–40 ποιήσομεν (subjunct.) is an easy change from 438 ἐνεποίεον, where, however, ἐν δ' αὐτοῖσι properly belongs. Final confirmation of the priority of 435–9 is provided by εἴη in 439 = 340 (where Hermann's εἴη as a rare form of the subjunct. is improbable), since the optative is correct after the past tense of ἔδειμαν but anomalous, even though loosely retained, after δείμομεν.

341–2 The trench is to be close to the wall, ἐγγύθι (or ἐπ' αὐτῷ at 440), though 8.213f. and 9.87 envisage quite a space between the two, cf. also 10.126 and 194. ἵππον, the vulgate reading in 342, is a collective singular as in Herodotus and Attic, but a few MSS and Eustathius have ἵππους and it is simplest to emend with Ameis–Hentze. ἀμφὶς ἐοῦσα, 'being all round' the camp, is acceptable, even though ἀμφίς strictly implies 'on both sides of'. See further on 441.

344–78 The frequency of standard vv. and half-vv. remains high as the singer turns from Achaean council to Trojan assembly, as does the proportion of awkward locutions in the parts that are not formular. There is a strong typical element in the speeches themselves; thus Antenor urges a disagreeable course of action on Paris just as Pouludamas does on Hektor at 12.210ff. and 18.249ff., to be met with violent refusal by Hektor beginning with the same words as here (12.231–4 = 357–60 and 18.285–357, with a different vocative of course); and Priam's conciliatory address bears a functional resemblance to that of Nestor at 1.247ff.

344–6 344 = 9.710; for the assembly outside Priam's house on the citadel (cf. 6.317 with n.) compare that at 2.788, ἐπὶ Πριάμοιο θύρῃσι. Here it is described as δεινὴ τετρηχυῖα, a curious phrase involving some strained adaptation. At 2.95 the Achaeans rushed to assembly, τετρήχει δ' ἀγορή ('the assembly was in disturbed motion', intrans. perf. of ταράσσειν), and the earth groaned beneath as the people sat – a highly metaphorical description of an especially tumultuous gathering. Here the assembly is simply 'disturbed', with none of the antecedents which might explain how; moreover it is δεινή, presumably to fill the cumulated hemistich – but how can an assembly or gathering be 'terrible', for the term can mean little less? Helen calls Priam δεινός at 3.172 (see n.), but as a reinforcement of αἰδοῖος; perhaps that is the source of this admittedly emotive epithet. Again the impression is given that the composer of this whole section is a little slapdash in adaptation where he cannot exactly repeat typical material.

347 Antenor is Priam's chief counsellor (see on 3.146–8) and had acted as host to Odysseus and Menelaos when they came to Troy to try and retrieve Helen at an earlier stage (3.207). He is thus a suitable person to make the present proposal.

348–9 348 is a standard v. of address, 3 × *Il.*; 349 is also formular, 4 × *Il.* (all in bks 7 and 8), 5 × *Od.* Priam will begin with the same two vv. at 368f.

350 | δεῦτ(ε), a ps.-imperative formed after δεῦρο, is relatively frequent and reinforces ἄγε(τε) here and at *Od.* 8.11, being stronger and more persuasive than the usual | ἀλλ' ἄγε(τε). Helen and her possessions were much mentioned in similar or identical language in bk 3, where they were the object of this first formal duel; 'Αργείην... αὐτῇ recurs at 3.458. At 363 the possessions will be further described by Paris as 'those I brought home from Argos'.

351–3 Strong internal breaks now bring a sense of urgency to Antenor's proposal. 'We are fighting after cheating over the oaths' must mean the oaths attending the duel in bk 3; as bT comment, he softens the criticism by including himself among the offenders. ὅρκια is acc. 'of respect' rather than direct object, which would be unique in Homer with ψεύδομαι. Aristarchus (Arn/A) athetized 353 (in which ἵνα is illegitimately used as though it were Attic ἐάν) as an attempt to supply a verb for 352. Modern commentators have followed suit, with Page (*HHI* 339) objecting to ἵνα μή as 'a miserable piece of prosody' rather than on grammatical grounds. That is indeed the chief difficulty; I am not clear that ἵνα is otherwise impossible. It is found 25 × in Homer, mainly to mean 'where' in a local sense; but the present use involves a relatively easy extension from local to circumstantial, or concrete to abstract, application: 'therefore I do not expect any beneficial result for us where we do not act as I suggest'. ἵνα + subjunct. is already beginning to develop a purposive sense in Homer (Chantraine, *GH* II, 268), and this different metaphorical application, also with the subjunctive, is not to be totally dismissed. To press for a directly conditional sense is in any event unnecessary, and Aristarchus' ἵν' ἄν for ἵνα (Did/A), though metrically advantageous, is otherwise peculiar (so Leaf; Chantraine 269 is not so sure). One thing is certain: that understanding ἔσται with κέρδιον, as a result of totally omitting 353, is difficult and not a normal Homeric idiom.

357–64 After predictably standard language for the succession of speakers Paris begins with a 4-v. rebuke that recurs at 12.231–4, its opening v. also at 18.285. In both those cases Hektor is reproaching Pouludamas for a similarly displeasing suggestion; the theme is a typical one. After 5 smooth whole-sentence vv. Paris delivers the punch-line in the contrastingly interrupted 362, with further variation to mark the close in a tightly enjambed final couplet.

357–60 The reproach is sarcastic but ostensibly respectful: οὐκέτ' in

357 implies that Antenor's advice is usually welcome – surely he could do better this time? But if that is what he seriously thinks, then the gods must have destroyed his wits.

358 οἶσθα...νοῆσαι: 'you know how to think of' something better.

360 The emphatic ἐξ (with ὤλεσαν), the repetition of δή after 359 εἰ δ' ἐτεὸν δή and the reduplication in ἄρα and ἔπειτα together form a complex and almost explosive preamble, in contrast with the bland and formally simple statements that have preceded.

362 The core of his reply is given with succinct brutality in words freshly deployed for the occasion. ἀντικρύ occurs 26 × *Il.*, normally of a weapon's path 'straight on' through the body, only here in this striking abstract sense. For ἀπόφημι cf. ἀπόφασθε at 9.422 and 649.

363–4 The possessions have been described before (see on 350), but Paris varies the language used so far. (Argos is of course the Achaean land or the Peloponnese, not the city.) The offer to add to what he and Helen had removed from Lakedaimon, thus meeting part of the terms set by Agamemnon at 3.286f. (q.v. with n., and cf. 3.459), is conciliatory up to a point but plainly unacceptable.

365–9 The repetition of 365 directly after 354, of 367 so soon after 326, followed by 368f. (omitted by many MSS) after 348–9 (see n. there), makes an arid and automatic impression. These functional formulas of address and so on were not subject to the normal rules of economy and are usually varied somewhat, more at least than this.

366 θεόφιν μήστωρ(') ἀτάλαντος -ν recurs twice, of Peirithoos and Patroklos, neither especially renowned for counsel (cf. Chantraine, *Dict.* s.v. μήδομαι); compare Διὶ μῆτιν ἀτάλαντος (etc.), 6 × *Il.*, of either Odysseus or Hektor. The -φι termination is old in its special locative and instrumental senses, but not necessarily so when substituting for a simple gen. or, as here, dative.

370–8 Priam ends the discussion with some practical instructions. Almost wholly compounded of vv. from elsewhere and stylistically un-exciting, they are notable for his failure to apply further pressure on Paris and for his independent suggestion about the battlefield dead, closely similar to Nestor's but specifically mentioning a truce.

370–1 = 18.298f., with the substitution of the formulas κατὰ πτόλιν and ὡς τὸ πάρος περ for κατὰ στρατὸν ἐν τελέεσσι. The Trojans are here gathered within the city and can hardly be imagined as rushing out onto the plain to spend the night there; moreover they will eat in Troy itself as 477 shows. That *this* is the adapted passage is shown by the inappropriateness of 371 to present circumstances, since they are hardly about to stay awake all night when inside the city walls. — ἐγρήγορθε is perf. imper. middle of ἐγείρω, cf. 10.67.

372–4 The first two vv. are heavily formular; the third = 3.87, but (in contrast with what was said on 370–1) it is that application, rather than this, that seems secondary.

375 On καὶ δέ (also at 173), 'introducing the last item of a series', see Denniston, *Particles* 202. πυκινὸν ἔπος (4× *Il. sic*) confirms Priam's suggestion as independent of Nestor's; αἴ κ' ἐθέλησι (etc.) is formular in this position.

376–8 For 376 cf. 3.112; Priam summarizes Nestor's corresponding proposal (at 331–3, but the singer does not attempt to follow his language too closely). 377f., by contrast, are a repetition of Hektor's words to Aias at 291f., but with | κήομεν for | σήμερον; see on 290–3. The repetition of εἰς ὅ κε, especially after 375 αἴ κ', and the three successive integral enjambments may be largely fortuitous but give Priam's closing words a certain liveliness in comparison with his earlier remarks.

379–80 379 is another formular verse. 380 is omitted by a minority of MSS including A and in many modern texts (though not OCT); the objection to it is clear, that as a close version of 18.298 it contradicts 370. Obviously the Trojans dine in the city and not 'in the army, by regiments [*or* at their posts]'. The alternative to omission is to restore κατὰ πτόλιν ὡς τὸ πάρος περ as in 370; that seems preferable, since some statement that the instruction was followed, and in the same terms, is in the oral style. Curiously the ancient critics do not seem to have concerned themselves much with the discrepancy, though κατὰ στρατόν was an ancient variant for κατὰ πτόλιν at 370 (Did/A).

381–2 381 repeats 372 with necessary adaptation. The night has now passed; ἠῶθεν must mean at the first appearance of dawn, before sunrise, in view of 421 where the sun's rays first strike the fields (so Ameis–Hentze). Why the Achaeans are already assembled at this unlikely hour is not made clear – another sign, perhaps, of the rather casual construction of this whole episode. Analytical theories that this assembly has been displaced from elsewhere, for example the aftermath of the duel in bk 3, cannot be entirely discounted.

383 That they should have gathered by the stern of Agamemnon's ship, and therefore close to his hut, is not unnatural in the circumstances; 11.806–8 states that by Odysseus' ship, i.e. in the centre of the line of ships according to 8.222f., was the regular meeting place.

384 ἠπύτα is found only here in Homer; the -ᾰ termination (as in ἱππότα, ἱππηλάτα etc.) is probably based on the vocative, cf. Chantraine, *GH* I, 199, and apparently ancient; yet other such epithets always belong to a proper name, and ἠπύτα κῆρυξ is unique in this respect. It is not an old formula, therefore, but is created by analogy for an exceptional metrical context, κῆρυξ being found 13 × *Il.* but only 3 × at the v-e, in the other two instances without an epithet. ἠπύτα from ἠπύω, 'speak loudly', is an appropriate creation since it defines a typical heraldic rôle, sometimes reflected in their names, cf. Thootes at 12.342 and von Kamptz, *Personennamen* 26. The model here may be Eputides as father of the herald Periphas at 17.323f.; but the influence of the formula ἱππότα Νέστωρ is also probable, occurring as it does in the otherwise identical v. at 9.52, τοῖσι δ' ἀνιστάμενος μετεφώνεεν ἱππότα Νέστωρ.

385–97 Idaios' speech is mainly made up of vv. reported from Paris and Priam just before, but is enlivened by his personal additions, see on 387 and 392–3.

387 Compare εἰ δ' αὖ πως τόδε πᾶσι φίλον καὶ ἡδὺ γένοιτο in an unusually polite address by Zeus to the other gods at 4.17. Messengers do not usually add their own comments or excuses, but Idaios' attempts to be ingratiating add an element of drama to an otherwise foregone conclusion.

388 This v. appeared also at 3.87 (see n.), where, however, it was awkwardly constructed after κέκλυτε. The present use is not therefore directly derived from there.

389–90 The central placing of the heavy name makes 389 a rising threefolder, in which the metrical lengthening of μέν is aided by colon-division. | ἠγάγετο Τροίηνδ' recurs at 22.116 in Hektor's final soliloquy, and for ὡς πρὶν ὤφελλ' ἀπολέσθαι cf. Helen's ὡς πρὶν ὤφελλον ὀλέσθαι as she mourns him at 24.764 – our poet was clearly familiar with the narrative of Hektor's death and its aftermath (and may, of course, be responsible for both). At 3.40 the subject of ὤφελλ', in Idaios' second interjection, is confirmed as Paris and not the κτήματα; for Paris' general unpopularity see also 3.453f.

392–3 Paris had stated baldly at 362 that 'the [*or* my] woman I will not give back'; Idaios fulsomely translates her into 'glorious Menelaos' lady wife'. He also implies that Antenor's proposal of 348ff. had received wide acclamation, though that is not stated there.

394–7 Priam's words of 375–8 are reported exactly, except for necessary adaptation of 375. The MSS here have the 'quite abnormal' (Shipp, *Studies* 260) ἠνώγεον, presumably a bastard imperf. formed after pluperf. ἠνώγει as in 386; Bentley's ἤνωγον is a simple emendation, with lengthening of -ον facilitated by colon-break as well as the digamma of (ϝ)ειπεῖν.

398–411 The reactions of both Diomedes and Agamemnon, predictable in themselves, are expressed with some dramatic turns of phrase.

398–9 The formular v. 398 has already occurred at 92, followed as here by ὀψὲ δὲ δή in 94 (itself recurring at 9.31 and 696). Diomedes as always is the hero least overawed by circumstances, reacting with typical incisiveness to criticism, bad news or an important new suggestion as here. See also on 8.28–30.

400–2 His advice is rhetorically phrased as well as succinct: let no one accept the offered treasure – or Helen herself, he adds for good measure, even though she has definitely *not* been offered. Gen. Ἀλεξάνδροιο is ablatival, 'accept from A.', cf. 1.596. For 401 γνωτόν = 'self-evident' cf. *Od.* 24.182; γνωτὸν δὲ καὶ ὅς... entails either understanding ⟨ἐκείνῳ⟩ ὅς or taking ὅς as equivalent to εἴ τις as at 14.81, but the crucial observation is that καὶ ὅς μάλα νήπιός ἐστι recurs (in a regular construction with κε... γνοίη) at 17.629 and is bodily transferred from such a context to here. For the ὀλέθρου πείρατα that in 402 are 'fastened onto' the Trojans see 6.143n.

403–4 = 9.50–1, with μῦθον ἀγασσάμενοι 4× *Il.* (but not *Od.*) elsewhere; on ἄγαμαι see 41n.

406–8 Achaean applause speaks for itself but Agamemnon is careful to make plain that his own approval is also necessary, ἐμοὶ δ' ἐπιηνδάνει οὕτως. His assertive attitude is confirmed by 408 οὔ τι μεγαίρω – I do not grudge it, i.e. it is also *my* decision.

407 ὑποκρίνονται was noticed by Aristarchus (Arn/A); elsewhere in Homer (at 12.228 and 3× *Od.*) the verb means 'interpret' and not 'reply' as in subsequent Ionic (often in Herodotus; ἀποκρίνεσθαι is Attic), and should be so understood here: the Achaeans by their cries, 403 ἐπίαχον, rather than by any direct μῦθος, are interpreting their feelings for you, τοι.

408 Aristarchus (Nic/A) noted a pause (which could be marked by a comma in a modern text) after νεκροῖσιν: 'about the corpses, I do not at all grudge burning them'.

409–10 The syntax is imprecise and proverbial but clear in implication (neither it nor e.g. φειδώ being particularly 'late'): 'there is [*i.e.* should be] no sparing, in the matter of dead corpses, over quickly propitiating them in the matter of fire' – both gens. being loosely partitive. ἐπεί κε θάνωσι is to be taken closely with ὦκα rather than as a mere reinforcement of νεκύων κατατεθνηώτων (Ameis–Hentze).

411 ἴστω of a god means literally 'let him know', i.e. let him be witness; this use with ὅρκια as direct object is a unique extension, the normal construction being with μή, ὡς or acc. + inf. The oaths are those that would be necessary for the truce, despite Nestor's remarkable failure to mention them (331n.).

412–41 Both sides gather up and cremate their dead; the Achaeans carry out Nestor's plan of using the occasion to build a wall and trench before their camp

412 Similarly at 10.321 Dolon tells Hektor to hold up his staff (τὸ σκῆπτρον ἀνάσχεο, likewise with the developed def. article) and swear. For Agamemnon's staff or sceptre as especially potent in oaths see on 1.233–44 and 234–9. Zeus as object of invocation is sometimes reinforced by the gods in general, see e.g. on 6.476–81.

413 | ἄψορρον (5 × *Il.*) is strongly emphatic: 'back once again' to the city.

414–18 A strikingly cumulative sentence which technically could end at 414, 415, 416 or 417. V. 416 makes a naive impression with the repetition of Idaios' name and of ἦλθε after ἔλθοι; but it generates 417, in which στὰς ἐν μέσσοισιν, unnecessary in itself though corresponding to 384, allows the introduction of new and essential information in the second hemistich, namely that they then prepared themselves – itself expanded and analysed in 418.

414 The patronymic Dardaniones occurs only here and at 8.154 in an identical hemistich. Dardanos' descendants are the Dardanoi or Dardanioi, sometimes signifying Trojans in general but sometimes distinguished from the Τρῶες as descendants of Assarakos, whose branch of the family, including Aineias, continued to count Dardanie (a non-urban settlement up in the foothills of Ida) as home rather than Ilios, the citadel by the sea; see 20.215ff. and 2.819–20n.

415 This v. is mainly composed of formular elements, cf. 2.789 and 794.

416 'Speak out' is a common sense of ἀποειπεῖν (which can also mean 'refuse' as at 1.515, 9.675), cf. Paris' ἀπόφημι at 362. The poet opts for summary ἀγγελίην ἀπέειπε rather than prolonging this already fragmented account by a direct report of what was said.

418 Division into two groups with distinct functions is precise and logical, unlike the syntax which is deliberately varied by ἕτεροι δέ...

419–20 ...which, however, resonates with ἑτέρωθεν in another dichotomy between Trojans and Argives, here described in exactly balanced terms. νέκυς (as at *Od.* 24.417) has to be substituted for νέκυας to accommodate Aristarchus' ὀτρύνοντο (Did/A), 'made haste', for vulgate ὄτρυνον; that is certainly right in view of 419 εὐσσέλμων ἀπὸ νηῶν, i.e. they hastened from the ships to do these tasks (rather than urged, from the ships, unspecified others to do them). Leaf felt 420 to be an added elaboration, which is unlikely, especially in a heavily cumulated passage; cf. the corresponding repetition in 428–32.

421–32 The description of collecting and disposing of the dead is plain, almost severe, but with touches of pathos: the brevity of 423 οἱ δ᾽ ἤντεον ἀλλήλοισιν as well as their silence in 427, underscored by the sole integral enjambment after σιωπῇ |.

421–2 = *Od.* 19.433f., likewise signifying a time well after dawn itself (which has already been mentioned, there at 428 as here at 381 ἠῶθεν). But this relatively short interval, a couple of hours at most, now has to accommodate Idaios' going to the ships and back again, apart from the actual discussions. The couplet is a striking one, rarely used since the discrimination of this after-dawn period is only rarely needed. ἀκαλαρρείταο comes only here and in the identical *Od.* passage; it is apparently compounded from ἀκαλά as adverbial neuter plur. of ἀκαλός = 'peaceful', 'gentle' (so Hesychius), as in Hesiod frag. 339 M–W, Sappho frag. 43.5 L–P; cf. Chantraine, *Dict.* s.v. ἀκή. The streams of Okeanos were free from storms according to the D-scholium.

424 For the occasional Homeric use of εἶναι with an adverb cf. 6.131 δὴν ἦν, 9.551 κακῶς ἦν.

425–6 The second half of 425 and first of 426 are both formular, cf. e.g. 14.7, 16.3. ἀλλ' in 425 continues the sense of the previous v.: it was difficult to tell whether the corpses were Trojan or Achaean, but by washing them they did so, and were able to lift them onto their own wagons.

427 Both sides wept as they lifted the dead (426), but Priam (who had naturally left the city to preside over the cremation) forbade further, perhaps ritual, lamentation (though they were still ἀχνύμενοι κῆρ, 428) as the Trojans piled them on the pyre. No distinction seems intended between barbarian laments and Greek self-restraint (*contra* AbT), and the Achaeans are probably to be imagined as performing equivalent acts in silence at 431.

428 There is some doubt over the reduplicated form ἐπενήνεον, only here and in 431; Aristarchus did not query it and it was the vulgate reading, but 23.139 νήεον (+ 2 × elsewhere) suggests ἐπενήεον, accepted by Payne Knight, Leaf, Schwyzer, LSJ, cf. Chantraine, *Dict.* s.v. νηέω.

430–2 The parallel actions of the two sides are again stressed by ἑτέρωθεν (as at 419) and by repetition of 428f. as 431f. (except for their different destinations).

433 A unique v.: it was not yet dawn, night was ἀμφιλύκη, i.e. with a hint of daylight (cf. Chantraine, *Dict.* s.v. * λύκη, related to λεύσσω, λύχνος, Lat. *lux*). 23.226f. depicts a slightly later phase immediately before dawn itself; whereas at 24.788f. the people gathering at dawn round Hektor's pyre are described in otherwise similar language,

> ἦμος δ' ἠριγένεια φάνη ῥοδοδάκτυλος Ἠώς,
> τῆμος ἄρ' ἀμφὶ πυρὴν κλυτοῦ Ἕκτορος ἔγρετο λαός.

Here it may be the need to conceal their further actions that makes the Achaeans begin at the earliest possible moment, when there is just enough light for them to see (though the task will continue all day); but Trojan failure to protest or comment at any stage is peculiar in itself. There is in any case something casual and untypical about the timing of events: the Trojan assembly at nightfall (345) and the Achaean assembly the following dawn (381f.); Idaios' journeys to and fro, and the first preparations for gathering the dead, all by soon after sunrise (421–3); the failure to suggest nightfall (either directly, or by the mention of an evening meal or going to sleep) at the end of that day; and the present pre-dawn activity (432f.). But there can be no doubt that the decision to gather the dead, and its performance, occupies *the whole of one day*, with the building of the mound and the associated wall and trench (during which nothing is heard of the Trojans), followed by the arrival of the ships from Lemnos, *the whole of the next* (cf. 465–82).

434 ἤγρετο must be read for MS ἔγρετο: the meaning must be that they gathered (ἀγείρομαι), not that they woke up (ἐγείρομαι) – clearly the group in question did not sleep by the pyre, indeed (all) the Achaeans went back to the ships after burning the dead (432). Why this κριτός... λαός, select host, should be specified is not clear; they might be special mourners, but it is they who apparently build not only the mound but also the wall and trench (435–7). Nestor at 336ff. had simply proposed 'let us build...', obviously meaning the Achaeans in general, and all available forces would be needed for such a huge task – yet its accomplishment in a single day shows that realistic criteria cannot in any case be invoked. Could κριτός be affected by the not dissimilar-sounding κλυτοῦ in the similar 24.789, quoted in the preceding n.? Or by 436 ἄκριτον? Or by the special activity implied in 334f. (but that is probably an Athenian addition)? The difficulty remains; but perhaps the v. is indeed modelled after 24.789 *vel sim.*, with κριτός not specifically thought out in context.

435–40 ~ 336–41 where Nestor proposed the present actions in the same words, except for necessary adjustments of number, tense etc. Yet two variations show, surprisingly enough, that the present passage was conceived first, and the earlier proposal adapted from it: (i) the inclusion of τεῖχος in 436 (see on 338 for the difficulties of its omission there); and (ii) the optative εἴη which is regular in 439 but anomalous at 340 (see comment there).

435–6 On the probable meaning of ἐξαγαγόντες, in the light of Aristophanes' ἐν πεδίῳ here, see on 336–7.

441 = 9.350, where Akhilleus refers slightingly to the ditch; the stakes, which are important, are also prominent at 12.55f. Nestor had used a different and more general description at 341f., one that would be less appropriate to the present factual narrative.

442–82   After a brief diversion to Olumpos for a (doubtfully authentic) complaint by Poseidon, wine-ships arrive from Lemnos and the Achaeans feast after their labours, after nightfall, but fearfully as Zeus thunders ominously

443–64 There is a sudden switch to Zeus's residence on Olumpos. This scene of protest by Poseidon and conciliation by Zeus is broadly paralleled at *Od.* 13.125ff., where Poseidon insists on turning the Phaeacian ship to stone. It also appears to duplicate 12.3–33, where the poet will describe how the wall and trench will be obliterated by Poseidon and Apollo turning the local rivers against them after the fall of Troy. Zenodotus, Aristophanes and Aristarchus (Arn, Did/A) all found the present scene to be the interpolation (in an 'unusual consensus', Bolling, *External Evidence* 99); though its inclusion of many vv. found elsewhere says little, and Shipp's judgement that it is 'unusually crammed with abnormalities' (*Studies* 261) is far too strong, see on 447 and 452–3 *ad fin.* More to the point, it interrupts a generally workmanlike narrative and is anticlimactic in itself, while the new Achaean wall can hardly be seen as a serious rival to the huge enceinte of Troy (452f.). Moreover by specifically linking Apollo with the earlier wall-building it directly contradicts 21.446–9, where Poseidon builds the wall and Apollo tends Laomedon's herds. Almost the only thing in its favour is that it lends more emphasis to this whole cursorily introduced affair of the wall and trench – though see further de Jong, *Narrators* 153. Both this and the bk 12 version make the same point about the Achaean failure to offer hecatombs (450 = 12.6), but there it is taken more seriously, including by Zeus himself. On balance the evidence suggests that the present scene *is* an addition, developing the narrative of 12.3ff. after the dramatic model of the discussion between Poseidon and Zeus in *Od.* bk 13. If so, it is likely to have been developed not by Homer himself but by another ἀοιδός, a close follower perhaps, rather than by a fully-fledged rhapsodic elaborator whose uncertainties of taste might have shown up more clearly.

446–53 Poseidon's words are rhetorically phrased and rhythmically varied, with the double integral enjambment of 448–50 leading to the curt assertion of 451.

447 ἐνίψει is clearly intended as fut. of ἐνέπειν = 'tell' rather than ἐνίπτειν = 'blame', perhaps after *ἐνέψω as Chantraine suggests, cf. *Dict.* s.v. ἐννέπω.

450 It is true that sacrifices were not mentioned when the fortification works were undertaken; but the Achaeans were in a hurry, and it is not clear that offerings were *de rigueur* before all such tactical enterprises. Poseidon is of course on his dignity here, but the same criticism is made more objectively at 12.6.

451 'As far as dawn spreads' means 'over the whole earth', cf. 8.1 Ἠὼς μὲν κροκόπεπλος ἐκίδνατο πᾶσαν ἐπ' αἶαν.

452–3 See on 443–64 for whether or not Apollo actually helped build the wall; there were obviously two versions, but Apollo's herding may be due to conflation with the separate tale of his servitude to Admetos. — The dissyllabic dat. ἥρῳ recurs at *Od.* 8.483 | ἥρῳ Δημοδόκῳ (see Hainsworth *ad loc.*) and is an acceptable alternative to ἥρωϊ (8 × *Il.*); ἀθλήσαντε is a no less acceptable contraction, as is shown by 9.124, πηγοὺς ἀθλοφόρους, οἳ ἀέθλια ποσσὶν ἄροντο. More probably 'late' is πολίσσαμεν meaning 'build' in general, not of building a πόλις as in the verb's only other Homeric occurrence at 20.217.

455 Here will address Poseidon similarly at 8.201; here εὐρυσθενές has special force in view of 458.

456–8 A weaker god might 'fear this thought', an imprecise phrase unparalleled elsewhere, but Poseidon's fame is world-wide. The conversion of 451 into 458 by substituting | σόν for | τοῦ is too obtrusive to be wholly satisfying, and Zeus's point that Poseidon need not bother about such minor matters could be made more forcibly in quite different terms.

459 For ἄγρει μάν see on 5.765–6.

461–3 This appears to be a version of the more detailed and powerful description at 12.27–32 (462 being identical with 12.31). There Poseidon turns all the rivers against the wall and smashes its foundations with his trident, then covers all the shore with sand, 32 τεῖχος ἀμαλδύνας (cf. 463 here, μέγα τεῖχος ἀμαλδύνηται). ἀμαλδύνειν, 'efface' or 'wipe out', not uncommon in Ionic poetry later, occurs only in these two contexts in Homer (cf. *HyDem* 94).

465 | δύσετο δ' ἠέλιος is an established Odyssean formula (9×, of which 7 × followed by σκιόωντό τε πᾶσαι ἀγυιαί), not found elsewhere in *Il.* The phrase τετέλεστο δὲ ἔργον is also (lightly) formular, elsewhere (1 × *Il.*, 1 × *Od.*) at the v-e. The resulting v. is plain and dignified.

466–82 The arrival of wine-ships from Lemnos and the Achaeans preparing their festive meals make a strong ending, one that conveys a feeling of accomplishment after the day-long task of building wall and trench – at least until Zeus's thundering begins. The next Book, too, will end with a similarly striking and threatening image as Trojan watch-fires burn night-long across the plain.

466 The verbal form βουφονέω is found only here in the whole of Greek; that is accidental, no doubt, since the Bouphonia at Athens (as part of the festival of Dipolieia) was well known, as was the month-name Bouphonion at Delos and Tenos; moreover the adjective βουφόνος occurs at *HyHerm* 436 and elsewhere. Yet φόνος etc., unlike σφάζειν etc., always implies slaughter with the implication of murder; that is what the Bouphonia was concerned with, and βουφονεῖν is an unexpected term for the butchering of oxen either in a normal religious or in a secular context – AbT were wrong in saying it was appropriate for the latter. Apart from this difficulty, which should not be exaggerated, the rising three-folder is neat enough; δόρπον ἕλοντο will be aptly amended to 'prepared a rich feast' at 475.

467–9 Euneos son of Iason is mentioned at 23.745–7 as buying Akhilleus' prisoner Lukaon from Patroklos with a silver mixing-bowl given by Phoenicians to his grandfather Thoas. He has a 'speaking name' apt for a despatcher of ships to Troy, and is probably a Homeric fiction (Shipp, *Studies* 261, untypically called him Euenos and made him an Atticism). Lemnos was famous for the Argonauts stopping there on their voyage, and being ardently received by the Lemnian women who had been abandoned by their husbands. Jason slept with king Thoas' daughter Hupsipule, and it is natural that their offspring should succeed to the throne; otherwise the Argonautic saga is alluded to only at *Od.* 12.69–72. Yet Lemnos itself is part of the background of the Trojan venture; aside from the present context, the Achaeans had feasted there on the way to Troy (8.230–4) and left Philoktetes behind there (2.727).

470–2 Euneos sends a thousand measures of μέθυ (sweet wine, as at 9.469) for the Atreidai, but the Achaean troops at large have to barter for theirs: ἔνθεν in 472 means 'from the ships', and οἰνίζοντο implies 'produced wine' rather than 'prepared' it as at 8.546.

473–5 The fivefold repetition of ἄλλοι gives an effect of busy and diverse activity, if in a rather mechanical way. αἴθωνι σιδήρῳ | is formular, 3 × *Il.*, 1 × *Od.*; the epithet must mean 'bright' here (cf. e.g. αἰθήρ as bright sky), rather than having its stricter and more usual sense of 'flame-coloured', as of lions or horses, or 'blazing'. It is 4 × applied to cauldrons, and they are surely of bronze. Other formulas for iron are πολιόν τε σίδηρον | and πολύκμητός τε σίδηρος |; iron is grey not tawny, and the present phrase, a less precise addition to the system, could refer to 'finish', in artefacts as against the raw state, rather than colour.

Verse 474 adds another related pair of barter-goods, hides and 'cattle themselves'; one might expect the latter to be reserved for feeding the army as a whole. The next item, ἀνδραπόδεσσι, is as remarkable for the term itself as for the idea of war-captives belonging to ordinary troops: ἀνδράποδα (here with a heteroclite ending) does not recur in epic though it is common in Herodotus, Thucydides and Xenophon. Aristarchus consequently followed Zenodotus and Aristophanes in athetizing the v. (Arn/AT), though the fifth ἄλλοι, to which he also objected, is acceptable and the second hemistich a desirable summary (and extension of 466 δόρπον ἕλοντο) after the wine-ships detail. The regular Homeric term for slaves, including captives, is δμῶες, δμωαί, with δούλιον etc. implying more degraded rôles. One cannot be certain that ἀνδράποδα (formed evidently on the analogy of τετράποδα, cf. Chantraine, *Dict.* s.v. ἀνήρ A (b)) was not available to singers; it is certainly not specifically Attic, *contra* Shipp after Wackernagel; but the idea of this v. as an addition cannot be excluded.

476–82 The lively *genre* scene of the wine-ships and the bartering can now be seen as preparing the way for a powerful and brilliant *dénouement*, as night-long thundering from Zeus makes a sinister accompaniment to the feasting and fills the troops with fear.

476–8 παννύχιοι μὲν ἔπειτα (also at 18.354) leads to | παννύχιος δέ in 478, where most editors take σφιν to refer to the Achaeans only; admittedly 477 Τρῶες…ἐπίκουροι could be understood as parenthetical, but Leaf seems correct in taking the thunder to be terrifying to both sides.

479 | σμερδαλέα κτυπέων is based on | σμερδαλέα ἰάχων, 7 × *Il.*; cf. 8.170 κτύπε, where Zeus thunders to encourage the Trojans.

480 One of the surprisingly few Iliadic references to libation (cf. p. 10); the action will turn out to be ineffectual.

482 This v. was omitted by Zenodotus on unpersuasive grounds (Arn/A, here and on 8.1); a standard way of marking the end of a day's action (cf. 9.713, *Od.* 16.481, 19.427), it makes a rather bland conclusion, though not entirely devoid of irony.

BOOK EIGHT

The eighth Book is unusual in several respects. Known in antiquity as the Κόλος Μάχη or Curtailed Battle, it describes the fighting over one complete day, which begins with Zeus forbidding the gods to interfere and ends with the Trojans encamped threateningly in the plain. Their success is due to Zeus's support for Hektor, for he has at last decided to implement his promise to Thetis in bk 1 and avenge Agamemnon's insult to Akhilleus. Athene and Here are naturally unhappy at Hektor's success, and their frustrated attempt to set out for the battlefield against him is a major episode, clearly related to their similar but successful intervention in aid of Diomedes at 5.711ff. It is characteristic of the Book as a whole that most of its actions and initiatives, whether divine or human, are soon abandoned or reversed. Only Zeus's initial determination is ultimately maintained, to produce the sense of crisis needed to motivate the Embassy in bk 9.

Book 8 maintains something of the quality of its predecessor, halting or repetitive at times but with intermittent brilliance of detail and description. Similar doubts are raised about the degree to which certain episodes have been added as a whole or subjected to elaboration. Here those doubts may be increased by (i) a greater than usual number of vv. suspected by the Alexandrian critics; and (ii) a greater than average proportion of plus-verses. These are obvious post-Homeric repetitions and additions which did not survive the Aristarchan recension of the text. The chief witness here is the pre-Aristarchan Hibeh papyrus P 7, which adds at least 25 extra vv., supported neither by Aristarchus or the medieval vulgate nor by their general appropriateness, to the first 258 vv. of the Book (of which it records a mere 90, between gaps). Yet it should be noted on (i) that of the 45 or so vv. athetized by Aristarchus (nearly half also proscribed by Zenodotus), most look innocuous and are the target of apparently pedantic criticism; and on (ii) that pre-Aristarchan papyri cover only a small proportion of the epic as a whole, and that the survival of P 7, which is unparalleled in its proportion of added vv., could place bk 8 in a misleading light. Yet the norm is suggested by another papyrus from Hibeh of similar date (mid- 3rd cent. B.C.), P 41, which covers parts of bks 3, 4 and 5 and contains only a single plus-verse (4.69a) out of 74 vv. preserved (cf. S. West, *Ptolemaic Papyri* 64–7), as opposed to P 7's 25 out of 114.

Even so, it is clear that the exceptional number of vv. and passages in this Book, even after the Aristarchan recension, which recur elsewhere in the

293

Iliad, together with its episodic quality, made it both tempting and unusually easy both to add to and to subtract from the total *numerus versuum*. Dr S. West put the matter with typical clarity: 'The proportion [*sc.* of plus-verses] depends partly on the context: passages containing many *versus iterati*, like Θ...or a summary of a typical scene described elsewhere in greater detail...attracted plus-verses, while a passage for which there are no close parallels elsewhere in Homer was likely to remain free from them. Concordance interpolation exercised a powerful attraction: thus a line or group of lines which follow a particular formula in one place are inserted after it in another passage where they may be rather less suitable' (*op. cit.* 12f.). She added on p. 75 that bk 8 'in any case contains a great number of lines which recur elsewhere, and there would be a strong temptation to expand it with further borrowings'.

Neither the plus-verses nor Aristarchus should deter the commentator from using other criteria – of consistency, relevance and taste – which may suggest certain vv. and passages as inauthentic in some sense. Even the most conservative editor may feel that in bk 8 there are at least two or three places where a short section, not always cast into doubt by Aristarchus, needs to be identified as a probable accretion. Yet Ameis–Hentze went too far in bracketing no fewer than 43 vv. in all (not counting 547*a* and 549*a–c* in the OCT numeration), some on the grounds that they are omitted by some of the better MSS. Most of these might at best be seen as concordance interpolations, to use the convenient term explained in the quotation from Dr West in the preceding paragraph, about which certainty must often lie out of reach. Possible confusions and disagreements in this respect are illustrated in Bolling, *External Evidence* 100–16, cf. A. Shewan, *Homeric Essays* (Oxford 1935) 357–68. Yet part at least of 28–40 is open to a different kind of objection, as to a lesser degree are 524–8 and 538–41. These and other possible additions are discussed in the commentary, and confirm that bk 8 as a whole has been peculiarly subject to fluctuations of length in the course of transmission. Chantraine (*REG* 47, 1934, 281ff.) concluded that, in Dr West's words, 'the text remained fluid in this part of the Iliad later than elsewhere'. She herself felt the variations to be too superficial to justify such a view (*op. cit.* 75), but it remains possible that bk 8 (and possibly also 7) was still under refinement at the time of Homer's retirement or death.

1–52   Early next day Zeus warns all the gods, with elaborate threats, not to interfere in the fighting down below; after which he travels from Olumpos to Ida in his divine chariot

1   ~ 24.695, with the first hemistich as in 19.1, cf. also 23.227. 'Saffron-robed' is typical of the lyrical language applied in the epic tradition to

Dawn, who is also 'rosy-fingered', 'early-born', 'divine', 'fair-throned', 'golden-throned', 'fair-tressed', 'bringing light to mortals' and 'rising from Tithonos' bed'; except only that it is absent from the *Odyssey*. In 3/4 occurrences the dawn that is κροκόπεπλος is *spread over* earth or sea, cf. 485–6n.; but 19.1 lacks this detail and shows that the epithet could be similar in implication to ῥοδοδάκτυλος, for which see on 1.477 *ad fin.* πᾶσαν ἐπ' αἶαν | is formular, 4 × *Il.*, 1 × *Od.*

2 ἀγορὴν ποιήσατο *sic* recurs at 489 with Hektor as subject.

3 = 1.499, 5.754 (see nn. there), where the previous v. makes clear that Zeus is sitting apart from the other gods, i.e. from their regular haunts and dwelling-places. These are not on the 'highest peak' of Olumpos, where he evidently had a sanctuary equivalent to that on Gargaros, a high peak of Ida, mentioned at 48. In envisaging all the gods as meeting there, and Zeus preparing his chariot there at 41–5 as though outside his palace, this singer has been a little careless. The anomaly is remarked by modern editors but not Aristarchus (who made other minor comments on the v., Arn/A), and is not reflected in the medieval MSS.

4 Though composed of formular elements (e.g. ἀγόρευε and ἄκουον *sic*, cf. πάντες ἄκουον | at 12.442), this v. does not exactly recur.

5–27 Zeus's speech is highly figurative but also carefully logical; untypical in content, it makes little use of the repeated vv. and half-vv. that otherwise predominate. It is, of course, central to the whole purpose of this Book in its development of the *menis*-plot and of Zeus's promise to Thetis. Rising threefolders are conspicuous (5, 7, 10, 15, 27, perhaps 17); several of the sentences are of some length, and enjambment is progressive (6, 13, 14, 15), periodic (10, 11, 19, 23) and integral (7, 8, 21, 25) in equal measure. The greater than usual amount of periodic enjambment (cf. vol. I, 33), together with the virtual confinement of progressive enjambment to the cumulative description of Tartaros in 13–16, reflects a style that is elaborately explicit rather than strongly impassioned. Zeus conveys the force of his inhibition (which is never directly stated, see on 7–9) through a vivid and unusual description of the underworld depths to which rebels might find themselves confined, followed by a fantastic offer, again of cosmic dimensions, of testing his physical strength against that of the other gods combined.

5–6 = 19.101–2 (where most MSS, probably wrongly, have ἀνώγει for κελεύει); 6 is formular, 5 × *Il.*, 5 × *Od.* Verses of address beginning, like 5, with κέκλυτε or κέκλυτέ μευ are common enough (11 × *Il.*, 20 × *Od.*; it is perverse of Shipp, *Studies* 262n., to question their traditionality), and no fewer than nine of them are followed by | ὄφρ' εἴπω as in verse 6. Yet twenty-two such vv. are *not* so followed, and the absence of 6 in many MSS including A, as well as in P 17, is hardly significant – certainly not sufficient reason for bracketing, with Ameis–Hentze. The rhythm of the present passage may be better with 6 in place to separate the rising threefolders 5 and 7.

7–9 These vv. are specially composed for their context, though obviously with formular elements (e.g. τελευτήσω -αι τάδε ἔργα, 2 × *Od.*). οὖν in 7 is used for emphasis in the first part of a negative disjunction (Denniston, *Particles* 419); γε stresses a pronoun as at 5.301 (Denniston 121f.); τό refers forward to διακέρσαι, *hapax* in Homer (though cf. 15.467 ἐπὶ...κείρει), literally to cut through, here metaphorically to negate or frustrate. Zeus specifies both male and female gods (Shipp's objections, *Studies* 263, both to θήλεια and to θέαιναι in 5 and 20 are unconvincing), not just as a 'polar' construction to convey the wide range of his ban but also with covert reference to Here and Athene, the usual trouble-makers. He never positively describes the 'deeds' to be accomplished, but leaves them to the imagination.

10–11 10 belongs to a set of vv. with ingenious variations in their second halves:

1.549   ὃν δέ κ' ἐγὼν ἀπάνευθε θεῶν ἐθέλωμι νοῆσαι
8.10   ὃν δ' ἂν ἐγὼν ἀπάνευθε θεῶν ἐθέλοντα νοήσω...
2.391f.   ὃν δέ κ' ἐγὼν ἀπάνευθε μάχης ἐθέλοντα νοήσω | μιμνάζειν
15.348   ὃν δ' ἂν ἐγὼν ἀπάνευθε νεῶν ἑτέρωθι νοήσω.

V. 11 recurs at 13.9 (of the same situation), where ἐλθόντ' is less awkward; but the jingle with ἐθέλοντα may have seemed attractive.

12–13 The hypothetical offender will be struck by Zeus's thunderbolt – he elaborates the threat at 402–5 and 455f. – and so return in poor shape to Olumpos, or be hurled down into Tartaros. οὐ κατὰ κόσμον, a sinister understatement, is to be taken closely with ἐλεύσεται (Nic/A); the phrase is used of Thersites' insults at 2.214.

13 Flinging disobedient deities out of Olumpos is a favourite punishment by Zeus. At 15.18–24 he reminds Here of how he hung her up with anvils tied to her feet for an earlier offence, then threw (ῥίπτασκον) down to earth anyone who came to her aid; it was probably on this occasion that he cast Hephaistos down to Lemnos according to 1.590–4 (cf. 1.586–94n.). A variant of the motif is used at 18.394–9, where Here does the throwing, but again of Hephaistos; now the fall is to be not merely to earth but to Tartaros itself deep below. Tartaros, to be further described in the next three vv., is ἠερόεντα (cf. Hesiod, *Theog.* 119 and 682), i.e. filled with ἀήρ and so darkness; compare 478–81, where Zeus renews his threat to Here and implies that she might come 'to the lowest boundaries of sea and earth, where Iapetos and Kronos [cf. 14.203f.] rejoice neither in the rays of the Sun nor in the breezes, but deep Tartaros lies on every side'. In fact

Tartaros (a word of unknown, probably oriental, etymology according to Chantraine, *Dict.* s.v., though West, *Theogony* p. 195, prefers AbT's association with ταράσσειν) is mentioned in the whole of Homer only on these two occasions in the present Book (cf. Schmidt, *Weltbild* 105f.). Erebos, on the other hand, is named 3 × *Il.* (including 368), 4 × *Od.*

14 τῆλε is first word in 5/14 Iliadic occurrences, here emphasized by μάλ' (which belongs to speech rather than to narrative, so too superlatives like βάθιστον, see p. 31). The only Homeric occurrences of βέρεθρον, Attic βάραθρον, are here and at *Od.* 12.94; it implies a gulf, pit or recess which devours anything that penetrates it, from the same root as e.g. βιβρώσκειν and Lat. *vorare* (Chantraine, *Dict.* s.v. βάραθρον). At Athens criminals were cast into the *barathron* (cf. e.g. Herodotus 7.133), a special cleft, but it is doubtful whether there is any such specific overtone here. The term does not recur in any of Hesiod's quite full descriptions of the underworld, see next n.

15–16 Each v., like 14, is cumulated in progressive enjambment. Descriptions of the underworld were perhaps especially susceptible to catalogue-like expansions – compare the complex and sometimes repetitive descriptions in Hesiod, *Theog.* 717–819, where even the generally conservative M. L. West allows a degree of rhapsodic elaboration; but there is nothing to suggest anything of the kind in the present Homeric context, which is both clear and logical.

V. 15 recurs at Hesiod, *Theog.* 811, though with ἔνθα δὲ μαρμάρεαι for ἔνθα σιδήρειαι. The latter term is clearly the more appropriate, since μαρμάρεος in epic means 'sparkling'; also more consistent with the brazen threshold, for which compare Tartaros' brazen gates and threshold at *Theog.* 733f. and 749f. The gate and its threshold are perhaps to be envisaged as on the floor of Tartaros rather than in its upper part, see next para., (ii). West, *Theogony* p. 358, considers it possible that the 'four-storey' universe implied by 16 is 'an attempt to outdo' the three-storey one of Hesiod; see vol. I, 10 for his conviction that Hesiod is earlier than Homer. Yet Hesiod's statement at *Theog.* 720 that the Titans' place of confinement (i.e. Tartaros, whether or not one accepts 721, on which see P. Mazon's introduction to the Budé Hesiod, pp. xviiif.) is 'as far *below earth* as sky is from earth', substituting ὑπὸ γῆς for Ἀΐδεω, looks like an attempt to make the Homeric description more symmetrical, both ἔνερθ' ὑπό and γῆς with γαίης showing signs of strain (correctly Shipp, *Studies* 265). Admittedly Hades is normally the king rather than the place as here, but the formula πύλας Ἀΐδαο περήσειν | (etc.), as at 5.646, encouraged or exemplified a broader application of the term.

In any case the schematic drawing accompanying AT's scholium on 13 (and reproduced in Erbse *ad loc.*):

Book Eight

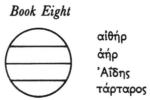

gives a clearly misleading interpretation of the *textus receptus* and should look more like this:

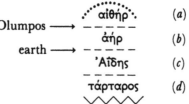

since (*d*) = (*a*) + (*b*), provided (i) that οὐρανός implies the *upper part* of αἰθήρ (as οὐρανόθεν in 19 and 21 suggests), and (ii) that the *lower parts* of Tartaros are meant, and that the iron gate of 15 is envisaged as there. Such a scheme does not possess the symmetry of the scholiasts' (Aristarchan?) interpretation, or of the Hesiodic version; yet it accurately reflects the ideas of Hades as immediately below the earth and of Tartaros stretching down almost indefinitely as in Xenophanes frag. 28 D–K.

17 Can be phrased either as a rising threefolder or, less plausibly, with regular central caesura. If the former, it would balance the rising threefolder at 10, thus marking beginning and end of the first part of Zeus's threat: 27 is also relevant, see next n.

18 One cannot be sure how ancient singers would articulate this v. with its parenthetical vocative θεοί, but since the conclusion of the threat's second part is a rising threefolder at 27, so its introduction may be too: εἰ δ' ἄγε πειρήσασθε θεοί ἵνα εἴδετε πάντες. The rhetorical disposition of four rising threefolders in this manner (i.e. at 10, 17, 18, 27) would be quite striking, well within the powers and ambitions of this singer (surely Homer himself) in such a remarkable pronouncement. The v. is otherwise similar to 1.302, εἰ δ' ἄγε μὴν πείρησαι, ἵνα γνώωσι καὶ οἵδε. For the sarcastic and threatening use of εἴδετε compare Agamemnon's boast from the same Book, 1.185f., ὄφρ' εὖ εἰδῇς | ὅσσον φέρτερός εἰμι σέθεν.

19–20 Should the major pause follow κρεμάσαντες in 19 rather than πάντες in 18? The former was urged by Nicanor according to bT, followed e.g. by Leaf, and allows the δ' of 20 πάντες δ' to be kept. The latter is adopted in OCT, with consequent emendation of δ' to τ' (the change being nugatory in itself), which makes the challenge more dramatic and is perhaps correct. — The other gods are to suspend a golden cord 'from the sky', ἐξ οὐρανόθεν (a pleonastic coalescence of ἐξ οὐρανοῦ and οὐρανόθεν, also in 21 and 2 × elsewhere *Il.*, 2 × *Od.*), in which 'sky' might refer either to the top of Mt Olumpos, just above the clouds where the gods normally dwell, or to the vault of heaven itself, the χάλκεος οὐρανός of 17.425. Either would suit the first part of the scene Zeus is imagining, down to 22, but see further on 25–6. ἐξάπτεσθε, 'attach yourselves from it' preparatory to pulling.

21 πεδίονδε: either to the earth's surface or to the divine surface of Olumpos, cf. previous comment.

22 The first hemistich recurs at 17.339; here Zeus refers to himself by name and with a grand title (much as he will term himself Κρονίωνα at 470), to give a touch of dignity to this otherwise rather comical, if unnerving, suggestion.

23–4 'But as soon as I, too, *really* wanted to pull, I should pull ⟨you up⟩ together with earth itself and sea itself' (for the sociative datives cf. e.g. 9.542). Sea is joined to earth, of which it is a part, for rhetorical effect.

25–6 | σειρὴν μέν κεν ἔπειτα continues the brilliant rhetoric, with | σειρὴν μέν echoing the spondaic and ponderous | αὐτῇ κεν of the preceding v., then suddenly lightened by the dactylic run of κεν ἔπειτα, reflecting Zeus's ease, perhaps, in contrast with the weight he has lifted. Now, for certain, Olumpos is seen as where Zeus is, the divine mountain-top complete with spur (ῥίον) rather than heaven or the upper air itself; for it is from Olumpos that he ties the cord, and 'all that', τὰ δέ... πάντα (i.e. earth and sea rather than the other gods themselves), would be μετήορα, floating (cf. 23.369; from μετ-αείρειν, 'lift up'). Clearly there is a certain conflation, which has perturbed critics, of the two views of οὐρανός, since Olumpos, regarded as the Thessalian mountain, rises from earth itself and yet is here imagined as separate from it: that is, in the sky. This is hardly out of keeping with the fanciful nature of Zeus's proposal, though it probably arises from an underlying ambivalence about the divine dwelling-place (see on 5.749–52). Zenodotus averted the difficulty by athetizing both vv. (Arn/A); Aristarchus (Arn/A on 19, Arn/bT on 25) evidently thought that Zeus tied the cord to Mt Olumpos *below* (i.e. he was in the οὐρανός above Olumpos), and so hauled the mountain, with earth and sea attached, into mid-air. That must depend on the valuation of ἔπειτα in 25: its most obvious meaning is 'next in sequence', but Aristarchus had to take it to mean 'at that moment' ('when I want to pull', Arn/A), which is ingenious but unconvincing.

27 The rising threefolder emphasizes the completion of the argument, closing the ring after 17 which it may also balance rhythmically – see the nn. on 17 and 18. Here (unlike 7) the polar expression is purely rhetorical, since Zeus's superiority to *men* hardly needs proving.

28–40 Zeus's threat, though not untypical in tone (cf. e.g. 15.14 and 137, Fenik, *TBS* 219), has been unique in detail and expression. What follows, down to 72 at least, is by contrast almost entirely composed of vv. and passages found elsewhere in Homer and mainly in *Il.* That does not necessarily brand it as interpolated or due to post-Homeric elaboration; but these first 13 vv., in which Athene complains and Zeus apparently relents, are open to the strongest suspicion. That is because his relenting undermines his whole position, making his spectacular threats pointless, even absurd, and being contradicted by his undiminished hostility to the two goddesses later in the Book (cf. e.g. 447–56). Yet the difficulty cannot be cured simply by omitting 38–40, since ὡς εἰπών in 41 shows that Athene's complaint was in fact answered. Therefore if Zeus's words at 39f. are unacceptable here (as opposed to 22.183f., where they recur), then the whole of Athene's complaint at 30–7 has to be surrendered likewise – as indeed do 28f., for none of this can justify ὡς εἰπών in 41, a phrase that cannot plausibly be emended away. The only other possibility would be that Zeus made some *unfavourable* reply to Athene (much as he replies unfavourably to Here making the same complaint at 463–8), for which 39f. were somehow substituted. Yet there is no reason for such a change (neither type of reply being substantially more 'typical' than the other, *pace* Fenik 202f.), nor is there any evidence for it in the tradition. — The whole sequence of 13 vv. was athetized by Aristarchus (Arn/A), initially on the ground that 'they have been moved here from other places', ὅτι ἐξ ἄλλων τόπων μετάκεινται; then that 39f. 'are at odds here with the context', ἐναντιοῦνται δὲ ἐνθάδε τοῖς ὑποκειμένοις. The Hibeh papyrus P 7, on the other hand, evidently contained the whole passage (though 33–7 are missing).

28–30 These vv. are not open to objection in themselves (i.e. apart from the contextual argument against them in the preceding n.), since the divine reactions are natural and their expression typical; 28 is formular (followed by ὀψὲ δὲ δή as at 7.399 and 3 × in bk 9) and 29 = 9.694, cf. 9.431, with | μῦθον ἀγασσάμενοι 6 × *Il.* Together the 3 vv. down to μετέειπε recur at 9.430–2; ἀγόρευσεν here replaces ἀπέειπεν there, but that is hardly a sign of secondary adaptation (*contra* Shipp, *Studies* 265) – indeed it has the merit of avoiding an undesirable echo with μετέειπε as in 9.431f.

31 Athene addresses Zeus in these same terms 3 × *Od.*

32–7 Here will say exactly the same thing at 463–8 when she and Athene have been forced by another drastic threat from Zeus to return to Olumpos. There her words are thoroughly appropriate, some reply to Zeus's taunts being needed to elicit his further threats for the following day and his longer-term prophecy of events including Patroklos' death (470ff.) – a powerful and unusual sequence which there is no reason for regarding as superfluous or inauthentic. Here, on the other hand, these vv. are unnecessary in themselves and unacceptable in context (28–40n.);

moreover substantial *verbatim* repetition by two different characters, except in the case of messengers etc., is unusual even in the oral style. For the details of this complaint see on 463–8.

38–40 ~ 22.182–4, where Zeus has just mooted the idea of saving Hektor; Athene objects, and Zeus conciliates her with these words, then tells her to proceed with her plan of supporting Akhilleus. See on 28–40 for the objection to these vv. in the present context; they are better in place in bk 22, even if not perfectly so as Leaf claimed – for even there the ethos of Zeus's comment that he was not speaking seriously, θυμῷ | πρόφρονι, whether ironical or not (cf. the A-scholium on 40), is surprising. At least ἐπιμειδήσας (for which see on 4.356–7; P 7 had a different version with μείδησεν, adding 1.361, cf. Bolling, *External Evidence* 102) is replaced there by the innocuous ἀπαμειβόμενος. For Τριτογένεια see on 4.513–16.

41–52 Now follows another episode, Zeus's journey to Ida, composed of vv. found elsewhere; but this passage, or something like it, is necessary in context, moreover it is charming and impressive in itself, with the cumulated vv. (every other one: 42, 44, 46, 48, 50, 52) conveying a sense of divine ease and luxuriance.

41–4 ~ 13.23–6, where Poseidon, after leaving the peak of Samothrace and reaching his underwater palace at Aigai (hence ἔνθ' ἐλθών for 41 ὡς εἰπών), yokes his horses and mounts his chariot – *his* horses skim the waves whereas Zeus's fly swiftly (42 ὠκυπέτα) through the air, but this part of the description can apply brilliantly to both.

41 τιτύσκομαι commonly in Homer means 'aim', of weapons, metaphorically 'intend' or 'purpose' at 13.558f.; but 'prepare' or 'arrange' of a chariot here (= 13.23) and a fire at 21.342. Cf. Trümpy, *Fachausdrücke* 110f., Chantraine, *Dict.* s.v., who compares the corresponding senses of τυγχάνω and τεύχω. — Gold is everywhere, but a touch of realism persists; gold would be too soft for hooves as for an axle, which is likewise of bronze in the continuation of this passage at 13.30.

43 Golden armour is fitting for Zeus in majesty; it may be more immediately necessary for Poseidon as he approaches the battlefield at 13.25, but Ameis–Hentze were wrong (in more ways than one) in concluding that the bk 13 passage must therefore be the original and this a copy. — γέντο, 'grasped', 5 × *Il.*, not *Od.*, from a probable root γεμ-, cf. Chantraine, *Dict.* s.v.

45–6 The two contexts diverge now as Poseidon drives over the waves, Zeus through the air; but our singer is able to draw on other typical vv. and parallel scenes for his continuation. V. 45 is formular, usually with ἐλάαν as here but 3 × *Il.* with ἵππους instead, i.e. where horses have not so far been mentioned. The couplet recurs, with that difference, at 5.768f. where Here drives from Olumpos down to Troy. 46 is formed from typical elements: | μεσσηγύς 4 × *Il.* elsewhere, not *Od.*, and οὐρανοῦ (etc.) ἀστερόεντος | 5 × *Il.* elsewhere, 4 × *Od.*

47–8 Verse 47 recurs at 14.283 and 15.151 of other gods coming to Ida. It is indeed rich in springs like other well-wooded mountains (though πολυπίδακα etc. is peculiar to it in Homer, 8 × *Il.*), as in wild life: J. M. Cook (*Troad* 306) was told in 1968 of hares, jackals, boar, badgers, deer, wild cats, partridge, bears, even leopards. For μητέρα θηρῶν cf. also μητέρα μήλων 3 × *Il.*, 1 × *Od.* — Γάργαρον is placed in apposition to specify a particular part of the whole massif. Its gender is unclear, and ancient and modern critics veer between Γάργαρος, Γάργαρον and even Γάργαρα. For ἀνὰ Γαργάρῳ ἄκρῳ at 14.352 and 15.152 cf. ἄκρῳ 'Ολύμπῳ at 13.523; its remaining appearance is 14.292 Γάργαρον ἄκρον – that is, it could be masc. in all 4 Homeric occurrences. Homer surely envisages it as Ida's highest peak (cf. 51 ἐν κορυφῇσι), whichever that might have been thought to be; actually it is Baba Dağ at the western end of the long E–W ridge known as Kaz Dağ (Cook, *Troad* 304–7). The later settlement called Gargara has been identified by Cook (257f.) near the much lower and separate peak of Koca Kaya, a few miles N–E of its mother-city Assos, its name perhaps due to a misidentification from Lesbos; at any rate the battlefield of Troy is not visible from there as it is from Baba Dağ (cf. Leaf, *Troy*, London 1912, 10).

At 22.170f. Zeus pities Hektor who 'burned many an ox-thigh for me on the peaks of rugged Ida'. τέμενος βωμός τε θυήεις recurs at 23.148, *Od.* 8.363, of other deities, with θυήεις referring to burnt offerings in general, strictly non-animal ones (see on 6.269–70); 'fragrant' is a mistranslation here, though correct for 15.153 θυόεν and for θυώδης, 3 × *Od.*

49–50 Again the actions – of halting and unharnessing the horses, then concealing or alternatively feeding them – are typical, so in more or less the same words of Iris at 5.368f., Here at 5.775f., Poseidon at 13.34.

51–2 Finally Zeus takes his seat in his sanctuary on the mountain-top (an allusion to a 'rock throne', as Ameis–Hentze assumed, being just possible), 'exulting in glory' (for which see on 1.405 and 5.906) and gazing at Troy and the Achaean camp below – he will do so again at 11.81f., but it is an undeniably majestic conclusion to his monotheistic *tour de force* here.

53–171   The troops march out after dawn; fighting is even at first, then Zeus favours the Trojans. Nestor is saved by Diomedes when one of his horses is killed; together they face Hektor, but retreat when Zeus hurls a thunderbolt in front of their chariot and then thunders again in support of the Trojans

53–9 The cumulative style continues as both sides emerge for battle, with 54, 56f. and 59 adding detail to the main statements of action.

53–4 At the end of bk 7 the Achaeans slept in fear after feasting for much of the night. Now after dawn they take another meal, δεῖπνον (see on 2.381), before the day's fighting. | ῥίμφα and κατὰ κλισίας are formular, though not combined elsewhere; θωρήσσοντο | is found *sic* 6/8 × *Il*. The untraditional phrase is ἀπὸ δ' αὐτοῦ, with unusual temporal sense; τοὶ δ' αὐτόθι was an ancient variant (Did/A). The 'wild' P 7 attempted to fill out the description with details taken from other scenes; here it added four plus-vv. after 54, of which the last three = 2.477–9, a description of Agamemnon marshalling the host.

55 ἑτέρωθεν continues to set the scene in terms of a clear visual opposition between Achaeans on the one side, Trojans on the other; | Τρῶες δ' αὖθ' ἑτέρωθεν 5 × *Il*., cf. | Ἀργεῖοι δ' ἑτέρωθεν 4 ×. ὁπλίζοντο clearly corresponds with 54 θωρήσσοντο, though normally it means 'prepare' in a more general sense. Now P 7 adds 11.57–60, an obvious concordance interpolation since 11.56 ~ 55 here.

56–7 μέμασαν...μάχεσθαι: cf. 7.3 μέμασαν πολεμίζειν ἠδὲ μάχεσθαι and 2.863 μέμασαν δ' ὑσμῖνι μάχεσθαι. The lesser number of Trojans (allies apart) and, in the next v., the need to defend wives and children, are typical motifs (cf. Fenik, *TBS* 219), though not exactly so expressed elsewhere. χρειοῖ ἀναγκαίῃ, of which the second term must be adjectival, is unique. The poet of this Book, though his main *forte* is for deploying vv. and half-vv. from elsewhere, is also capable of making his own formular adaptations and creating, from time to time, novel if not especially elegant phrases.

58–9 These vv. repeat the description of 2.809f., when the Trojans, after hastening to arms, issue from the city; see nn. *ad loc.* (the former on πᾶσαι as meaning what it says, i.e. more than one gate).

60–5 These vv. repeat the description of 4.446–51 when battle is first joined; see comments there, including on the clash of shields and on the powerful and rhetorical style. There the generic narrative is reinforced by a developed simile. P 7 gratuitously added 18.535–7 after 65, a description of Eris and other allegorical figures, perhaps to correspond with 4.440ff.

66–7 These vv. recur at 11.84f., similarly of a new day's fighting which remains evenly balanced until midday, when one side or the other gains the ascendancy (cf. Fenik, *TBS* 81).

68 There, that idea is expressed by the hour when the woodcutter takes his dinner. Here and at 16.777 the sun's position is given as he 'bestrides' the middle part of the vault of heaven, cf. similar expressions for evening in terms of the setting sun at e.g. 1.475, 11.194, 16.779.

69–72 Zeus weighs the fates twice in *Il*., here and at 22.209–13 (q.v. with nn.). The couplet in which he stretches out (ἐτίταινε, a form of τεῖνε) the golden scales, then places two dooms of death in them, is identical in each case; then follows a v. defining the owners of the doom (Trojans and

Achaeans here, in the formular v. 71, Akhilleus and Hektor there), then a lightly varied description of holding up the scales and the sinking of 'the day of destiny' of one or the other:

8.72 ἕλκε δὲ μέσσα λαβών,   ῥέπε δ' αἴσιμον ἦμαρ Ἀχαιῶν
22.212 ἕλκε δὲ μέσσα λαβών,   ῥέπε δ' Ἕκτορος αἴσιμον ἦμαρ.

The expression so far is accomplished and probably traditional.

70 τανηλεγέος θανάτοιο: an old formula, 2 × *Il.*, 6 × *Od.*; the epithet's meaning is disputed, cf. Chantraine, *Dict.*, with Blass, Bechtel and Leumann (*HW* 45) arguing for (τ)αν-ἀλέγειν, Szemerényi defending traditional τανϝ-ἀλέγειν, cf. τανύ, 'of long concern'.

73–4 At 22.213 the sinking of Hektor's doom is described in a brief appended clause, | ᾤχετο δ' εἰς Ἀΐδαο, meaning that the scale sank down toward the underworld. ῥέπε, 'turned' or 'leant', especially of the movement of a balance, has already implied that the significant direction is being taken, presumably downward since the heavier doom is the predominant one. Now this is made absolutely clear, with the added implication that Hades is where Hektor himself will end up. In the present bk 8 version, however, this concise and pregnant expression is apparently expanded into two vv. athetized by Aristarchus and assigned to a *diasceuast* (Arn/A). For the Achaeans' doom now becomes plural, κῆρες, which strangely takes a dual verb ἐζέσθην (for which the ancient variant -εν is a desperate remedy); moreover the desired meaning is not that the scale actually *settles* on the earth (whose standard epithet 'much-nurturing' is, admittedly, quite ironic here), but merely that it moves towards it. Yet κήρ could surely become multiple for a collective subject when required; and the dual verb could refer loosely to the two scales rather than the κῆρες themselves. This apparent expansion of the simple 'went towards the house of Hades' is ungainly and could be rhapsodic, but one cannot (of course) be sure. Metaphorical references to Zeus's balance at 16.658 and 19.223 show the concept to be a typical one, subject no doubt to variant expression even within the aoidic phase. Despite possible borrowings and adaptations, the whole of the present passage down to 77 is vigorous and clear.

75–7 μεγάλ' (μέγα δ') ἔκτυπε *sic* is formular, 3 × *Il.*, 1 × *Od.*; so is χλωρὸν δέος εἷλεν (etc.), 4 × *Il.*, 6 × *Od.*, but 'blazing flash' for lightning is found only here.

78–91 The tale of Nestor's rescue by Diomedes is original in content (so far as *Il.* is concerned) and told in a straightforward, not especially derivative, narrative style. Neoanalysts have argued (but cf. Kullmann, *Quellen* 45) that the *Aithiopis* episode where Nestor's son Antilokhos rescued his father from a similar predicament (also caused when a horse is wounded by an arrow-shot from Paris), at the cost of his own life, is the model from which the present episode is derived. There is no evidence for this rather than other possibilities: that this is the model for the later poem, or more probably – in view of deficiencies in the present account – that both are versions of a lost, typical exemplar. See further p. 27 and M. W. Edwards' discussion of Neoanalysis in vol. v, ch. 2 (ii).

78–84 Nestor is οὖρος Ἀχαιῶν, 'watcher over' them, here and 3 × later in the poem (and once *Od.*). The narrative is tense and rhetorical, with increasing subordination and varied enjambment: neither Idomeneus nor Agamemnon dared remain, nor the Aiantes – only Nestor stayed behind, not willingly, but his horse was hurt, which Paris struck with an arrow on the head where the mane begins, a fatal spot.

81 ἐδάμνατο was read for ἐτείρετο in some commentaries according to Did/A, presumably because the wound was fatal; but not immediately, cf. 86, and ἐτείρετο can stand.

82 This is the regular description of Paris when he has to fill the whole v. (sometimes with another word in place of | δῖος), i.e. he is type-cast, in accordance with the demands of the epic as a whole, as Helen's husband rather than e.g. as good archer or prince of the Trojans.

85–6 The sudden pain made him rear up (ἀν-επ-αλτο rather than from ἀναπάλλομαι), the arrow entered his brain, he threw the two yoke-horses into confusion in his death-agony ('as he rolled around with the arrow in him').

87–91 The dramatic narrative continues: while the old man rushes (down from the chariot) to cut the traces, Hektor's horses come through the tumult with their bold rider – Hektor himself, that is; and the old man would have lost his life had not Diomedes keenly noticed. On παρηορίαι and the concept of παρήορος = 'trace-horse' see 7.155–6n. The only other mention of a trace-horse in *Il.* is the fuller one of the wounding and death of Patroklos' trace-horse Pedasos at 16.467–77, where the two yoked horses are confused and the charioteer Automedon cuts Pedasos loose. The point is much the same, yet the expression here is evidently independent (though ἀΐσσειν occurs both at 8.88 and at 16.474). In reality trace-horses would have been a particular liability in battle, and like many other details of chariot-tactics were probably the product of misunderstandings in the poetical tradition; the matter is convincingly discussed by Delebecque, *Cheval* 98–102. The single trace-horse looks particularly impractical, and might have been imported from chariot-racing. Delebecque makes the important point (101) that only two horses are killed or wounded in the whole of the *Iliad*, and they are precisely these two trace-horses of bks 8 and 16. The disabling of one of the regular, yoked pair would have had drastic and immediate consequences for those in the chariot; this aspect of Homeric warfare is suppressed, therefore, and the trace-horse introduced precisely because he can create a crisis but still be cut free, when a character needs to be threatened in a particular way as Nestor is here.

87–90 Hektor's arrival is described through that of his chariot and horses, no doubt as a contrast with Nestor's disabled team; the mention of his name in the gen. at 88 slightly detracts from emphatic runover | Ἔκτορα in 90. As Aristarchus noted (Arn/A), he is not strictly ἡνίοχος – Eniopeus is that, 119f. Commentators have noticed that θρασύς is predominantly applied to Hektor, but that is mainly a function of the formula θρασὺν Ἔκτορα before the bucolic diaeresis, 6 ×, which is part of his name–epithet system. It is more remarkable that the term is 4 × used of a ἡνίοχος, all in this Book. Another idiosyncrasy is ἰωχμός (related to ἰωκή, διώκω), only here and at 158, also Hesiod, *Theog.* 683.

90–1 For the common syntactical pattern καί νύ κεν... | εἰ μὴ ἄρ' ὀξὺ νόησε see on 3.373–5.

92–8 Diomedes notices Nestor's predicament and calls on Odysseus to help, in an apparently pointless little digression. Odysseus was not mentioned among the leaders in flight at 78f., being perhaps reserved for here. Calling on a companion to join one in an enterprise is a typical motif, but Diomedes' words are (a) derogatory and (b) ignored. (a) can perhaps be paralleled by Agamemnon's insulting exhortations in the Epipolesis, not only of Odysseus and Menestheus (4.340 τίπτε καταπτώσσοντες ἀφέστατε...;) but also of Diomedes himself (4.371 τί πτώσσεις...;); but (b) is unique (since e.g. Hektor's ignoring of Sarpedon at 5.689f. has a motive). The possibility that these few vv. were added in the post-Homeric period, when a malicious interpretation of Odysseus' qualities was beginning to gain ground, cannot be entirely discounted; but see also on 261–5.

94 Does κακὸς ὥς go with μετὰ νῶτα βαλών (not elsewhere in Homer) or ἐν ὁμίλῳ? The colometry of this rising threefolder confirms Aristarchus' view (Nic/A) that the latter is correct.

95 A more traditional v. and a more effective one, cf. e.g. 258, 22.283.

96 ἄγριον ἄνδρα | recurs at 21.314 of Akhilleus raging in the river; Hektor is little less dangerous.

97–8 Odysseus does not heed Diomedes' words but rushes past (παρήϊξεν, cf. 5.690) toward the ships. Does he simply not hear in the confusion, or does he deliberately ignore them? This is how Aristarchus took it (Arn/A), and it would make his behaviour positively disgraceful – and the chance of interpolation higher. The compound ἐσάκουσε is unique in Homer; later uses can have either implication, but Leaf drew attention to Platt's observation that Thucydides 4.34.3, ὑπὸ δὲ τῆς μείζονος βοῆς τῶν πολεμίων τὰ ἐν αὐτοῖς παραγγελλόμενα οὐκ ἐσακούοντες, appears to provide a close parallel, with the force of the compound ἐσακούειν being '*properly* hear'. That would allow Odysseus to be more or less exonerated.

99–100 Diomedes approaches Nestor on his own (that is, without Odysseus; he has Sthenelos as charioteer according to 109 and 113f.); αὐτός ~ μόνος is commoner in *Od.*, though cf. 13.729. Less satisfactory is προμάχοισιν ἐμίχθη, a thrice-used formula quite inappropriate here, where there are no 'front fighters', either Trojan or Achaean, for him to mingle with. It seems that 5.134, Τυδεΐδης δ' ἐξαῦτις ἰὼν προμάχοισιν ἐμίχθη, has been carelessly reused, with the substitution of the similar-sounding αὐτός περ ἐών for ἐξαῦτις ἰών.

102–11 His words to Nestor are relaxed in tone and the sense of crisis has disappeared; indeed he makes no reference to the dead trace-horse and seems to assume that Nestor has simply been delayed through slowness and age. His three sentences are of 3, 4 and 3 vv. respectively; integral enjambment increases after the first sentence, with internal stops relatively frequent. Their placing is different in each of the first 5 vv.; then 107, like the closing 111, is uninterrupted, with the 3 intervening vv. balanced by perceptible pause at the bucolic diaeresis.

102 ἦ μάλα δή is very emphatic, cf. 6.255–7n. and 22.229, here with a touch of affectionate irony.

103–4 γῆρας ὀπάζει | is lightly formular, cf. also 23.623 χαλεπὸν κατὰ γῆρας ἐπείγει |; the rest is evidently freshly composed. Nestor's great age is stressed; his horses are notoriously slow, as in the chariot-race at 23.309f., and even his charioteer is ἠπεδανός, only here in *Il.*, 'a weakling'.

105–7 These vv. were addressed by Aineias to Pandaros at 5.221–3, q.v. with n., before these famous horses were captured by Diomedes, in whose mouth the words assume an especially complacent ring.

108 For the half-divine horses as μήστωρε φόβοιο see 5.270–2n.

109–10 The two charioteers are to take Nestor's pair of horses back, while this pair, i.e. the speaker's, are to be driven against Hektor. The five dual forms in 109 are curiously unobtrusive; κομείτων and 113 κομείτην, as distinct from κομίζειν etc., are found only here in *Il.* against 6 × *Od.* Sthenelos, himself no mean warrior, is unusually inconspicuous and is now despatched with the feeble Eurumedon (who is nevertheless ἀγαπήνωρ at 114); he would of course have been more use than Nestor in the venture against Hektor, itself improvised by Diomedes out of an intended rescue; but the whole episode is particularly weak in practical terms.

110–11 ὄφρα καὶ Ἕκτωρ | εἴσεται recurs at 16.242f., cf. χεῖρες... μαίνονται later in that same sentence; for the *spear* raging see rather 16.74f., Διομήδεος ἐν παλάμῃσι | μαίνεται ἐγχείη (with 13.444 and comment). The expression here sounds natural, nevertheless, not derivative.

113–14 The two charioteers drive Nestor's horses back to safety; that they are mares is shown by Νεστορέας – they are the Νηλήϊαι ἵπποι of 11.597, cf. 615 (though treated as male in the Funeral Games, e.g. at

23.309f., so bT). Nestor's 'feeble' charioteer of 104, q.v. with n., is now named as Eurumedon, who reappears at 11.620; Agamemnon had a charioteer of the same name, but further described as son of Ptolemaios son of Peiraios, at 4.228. Bk 11, on which the present Book apparently draws on several occasions, focuses attention on Nestor from 500 on.

115–17 Nestor takes the reins of Diomedes' chariot (in regular formular language) and they rapidly approach Hektor – who must have been very close at hand if he was imminently threatening the old man at 89f.

118–23 Diomedes looses off a spear as Hektor charges, hitting not him but his charioteer Eniopeus (not mentioned elsewhere, though cf. 14.444), who falls dead from the chariot. The motif is typical (cf. e.g. 16.463 and Fenik, *TBS* 221), but here and in the repeated version at 311ff. the encounter is interrupted in a special way as Hektor drives off to find a new charioteer. The whole incident appears to be not very precisely visualized.

121 | ἵππων ἡνί' ἔχοντα recurs at 16.739. The doublet version at 313 is preferable with | ἱέμενον πόλεμόνδε instead, perhaps because ἡνιοχῆα immediately precedes; but that would not suit the present context.

122–3 The former v. recurs at 15.452 (as well as 314 here), the latter at 5.296 (as well as 315).

124 ~ 17.83 (and = 316 here); πύκασε, 'enveloped', 'closely covered'.

126–9 Hektor seeking a substitute charioteer is described in tenser rhythms than the death itself, with successive stops at the bucolic diaeresis and consequent integral enjambments. His necessary haste is confirmed by οὐδ' ἄρ' ἔτι δήν and αἶψα, and perhaps suggested too by peremptory ἐπέβησε, 'made him mount'.

126–7 κεῖσθαι is a useful if inessential runover-word, not needed in the corresponding passage after 317. μέθεπε, 'drove ⟨his horses⟩ after', cf. 5.329. That they 'did not long lack a driver' is an original application of σημάντωρ, elsewhere 'commander'.

128 Arkheptolemos is unmentioned elsewhere except when he in turn succumbs in the doublet at 312ff.

130–2 Now occurs one of the abrupt changes of direction typical of this Book: Diomedes and Nestor are still on the attack, but Hektor has equipped himself with a new charioteer and is presumably ready to renew the combat, no less formidable than before. Yet had not Zeus intervened violently at 133 the Trojans would have been completely routed and penned up in the city like sheep – 130 recurs of the Achaeans at 11.310 (referring to terrible things that would have happened to them, not to an unacceptable reversal of Zeus's intentions as Willcock thought), but is expanded here by the brilliant new simile of 131. Cf. 17.319ff., where the Trojans would have been driven back into the city (with better cause) had not Apollo intervened.

133–6 Zeus thunders and delivers a thunderbolt just in front of Diomedes' chariot, in a more specific version, unparalleled in *Il.*, of his action at 75f. after weighing the fates. The flames from the burning sulphur rise up terribly – again a vivid expression, perhaps after 14.415, as the horses crouch down in fear ὑπ᾽ ὄχεσφι, presumably close to the chariot, cf. 41 (though it is not clear how this was done; one would expect them to rear up, rather).

137–9 Nestor at least is afraid, and drops the reins he had grasped, in corresponding terms, at 116. His words to Diomedes at 139 hardly imply, as Ameis–Hentze thought, that the latter must have taken the reins himself, since he is in any event clearly in charge.

139–44 Nestor's address is emphatic but reasonable in tone; the thunderbolt is dramatic testimony to Zeus's wishes, but the point has to be hammered home, with someone like Diomedes, even so. The conversation is 'unlike any other' (Fenik, *TBS* 222) in detail, but the basic idea of the futility of fighting when a god is clearly against one is typical, cf. Fenik 164 – yet another instance of the epic interplay between creative and traditional.

140–2 The language is traditional: οὐχ ἕπετ᾽ ἀλκή | is loosely formular, cf. οὐδέ τις ἀλκή | (4 × *Il.*), γίγνεται ἀλκή | (2 ×), ἐστὶ καὶ ἀλκή | (2 ×). In 141 Ζεὺς κῦδος ὀπάζει is found 3 × *Il.*, 1 × *Od.*; in 142 αἴ κ᾽ ἐθέλῃσι (etc.) is formular at the v-e, and | σήμερον· ὕστερον was used at 7.30.

143 Here, however, the formula Διὸς νόον αἰγιόχοιο | (4 × *Il.*) is adapted, with εἰρύσσαιτο replacing the conventional epithet: harmless in itself, but the usage of the verb is idiosyncratic none the less. The comment of bT was λείπει ἡ μετά, i.e. one would expect a compound, μετ- or παρ-, to make the meaning ·clear: 'draw aside' or 'divert', from ἐρύω, in contrast with the apparently similar 1.216 εἰρύσσασθε, 17.327 εἰρύσσασθαι which both clearly mean 'preserve' and are from a different verb, ἔρυμαι, cf. Chantraine, *Dict.* s.vv.

144 The second hemistich is straightforwardly formular, recurring at 211, also of Zeus, and elsewhere.

146–50 Diomedes accepts the force of Nestor's argument but cannot bear the thought of Hektor gloating over him; for heroic shame over prudent retreat compare Hektor's own words to Andromakhe at 6.441–3. Vv. 146 and 147 are formular and the second half of 150 recurs in 4.182; on ἀπειλήσει see 7.224–5n.

152–6 Nestor counters with a brief but telling comment, full of familiar phrases and half-vv. but rhetorically persuasive, reminding Diomedes that whatever Hektor may say there are plenty of Trojans who have cause to disagree.

153–4 | εἴ περ γάρ followed by a subject or object emphasized by γε, then by an apodosis beginning with emphatic ἀλλά in the next v., is a regular idiom, cf. 1.81f., 19.164f. (and with δέ rather than initial ἀλλά at 4.261f., 12.245f.). On Δαρδανίωνες see 7.414n.

155–6 The addition of Trojan widows and the pathetic contrast of θαλερούς and ἐν κονίῃσι lend further rhetorical force to Nestor's words.

157–9 Nestor turns the horses to flight and the Trojans 'pour missiles over them'; there is no longer any sense that Hektor and Diomedes are more or less isolated. For ἰωχμόν see 87–90n. *fin.*; 158 ἐπὶ δέ to 159 recurs at 15.89f.; ἠχῇ θεσπεσίῃ is formular, 7 × *Il.*, including three similar instances which show the noise here to be the war-cry.

161–6 Hektor's derision must be almost worse than Diomedes had feared: the Achaeans will dishonour him, he is no better than a woman, a cowardly puppet.

161–2 Present honour is outlined as a rhetorical contrast to future dishonour. V. 162 recurs at 12.311 of Sarpedon and Glaukos; for full drinking-cups see also Agamemnon's words to Idomeneus at 4.257ff.

163 ἄρ', 'as I now see' (Ameis–Hentze) rather than 'after all' (Leaf). It is hard to say why γυναικὸς...ἀντὶ τέτυξο is such a peculiarly insulting form of words: 'you always were [pluperf. with imperf. sense] a woman at heart' – a neat formulation, unparalleled elsewhere.

164–6 The insults continue with ἔρρε, cf. 238–9n. γλήνη is literally 'eyeball' as at 14.494, *Od.* 9.390, usually understood here as a doll-like creature like one reflected in the pupil, just as κόρη, 'girl', came to mean pupil; γλήνεα as treasures or trinkets at 24.192 do not seem relevant. Aristarchus evidently did not waste time discussing these vv. in detail (Diomedes must have been small-eyed according to bT!), since like Aristophanes he athetized them (Arn, Did/A), adding that they were artistically inferior and unsuited to the characters, and that δαίμονα δώσω is simply not Homeric. His first two reasons can be rejected; style and language throughout are vigorous and rather original (including 'you shall not set foot on our defences', see on 7.338 for πύργοι as walls), and the insulting content is only to be expected. Yet δαίμονα δώσω, neat as it sounds, is indeed hard to stomach; δαίμων meaning 'destiny' is post-Homeric, not even *Od.* 11.61, δαίμονος αἶσα κακή, being really close. Zenodotus (Did/AT) substituted πότμον ἐφήσω, cf. 4.396, probably a conjecture; the 3 vv. can simply be omitted without destroying the basic sense, but perhaps on this occasion Zenodotus is right.

167–8 Logically the alternatives considered when someone διάνδιχα μερμήριξεν are set out in an ἤ...ἦε disjunction as at 1.189–92, 13.455–7; so too without διάνδιχα at 5.671–3. Here only one course is named; Aristarchus rightly rejected the crude addition ἢ μήτε στρέψαι μήτ' ἀντίβιον μαχέσασθαι mooted by some (Arn/A), but his own defence of the text, that διάνδιχα covers the two elements of στρέψαι καὶ...μαχέσασθαι, is clearly impossible. For a simple infinitive after μερμήριξα (etc.), without διάνδιχα, cf. *Od.* 10.152, 10.440, 24.236; our poet seems to have conflated this Odyssean idiom with the fuller Iliadic one.

169–71 Yet another idiom is mildly distorted: τρὶς μέν (followed by τρὶς δέ) is always elsewhere applied to concrete acts of rushing forward, etc., as at 5.436, 11.462, 16.702, 16.784, 18.155, 18.228, 20.445, 21.176. 'Pondering' or 'wondering' three times is unparalleled and a trifle bizarre, perhaps intentionally naive. There follows on each occasion a clap of thunder from the direction of Ida, not it seems in response to Diomedes but as encouragement for the Trojans – from which, admittedly, Diomedes can draw his own conclusions (see also Stockinger, *Vorzeichen* 24f., 139). Finally σῆμα τιθεὶς Τρώεσσι is straightforward in itself (it happens not to recur, but cf. e.g. σήματα φαίνων, 3 ×) – but νίκην is not easily taken as simply appositional to it (as e.g. by Willcock; a 'slight zeugma', Leaf; Aristarchus was perhaps not entirely happy, cf. Nic/A). ἑτεραλκέα νίκην is formular, 3 × *Il.* elsewhere, twice with μάχης; on the epithet see 7.26–7n. No obvious emendation offers itself, σημαίνων having a slightly different connotation in Homer. The combination of the two phrases seems thoroughly clumsy, and with the preceding 4 vv. typical of this composer at his hastiest.

172–252 Hektor urges on the Trojans, and Here fails to persuade Poseidon to intervene; they are breaking into the camp when Agamemnon temporarily rallies the Achaeans and prays to Zeus for salvation; he sends a favourable omen and the Achaeans recover for a time

173–83 Hektor's *parainesis*, by contrast, is regular in language and content. This is the first of four uses of the initial exhortation, with 172–4 = 11.285–7, 15.485–7, 17.183–5. Three points are then made: (i) Zeus has guaranteed me victory; (ii) the new wall and trench will not keep us Trojans out; (iii) so let fire be at hand when I reach the ships.

175 He recognizes, γιγνώσκω, Zeus's support, just as Nestor had called on Diomedes at 140 to recognize its opposite; it is unclear whether the verb carries a technical mantic sense here. His main indication is obviously the three claps of thunder; it is not quite clear why that should necessarily be taken as a sign of support for the Trojans, even if he can see Diomedes and Nestor continuing their retreat thereafter.

177–9 The reference to the new Achaean defences (cf. 7.436–41) is unexpected and gives the first indication that the Trojans are now close to the naval camp itself. Poseidon at 7.451 had found the wall and trench substantial enough; now Hektor scorns them. μηχανόωντο suggests the care the Achaeans had devoted to building them; ἄβληχρ᾽ οὐδενόσωρα directly following is a startling assessment of their real value. On the former epithet see 5.336–8n.; the latter is from ὥρη = 'consideration', the compound with οὐδενός occurring only here (and in Oppian) as a relatively late formation, cf. Attic ὀλιγωρεῖν.

180–2 The injunction concerning fire foreshadows Hektor's cry οἴσετε πῦρ at 15.718, when after much further fighting he really is among the ships. The closest parallel to μνημοσύνη τις...γενέσθω, and then not really very similar, is 7.409f. τις φειδώ...γίγνετ'. Abstract formations are relatively common in speeches (see pp. 30–3), and no doubt the ponderous periphrasis, rather than a simple τις...μνησάσθω as at 17.670f., is chosen for reasons of emphasis.

183 Omitted by most MSS and two papyri (cf. S. West, *Ptolemaic Papyri* 84f.), and ignored in the scholia, this has the appearance of an addition. Yet the Achaeans being bewildered by smoke is an untypical detail (perhaps borrowed, however, from 9.243), and the cumulative style encouraged such clarifications. Perhaps the strongest argument against the v. is that it is a rhythmical anticlimax after the rising threefolder 182.

184–97 Hektor now addresses his horses; 184 recurs in the chariot-race at 23.442, where Menelaos similarly follows a speech to Antilokhos with equine exhortation, the latter having already urged on his own horses at 402ff. Such a speech is possible, then, by Homeric standards, indeed could be considered as a typical motif; but two anomalies of content will give grounds for suspicion (see on 185, 191–7), even though untypical details are relatively common in this Book. The whole address is inorganic and its purpose questionable, except of course to emphasize Hektor's preparations, and his formidable quality, still further.

185 He is conceived as driving four horses, which is unique for a war-chariot in Homer (since 11.699 and *Od.* 13.81–3 describe racing teams). Aristarchus athetized (Arn/A) on this ground, correctly, also because of the dual verbs in 186 and 191. No cure is possible, e.g. by counting two of the four either as adjectival or as trace-horses (Akhilleus has a single trace-horse at 16.152, like Nestor earlier in this Book). The names are culled from other Homeric contexts: Xanthos is one of Akhilleus's divine pair borrowed by Patroklos at 16.149, Podargos and Aithon (*sic*) belong to Menelaos and Agamemnon respectively at 23.295 (and Podarge is mother of Akhilleus' pair), Lampos is one of the Sun's horses at *Od.* 23.246. Clearly Hektor is addressing two horses only, as regular Homeric practice and the subsequent duals confirm. Either, therefore, this v. has replaced one in which only two names were given, or it is a probably rhapsodic addition. Leaf's comment that 'The speech would begin very badly without the opening line' is unpersuasive, cf. e.g. 23.403.

186–90 Commentators from antiquity on have made heavy weather of

Book Eight

this sentence, finding its syntax confused and 189, athetized by Aristophanes and Aristarchus (Did/A), impossible. Yet (i) syntax is explained if (and only if) 186 κομιδήν is understood concretely, i.e. as 'provisions' rather than 'care', as at *Od.* 8.232f., ἐπεὶ οὐ κομιδὴ κατὰ νῆα | ἦεν ἐπηετανός. The sense is: 'Now pay me back for the provisions which Andromakhe set by you in great abundance, honey-sweet corn, mixing in wine to drink when her spirit bade her, even before ⟨those which she set by⟩ me.' μελίφρονα, elsewhere (4 × *Il.*, 4 × *Od.*) of wine, is literally 'honey-hearted', cf. 10.569 μελιηδέα πυρὸν ἔδοντες |. (ii) 189 has an apparently superfluous τ' which is irregular, but cf. Denniston, *Particles* 502 (g) and especially Pindar, *Py.* 6. 44–6, Θρασύβουλος πατρῴαν μάλιστα πρὸς στάθμαν ἔβα, πάτρῳ τ' ἐπερχόμενος ἀγλαΐαν ἅπασαν. Aristarchus accepted this but found the idea of horses drinking wine highly ridiculous; he is controverted by Delebecque, *Cheval* 59, who makes the essential observation that ἐγκεράσασα probably means that the wine was mixed *with the corn* (and not in a mixing-bowl, with water, the usual application of κεράννυμι); that is a possible though not a necessary implication of the compound form. Willcock cites Columella 6.30 for such special treatment for medical reasons. As for πιεῖν ὅτε θυμὸς ἀνώγοι, it is a wine-drinking formula, cf. 4.263 and *Od.* 8.70, here probably half-humorously reinterpreted so that the horses remain subject of πιεῖν (as though they were drinking wine by itself), whereas the θυμός belongs to Andromakhe.

191–7 Aristarchus did not athetize these vv., but they are more open to suspicion than 189. Nestor's shield, which is 'all gold, handgrips and itself', has not been heard of before and will not be heard of again; the same is true of Diomedes' divinely-made corslet (which clearly has nothing to do with the golden one he is supposed to have got from Glaukos at 6.235f., *contra* Arn/A). These unlikely accoutrements are plainly invented to add weight to an erratic occasion, as indeed was the address to the four horses at 185; I suspect rhapsodic influence again, rather than (e.g. with Willcock) a flight of fancy by the main composer of this Book, extravagant as his tastes sometimes are. The passage is largely made up of half-vv. derived from elsewhere in either epic: 191 (as far as σπεύδετον) is addressed by Antilokhos to his horses at 23.414; for 192 second half cf. *Od.* 9.20; for 193 first half cf. 14.351, 18.562; for 195 second half cf. 2.101 (of Agamemnon's sceptre), 19.368 (of Akhilleus' new armour); 196 first half = 5.273 (Diomedes speaking of Aineias' horses), 197 ~ *Od.* 9. (again!)101, with ἐπιβησέμεν transitive.

191 The corresponding v. at 23.414 ends with ὅττι τάχιστα, which also concludes the sentence. It is conceivable that the present passage also ended similarly, and was then converted to ὄφρα λάβωμεν... (for which αἴ κε λάβωμεν was an ancient variant, Did/A) to accommodate the exotic spoils.

193 Compare the early 6th-cent. B.C. inscription on the base of the colossal Naxian statue of Apollo at Delos, τό αὐτό λίθο ἐμὶ ἀνδριάς καὶ τό σφέλας.

196–7 The capture of these two pieces of armour would not of itself put the Achaeans to flight; even if their wearers were killed in the process, Hektor's intention at 182f., of firing the ships and killing the Achaeans among them, is directly contradicted (so Ameis–Hentze).

Hibeh papyrus P 7, which covers some of this part of the Book, adds a v., too fragmentary to be restored, after 197. Like 199*a* (whatever its form; cf. Gerhardt's restoration as χερσὶν δ' ἀ]μφοτέραισιν ἐ[ὼ πεπλήγετο μηρώ *ap*. Bolling, *External Evidence* 107), this need not be a direct concordance interpolation, though S. West, *Ptolemaic Papyri* 87f., notes that similar gestures of grief or indignation were added after 11.272 (by P 432) and 23.136 (by P 12).

198–212 Herē is indignant at Hektor's boasting; she rallies Poseidon and proposes that the pro-Achaean gods ignore Zeus's ban and turn the Trojans back. Poseidon strongly rejects the idea, and the episode is soon at an end. This is typical of the stops and starts, the aborted enterprises, of this Book, its only obvious purpose to fill the gap between Diomedes and Nestor retreating before Hektor (implied at 170f.) and the Achaeans fighting desperately in the trench at 213ff. Yet Fenik (*TBS* 223) notes that 'this scene seems to be a prelude or preview of 8.350 where Hera persuades Athena to help her intervene', and refers to a 'stylistic habit', discussed by him on pp. 213f., of preceding a decisive action or encounter by a brief anticipatory scene – for example Hektor's first, interrupted encounter with Akhilleus at 20.419ff. before the final one in bk 22, or Meriones' two encounters with Deiphobos, the second one successful, at 13.156ff. and 526ff. It is doubtful whether such a 'habit' justifies Herē's attempt here, since it loses more in immediate dramatic terms, being such a weak and anti-climactic episode in itself, than it can gain by showing Herē's typical response to Achaean defeat or temporarily reminding the audience of Zeus's ban.

198 Athene protested against the ban at 30f.; now her confederate becomes indignant – immediately at Hektor's inconsistent boast about driving away the Achaeans that night, more generally at his undoubted success so far.

199 The motif of Olumpos shaking, majestically stated at 1.530 when Zeus nods his ambrosial locks for Thetis, is now made almost ridiculous – Herē is simply not that kind of deity. At 442f. Zeus, again, will shake

Olumpos as he sits on his golden throne after asserting his will against the two goddesses; that has its own magnificence and may be the model here, where 15.150 | ἕζετο δ' εἰνὶ θρόνῳ, likewise of Here, is also relevant. For 199a see on 196–7.

200 ἀντίον ηὔδα is normally used of replying to a previous speaker; here and at 24.333, *Od.* 5.28 ἀντίον simply implies 'directly', harmlessly enough.

201–5 Here's address contains several hemistichs from elsewhere, as one might expect in this Book: 201 ~ 7.455 + 15.553, 202 (first half) = 353 (with ἐν φρεσὶ θυμός twice elsewhere), 204 (first half) = 9.599, 205 (first half) = 2.123 (and for the second half cf. ὅσοι Τρώεσσιν ἀρωγοί |, 2 ×). Nevertheless her argument is tightly articulated, e.g. 201 (better taken as a question) | οὐδέ νυ σοί περ…, 'does not even *your* heart grieve?' with 203 | οἱ δέ τοι…, 'and yet they bring you…'

202 At least two plus-vv. are found in P 7. Vv. 202*a* and *b* are clear concordance-interpolations, with 202*a* = 34, 354, 465, each of which, as here, follows a v. mentioning grief for the Achaeans or their being destroyed; whereas 202*b* = 355, itself following directly on the equivalent of 202*a*.

203 Helike recurs only at 2.575, not specifically in relation to Poseidon (who had, however, a cult there); he had a palace beneath the waves at Aigai according to 13.21, *Od.* 5.381. He is Helikonios at 20.404, but that (*pace* most commentators) is nothing to do with Helike; it must mean 'of Helikon' and is a probable reference to the cult of Poseidon Helikonios at the Panionion on Mt Mukale, cf. Herodotus 1.148.1, Burkert, *Religion* 136–8. The ancient critical tradition was understandably confused, and that is probably reflected in *Hy* xxii.3. More to the point, unless he shared this confusion our singer is not completely indebted to other Homeric passages for this v.; ἀνάγουσιν is an untraditional compound *metri gratia*, though the idea and expression depend on 1.390 ἄγουσι δὲ δῶρα ἄνακτι (where the lord is Apollo and the gifts, as presumably here, a hecatomb).

204 βούλεο is either imperative or imperf. indic., probably the latter.

206 The v-e formula εὐρύοπα Ζεύς is designed for the nominative (9.× *Il.*) but can be converted to the acc. by using the archaizing form Ζῆν (rather than Ζῆν' in synaliphe with the next v. as Aristarchus thought, Arn/A); so too at 14.265, 24.331.

207 αὐτοῦ κ' ἔνθ', inelegantly, cf. e.g. 23.674 ἐνθάδ' ἀολλέες αὖθι μενόντων; 'he would be sorry at sitting there all by himself on Ida'.

209–11 Poseidon's violent rejection is reflected in the unique ἀπτοεπές, of debated etymology: probably from *ἀ-ϝεπτο-ϝεπής, 'speaking a word that should not be spoken' (Wackernagel), cf. Chantraine, *Dict.* s.vv.

ἄαπτος, ἄεπτος. The rest of his reply is closely related to what he tells her on another occasion when she tries to get him into action, part of the prelude to the Theomachy, 20.134f.:

οὐκ ἂν ἔγωγ' ἐθέλοιμι θεοὺς ἔριδι ξυνελάσσαι
ἡμέας τοὺς ἄλλους, ἐπεὶ ἦ πολὺ φέρτεροί εἰμεν.

Yet the sense there is forced and unclear, suggesting that it is not a direct model for the present version.

213–14 Meanwhile the Achaeans have been driven back through the trench – a more drastic consequence than the preceding Diomedes–Nestor narrative might suggest, but reverting, rather, to the general situation at 76–9. V. 213 is notoriously difficult, though its import is not in doubt. | τῶν δ' brings the listener down from Olumpos to earth: 'with them, i.e. the Achaeans, was filled the space...' (πλῆθεν, imperf. of πλήθω, which takes the gen.); the difficulty lies in ὅσον ἐκ νηῶν ἀπὸ πύργου τάφρος ἔεργε: 'as much (space) as, from the ships, the trench separated from the wall [lit. tower]'. ἐκ νηῶν presumably means 'away from the ships' and has little force except to stress, what is obvious, that the trench was on the outer side of the wall. It certainly cannot mean what bT reported some as understanding, namely the wall which *resulted from* (the defence of) the ships. ἀπό could be in tmesis with ἔεργε or it could govern πύργου, with little effect on meaning. That which the trench separated from the wall must be the space between the two: the Achaeans, therefore, have been driven back through the trench, the dangers of which (cf. e.g. 12.63f.) are here ignored, and are fighting just below the wall. When they rally at 252ff. Diomedes is the first to drive his chariot out of the trench (254f. ἵππους | τάφρου τ' ἐξελάσαι); then when Zeus turns against them again they are pushed back towards the trench at 336 and flee through it at 343f. The use made of the newly-constructed defences is typically rather casual in this Book, and it is striking how the trench and the wall and the obstacle they present both to fleeing and to attacking troops, especially to chariots, are not nearly so keenly visualized as they will be later, in bks. 11 and 12, 15 and 16.

215 εἰλομένων is a typical runover participle (cf. 1.2 οὐλομένην) leading on to additional information, here that Hektor was the main cause of their predicament. Elaborating or explaining the participle with a repetition of the verb in εἴλει is another Homeric idiom, cf. e.g. 16.105, 18.227, 19.376, 20.317, 22.464f. (so Ameis–Hentze).

216 This v. is followed by a plus-v. in P 7, probably = 130 and 11.310, syntax-generated by succeeding καί νύ κ' in each case.

217 Shipp, *Studies* 263, objected that πυρὶ κηλέῳ regularly comes at the v-e; but the formula is not nearly frequent enough (5 × *Il.*, 2 × *Od.* at most) to make displacement or adaptation seem irregular, especially in view of 15.744 |.σὺν πυρὶ κηλείῳ. On the relation of κηλέος, 'burning', to καυαλέος see Chantraine, *Dict.* s.v.

218 This v. resembles 1.55, with its first half = *Od.* 5.427. Herē implants the idea in Agamemnon of rallying the Achaeans (why had he not thought of it before?); for divine motivation of this kind cf. 467, 5.676, 7.44.

219 ποιπνύσαντι, 'bustling' or 'hastening', perhaps from πνέω as causing one to breathe heavily; cf. Hephaistos at 1.600 and, more majestically as here, Poseidon at 14.155. The urgency is stressed also by θοῶς.

220–1 Agamemnon passes among the ships and huts holding a great red cloth in his hands – a unique idea, the cloth obviously to be waved to draw attention to his words (rather than to shoo back those fleeing in through the gates as bT suggest). That the cloth is a cloak is probable, not certain; φᾶρος means that at 2.43, when Agamemnon wakes after the deceitful dream and puts on first a tunic, then a great φᾶρος, also at *Od.* 3.467; but at 18.353 a white φᾶρος or coverlet, rather, is spread over Patroklos' shroud.

223–6 He stands on Odysseus' ship, obviously so as to be both seen (as he waves the cloth) and heard. Are we to suppose that the ship towers over the wall, on the other side of which most of the Achaeans must still be penned? Probably the singer did not consider this, especially since he is apparently using a passage – 222–6 here = 11.5–9, q.v. with nn. – where Eris similarly shouts to the Achaeans; moreover she holds in her hands a 'portent of war', πολέμοιο τέρας, at 11.4, rather like Agamemnon with his red φᾶρος, confirming the connexion between the two passages: see Fenik, *TBS* 224. Yet the last 3 vv., 224–6, are retained by only a minority of MSS (P 7, lacunose here, would presumably have had them), and are ignored in the scholia. They name, and account for, the extremes of the Achaean lines, i.e. the huts of Aias at one end and Akhilleus at the other. Interestingly enough their omission here is justified by the special circumstance that Agamemnon, unlike Eris, is not shouting to his troops along the whole line of ships from extremity to extremity, but as they bunch up, around the gates perhaps, on the other side of the wall.

227 A standard v., 5 × elsewhere, with διαπρύσιον meaning 'penetratingly' *vel sim.*, cf. 17.748; the etymology of -πρύσιον is disputed, cf. Chantraine, *Dict.* s.v.

228–44 Agamemnon's *parainesis*, expansive after the initial rebuke, develops two minor motifs in an original way: (i) the need to live up to earlier boasts (229–35); (ii) previous piety should be rewarded (236–41).

228 = 5.787, q.v. with n. Aristarchus (Did/A) read ἐλεγχέες there, but ἐλέγχεα is a valid alternative, cf. 2.235.

229 πῆ ἔβαν: cf. 2.339, 5.472, 24.201; εὐχωλαί, 'boastings'. Agamemnon tactfully associates himself with these through φάμεν, but soon distances himself from them, 230 ἠγοράασθε.

230 The Achaeans stopped in Lemnos and abandoned Philoktetes there (2.722; *Cypria*, OCT Homer v, 101); the wine they drink at 232 recalls the Lemnian wine-ships of 7.467. For boast or threats before the event cf. 13.219, or, over wine, 20.83–5; Fenik, *TBS* 224. I agree with Willcock that the simplest way to avoid anacoluthon here is to take ὁπότ' ἐν Λήμνῳ as meaning 'when ⟨you were⟩ in Lemnos' (cf. bT and *Od.* 10.176), though Leaf found this 'harsh', Chantraine (*GH* II, 362n.) 'hardly probable'. κενεαυχέες is found only here and in late-Greek imitations; αὐχέω itself is post-Homeric, but Wackernagel and Risch (refs. in Shipp, *Studies* 264 n. 1) supposed the compound to represent *κενεευχέες, giving real point (*pace* Shipp) after 229 εὐχωλαί.

231–2 With their crudely matching initial participles devoid of connection or emphasis, these 2 vv. make an arid impression different from that of most Homeric cumulations. Aristarchus athetized 231 (Arn/A), but because drinking, rather than eating, causes boasting; yet the omission of either v. would be an improvement, and 231 is certainly easier to drop in terms of sense. The difficulty is that, whereas its expression is harmless if comically grandiose (oxen are 'with upright horns' elsewhere, but only when they are visualized directly rather than as source of meat), its successor, apparently approved by commentators, is strictly nonsensical. It is a patent adaptation of *Od.* 2.431, στήσαντο κρητῆρας ἐπιστεφέας οἴνοιο (cf. *Il.* 1.470, 9.175); but whereas setting up mixing-bowls, i.e. setting them in place, makes sense, *drinking* them, or even *from* them, does not (and drinking the whole of their contents is not a possible meaning). On this occasion, then, the poet of this Book, who tends to be derivative, original and slapdash by turns, may have gone too far; though the possibility of rhapsodic elaboration through both vv. cannot be discounted.

233–4 Aristarchus left ἀνθ' unaccented, i.e. from ἀντί (Arn/A); some grammarians disagreed, and Herodian himself took it to represent ἄντα and therefore accented on the first syllable (Hrd/A). The former would mean '(the boasts you uttered) that each would stand in battle against a hundred or two hundred Trojans', the latter that 'each would stand...in place of (i.e. as equivalent to) a hundred...' Either 'in face of' or 'in place of' makes sense; what does not seem possible is to understand στήσεσθαι in the latter case as meaning 'weigh', i.e. count for as much as, since while trans. ἵστημι with that sense is found in Homer, at least at 24.232, the intrans. middle is not so found, or indeed (as Leaf remarked) in later Greek either. If anything, ἄξιοι later in the v. supports ἀντί rather than ἄντα.

235 Both Aristophanes and Aristarchus athetized (Did, Arn/A), the latter on the ground that it weakens the preceding οὐδ' ἑνός to make it refer to a particular person (he added that an alternative reading, ᾧ δὴ κῦδος Ὀλύμπιος αὐτὸς ὀπάζει, would undermine the rebuke even further). The v. does somewhat weaken the force of the rhetoric, yet it is just the sort of cumulative elaboration by afterthought that singers often indulged in, sometimes with a loss in accuracy as well as concision.

236–7 The thought of imminent danger to the ships makes him turn to Zeus in a familiar mixture of rebuke and supplication, combined with the kind of self-pity that is typical of Agamemnon. His habit of blaming Zeus for deluding him, also seen at 2.111, 9.18, 19.86ff., is accurately portrayed here. His ἄτη lies in thinking Zeus would respond to his sacrifices, and he complains that no other king has been treated so badly. The singer handles all this with notable skill.

238–41 That Agamemnon made sacrifice to Zeus on every altar of his that he passed on his way to Troy, on behalf of the expedition's success, is a new and intriguing idea. Compare *Od.* 3.177ff., where Nestor tells how on his way back across the Aegean he put in by night at Geraistos, southern promontory of Euboia, and offered many thighs of bulls to Poseidon (who had a sanctuary there).

238–9 οὐ μὲν δή ποτέ φημι... is exceptionally emphatic, maintaining the indignant rhetoric of 236 ἦ ῥά τιν' ἤδη. Resentment may be continued in ἐνθάδε ἔρρων (also at 9.364), since this verb, of unknown etymology, seems properly to imply going *in an unfortunate or ill-omened manner* – which is why ἔρρε etc. (4× *Il.*) means something like 'go to the devil'. Yet 18.421f., of Hephaistos ἔρρων | πλησίον, *sc.* to Thetis, does not have this connotation, and the same could be so here.

240 There is an ironic parallel with Hektor's pious behaviour, which is taken more seriously by Zeus and makes him wish to save him from death; indeed the language here is obviously related to that of 22.170, Ἕκτορος, ὅς μοι πολλὰ βοῶν ἐπὶ μηρί' ἔκηεν.

242–4 The prayer is conventionally expressed but given special intensity by the repeated περ: 'grant this prayer, at least... ⟨if we cannot take Troy⟩ then at least let us ourselves escape'. The redundance of 243 ὑπεκφυγέειν καὶ ἀλύξαι (also 1× *Od.*) is for emphasis: Ameis–Hentze noted the contrast of aor. ἔασον and present ἔα, continuative, in 244 (= 17.376, cf. 5.465 and n.): 'Do not leave the Achaeans to the Trojans to be thus brought low.'

245–6 Zeus reacts immediately and sympathetically, in accordance with the tendency to volte-face in this Book. 245 will recur at 17.648, where it is natural for the god to respond favourably to Aias' pathetic plea ('kill us in daylight'); here Agamemnon is indignant and legalistic, rather, his tears reflecting frustration as much as sorrow. Zeus's acquiescence goes against his intention of helping the Trojans; yet neither he nor the poet (let alone the whole epic tradition and the audience) can allow the Achaeans to be wiped out.

247–52 Portents continue (after 75–7, 133ff., 170f.); here 247 = 24.315, where Zeus sends the eagle to encourage Priam in his move to recover Hektor's body. There the eagle (τελειότατον, most fulfilling as a portent) impresses by its huge size and by appearing on the right (317–20). Here the elaboration is different; the eagle carrying prey which it then lets go is a motif recurring at 12.200–9 (it drops, κάββαλ(ε) as here, a snake which has bitten it, among the Trojans); but the Achaeans are treated to an almost more extreme demonstration, as the bird drops a young deer right beside Zeus's own altar. That confirms, if confirmation is needed, that the omen comes from Zeus.

249–50 Nothing is heard of this altar elsewhere, though it must be prominent among those near Odysseus' headquarters (namely in the centre of the line of ships, cf. 223f.) which are mentioned at 11.807ff. as in the main assembly-place of the Achaeans. Nowhere else is Ζεὺς πανόμφαιος mentioned; ὀμφή (cf. 2.41 and n.) is the voice of a god, and presumably Zeus as thunderer and sender of other portents is aptly so called, though in cultic terms it remains odd. The epithet itself recurs in Simonides and elsewhere.

251 The deer is not especially associated with Zeus (with Artemis, rather), but the eagle and the altar show the portent to be his.

252 This v. comes twice elsewhere, more suitably since μᾶλλον here suggests that the Achaeans are already advancing, which is not the case (Ameis–Hentze). P 7 added two extra vv.; neither is found elsewhere, and together they form a pointless anticlimax.

253–349 Diomedes initiates the Achaean counter-attack; Teukros has a run of successes with his bow but cannot hit Hektor, who disables him with a stone-throw. Zeus inspires the Trojans to advance once again, and the Achaeans are thrown back once more through the trench

253–5 The expression is idiomatic and rhetorical; ἔνθ' οὔ τις, also at 23.632 and 2 × *Od.*, comes only here in this particular use with πρότερος: 'None of the Achaeans, many as they were, could claim sooner than Diomedes to have steered their swift horses so as to drive out of the trench and fight strongly back.'

256–60 Diomedes, still essentially formidable, kills Agelaos, not heard of elsewhere, with a spear-thrust in the back as he turns his chariot to flee – on this and other typical motifs see Fenik, *TBS* 225. Language is also

Book Eight

typical throughout, with 258f. = 5.40f., 11.447f. (and 259 another 3 ×
elsewhere); on 260 see 5.294n.

261–5 The predicate is understood from 255: these leaders followed
Diomedes in fighting back, though no specific victims are assigned them.
Again the language is standard, with the whole list from 262 to 265 already
occurring at 7.164–7, where these same heroes are among those that sprang
up to face Hektor's challenge after Nestor had rebuked them. There,
Agamemnon and Diomedes headed the list at 162f., and Thoas and
Odysseus were added at 168; see nn. on 7.161–8, 164 and 165, in the first
of which it was concluded that these 4 vv. 'are hardly typical and
traditional, and one or other context is borrowing from the other', with bk
8 as *prima facie* candidate as borrower. The total of nine warriors is
emphasized in each case (at 7.161, 8.266); what is surprising is the omission
of Odysseus here – he was ninth and last to be mentioned, after the
relatively less important Thoas, at 7.168. It is hard not to sense a
connexion, as Aristarchus did (Arn/A on 266), with the apparently
disparaging treatment of him at 92–8, where he failed to hear, or ignored,
Diomedes' call for assistance. Incidentally that is the only mention of him
in this Book (except for the reference at 222 to the position of his ships).

266 Teukros is included since he is to have a brief *aristeia* immediately
after; perhaps Thoas and Odysseus are discarded to make room for him,
though see last n. *ad fin.* He draws his bow (as distinct from merely holding
it as at 15.443) as he advances, which is impractical and perhaps even
slightly absurd – this is a genre conception of the threatening archer, as of
Apollo in different circumstances at *HyAp* 4.

267–72 The use of repeated vv. and half-vv. declines noticeably in the
Teukros-*aristeia*. Here is a unique description of him operating from behind
the protection of Aias' great shield (he is usually envisaged as fighting close
at his side, notably at 15.442–4 (ἄγχι παρέστη), cf. 12.349f. = 362f.). He
stands, i.e. crouches, under it (267), Aias draws it aside (268 ὑπεξέφερεν),
Teukros takes a keen look round (269 παπτήνας) and shoots, then draws
back again under the protection of the shield (271f.). Leaf was right to
describe these tactics as 'characteristically oriental'; Lorimer, *HM* 183,
agreed (see further Y. Yadin, *The Art of Warfare in Biblical Lands*, London
1963, 295f.). She also observed, p. 197, that Teukros is shown by 325 as
using the oriental (i.e. Scythian and Assyrian) draw to the shoulder, but
denied that he necessarily crouches. That is not entailed by the mother-
and-child simile of 271, q.v. with n., but seems probable nevertheless.
Fenik, *TBS* 225f., notes a similar close liaison, though less extreme, between
Aias and his lesser namesake fighting side by side as spearmen at 13.701–8,
significantly after a list of warriors as here. — Enjambment is heavy and

internal punctuation varied from 268 on, with the parataxis of 270 ὁ μὲν...ὄλεσσεν emphasizing the graphic switch from archer to victim and back.

270 A minority of (late) MSS have ὄλεσκεν, an ill-judged attempt (since the action of ὁ μέν falling is typical not repetitive) to match the frequentatives δύσκεν and κρύπτασκε (for which -εσκε might be restored, cf. Chantraine, *GH* I, 323).

271 The touching image of the child clinging to its mother hints at Teukros' fragility as well as his dependence.

273–6 Now follows another list, this time of Teukros' victims, introduced by a rhetorical question which is a shortened form of 5.703 (q.v. with n.), 11.299, 16.692 – a question not necessarily addressed to the Muse(s) like the more elaborate version at 2.484, 11.218, 14.508. The eight names are carefully disposed between the 3 vv., with decorative epithet in 275 and patronymic in 276 to lend variety. The victims are created for the occasion, the first three names and Melanippos being assigned to Trojan or allied casualties elsewhere. Daitor, Lukophontes and Amopaon (= ἀμ-οπάων) occur only here, while there are at least two men called Khromios on either side, see 4.295–6n.

277 = 12.194, 16.418, where the v. supplies an essential main verb for a preceding list of victims. Here it is inorganic and omitted by the majority of MSS (including all the most reliable), which could be right.

278 This v. was used at 4.255 (with τούς for τόν) in the Epipolesis, where Agamemnon praised Cretan preparations. The ethos of the present passage is not dissimilar, with fulsome praise from Agamemnon winning less than wholehearted gratitude from the recipient.

279 For τόξου ἄπο κρατεροῦ...ὀλέκοντα cf. 4.605 πέφνεν ἀπ᾽ ἀργυρέοιο βιοῖο.

281–91 Agamemnon uses the two typical heroic inducements, glory (especially for the father) and material reward.

281 The successive vocatives are coaxing, almost lover-like. The head stands for the whole person as at 15.39, with φίλη κεφαλή, 'beloved one', used of the dead Patroklos by Akhilleus at 18.114.

282–3 Teukros is to be φόως, 'light', for the Achaeans and his father; the metaphor has slightly different values in each case – relief for the former, as regularly (so too when αἴ κεν...γένηαι is repeated at 11.797, cf. 16.39), but glory, cf. 285 εὐκλείης, for the latter.

284 This v. was omitted by Zenodotus, athetized by Aristophanes and Aristarchus (Did/AT), apparently because bastardy was not flattering but the reverse (Arn/A). Teukros' mother was Hesione daughter of Laomedon in later accounts (cf. the D-scholium in A), though Homer does not anywhere suggest that, cf. e.g. 15.439 with n.

Book Eight

285 Telamon's distance is merely to suggest how great will be the fame that can reach him there. ἐπίβησον, 'move him towards', i.e. bring him into the sphere of, glory is a regular idiom, cf. 2.234 with n., also 2 × *Od.*

287 Athene is similarly associated with Zeus at 10.552f. and 2 × *Od.*; there she is a special protectress, here too Agamemnon must feel that she is on the Achaean side, with Zeus as final arbiter.

289–91 A special reward of honour (πρεσβήϊον only here) is otherwise offered only among Trojans; naturally the king intends to reward himself first. For the relative value of such prizes see 23.702–5 (where a woman, useful rather than desirable as here, comes second to a tripod-cauldron) and *Od.* 15.84f. (where such a cauldron is worth about as much as two mules).

293–6 After the first three enjambed and internally punctuated vv., uninterrupted 296 brings the usual sense of completion or climax – and in this case of the continuity of his attack. δεδεγμένος implies lying in wait as at 4.107, not that they are moving towards him (which is not the case, cf. 295).

297–9 A vigorous and graphic reply, not unlike Pandaros' to Aineias at 5.18off.: 'Eight long-pointed arrows have I shot, and all were fixed in the flesh of stalwart warriors; but this mad dog I cannot hit.' τανυγλωχῖνες comes only here; 15.315 (of spears) is the probable model for 298, ἄλλα μὲν ἐν χροῖ πήγνυτ' ἀρηϊθόων αἰζηῶν; for λυσσητῆρα cf. 13.53 λυσσώδης, also of Hektor. Homeric Greek for what we call flesh is χρώς, 'skin', 52 × *Il.* in one sense or the other; cf. e.g. 4.237 τέρενα χρόα γῦπες ἔδονται. σάρξ (or rather σάρκες) occurs only 2 × *Il.*, once at 380 to distinguish lean meat from fat in a sacrifice. Its 4 Odyssean uses, one of a wound, show a certain development; see further Chantraine, *Dict.* s.v.

300 Only here and in the similar 309 is ἴαλλε used of despatching a missile, for which one might have expected it to be traditional ('sending it speeding away'; it is probably connected with ἄλλομαι, 'leap'). Its commonest use, on the contrary, is in the formular v. οἱ δ' ἐπ' ὀνείαθ' ἑτοῖμα προκείμενα χεῖρας ἴαλλον, 3 × *Il.*, 11 × *Od.*

302–5 By a typical turn of events Teukros now misses Hektor and hits someone else – Gorguthion, one of Priam's many sons, not heard of elsewhere. His name at least has a certain actuality, being probably related to that of the Gergithes of the northern Troad (von Kamptz, *Personennamen* 322). His mother Kastianeira came from Aisume (so MSS, though Alexandrian critics favoured Aisumne, Did/A), speculatively identified by Stephanus of Byzantium with a town in Thrace; ὀπυίω implies legitimate marriage (until late Greek), which is puzzling, though according to 21.88 he had Laothoe as wife 'and many others'.

306–8 Gorguthion let his head fall to one side like a poppy, 'which in

323

a garden ⟨does so⟩ when weighed down with seed and spring showers'; but note the parataxis in the Greek. In the resumption at 308 editors take ἤμυσε as trans., only here, to balance it exactly with 306 βάλεν; more probably the verb is intran., as regularly, and κάρη now subj. not obj.: 'so did his head incline to one side'. The explanation that it is weighed down with the helmet is hardly necessary, a further piece of poetical pseudo-realistic fantasy – for the body would tend to collapse all at once, and the sagging of the head not stand out from the rest. At 16.341 a victim's head similarly slumps sideways, but because it has been almost severed.

309–10 ~ 300f., marking Teukros' second unsuccessful attempt as deliberately balanced with the first.

311 ἀλλ' ὅ γε καὶ τόθ' ἄμαρτε is an effortless adjustment of 302 καὶ τοῦ μέν ῥ' ἀφάμαρτε; now it is added that Apollo diverted the shot – probably the god is envisaged as acting directly, rather than figuratively as patron of archery.

312–19 Arkheptolemos had been sought out at 127f. to replace Hektor's charioteer Eniopeus, killed by a spear-throw from Diomedes; now it is his turn to die. The language of these parallel scenes is closely similar, with 313 βάλε – 317 = 121 βάλε – 125; now Hektor's half-brother Kebriones is installed at 318f., with less detail and tension than his predecessor at 126–9; he in turn will succumb, but not until 16.737ff. Being Hektor's driver, as bT noted, is no sinecure.

320–2 Once his replacement charioteer has the reins, Hektor leaps down with a shout, picks up a stone, and goes straight for Teukros. 320 recurs at 23.509 of the chariot-race, where 'all-gleaming' may be more appropriate (Diomedes' chariot being overlaid with gold and tin at 23.503); yet παμφανόωντος etc. is an all-purpose decorative epithet used of spears, helmets, armour in general, even walls at 435 and 13.261. V. 321 = 5.302, 20.285, in both of which ἰάχων describes one warrior, ὁ δέ... λάβε another. Here, rather, as Leaf noted, ὁ δέ introduces, as often, 'a fresh action of the subject of the preceding clause'. For σμερδαλέα and χερμάδιον see 5.302–4n.

322 Does not recur exactly, though | βῆ (βάν) δ' ἰθύς and θυμὸς ἀνώγει | are formular; for the second hemistich cf. 301 βαλέειν δέ ἑ ἵετο θυμός.

323–5 Teukros had taken an arrow from his quiver (φαρέτρης is metrically unsuitable), placed it on the bow-string, and was drawing it past his shoulder. The stance of Homeric archers provoked much discussion among ancient critics; Neoteles wrote a book on it, cf. Porph. 1.123.11 (quoted by Erbse, ii p. 359). As Willcock notes, Teukros stands sideways on to his target and shoots along the line of his body with the string drawn back to his chest as at 4.123.

325–8 τῇ in 327 refers to 325 ὅθι...: Teukros drew the string past his shoulder, and it was there that the stone struck him, where collar-bone separates (i.e. connects) neck and chest – actually neck and shoulders, as more accurately of Hektor's death at 22.324. That spot is said to be μάλιστα... καίριον; the formula was used of a vulnerable place for horses at 4.185, and is in any case not wholly appropriate here, where death does not supervene. The idea, not the expression, seems to stem from Hektor's death-scene, since at 22.325 it is again near the collar-bone, though in the throat, that 'the life-spirit's destruction is swiftest'.

327 The first half recurs of Hektor's fatal wounding at 22.326; see previous n. Again that usage seems more 'original', since ἐπὶ οἷ μεμαῶτ(α) suits that context, where Hektor is rushing at Akhilleus with his spear, and not this one, where Teukros must be standing still to make his bow-shot. μεμαῶτα etc. can mean simply 'being eager', 'being aggressive' when used by itself (as at 14.375) or with an inf. as in the formula μεμαῶτε μάχεσθαι, but with ἐπί or ἰθύς it must imply motion against.

328 It is not the wrist holding the string and arrow-butt that is struck and numbed, but the one holding the bow itself. His whole left arm is paralysed by the breaking (presumably) of the collar-bone.

329 The second hemistich recurs at 15.465, where the mere snapping of the string causes Teukros, again, to drop the bow. For the rest see on 5.309–10.

330 Teukros has not completely collapsed (cf. 329), and πεσόντος is used loosely.

331–4 These vv. recur at 13.420–3 where Antilokhos protects the corpse of Hupsenor; for the action cf. 5.299, 17.4, 17.132f. It was noted by bT that Aias here did not need to run, θέων, from far off, in view of 267–72. Yet the Antilokhos description seems derived from here rather than vice versa, nevertheless, since Hupsenor was plainly killed there (at 13.411f., by a spear-shot in the liver) and can hardly be groaning still, στενάχοντα, as at 423, see n. there. The names of the comrades who lift the victim are stock ones and do not help: Alastor (with Khromios) is admittedly a Pylian, like Antilokhos, at 4.295 – but a Lycian (again with Khromios!) at 5.177; whereas this Mekisteus must be the one, of unknown local origin, killed together with Ekhios (here, his father) at 15.339, and not the different one, father of Argive Eurualos, at 2.566 etc.

335–49 The Achaeans are driven back again through the trench and into the camp. Teukros' wounding and withdrawal has affected the tactical situation, but not to that extent, and the sudden switch of fortunes is ascribed once more to Zeus. The narrative style continues smooth and effortless, but there is substantial repetition and borrowing, especially perhaps from bk 15.

337 σθένεϊ βλεμεαίνων -ει 6 × *Il.*; the verb is of unknown derivation and debatable meaning; 'exult' is a contextual possibility, cf. κύδεϊ γαίων,

favoured in some scholia. μενεαίνω from μένος suggests βλεμεαίνω from
* βλέμος (Chantraine, *Dict.*); ἀβλεμές means 'feeble' according to
Hesychius. Much remains obscure.

338–42 The simile has a structural resemblance to 11.172–8, where
Agamemnon is like a lion who panics the cattle but concentrates on one
victim; the closing v. there = 342 here. Here it is the lion – or boar, more
suitably – that is in flight; the dog snapping at his hindquarters as he
swerves to avoid him, ἑλισσόμενον (rather than 'turns to fight', Willcock),
is sharply observed.

339–40 ἰσχία τε γλουτούς τε are not direct object of ἅπτηται, which
regularly takes the gen., but specify κατόπισθε, being epexegetic (Ameis–
Hentze) rather than 'of the part affected' (Leaf). The verb is conative ('try
to make contact'); subjunct. after ὡς δ' ὅτε is not maintained in δοκεύει, but
that is a separate, paratactic observation. ποσὶν ταχέεσσι διώκων in 339 is
perhaps a slight anticlimax here, stronger in its 3 occurrences in bk 22.

341 ὥπαζε, 'followed closely', cf. ὀπάων, ἕπομαι; and ἕφεπε in the
corresponding v. at 11.177.

343–7 The first 3 of these vv. recur with necessary adjustments as the
opening of bk 15. There it is the Trojans that are driven back through the
trench (therefore Δαναῶν ὑπὸ χερσίν in 2) and find themselves παρ'
ὄχεσφιν (in 3) rather than παρὰ νηυσίν as here. These are not typical vv.,
and it is fair to suppose that the two passages are specifically related –
probably that one is derived from the other. Bk 8 is *a priori* more likely as
borrower, yet holding back from further flight (ἐρητύοντο) *among the ships*
makes better sense than doing so *by the chariots*. The Achaeans had no
alternative but to fight among the ships, the Trojans could and should have
mounted their chariots and retreated out of reach. But 8.345 is also
repeated as 15.367 (with | ὡς οἱ μέν for | οἱ μὲν δή, but νηυσίν not ὄχεσφιν),
where, moreover, it is followed by two vv. identical with 8.346f. here
describing supplications to the gods. It seems as though the poet of bk 15,
having to describe two separate retreats through the trench (one by Trojans
and the other by Achaeans), adapted a v. from his second description and
applied it less than appropriately, with chariots substituted for ships, to his
first. In that case the bk 8 poet (whether or not the same) combined vv.
from both those scenes.

346–7 The enjambment is developed awkwardly but the sense is clear;
εὐχετόωντο should really be a participle co-ordinate with κεκλόμενοι, but cf.
3.80. They stayed there calling out (*sc.* in dismay) to each other and
beseeching the gods with raised arms.

348–9 Hektor, behind them, whirls his chariot here and there, a unique
and powerful expression; his remounting it after 320 has not been
mentioned, but that kind of detail is often omitted. He is like the Gorgon

or Ares in his glance – at 11.37 the Gorgon on Agamemnon's shield is δεινὸν δερκομένη, and at 15.605–8 Hektor rages like Ares, his eyes gleaming terribly; here the two ideas are rather perfunctorily combined.

350–484 Athene and Here view the Achaean rout with perturbation, and are driving out of Olumpos to intervene when Zeus sees them from Mt Ida and sends Iris to warn them, with heavy threats, to desist; Here persuades Athene that they should do so. Zeus returns to Olumpos and rebukes the goddesses, revealing that Hektor will remain victorious until after Patroklos' death

350–484 The episode begins with an initial indignant conversation between the two goddesses (350–80) and ends with Zeus rebuking them and reasserting his intention of continuing support for the Trojans on the next day (438–84). Nearly two-thirds of the whole, 86 vv. out of 135, consists of speech. The incident is remarkable in two ways: (i) the goddesses' preparations repeat those of bk 5, with omissions, when they drove down to the battlefield to stop Ares; (ii) this enterprise, unlike that one, comes to nothing and is aborted by Zeus almost as soon as it has begun. On (i), it was shown in the commentary on bk 5 (on 719–52, 719–21 and 734–7) that the version of the divine preparations is an expansion of bk 8 here rather than the latter an abbreviation of the former, as one would expect. This strengthens the impression that this Book, despite its many repeated vv. and half-vv. and its sometimes spasmodic construction, is much more than a mechanically formed and derivative afterthought. On (ii) one naturally seeks some literary and dramatic point for such an inconclusive episode. Is it not to give final confirmation of the Book's central theme, namely that Zeus's will is paramount, that the other gods cannot frustrate it, and that it points towards Trojan dominance and Achaean crisis until Akhilleus' wrath is assuaged? At 198–211 Here had unsuccessfully tried to get Poseidon to intervene, contrary to Zeus's edict; now a renewed threat from Hektor makes her turn to her old ally Athene, with the audience strongly reminded of their earlier successful foray against Ares. Seen against that model, the inglorious termination of their present rash attempt is all the more dramatic.

350 A god seeing a mortal or mortals suffering, and pitying them, is a typical device (cf. 15.12, 16.431) for introducing a fresh divine initiative; but the idea of divine pity as such should not be underrated.

352 | ὢ πόποι (29 × *Il.*) as usual conveys surprise or indignation; Here repeats the address at 427, this time alarmed by Zeus's threat.

353 κεκαδησόμεθ' from κήδομαι: 'shall we no longer feel concern for the Danaans ὑστάτιόν περ, even though at the last minute?'

355–6 Hektor's aggression is described in strong but formular terms, except for the powerful ῥιπῇ which is used elsewhere of rushing wind, fire, or missiles. 'Raging unendurably' is how Odysseus describes the Cyclops at *Od.* 9.350.

358–73 Athene too wishes Hektor would drop dead, but does not directly reply to Here's implied invitation to intervene. Her digression on Herakles is a brilliant device to enable her to ignore the issue of Zeus's ban at 5ff.

358 | καὶ λίην (3 × *Il.*) is extremely emphatic. The otherwise awkward addition of μένος to formular θυμόν (cf. ἀπὸ θυμὸν ὀλέσσαι etc.) may contain an etymological reference to 355 μαίνεται (so Leaf), especially in view of 6.100f. (of Diomedes) ἀλλ᾽ ὅδε λίην | μαίνεται, οὐδέ τίς οἱ δύναται μένος ἰσοφαρίζειν.

359 The artificial lengthening of the last syllable of φθίμενος is harsh in this position when not supported by colon-division. It is arguably helped by the analogy of (φίλη) ἐν πατρίδι γαίῃ, itself based on the common φίλην ἐς πατρίδα γαῖαν.

360–1 The transition to another who is mad or raging, μαίνεται, is abrupt, and that Zeus should be the new subject surprising. φρεσὶ...ἀγαθῇσι is not exactly paralleled (though cf. Zeus's counter-accusation at 423); the abuse seems clearly related to Dione's description of Herakles at 5.403 (see n.), σχέτλιος, ὀβριμοεργός, ὃς οὐκ ὄθετ᾽ αἴσυλα ῥέζων, and the presence of Herakles in both contexts seems significant. ἀλιτρός | recurs, awkwardly, at 23.595; ἀπερωεύς, 'thwarter', is *hapax*, a surprising term in a curiously clumsy phrase, not least in the plural form of ἐμῶν μενέων – only here in the gen. and hardly justified by the formula μένεα πνείοντες.

362–9 Athene's repeated help for someone Here detested would be a tactless subject were she not acting under Zeus's instructions (365).

363 ὑπ᾽ Εὐρυσθῆος ἀέθλων recurs at 19.163. References to Herakles' doings are broadly scattered through the poem, from his birth (14.323f., 19.96–133) to his labours under Eurustheus, cf. also 15.639f. (Kerberos here is the only one specified, though not so named; the canon of twelve is post-Homeric), to his attacks on Troy to punish Laomedon (5.640–2, 20.145–8) and on Pulos with the wounding of Hades (5.395–404, 11.690–3), to Here's persecution of him and his wounding her (14.250–5, 15.25–30, 18.117–19, 5.392–4). For possible sources used by the Homeric tradition see on 5.396–7.

364–5 πρὸς οὐρανὸν...ἀπ᾽ οὐρανόθεν echoes the correspondence between Herakles' appeals and Athene's immediate responses to them, cf. the frequentatives σώεσκον...κλαίεσκε with the continuative imperf. προΐαλλεν.

366–70 A complex sentence, progressively enjambed, with three subordinate clauses each occupying a v., then the main clause. It is graphically expressed; Hades (understand δῶμα) is πυλάρταο, 'fastener of the gate' (i.e. preventing escape from the underworld), twice elsewhere (also two minor Trojans are so named); he is στυγερός, thrice of Ares, only here. That is clearly to produce a play with Στυγός and στυγέει in the next 2 vv.: 'Now, though I saved his son from that hateful realm and those hateful waters, it is me he hates.' αἰπὰ ῥέεθρα recurs at 21.9 of Skamandros; for the form of the adj. cf. πόλιν... αἰπήν (5 × *Il.*), Shipp, *Studies* 75; the 'steep' waters have general force but also suggest the difficulties of recrossing.

371–2 These vv. were omitted by Zenodotus and athetized by Aristarchus (Arn, Did(?)/A) as a needless summary of the scene at 1.500–2; but they are not an exact repetition (and substitute kissing the knees for clasping them), and the elaboration of the bare reference to Thetis in 370 is typically Homeric, *contra* Bolling, *External Evidence* 109.

373 After two flowing and heavily subordinated sentences this blunt and asyndetic boast rounds off Athene's passionate digression: 'the time will come when he calls me his dear grey-eyed one again'. The implication is not so much (with Ameis–Hentze) that Zeus will need something else from her and she will refuse, as that his displeasure is never permanent, and therefore she can disobey him now.

374–6 Athene as a war-goddess is obviously to do the fighting, Here is charioteer as at 5.720ff. For 376 τεύχεσιν... θωρήξομαι cf. 388 = 5.737. Are they already in Zeus's palace? V. 375 suggests not, though Ameis–Hentze may be right that καταδῦσα means she will go into an inner room there; and the bk 5 version, which lacks such a statement of intent and proceeds directly to her shedding her robe on Zeus's floor (733f. = 384f. here), suggests that she is already there. It is in Zeus's house that they rejoin the other gods at 436f.

378 One ancient reading was προφανεῖσα, agreeing with 376 ἴδωμαι, but Aristarchus (Did/A) favoured προφανέντε which is probably correct, the masc. for the fem. dual form being supported by 455 πληγέντε. Zenodotus and, curiously, the majority of MSS had the impossible προφανεῖσας (with Hesiodic -ᾰς) to avoid this problem (and, perhaps, the harmless hiatus); he followed it by ἰδὼν ἐς δοῦπον ἀκόντων, an awkward conversion of 11.364 ἰὼν δ᾽ ἐς δοῦπον ἀκόντων, presumably to avoid the acc. after γηθήσει – for which, however, 9.77 provides adequate parallel. For the 'bridges' of war see on 4.371, 5.87–8.

379–80 ~ 13.831f. (cf. 17.241), with | ἦ τις καί for | – ∪ ἀτάρ there; this brings another long and quite eloquent sentence to a forceful close.

381–96 Athene's arming repeats much of the equivalent scene in bk 5, though without her heavily-decorated aegis and helmet; Here's (and

Hebe's) detailed preparation of the chariot, described at 5.722–32, is completely omitted. Thus 381–3 here = 5.719–21, 384–96 = 5.733–7 + 745–52. For the relationship of the two contexts see on 350–484, also on 5.719–52, 719–21 and 734–7.

381–3 See on 5.719–21.

384–8 See on 5.734–7, also on 375 above. Vv. 385–7 were unjustifiably athetized by Aristophanes and Aristarchus and omitted by Zenodotus (Arn, Did/A), as unnecessary here since Athene will not see action.

389–96 See on 5.745–7, 5.748 and 5.749–52. Aristarchus (Arn/A) athetized 390f., see previous n. On 395 see further Apthorp, *MS Evidence* 197.

397–8 Here the two accounts diverge: at 5.753ff. the goddesses find Zeus on Olumpos' highest peak and receive his permission to intervene down below; here Zeus sees them from Ida and is furious. The language is formular (with 398 = 11.185), except for the placing of ἐπεὶ ἴδε directly before the formula χώσατ᾽ ἄρ᾽ αἰνῶς, which cleverly conveys the immediacy of his wrath (so Ameis–Hentze).

398 Iris is 'golden-winged' here and at 11.185; no other Homeric deity is winged, though Hermes has winged sandals in *Od*. Zeus is on Ida, but she appears instantly.

399–408 Zeus tells Iris to turn the goddesses back (399f.) and adds what will happen if they do not obey. Elsewhere the same address, βάσκ᾽ ἴθι, Ἶρι ταχεῖα is followed by specific instructions to pass on a message; so at 11.186 (τὸν Ἕκτορι μῦθον ἔνισπες), 15.158f., 24.144f. That helps explain why she there merely repeats his words (after brief encouragement at 24.171–4), whereas here she will add her own more trenchant comments, no doubt to ensure that her mission as a whole is successful. See also on 7.385–97 and 7.387.

399–400 'Let them not come ἄντην, against me', i.e. by coming to the battlefield below Mt Ida where Zeus is; 'for it is not good that we should clash in war' – or rather (in view of the γάρ clause which follows) 'our clash in war will not be a happy one' (i.e. for them). πτόλεμόνδε is a more graphic substitute, no doubt partly *metri gratia*, for the dat., cf. 11.736 συμφερόμεσθα μάχῃ.

401 An emphatic formular v., 3 × *Il*., 2 × *Od*.

402–5 Zeus's threat is a picturesque expansion of his initial warning at 12, πληγεὶς οὐ κατὰ κόσμον ἐλεύσεται Οὔλυμπόνδε. Here he will cripple their horses, smash their chariot, hurl them out of it, inflicting wounds with his thunderbolt that will take more than ten years to heal; ἐς ... δεκάτους ἐνιαυτούς is a useful conflation of ἐς δέκα ἐνιαυτούς and δεκάτῃ ἐνιαυτῇ. ἀπαλθήσεσθον after κεν is conditional fut., 'they will not heal the wounds ⟨if all this happens⟩'.

406 Something like 'the consequences' is to be understood as object of ἴδῃ.

407–8 Athene is Zeus's main culprit; now these vv. are added, a little lamely perhaps, to take account of Here (who is, however, to suffer the same punishment). For the combination of νέμεσις and χόλος cf. 6.335. ἔωθεν, as in Herodotus, is for εἴωθεν; ἐνικλᾶν, again only here and in 422, then Hellenistic, is a rather mysterious compound of κλάω, here 'frustrate'. Aristarchus accepted these vv. (and favoured ὅττι κεν εἴπω over ὅττι νοήσω which became the vulgate, Did/A), but it is hard not to suspect later, even post-rhapsodic, elaboration.

409–10 409 recurs twice in bk 24; ἀελλόπος, 'storm-footed', is a stronger version of Iris' common epithet ποδήνεμος (10 × *Il.*). 410 recurs at 15.79 (cf. 11.196, 15.169), where Aristarchus fussily read ἐξ rather than κατά, which remained the vulgate reading; the v. is omitted here by important MSS (A,B,C), perhaps because of the repetition of Olumpos again in 411, but should probably be retained.

411 πρώτῃσιν...πύλῃσι: at the outer part of the gate, i.e. just as they were leaving.

412 She 'told them Zeus's word' but will also add her own comments; see on 399–408.

413–15 Compare Athene's own claim at 360 that Zeus φρεσὶ μαίνεται οὐκ ἀγαθῇσι. In 414 οὐκ ἐάᾳ is a deceptively mild way of expressing total prohibition, cf. 428. ἦ τελέει περ in 415 summarizes Zeus's τὸ δὲ καὶ τετελεσμένον ἔσται of 401.

419–20 Iris turns to *oratio recta*. Aristarchus (Arn/A) athetized the last 5 vv. of her speech, from 420 on, the first 3 as unnecessary, the last 2 (see next n.) as unsuitable.

423–4 Iris' final contribution is surprisingly violent as she develops Zeus's criticism of his daughter. αἰνοτάτη is a term applied by Here to Zeus himself in the formular v. αἰνότατε Κρονίδη, ποῖον τὸν μῦθον ἔειπες (6 × *Il.*, including 462); that is acceptable, but κύον ἀδεές (ἀδϝεές), 'fearless bitch', belongs rather to the crude abuse of the Theomachy, where Here applies it to Artemis at 21.481. — Actually Athene had had no intention of raising her spear against Zeus, Διὸς ἄντα; Iris is developing Zeus's own idea of what might happen, cf. 406 ᾧ πατρὶ μάχηται reported as 420 σῷ πατρὶ μάχηαι.

427–31 Here immediately and prudently gives in; her opening words to Athene comically recall her initial indignant address of 352, after which she develops her new position in carefully enjambed and rhythmically varied phrases. οὐκέτ' ἔγωγε | νῶϊ ἐῶ is emphatic, cf. 414 οὐκ ἐάᾳ Κρονίδης. The futility of gods suffering βροτῶν ἕνεκα is a recurrent theme: men can die or not as they please. The epigrammatic style continues in the closing concession: 'let him have his own ideas and make judgement between Trojans and Danaans as is fitting'; Leaf detected a contemptuous note in τὰ ἃ φρονέων, 'those plans of his', but that is questionable in view of ὡς ἐπιεικές (5 × *Il.*).

432 ~ 157, where the charioteer (Nestor) likewise turns the horses after urging retreat, and without waiting for a reply.

433-5 The Horai, whose gates opened for the two goddesses at 393, now unharness their horses and deal with the chariot (as Poseidon will for Zeus at 440f.). Their guardianship of the gate of Olumpos is probably an invention of the Homeric tradition, see on 5.749-52; here their duties are extended further. These are routine tasks; 434f. = *Od.* 4.40, 42, except that the stalls are ambrosial here. At 5.722 it was Hebe who prepared the chariot for these goddesses, but perhaps it was too complicated to introduce her here for the dismantling process. For παμφανόωντα see 320-2n.; it is idle to speculate whether it was polished wood or stucco that made these walls shine.

436-7 θρόνος is the usual word for a divine seat; κλισμοί suggests something smaller, but these too are golden, like Zeus's θρόνος at 442. φίλον τετιημένος -η ἦτορ recurs 6 × *Od.*, in *Il.* only at 11.555 and without φίλον.

439 θῶκος only here in *Il.* (which however has θάασσε twice) but 3 × *Od.*, including 5.3 οἱ δὲ θεοὶ θῶκόνδε καθίζανον; the word is of unknown etymology, cf. Chantraine, *Dict.* s.v. θᾶκος, but evidently meant much the same as θρόνος. δίωκε meaning 'drove swiftly' (so Arn/A) is a relatively late development, cf. *Od.* 13.162.

440-1 Poseidon deals with his elder brother's chariot and horses, evidently as a mark of respect. For covering the chariot with a cloth see on 5.194-5; it is placed on a stand, probably after the removal of its wheels (cf. 5.722-3n.) – compare the use of βωμός, normally 'altar', for a statue-base at *Od.* 7.100.

443 Olumpos shakes as Zeus sits down, see on 199; his majestic demeanour increases the contrast with the disgruntled goddesses.

444-5 Διὸς ἀμφίς must mean apart from Zeus, not one on each side of him; that is shown by οἶαι, 'alone of all the gods', as well as by their sitting close to each other at 458.

446-56 Zeus can hardly help noticing Athene's and Here's sitting apart and refusing to greet him, so he proceeds at once to a sarcastic reference to their attempt and renewed threats about what might have happened. The style is relaxed, with sentences of moderate length and mainly progressive enjambment; indeed this whole episode is narrated in an easy and accomplished manner, both in the combination of formular and repeated elements and in the development of original vv. and sentences.

447 τετίησθον: cf. 437 τετιημέναι ἦτορ.

448 'So you did not tire yourselves, then, in glorious battle...': θήν is equivalent to δή, 'sometimes with a note of contempt', Denniston, *Particles* 288f., who compares 13.813.

450–1 Zeus began and will end with the goddesses' failure and what would have happened had they persisted; now he interjects a general assertion of his physical supremacy over all the gods, with clear reference to his proclamation at the beginning of the Book. | πάντως, very emphatic, occurs only here and at *Od.* 19.91.

452–3 'But *your* glorious limbs (φαίδιμα γυῖα | 8 × *Il.*, here ironic) were seized with trembling before ever you saw fighting.' The repetition πόλεμόν... πολέμοιο emphasizes their avoidance of it.

454–6 Zeus repeats his affirmation of 401, then refers in a rather alarming way to his threat of 402f.: they would have been brought back home as stretcher-cases, thunderbolt-struck, their own chariot (he means) smashed to pieces under them. The closing v. is not, as often, rhythmically different, but the ruminative and slightly ironic addition of ἵν᾽ ἀθανάτων ἕδος ἐστίν makes a distinctive ending.

457–62 = 4.20–5; the scene is a memorable one as the two goddesses sit side by side muttering threats against Troy. Athene glowers at Zeus but does not address him; Here cannot contain her wrath, and after a standard indignant address...

463–8 ...utters words already assigned to Athene at 32–7. The comment on 28–40 showed why that protest, since it elicits an unlikely concession from Zeus, must be regarded as out of place there. Here it is unobjectionable, its tone of modified defiance providing a motive for Zeus's further threat at 470ff. of what he will do on the morrow.

463 The vulgate gives ἐπιεικτόν (for which see on 5.892) as at 32, though Aristarchus (Did/A) and a few MSS read ἀλαπαδνόν here, as in τῶν τε σθένος οὐκ ἀλαπαδνόν, twice in similes of wild boars.

466–8 These vv. are omitted here by the majority of MSS, though for no clear reason. Aristarchus appears not to have commented on 466f. (see Erbse *ad loc.*, van der Valk, *Researches* II, 428); though 37 (= 468) was omitted by Zenodotus and perhaps athetized by Aristophanes and Aristarchus because of ὀδυσσαμένοιο τεοῖο (Arn/T). Zeus's angry riposte is perhaps better motivated if Here has said that she and Athene will continue to advise the Achaeans, rather than merely pitying them. See further Apthorp, *MS Evidence* 23f.

468 τεοῖο is 'a quite impossible form', Leaf; 'not certainly late', Shipp, *Studies* 79. τεός is a possessive adjective, probably an Aeolism; it must be intended as a pronoun, 'through you hating them'. The phrase, although strange and awkward, is rhetorically forceful, and has some claim to be accepted as Homeric.

470–2   At 465 and 468 Here has talked of the destruction, ὄλωνται, of the Achaeans; now Zeus tells her that she can see him ὄλλυντα even more on the next day, if she wishes (on which see 4.353n.). Again the tone is determined and somewhat contemptuous. πουλύν seems weak here, but cf. 10.517 κατεδύσετο πουλὺν ὅμιλον.

475–6   Aristarchus athetized (Arn/A) as an unnecessary and inaccurate development of 474; for Patroklos is to die on the very next day (whereas ἤματι τῷ suggests a more distant day, cf. 22.359), and not among the ships but in the open plain. Most editors reject these objections, and Schadewaldt (*Ilias-Studien* 110 n. 3) observed that imprecisions in predictions of future events are not uncommon in *Il.* Ameis–Hentze, however, agreed with Aristarchus, noting also the lack of a balancing δέ-clause after 475 οἱ μέν, and bracketed not only these vv. but also the previous two, which lets 477 ὡς γὰρ θέσφατόν ἐστι refer to the general destruction of Achaeans in 472 and thus implicitly to Zeus's weighing of the fates at 69ff. That has its attractions, though the only substantial difficulty is the inconsistency over Patroklos' death.

477   θέσφατον means 'divinely decreed', but its usage is not clear enough (it only recurs once in *Il.*) to indicate weighing the fates of the two armies (see previous n.) rather than his own general will and foreknowledge of future events. His divine confidence heightens the contrast between σέθεν and ἐγώ and his indifference to her anger (478 χωομένης being cumulated onto Agamemnon's σέθεν... ἀλεγίζω of 1.180).

477–83   The climax comes in precise ring-form: 'I do not care if you are angry, even if you go to the lowest boundaries... even if you go there, I do not care if you are angry.' Zeus's vision of where she might go becomes ominously clearer; at first one might think he means the farthest bounds of earth (which is where at 14.200 and 301f. her friends Okeanos and Tethus dwell); but then the addition of καὶ πόντοιο shows that νείατα, after all, has its strict sense of 'lowest', and that these are the springs, boundaries and roots (as Hesiod terms them at *Theog.* 736ff. and 807ff.) of earth, sea and sky in Tartaros itself. It is there that Iapetos father of Prometheus and Kronos father of Zeus himself, representing the Titans, sit (480 ἥμενοι, i.e. in imprisonment) and enjoy neither sunlight nor breezes, but 'deep Tartaros surrounds them on all sides'. In v. 482 ἀλωμένη adds a final note of ambiguity: why should her wanderings take her so far? Perhaps that is the farthest anyone could penetrate, or she might be trying to enlist sympathy from Zeus's most recent enemies, the Titans; but there may be a hint that she might find herself imprisoned there one day, in accord with Zeus's threat of 12–16 that any god who disobeyed him would either be struck by thunderbolt (12 πληγείς, cf. 455 πληγέντε) or flung down into Tartaros.

480 Huperion recurs in *Il.* only at 19.398, παμφαίνων ὥς τ' ἠλέκτωρ Ὑπερίων (whereas ἠλέκτωρ by itself means 'sun' at 6.513, q.v. with n.). In *Od.* it is more fully established as an epithet of Helios (5 ×), but at 1.24 simply means 'sun' by itself. In origin a comparative of ὕπερος (cf. N. J. Richardson on *HyDem* 26), Ὑπερίων could itself be seen as a patronymic form, or more simply as 'who goes overhead'; the idea of Huperion as father of the sun seems to be developing just at the end of the Homeric tradition, cf. *Od.* 12.176 Ἠελίου τ' αὐγὴ Ὑπεριονίδαο ἄνακτος, and is unambiguously exemplified in Hesiod, *Theog.* 374, and *HyDem* 26.

483–4 A final compliment is appended once the ring is complete: 'I care not, since nothing is more bitch-like than you', with οὐ σέο taking up οὔ σευ in the previous verse. Herē accepts this in silence.

485–565 Darkness interrupts the fighting; Hektor gives orders for the night and encourages his troops, predicting success on the morrow. They burn countless fires on the plain and await the dawn

485–6 Sunset eases the transition from Olumpos back to affairs on earth. It is described in unusual terms, as the typical language of 1.605, αὐτὰρ ἐπεὶ κατέδυ λαμπρὸν φάος ἠελίοιο, or (of dawn) 7.421f., Ἠέλιος μὲν ἔπειτα νέον προσέβαλλεν ἀρούρας, | ἐξ ἀκαλαρρείταο βαθυρρόου Ὠκεανοῖο, is elaborated into the sun *falling* into Okeanos and *dragging* night over the land. 'Black night' is a common formula, though at the v-e; 'grain-giving ploughland' recurs at 20.226 but 9 × *Od.* Most of the descriptive elements are familiar, but the new image is a brilliant one with darkness *drawn over* the land – progressively, that implies. This suggests, if not a spherical earth, at least a more complex and accurate view of nightfall than elsewhere in Homer.

487–8 Trojan disappointment is played down to heighten Achaean relief: for τρίλλιστος, 'thrice prayed-for', cf. τρισμάκαρες, 2 × *Od.*

489–91 Hektor assembles his troops by the Skamandros – away from the ships, 490 νόσφι νεῶν, though still quite close, ἐγγύθ', ἐγγύς, according to 9.76 and 232. V. 491 recurs at 10.199, where it has more point (see n. there); it also suggests a smaller space than would be needed for a whole army. Neither Aristarchus (who related it to the question of the νεκρῶν ἀναίρεσις in bk 7, Arn/A) nor the MSS cast doubt on it, but other and more demonstrable additions to the closing part of this Book make concordance-type interpolation seem not improbable here too.

492–5 A clumsy adaptation of 3.265, cf. 24.459, leads to a near-repetition of 6.318–20 (with τόν ῥ' Ἕκτωρ ἀγόρευε here for ἔνθ' Ἕκτωρ εἰσῆλθε). See the discussion of 6.319–20; Aristarchus found the passage better in place here, Zenodotus the contrary (Arn/A). It is indeed inessential in its bk 6 context, but in neither case does this apparently typical description appear to be used to best effect.

496 = 2.109, where Agamemnon, who has been holding his ancestral staff, now leans on it. In both cases one might expect staff or spear to be held upright in a formal pose or moved to and fro to emphasize an argument, cf. 2.109n. See further Bolling, *External Evidence* 111.

497–541 Hektor's long speech to his troops is curiously rambling and repetitious, especially in its latter part. Willcock (on 523–41) sees this as perhaps a sign of his 'blustering and trying to convince himself', and that may be true to an extent, although he has been filled with confidence until now. Rhapsodic elaboration or insufficient revision, rather, may be the main factor. His successive points are as follows:

(1) I expected to drive them away, but night has intervened (498–501).

(2) So unharness and feed your horses and bring wine and food from Troy, making fires so that the Achaeans do not escape. If they try, they will not do so unharmed (502–16).

(3) Let the heralds tell young and old in the city to bivouac on the walls and the women to light fires in their houses, to avoid a raid while the army is away (517–22).

(4) These are my instructions for now; more will follow tomorrow; and I pray to Zeus to drive the curs away (523–8).

(5) So let us keep watch tonight, and at dawn engage them by the ships; then I shall know whether Diomedes will win, or I; I am confident he will fall tomorrow at dawn (529–38).

(6) Would that I were as sure of being immortal and honoured like a god as I am that this day brings evil for the Argives (538–41).

498 A possible rising threefolder, something rare in the bland and unemphatic style of the whole latter part of this Book. ἐφάμην, 'I thought'.

499 = 12.115, with its two halves also formular.

501 Zenodotus read ἐπεὶ Διὸς ἐτράπετο φρήν for the formula in the second hemistich (Arn/A), making it identical with 10.45; that looks like a concordance-type conjecture and Aristarchus dismissed it as unsuitable, though the resulting sense is neither impossible nor inappropriate.

502–3 = 9.65f. (down to ἐφοπλισόμεσθα), cf. *Od.* 12.291f.; also 7.282 and 293, ἀγαθὸν καὶ νυκτὶ πιθέσθαι.

505–7 βόας καὶ ἴφια μῆλα is formular (2 × *Il.* elsewhere + 8.545, 6 × *Od.*), typical prey for a raiding force rather than material for an impromptu meal as here. The description may be influenced by the Achaean meal at the end of bk 7 (cf. 7.466 βουφόνεον, 7.472 οἰνίζοντο), but that was behind their new defences. καρπαλίμως is a typical runover-word transition; οἰνίζεσθε here means simply 'get wine' rather than buy it as in the bk 7 context, and σῖτον seems to be generated, unnecessarily after the mention of meat, as a polar contrast to the wine (though cf. *Od.* 20.312f.).

508–9 For παννύχιοι cf. 554 and 7.476; μέσφ(α) for μέχρι is unique in Homer; ἠοῦς ἠριγενείης | seems to be based on the mainly Odyssean formula ἦμος δ' ἠριγένεια φάνη ῥοδοδάκτυλος Ἠώς, see on 1.477. ἠοῦς (contracted) also at 470 and 525; see 530, 535, 538 for further emphasis by Hektor on the crucial next day. The fires, to be memorably described at 554ff., are mainly to show the Achaeans that the enemy are still there.

510–11 On | μή πως καί see 20.301n. Later that night, at 9.27, Agamemnon does propose flight, despite all the fires on the plain.

512–13 'Let them not board the ships at will and without difficulty, but in such a way that some of them have a missile to digest even at home.' πέσσειν is applied to anger or cares in *Il.*, even to γέρα or rights at 2.237; here the metaphor is especially vivid, and need not be translated into exact terms, 'brood on', 'cure' (of the wound) or whatever. — Hektor had previously envisaged slaying all the Achaeans, e.g. at 498; his present talk of survivors is to make the point that they will be a living reminder of the danger of attacking Troy in future (515f.).

514–16 The first two vv. represent successive cumulations to develop and explain the βέλος in 513. For the second half of 515 cf. τόν τε στυγέουσι καὶ ἄλλοι, 3 × *Il.*, with 516 recurring at 19.318.

517–21 Untraditional compounds proliferate, with πρωθήβας, πολιο-κροτάφους and θεοδμήτων all *hapax* in Homer, if plain in meaning. The boys and old men are to camp out (λέξασθαι from λέχομαι, cf. λέχος) on the walls (which is what πύργων connotes here; they are god-built, i.e. by Apollo and Poseidon for Laomedon, cf. 7.452f.). θηλύτεραι of γυναῖκες, only here *Il.* but 5 × *Od.*, is presumably to emphasize the functional differentiations of age and sex. Each is to build a great fire at home, obviously to suggest activity and wakefulness while watch is kept from the walls.

523 'Let (all this) be as I declare'; the instructions have been complex enough to warrant such a conclusion, though bT found it tyrannical rather than regal. Plur. μεγαλήτορες is untypical, being applied to the Trojans sardonically at 21.55, then once each to Phlegyans, Paphlagonians and Myrmidons.

524–5 Aristarchus athetized (Arn/A), mainly because of lack of connexion with what follows; they certainly look like a loose elaboration of 523. The sense is 'let this speech suffice for now; the second one I shall deliver at dawn' – that is, all that concerns tonight's arrangements has been said, what concerns tomorrow will come later. ὑγιής of a μῦθος, meaning 'beneficial' or 'relevant', is peculiar, and the separation of today's orders from tomorrow's suggests scholarly pedantry rather than military precision. In 525 ἠοῦς can be taken with ἀγορεύσω rather than τὸν δ', *contra* Leaf, thus eliminating an Atticism, but even so the style is clumsy.

526-7 The asyndeton is violent and perhaps hard to justify – and why does Hektor choose to interpose such a prayer at this point? Aristarchus, Arn/A (against Zenodotus' ἔλπομαι εὐχόμενος, supported by e.g. Leaf and Willcock), took the sense to be 'I claim, being given good hope by Zeus and the other gods, that I will drive out...', which is surely impossible; the obvious 'I pray in good hope...to drive out' is better. The (foreign) dogs are 'carried here by dooms of death' – at least the succeeding v. 528 gives a more plausible interpretation than several modern editors, though Aristarchus (Arn/A) was right to bracket it (and Zenodotus to omit, Did/AT) as superfluous; it has all the appearance of a later versified gloss, not least in the present tense of φορέουσι. Editors of all complexions have bracketed several vv. hereabouts; it is indeed hard not to suspect almost every component of 523-8 inclusive.

529-32 If they are omitted, then 529 follows directly on 522: old men and boys are to keep watch, the woman are to burn fires to deter ambush, while we stay on guard through the night and tomorrow renew battle against the ships.

532-4 Hektor singles out Diomedes as key to victory or defeat, in harmony with his major rôle from bk 5 on. ὁ Τυδεΐδης κρατερὸς Διομήδης recurs at 11.660 and 16.25 (after βέβληται μέν; the asyndetic opening here is less elegant), making a rising threefolder. The τεῖχος is of course that of Troy. These vv. are probably authentic, see next n.

535-7 Aristarchus is reported (Arn, Did/A) as debating whether these three vv. should be athetized, or whether it should be the following three (i.e. 538-40), 'because they are expressions of the same idea'. Experts have devoted much discussion to this (see Erbse *ad loc.* for refs., also Bolling, *External Evidence* 112-14), but only Wolf and Wecklein observed that it is these 3 vv. *and the preceding three* (i.e. 532-4, not 538-41 (*sic*), where the fourth v. is integral and which have a quite different sense) that are doublets. The scholium, in any case corrupt (cf. Bolling 113), distinguishes the two sets by diacritical signs: these three carry the antisigma in A, then 538-40 the stigmē or point. It seems that those points have become misplaced and should be written against 532-4. The latter part of the scholium would then make sense: 'Aristarchus condemns the second set [i.e. 535-7] because the words are excessively boastful.'

Even without the scholium, 535-7 is clearly recognizable as a repetitive doublet: (532-4) 'I shall know whether Diomedes will drive me back, or I kill and plunder him; (535-7) he shall find out whether he can resist my attack, but I believe I shall kill him and many companions.' The interpolation is certainly of 535–7 not 532–4, since the former's expression is suspect in several respects: (i) διαείσεται with ἣν ἀρετήν is an apparent misunderstanding of 13.277; (ii) | μείνῃ (etc.) ἐπερχόμενον, 3 × *Il.* elsewhere, takes a personal direct object, not 'spear' as here (7.262 being no support for this, *pace* Ameis–Hentze); (iii) ἀλλ' ἐν πρώτοισιν, ὅϊω recurs in a quite different sense at *Od.* 8.180; that may be irrelevant since both ἐν πρώτοισι(ν) and ὅϊω | are formular, but the martial sense of ἐν πρώτοισιν is in any case unsuitable here; (iv) 537 κείσεται οὐτηθείς should mean 'shall lie wounded', not dead; and (v) 'lie' has to be understood with πολέες δ' ἀμφ' αὐτὸν ἑταῖροι also, though a verb is expressed in the following v. in more regular uses of this formula at 2.417f. and 19.5f.

538–41 Irrespective of Aristarchus' misreported opinions on 535–7, these 4 vv. probably stand or fall together: 538 εἰ γὰρ ἐγὼν ὥς is needed before εἴην, with ἠελίου... αὔριον cumulated to fill the first part of the verse. 540f. are identical with 13.827f., and that context provides the main model:

13.825 εἰ γὰρ ἐγὼν οὕτω γε Διὸς πάϊς αἰγιόχοιο
  εἴην ἤματα πάντα, τέκοι δέ με πότνια Ἥρη,
  τιοίμην δ' ὡς τίετ' Ἀθηναίη καὶ Ἀπόλλων,
  ὡς νῦν ἡμέρη ἥδε κακὸν φέρει Ἀργείοισι,

with *Od.* 5.136 = 7.257 = 23.336, θήσειν ἀθάνατον καὶ ἀγήρων ἤματα πάντα, suggesting the simplification of the first two vv. Bolling, *External Evidence* 114, followed Christ in thinking that Hektor's speech originally ended with 534, and that 538–41 and the doublet 532–4 are later elaborations. 534 does indeed make a reasonable conclusion, and the present passage does not fit so well here as its probable model does in bk 13; it contains, moreover, a specific fault discussed in the next comment.

538 ἠελίου ἀνιόντος recurs, though at the v-e, at 22.135; ἐς αὔριον recurs at *Od.* 11.351, but after ἐπιμεῖναι (and αὔριον ἐς at *Od.* 7.318, again with some sense of 'until'). It seems to be an inept verse-filler here, with ἐς meaningless.

541 After Hektor's repeated emphasis on action at dawn the next day (quite apart from αὔριον in the suspect 535 and 538), it is at first surprising to find him referring to *this* day as the one that brings grief to the enemy. Obviously this is caused by failure to adjust 13.828, where 'today' is in place; but the sense is clear enough, even quite dramatic.

543–7 Hektor's instructions of 503–7 are now carried out; the treatment of the horses is described in different terms (with 543 = *Od.* 4.39, the use of Odyssean phraseology being noticeable hereabouts), but the rest is exactly repeated except for necessary conversion of imperatives, i.e. 545–7 ~ 505–7. ἄξοντο in 545 is an artificial aor. (for ἀγάγοντο) created after 505 ἄξεσθε.

548–52 Only 549 belongs to the vulgate text; the other 4 vv. were quoted as Homeric, and with reference to the Trojans camping out, in the ps.-Platonic *Alcibiades* II, 149D, together with a paraphrase of 549. They were mistakenly accepted into the text by Barnes followed by Wolf but are nowadays universally rejected (being assigned by Wilamowitz to the Cyclic *Little Iliad*, cf. Bolling, *External Evidence* 115). Most are assembled from other contexts: thus 548 ~ 1.315, 2.306; 551f. ~ 24.27f., cf. 4.47. Only 550 τῆς δ' to 551 οὐδ' ἔθελον cannot be strictly paralleled, and these words are opposed to the whole Homeric concept of sacrifice; for Homer's gods do not feed on sacrifices, and even their absorption of the κνίση has been suppressed as part of the progressive de-carnalization of these deities – see the full discussion on pp. 10–13. δατέοντο, 'divided up', is strange when applied to the savour, and probably presupposes a model in which the gods divided up the meat itself. Finally the idea that the gods in general were hostile to Troy is of course absurd in view of the *Iliad*'s position on Here, Athene and Poseidon, and is due to failure to adapt e.g. 24.27. Cf. 541n. for a similar fault.

549 This v., on the other hand, appears in the medieval MSS and was apparently not questioned by Aristarchus (though included in paraphrase in the ps.-Plato quotation). It is similar in content to 1.317 (with οὐρανὸν εἴσω | 2 × *Il.* elsewhere), and without it the δέ of 553 οἱ δέ is awkward. Whether it was necessary to indicate that a meal was taken and the gathered fuel put to use in that respect is debatable. Leaf's 'a hasty bivouac on the plain is no time for a solemn sacrifice' has little force; rather Hektor's failure to mention the meal itself, let alone a sacrifice, after 507 may suggest that it would not be specified here either. Doubts remain.

553–65 The Book ends with a brilliant vision of the Trojan camp-fires shining like multitudinous stars on a clear night.

553 μέγα φρονέοντες, 'with high confidence'. Most MSS read γεφύρῃ, which had support from Aristarchus (Nic, Did/A), perhaps in view of ἐπί which was also the vulgate reading; but the regular ἀνὰ πτολέμοιο γεφύρας, as in 378, should be restored.

555–61 One last problem, typical of this Book, remains, over how much of this resplendent simile properly belongs here. Aristophanes and Aristarchus athetized, and Zenodotus omitted, 557–8 (Arn, Did/A) as taken from 16.299f. where they recur. That is in a different simile where they are undeniably more appropriate:

> 16.297 ὡς δ' ὅτ' ἀφ' ὑψηλῆς κορυφῆς ὄρεος μεγάλοιο
> 298 κινήσῃ πυκινὴν νεφέλην στεροπηγερέτα Ζεύς,
> 299 ἔκ τ' ἔφανεν πᾶσαι σκοπιαὶ καὶ πρώονες ἄκροι
> 300 καὶ νάπαι, οὐρανόθεν δ' ἄρ' ὑπερράγη ἄσπετος αἰθήρ,

301 ὡς Δαναοὶ ...
302 τυτθὸν ἀνέπνευσαν ...

'As when from the high peak of a great mountain Zeus the lightning-gatherer moves thick cloud, and all the look-out places show up and the jutting ridges and valleys, and limitless upper air is broken open from heaven downward, so did the Danaans ... draw breath for a while.' There, the high places show up (ἔκ τ᾽ ἔφανεν, aor.) as the cloud moves away – the break in the clouds is a sudden event (ὑπ-ερράγη, aor. again), and just so are the Danaans suddenly given a breathing-space. Here, by contrast, all the stars are clearly seen and the upper air is windless (that is, on a calm night and when clouds are plainly *not* being moved onto and away from the mountain peaks): just so, and so many, are the Trojan fires on the plain. The description of this sudden break in the clouds is out of place, in literal terms at least; yet it is a mark of the oral formular style that descriptions can be repeated even though some detail is not quite consistent with the new context (so Willcock *ad loc.*). It is possible, after all, that the idea of φαίνετ᾽ in 556 of itself brought ἔκ τ᾽ ἔφανεν etc., from a roughly similar context, into the singer's mind. It has been objected that the omission of the 2 vv. leaves ἄστρα in 555 and 559 too close together; but such repetition is especially typical of similes, and αἰθήρ | in 556 and 558 are equally close if the vv. are left in place. H. Fränkel (*Die homerischen Gleichnisse*, Göttingen 1921, 34n.) could not decide whether 557f. should be considered an interpolation or not; that seems a reasonable position to take.

555 Ancient critics were exercised over this bright moon, but decided that the epithet is a generic one and does not mean that the moon was full. It is perhaps mentioned as a feature of the clear night sky more than to single out the circumlunar stars in particular.

559 This v. is of course genuine (*contra* Bolling, *External Evidence* 115, who was misled by an obvious textual corruption in the T scholium on 557–8, cf. Erbse *ad loc.*); the herdsman's reaction is typical, cf. 13.493 γάνυται δ᾽ ἄρα τε φρένα ποιμήν and 3.10f., with *Od.* 6.106 γέγηθε δέ τε φρένα for the present phrasing.

560–1 It is the number, τόσσα, rather than the clarity and brilliance of the fires that is chosen as specific point of comparison (though τοῖα and ὡς τά were ancient variants, Did/A), and this idea is developed in the next 2 vv. Ἰλιόθι is strictly locative with πρό adverbial, but in effect counts as gen. with πρό prepositional.

562–4 A thousand fires (Zenodotus, Arn/A, read μυρί᾽, 'ten thousand') burn in the plain with fifty men round each, making a good poetical number for Trojans and allies together. σέλα is contracted from σέλαϊ.

564–5 A closing couplet reminds us once again that, among much that appears unrefined or casually assembled in this Book, there are many flashes of Homeric brilliance; for now, to complete the descriptive ring after 543f., attention is focused on the horses as they munch their barley and spelt (in the language of 5.196, q.v. with n.), and like the whole army assembled there await the dawn.

INDEX

The Index is not fully comprehensive; minor Homeric characters can be traced through the index of OCT. A fuller index of Greek words will be provided at the end of the whole Commentary.

Lightning Source UK Ltd.
Milton Keynes UK
UKHW010643150921
390330UK00009B/123